ROUTLEDGE INTERNATIONAL COMPANION TO EDUCATION

ROUTLEDGE INTERNATIONAL COMPANION TO EDUCATION

EDITED BY

BOB MOON, MIRIAM BEN-PERETZ AND SALLY BROWN

London and New York

First published 2000
by Routledge
11 New Fetter Lane, London EC4P 4EE

Simultaneously published in the USA and Canada
by Routledge
29 West 35th Street, New York, NY 10001

Routledge is an imprint of the Taylor & Francis Group

© 2000 Routledge

Typeset in Ehrhardt by RefineCatch Limited, Bungay, Suffolk
Printed and bound in Great Britain by
TJ International Ltd, Padstow, Cornwall

British Library Cataloguing in Publication Data
A catalogue record for this book is available from the British Library

Library of Congress Cataloging in Publication Data
A catalog record for this book has been applied for

ISBN 0–415–11814–X

CONTENTS

v

PART II: PROCESSES

PART III: SUBSTANTIVE ISSUES

CONTRIBUTORS

THE EDITORS

BOB MOON is Professor of Education at The Open University, England, where he directs the Centre for Research and Development in Teacher Education. Prior to this he was a teacher and Headteacher of two urban secondary comprehensive schools. He has written extensively on curriculum and teacher education and has a particular interest in comparative and international education. He is editor of the International Developments in School Reform series, published by Routledge. He has also acted as adviser to a number of national governments and international organisations, including OECD, UNESCO and the World Bank.

MIRIAM BEN-PERETZ is Head of the Center for Jewish Education in Israel and the Diaspora at the University of Haifa, Israel, and is visiting Professor at several universities internationally. She has been Dean of the School of Education at the University of Haifa, and President of Tel-Hai College. Among her numerous publications are *The Teacher-Curriculum Encounter: Freeing Teachers from the Tyranny of Texts* (SUNY, 1990) and *Learning from Experience: Memory and the Teacher's Account of Teaching* (SUNY, 1995). In 1997 she was awarded the Lifetime Achievement Award by the American Educational Research Association, for contributions to curriculum studies.

SALLY BROWN is Deputy Principal and Professor of Education at the University of Stirling, Scotland. She was previously Director of the Scottish Council for Research in Education. She has wide-ranging research interests, including assessment, special educational needs and the nature of teaching. Among her publications are *What Do They Know? Criterion Referenced Assessment* (1980), *Making Sense of Teaching* (1993) and *Special Educational Need Policy in the 1990s* (1994).

THE CONTRIBUTORS

LEN ALMOND
Loughborough University

TONY BECHER
University of Sussex

MARVIN W. BERKOWITZ
University of Missouri–St. Louis

DOUGLAS G. BOUGHTON
Northern Illinois University

JILL BOURNE
University of Southampton

OLIVER BOYD-BARRETT
California State Polytechnic
University

KEVIN J. BREHONY
University of Reading

NICHOLAS C. BURBULES
University of Illinois at
Champaign/Urbana

TONY BUSH
University of Leicester (EMDU)

DAVID CARR
University of Edinburgh

SIMON CATLING
Oxford Brookes University

ANNA CHRONAKI
Open University, UK

MARC J. DE VRIES
Eindhoven University of
Technology

ROSEMARY DEEM
Lancaster University

CHARLES DESFORGES
Exeter University

DAVID M. DONAHUE
Mills Cares Center

SHARON FEIMAN-NEMSER
Michigan State University

COLIN FLETCHER
University of Wolverhampton

ROBERT E. FLODEN
Michigan State University

KRISTIN DONALDSON GEISER
College of Notre Dame

DAVID GILLBORN
London University, Institute
of Education

ESTHER E. GOTTLIEB
West Virginia University

JACKIE GREEN
Leeds Metropolitan University

MADELEINE GRUMET
University of North Carolina at
Chapel Hill

BJØRG B. GUNDEM
University of Oslo

CHARLES HAUSMAN
University of Utah

DEVORAH KALEKIN-FISHMAN
University of Haifa

JENNY LEACH
The Open University, UK

ROY LOWE
University of Wales

ALASTAIR MACBETH
University of Glasgow

ROBIN MASON
The Open University, UK

ROBERT MCCORMICK
The Open University, UK

KATE MCCOY
John Jay College, CUNY

DONALD MCINTYRE
University of Cambridge

SUSAN L. MELNICK
Michigan State University

NEIL MERCER
The Open University, UK

ROSAMOND MITCHELL
University of Southampton

JOSEPH MURPHY
Vanderbilt University

PATRICIA MURPHY
The Open University, UK

PEARLA NESHER
University of Haifa

JON NIXON
University of Stirling

PATRICIA J. NORMAN
Michigan State University

PATRICIA P. OLMSTED
High/Scope Educational Research
Foundation, Michigan

CHRISTOPHER OULTON
University College Worcester

RICHARD J. PAXTON
University of Wisconsin Oshkosh

BRIDIE RABAN
The University of Melbourne

BETTY A. REARDON
Teachers College, Columbia
University

DAVID REYNOLDS
University of Exeter

SCOTT M. RICHARDSON
Close Up Foundation, Virginia

ANNA ERSHLER RICHERT
Mills College

SHEILA RIDDELL
University of Glasgow

IAN ROBOTTOM
DEAKIN UNIVERSITY

MURRAY SAUNDERS
University of Lancaster

SHIFRA SCHONMANN
University of Haifa

WILLIAM SCOTT
University of Bath

TOM STEELE
University of Glasgow

SIDNEY STRAUSS
Tel Aviv University

KEITH SWANWICK
London University Institute
of Education

PINCHAS TAMIR
Hebrew University

TONY TAYLOR
Monash University

CHARLES TEDDLIE
KEITH TONES
Leeds Metropolitan University

HARRY TORRANCE
University of Sussex

MUN C. TSANG
Columbia University

MARY JANE TURNER
Close Up Foundation, Virginia

STEVEN WEILAND
Michigan State University

RICHARD WHITE
Monash University

DYLAN WILIAM
King's College London

SAM WINEBURG
University of Washington

ACKNOWLEDGEMENTS

The contributors and publishers would like to thank the following for permission to reprint material used in this book: Sujata Bhatt and Carcanet Press Limited for permission to reproduce an extract from 'Search for My Tongue', taken from *Point to Point* (1997); Myles Cambeuil for permission to reproduce the poem 'Cànan', first published in *Verse*, volume 11, number 2. Table 44.1 and Figure 44.5 were reproduced from *What is English Teaching?* by Chris Davies (Open University Press, 1996), reproduced by permission of Chris Davies and The Open University Press; Figures 44.1 and 44.2 are taken from *The Future of English* by David Graddol (The British Council, 1997), reproduced by permission of David Graddol and The British Council; Figure 44.4 is taken from *Using English: Conversation to Canon* by Janet Maybin and Neil Mercer (Routledge/Open University Press, 1996), reproduced by permission of Janet Maybin and Neil Mercer.

Every effort has been made to contact copyright holders for their permission to reproduce material in this book. The publishers would be grateful to hear from any copyright holder who is not here acknowledged and will undertake to rectify any errors or omissions in future editions of this book.

INTRODUCTION

The world of education is constantly in the process of transformation. This represents a challenge to any attempt to review the field as a whole. In many senses this has always been the case. Educationalists in 1900 would have looked with some awe at the expanding educational systems of the industrialised world. In 2000, expansion continues apace. The twenty-first century is likely to be dominated by the proliferation of new structures and organisations providing formal and informal opportunities for teaching and learning in forms that would have been undreamt of a century ago.

In planning the *Routledge International Companion to Education* we have attempted to capture the stimulus, even excitement, that comes from new work around the key educational debates. We sought out authoritative authors who could provide a contemporary analysis of work in particular fields but could also look forward to where new inspiration and new insights might come from. We also wanted, within the inevitable limitations of language and geography, to ensure an international coverage of the themes we identified. Many of the chapters, therefore, look beyond national boundaries. And where we wanted to ensure a more global orientation, we have asked for more than one contributor to set out their ideas.

The volume is divided into five topic fields: Foundations, Processes, Substantive Issues, Sectors and Subjects. In Foundations, key concerns that relate to all educational endeavours are addressed, contemporary ideas about the nature of learning and the role of language are two examples. Processes refers to the means by which educational purposes are enacted; pedagogy and assessment are two of the topics reviewed in this section. We have chosen, in the third section, a number of Substantive Issues that attract debate and discussion in most, if not all, parts of the world. The challenge of environmental education, the interrelation of gender and education, and the role of parents exemplify the types of issues selected. The structure of education varies considerably from one system to another. We felt, however, that it was important to give voice to the discourse around the general phases of education, the pre-school, primary, secondary, and so forth. Finally, we review all the major subject areas that shape so much educational experience at all levels, formal and informal. The discussions within and between each of these five sections inevitably overlap. We see this as a strength in the volume and we have given particular attention to indexing that permits the reader to look across the book as a whole.

We envisage the volume will be valuable to a wide range of audiences. Students who sought an overview of their area of interest, policy-makers wanting an immediate access to state-of-the-art thinking around a topic of current concern, and academics working in education and related areas who seek an insight into the movement of ideas around their own or adjacent fields of study. A further audience is the growing number of parents and others in local communities with an active interest in education.

It is also our intention that the volume should provide inspiration to delve yet more deeply into the literature and the debates that underpin each chapter. Each author, therefore, has developed a select bibliography to encourage this process. The volume is an exploration of the field as a whole and a starting point for further enquiry.

Miriam Ben-Peretz, Haifa, Israel
Sally Brown, Stirling, Scotland
Bob Moon, Oxford, England

January 2000

Part I

FOUNDATIONS

1

PHILOSOPHY OF EDUCATION

Nicholas C. Burbules

ASKING THE QUESTION: 'WHAT IS PHILOSOPHY OF EDUCATION?'

An essay on the topic 'philosophy of education' might be expected to begin with a simple definition of the subject, followed by a delineation of its major branches of thought. Several writers have undertaken such a project in recent years (Chambliss, 1996; Ericson, 1992; Noddings, 1995; Phillips, 1994; Senchuk, 1995; Smeyers, 1994; Smeyers and Marshall, 1995). In reading these accounts, one finds that a central theme is the essentially contested status of what philosophy of education is (a point illustrated, much earlier on, in the collection *What Is Philosophy of Education?*, edited by Christopher Lucas in 1969). Indeed, proposing and arguing for competing conceptions of the field has been one of the reliable cottage industries for its scholars and an arena of debate over criteria for participation in the professional organisations, academic departments, and journals that take on the label (Burbules, 1991; Giarelli and Chambliss, 1991). The most striking characteristic of 'philosophy of education', then, has been that from the very first uses of the term the negotiation of what the field itself is has been one of its primary objects of preoccupation (see especially Maloney, 1985). Such debates have had a principled philosophical dimension, but have also had specific consequences for the inclusion and exclusion of potential participants.

For this reason, any new attempt to stipulate a definition of 'philosophy of education' – even one that attempts to be even-handed and comprehensive – is itself implicated within such contests of boundary maintenance. Encyclopedia entries tend to encourage such disputes, as in the competing entries on 'phenomenology' written by Husserl, and then Heidegger, for successive editions of the *Encyclopaedia Britannica*, through which they expressed their struggle over the meaning of that philosophy. Thus a very different way of sketching the meaning and scope of a field might be to recount its contests of boundary maintenance, highlighting them *as such* and not merely as philosophical disputes. Such debates in philosophy of education, which are ongoing to this day, have become a perennial feature of professional meetings, hiring decisions, and so forth – the institutionalised conditions of practice that give shape to a discipline, and an important reference point for speculations about where philosophy of education might be headed in the future.

An ironically inclined reader will be amused, I suspect, that only a philosopher would be so chronically self-questioning and obstinate as to resist even the simple question of what his field of study is. Yet, perhaps, at the level of enactment this *is* an explanation – or demonstration – of what the field is and of what philosophers of education try to do. Rather than taking the task of offering a definition for granted, one might question the possibility of defining the discipline and explore the implications of offering a definition when the consequence of doing so is to rule in or out work that different groups may believe is philosophically worthwhile. For a reader wanting a more literal definition, and not a performative one, I would recommend any of the excellent overviews of the field cited above.

The first difficulty in tracing the development of the term 'philosophy of education' is that throughout most of Western thought what might be regarded broadly as philosophical reflections on education were never seen as constituting a distinct discipline or branch of philosophy. On the one hand, for most of the great writers in the philosophy of education pantheon (such as Plato, Aristotle or Rousseau) such reflections were continuous with their accounts of epistemology, ethics, politics or human nature. It would never have occurred to them that a philosophy of education could be developed that was not, at heart, an elaboration of such 'purely' philosophical themes. (Though in some cases the ruminations of philosophers on education have had little or nothing to do with their actual philosophical positions and have merely expressed their own predilections.)

At the same time, and from what might be termed the opposite direction of the theory–practice dialectic, what today is called 'philosophy of education' has also long been regarded as continuous with the serious reflections of practising educators, curriculum theorists and educational policy-makers. Having a 'philosophy of education', in this sense of the term, is simply a phrase for the process in which educational practitioners or reformers develop thoughtful, and to varying degrees systematic or coherent, justifications for their educational practices and commitments (something with which, not surprisingly, few academic philosophers have had very much experience or direct concern).

Hence, while in the contemporary context a central tension within philosophy of education has been between its philosophical, disciplinary aspirations and its relevance to educational policy and practice, at earlier points in its development this dichotomy would not have been recognised, either from the perspective of the philosopher or from the perspective of the educationist.

These continuities are particularly striking when viewed in an international context, where philosophy of education has been a less professionalised and institutionalised endeavour (Phillips, 1994) and where, as a consequence, it has been less isolated from other educational concerns. In European thought, for example, education has consistently been considered in a broader context apart from schooling, and so a 'philosophy of education' has usually been regarded as continuous with concerns about child-rearing generally (Smeyers, 1994; Smeyers and Marshall, 1995). In many non-European traditions, issues of intellectual development are frequently not regarded as separate from matters of spiritual, moral or cultural development. Here, something that could be termed a 'philosophy of education' would need to be also a philosophy of faith or duty to some larger source of identity and identification.

The repeated use of quotation marks here is therefore necessary because in fact the phrase 'philosophy of education' rarely comes up in such contexts: in many European contexts, for example, the phrase 'pedagogical science' or 'theory' encompasses many of the same activities that philosophers of education take as their domain. This is revealing, first, in helping to introduce the question of what the very name 'philosophy of education' assumes about the nature of philosophy and its relation to educational concerns and, second, in leading us to ask where the phrase does come from, and why it has gained the meanings, particularly in English-speaking contexts, that it has.

This becomes a particularly delicate, even intractable, problem when attempting to offer an institutionalised perspective on a field, as in this chapter. In both contexts across nations and contexts across disciplines of practice, many people are involved in teaching and writing about issues that could be called, in the broadest sense, 'philosophies of education' (rather like 'philosophies of life', one might say). Yet only a portion of these are identified with the organisations, graduate programmes and journals that use this particular label and hence authorise what counts as official knowledge in this field. Should a proposed account of philosophy of education be drawn broadly enough to encompass all activities that might be identified as such, or narrowly in terms of a label that has professional and institutional authorisation? I have settled for the more narrow, institutionalised account, largely because it is a story that deserves to be considered for its own sake, but also because documentation is more easily available to substantiate it. As a result, I am dealing with philosophy of education within the context of a particular history of concepts and debates, which is a subset of all the possible activities that might be classified as part of it. Others would certainly offer a different criterion of demarcation.

CREATING A DISCIPLINE: THE FORMATION OF PHILOSOPHY OF EDUCATION

The origins of philosophy of education as a distinct discipline arrived with the nineteenth century in English-speaking countries, most notably the United States (Chambliss, 1996). First of all, they accompanied the spread of an Enlightenment faith in the reasoned formulation of public policy, the attempt to ground policy on a systematic, consistent foundation of purposes and justifications. At the same time, they accompanied a growing institutionalisation and professionalisation of the teaching endeavour itself, especially as it was expressed in the ideals of public education and the common school. In this context, a philosophy of education was intimately linked with the argument for a conception of personal betterment and social perfectibility that would serve on the one hand to initiate, guide and inspire practitioners, and, on the other hand, to justify this set of aims to a broader public that was being asked to support and fund educational programmes on an unprecedented scale. While still not described by the name 'philosophy of education', such formulations of purpose and justification can be seen as the first explicit attempts to develop a reasoned, general account of the meaning and aims of education. And what is most significant about this development is the assumption, difficult for us to recognise today as it has become so widely accepted, that it is either possible or desirable to provide such a general account.

Soon, having a philosophy of education was seen as an indispensable dimension of competent, responsible practice in education. Such a belief was centrally established on the uneasily with many members of JDS and, indeed, with Dewey himself (see Kaminsky, 1993, 1996; Giarelli and Chambliss, 1991).

Over time, these concerns were manifested in the formation of a new, separate organisation, the Philosophy of Education Society (PES), in 1941. In many respects, this event marks a crucial turn in the development of philosophy of education as a discipline (indeed, of its aspiration to regard itself as a distinct discipline). R. Bruce Raup and the other founders of PES were quite explicit about defining their organisation, in contrast with JDS, as a professional society and not an advocacy group (Burbules, 1991; Giarelli and Chambliss, 1991; Kaminsky, 1993, 1996). This insistence took the form of, first, a self-selected charter membership of initially 34 persons who explicitly distanced themselves from the policies and views of JDS; second, establishing strict criteria of membership, and levels of membership, that would ensure that 'professional' philosophers of education would always constitute a voting majority of the organisation; and, third, proclaiming that philosophical method was the disciplinary core that provided the field with its substance and credibility. It is important to see the fundamental interdependence of these three choices: of excluding activism and partisanship, of establishing strict 'professional' criteria of membership, and of proclaiming a disciplinary method as the principle uniting PES's members. Choices about intellectual method or the scope of a discipline need to be seen, in this context, as implicated in decisions about the inclusion and exclusion of people and their points of view. Soon after this, in 1954, a select PES committee sought to formalise philosophy of education as a discrete discipline, based on suitable philosophical methods (Maloney, 1985).

The formation of PES was followed, in Great Britain, by the formation of a similar society, the Philosophy of Education Society of Great Britain (1966), which was seen as heralding a 'revolution in philosophy of education', involving a 'greater consciousness of and involvement with the methods and results of philosophy as an academic discipline' (Dearden, 1982, p. 60). Partly because of the dominance of the influence of R. S. Peters and P. H. Hirst, and their analytic conception of philosophy of education, Kaminsky (1993, p. 191) calls PESGB during this period a 'profoundly conservative' organisation, characterised by a narrow preoccupation with that analytic approach to philosophical method. The force of this hegemony was so strong that a commentator such as Dearden (1982, pp. 66–67) could say, with no sense of self-contradiction, that 'I do not myself think that philosophy of education stands in need of a single paradigm', then follow this by saying that whatever it is, philosophy of education must be concerned with 'general concepts, principles, positions and practices'; that it should make 'necessary distinctions to clarify meaning', should 'explore conceptual possibilities', 'identify what is necessary and what is contingent', 'expose question-begging . . . and inconsistency', 'draw implications', 'reveal absurd consequences', 'test assumptions', 'probe the validity of justifications', and so forth – all activities which, whatever their merit, clearly express the orientations of a particular conception of philosophical method.

The prominence of R. S. Peters in Britain, his influence on contemporaries such as Hirst and Dearden, and his many students who carried forth his reputation and commitment to analytic philosophy, make him a pivotal figure in the philosophy of education. His argument that the term 'education' itself required analysis, and the results of his investigations – that the term refers to a process of 'initiation' into a form of life, and that to call something 'educational' is to valorise the means and ends of that process (as opposed to socialisation into norms that may be instrumentally beneficial but not of intrinsic value) – defined an agenda of questions, and a method of enquiry, that helped shape the approach of a generation of philosophers of education throughout the English-speaking world.

At the same time, during the 1960s and 1970s, the analytic approach gained predominance in the USA as well, especially through the influence of Israel Scheffler (although he was never active in PES). Scheffler, even more than Peters, focused on the justifiability of the means and ends of education from an epistemological point of view: Do the activities of teaching support the development of reason, both as a process of learning and as an educational aim itself? Where do relativism and activism in education threaten this ideal of rationality? How can the analysis of educational language detect the effects of slogans and ideologies of belief? In many respects, the faith in analytic methods in philosophy of education was stronger and more absolute in the USA than in Britain.

Hence, although it is often assumed that the influence of the analytic school ran from the British side of the Atlantic towards the USA, a good argument can be made that the main influences actually ran in the other direction (Beck, 1991). Either way, in both contexts analytic work in philosophy came to dominate the articles found in the respective journals sponsored by PES and PESGB. *Educational Theory*, originally established by JDS in 1951 but soon co-sponsored by PES as well, came to represent what Kaminsky (1993, p. 72) calls a 'thoroughly professional version' of philosophy of education. The *Proceedings* of the PES meetings during these years show a similar convergence around specific issues and styles of philosophical argumentation. (In 1995, the *Proceedings* became the edited yearbook of PES, *Philosophy of Education 19XX*. For PESGB, their *Proceedings* were retitled the *Journal of Philosophy of Education* in 1978, and opened to general submissions as well as selected conference papers.) At the height of this analytic period, as Kaminsky (1993, p. 89) tells it, 'At the 1971 meeting of the Philosophy of Education Society, [Jonas] Soltis declared that "we are all analytical philosophers", and no one laughed.'

In yet another English-speaking context, Australia and New Zealand, the Philosophy of Education Society of Australasia (PESA) was formed in 1970. *Educational Philosophy and Theory*, which was to become its sponsored journal, actually preceded the formation of PESA by one year. While the influence of analytic work was felt strongly in these countries as well (and one might argue [see Beck, 1991] that the influential work of C. D. Hardie brought analytic method to philosophy of education there long before its influence was much realised in either the USA or Great Britain), in both Australia and New Zealand there was from the very beginning a more sceptical attitude towards the dominance of analytic philosophy (expressed most directly, perhaps, in the work of Kevin Harris, Michael Matthews and Jim Walker) and, during the 1970s, a much wider acceptance of Left scholarship as legitimate terrain for philosophers of education, although this perspective was also seen increasingly in work presented at PES (which came to see itself increasingly as an international organisation, comprising not only scholars from the United States and Canada, but from around the world) and at PESGB.

DISCIPLINING THE DISCIPLINE: THE METHODS OF PHILOSOPHY OF EDUCATION

This account reveals a particular consequence of the professionalisation of philosophy of education, as it was expressed in the aspiration to ground itself on philosophical method. It meant, during the period being described here, a desire to establish standards of rigour and tough-mindedness that could help this emergent field attain academic credibility. The methods of philosophical analysis were ideally suited to a stance of clear-eyed scepticism in the face of educational claptrap; of reasoned, balanced objectivity in the face of highly contested educational disputes; and of providing a helpful, elucidative service that colleagues in education – whether in pedagogy, policy or research – could find amenable to their concerns. Without neglecting the philosophical arguments that were posed in favour of analytic method, to which I shall turn in a moment, there can be little doubt that these stances also suited the professional self-interest of a discipline seeking academic credibility as philosophically rigorous, in part through stronger affiliations with professional associations in philosophy (Macmillan, 1991). They also reinforced a position of nonpartisanship in the constantly shifting arena of competing educational fads and trends.

Analytic philosophy of education made substantial contributions in elucidating such concepts as 'authority', 'indoctrination', and even the terms 'teaching' and 'education' themselves. This method specialised in offering fine-grained distinctions and typologies; diagnosing hidden equivocations or blurriness in the ordinary concepts found within educational slogans or clichés; and criticising faulty logic or misleading uses of statistics or other evidence. In many cases, educators found such analyses salutary and helpful: this was philosophy in the service of plain speaking and no nonsense.

This analytic movement within philosophy of education followed (though lagging by several years) developments within Anglo-American philosophy: notably the movement of logical positivism (especially the work of A. J. Ayer) and various forms of linguistic philosophy (especially the work of Gilbert Ryle). But the arguments raised in favour of analytic methods had the widespread appeal that they did within philosophy of education, in large part, because of their congruence with other imperatives within the field as an increasingly professionalised discipline.

First, as Maloney points out, there is a certain ambivalence that has often accompanied philosophy of education: on the one hand seeking credibility in relation to the traditions of philosophy; on the other seeking legitimacy within the often-utilitarian climate of schools of education. This tension tends to pull philosophy of education in competing, incompatible directions and helps to account for what she calls (Maloney, 1985, p. 252) the relentless need to *explain* and *justify* the discipline – hence the perennial business of negotiating and renegotiating just what philosophy of education is. Analytic method seemed to hold promise as the indisputably philosophical core that would uncontroversially link the discourses of philosophy of education with mainstream philosophy. At the same time, its appeal to clarity and logic meant that philosophers of education would not have to endure the accusations of abstraction, obscurantism and irrelevance they often heard within schools of education – here, finally, was something *useful* that philosophers could offer policy-makers and practitioners.

Second, the rise of analytic method clearly severed the chains joining philosophy of education, especially in the USA, to the ghost of Dewey. While the polymorphous Dewey continued, and continues, to be read and reread in the light of shifting philosophical trends (so that topics such as 'Dewey and Marxism', 'Dewey and Karl Popper', 'Dewey and Feminism', 'Dewey and Foucault' and so on, remain a hardy staple of scholarship in the field), the analytic period established the independence of philosophy of education (and, in the USA and Canada, the Philosophy of Education Society) from progressivism (and the John Dewey Society). Once again, there were both professional and philosophical reasons for this split.

Third, the analytic movement in philosophy of education took a particular shape in opposition to the movement that had preceded it, the so-called 'isms' approach: the recounting of traditional philosophical positions (realism, idealism, pragmatism) – with varying degrees of philosophical depth and accuracy – then tracing their 'implications' for education. One of the central tenets of the analytic school, repeated often, was that there were no direct implications of substantive philosophical positions for education: that a person may believe in realism, for instance, but still favour any of a variety of educational aims and practices (Chambliss, 1996; Phillips, 1994). The attempt to provide encapsulated summaries of complex, difficult philosophical positions, and then to read off from them neat implications for practice, was regarded as being philosophically sloppy, first of all, and as over-promising what philosophy could provide to education. This debate and transition away from the 'isms' approach can be traced across a series of NSSE (National Society for the Study of Education) Yearbooks devoted to philosophy of education, published in 1942, 1955, 1972 and 1981. Yet, not incidentally, this rejection of the 'isms' approach and the attendant view that philosophies had implications for education, also put at one more remove the concerns of professional philosophy of education from those of practitioners. No longer would a required course for teachers, for example, promise to help students acquire or formulate their own 'philosophy of education' – instead, these courses promised to help them 'think philosophically' about their educational aims and practices, whatever they were. This transition to a philosophically grounded discipline reached its apotheosis in the subtitle of the 1981 NSSE Yearbook: 'Philosophy *and* Education' (emphasis added). Similarly, the journal *Studies in Philosophy and Education*, which ran from 1960–1976, then lay dormant until 1989, was acquired by a commercial publisher and resuscitated as a journal with an emphasis on 'clarity and excellence in philosophical argumentation' as its chief editorial criteria (Nelson, 1996, p. 474).

CHALLENGING THE DISCIPLINE: NEW PERSPECTIVES IN PHILOSOPHY OF EDUCATION

Yet this evolution had other, less intended, consequences. Over time, the desire to seek a grounding for philosophy of education in philosophy meant that more and more scholars, including students studying for graduate degrees in the field, went into philosophy departments or the relevant aisles in libraries and bookstores and started reading (or, in some cases, returning again to) works in existentialism, phenomenology, and other 'Continental' philosophies. It meant that many philosophers of education read or reread primary sources in philosophy (from the pre-Socratics to Nietzsche, Heidegger, de Beauvoir, or Wittgenstein) and looked increasingly outside Anglo-American philosophy to more international sources. They also turned to texts on the margins of what had been counted as 'philosophy' before: critical theory, feminism, and those (such as Foucault) who would later be termed 'post-modern' writers. Their scholarship made substantial contributions to understanding such topics as power and inequality in education, and the critique of cultural intolerance in both the tacit and the 'hidden' curricula. In many ways returning to the older vision of phil-osophy of education as necessarily implicated in issues of politics, critique and reform, these philosophers eschewed the methods of analysis but, even more profoundly, rejected its vision of philosophy of education as an exercise in rational or objective reconnaissance.

Hence, no sooner did it happen that Jonas Soltis offered his widely accepted characterisa-tion of philosophy of education in 1971 than, within a year, essays were already appearing with titles like 'Analytic philosophy of education at the crossroads' (Edel, 1972). Criticisms of analytic philosophy, some though not all from critical theory or feminist points of view, gained wider credibility during this decade. These criticisms included, chiefly, the question of *whose* concepts were being taken for granted; the criticism that the methods of analysis, ostensibly neutral and objective, in fact imported substantive value commitments; the argument that the view of language undergirding this method was culturally bounded and ahistorical; and the complaint that its focus on 'merely verbal' concerns often made its results trivial and irrelevant (Barrow, 1994; Ericson, 1992; Phillips, 1985, 1994. See also Maloney, 1985, pp. 245–250 and Noddings, 1995, pp. 41–57).

Even such sympathetic commentators as Barrow, Ericson and Phillips give some weight to these criticisms, though they differ in their assessments of analytic philosophy of educa-tion today. For Barrow (1994, p. 4444), these criticisms are mostly 'irrelevant' and the 'objections can be met'. For Phillips (1994, p. 4454), on the other hand, 'antisepsis tri-umphed' as 'analytic philosophy became more technical and more inward looking, directed at issues of interest to other philosophers of education to the neglect of issues of relevance to a broad range of educationists'. For Ericson (1992), the criticisms held weight, but a 'second generation' of analytic philosophy of education still survived. This second gener-ation of analytic philosophers, including many of these selfsame authors (as well as Robert Ennis and Harvey Siegel) made substantial contributions to understanding issues of critical thinking, the forms of knowledge, and philosophical problems in educational research, for example. What is unmistakable, however, is that by the end of the decade of the 1970s, no one could say any longer 'we are all analytical philosophers of education'.

The philosophical work in education from critical theory or neo-Marxist, feminist and post-modern perspectives, beginning during this period and expanding to the present day, brought not only a shift in philosophical perspectives and methods, but a more explicitly political commitment. The tone of speakers and writers changed. Issues of class, gender, race, and other dimensions of disadvantagement and exclusion became explicit topics of investigation and focal points of advocacy. As we shall see in a moment, these issues were raised, reflexively, as points of critique against the field of philosophy of education itself.

These shifts in philosophical outlook, in turn, shaped and were shaped by the articles published in the professional journals of the field, and in the papers presented at confer-ences. Such manifestations have a dual relation to the scope and content of a field: repre-senting the work with which people are actually engaged, yet also reflecting back to the field what literatures, topics and perspectives are of current interest or importance. To the extent that scholars, especially younger scholars, are influenced by what they read and by what they find is publishable, such shifting trends play an active part in encouraging and giving legitimacy to new styles of work. This is a role about which journal editors and conference organisers are usually quite aware, and lends a responsibility to them, and to their reviewers, that goes beyond simply filtering and selecting 'the best' from the work that is submitted to them. For at the same time, they are helping to define, either narrowly or broadly, the field that they are representing. The circular process by which a field becomes what it is thought to be, in the minds of its members – and this can either be a highly conservative and static or a highly experimental and fluid intellectual process – is exemplified practically in these activities of peer review and selection (just as they are also exemplified in the courses and degree requirements of graduate programmes that prepare students with the imprimatur of the field upon their degrees). For philosophy of education in the post-analytic period, the contents of leading journals and conference publications (such as those sponsored by PES, PESGB and PESA) became increasingly eclectic, interdisciplinary and iconoclastic towards traditional conceptions of 'the field'. That this partly was an indication of a changing state of affairs, and partly a cause of it, was quite apparent to those involved in making such selections.

Something else momentous was happening to philosophy of education during this period, I believe, represented by two related sets of changes. The first concerned the demographics of the field, especially during the 1970s and into the 1980s, as more and more women entered what had been virtually all-male organisations or, among those women who were already participants, as more shifted their interests away from analytic philosophy or other traditional topics towards women's status within education (this list must especially include Maxine Greene, Jane Roland Martin and Nel Noddings). The second was the rise of feminism as a perspective on philosophical and professional issues within philosophy of education (Leach, 1991). Feminists pointed out that the questions of who was part of certain philosophical debates, and what philosophical language those debates privileged, were interdependent issues. They argued that the forms of philosophical argumentation, in which rigorous, aggressive debate was assumed to be the best way of testing new propositions, had the effect of narrowing the range of perspectives available for discussion and actively intimidating or silencing those who did not debate their points in that manner. They argued that the methods of analytic philosophy, such as the tendency to isolate conceptual issues from actual contexts, gave an artificiality to philosophical discussions, notably in cases of ethics where, they believed, situated, interpersonal factors needed to be topics of philosophical consideration from the very start (Noddings, 1995).

In these and other ways they argued the interdependence of issues of *content* and issues of *representation*. Which philosophical issues were being discussed, how they were discussed, and which issues were never discussed directly influenced and were influenced by the fact of who was part of those conversations, and who was not. Initially, this concern spoke directly to the under-representation of women in the professional organisations and journals of the field; eventually, such concerns began to be extended to other under-represented groups as well – including, once again, the question of the relevance of philosophy of education to the concerns, needs and interests of teachers (most of whom, of course, are female). One concrete manifestation of this shift has been a resurgence of interest in moral education, literature and more relational views of personhood.

These changes – the increased eclecticism of philosophical sources seen as relevant to philosophy of education, and the increased awareness of the interdependence of issues of content and of representation – are fundamentally transforming the field today. Chambliss summarises the contemporary scene in this way:

> In the last decade of the twentieth century, philosophy of education scarcely resembles a discipline with a distinct purpose and a clearly established agenda. It is more accurately characterized as a field of study defined by the variety of its research and interpretive projects.
>
> (Chambliss, 1996, p. 472)

What is most interesting about this characterisation is the implication that philosophy of education ever was a 'discipline with a distinct purpose and a clearly established agenda'. As noted, the very idea of 'philosophy of education' as a distinct discipline is an artefact of a particular set of philosophical and institutional conditions, ones more typical of certain English-speaking contexts. Beyond this, the idea that this discipline ever had a unified purpose and agenda fits only certain brief periods of its development (notably, during the period of progressivism and the period of analytic dominance) – yet even these periods were characterised by a good deal of internal friction and resistance to such unifying trends, and were followed by periods of reaction that explicitly challenged the boundaries established to define what truly counted as philosophy of education and what did not (Greene, 1991, 1995; Kohli, 1995).

RETHINKING THE DISCIPLINE: THE FUTURES OF PHILOSOPHY OF EDUCATION

Today, this reflexive awareness of how such philosophical boundaries also have institutional effects, and how these boundaries of inclusion and exclusion, in turn, feed back on which philosophical issues and perspectives are or are not represented within what officially counts as 'philosophy of education', has ushered in a new period for the field. What Chambliss characterises as a diffuse focus, or lack of focus, can be characterised just as accurately as a period of experimentation and expansion in philosophy of education. Consider, for example, Phillips's alternative characterisation:

> The situation in the 1990s is complex, and relatively healthy – philosophers are working with a variety of approaches, in a variety of fields, and the discipline is marked by an eclecticism perhaps unrivaled in previous periods.
>
> (Phillips, 1994, p. 4456)

There are paired centripetal and centrifugal forces at work in the field today, matching philosophers of education who prefer to draw the boundaries of the field more narrowly, around a strict disciplinary view of philosophical method (and within this view of philosophy a primary focus on matters of logic, epistemology, philosophy of science and philosophy of mind), and those drawing the boundaries more broadly, blurring distinctions of philosophy and theory, and emphasising the interdisciplinary cross-fertilisation of philosophy with literary interpretation, political theory, women's studies and other fields. These debates, it should be emphasised, arise as much from different views about who is a philosopher of education, who belongs at professional meetings, or who should be published in sponsored journals, as they do from the relative merits of disciplinary and interdisciplinary perspectives on the field. Yet, as Chambliss's assessment also reveals, if there is no disciplinary core whatsoever, is there anything that *does* characterise and unify philosophy of education as a field today? I shall return to this question in a moment.

A related issue about such boundary-drawing is the effect of the professionalisation of philosophy of education upon the involvement of philosophically minded practitioners and their concerns. As noted, from the very beginnings of the Philosophy of Education Society, for example, structures were put in place that would limit the involvement and influence of those without academic credentials in philosophy. While one can say that philosophers of education should continue to focus on issues of educational practice (Feinberg, 1995), this position stands in tension with actual policies that discourage the participation of those who hold these concerns closest to heart (Giarelli and Chambliss, 1991; Tozer, 1991). In the case of PES, for example, this tension is expressed in the uncomfortable, and occasionally alienated, relation between the national organisation, which is the most philosophically sophisticated and professionally oriented, and which has the strongest representation in the major sponsored publications of the field, and the ten or so 'regional' branches of the Society, many of which have a much higher rate of participation by colleagues in other fields of educational scholarship and practice – many of whom rarely attend, or would even consider attending, the national meeting. Similar interactions undoubtedly arise in other national contexts as well.

As a result of these dynamics, philosophy of education is once again in a period of self-examination about its scope and mission. The lead article in a recent collection of essays chosen to survey the field (Kohli, 1995), written by Maxine Greene, is entitled 'What counts as philosophy of education?' The responses by Feinberg and Phillips show how far from a consensual answer the field remains today. Yet the title of that collection, *Critical Conversations in Philosophy of Education*, and its design as a series of constructive engagements around a set of educational concerns, gives a different and, I think, more hopeful characterisation of the field. For if disciplinary boundary-drawing is regarded with more suspicion today, and if any prospective philosophical criteria for what counts as 'philosophy of education' have come to be scrutinised partly in terms of which voices and perspectives they privilege and which they disadvantage or exclude, then the only alternative demarcations of the field must be more procedural and 'boot-strapped'. In this sense, philosophy of education today represents those engaged in ongoing conversations, in person or in print, about certain issues, in full awareness of their diversity and eclecticism of method, while retaining a degree of openness about who else might need to be drawn into those conversations. What counts as philosophy of education is simply what these collective processes of deliberation, paper reviewing and public discourse acknowledge and accept as pertinent to a set of shared concerns. At the same time, these processes tacitly invite or exclude different participants, and even set the standards of what it means to *be* involved. Hence adopting or changing these processes is a decision with immediate consequences for who is to be involved; and the converse is also the case. The identification of those concerns, the boundaries of the discipline, and the representation of participants in professional societies, graduate programmes and publications, are shifting, interdependent strands of what is the field, each changing in response to the others.

Such a perspective itself raises a new challenge to the field, however, which is how this dynamic of self-examination and redefinition can maintain a sense of continuity; how a discipline that is continually remaking itself can respect the cumulative gains of sustained lines of enquiry, without discarding substantial bodies of scholarship as simply the outmoded musings of philosophical paradigms that have been transcended or surpassed. Will contemporary philosophers of education read earlier academic work with respect and interest, for example? Or will each new generation of philosophers of education become amnesiac about their predecessors? Will the suspicion towards 'canonical texts' mean that reading lists and syllabuses are continually discarded with each passing fashion? Or will traditions of enquiry in such areas as ethics, democratic theory, what counts as 'knowledge', and so forth, continue as sustained conversations among diverse texts and perspectives, to which each is regarded as making a distinct contribution?

Finally, within this decentred characterisation of philosophy of education, what trends stand out for the future? Without stipulating what the changing boundaries of the field will look like (a process I have obviously, painstakingly resisted throughout this essay), are there good guesses that can be offered about the future of philosophy of education? One avenue, I have suggested, is to recognise how current topics of interest such as identity, difference, power, a suspicion towards 'metanarratives', and so on, have become not only issues for philosophical investigation, but leverage points for reflection and critique within the field of philosophy of education itself.

How difficult and sensitive this process has become can be seen in the dynamics surrounding the reception of Harvey Siegel's Presidential Address to a joint meeting of the Philosophy of Education Society and the Philosophy of Education Society of Australasia in 1995 – an interchange that perfectly crystallised some of the key issues at debate today, and an event that might come to be regarded, with hindsight, as a kind of watershed for the field. At heart an appeal to and argument for 'inclusion', Siegel's account was sharply criticised for assuming as criteria for whom should be included, factors that are in fact exclusionary (some of these comments came from the responses of Bailin, 1995 and Morgan, 1995; others came from the floor). Yet, of course, all criteria are exclusionary – or else they would not be criteria. For certain philosophers, such as Siegel, the question of standards of philosophical merit, and the matter of their social effects, are entirely separate issues – and a perspective excluded as being nonphilosophical, if it 'is' nonphilosophical, need not be of concern to an organisation devoted to establishing and maintaining standards of integrity and excellence within the discipline. If prospective participants lack these criteria, the goal should be to find ways to help people acquire them, not to question the criteria. In criticism of this view, it was argued that the persistent effects of such standards, in terms of the exclusion of people, groups and their perspectives, *must* be taken into account if a field is not to become increasingly hermetic and self-rationalising – to say nothing of the possible effects of personal or professional harm upon those persons and groups by excluding them. Where there are important cultural or historical reasons why prospective participants have not acquired the characteristics defined by particular institutions as criteria of participation, one must consider the nature of those criteria as one potential factor.

Hence, as the boundaries of philosophy of education are being stretched and blurred, considerations of their role in including and excluding participation are becoming a topic of explicit, reflexive concern. If all criteria exclude someone, then the question of which exclusions will be found livable, and which ones not, is an element in weighing their relevance and merit. In my view, this is not a matter of abandoning all philosophical criteria, or of focusing solely on the question of inclusion and exclusion, but of becoming more sensitive to the complex interaction between them, and judging each in terms of the other. To the extent that professional organisations, graduate programmes, and journals and other publications are the institutional embodiment of the field, their decisions along these lines have profound implications for the intellectual and moral qualities of what the field turns out to be. This is particularly true in assessing the consequences of particular philosophical methods and content for attracting the interest and participation of educators from the arenas of policy, research or practice.

The time has passed when the demographics of a field can be regarded as irrelevant to its diversity and vitality. Just as women, once and for all, made the question of who was, and who was not, part of disciplinary conversations a matter of professional *and* philosophical concern, the field of philosophy of education must stand today in awareness of its roots in a particular conception of 'philosophy of education' that emerged from predominantly English-speaking countries; and recognise that in certain contexts its participants are still predominantly male, and, even where more equally male and female, almost entirely white. The increased globalisation of academic work, brought about by relative ease and speed of travel; the growth of international organisations and conferences (such as INPE, the International Network of Philosophers of Education, formed in 1990); the increase in contact among a multicultural group of colleagues; and the widespread use of the Internet as a means of global communication and electronic publication of scholarship, all portend a time when diversity and difference will move centrally onto the agenda of issues of concern to educational philosophers – including, naturally, the question of who is being respected as such. As new partners enter the conversation, further questions of how, where, and under what terms that conversation is occurring will inevitably become objects of philosophical reflection. This shift is already taking place, and provides, I suggest, the best indicator of where the field called 'philosophy of education' is headed. What this label will be taken to delimit, and by what criteria, will be the determination of *that* shifting population, as it has been for many previous generations of participants in the field. The one lasting change may be that the question, 'What is philosophy of education?' will never again be asked in the expectation that a single, unified definition is either possible or desirable.

ACKNOWLEDGEMENTS

This essay benefited from the good counsel and informed criticisms of many readers, including Joyce Atkinson, Miriam Ben-Peretz, Walter Feinberg, James Giarelli, James Kaminsky, Mary Leach, Ralph Page, Harvey Siegel, Paul Smeyers and John White.

REFERENCES

Bailin, Sharon (1995) 'Inclusion and epistemology: The price is right'. In Alven Neiman (ed.), *Philosophy of Education 1995*. Champaign, IL: Philosophy of Education Society, 23–26.
Barrow, Robin (1994) 'Philosophy of education: Analytic tradition'. In T. Husen and T. Neville

Postlethwaite (eds), *The International Encyclopedia of Education*, 2nd edition. Oxford: Pergamon Press, 4442–4447.

Beck, Clive (1991) 'North American, British, and Australian philosophy of education from 1941–1991: Links, trends, prospects', *Educational Theory*, 41 (3), 257–263.

Burbules, Nicholas C. (1991). 'Continuity and diversity in philosophy of education', *Educational Theory*, 41 (3), 257–263.

Chambliss, J. J. (1996) 'History of philosophy of education'. In J. J. Chambliss (ed.), *Philosophy of Education: An Encyclopedia*. New York: Garland Publishing, 461–472.

Dearden, R. F. (1982) 'Philosophy of education, 1952–82', *British Journal of Educational Studies*, 30 (1), 57–71.

Edel, Abraham (1972) 'Analytic philosophy of education at the crossroads', *Educational Theory*, 22 (2), 131–152.

Ericson, David (1992) 'Philosophical issues in education'. In Marvin Alkin (ed.), *Encyclopedia of Educational Research*. New York: Macmillan, 1002–1007.

Feinberg, Walter (1995) 'The discourse of philosophy of education'. In Wendy Kohli (ed.), *Critical Conversations in Philosophy of Education*. New York: Routledge, 24–33.

Furner, Mary (1975) *Advocacy and Objectivity: A Crisis in the Professionalization of American Social Science, 1965–1905*. Lexington, Kentucky: University of Kentucky Press.

Giarelli, James M. and Chambliss, J. J. (1991) 'The foundations of professionalism: Fifty years of the Philosophy of Education Society in retrospect', *Educational Theory*, 41 (3), 265–274.

Greene, Maxine (1991) 'A response to Beck, Giarelli/Chambliss, Leach, Tozer, and Macmillan', *Educational Theory*, 41 (3), 257–263.

Greene, Maxine (1995) 'What counts as philosophy of education?' In Wendy Kohli (ed.), *Critical Conversations in Philosophy of Education*. New York: Routledge, 3–23.

Haskell, Thomas (1977) *The Emergence of Professional Social Science*. Urbana: University of Illinois Press.

Henry, Nelson B. (1942) *Philosophies of Education: 41st Yearbook of the National Society for the Study of Education, Pt. 1*. Chicago: University of Chicago Press.

Henry, Nelson B. (1955) *Modern Philosophies of Education: 54th Yearbook of the National Society for the Study of Education, Pt. 1*. Chicago: University of Chicago Press.

Kaminsky, James S. (1993) *A New History of Educational Philosophy*. Westport, CT: Greenwood Press.

Kaminsky, James S. (1996) 'Professional organizations in philosophy of education'. In J. J. Chambliss (ed.), *Philosophy of Education: An Encyclopedia*. New York: Garland Publishing, 475–481.

Kohli, Wendy (1995) 'Contextualizing the conversation'. In Wendy Kohli (ed.), *Critical Conversations in Philosophy of Education*. New York: Routledge, xiii–xvi.

Leach, Mary S. (1991) 'Mothers of in(ter)vention: Women's writing in philosophy of education', *Educational Theory*, 41 (3), 287–300.

Lucas, Christopher J. (1969) *What Is Philosophy of Education?* New York: Macmillan.

Macmillan, C. J. B. (1991) 'PES and the APA – An impressionistic history', *Educational Theory*, 41 (3), 275–286.

Maloney, Karen E. (1985) 'Philosophy of education: Definitions of the field, 1942–1982', *Educational Studies*, 16 (3), 235–258.

Morgan, Kathryn (1995) 'We've come to see the Wizard: Revelations of the Enlightenment epistemologist'. In Alven Neiman (ed.), *Philosophy of Education 1995*. Champaign, IL: Philosophy of Education Society, 27–35.

Nelson, Thomas W. (1996) 'Literature in philosophy of education'. In J. J. Chambliss (ed.), *Philosophy of Education: An Encyclopedia*. New York: Garland Publishing, 472–475.

Noddings, Nel (1995) *Philosophy of Education*, Boulder, CO: Westview Press.

Phillips, D. C. (1985) 'Philosophy of education'. In T. Husen and T. Neville Postlethwaite (eds), *The International Encyclopedia of Education*. Oxford: Pergamon Press, 3859–3877.

Phillips, D. C. (1994) 'Philosophy of education: Historical overview'. In T. Husen and T. Neville Postlethwaite (eds), *The International Encyclopedia of Education* (2nd edn). Oxford: Pergamon Press, 4447–4456.

Phillips, D. C. (1995) 'Counting down to the millennium'. In W. Kohli (ed.), *Critical Conversations in Philosophy of Education*. New York: Routledge, 34–42.

Senchuk, Dennis M. (1995) 'Philosophy of education'. In Robert Audi (ed.), *The Cambridge Dictionary of Philosophy*. New York: Cambridge University Press, 583–584.

Siegel, Harvey (1995) 'What price inclusion?' In Alven Neiman (ed.), *Philosophy of Education 1995*. Champaign, IL: Philosophy of Education Society, 1–22.

Smeyers, Paul (1994) 'Philosophy of education: Western European perspectives'. In T. Husen and T. Neville Postlethwaite (eds), *The International Encyclopedia of Education* (2nd edn). Oxford: Pergamon Press, 4456–4461.

Smeyers, Paul and Marshall, James D. (1995) 'The Wittgensteinian frame of reference and philosophy of education at the end of the twentieth century'. In Paul Smeyers and James D. Marshall (eds), *Philosophy and Education: Accepting Wittgenstein's Challenge*. Boston: Kluwer, 3–35.

Soltis, Jonas (1971) *Philosophy and Education: 80th Yearbook of the National Society for the Study of Education, Pt. 1*. Chicago: University of Chicago Press.

Thomas, Lawrence G. (1972) *Philosophical Redirection of Educational Research: 71st Yearbook of the National Society for the Study of Education, Pt. 1*. Chicago: University of Chicago Press.

Tozer, Steven (1991) 'PES and school reform', *Educational Theory*, 41 (3), 301–310.

2

EXPLORING THEORY AND PRACTICE IN MORAL EDUCATION

David Carr

ETHICS AND MORAL DEVELOPMENT

Human interest in moral education probably has its source in a general concern with inducting the young into socially acceptable forms of conduct, which is as old as recorded history. But, of course, whilst any such process is ostensibly a practical matter, the smallest reflection upon it must give rise to awkward theoretical questions. How, for example, do we determine the extent of what is socially acceptable; must all agree, must most agree, must none disagree? Moreover, if all do not agree, what room is there for legitimate dissent from the majority view? More seriously, might not reflective dissent open the possibility that social consensus or obedience to custom does not necessarily determine what is right in some deeper moral sense? Indeed, it was arguably the greatest insight of the Greek philosopher Socrates – the effective founder of Western ethics – to have held against the pre-Socratic Sophists that a good human life is a matter neither of conformity to convention nor the pursuit of self-interest, but of obedience to a knowledge of the right or the good accessible only to the operations of reason. At all events, Socrates was probably the first to observe a clear distinction between what is socially acceptable and what is morally right which, whilst frequently blurred in subsequent thought, is nevertheless of the highest importance for clear thinking about moral education.

However, it is perhaps the question of the precise role of reason in moral life and education which most divides Socrates' ethical successors – not least his immediate heirs Plato and Aristotle, for both of whom issues of moral education are of profound social and political importance. Effectively, Plato presses the Socratic identification of virtue with knowledge into the service of a highly paternalist and counter-democratic conception of justice and civil order which prescribes a moral training in the observance of myth and custom for the unenlightened masses, reserving intellectual initiation in the abstract complexities of moral reason for a governing meritocratic elite of potential legislators and administrators. For Aristotle, on the other hand, since moral reason is a matter of practical and experiential rather than theoretical or abstract deliberation, it is implicated in the development of a range of sensibilities and qualities of character which are well within the reach of any rational agent; indeed, for him, such development is a *sine qua non* of responsible citizenship in the admittedly limited form of democratic order which he not unreservedly appears to endorse. Both Plato and Aristotle had much to say about the practical mechanics of moral education – construed as a curious mixture of dialectic and gymnastics by the former and something more akin to skill acquisition by the latter. Roughly, thought on these and other matters was dominated in the early middle ages by Plato and in the later – so-called Scholastic – medieval period by Aristotle.

With the advent of modernity – marked philosophically by the emergence of the new scientifically informed epistemology of Descartes – old ethical concerns take on a somewhat different complexion and new views of moral reason and education emerge in response to them. Almost certainly the greatest problem engendered by post-Cartesian faith in scientific method is the effective displacement of tradition – especially revealed religion – as the ultimate source of authority concerning right conduct. Perhaps the most conspicuous response to these new doubts about the rational basis of moral life is a curious reworking of ancient sophistical ideas – of self-interest as the only potent source of human motivation and obedience to social convention as the only source of civil order – into the view that morality and civil society are essentially matters of obedience to contract grounded in rational self-interest. Thus, for Hobbes, the founding father of contract theory, entry into morality and civil society is a matter of rational abdication of a basic human right to pursue interests that may trespass upon the security of others, in exchange for protection against similar trespasses against oneself; morality and civil order amount essentially to a loss of freedom – as the price for security.

It took the genius of Jean-Jacques Rousseau to conceive a version of contract theory which questioned Hobbes's arguably pessimistic and negative conception of human nature and moral motivation. Rousseau's influence upon subsequent moral and other educational thought is, moreover – like Plato's – inestimable. First, most obviously, as the recognised founding father of educational progressivism, Rousseau is the ultimate intellectual source of those modern ideas about education for democracy and schools as democratic self-governing communities discernible in the work of Homer Lane, A. S. Neill and others. Second, the highly influential contemporary work on cognitive moral development of Lawrence Kohlberg, considered shortly, would have been unthinkable bar the colossal debt of his mentor Piaget to Kant – and, in turn, Kant's acknowledged intellectual debt to Rousseau. Briefly, Rousseau's most significant contribution to the theory of moral education is a constructivist account of moral and social development grounded in the idea of autonomous self-legislation. Against Hobbes, who held that freedom is self-interested anarchy, and that moral observance – to the extent that it consists in submission to the rules of civil society – is bondage, Rousseau argued, via a rejection of Hobbes's asocial view of human motivation, that real self-interest is rooted in a free and enabling rational concern for the common good; moral conduct is essentially enlightened autonomous observance of a universal moral law accessible to any reason untainted by traditional prejudices. For this reason, Rousseau notoriously advocated a radically non-interventionist education designed to shield the young from the corruption of such prejudices.

One more issue to be noticed in this thumbnail sketch of pre-modern and early modern debates about moral formation arises from a major challenge – posed by the great empiricist philosopher David Hume – to the very idea that morality is a rational affair. Hume's radical empiricism – expressed centrally in the idea that reason is limited exclusively to the passive registering of facts and definitions – led him to deny not only the meaningfulness of evaluative discourse but also any effective role to the intellect in human agency; 'reason is and ought only to be', he maintained, 'the slave of the passions'. By arguing that familiar discourse of the good and the bad has no descriptive role, is merely expressive of our tastes and preferences and that only the desires inherent in such preferences can be effective in agency, then, Hume set the stage for later influential non-cognitive theories of ethics. And whilst there is dispute as to whether Hume should be regarded as thoroughly endorsing the moral subjectivism of his non-cognitivist heirs – since he also appears to have held that moral discourse serves an important social function in reinforcing those benign human sentiments which are objectively conducive to positive human association – he is the main source of those distinctions between *fact* and *value* and *is* and *ought* often held hostage to the fortunes of moral subjectivism.

It required nothing less than the enormous resources of Immanuel Kant's labyrinthine *Critique of Pure Reason* and *Critique of Practical Reason* to reply adequately to Hume's devastating critique of the very idea of moral reason. Although it is difficult to put Kant's complex ideas in a nutshell, his response to Hume's challenge was essentially to pioneer a pragmatics of discourse which brilliantly anticipates the work of much later 'use theorists' of meaning. In his first great Critique, Kant happily concedes to Hume and empiricism in general that the deliverances of sense experience set the bounds of what may be intelligibly thought and said about the world – though for Kant reason plays a significantly active role in structuring that experience. He is therefore bound also to agree that moral judgements lie beyond the bounds of theoretical or descriptive sense. But such judgements may still be considered rational in virtue of their distinctive prescriptive or action-guiding role in human practical affairs. Moreover, just as moral reasons are not a bogus kind of theoretical reason, so they are not merely expressions of natural impulses – for the sense of what we ought morally to do more often than not conflicts with natural inclinations. In view of this, Kant distinguishes moral or 'categorical' imperatives from other practical imperatives as grounded in a sense of duty focused on ideas of reciprocity and respect for persons – an explicit elaboration of that idea of a universal moral law prefigured in the work of his chief intellectual inspiration Rousseau. Indeed, contrary to Hume's view that practical agency is slavery to the passions, Kant follows Rousseau in arguing that true human freedom is only possible via development of a capacity for autonomous conduct which fundamentally con-sists in obedience to the moral law; and this idea – as we shall see – has had unparalleled influence upon modern theorising about moral education.

MORALITY, EDUCATION AND SOCIETY: SOCIOLOGICAL PERSPECTIVES

As just seen, past philosophers such as Plato, Aristotle and Rousseau explicitly acknow-ledged the crucial role of education – conceived in broadly moral terms as a matter of influencing for the good the values of the young – in accommodating individuals to some actual or ideal social or political order. From a modern perspective it might be said that if this is a legitimate function of education in general and moral education in particular, we might stand to learn much about it from the theoretical and empirical enquiries of modern social scientists – and, despite the obvious conceptual dangers of assuming any possibility of recourse here to 'empirical' social data entirely innocent of ethical or evaluative presuppositions, it is true that social theory more or less informed by philosophy has greatly influenced modern thinking about moral education.

Modern social sciences are mainly offshoots of a more generalised body of nineteenth-century enquiry into economic and other relations between individual, society and state known as political economy. In the broadest terms, of course, there are two main approaches to understanding human identity with respect to questions of spiritual, cultural and material flourishing: one can regard human identity as an essentially individual affair, and society as no more than some atomic assembly of otherwise separate individuals; or one can regard society and culture as in some sense prior to any conception of human individuality. The first approach, taken to extremes by Hobbes, is deeply entrenched in the empiricist tradition and was to reach its zenith in the work of economists such as David Riccardo and Adam Smith and in the philosophy of utility. At all events, the basic idea that human prosperity consists in individual self-development – which is apt to be fostered by liberty and free enterprise and impeded by overmuch state governmental regulation of individual affairs – informs the theory of liberalism and (less obviously) the utilitarian 'greatest happiness principle' which were to receive their clearest statements in the work of John Stuart Mill. And whilst utilitarianism is a strongly contested moral theory – though still vigorously defended in some quarters of analytical ethics – one form or another of liberalism has dominated twentieth-century social, political and economic theory. However, to the extent that the ethics of utility is difficult to square with any extreme form of liberal individualism, it has been more usual for contemporary liberals such as John Rawls to ground liberal ethics in some or other contractarian form of Kantian-derived deontology rather than in utilitarianism. Again, moreover, although few liberal philosophers have written directly on moral education, their impact on this field – particularly on work concerning education in tolerance and respect for alternative views – has been enormous.

The other approach to understanding the relationship of social unit to society, however, conceives it less in terms of external political or economic constraints on individual rights and liberties – indeed, it maintains that without reference to processes of socio-cultural formation, little sense may be made of human personal individuality or freedom – and more in terms of pre-contractual common bonds of human attachment and co-operation by which biologically separate individuals acquire common goals and purposes. Some such conception is already at work in the social theories of Aristotle and Rousseau, but it is developed in often extremely corporativist forms by idealist – particularly Hegelian – heirs to the rationalist side of Kant's metaphysics. Clearly, for example, the social theory of Karl Marx and his followers – in its explicit repudiation of the asocial philosophy of mind of classical empiricism – stands squarely in this tradition. However, in endorsing a class-conflict conception of social evolution – influenced by Hegelian dialectic – and a pessimistic Rousseauesque view of the adverse effects of social conditioning, Marx and his followers view formal education as little more than an instrument of class oppression or indoctrination and their views have not greatly contributed to positive theories of education or moral education.

We need rather to turn to the mainstream sociological offshoot of political economy for substantial development regarding the theory of moral education as such. Here, in contrast with the 'conflict' theories of (perhaps) Marx and others, so-called 'consensus' theorists and structural functionalists have been more inclined to emphasise the positive role of education in value transmission and its powerful potential for social cohesion. From the present perspective, moreover, there can be no doubt that the most important figure in this broad tradition is Émile Durkheim whose work *Moral Education* has had enormous influence – particularly with regard to the pervasive modern problem of establishing a basis of common moral values in circumstances of the secular erosion of traditional, religiously based belief systems. Briefly, Durkheim took the view that moral norms are at heart a species of social rule and argued, notoriously, that in any modern secular moral system 'Society' should occupy roughly the role played by 'God' in traditional moralities. Effectively, Durkheim worked out a detailed, though not unproblematic, view of the nuts and bolts of moral education – as involving the promotion of discipline, social attachment and autonomy – on the basis of a sociological reconstruction of Kantian deontology.

Though neither social scientist, nor someone who wrote directly on moral development as such, it may nevertheless be appropriate to mention John Dewey in this section as a thinker whose work has a strongly social-theoretical flavour, and has also been highly influential on the moral educational theory and practice of others – particularly in North America. Arguably, given its persistent emphasis on the promotion of capacities for democratic association as the pre-eminent aim of education, Dewey's work constitutes little more than an extended, albeit implicit, treatise on the overriding importance of moral education for individual and social human flourishing. True to the spirit of the holistic pragmatic instrumentalism he pioneered, however, Dewey would not appear to have regarded moral education as a distinct curricular component to be conceived separately from other aspects of human civic, social and educational development. All the same, whilst one might readily endorse this general holistic position, there is also considerable room for dissent from the particular instrumentalist form it assumes in the work of Dewey and his widespread modern following.

PSYCHOLOGY – AND THEORY INTO PRACTICE

However, though many ancient and modern philosophers and social theorists have had much of interest to say about the practical mechanics of moral education, it is hardly surprising that protracted attention to the actual dynamics of moral association had, by and large (and for better or worse), to await latter-day attempts to develop psychology as a form of empirical scientific enquiry. In this regard, moreover, Freud's initial trail-blazing work on the psychopathology of deviance and personality disorder might well have been expected to exercise considerable influence on thinking about moral formation. In the event, however, any such impact has been slight and confined almost exclusively to the work on the rehabilitation of problem children of such interesting pioneers of educational progressivism as Homer Lane and A. S. Neill.

Moreover, with regard to implications for the theory and practice of moral education, matters hardly fared better with the extensive behaviourist programme which dominated scientific psychology for at least the first half of the present century. Despite its influence on educational innovators as diverse as John Dewey and Bertrand Russell, not to mention its undoubted impact on mainstream pedagogical developments, theories of behavioural conditioning have not generally appeared compelling from the perspective of understanding moral life and education. The reasons for this, moreover, are much the same in the case of behaviourism as in that of depth psychology – that such theories deal, by and large, with the external or pathological causes of desirable or undesirable human behaviour and are therefore disinclined or unable to account for those characteristics of voluntary and rational agency which, as all major traditional philosophers have argued, are virtually ineliminable from any plausible story about moral life. By the same token, the practical attempts of behavioural engineers to construct moral rescheduling programmes for those considered deviant from a range of evaluative perspectives, have readily attracted censure on grounds that they are morally coercive and manipulative; for, who can say – especially with regard to 'deviant' behaviour which is not obviously harmful to others – that one person's moral correction is anything more than another's social control?

At all events, the most influential psychological theory of moral education and growth of modern times is without doubt that developed in the context of cognitive psychology – a movement itself partly definable as a reaction to behaviourism – by Jean Piaget, Lawrence Kohlberg and their numerous followers. The early exploration of ideas of moral education and reasoning of Piaget, of course, was part and parcel of a larger enquiry into the development of principled deliberation as such, and it follows that general pattern. Proceeding in tune with a psychological reconstruction of Kantian epistemology, Piaget argues, in a manner reaching back even further to Rousseau's idea that 'childhood has its own ways of seeing, thinking and feeling'; that intellectual development in general is essentially a matter of progress through a number of qualitatively distinct, age-related stages of cognitive processing, proceeding roughly from a focus on the more concrete and particular aspects of experience to the more abstract and general. In the case of moral development, this comes down to progress from a state of solipsistic egocentricity, via a stage of heteronomous observance of externally imposed rules, to a capacity for Kantian practical moral decision-making in the light of autonomous rational principles. Crucially, moreover, Piaget claimed that these stages were identified on the basis of actual empirical observation of the different modes of reasoning of children of different ages.

Piaget's initial explorations of moral understanding, whilst no doubt suggestive, clearly cried out for rather more precise detailing of the fine grain of moral stage transitions and this was not long forthcoming at the hands of the late American cognitive psychologist Lawrence Kohlberg and the generations of students who followed in his wake. Kohlberg began by elaborating Piaget's two or three basic stages into a more complex taxonomy of six stages divided into three levels. The overall drift of development, however, is much the same as in Piaget: progress from relatively egocentric, 'pre-moral' modes of response, through various styles of conformity to convention, to moral reasoning of a more independent and principled sort. In fact the moral developmental ideal for Kohlberg, as for Piaget, is the attainment of a capacity for autonomous moral decision-making of a psychologised, Kantian kind which strongly resembles the moral prescriptivism developed by liberal Oxford philosophers in the immediate postwar period; on this view, moral maturity consists in an ability to self-legislate for consistent moral commitment on the basis of universalisations regarding what is or is not acceptable human conduct. However, though Kohlberg also devised an ingenious diagnostic cum pedagogical programme – focused on the discernment and resolution of specific 'moral dilemmas' – for identifying moral stages and assisting progress from one stage to another, his research also convinced him that few individuals ever progress beyond the lower heteronomous stages of moral understanding to the higher stages of principled autonomous reasoning.

Perhaps the greatest edge of Kohlberg's account – which has exercised enormous influence on the theory and practice of moral education for something like three decades – is that it purports to reconcile two ostensibly inconsistent moral intuitions: first, the idea that moral judgements may be principled, objective and rationally grounded; second, the idea – apparently supported by evidence of cultural pluralism – that there may be principled and apparently irresolvable disagreement between different moral views. The reconciliation is sought in the claim that although moral judgements may indeed vary in content, opposed or inconsistent judgements may nevertheless be considered objective to the extent that they are based on invariant principles of rational deliberation. Moreover, whatever the plausibility of this story, it seems to give the theory a certain advantage over its two main postwar rivals in the theory and practice of moral education. On the one hand, then, the influential Values Clarification movement developed in the 1960s and 1970s by such American theorists as Raths and Kirschenbaum emphasises the individual commitment aspect of evaluative life, and the importance of avoiding indoctrination, at the price of a personal exploration view of values education which many have considered dangerously subjective or relativistic. But, on the other, the Character Education movement, which has more recently been gaining ground in the United States, has sometimes been regarded as erring more on the side of an intolerant and coercive objectivity – especially in so far as cruder versions have been associated with the more reactionary profiles of right-wing politics and fundamentalist religion. However, there are more or less balanced versions of this rather broad movement, and – as we shall see – it is likely that a very reputable ancient view to the effect that moral education is at heart a matter of character development represents the most serious contemporary rival to Kohlbergianism.

All the same, Kohlberg's theory attracted criticism from the very outset – and Kohlberg and his followers have been perennially faced with the problem of answering such criticisms with only doubtfully consistent amendments of the theory. For example, it is a fair complaint against the individualist prescriptivism at the core of Kohlberg's account that it dangerously fails to do justice to the important social and interpersonal dimensions of moral life; it was in response to such criticism, therefore, that Kohlberg supplemented his account with developments focused upon the idea of a *community of justice*, doubtless influenced by a blend of Deweyan and contractarian ideas – though it is by no means clear that the prescriptivism sits easily with the contractualism. Again, although Kohlberg readily derided what he called the 'bag of virtues' approach to moral development advocated by proponents of character education, he was himself forced to acknowledge the importance of certain 'executive virtues' in order to account for the problem of weakness of will to which his basic theory is vulnerable – though it is again unlikely that any such supplement plugs the gap effectively. More recently, however, feminist and other theorists of 'care' such as Carol Gilligan and Nel Noddings have clearly highlighted the extent to which Kohlberg's theory marginalises the important affective sources of moral motivation. Although Kohlbergians have sought a way round this problem, any such solution seems highly unlikely in the terms of a neo-Kantian ethics of personal commitment which explicitly denies moral significance to non-cognitive states and dispositions.

Failing any satisfactory resolution of these potentially mortal theoretical and practical problems, it is not clear that the ambitious Kohlbergian programme is any longer sustainable; in which case the pressing question is that of whether any coherent alternative position may be available. Moreover, I believe that any such position would need to be one that basically questions each and every ingredient in the particular blend of liberal assumptions (Kantian, deontological, prescriptivist, contractualist and so on) lying at the heart of Kohlberg's theory, and the best candidate here is liable to be some moral-educational analogue of the neo-Aristotelian 'virtue-theoretical' critique of liberal ethics mounted by 'post-analytical' and communitarian social and moral philosophers such as Alasdair MacIntyre, Charles Taylor and Martha Nussbaum over the last couple of decades. A potential gain of any such line of enquiry might be that the traditional focus from Aristotle onwards on the ethical centrality of virtues as qualities of moral character is a source of powerful psychological insight into precisely those problems of moral motivation and affectivity with which Kohlbergians seem unable to deal. Moreover, though the spectres of both vicious ethical relativism and an intolerant moral conservatism have been observed to lurk behind a 'rival traditions' account of virtue such as MacIntyre's, the development of a basically Aristotelian 'culturally internalist' model of practical deliberation which is both critically self-reflexive yet tolerant of other moral perspectives cannot be ruled out. However, although there have been significant recent attempts to construe moral education in virtue-theoretical terms, such attempts are as yet in their infancy and it is probably much too early to weigh the prospects of their success.

A word should also be said, in this woefully inadequate thumbnail sketch of the practical end of thinking about moral education, about the place of moral education in the school curriculum. Two main views about how moral values are to be promoted to children would seem to be: first, that they are best explicitly taught or 'caught' from the ethos of the school or the so-called 'hidden curriculum'; second, that they might be a specific object of curricular attention – which, of course, may mean direct exploration of morally focused curriculum materials explicitly designed for the purpose. However, though it is likely that most educationalists generally would regard moral education as a matter of balanced interplay between explicit instruction, open critical discussion of moral issues and more covert positive influence, whereas character educationalists and virtue theorists emphasise the importance – at least for basic moral grounding – of the former, Kohlbergians and value clarificationists would be more inclined to see open critical questioning as the focal point for true moral development. It is for this reason that character educationalists have often laid most professional emphasis on the importance of 'good' teacher example – on the part of *all* teachers – for moral education, whereas Kohlbergians and other liberals have sometimes stressed the need for 'neutral' teachers who have specialist skills for the promotion of moral questioning on the part of pupils. With regard to this last enterprise, the development of explicit curriculum materials designed to assist the progress of moral cognitive strategies has been something of a major modern industry; these developments, mostly predicated upon the questionable Kohlbergian assumption that moral growth is centrally concerned with dilemma resolution, are far too extensive to detail here – but the UK work of Peter McPhail and colleagues provides a not unrepresentative sample.

The significance for the promotion of enquiry into moral education of various contemporary professional associations and organisations should also not go unnoticed in this brief review. Thus, though much moral educational theorising and practice in North America had its origins in psychological theory, it has mostly in the UK occurred within the province of educational philosophy, and the *Journal of Philosophy of Education* founded by R. S. Peters – himself a prolific and influential writer on moral education who sought to develop a liberal educational position not at all unsympathetic to Kohlberg's – has been over the years one of the leading educational philosophical outlets for original thinking in the field. Again, John Wilson, another British advocate of a very comprehensively developed philosophical view of moral education of a broadly liberal turn has been associated since its origins with the UK *Journal of Moral Education*, which is perhaps the leading international multidisciplinary outlet for contemporary ideas concerning moral and values education. In turn, the *Journal of Moral Education* has enjoyed a close and fruitful association with the North American *Association for Moral Education*, now into its third decade of annual conferences in the United States and Canada, and which – whilst still something of a Kohlbergian bastion – has nevertheless for many years been highly hospitable to the broadest possible range of moral-educational views.

SELECT BIBLIOGRAPHY

Aristotle (1925) *The Nicomachean Ethics*, Oxford: Oxford University Press.

Carr, D. (1996) 'After Kohlberg: Some implications of an ethics of virtue for the theory of moral education and development', *Studies in Philosophy and Education*, vol. 15.

Carr, D. and Steutel, J. (1999) *Virtue Ethics and Moral Education*, London: Routledge.

Dewey, J. (1961) *Democracy and Education*. New York: Macmillan.

Durkheim, E. (1961) *Moral Education: A Study in the Theory and Application of the Sociology of Education*, New York: Collier-Macmillan.

Gilligan, C. (1982) *In a Different Voice: Psychological Theory and Women's Development*, Cambridge, MA: Harvard University Press.

Halstead, J. M. and McLaughlin, T. H. (eds) (1999) *Education in Morality*, London: Routledge.

Hirst, P. H. (1974) *Moral Education in a Secular Society*, London: London University Press.

Kant, I. (1948) *Groundwork of the Metaphysic of Morals*, trans. by H. J. Paton under the title of *The Moral Law*, London: Hutchinson.

Kirschenbaum, H. (1977) *Advanced Values Clarification*, La Jolla, CA: University Associates.

Kohlberg, L. (1981) *Essays on Moral Development: Volumes I–III*, New York: Harper Row.

Lickona, T. (1996) 'Eleven principles of effective character education', *Journal of Moral Education*, 25 (1).

MacIntyre, A. C. (1991) *How to Appear Virtuous without Actually Being So*, University of Lancaster: Centre for the Study of Cultural Values.

Mill, J. S. (1970) *On Liberty*, in M. Warnock (ed.), *Utilitarianism*, London: Fontana.

Noddings, N. (1984) *Caring: A Feminist Approach to Ethics*, Berkeley, CA: University of California Press.

Peters, R. S. (1981) *Moral Development and Moral Education*, London: George Allen & Unwin.

Piaget, J. (1932) *The Moral Judgement of the Child*, New York: Free Press.

Plato (1961) *Meno, Gorgias, Protagoras and Republic* in E. Hamilton and H. Cairns (eds) *Plato: The Collected Dialogues*, Princeton, NJ: Princeton University Press.

Rawls, J. (1985) *A Theory of Justice*, Cambridge, MA: Harvard University Press.

Rousseau, J. J. (1974) *Emile*, London: Dent.

Simon, S. and Olds, S. (1976) *Helping Your Child Learn Right from Wrong: A Guide to Values Clarification*, New York: Simon & Schuster.

Spiecker, B. and Straughan, R. (eds) (1988) *Philosophical Issues in Moral Education*, Milton Keynes and Philadelphia: Open Court Press.

Straughan, R. (1982) *Can We Teach Children to Be Good?*, London: Allen & Unwin.

Taylor, M. (ed.) (1975) *Progress and Problems in Moral Education*, Slough, Berks: NFER Publishing Co.

Wilson, J. (1990) *A New Introduction to Moral Education*, London: Cassell.

Wright, D. (1971) *The Psychology of Moral Development*, Harmondsworth: Penguin.

3

THEORIES OF COGNITIVE DEVELOPMENT AND LEARNING AND THEIR IMPLICATIONS FOR CURRICULUM DEVELOPMENT AND TEACHING

Sidney Strauss

The focus of this chapter is on one aspect of developmental psychology: cognitive development. So as to put the chapter into a framework, a few words about the state of contemporary psychology and child development are in order.

CONTEMPORARY PSYCHOLOGY

Human beings are too complex to understand and research in their entirety. For sake of convenience, we divide humans into parts that seem reasonable to us today. These parts are the domains we study in contemporary psychology. Table 3.1 presents a view of what those domains are, the theories we have constructed to describe those parts, and the major theoreticians who have developed those theories.

Contemporary psychology is undergoing rapid and far-reaching changes. There were periods when little change was the order of the day, e.g. behaviourism held sway in Anglo-American psychology for the first 50 years of this century. A major reason for the deep changes in contemporary developmental psychology is the cognitive revolution that began in the mid-1950s. Areas now under the modern rubric of 'cognitive psychology' were once a bastion of psychology. Learning, memory, sensory processes and other subdomains were the hard science research parts of psychology. Today, these subdomains are being studied in departments of cognitive sciences, which include the wet mind (brain sciences), philosophy, linguistics, mathematics, computer sciences (especially artificial intelligence) among others.

Another several decades of this trend might end up with psychology departments devoid of this area or psychology departments may combine with others, keeping the title cognitive psychology in the psychology departments. An example of the former comes from MIT whose psychology department, which was almost exclusively in the cognitive sciences, disbanded and became integrated into a new department of cognitive and brain sciences.

Although prophecy is fraught with problems, I believe that the future of psychology will see this parting of the ways continue, where cognitive psychology will become part of other departments and the remainder of psychology will have more of a helping professions flavour to it.

DEVELOPMENTAL PSYCHOLOGY

Table 3.1 was prepared with an eye towards developmental psychology's place in the larger scheme of psychology. Notice that in Table 3.1, the developmental part is above the others. This is because development is not content-free. Something develops. There is physiological development, personality development, cognitive development, etc.

The changes in psychology, described above, are being felt in developmental psychology and are leading to a split in the ranks. The result is two major variants of developmental psychology.

One variant is based on a positivist, laboratory experimental approach to cognition, where

Table 3.1 Subdomains of psychology

Schools of thought	*Areas of development*						
	Psychological	*Social*	*Cognitive*	*Personality*	*Moral*	*Motivational*	*Emotional*
Nativism			Chomsky Fodor				
Behaviourism		Bandura Mischel	Skinner Estes	Miller	Berlyne		Skinner
Structuralism		Damon	Piaget Werner	Mehrebian	Kohlberg Turiel		Greenspan
Information processing			Klahr Siegler				
Socio–historical			Vygotsky Cole Wertsch				
Neo–Piagetian			Case Fischer Halford				
Non–universal			Feldman				
Naive theories			Carey Gelman Keil Wellman				
Representational redescription			Karmiloff–Smith				

the search is for cognitive universals. One recent lead in this realm is taken by adherents of information-processing theories (Elman *et al.*, 1996). Here there is an attempt to describe cognitive development in terms of connectionist models of psychology and brain functioning.

The second variant is a cultural psychology that bears witness to the influences of Vygotsky's socio-historical approach on our understanding of development (Shore, 1996; Stigler *et al.*, 1990). Here the view is post-modern in nature, where narratives and texts play a central role in understanding human development. The search is for contextual influences on human behaviour and development, where universals are eschewed.

In this chapter I deal with one aspect of the general area of child development: cognitive development. Within the area of cognitive development, I deal with learning and development. I also address the nature of the relations between curriculum development, teaching, and theories of learning and development.

CURRICULUM DEVELOPMENT

Elsewhere (Strauss, 1997), I defined curriculum as the external manifestation of an underlying conceptual system about: (a) the nature and structure of subject matter that is being taught, (b) children's conceptions (sometimes preconceptions or misconceptions) of that subject matter, and (c) mechanisms of cognitive change, i.e. learning and development.

As for the mechanisms of cognitive change, buried in curricula are assumptions curriculum writers have about how learning and development occur in children's minds. Generally, these assumptions are uninspected. They are tacit and between the lines. But investigators can unearth these assumptions through hermeneutic text interpretation.

A simple example here might be helpful. Often one sees in mathematics curricula the following: a problem type is presented; solutions to two problems are demonstrated; and the children who are studying from the curriculum are presented with 15 similar problems for solution. One could surmise from this rather familiar description that the curriculum developer believes that children learn through demonstration and practice. I do not quibble with that implicit description of the nature of the mechanism that leads to learning. Instead, I use this as an example of how one could analyse a section of a curriculum to determine the nature of the curriculum developer's implicit model of children's learning and development.

One purpose of the present chapter is to elaborate on different theories of learning and development which cognitive development psychologists have constructed and then to show their potential influence on curriculum development. In the discussion section, I return to curriculum development in the light of the exposition of these theories.

TEACHING

Teachers, when teaching subject matter, have conceptual systems that describe children's minds and how learning and development take place in those minds. Research indicates that teachers have two main kinds of conceptual systems, called mental models (Johnson-Laird,

1983; Norman, 1983), that guide their behaviours (Mevorach and Strauss, 1996; Strauss, 1993a, 1996).

Kinds of mental models

The first is an in-use mental model (Schon, 1983). This is the mental model teachers have about children's learning that is exhibited when they actually teach in the classroom. The second is an espoused mental model (Schon, 1983). This is the mental model teachers show when they speak about how they teach. Both kinds of mental models are claimed to lead to behaviours: actual teaching behaviours in the case of teachers' in-use mental models and their verbal descriptions of how they would teach in the case of their espoused mental model.

How espoused mental models are inferred

We infer implicit espoused mental models from what teachers say explicitly about how they teach. We do not ask teachers what they think children's minds and learning are because when we have done that, teachers tell us what they remember about Piaget and Vygotsky from their university courses. Instead, we ask them how they teach difficult material and infer from what they tell us what we believe are their implicit mental models of learning. This inference is reasonable because teachers teach so that learning will take place in children's minds.

An example might be helpful here. In discussions with teachers about how they teach difficult subject matter, they might say that complex material is difficult for children, and that breaking up the complex materials into parts makes the material easier to learn. This is the explicit part of what teachers say. We infer from that explicit statement that a part of the teacher's implicit mental model holds that smaller pieces of knowledge can get into the mind more easily than larger pieces of knowledge. This is implicit because it was not what the teacher said, but what we inferred had organised that statement. Teachers' implicit espoused mental models underlie their explicit statements.

The espoused mental model of children's minds and learning we found among teachers bears a family resemblance to 1960s information-processing models such as that of Atkinson and Shiffrin (1968). In the discussion section of this chapter, I elaborate on the topic of teaching, the nature of the espoused mental model, and its connections to theories of learning and development, the topic of our next section.

THEORIES OF LEARNING AND DEVELOPMENT

Debate abounds concerning definitions of learning and development and their places in theories of cognitive developmental psychology and educational theory and practice (Kuhn, 1995; Liben, 1987; Strauss, 1993a). Notions of learning and development are neither fixed nor agreed upon. Instead, they are defined by the theory in which they are embedded. In other words, much of what is said about definitions of learning and development depends on the theory of the speaker's persuasion. In this section, I lay out various positions about learning and development as they pertain to theories that imbue cognitive and developmental psychology.

Debate about learning and development has energised the fields of cognitive and developmental psychology and education over the distant and not too distant past. Theorists' positions about learning and development result from the various stances taken with respect to the following issues: origins (i.e. with what do infants come into the world?); how what infants are born with changes over time; relations between the individual and the environment; and domain-general versus domain-specific knowledge.

As for this last issue, there has been considerable controversy over the years about what cognitive and developmental psychologists should search for: domain-general or domain-specific systems. As for domain-general systems, diverse data and phenomena that can be described by a single model fulfil the sought-after criteria of parsimony and power. That description has been the aim of most cognitive and developmental psychologists. As for domain-specific cognitive systems, research findings in neuropsychology, the effects of brain damage for cognitive functioning, representations of experts in a domain, and more all point to a certain encapsulation or domain-specificity of cognitive entities.

To anticipate some of what follows in this chapter, I believe this either-or view of domain-general versus domain-specific knowledge restricts debate, but that is the way many people in the field often cast it these days. There are exceptions, though. Case (1985, 1992, 1993), Feldman (1994, 1995), and Karmiloff-Smith (1992, 1994) attempt to find ways to include both domain-general and domain-specific systems in their theories.

I briefly summarise these issues with respect to nine theories: nativism, behaviourism, structuralism, information-processing, the socio-historical approach, and four interstitial theories: a neo-Piagetian theory, a theory of non-universal development, the naïve theories approach, and the representational redescription approach.

Nativism

Nativists are influenced by the rationalist philosophical tradition. Radical nativists, such as Fodor (1980, 1983), argue that infants are born with complete and abstract knowledge about aspects of their world. Using language as an example, the argument is that infants are born with a universal grammar (UG). They are also born with learning devices that allow any child to learn, in my example, any language.

The arguments posed by Fodor (1980, 1983) about human cognition have had serious consequences for cognitive developmental psychologists. He has claimed, in so many words, that human cognition does not allow for development. Fodor's (1983) thesis about the modularity of mind is the basis for this claim.

He argues that the mind is genetically specified and has independent modules that are specified for the kinds of inputs that come to it from the environment. A language module, for instance, is specified for language input. Domain-specific transducers deal with the domain-specific environmental information. Holding a picture to our ears will not activate language transducers. In this view, then, cognition is modular, domain-specific and genetically hard-wired in the neuronal architecture. These modules are self-contained and need no recourse to general, domain-general cognitive goals. They allow automatic outputs that are driven by environmental stimuli.

He does allow for central processing, however, which he claims is domain-general. Computations in the central processing part of cognition lead to beliefs about the world. These beliefs are what are in long-term memory concerning the environment. They concern belief fixation (also see Fodor, 1980), the accumulation of declarative beliefs about the world, and procedural planning of actions in that world. Fodor (1983) claims that the search for central processing components and processes is the pursuit for an after-the-important part of human cognition. In his view, the work done by the modules and their transducers are the significant part of cognitive work. When what gets worked out at the modular level gets passed on to the central processing system, the interesting part of cognition has already happened. As a consequence, he argues, much research and theory in cognitive psychology gets in at the wrong place.

A second reason radical nativists argue that, in principle, there is no development is that, in their view, it is impossible to get from less to more powerful mental structures (Fodor, 1980). Because this is impossible, one must engineer an infant who has the most powerful structures from birth. The moment radical nativists take that position, there can be no development because the most powerful structures are in place from the very beginning.

Change that takes place, then, must be learning, and learning must be deductive. Here the argument is that, very roughly, children deductively test hypotheses about their environment (e.g. their language) and get feedback about whether or not their hypotheses are confirmed or disconfirmed. And where can these hypotheses come from? From the complete UG with which they are born.

Radical nativists place the greatest emphasis on the individual and the innate knowledge each of us is born with. The environment is the place where the hypotheses about the world get tested. It has been argued that this environment is, by definition, impoverished. In short, the radical nativists argue that children are born with complete, abstract knowledge; that in principle, development cannot occur – deductive learning is the explanation for change; learning is domain-specific; and the individual's innate modular and encapsulated knowledge is the main part of the individual–environmental interactions.

Behaviourism

The radical version of behaviourism (Bijou and Baer, 1961, 1965; Skinner, 1953) is that infants are born with neither knowledge (*tabula rasa*) nor organisation. With respect to what knowledge and cognitive equipment the infant brings into the world, radical behaviourism occupies the pole at the other extreme of the continuum occupied by the radical nativists. Behaviourists claim that infants are born with capacities to discriminate aspects of the environment, respond to it, generalise, and so on.

Because their position is that infants are born without knowledge and, as a result, they are unstructured with respect to knowledge, radical behaviourists are unlikely to claim that the child will eventually have mental structures. This is because such a claim would force them to find an explanation as to how an unstructured mental system becomes structured.

Because there is no restructuring, there is no development. Cognitive change that does take place, then, is learning.

Ironically, the position that there is no development but only learning is common to the radical nativists and the radical behaviourists. The nature of learning is very different, of course, for advocates of the two theories. For the nativists it is deductive hypothesis testing, whereas for the behaviourists it is inductive. I elaborate a little on the behaviourist position here.

Radical behaviourists argued that learning – the capacity to form associations inductively in a lawful way – is the basis for the knowledge gained about the world. The environment impinges on us, and we form associations about it in such a way that the more we are exposed to a particular environment, the stronger the association; and the closer the aspects of the environment are in time and space, the more likely the association will be formed. The former is called the law of frequency, and the latter is called the law of contiguity.

Behaviourists have the environment as the main element in the relations between the individual and the environment. The external environment is what is to be noted and copied internally.

In short, radical behaviourists claim that infants are born without knowledge; development does not occur because there are no cognitive constraints on the initial (knowledge-free) system; laws of inductive learning are the sole explanation for cognitive change; the search is for domain-general mechanisms of learning; and the environment is the main part of the individual–environment interactions.

Structuralism

Structuralists, such as Piaget, argue that infants are born with a weak structure of reflexes that transforms itself over time. Relations between the structure of reflexes and mental structures on the psychological plane have to do with the biological roots of psychological development. How one goes from one to the other is, of course, a puzzle yet to be solved by structuralists.

Because structuralists posit that infants begin life with a structure, the likely ensuing position is that their future cognitions will also be structured. The issue then turns to the direction and nature of development that proceeds from relatively weak to relatively powerful mental structures (Fodor, 1980). The position taken by Piaget and his followers is that this development takes the form of qualitatively different structures that are transformed in an invariant sequence.

Learning, in the structuralist view, is the application of mental structures to new content. Mental structures limit what can be learned because one cannot apply a mental structure that does not exist or has not yet been constructed. In this sense, development sets constraints on learning.

Structuralists maintain an intermediate position between the radical nativists and the radical behaviourists about individual–environment relations. They are avowedly interactionist in the sense that there is a subtle give and take between the environment and the structure. Assimilation, accommodation, and the equilibration of mental structures are major organising principles for Piaget (1970).

One of the purposes of these structures is to maintain a state of equilibrium with the environment (adaptational equilibrium) and with itself (organisational equilibrium). The mechanism of cognitive development is disequilibrium of the two types just noted. In the case of adaptational disequilibrium, the mental structure cannot completely account for discrepant environmental information. Organisational disequilibrium occurs when the child contradicts herself, where the contradiction is the result of conflicting mental structures the child has developed. I have more to say about this in the section on Curriculum Development and Theories of Learning and Development.

Despite this principled interactionist position, which Piaget thought separated him from the radical nativists and radical behaviourists, Karmiloff-Smith (1992, 1994) recently claimed that there is a common view held by radical behaviourists and Piagetian structuralists. Both claim that infants are born without knowledge. If infants are without knowledge, how do they acquire or construct it (choose your theory when you choose your term)? Both give the same answer: through domain-general devices. As stated above, for the radical behaviourists, the device includes the capacity to discriminate environmental features, generalise, and form associations inductively. For the structuralists, the device is the assimilation–accommodation–equilibration complex as it gets expressed through the structures.

The domain-general system Piaget posits does not allow for domain-specificity in infancy and afterwards. He argues that domain-specific and innately specified modules do not format environmental input. Instead, that input gets acted upon by the same mechanisms, regardless of the nature of the data from the environment. These mechanisms are controlled by the representational structures that are posited to develop over time in the now-famous sequence Piaget argued describes the cognitive development of mental structures.

In sum, structuralists claim that development occurs, and that what develops is structures. Learning, then, is constrained by development. Infants are born with a domain-general structure of reflexes that have no domain-specific modularity. The individual–environment relations are interactionist. It is in these interactions that the child's actual developmental trajectory gets worked out and is the result of a mixture of what the structure offers as possibility and what the environment affords as reality.

Information-processing approaches

Information-processing theories are somewhat atheoretical. They are, of course, part of a general worldview, but they are not explicitly ideological in the sense that the three previous theories are.

The theories I present emphasise developmental aspects of information-processing, but these aspects are not a prerequisite for information-processing approaches. Information-processing approaches that do deal with development are quite varied: production systems (Klahr, 1984), rule assessment (Siegler, 1981), skill acquisition (Fischer, 1980) and so on. There does not seem to be consensus among these approaches about how much knowledge the child is born with and how it is organised. Yet, there are some unifying themes to which most information-processing advocates adhere. One is that thinking is information-processing. Others are the emphasis placed on the ways children represent knowledge, how they transform information, and the processing limitations that constrain the inductive inferences they can make about their world.

What develops according to these approaches? The answer depends on the approach, of course, and given space limitations, I can only hint at what answers have been offered to this question.

The novice–expert shift is a candidate for what develops. Domain-specific knowledge representation has been described in terms of novice–expert dimensions. The novice's domain-specific knowledge representation differs from the expert's on a number of dimensions: its knowledge base, organisation, problem-solving, and so on. These dimensions set limits on what and how much can be learned. For example, a child who has a larger knowledge base about a particular domain and whose knowledge representation is deeper than another child's will learn more about new material when it is presented.

Another candidate for what develops is working memory limitations. There is controversy about whether or not working memory changes. Among those who believe there are age-related working memory changes is Case (1993). The argument is that working memory limitations set constraints on the inductive inferences that can be made. And as working memory increases with age, so do the kinds of inferences children can make.

In these two examples, the developmental aspect pertains to constraints placed on the information-processing system, be they processing constraints on knowledge representation and organisation or on working memory constraints.

Learning can be the result of several processes that occur alone or in concert. Among them are strategy construction (Siegler and Shipley, 1987), automatisation (Case, 1984), encoding (Siegler, 1981, 1984), generalisation (Klahr, 1984), and analogy construction (Gentner, 1983).

Automatisation can be used to demonstrate what learning mechanisms might be. Case (1984) argued that within the information-processing constraints on working memory, children are able to learn new material through automatisation. When automatisation occurs, space is freed up in working memory for other information to be taken into account. Notice that the information-processing capacity has not changed here. Instead, within the constraints of that capacity, one can deal with more information by, say, automatising processing.

The bulk of the information-processing approaches place the burden of the individual–environment relations on the environment. Physical input from the environment gets transformed as it makes its way to the place where it is eventually stored. But there is no question that the individual also plays a role here in that knowledge representation of the new material will influence what and how much will get learned.

In sum, information-processing approaches are somewhat atheoretical. Many do not make claims about the nature of the knowledge and its organisation which infants are born with. Some approaches claim that development occurs with respect to changes in the constraints on the information-processing system that limit the kinds of inferences that can be made. These constraints are at the working memory level. And, to use Fodor's terminology, they are part of the central processing system, not at the level of transducers. Learning overcomes processing constraints via mechanisms such as strategy construction, automatisation, encoding, generalisation and analogy construction. And the environment is the dominant factor in environment–individual relations.

The socio-historical approach

The socio-historical position, as advanced by Vygotsky (1978, 1987), maintains a two-track position about human cognitive processes: the natural and the cultural. Natural processes follow the path of maturational underpinnings and the environment supplies information for those underpinnings to get played out. These lower mental processes are not reflective and are the result of direct, personal experience with the environment.

For the cultural track, the social environment is crucial, as are the tools that are used for understanding and engaging the environment. There are two basic kinds of tools: material and psychological. Material tools mediate between the individual and nature. For example, a hoe has a handle designed to fit the individual's hand and a plate built to fit the material world. The hoe mediates between the individual and nature, both literally and metaphorically.

Psychological tools mediate between individuals in their social interactions. These are signs, symbols and discourses. These semiotic systems are also used by individuals to change their own psychological processes. Languages we have constructed come to organise the ways we understand our environment, others and ourselves. This idea gets picked up in the Discussion section where I present how theories of learning and development can effect curriculum development. This is the kernel of Vygotsky's (1987) general genetic law of cultural development. He claimed that all functions appear twice: first among people as an interpsychological category and then within the child as an intrapsychological category (Wertsch and Tulviste, 1992).

I now turn to the roles of learning and development according to this approach. I begin with a caveat. There are at least two main understandings of these terms: Vygotsky's (1987) and his modern-day interpreters.

In Vygotsky's (1978) view, learning goes beyond development and draws development in its wake. An individual's developmental level is her mature knowledge as expressed when she works alone. Vygotsky (1987) called this the individual's actual knowledge. Learning in social interactions among individuals happens in the zone of proximal development (ZPD). What is learned in concert with others comes to be internalised, and what is learned becomes the new actual knowledge or the new developmental level. This learning with others creates and actualises potential knowledge as individuals move towards a new developmental level. In this sense, learning is the leading edge of development. It creates new developmental levels.

One area where Vygotsky's modern-day interpreters differ from Vygotsky is in the sense in which the terms development and learning are used: they believe the terms are inadequate to describe what they have in mind. One reason for this has to do with the unit of what they believe changes with age. Newman, Griffin and Cole (1989), for example, suggested that the unit of analysis for cognitive change is neither the invariant mental structures (as Piaget would have it) nor the mental processes that transform information (as appealed to by information-processing people). Both exist in the mind of individuals. Neither is it in the environment. Instead, the unit is in the social interaction between individuals and between them and the environment.

This unit requires a language of description different from the ones we currently use. The alternative suggested by Vygotsky's interpreters is to view learning as a social practice, an activity that takes place among people in social contexts. The unit of analysis is located in that nexus. When one takes this view, the notions of learning and development lose their usual meaning.

The emphasis on individual–environment interactions for learning and development leans strongly towards the social activity that is between the individual and the environment. However, Wertsch and Tulviste (1992) noted problems with this emphasis, mostly because of the lack of construction in the ZPD, as Vygotsky (1978) described it. Vygotsky's view of internalisation has a ring of absorption, rather than the sound of reconstruction. Contemporary adherents of the socio-historical approach have added constructivism to Vygotsky's theory, so as to bring it more in line with current views of cognitive functioning, even though those views are not derived from the original socio-historical approach.

In sum, the socio-historical approach engineers infants with two tracks – the natural and the cultural – without making claims about how much knowledge the infant is born with. Vygotsky claimed that learning proceeds in advance of development as the zone of proximal development is created. Some contemporary socio-historical theorists and researchers believe that these terms are obsolete and no longer useful. And Vygotsky places great emphasis on the roles of social activity in the ontogenetic development of cognition.

Interstitial theories

Four interstitial theories have taken some positions from different theories: Case's (1985, 1993) neo-Piagetian theory, Feldman's (1994) theory of non-universal development, the naïve theories approach (Carey, 1985; Spelke, 1990, 1991) and representational redescription theory, developed by Karmiloff-Smith (1992, 1994).

Neo-Piagetian theories

Neo-Piagetians blend structuralist tenets with those of information-processing. Among the neo-Piagetians are Case, Demetriou and Efklides, Fischer, Halford and Pascual-Leone. I use Case's work (1984, 1985, 1992, 1993) to illustrate what neo-Piagetians are up to.

Case's approach is structuralist in that he seeks general structural organisations that have properties of stage-like development. For example, their development is sequential. They are qualitatively different from each other. They are domain-general. The forms of learning are modified by the structures children construct. And cognition is influenced by general developmental rules.

The point of departure from the structuralist approach in Case's theory is that he uses an information-processing frame to describe the processes that occur when the mental organisation deals with information. The move from describing mental structures via logical and mathematical structures, as did Piaget (1970), to describing them in terms of information-processing systems, as does Case, led Case to descriptions of cognition and development that are different from Piaget's.

These differences are inspired by contemporary learning theory as advanced by information-processing adherents. One difference is that, in addition to the structures being domain-general (which is Piagetian), they also cover domain-specific knowledge (which is aligned with information-processing approaches). Also, although there are general developmental cognitions that are restructured (Piagetian), Case posits that cognitive change also occurs because of specific experiences (information-processing).

In short, neo-Piagetians seek to determine general cognitive structures and their developmental sequences while, at the same time, they search for domain-specific knowledge organisations that are the products of specific experiences with the environment.

In sum, Case's version of neo-Piagetian theory posits that infants are born with M-power and it develops. There are radical shifts in the levels at which children's M-power gets structured in mental organisations. The content and organisation of these structures are not determined only by experience. The structures apply across a very broad range of domains. And these structures are part of children's general developmental level and are not acquired solely by formal schooling or specific experiences. Learning and development, then, are both domain-specific and domain-general.

Non-universal development

Feldman's (1994, 1995) interstitial theory of non-universal development has elements of both the structuralist and the socio-historical approaches. He argues that most of cognitive development is about non-universals, yet cognitive developmentalists attempt to describe universal development. Ontogenesis proceeds in the following order of intellectual achievements: universal (e.g. early Piagetian stages), pancultural (e.g. quantity), cultural (e.g. arithmetics), discipline-based (e.g. mathematical psychology), idiosyncratic (e.g. mathematical models that describe formal operations in Piaget's 1970 theory), and unique (e.g. those creative changes in models made by an individual that lead to a reorganisation of understanding the formal operations stage, a reorganisation that is accepted by experts in the field).

The development of societies proceeds in the reverse order, beginning with the unique achievements of individuals who make an impact on their subfields, perhaps on their fields, and, in rare cases, on their cultures.

Several matters arise when one takes Feldman's (1994) position.

1 He takes the structuralist position that structures and developmental sequences do exist. Individuals develop through these stages. The sequence of development, however, is in the domains through which individuals develop.
2 Developmental transitions are powered by the same mechanisms that Piaget and his followers claimed underlie cognitive development: structural conflict of the adaptational and organisational varieties.
3 Developmental sequences are expressed in cultural domains. For example, in baseball, there are a number of levels of expertise through which to develop, from the level of the sandlot novice through A, AA and AAA levels arriving, possibly, to the major leagues.
4 All non-universal developments take into account individual differences, creativity and motivation, and require the arrangement of special situations in order for learning to occur, such as schools, private lessons and so on.

This opening up of cognitive developmental theory to the acquisition of non-universals makes structuralist theory, at least this variant of structuralist theory, more amenable to discussing its implications for education.

Feldman does not couch his theory in these terms, but it includes both domain-general and domain-specific organisations. The domain-general part pertains to universal developmental achievements, whereas the domain-specific part concerns the expressions of these domain-general cognitions in achievements in culturally organised, domain-specific areas.

In sum, the theory of non-universal cognitive development does not make claims about origins of structures and knowledge in the infant. Structures are the cognitive entities that develop, and their sequence is the result of a subtle blend between these structures' properties and the structure of the domain in question. Developmental sequences are as much in domains of cultures as they are in the minds of individuals. And there are both domain-general and domain-specific aspects to the theory.

Naïve theories approaches

Those who advocate the naïve theories approach usually uphold an amalgam of nativism and structuralism (Carey, 1985; Gelman, 1990).

Radical nativism, it will be remembered, seeks a description of innate domain-specific modules. Adherents of that approach argue that central processing, which is where domain-general beliefs get fixated, is the wrong level to seek lawful cognition and knowledge acquisition. As I have shown, radical nativism also shuns a developmental position.

There are nativists of another stripe, those who are not advocates of the radical position (Carey, 1985; Gelman, 1990). They claim that infants are born with considerable innately specified knowledge about their world, that learning takes place within the constraints set by those specifications, and that mental constructions occur within these constraints.

Advocates of the naïve theories approach, then, seek out innate domain-specific characteristics of cognition, which aligns them with that aspect of radical nativism, while seeking rules of constructivist development, which is associated with structuralism. In short, this emerging position suggests that one can be both a nativist and a constructivist or, to use Gelman's (1990) terminology, a 'rational constructivist'.

Within the naïve theories approach to cognitive development and learning, Carey (1985) proposed a rather advanced theory. She claimed that children have theory-like conceptual structures. Abstractness and law-like coherence characterise theories, the phenomena in their domains, their explanatory mechanisms, the ways they produce interpretations of evidence, and more. The number of such domains is limited: biology, physics, language, space, number and a few others.

Carey de-emphasises domain-general knowledge and places great emphasis on domain-specific knowledge. The latter is within domains, such as biology, physics, language, etc. The wired-in, innately specified cognitions are domain-specific. Carey (1985) further claimed that concepts in particular domains are part of larger naïve or lay theories about that domain. One of the tasks of developmental psychologists who adhere to this theory is to determine the nature of these naïve theories about the domains under study.

Carey also claimed that because concepts are embedded in naïve theories, conceptual change, which can be understood as development, can be viewed as similar to theory change in domains. For example, aspects of theory change in the sciences serve as a way to think about how the development of lay theories occurs in children (and adults).

The educational implications of the naïve theories approach is that we can view learning through instruction, in the widest sense of this term, as the engine that drives development. Instruction, both formal and informal, leads to knowledge acquisition that leads, in a yet undetermined manner, to cognitive development.

In short, the perspective here is that infants are born with innately specified knowledge about their world, which sets both information-processing and theory structural constraints on their learning. Hence, there is emphasis on domain-specific knowledge. Children form concepts within large domains that have theory-like qualities. The development of concepts occurs in ways that resemble theory change in disciplines. Learning through instruction may lead to development. And the environment–individual complex is subtlely interactive.

A theory of representational redescription

Karmiloff-Smith (1992, 1994) recently presented a theory of cognitive development that combines aspects of nativism, the socio-historical approach and structuralism. The nativist part that remains in her theory is the notion that human beings are born with domain-specific predispositions.

Mental constructions, thought to be built off the innate knowledge, are the re-representations that humans construct about their world. What this means is that people internally represent their external environment (i.e. we mentally appropriate it). We then represent our representations (or re-represent our environment) via various languages. These languages are cultural artefacts and, thus, are within the province of Vygotsky's socio-historical approach. Part of the re-representation includes changes from implicit to explicit representations. The emphases placed on these changes also have a socio-historical ring to them. The structuralist part, inherent in her theory, is that these re-representations are constructed, which is consistent with the constructivist position held by Piaget.

When melding theories that are quite different in their stances about essentials in human cognition, it is important to avoid producing a theory that is an eclectic patchwork quilt with parts taken from here and there, where these parts are slapped on to each other. Karmiloff-Smith has managed to avoid that. To resolve the essential tensions between the nativist and structuralist approaches, she added a notion that allows both to sit side-by-side without serious conflict: representational redescription.

Karmiloff-Smith took on Fodor's (1983) claims about the modularity of cognition and argued against his notion in two main ways. First, she argued against the notion that innate modules are prespecified in detail. She made them more epigenetic than Fodor made them out to be. Second, she fuzzed up the sharp distinction Fodor made between prespecified modules and central processing.

Similarly, Karmiloff-Smith took issue with some of Piaget's claims. Most important among the issues she chose to address is Piaget's position about domain-generality. She argued that it is difficult to hold Piaget's domain-general position alone with respect to infants' mental equipment: there is simply too much evidence from different quarters showing us that cognition is modularised. So she rejected Fodor's claims for the notion of cognitive modules being encapsulated. Similarly, she rejected Piaget's notion of domain-general cognition, where the same mechanisms of data processing occur without regard to the nature of the environmental input.

What does she offer as an alternative? First, she accepts the nativist idea of domain-specificity, but she includes the development of these modules, a notion that is unacceptable to radical nativists. And she accepts the structuralist notion of constructivism. Her alternative offers a way to put domain-specificity and constructivism together. To do so she had to change, somewhat, the definitions Fodor gave of domain-specificity and modules and Piaget's domain-general constructivism. And in so doing, she invented the notion of representational redescription.

Karmiloff-Smith (1992, 1994) includes domain-specificity of human cognition, where domains are physics, mathematics, biology, language, psychology, etc. She also allows what she terms 'microdomains', which are subdomains such as addition in the domain of mathematics and psychological causality in the domain of psychology. Her major addition here is that she developed a recurrent phase change model that occurs at different times and for different microdomains and within each domain. One of the reasons for this move on her part is that it can account for both domain-specific and domain-general cognition. It also addresses how children's representations become increasingly flexible, an area that is missing in Fodor's (1983) account of cognition.

In her recurrent phase change model, Karmiloff-Smith (1986, 1992, 1994) argues that development involves three recurrent phases:

1 The first learning phase is data driven and connected to the immediate environment. Children's performances here are successful in that they get to a level of behavioural mastery.
2 The second learning phase is more internally focused. Children's internal representations of knowledge in a microdomain have precedence over environmental data. The shift from phase 1 to phase 2 can lead to a drop in performance. The drop is in performance and not in the representational system that leads to that performance and, as a result, this is a case where a drop in performance signifies cognitive advance.
3 The third learning phase involves an integration of external environmental input and internal mental representations. This learning phase leads to children's correct productions but, although they are similar or even identical to the performances from phase 1, they are different in that they have different representational systems underlying them.

In addition to the learning that takes place in recurrent phase change, children's internal representations are formatted on at least four levels: one level of implicit representation and three levels of explicit representations. These redescriptions of representations are redescriptions at a new format level and language of what was previously described at a lower format level. Among other characteristics, movement through the format levels involves increasing consciousness of one's representational systems.

In short, Karmiloff-Smith's theory of representational redescription posits innate domain knowledge that is not modularised. Development involves an increasing modularisation of representational systems and their increasing explicitness. As for the environment–individual interaction, both are important in different ratios at various phases of development. And the theory posits importance for both domain-general and domain-specific representations.

Summary

The brief discussion of nine major theories attempted to show that the position one takes about the origins of knowledge (i.e. what the child is born with) and issues related to domain-generality and domain-specificity has potential to constrain what theorists say about relations between learning and development, mechanisms of learning and development, and the nature of the relations between the individuals and their environment. I now briefly turn to what this has to do with curriculum development and teaching.

CURRICULUM DEVELOPMENT AND THEORIES OF LEARNING AND DEVELOPMENT

In the introduction I defined curriculum as the external expression of an underlying implicit conceptual system held by the curriculum developer about the nature of the subject matter being taught, children's preconceptions of that subject matter, and mechanisms that govern learning and development. Given my review of theories of learning and development, it is appropriate to ask how the curriculum developer can engage them.

The main point here is that the understanding the curriculum developer has about the nature of children's learning guides her choices about which curriculum activities to include in the curriculum. An example might be useful here. Research on children's developing understandings of the concept of temperature can serve as a case in point.

Children's developing concepts of temperature

An aspect of the concept of temperature can be tested by giving children two tasks: a qualitative and a numerical task. For the qualitative task, children are presented with two cups of water and are told that they are cold and are the same temperature. The experimenter then pours the water from the two cups into a third, empty cup and asks the children what the temperature of the mixed water is. The numerical task is identical to the qualitative task, except that the children measure the water's temperature in the two original cups and determine that they are both 10°C.

The developmental trajectory of children's solutions to the two tasks was found to be quite different. The qualitative task was solved correctly by most young children (ages 4–6); many older children (ages 7–9) solved it incorrectly; and still older children (ages 10 and older) solved it correctly. This unusual U-shaped behavioural growth curve, which was found for the qualitative task, and the drop in correct responses over age was interpreted by Strauss and Stavy (1982) to be a sign of cognitive advance.

The solutions children offered to the numerical task had a different behavioural growth curve. It was found that very few children solved the 10°C + 10°C task correctly, as most children argued that the mixed water was 20°C. It was only at age 11 that approximately 25 per cent of the children solved that task correctly. A much lower percentage of children solved that task correctly at earlier ages.

The question before us is as follows: How would a curriculum developer construct activities whose main purpose is to foster learning so that children with incorrect understandings of the numerical problem would have a more adequate understanding of that problem after they did the activities of the unit's worksheets?

The structuralist curriculum developer

If the curriculum developer were a structuralist, she might attempt to create organisational conflict within the child. For example, she could build the activities in the following manner. She could ask the children to: (a) mix same-temperature cold water, as in the qualitative task, (b) judge the temperature of the mixed water, and (c) note, on a qualitative thermometer (i.e. a thermometer that has qualitative readings on it, such as cold, tepid, hot) drawn on the worksheet, what the temperature of the mixed water was. She might then ask children to: (a) mix same-temperature water that was originally 10°C, (b) judge what the resulting temperature should be when the original water was mixed, and (c) note on a numerical thermometer (i.e. the usual thermometer that has numerical readings of temperature) what the temperature of the mixed water was. Were the children who studied with these worksheets similar to those found in Strauss and Stavy's (1982) research, they would mark the temperature of the mixed water on the qualitative thermometer as cold, whereas they would mark the temperature of the mixed water on the numerical thermometer as 20°C.

The structuralist curriculum developer, in an attempt to create organisational conflict, could then pit these two ways of thinking in the hope that the children would realise that they are producing conflicting judgements. That could be done by asking the children to compare their markings on the qualitative and numerical thermometers and to see if they are marked at the same location. They could also suggest to the children that they might discuss the implications of their markings being at the same or different places. For a description of research that studied the above, see Stavy and Berkowitz (1980) and Strauss (1987).

The point here is that the structuralist curriculum developer could construct worksheets that would attempt to lead children to understand that they are producing conflicting judgement, which the curriculum developer believes comes from different mental structures.

How would a socio-historical curriculum developer create a curriculum unit to teach a better understanding of the numerical concept of temperature?

The socio-historical curriculum developer

An adherent of the socio-historical approach, in an attempt to help children gain a better understanding of the numerical task for the temperature concept, would construct worksheets that are quite different from those constructed by the structuralist curriculum developer, expressing, of course, her socio-historical understanding of how children come to learn.

A starting-point for the worksheets might be grounded in the nature of the symbolic systems being used to describe the water's temperature. After all, the qualitative and numerical tasks are identical in terms of physics. What makes them different, then, is the language used to describe the physical phenomenon we are studying.

We feel water's temperature sensorally. And we give those sensations names, depending on the language we use: we can call the water cold, hot or tepid. Those are words from natural language and they are classificatory, nominal. We can also use comparative terms, such as 'more', 'less' and 'same', all of which allow us to compare temperatures of water. And we can describe the water's temperature numerically by using the numerical scale etched on the thermometer, which is an instrument that was constructed for the purpose of measuring temperature. Carnap (1966) discusses these three measurement languages in a philosophical treatment of physics.

Our hypothetical curriculum developer of the socio-historical persuasion might build worksheets that have the children discuss the similarities and differences between the two tasks in terms of the languages we use to describe them. For instance, the worksheets might have the children discuss among themselves that the physics of the problem is identical but the languages used to describe the physics is different. The children could also discuss what the two languages give us in terms of (a) precision, (b) a sense of 'closeness' to our intuitive knowledge, etc. And there could be discussions about the idea that humans constructed both languages and can be seen as alternative descriptions of the same physical phenomenon.

The worksheets were built to help children to understand that:

1 the two tasks of pouring water are identical,
2 the physics of the two tasks is identical,
3 two languages (natural and mathematics) can describe the same phenomenon,
4 the two languages have differences and similarities,
5 the two languages, as different as they are, should allow the same solution to the tasks because the tasks tap the same physics phenomenon.

Summary

The above intended to indicate how curriculum developers who are proponents of the two approaches to learning and development might construct worksheets when they have before them identical developmental data, i.e. children solve differently (U-shaped and a gradually increasing curve) two tasks (qualitative and numerical) that tap an aspect of children's conceptions of temperature.

The structuralist curriculum developer believes that learning and development occur as a result of conflict and, as a result, the worksheets are constructed to induce, in our case, organisational conflict. The socio-historical curriculum developer believes that the semiotic system and consciousness about it and about our own cognition help foster learning. As a consequence, the worksheets might have the children discuss the two semiotic systems (natural language and mathematics) and their relations to the identical physics task.

We now discuss a second arena where theories of learning and development influence educational matters: teaching.

TEACHING AND THEORIES OF LEARNING AND DEVELOPMENT

Teaching is carried out to foster children's learning. When a teacher speaks about how she teaches or when she actually teaches, she indicates her understanding of the nature of children's minds and how learning occurs in those minds. This understanding is generally implicit, but it is there none the less.

In this section I describe how teachers hold a particular view of children's minds and learning – an information-processing view. I then show how a socio-historical view of children's minds and learning leads to different teaching.

The information-processing teacher

In the introduction I outlined teachers' implicit espoused mental model of children's minds and learning. I now very briefly elaborate on it.

The mental model of children's minds and learning shows an engineering vision on the part of the teachers (Strauss and Shilony, 1994; Strauss *et al.*, 1998). The basic premise of this model is that the teacher possesses knowledge, and it is external to children's minds. Once one takes that position, two engineering problems follow: First, how does one get the external information inside the child's mind? And second, once it gets there, how can one move it along to the place where it gets stored or, in other words, gets learned?

In order for learning to occur, the content must first enter children's minds, and teachers conceive of children as having openings of a certain size that allow information to enter. Their notion of 'opening size' recalls the notion of working memory capacity. Teachers believe that good pedagogy involves serving up knowledge in chunk sizes that can 'get through' the openings. For example, teachers said that what makes some subject matter difficult is that it is too complex and, as a result, it may not be able to get 'in' the mind. Here teachers see their task as reducing this complexity by breaking the material into component parts so that it will be able to enter the mind's opening. However, even were the material to be of the right complexity, it may never enter the mind if the child's affective states are not primed to receive the content. Conceived metaphorically, the entrances to children's minds have 'flaps' that are open when children are attentive. If children are uninterested or unmotivated, the flaps go down and the material cannot enter the mind.

Teachers believe that once content gets through, it must somehow connect up with already existing knowledge by means of analogies, associations, familiar examples and so on. This corresponds to an elaborative-processing model. Accordingly, teachers believe they should facilitate connection-making between new and old knowledge. If there is no existing knowledge to get connected to, the new knowledge can get driven into memory through repetition, rehearsal and practice. This new knowledge now becomes part of already learned knowledge. How does the new knowledge affect the prior knowledge? Teachers believe that there are changes in the amount and organisation of prior knowledge, the prior knowledge gets broadened and generalised, it is at higher levels of abstraction that what was in previous knowledge, and more.

These are some of the solutions to the two engineering problems that result from teachers' mental models of the structure of children's minds, how learning takes place in those minds, and how instruction fosters that learning. These solutions are seen within teachers' implicit information-processing mental model of children's minds and learning. But, as shown, there are other models of children's learning and development and they, too, can be expressed in teaching. We now turn to a version of learning that is based on the socio-historical view.

The socio-historical teacher

The socio-historical view of learning has a strong social component to it. Social interactions lead to learning and it is that very learning that draws development in its wake. Social interactions are of two sorts: social interactions between individuals, as in conversations, and social interactions between individuals and their culture, including artefacts.

As mentioned, the zone of proximal development was one of Vygotsky's many legacies that have significance for our ideas about learning and teaching. The idea here is that children have knowledge about the topic you want to teach them before you teach them. Teachers assess that mature knowledge, which is knowledge they have constructed with the assistance of others but which they hold autonomously at the time of assessment. Vygotsky (1987) termed this: children's actual knowledge.

Instruction is intended to help guide children from their actual knowledge to what Vygotsky termed their potential knowledge. This is the knowledge children and teachers co-construct as they engage in learning. The distance children travel from the actual knowledge to the potential knowledge is the zone of proximal development.

The conversations teachers have with children in this construction zone involve scaffolding. One important part of scaffolding, but not of the sort where teachers scaffold and children have their knowledge constructed for them, is co-guiding. Teachers can assess what children's actual knowledge is and they have a lay of the land in terms of the places to which they want to help children move. Children do not have that lay of the land. If they had it, they would most probably be where the teachers want them to be. On the other hand, there are different routes to get to the places teachers have determined are worthwhile. Teachers cannot know which route is best for any one child, but the children know what is working during teaching, and what is not. In this understanding of teaching, the learner and teacher are partners who guide each other. For an elaborated version of teaching inspired by the socio-historical approach, see Newman *et al.* (1989). This socio-historical view of teaching is clearly different to the information-processing view that was found to be the dominant view held by teachers (Strauss and Shilony, 1994; Strauss *et al.*, 1998).

SUMMARY

I presented nine major theories of child cognitive development, with emphasis on how they view learning and development. The differences between the theories were shown to be rather large. I then showed how some of these theories have consequences for two aspects of educational practice: curriculum development and teaching. In usual practice, curriculum developers and teachers are not aware of the theories of learning and development that guide their practice. I showed that were these two educational practitioners to be aware of the theories they hold and the nature of alternative theories, their curriculum development and teaching decisions would most likely be richer than those they make without that awareness.

REFERENCES

Argyris, C. and Schon, D. (1974) *Theory in Practice: Increasing Professional Effectiveness*. San Francisco: Jossey-Bass.

Atkinson, R. C. and Shiffrin, R. M. (1968) 'Human memory: A proposed system and its control mechanisms'. In K. W. Spence and J. Spence (eds), *The Psychology of Learning and Motivation: Advances in Research and Theory*, vol. 2. New York: Academic Press.

Bijou, S. W. and Baer, D. M. (1961) *Child Development 1: A Systematic and Empirical Theory*. New York: Appleton-Century-Crofts.

Bijou, S. W. and Baer, D. M. (1965) *Child Development 2: Universal Stage of Infancy*. New York: Appleton-Century-Crofts.

Carey, S. (1985) *Conceptual Change in Childhood*. Cambridge, MA: Bradford Books/MIT Press.

Carey, S. and Spelke, E. (1994) 'Domain-specific knowledge and conceptual change'. In L. Hirschfeld and S. A. Gelman (eds), *Mapping the Mind: Cognition and Culture*. New York: Cambridge University Press, 169–200.

Carnap, R. (1966) *Philosophical Foundations of Physics*. New York: Basic Books.

Case, R. (1984) 'The process of stage transition: A neo-Piagetian view'. In R. J. Sternberg (ed.), *Mechanisms of Cognitive Development*. San Francisco: Freeman, 19–44.

Case, R. (1985) *Intellectual Development: Birth to Childhood*. New York: Academic Press.

Case R. (1992) *The Mind's Staircase: Exploring the Conceptual Underpinnings of Children's Thought and Knowledge*. Hillsdale, NJ: Erlbaum.

Case R. (1993) 'Theories of learning and theories of development'. *Educational Psychologist*, 28, 219–233.

Demetriou, A. and Efklides, A. (1988) 'Experiental structuralism and neo-Piagetian theories: Toward an integrated model'. In A. Demetriou (ed.) *The Neo-Piagetian Theories of Cognitive Development: Toward an Integration*. Amsterdam: Elsevier, 137–173.

Demetriou, A., Efklides, A. and Platsidou, M. (1993) (eds) 'The architecture and dynamics of developing mind'. *Society for Research in Child Development Monographs*, 58.

Elman, J. L., Bates, E. A., Johnson, M. H., Karmiloff-Smith, A., Parisi, D. and Plunkett, K. (1996) *Rethinking Innateness: A Connectionist Perspective on Development*. Cambridge, MA: MIT Press.

Feldman, D. H. (1994) *Beyond Universals in Cognitive Development*. Norwood, NJ: Ablex.

Feldman, D. H. (1995) 'Learning and development in nonuniversal theory'. *Human Development*, 38, 315–321.

Fischer, K. W. (1980) 'A theory of cognitive development: The control and construction of hierarchical skills'. *Psychological Review*, 87, 477–531.

Fodor, J. (1980) 'On the impossibility of acquiring "more powerful" structures'. In M. Piatelli-Palmarini (ed.), *Language and Learning: the Debate between Jean Piaget and Noam Chomsky*. Cambridge, MA: Harvard University Press, 146–162.

Fodor, J. (1983) *The Modularity of Mind*. Cambridge, MA: MIT Press.

Gelman, R. (1990) 'Structuralist constraints on cognitive development: Introduction to a special issue of *Cognitive Science*'. *Cognitive Science*, 14, 3–9.

Gentner, D. (1983) 'Structure mapping. A theoretical framework for analogy'. *Cognitive Science*, 7, 47–59.

Halford, G. S. (1982) *The Development of Thought*. Hillsdale, NJ: Erlbaum.

Halford, G. S. (1995) 'Learning processes in cognitive development: A reassessment with some unexpected implications'. *Human Development*, 38, 295–301.

Johnson-Laird, P. N. (1983) *Mental Models: Towards a Cognitive Science of Language, Inference, and Consciousness*. Cambridge, MA: Harvard University Press.

Karmiloff-Smith, A. (1986) 'From metaprocess to conscious access: Evidence from children's metalinguistic and repair data'. *Cognition*, 23, 95–147.

Karmiloff-Smith, A. (1992) *Beyond Modularity: A Developmental Perspective on Cognitive Science*. Cambridge, MA: MIT Press.

Karmiloff-Smith, A. (1994) Precis of *Beyond Modularity: A Developmental Perspective on Cognitive Science*. *Behavioral and Brain Sciences*, 17, 693–707.

Klahr, D. (1984) 'Transition processes in quantitative development'. In R. J. Sternberg (ed.), *Mechanisms of Development*. San Francisco: Freeman, 101–140.

Kuhn, D. (1995) (ed.) 'Development and learning: Reconceptualising the intersection'. (Special issue). *Human Development*, 38.

Liben, L. (1987) (ed.) *Development and Learning: Conflict or Congruence?* Hillsdale, NJ: Erlbaum.

Mevorach, M. and Strauss, S. (1996) 'Teachers' in-action mental model of children's minds and learning'. Unpublished manuscript, Tel Aviv University, Tel Aviv, Israel.

Newman, D., Griffin, P. and Cole, M. (1989) *The Construction Zone: Working for Cognitive Change in Schools*. New York: Cambridge University Press.

Norman, D. A. (1983) 'Some observations on mental models'. In D. Gentner and A. L. Stevens (eds), *Mental Models*. Hillsdale, NJ: Erlbaum, 7–14.

Pascual-Leone, J. (1970) 'A mathematical model for the transition rule in Piaget's development stages'. *Acta Psychologica*, 32, 301–345.

Pascual-Leone, J. (1988) 'Organismic processes for neo-Piagetian theories: A dialectical causal account of cognitive development'. In A. Demetriou (ed.), *The Neo-Piagetian Theories of Cognitive Development: Toward an Integration*. Amsterdam: North Holland, 25–65.

Piaget, J. (1970) 'Piaget's theory'. In P. H. Mussen (ed.), *Carmichael's Manual of Child Psychology*, vol. 1, 3rd edition. New York: Wiley, 703–732.

Rogoff, B. and Wertsch, J. V. (1984) (eds) *Children's Learning in the Zone of Proximal Development*. San Francisco: Jossey-Bass.

Schon, D. A. (1983) *The Reflective Practitioner: How Professionals Think in Action*. London: Temple Smith.

Schon, D. A. (1987) *Educating the Reflective Practitioner*. New York: Basic Books.

Shore, B. (1996) *Culture in Mind: Cognition, Culture, and the Problem of Meaning*. Oxford: Oxford University Press.

Shulman, L. S. (1986) 'Those who understand: Knowledge growth in teaching', *Educational Researcher*, 15, 4–14.

Siegler, R. S. (1981) 'Developmental sequences within and between concepts'. *Monographs of the Society for Research in Child Development*, 46, (2, Serial No.189).

Siegler, R. S. (1984) 'Mechanisms of cognitive growth: Variation and selection'. In R. J. Sternberg (ed.), *Mechanisms of Cognitive Development*. San Francisco: Freeman, 141–162.

Siegler, R. S. (1989) 'Mechanisms of cognitive development'. *Annual Review of Psychology*, 40, 353–379.

Siegler, R. S. and Shipley, C. (1987) 'The role of learning in children's choice strategy'. In L. Liben (ed.), *Development and Learning: Conflict or Congruence?* Hillsdale, NJ: Erlbaum.

Skinner, B. F. (1953) *Science and Human Behavior*. New York: Macmillan.

Spelke, E. (1990) 'Principles of object perception'. *Cognitive Science*, 14, 29–56.

Spelke, E. (1991) 'Physical knowledge in infancy: Reflections on Piaget's theory'. In S. Carey and R. Gelman (eds), *Epigenesis of Mind: Studies in Biology and Cognition*. Hillsdale, NJ: Erlbaum.

Stavy, R. and Berkowitz, B. (1980) 'Cognitive conflicts as a basis for teaching quantitative aspects of the concept of temperature'. *Science Education*, 64, 679–692.

Stigler, J. W., Shweder, R. A. and Herdt, G. (1990) *Cultural Psychology: Essays on Comparative Human Development*. Cambridge: Cambridge University Press.

Strauss, S. (1987) 'Educational-developmental psychology and school learning'. In L. Liben (ed.), *Development and Learning: Conflict or Congruence?* Hillsdale, NJ: Erlbaum, 133–158.

Strauss, S. (1993a) 'Teachers' pedagogical content knowledge about children's minds and learning: Implications for teacher education'. *Educational Psychologist*, 28, 279–290.

Strauss, S. (1993b) (ed.) 'Learning and development'. (Special issue). *Educational Psychologist*, 28 (3).

Strauss, S. (1996) 'Confessions of a born-again structuralist'. *Educational Psychologist*, 31, 15–21.

Strauss, S. (1997) 'Cognitive development and science education: Towards a middle level model'. In W. Damon (series ed.), I.E. Sigel and K. A. Renninger (vol. eds), *Handbook of Child Psychology: Vol. 4. Child Psychology in Practice*. New York: Wiley, 357–399.

Strauss, S. and Shilony, T. (1994) 'Teachers' mental models of children's minds and learning'. In L. Hirschfeld and S. A. Gelman (eds), *Mapping the Mind: Cognition and Culture*. New York: Cambridge University Press, 455–473.

Strauss, S. and Stavy, R. (1982) 'U-shaped behavioral growth: Implications for developmental theories'. In W. W. Hartup (ed.), *Review of Developmental Research*. Chicago: University of Chicago Press, 547–599.

Strauss, S., Ravid, D., Magen, N. and Berliner, D. C. (1998) 'Relations between teachers' subject matter knowledge, teaching experience, and their mental models of children's minds and learning'. *Teaching and Teacher Education*, 14, 579–595.

Vygotsky, L. S. (1978) *Mind in Society: The Development of Higher Psychological Processes* (M. Cole, V. John-Steiner, S. Scribner and E. Souberman, eds), New York: Plenum.

Vygotsky, L. S. (1987) *The Collected Works of L. S. Vygotsky. Volume 1: Problems of General Psychology* (R. W. Rieber and A. S. Carton, eds), New York: Plenum.

Wellman, H. M. (1990) *The Child's Theory of Mind*. Cambridge, MA: Bradford Books/MIT Press.

Wellman, H. M. and Inagaki, K. (1997) (eds) *The Emergence of Core Domain of Thought: Children's Reasoning about Physical, Psychological and Biological Phenomena*. (Volume 75 in New Directions for Child Development). San Francisco: Jossey-Bass.

Wertsch, J. V. and Tulviste, P. (1992) 'L. S. Vygotsky and contemporary developmental psychology'. *Developmental Psychology*, 28, 1–10.

4

COGNITION AND TEACHING

Richard White

Cognition concerns knowledge. It refers to both an act and a state. The act is the process by which the brain creates meanings from the impressions received by the senses, and the state is the knowledge that is the outcome of the act. Purposeful teaching and effective education require understanding of process and state.

Fundamental points follow from the truism that cognition occurs within an individual. The individual's physical, mental and emotional states influence cognition. Cognition is not independent of affect. Cognition occurs within a context, which will influence the person's purposes and goals. People differ in purposes, even when placed in the same situation, and an individual can change purpose, so different cognitions may follow from apparently similar contexts.

Cognition involves the construction of meaning. The meaning constructed for fresh information and experiences depends on what the individual knows already. Since prior knowledge is a factor in cognition, when two people receive the same information they are likely to form at least slightly different, though related, meanings from it.

Construction of meaning requires skills known as learning strategies. Some people are quicker than others to see implications and connections of information. An open debate continues on the extent to which training in strategies can improve a person's ability to learn.

Accounts of cognition include the operation of contexts, purposes and strategies in the construction of meaning. They also include models of how constructed meanings are stored in memory, and how they are recalled and used. Some models discriminate between types of knowledge. Most focus on networks of links between elements of information. Since neuro-physiology has not yet discovered how and where knowledge is stored, the models are speculative. They are, nevertheless, useful in derivation of principles of teaching.

EMERGENCE OF COGNITION IN MODERN PSYCHOLOGY

Accounts of the development of modern psychology commonly begin with Wilhelm Wundt, who is credited with separating psychology from philosophy and physiology in about 1879, when he opened his psychology laboratory in Leipzig. Wundt's principal research method was introspection. Both for those who agreed with him and those who differed, Wundt stimulated studies of the mind in North America as well as Europe. Echoes of the debates that followed can be heard in discussions today. William James, for instance, wrote of the active, dynamic mind that selects aspects of experience and creates its own perceptions of reality (James, 1890), principles that have been developed in depth in notions of metacognition and information-processing.

Though fundamental and stimulating, Wundt's methods encountered criticisms. Introspection did not produce knowledge that cumulated into a useful theory (Gardner, 1985). Concerns about the subjectivity, and hence the unreliability, of introspection and self-report methods led to a new movement, behaviourism, which largely buried for 40 years scholarly interest in the unobservable workings of the mind, including how it acquires knowledge. Although it began about a decade earlier, the landmark of the movement is the publication in 1924 of Watson's book *Behaviorism*.

Though subdued, interest in cognitive processes was not entirely dead. Indications of life were the Gestalt movement, led by Wertheimer (1912) and marked by Köhler's (1917/1925) book *The Mentality of Apes*, and the notion of schemata developed in Bartlett's 1932 classic, *Remembering*. Both the Gestalt theorists and Bartlett emphasised that humans organise their experiences into meaningful wholes, and that this organisation depends on what the individual already knows.

The resurgence of interest in cognition probably was delayed by the depression of the 1930s, the rise of totalitarian states and the Second World War. Several factors may have combined in the 1950s to promote it. Among them was recognition of behaviourism's inability to explain major parts of human experience. An example is acquisition of language. Linguists, such as Chomsky (1957), argued effectively that language is too complex to be acquired through stimulus–response learning. Then there was the discovery by English-speaking scholars of the work of Piaget, and their appreciation of his principle that cognitive growth is a consequence of interplay between the individual and the environment. Piaget's clinical interviews with children demonstrated the crucial nature of beliefs and their role in the construction of meanings for experiences. Also important was the invention of computers, and hence the analogy that could be made between the steps by which they processed information and the way in which humans learned. Information-processing became integral to notions of cognition. Gardner (1985) provides a detailed account of these influences.

From these factors emerged the major theme, that cognition involves a sequence of mental operations that result in the construction of meanings for experiences, and the subsequent storage in memory of those meanings. Further operations enable recall or reconstruction of stored meanings, and their use in coping with new situations. Concern remains that these operations cannot be observed directly, and so their nature remains speculative. As a result, much of the history of cognition is taken up with debates about alternative depictions of the operations, and with attempts to devise experiments that would discriminate between them. These debates and attempts continue, as does a further concern: what is the ultimate driver of the operations? What is the nature of the central processor, the self that controls the whole?

INFORMATION-PROCESSING

Though it is logically possible for there to be a model of cognition that does not parallel the operations of the electronic computer, this is hardly practical now, when the analogy with the computer pervades depictions of learning. Like all analogies, this one has shortcomings as well as advantages. Both should be kept in mind. Criticisms of the computer model, such as that of Searle (1992), might in time produce a change in the conception of cognition equally as revolutionary as the move from behaviourism. For now, however, the computer analogy dominates.

One of the best known of the many representations of how humans process information is that of Atkinson and Shiffrin (1968). The model is sequential, and begins with physical stimuli impinging on nerve receptors, and being held briefly in a sensory buffer. Sperling's (1960) experiments provide evidence for this buffer, and its holding period of a second or less. A common instance of the buffer is the persistence of the image when a torch light or a sparkling firework is swung around in the dark: we seem to see a line or circle of light. According to the model, some of the stimuli are translated into meaningful forms and selected for attention. The translation and selection are vital processes. Both have been studied extensively.

Translation involves pattern recognition, important in how we structure the world. We can read different typefaces, for instance, and (within limits) individual handwriting, in every case recognising the marks as specific letters and words; or we can recognise ranges of shapes as particular objects. Texts (e.g. Matlin, 1983; Reed, 1992) describe explanations of how we do this, such as matching what we experience with a template stored in memory, or picking out critical features. In whatever way it occurs, no cognitivist doubts that existing knowledge is the crucial element in translation. We cannot see what we do not know. Knowledge here, of course, involves parallels with familiar objects, so that if you are shown some new object, such as a specialised surgical instrument, you would perceive it as like something you already know about, such as a pair of pliers.

We attend to only some of the stimuli that impinge on us. The information-processing model has a portion of the entries into the sensory buffer passing on to a short-term memory store. Miller (1956) showed that this store has limited capacity, of about seven items. Broadbent (1975) later suggested that it is less, perhaps about four. Discussion of this raised the issue of what is an item. We collect our sensory impressions into meaningful wholes, or chunks. What constitutes a chunk, however, may differ from person to person. This is of importance in teaching. The teacher, being more familiar with a topic and more informed, is likely to perceive information in larger meaningful wholes and hence fewer chunks than the students can. It would be easy for the teacher to overload the students' short-term memories. Further, students will differ in their short-term memory capacities. Johnstone and El-Banna (1986) have shown how the capacity is related to ability to solve problems: once the problem requires the solver to hold more pieces of it in mind at once than the person's STM capacity, it cannot be done.

Information cannot be held in short-term memory for more than half a minute or so without rehearsal. It is either passed on to long-term memory or lost. Thus we do not keep memories of much of the experiences of a day – what we saw on the way to work, what we did at 11.30 am, and so forth. Much of what we process into long-term memory is a deliberate choice. That selection is affected by our purposes. Although for economy theories of cognition focus on knowledge and give less attention to motivation, they recognise that cognition is but one aspect of a complete organism. In this, cognitive theories return to James's view that behaviour is planned. Gardner (1985) identifies Lashley's argument at the Hixon Symposium in 1948 that rapid complex behaviours such as speech or playing music must be planned and organised in advance as a key moment in the shift from behaviourist to cognitive views. Prominent descriptions of how plans operate in information-processing include books by Miller *et al.* (1960) and Schank and Abelson (1977).

Although the notion of short- and long-term memories is widely used, in a frequently cited article Craik and Lockhart (1972) proposed an alternative in which information varies in the depth of its processing. Their model does not require separate stores. Consciousness, which in the Atkinson and Shiffrin model is a function of the short-term (or working) memory, here concerns whatever part of the total knowledge currently is activated. Although many cognitivists appreciate the depth-of-processing model, they continue to find the notions of short- and long-term stores convenient.

There are various portrayals of aspects of long-term memory, which have stimulated debate. One concerns the presence of images in memory. In opposition to behaviourism, Paivio (1971) restored imagery as an item in psychology. His experiments demonstrated that for many problems people use mental images rather than verbal reasoning. Luria (1968) describes a person with extreme powers of imagery. Few people deny that imagery is experienced, but there is debate over whether we recreate images much as a computer produces graphics as Kosslyn (1975; Kosslyn and Pomerantz, 1977) described, or create them from verbal propositions, which Pylyshyn (1973) argued.

Tulving (1972) made another distinction, between episodic and semantic memories. Episodic memory refers to knowledge located in time and place, involving memories of actual experience. In a sense all knowledge has episodic character, since we acquire it at a particular place and time. For much of what we know, however, we have lost the details of when and where we acquired it. Semantic memory does not necessarily have connections of time and place of learning. Neither Tulving nor Paivio postulated separate sites in the brain for the types of memory they distinguished.

As well as speculation about types of memory, there have been various accounts of the patterns of relations between the elements of knowledge. Frequently these accounts depict networks. An early instance is the Human Associative Memory system of Anderson and Bower (1973), which was strongly influenced by their goal of programming a computer so that it could answer logical inferential questions about stored information. For other examples see Quillian (1968) and Rumelhart *et al.*, (1972).

Networks consist of nodes joined by lines. In most models, the nodes are nouns, and the lines represent the relations between the nouns. An alternative, largely overlooked, is to have propositions as the nodes, with the lines being present whenever a pair of propositions contains a common term. This might accord better with the general acceptance that the units of information are individual propositions.

TYPES OF KNOWLEDGE

Although most network models include only propositional knowledge, that is statements of beliefs or facts, theorists propose other types such as images and episodes. Discrimination between types of knowledge is important in education, since the types may be learned differently and may produce different forms of understanding.

One important distinction made by Ryle (1949) is between knowing *that*, and knowing *how*. Where knowing *that* is propositional, knowing *how* is algorithmic, constituting the capacity to perform a rule-governed procedure such as telling the time from an analogue clock, substituting in a formula, applying rules of grammar, or finding a given word in a dictionary. Gagné and White (1978) proposed much the same forms of verbal knowledge (knowing that) and intellectual skills (knowing how), and added the further types of images, episodes, motor skills and cognitive strategies (equivalent to learning strategies, described below).

These classifications of types of knowledge run across the traditional scholarly separation of disciplines of history, mathematics and so on. Such distinctions are important, because they emphasise that different forms of knowledge are learned (and therefore should be taught) differently.

The types are relevant also to the notion of understanding. Virtually all descriptions of understanding, which could be characterised as knowing *why*, portray it as a perception of links between elements of knowledge. Episodes, recollections of experiences, provide a foundation for these links, since even a subject as sophisticated and abstract as mathematics requires experiences with shapes, objects and countable units. Different proportions of episodes and images linked to propositions and algorithms give different flavours of understanding.

The variation that White and Gunstone (1980) have shown exists between individuals' preferences for one type of knowledge or another has consequences for teaching. One implication is that teachers should use diverse but parallel forms of presentation, in part to give each student, whatever his or her preferential form, the maximum chance of forming an accurate meaning, and in part to encourage all to acquire a rich mix of the various types of knowledge and hence a more complete understanding.

SCRIPTS AND SITUATED COGNITION

We recall some events as singular episodes, but if an experience is repeated often enough we form from it a generalisation that Schank and Abelson (1977) term a script. Thus we have scripts for the supermarket, the theatre, catching a bus and so forth. With further experience a script can become more subtle and extensive, so that we have a deeper understanding of the event. In this way novices gradually become experts. Presumably, as Schon (1983) advocates, reflection assists their progress.

Scripts are relevant to the recent notion of situated cognition (Brown *et al.*, 1989). Lave (1988), Carraher *et al.* (1985), Scribner (1984) and others have found that people are far more competent at certain arithmetic problems in well-experienced situations such as bowling alleys or supermarkets than they are at identical problems in less relevant (though equally familiar) situations such as classrooms or at home. The relation between scene and capacity to cope surely extends beyond arithmetic. As Lave (1988) points out, cognition is a complex *social* phenomenon: the way we think and the way we use knowledge are functions of the situation. A major challenge for systems of education is to ensure that the knowledge learners acquire in classrooms is available to them in other settings. Choi and Hannafin (1995) point out that to meet this challenge teachers, curriculum designers and test constructors will have to alter fundamental aspects of their practice. Griffin (1995) provides an example of a short teaching procedure for situated learning. Anderson *et al.* (1996) warn against carrying enthusiasm for situated learning too far, and argue that there is still value in abstract instruction in formal settings.

CONCEPTS

Propositions, images, episodes and so forth are elements of knowledge. When a person links a number of elements with the name of an object or an idea, such as democracy or elephant, the collection of linked elements forms that person's concept for that object or idea. Among the elements may be the skill of distinguishing democracies from non-democracies, elephants from non-elephants. Since two people are unlikely to have identical episodes and images, or even propositions, about democracy, or elephants, it follows that their concepts differ. This has implications for future teaching, since it means that students begin each topic with varying knowledge (unless it is something for which none of them knows anything at all). It also has implications for assessment: Which elements are essential? Should credit be given for knowledge beyond the expected? Does the assessment over-emphasise propositions or algorithms?

CONSTRUCTION OF MEANING

Meaning is an outcome of relating new knowledge to old. Since people differ in what they already know, and select different things for attention, they will construct different meanings for events and information. Appreciation of this has led to a movement known as constructivism. Steffe and Gale (1995) provide a compilation of constructivist views.

Constructivism has become especially popular in science education, where research on children's explanations of natural phenomena expanded rapidly in the 1980s. Pfundt and Duit (1994) provide a bibliography of several thousand studies. The first phase of this research on alternative conceptions – so-called because it deals with notions that differ from scientists' depictions of nature – consisted of probes of beliefs. The research (e.g. Driver *et al.*, 1985; Osborne and Freyberg, 1985; Wandersee *et al.*, 1994) found that students often had formed explanations of phenomena such as motion and temperature that they retained despite being taught different, scientific explanations.

The next phase involved attempts to bring students' explanations in line with scientists'. This proved surprisingly difficult, with researchers often having no, or at best mixed, success (e.g. Brown and Clement, 1989; Gauld, 1986; Gunstone *et al.*, 1981). The difficulty drew attention to how alternative conceptions arise in the first place, which is the third phase of the research. Bliss and Ogborn (1994), Vosniadou (1994) and Tytler (1994) provide promising lines of research and theory.

Although the basic principle in constructivism is that each individual constructs a personal meaning from information and experience, this does not mean that all constructions are equally valid or useful, nor that mentors have no role in learning. Duit (1995) reminds us that the issue in teaching is one of balance between self-development and guidance. That is the essence of Vygotsky's (1978) much-cited notion of a zone of proximal development. Vygotsky noted that children can, with the help of a more knowledgeable person, solve problems that they cannot do on their own. The tutor does not solve the problem for them, but guides their thinking. For guidance to be successful, however, the learner must already have relevant knowledge on which the thinking can draw. In new learning, which can be regarded as a form of problem-solving, the guidance must help the learner to relate the new information to old. This notion of Vygotsky's is consistent with other writing on the construction of meaning, for example by Ausubel (1968) and Wittrock (1990). Rogoff and Wertsch (1984) and Oerter (1992) describe the application of Vygotsky's notion in teaching.

Meaning is constructed for something. White (1988) discriminated between various targets of understanding: single elements of knowledge such as a proposition; concepts; whole disciplines, such as nineteenth-century history or rational economics; extended communications such as a novel, play, painting or movie; social situations; and people. In all cases, construction of meaning involves the linking of new information to old, especially to scripts and episodes.

LEARNING STRATEGIES AND METACOGNITION

Learning strategies are conceived as the means by which one processes information, especially from short-term memory into long, and so constructs meaning. Various theorists have set out lists of strategies, which although they differ in details present an essentially similar conception of planned, purposeful, self-monitored thought. For examples see Nisbet and Shucksmith (1986), Holley and Dansereau (1984), Weinstein and Mayer (1986) and White (1988). In all of these examples, learning is analysed as a series of processes under the learner's control. Some entries in a list of commonly mentioned strategies compiled by Nisbet and Shucksmith (1986, p. 28) demonstrate this:

Planning: deciding on tactics and timetables
Monitoring: continuous attempt to match efforts, answers and discoveries to initial questions
Checking: preliminary assessment of performance and results.

These examples are typical of descriptions of learning strategies, in that they appear as purposeful acts. Thus although strategies could be thought of as innate, their very formulation implies that they are trainable. This holds out hope for significant improvement in the quality of learning.

The purposeful character of learning strategies implies that their use is deliberate and aware rather than automatic and unconscious. Certainly most training procedures focus on developing conscious use, and have become synonymous with the notion of metacognition.

Flavell (1976) defined metacognition as knowledge of thinking processes, awareness of one's own, and the ability to control them.

Initial research into metacognition (e.g. Brown, 1978; Paris *et al.*, 1983) concentrated on reading, where a major problem is inability to convert the symbols on the page into a meaningful whole. Poor readers may decode the words yet fail to see the meaning of the sentence or the overall theme of a passage.

Metacognition is not confined to reading. It extends to all learning, including the important context of lessons in schools. This context is more complex than reading, for it involves relations between students and between students and teacher, differences between teachers, the nature of the subject matter, characteristics of the educational system such as examinations and class sizes, and characteristics of society such as perceived purpose of education, respect for learning, employment prospects and divisions of social class. Such complexity makes training in metacognition, or learning strategies, complex and difficult to evaluate. There are, however, some encouraging projects.

TRAINING OF LEARNING STRATEGIES

Training of learning strategies promises to advance cognition. Since learning is a lifelong activity, training is appropriate for adults as well as children. It is not surprising, however, that most attempts occur in schools, where society concentrates organised learning.

Some programmes run as separate classes, and others as integral parts of subject teaching. A widely publicised example of separate classes is de Bono's CoRT programme (de Bono, 1988), in which training is given on strategies such as CAF: Consider All Factors – that is, to think about the situation for a while before reaching a decision. This strategy aims to overcome a common learning problem that Baird (1986) names premature closure.

Evidence for CoRT's effectiveness is equivocal. Edwards (1991) points out that evaluations of it have had weaknesses in design. Weaknesses are hard to avoid, since CoRT, like other programmes for training learning strategies, is lengthy, and it is difficult to create and maintain for the weeks required an experiment that meets all the criteria of strength. Thomas (1992) identified one of the troubles CoRT trainers experience, which can affect all strategies programmes but especially those run as separate classes: most students remain unconvinced that the effort is worthwhile. Even when students had practised the CoRT techniques, Thomas found that they tended to abandon them under pressure, such as in examinations.

Another separate-class programme is Feuerstein's Instrumental Enrichment. This, too, has had mixed success. See Shayer and Beasley (1987) for a review.

A key problem for separate-class programmes is getting students not just to learn the strategies but to transfer them to other lessons and to everyday situations. Integrated programmes, where strategies are promoted along with the teaching of content, avoid part of that problem. Their integration, however, makes them even more difficult to evaluate. So many events occur, and so many factors operate, in classrooms that it is hard to tell which is responsible for any effect.

The Project for Enhancing Effective Learning (PEEL) (Baird and Mitchell, 1986; Baird and Northfield, 1992) is a large-scale example of an integrated programme. It is a professional development programme rather than a research project. It has not been evaluated thoroughly, although White and Mitchell (1993) report marked increases in appropriate behaviours. PEEL developed from a research study of six months' duration, involving one teacher and three science classes (Baird, 1986). This prior study illustrates some of the issues for attempts to train strategies. Baird found that gains made in the science lessons could be negated by the learners' experiences with other teachers. This, of course, is also a problem for separate-class programmes. He also found that the teacher he worked with, though committed to encouraging students to question and say when they did not understand, often gave them no opportunity to do so because he felt obliged to teach a given amount of content even if the students failed to understand it. This is a significant point for strategies programmes and their evaluations: the social context has a powerful effect.

PEEL attempts to overcome both of the difficulties Baird encountered. In secondary schools it requires a collaboration of teachers of several subjects, so that students experience consistent practices during a year. In primary schools, too, it is preferable for teachers to work in partnerships, to support each other, and for the students to experience consistency from one year to the next. Concerning social context, the project requires acceptance by parents and support from school administration. There appears to be little difficulty about either: the intent of improving learning appeals to parents, and the teacher enthusiasm and more purposeful behaviour of students satisfy headteachers.

A problem for studies of cognition is that the processes are unobservable. They have to be inferred from indirect indicators. One of the useful outcomes from PEEL is teachers' specification of 25 Good Learning Behaviours, which Mitchell (1992) relates to the strategies of monitoring and of constructing meaning. Examples of Good Learning Behaviour on the part of a student include the following:

- When stuck, refers to earlier work *before* asking teacher;
- Seeks reasons for aspects of the work;
- Seeks links between different subjects;
- Challenges the text or an answer the teacher sanctions as correct.

Display of these behaviours has been observed at a rate of one per minute in PEEL classes, compared with about one-tenth as often in other classes (White and Mitchell, 1993).

The project Cognitive Acceleration through Science Education (CASE) (Adey and Shayer, 1994) fits somewhere between the separate-lesson programmes such as CoRT and the fully integrated ones such as PEEL. CASE consists of a series of science lessons, delivered by the students' usual teacher, but replacing one regular science lesson each fortnight. Like PEEL, CASE is a lengthy intervention. The experimental form, evaluated by Adey and Shayer, ran for two years of teaching, with monitoring of effects for up to three further years. Long, intensive intervention appears to be an essential in training people in strategies. This complicates research, for it is difficult to eliminate the possibility of interference from other factors, and difficult to maintain a consistent treatment.

Interventions on the scale of CASE are beyond the resources of individual teachers. The need for long involvement, however, puts teachers in a better position than outside researchers to carry out studies of cognition. Their own day-to-day experiences are a source of information, and they can implement, maintain and record effects of an innovative programme more easily than an outsider. Examples of teachers' programmes are Gove and

Kennedy-Calloway (1992); Jane and Jobling (1995); Osler *et al.* (1996); Swan and White (1994).

COGNITION AND AFFECT

Taking part in a lengthy study of cognition, or metacognition, brings home to a researcher the importance of students' motives and feelings. Yet, as Eisner (1994) points out, cognition is often contrasted with affect, and knowledge is considered independently of feelings. Education systems tend to maintain the distinction, and to emphasise cognition and neglect affect. We see this in the allocation of time to subjects, in which those primarily concerned with aesthetics, such as music and art, have a minor place in most systems. It is also evident in assessment, which in most subjects deals entirely with cognitive outcomes. This may be through lack of valid measures of affect, but it appears that little urgency exists to overcome that lack.

Affect is connected with class dynamics. Though cognition occurs in individuals' heads, those individuals experience a social context. Some contexts will foster cognition, some inhibit. Popular analogies with commercial enterprises invoke competition as desirable in the classroom, but the teachers in PEEL advocate co-operation. Other research supports them (Wentzel, 1991). Co-operation and prosocial behaviour may also be helpful in programmes of moral development (Oser, 1992; Solomon *et al.*, 1992).

Attempts to foster cognition, either through training in metacognition or otherwise, should consider affect. That consideration might well extend to probing learners' purposes. How internal are these purposes? Are they trying to learn better because of their appreciation of learning, or to impress their peers or please the authorities of teachers, parents and examiners?

FUTURE RESEARCH

It is now 40 years since cognition began again to be a focus of speculation and research. The initial psychological studies of perception and short-term memory have been followed by two diverging fields of work, one physiological, the other educational.

The physiological work involves a search for the neural mechanisms of learning and the manner in which the brain stores memory. The outcomes of this research may assist diagnosis of learning deficits and design of remedial mediation, but otherwise appear unlikely to be of major relevance to education. Learning will continue to occur in a social context, and educationists will need to understand the complexities of that context rather than the details of neural functioning.

The suggestions for lines of research that follow cannot be prescriptive. Each piece of research opens new lines, and each researcher sees particular needs and opportunities.

The model of information-processing includes a selection of events for attention and their translation into meaningful form. Research could look at the effects of multiple modes of presentation – words, symbols, enactments; visual and auditory; and whether the modes are experienced simultaneously or successively – on selection and translation. Individual differences in preferences for particular modes, or in abilities to cope with them, could be studied.

Most research on cognition attends to acquisition of information; the balance might shift to recall of information at need, either in a lesson or an examination or in everyday situations.

Although linking of elements of knowledge is a key aspect of models of cognition, there needs to be much more research into how teaching might promote that linking. An instance is the study by Mackenzie and White (1982) of the linking of episodes with propositions in geography and the resulting improvement in recall.

Classroom teachers could do much research on development and evaluation of training of specific strategies in cognition, such as organisation of extended answers or perception of alternative interpretations.

Diagnostic procedures are needed, to identify presence or absence of cognitive processes. As well as being useful for identifying students at risk, the procedures would assist evaluation of projects to train strategies. They would be particularly helpful in assessing replications of major programmes such as PEEL and CASE.

Longitudinal studies of cognition could influence the practice of education. They are rare, because difficult to conduct. In a search of 25 years of publications in four major journals of research on science education, Arzi (1988) found only 34 longitudinal studies. More common are cohort studies, which compare learners of different ages or educational levels. Though useful, cohort studies are not as effective as longitudinal ones in showing how an individual builds up a system of beliefs, or how particular events and aspects of context influence acquisition of knowledge, learning strategies, or motivation to learn. Linn and Eylon (1996) provide an example of a true longitudinal study.

REFERENCES

Adey, P. and Shayer, M. (1994) *Really Raising Standards: Cognitive Intervention and Academic Achievement*. London: Routledge.

Anderson, J. R. and Bower, G. H. (1973) *Human Associative Memory*. Washington, DC: Winston & Sons.

Anderson, J. R., Reder, L. M. and Simon, H. A. (1996) 'Situated learning and education'. *Educational Researcher*, 25 (4), 5–11.

Arzi, H. J. (1988) 'From short- to long-term: Studying science education longitudinally'. *Studies in Science Education*, 15, 17–53.

Atkinson, R. L. and Shiffrin, R. M. (1968) 'Human memory: A proposed system and its control processes'. In K. W. Spence and J. T. Spence (eds), *The Psychology of Learning and Motivation: Advances in Research and Theory*. New York: Academic Press.

Ausubel, D. P. (1968) *Educational Psychology: A Cognitive View*. New York: Holt, Rinehart & Winston.

Baird, J. R. (1986) 'Improving learning through enhanced metacognition: A classroom study'. *European Journal of Science Education*, 8, 263–282.

Baird, J. R. and Mitchell, I. J. (eds) (1986) *Improving the Quality of Teaching and Learning: An Australian Case Study – The Peel Project*. Melbourne: Monash University.

Baird, J. R. and Northfield, J. R. (eds) (1992) *Learning from the PEEL Experience*. Melbourne: Authors (Monash University).

Bartlett, F. C. (1932) *Remembering*. Cambridge: Cambridge University Press.

Bliss, J. and Ogborn, J. (1994) 'Force and motion from the beginning'. *Learning and Instruction*, 4, 7–25.

Broadbent, D. E. (1975) 'The magic number seven after fifteen years'. In A. Kennedy and A. Wilkes (eds), *Studies in Long Term Memory*. London: Wiley.

Brown, A. L. (1978) 'Knowing when, where, and how to remember: A problem of metacognition'. In R. Glaser (ed.), *Advances in Instructional Psychology: vol. 1*. Hillsdale, NJ: Erlbaum.

Brown, D. E. and Clement, J. (1989) 'Overcoming misconceptions via analogical reasoning: abstract transfer versus explanatory model construction'. *Instructional Science*, 18, 237–261.

Brown, J. S., Collins, A. and Duguid, P. (1989) 'Situated cognition and the culture of learning'. *Educational Researcher*, 18, 32–42.

Carraher, T. N., Carraher, D. W. and Schliemann, A. D. (1985) *British Journal of Developmental Psychology*, 3, 21–29.

Choi, J.-I. and Hannafin, M. (1995) 'Situated cognition and learning environments: Roles, structures, and implications for design'. *Educational Technology Research and Development*, 43, 53–69.

Chomsky, N. (1957) *Syntactic Structures*. The Hague: Mouton.

Craik, F. I. M. and Lockhart, R. S. (1972) 'Levels of processing: A framework for memory research'. *Journal of Verbal Learning and Verbal Behavior*, 11, 671–684.

de Bono, E. (1988) 'The CORT Thinking Program'. In J. W. Segal, S. F. Chipman and R. Glaser (eds), *Thinking and Learning skills: vol. 1. Relating Instruction to Research*. Hillsdale, NJ: Erlbaum.

Driver, R., Guesne, E. and Tiberghien, A. (eds) (1985) *Children's Ideas in Science*. Milton Keynes: Open University Press.

Duit, R. (1995) 'The constructivist view: A fashionable and fruitful paradigm for science education research and practice'. In L. P. Steffe and J. Gale (eds), *Constructivism in Education*, Hillsdale, NJ: Erlbaum.

Edwards, J. (1991) 'The direct teaching of thinking skills'. In G. Evans (ed.), *Learning and Teaching Cognitive Skills*. Melbourne: ACER.

Eisner, E. W. (1994) *Cognition and Curriculum Reconsidered* (2nd edn). New York: Teachers College Press.

Flavell, J. H. (1976) 'Metacognitive aspects of problem-solving'. In L. B. Resnick (ed.), *The Nature of Intelligence*, Hillsdale, NJ: Erlbaum.

Gagné, R. M. and White, R. T. (1978) 'Memory structures and learning outcomes'. *Review of Educational Research*, 48, 187–222.

Gardner, H. (1985) *The Mind's New Science: A History of the Cognitive Revolution*. New York: Basic Books.

Gauld, C. (1986) 'Models, meters and memory'. *Research in Science Education*, 16, 49–54.

Gove, M. K. and Kennedy-Calloway, C. (1992) 'Action research: Empowering teachers to work with at-risk students'. *Journal of Reading*, 35, 526–534.

Griffin, M. M. (1995) 'You can't get there from here: Situated learning, transfer, and map skills'. *Contemporary Educational Psychology*, 20, 65–87.

Gunstone, R. F., Champagne, A. B. and Klopfer, L. E. (1981) 'Instruction for understanding: A case study'. *Australian Science Teachers' Journal*, 27 (3), 27–32.

Holley, C. D. and Dansereau, D. F. (1984) *Spatial Learning Strategies: Techniques, Applications, and Related Issues*. Orlando, FL: Academic Press.

James, W. (1890) *The Principles of Psychology*. New York: Holt.

Jane, B. L. and Jobling, W. M. (1995) 'Children linking science and technology in the primary classroom'. *Research in Science Education*, 25, 191–201.

Johnstone, A. H. and El-Banna, H. (1986) 'Capacities, demands and processes – a predictive model for science education'. *Education in Chemistry*, 23, 80–84.

Köhler, W. (1925) *The Mentality of Apes* (trans. E. Winter). London: Routledge & Kegan Paul.

Kosslyn, S. M. (1975) 'Information representation in visual images'. *Cognitive Psychology*, 7, 341–370.

Kosslyn, S. M. and Pomerantz, J. R. (1977) 'Imagery, propositions, and the form of internal representations'. *Cognitive Psychology*, 9, 52–76.

Lave, J. (1988) *Cognition in Practice: Mind, Mathematics and Culture in Everyday Life*. Cambridge: Cambridge University Press.

Linn, M. C. and Eylon, B-S. (July, 1996) 'Lifelong science learning: A longitudinal case study'. In *Proceedings of CogSci96*, San Diego.

Luria, A. R. (1968) *The Mind of a Mnemonist* (trans. L. Solotaroff). New York: Basic Books.

Mackenzie, A. A. and White, R. T. (1982) 'Fieldwork in geography and long-term memory structures'. *American Educational Research Journal*, 19, 623–632.

Matlin, M. (1983) *Cognition*. New York: Holt, Rinehart & Winston.

Miller, G. A. (1956) 'The magical number seven, plus or minus two: Some limits on our capacity for processing information'. *Psychological Review*, 63, 81–97.

Miller, G. A., Galanter, E. and Pribram, K. (1960) *Plans and the Structure of Behavior*. New York: Holt, Rinehart & Winston.

Mitchell, I. (1992) 'The class level'. In J. R. Baird and J. R. Northfield (eds), *Learning from the PEEL Experience*. Melbourne: Monash University Faculty of Education.

Nisbet, J. and Shucksmith, J. (1986) *Learning Strategies*. London: Routledge & Kegan Paul.

Oerter, R. (1992) 'The zone of proximal development for learning and teaching'. In F. K. Oser, A. Dick, and J.-L. Patry (eds), *Effective and Responsible Teaching: The New Synthesis*. San Francisco: Jossey-Bass.

Osborne, R. J. and Freyberg, P. (1985) *Learning in Science: The Implications of Children's Science*. Auckland: Heinemann.

Oser, F. (1992) 'The pilot project "Democracy and Education in the School" (DES) in Northrhine-Westfalia'. *Moral Education Forum*, 17 (2), 1–4.

Osler, J., Flack, J. and Mitchell, J. (1996) 'Voices from "the swamp" – students' perspectives on an attempt to improve learning'. *Reflect*, 2 (2), 15–20.

Paivio, A. (1971) *Imagery and Verbal Processes*. New York: Holt, Rinehart & Winston.

Paris, S. G., Lipson, M. Y. and Wixson, K. K. (1983). 'Becoming a strategic reader'. *Contemporary Educational Psychology*, 8, 293–316.

Pfundt, H. and Duit, R. (1994) *Bibliography: Students' Alternative Frameworks and Science Education* (4th edn). Kiel: Institute for Science Education, University of Kiel.

Pylyshyn, Z. W. (1973) 'What the mind's eye tells the mind's brain'. *Psychological Bulletin*, 80, 1–24.

Quillian, M. R. (1968) 'Semantic memory'. In M. Minsky (ed.), *Semantic Information Processing*. Cambridge, MA: MIT Press.

Reed, S. K. (1992) *Cognition: Theory and Applications* (3rd edn). Pacific Grove, CA: Brooks/Cole.

Rogoff, B. and Wertsch, J. V. (eds). (1984) *Children's Learning in the "Zone of Proximal Development"*. San Francisco: Jossey-Bass.

Rumelhart, D. E., Lindsay, P. H. and Norman, D. A. (1972) 'A process model for long-term memory'. In E. Tulving and W. Donaldson (eds), *Organization of Memory*. New York: Academic Press.

Ryle, G. (1949) *The Concept of Mind*. London: Hutchinson.

Schank, R. C. and Abelson, R. P. (1977) *Scripts, Plans, Goals and Understanding: An Inquiry into Human Knowledge Structures*. Hillsdale, NJ: Erlbaum.

Schon, D. A. (1983) *The Reflective Practitioner: How Professionals Think in Action*. New York: Basic Books.

Scribner, S. (1984) 'Studying working intelligence'. In B. Rogoff and J. Lave (eds), *Everyday Cognition: Its Development in Social Context*. Cambridge, MA: Harvard UP.

Searle, J. R. (1992) *The Rediscovery of the Mind*. Cambridge, MA: Bradford.

Shayer, M. and Beasley, F. (1987). 'Does instrumental enrichment work?'. *British Educational Research Journal*, 13, 101–119.

Solomon, D., Watson, M., Battistich, V., Schaps, E. and Delucchi, K. (1992) 'Creating a caring community: Educational practices that promote children's prosocial development'. In F. K. Oser, A. Dick, and J.-L. Patry (eds), *Effective and Responsible Teaching: The New Synthesis*. San Francisco: Jossey-Bass.

Sperling, G. (1960) 'The information available in brief visual presentations'. *Psychological Monographs* 24 (11).

Steffe, L. P. and Gale, J. (eds) (1995) *Constructivism in Education*. Hillsdale, NJ: Erlbaum.

Swan, S. and White, R. (1994) *The Thinking Books*, London: Falmer.

Thomas, G. (1992) 'An investigation into the transfer of cognitive strategies'. Unpublished Master of Educational Studies thesis, Monash University, Melbourne.

Tulving, E. (1972) 'Episodic and semantic memory'. In E. W. Tulving and W. Donaldson (eds), *Organization of Memory*. New York: Academic Press.

Tytler, R. (1994) 'Consistency of children's use of science conceptions: Problems with the notion of "conceptual change"'. *Research in Science Education*, 24, 338–347.

Vosniadou, S. (1994) 'Capturing and modeling the process of conceptual change'. *Learning and Instruction*, 4, 45–69.

Vygotsky, L. S. (1978) *Mind in Society: The Development of Higher Psychological Processes*. Cambridge, MA: Harvard University Press.

Wandersee, J. H., Mintzes, J. J. and Novak, J. D. (1994) 'Research on alternative conceptions in science'. In D. L. Gabel (ed.) *Handbook of Research on Science Teaching and Learning*. New York: Macmillan.

Watson, J. B. (1924) *Behaviorism*. Chicago: University of Chicago Press.

Weinstein, C. E. and Mayer, R. E. (1986) 'The teaching of learning strategies'. In M. C. Wittrock (ed.), *Handbook of Research on Teaching* (3rd edn). New York: Macmillan.

Wentzel, K. R. (1991) 'Social competence at school: Relation between social responsibility and academic achievement'. *Review of Educational Research*, 61, 1–24.

Wertheimer, M. (1912) 'Experimentelle Studien über das Schen von Bewigungen'. *Zeitschrift für Psychologie*, 61, 161–265.

White, R. T. (1988) *Learning Science*. Oxford: Blackwell.

White, R. T. and Gunstone, R. F. (1980) *Converting Memory Protocols to Scores on Several Dimensions*. Australian Association for Research in Education Annual Conference Papers, 486–493.

White, R. T. and Mitchell, I. M. (1993) 'The promotion of good learning behaviours'. Paper presented at the conference of the European Association for Research on Learning and Instruction, Aix-en-Provence, France.

Wittrock, M. C. (1990) 'Generative processes of comprehension'. *Educational Psychologist*, 24, 345–376.

5

LEARNING

Charles Desforges

THE SIGNIFICANCE OF LEARNING

It is broadly agreed that societies are undergoing a period of rapid and dramatic change. It has been well said that economic and political dynamics are altering the structures of personal and social experience and placing new demands on the capacities persons need to flourish in society. The changes are of such a scale and pace as to carry both great threat and vaunting promise. There is the threat to stability and to the established order of things. At the same time there is the promise of undreamt of qualities of life. This has placed education at the centre of public policy with the core task of helping people transform how they think of themselves. The term 'learning society' captures the necessity for continuous and progressive adjustment to change and emphasises the need for an educational system based on a powerful and practical understanding of learning for people at all ages and stages of their development. Learning has the potential to permeate and enhance all aspects of our lives from the narrow issue of acquiring a corpus of schooled knowledge and skill to the broader matter of learning to be a person in society and through every aspect of social life including leisure, wealth creation, health, family, workplace and political life. The urgent need for productive and progressive adjustment to change places increasing burdens of relevance, efficiency and effectiveness on educational systems and imposes learning as the core concept of our time.

OVERVIEW

The central purpose of educational systems is to promote learning. Learning is the field's most basic concept. The verb 'to learn' may take an object. One always learns something. In educational terms this 'something' is defined by the curriculum whether this be formal (as in schooling) or informal (as in life's experiences). The matter of curriculum content is not treated here in any depth although it cannot be ignored. The focus here is on the process of learning and the structure of learning experience. The key questions are:

- How are learners most profitably engaged with the curriculum?
- How, once determined, is the curriculum best sequenced?
- What is the role of the learner?
- How is learning best managed?
- How can learning acquired in one setting be transferred to other settings (the problem of transfer)?

These issues are keenly debated by practitioners and managers in educational systems.

Until recently our understanding of these matters has been dominated, explicitly or implicitly, by psychological theories of learning. However, it has now become clear that the contribution of these theories to education has been disappointing. Fortunately, contemporary work emanating from cognitive anthropology and socio-psychological studies of learning in and out of school offer the promise of creating a theory of learning specifically designed from the outset to inform educational practice regarding the management of learning. An educational learning theory is in the offing.

In this essay I set out and comment on the learning theories which have, until recently, dominated thinking about learning in the field of education. The commentary surveys first the general structure of learning theory as applied to education and then specific reference is made to the following theories: associationism; constructivism; learning as problem-solving; and the most recent theory of connectionism. These theories have, by and large, focused on learning as a covert, individual, intellectual process.

Following this discussion of classical and contemporary psychological theories I survey some key issues relevant to the development of an educational learning theory. This includes a commentary on the effect of context on learning, including a discussion of learning out of school and learning in classrooms. Research on these topics indicates that for educational purposes learning must be conceived of as a covert intellectual activity and a social practice. Psychological theories of learning have focused on individual mental life. It has become clear, however, that the social setting is a significant determinant of the quality of learning. Factors that affect learning in this sense are surveyed, including the effects of the management of classroom work and classroom assessment processes.

Perhaps the single most important issue for education is ensuring that schooled learning (in its broadest sense) is usable beyond schooling. This is discussed as the issue of learning transfer. It is a matter of debate as to whether this is the central challenge or the most salient distraction for a theory of learning. This issue is discussed in terms of the contemporary theory of situated learning.

Students are, of course, not passive in the face of educational provision, nor does a body of students meet a given provision with a uniform response. The quality of learning and the nature of the learning experience is, to a degree, mediated by students' personalities, purposes, motives and approaches to learning. The students' role in learning is recognised and discussed in this section.

Finally, an educational learning theory is outlined.

UNDERSTANDING LEARNING: THE STRUCTURE OF LEARNING THEORIES

It is chastening to note that educational systems have a very deep problem in regard to learning theories. The *Encyclopaedia Britannica* (1996) entry states that, 'By the end of the 20th century learning theory seemed to consist of a set of hypotheses of limited applicability.' There is extensive evidence that students' conceptions are shallow and of limited utility whilst at the same time pupils and employers complain about the dull and often useless learning experience that pupils have endured.

Learning experiences in institutions are largely determined by the working practices of teachers which, in turn, are a function of professional traditions and cultures, pragmatic and practical considerations, available curriculum materials and the perceived demands of assessment systems, particularly high-profile, public assessment systems. It is difficult to assess the degree to which learning theory influences the practice of professional educators. Whilst such theory is evident and even perhaps salient in teacher education, it is well known that there is a vast gulf between theory and practice in education. That being said, it might be expected to be axiomatic that professional educators would be furnished with, and even use, powerful understandings of learning. Certainly, learning theorists have not been coy in their attempts to influence educational practice.

A number of perspectives or theoretical approaches to learning have been and are on offer to teachers. These have some common properties. There is a general structure to theories of learning. Each adopts a particular view about the nature of knowledge. Differences in these fundamental ontological assumptions are at the core of differences in the theories and generate all other idiosyncratic properties of the theory. Following from the fundamental assumptions about the nature of knowledge, each theory adopts a different model about what it means to be 'learned', about the difference between a novice and an expert. Equally, each theory adopts a distinctive view on how knowledge is acquired and on the form of knowledge representation. Each theory may be identified with a particular view on how learning acquired in one setting or context is used in another context – the issue of knowledge use or knowledge transfer. This is as far as learning theory goes, but from an educational point of view each theory may be seen to generate distinctive prescriptions for professional educators – prescriptions to be applied to the nature and structure of the curriculum and to the design of learning experiences, i.e. to the business of engaging pupils with the curriculum. It should be emphasised that implications for teaching, i.e. for the promotion of learning, have to be derived from psychological theories of learning. Implications for practice are not evident or axiomatic or empirically based. Rather, they are derived through creative interpretation from theories that differ fundamentally in one respect, that of the core assumption about the nature of knowledge.

In the following sections I survey, using the above structure, psychological learning theories as applied to education, tracing their impact on educational practice.

ASSOCIATIONIST LEARNING THEORY

In the associationist view, knowledge consists of connections or associations between small elements of experience. We link words with objects for example. All learning, however complex, is made up of associations. In mathematics, for example, long multiplication of 36×219 can be unpacked and be seen to be made up of dozens of links involving basic connections of 3×2; 3×1; 3×9; and so on together with connections of place value.

In the associationist view of knowledge, the difference between an expert and a novice in any field is that the expert has a larger and richer corpus of associations. Learning in the associationist view involves acquiring more links and having them at ready disposal. Research has established the 'laws of association'. These identify the conditions under which links between elements of experience are most readily made and sustained.

- The '*law of contiguity*' states that elements experienced close together in time are more likely to be associated.
- The '*law of practice*' states that repetition helps to establish and sustain links.
- The '*law of effect*' indicates that associations accompanied by favourable effects (e.g. reduction of needs such as hunger) are likely to be effectively established.

Because elements of association are so small, specific and particular, little transfer from one context to another is anticipated in the associationist view. The '*law of identical elements*' states in essence that an association made in one context might be expected to be evident in another to the degree that the contexts have elements in common. Since settings are very particular in almost all respects, transfer of learning might be the exception rather than the rule.

The associationist implications for education suggest that the curriculum in any subject area must be unpacked until the basic elements are identified. A learning sequence should then be devised which maximises the possibility of pupils and students building associations most effectively. This view has had considerable influence on the design of curriculum materials in subjects such as mathematics or physics, in which concepts may be perceived to be hierarchical. The associationist approach has been influential in programmed learning, computer-assisted instruction and in behaviour modification, in which technique unacceptable classroom behaviours are shaped using systems of reinforcement into prosocial behaviour. Associationist theory is also at the heart of most models of computer-assisted learning. The impact of IT, such as it is, in education is in essence the modern impact of associationism.

In the broad range of subjects in the curriculum it has not proved possible to establish hierarchies of concepts or associations. Understanding issues in the arts, or humanities, for example, is not readily perceived as being 'associative'. And teachers have found it extremely difficult to manage classroom contingencies to the degree necessary to modify behaviour according to the tenets of the associationist technology.

Once teachers have arranged the teaching sequence, or bought work books with material arranged in appropriate sequence, their job is to manage student practice with feedback so that associations are effectively and efficiently established according to the laws of association. Lessons would typically take the form of the teacher showing the association and then getting students to repeat it (e.g. spellings, vocabulary, number bonds). Associations may be compiled and practised as routines, e.g. mathematical problem-solving or design of experiments. Much modern classroom practice follows this rhythm.

As new associations are added to the repertoire, revision of old associations becomes necessary using practice with feedback. Little transfer to new problems is expected. Successful performance on a new problem depends, in the associationist view, on the degree of familiarity of the elements of the problem with associations already held.

Evidence suggests that learners show more transfer than is to be expected in a strict associationist view. In one study, of the performance of algebraic functions, pupils were taught to solve problems such as $(x + y)^2$. In a test of transfer they were given problems such as $(b_1 + b_2)^2$. In the former there were 6% errors whilst in the latter test condition there were 28% errors. Clearly, students had difficulty but were not so overwhelmed as the identical elements theory would suggest.

In summary, associationism is linked particularly to 'top-down' or curriculum-centred approaches to education, in which the learner engages in large amounts of carefully structured practice and repetition. It has its modern impact in computer-assisted learning. This is an exceptionally active field which, according to pundits, is set to revolutionise the delivery of education. There is very little evidence that it has yet done so, and, seen in the light of the following accounts of alternative revolutions, there is very little likelihood that it will.

CONSTRUCTIVISM

In this view little of any importance is learned through simple associations. Constructivists suggest that human learners have the capacity to invent or construct general theories about their experience. Knowledge is thus seen to be constructed through intellectual action on experience. Students in the constructivist view do not merely react to experience. They reflect on it and theorise it, developing mental structures or schemata for understanding it. For example, a pupil might learn that A is bigger than B and B bigger than C. They then work out that A must be bigger than C. Once this logical structure has been invented, it is applicable to any problem involving elements serially ordered whether the relationship be size or speed or mass. Knowledge consists of constructed schemata of this sort.

The difference between a novice and an expert in this perspective is qualitative rather than quantitative. The expert knows 'different' rather than 'more'. The expert has more powerful ways of structuring experience and these ways have more general application.

Acquisition of knowledge, i.e. the acquisition of more sophisticated schemata, is not straightforward. Learning consists of the restructuring of intellectual schemata. For example, if children aged about 5 are shown the array of counters depicted in Figure 5.1 and asked if there are the same number of black counters as white counters they, like older children, will say, 'Yes'.

If the extreme right black counter is moved an inch to the right and the question

Figure 5.1 Array of black and white counters used to assess children's conservation of quantity.

repeated, older children (aged 7/8 years) will say 'Yes', but younger children (5/6 years) will say 'No'. The younger ones, it is argued, judge the number of counters by the length of the line of distribution.

At some later stage children learn to count and to use counting to answer the question, 'how many?' When children in this stage meet the above test they hesitate, sometimes judging the array to be equal and sometimes the black row to show more. It is hypothesised that these children have two ways of answering the question: they look at extension and/or they count. These schemata give conflicting results.

At a later stage children reliably conclude that both arrays have the same number of counters regardless of their pattern of distribution. When asked for a reason for their answer, they argue that nothing has been added or taken away. The children have invented a way of looking at the problem which is independent of both counting and distribution. They have constructed the concept of conservation of number. They have invented the idea that some processes influence quantity (adding or subtracting items) and some processes do not (e.g. changing distribution).

Figure 5.2 indicates the general processes involved in learning through restructuring schemata.

In understanding this diagram it is useful to refer back to young children's acquisition of schemata of number conservation through a process of intellectual construction. Initially the child has a schema for number which causes no problems for him or her intellectually. The child is comfortable with it; he or she is in a state of intellectual equilibrium. Learning to count and being questioned provide the child with experiences that do not fit the schema. The experience causes disequilibrium. The child, for a period, might ignore this or learn to live with it. There is extensive evidence that this is what learners at all ages and stages frequently do in the face of evidence challenging existing schemata. In these circumstances no learning takes place as new data are ignored or dismissed. Even if conflicting data become salient, a new structure will have to be invented before an old schema is abandoned.

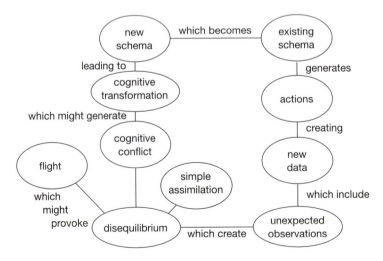

Figure 5.2 The processes of cognitive structuring

70

These processes are evident in the development of scientific theory as well as in the intellectual activity of young learners. The intellectual journey from existing schema to new schema is long and arduous. There are many easy routes off the track. Unexpected observations are easily dismissed as errors or 'blips'. Disequilibrium is easily avoided and new theories are difficult to construct. This stability has considerable survival value. Potentially new data are afforded continuously in everyday life. Persistent reconstruction of schema would lead to madness. Mental stability requires that we stick with what we know until conflicting evidence builds up to the degree that we can no longer ignore it.

Teaching from a constructivist point of view involves identifying a learner's existing schemata and then arranging experiences that challenge those schemata and that provoke the construction of more advanced intellectual structures. None of these tasks is easy, and learners have shown resistance to such challenging experiences.

In science, for example, most 6/7 year olds believe that shadows are projected by the observer's eyes and that they are rather like mirror images. A constructivist approach to teaching the established scientific view of shadows involves posing challenges to young learners' conceptions. They can be shown and asked to explain how shadows move even though the observer remains still, for example. These techniques are known to create disequilibrium but they do not necessarily lead to new constructions.

Once new constructions are created, however, they are expected to be very powerful and to be at the heart of knowledge transfer. For example, once a learner constructs a schema for the conservation of substance, the logic is expected to apply to all materials under any transformation: you only get more or less stuff if you add or take away material, all other transformations being irrelevant to quantity.

Evidence shows, however, that learners who confidently conserve quantity of, for example, plasticine as it is rolled or squashed seem readily to abandon the principle when a different material (e.g. sand) or a different transformation (e.g. cutting up) is used. Learners show a great deal less capacity for knowledge transfer than constructivists would predict.

In summary, constructivism is associated with learner-centred approaches to teaching in which the student is expected to be intellectually active in building their knowledge base. The theory is a considerable force in the development of curricula, and in particular the development of science and mathematics curricula. Extensive work is being done to identify students' conceptions of key ideas in these domains and, from these, into the development of learning experiences that challenge these conceptions, moving them in the direction of established theories in the subject. Important developments might be expected but work in this field has raised fundamental questions about the very purpose, for example, of science education. Should pupils learn established science as an esoteric and rapidly dating corpus of knowledge or should they learn methodology? Should they learn perhaps that, in contrast to everyday conceptions of the material world, there is an alternative, scientific point of view? These basic questions have been provoked by the rise of constructivism but they cannot be resolved without value judgements drawn from a much wider debate on educational purposes.

LEARNING AS PROBLEM-SOLVING

This view of learning owes much to the pragmatic philosophy of John Dewey and to Gestalt psychology. Knowledge in this perspective takes the form of strategies, that is to say, broad approaches to problem-solving. Bodies of knowledge and skill and general intellectual structures such as schemata are less important in this view than the capacity for reflective enquiry which is applied strategically to solve problems. No distinction is made between knowing (i.e. having theories) and doing (i.e. having associations). Learning through a problem-solving approach involves learners in analysing and defining the issue before them, in planning possible approaches, in making decisions about how to tackle the matter, and in monitoring, evaluating and reviewing the effects of any action taken.

In this view the difference between the novice and the expert is a qualitative difference in the degree of executive and intellectual control exercised by the learner in the face of the learning situation.

How are executive control and a strategic, problem-solving approach to learning acquired? This matter is hotly contested. Three approaches may be identified. First, there are those who advocate that 'problem-solving' can be taught disembodied from any particular context as a set of generic thinking skills. This 'stand alone' approach is extremely popular with publishers of 'how to do it' or 'teach yourself to learn' schemes. There is little persuasive evidence that this approach works.

Second, there are advocates for teaching problem-solving strategies within academic subjects. These advocates point out that first, no learning could take place without content and second, different academic subjects seem to be associated with predominantly different approaches to knowledge acquisition. Mathematicians, for example, are considered to favour deductive reasoning whilst scientists are considered to be more predisposed to inductive approaches to learning. This approach avoids the traditional 'content' versus 'process' debate in education by insisting that thinking (process) be taught in the context and on the back of academic subject material (content).

A newer approach, the 'immersion' approach, is currently being developed. This involves placing problem-solving at the heart of the curriculum – but implicitly so, i.e. the approach to learning as problem-solving becomes, in this view, a taken-for-granted, implicit part of the culture of learning. Thinking is so integral to the pursuit of meaning and learning that it, as it were, drops out of sight. Indeed, any focus on process distracts from the business of learning, as focus on syntax distracts from the flow of speech.

The perceived conditions for this approach to learning are (a) that pupils/students are free to pursue their own ideas and (b) that they are in possession of a relevant and rich corpus of ideas to pursue. In this view learning is driven by ideas. By way of concrete example, a class of 6 year olds was set the problem of finding the difference in height between two pupils, J at 62 ins. and P at 37 ins. Classically this would be treated as a routine subtraction problem to be solved (without any new learning taking place) by a routine previously demonstrated and established by the teacher. In this particular instance the children, encouraged by the teacher, represented the problem in many ways (using numbers, symbols, schematic or figurative diagrams for example). Each form of representation evinced a different way of looking at the problem and afforded different ways of solving it. The class shared and discussed their approaches. The example shows several key attributes of the learning as a problem-solving approach. First, perception plays an important role in shaping the problem and subsequent action on it. This is in contrast to the other views of learning, which focus on what happens to information once it is 'in the head' and in which perception is seen to be a passive process, something rather thrust on the mind. In the problem-solving approach, perception is where cognition and reality meet in the context of ideas brought to bear on the interaction.

A second key attribute of the immersion approach evident in the example is the role of ideas. Ideas shape action, are at the basis of modelling the problem, and drive the need for further evidence or operations. The key to teaching in the approach is to teach the core ideas of a subject so that their operation is implicit.

A third evident attribute is the role of discourse. Ideas are shared and debated. Nothing is ruled out or ruled in. The discourse is driven by the desire to share approaches. The rules of the discourse focus on explicitness. The deeper strategic processes of problem-solving are left implicit. The reflective enquiry approach is taken for granted. The immersion approach, as the metaphor implies, is rather like learning a first language. Learners use, participate, communicate and in so doing acquire an intuitive grasp of the syntax – in this case the syntax of reflective enquiry.

The teaching implications are profound, especially in the immersion approach which necessitates a major reorientation of the curriculum. The curriculum itself becomes 'problematised' by the pupils. Teachers must develop a global view focusing on the network of big ideas which define the subject. Pupils' ideas and representations must be taken as serious attempts to learn in the domain. The teacher's role is to expand the pupils' perception of the field through the extension of executive and critical thinking brought about through discourse emanating from the sharing of ideas. Reflective enquiry is a natural residue of this process.

The problem of transfer is radically altered in this perspective. It is perceived to be based on a fundamentally flawed distinction between acquiring and using knowledge, in the distinction between two artificial categories which once invented prove very difficult to bring back together. The distinction flows further, creating dichotomies of theory/practice; learning/doing; reason/experience. The concept of reflective enquiry moves beyond these distinctions. Transfer does not depend on decontextualisation of skills and knowledge, but rather on their contextualisation. Transfer depends on how well connected the network of ideas held by the pupil is both to the phenomenon in question and to its multiple representations. From a teaching point of view, in this perspective, the curriculum is not an object to be known, it is a site for setting problems to promote critical enquiry from which flows, as a residue of enquiry, deeper understanding.

At this juncture, little evidence can be brought to bear on the practical effectiveness of the perspective. There is very little evidence on the matter. What can be said is that it would present enormous difficulties for classroom practice, not the least of which would be establishing an appropriately powerful corpus of knowledge on the part of classroom teachers. The view also, at first sight, seems to set fearsome challenges for assessment and accountability and for that reason alone might be predicted to be politically unattractive.

CONNECTIONISM

In the theories described above there is an implicit assumption that higher forms of mental life (and in particular, the higher forms of thinking and learning which are the business of education) are rule based if not rule governed. The operation of rules seems evident, for example, in human language learning, production and comprehension. Most classical psychological theory of learning has been an attempt to discover the nature of these rules, to model them and to pass them on in educational settings. It is clear that there has been some success in this endeavour and yet severe misgivings are in order.

Perhaps the most serious reservation with the view that human learning is rule based is the observation that if a system operated to a set of rules, there is no way that it could generate a higher-level rule that could either control the system or advance it. Higher-level learning is thus rendered impossible. Consistent with this conclusion is the observation that systems for controlling complex mechanisms in nature do not seem to be hierarchically rule governed. Nature's way of handling complex tasks is more akin to swarming, i.e. such tasks (e.g. the regulation of heart rate) are achieved through multiple, overlapping systems. Even where the modelling of human intellectual processes has been successful, it is noteworthy that the easiest things for humans to do (e.g. pattern recognition) are proving the most difficult to model. Research has shown that humans use mental models rather than rule-based systems in problem-solving and are likely to use relatively untrustworthy heuristics, such as case studies, rather than formal principles in dealing with everyday statistical inferences (estimating the chances of winning a prize in a lottery for example).

None of this proves that human thought and learning are not rule governed or rule based but it does raise serious doubts on the matter and it has been well said that human cognition may be more makeshift and inelegant than classical wisdom would lead us to expect. This observation opens the door to radical alternatives central to which, in contemporary psychology, is connectionism. Connectionist theory aims to overthrow the long-held notion that cognition is based on rules.

Connectionism retains the basic assumption that mind produces and operates on representations of the world. In this perspective knowledge is a vast network of interconnected elements. Connectionism differs profoundly, however, from associationism. In the latter, links are stored between elements of experience, each of which has individual significance. In connectionism the individual elements signify nothing. 'All knowledge is in the connections', as Bereiter (1991) has forcefully put it. Learning and thinking operate through processes that do not involve rules as agents.

This core concept of connectionism is difficult to convey without a full and dedicated treatment. Any metaphor might be dangerously misleading. That being said, it is not uncommon to observe similar structures. For example, the strength of a cantilever bridge does not reside in any particular element, nor does it depend on it. The strength is in the interconnections of the elements. This, in connectionist terms, is saying more than that the whole is greater than the sum of the parts. Connectionism is more active and organic than that.

From a connectionist point of view, perception plays a significant role in cognition. It has been observed that rule-based systems start with theorem proving and work towards perception. Connectionism reverses that. Connectionist models so far have focused successfully on doing what humans do best – i.e. pattern recognition. The models approximate rather than embody rationality and proceed on best-guess approaches rather than definitive rules.

The expert/novice difference in connectionist terms perhaps captures the fundamental essence of this approach and in particular the position on the relationship between actual performance and the rules that are sometimes (and in connectionist terms, mistakenly) said to describe it. Bereiter has observed that for a novice cook, performance is a poor approximation to the recipe, whilst for an expert cook, the recipe is a poor approximation to performance. The difference between novice and expert is thus qualitative but is not well described in terms of rules.

From the connectionist point of view, rules neither describe nor govern human cognition. This has profound implications from an educational viewpoint. Again, following Bereiter, it does not mean that rules of or for intellectual processing are bound for the educational bin. Rationality is highly prized in our society. Currently educational systems are, to a significant degree, based on the assumption that intellect is rule governed and the purpose of schooling is to teach the rules. Whilst pupils are taught the rules, the evidence is that they rarely practise them, although they frequently refer to them to justify their approaches to learning and problem-solving. Rationality is thus a significant part of public discourse; it is how we talk about mental life even if it is not relevant to how we conduct mental life. Bereiter has concluded, 'Once we recognise that rules are a part of public discourse rather than lines of a mental programme we can afford to be entirely pragmatic about their use in education.' This is a profoundly disturbing suggestion, implying that the corpus of educational methods based on assumptions about rules, definitions and explicit processes stand on 'illusory psychological foundations'.

There has always been a school of thought in education which has stood in contradiction to this 'illusory foundation'. Famously articulated by Rousseau, it has emphasised the organic quality of human cognition and has promulgated models of learning more akin to biological growth than to technical design. The organic point of view has generated institutions such as the kindergarten and open education. These movements have lacked the scientific base seen as essential in contemporary society and have been and are dismissed as romantic. It could be that connectionism and the models of perception being generated will provide the conceptual rationale considered so lacking. If so, then there is some prospect of the generation of highly productive educational developments. It is too soon to say, as the 'connectionist revolution' has hardly started.

Connectionism could serve as a framework in which to critique and build on the rhetoric of naturalistic or organic views of learning and their related models of teaching. The so-called 'progressive' approaches to education, often seen as aimless by politicians anxious about measuring educational outputs, have long posed severe challenges to teachers. An organic model of learning has been taken to imply a 'gardening' model of teaching, with the teacher playing the role of soil, weather and other aspects of a suitably nurturing environment. This role was perhaps most clearly articulated in the Plowden Report of the mid-1960s. The role placed massive demands on teachers' subject and pedagogic knowledge, classroom management skills and, above all, capacity for nurturant interventions. So explicit was the challenge that the Report, intended to foster progressive methods, might very well have buried them. If connectionism is to promote teaching methods relevant to fostering natural human learning, it will do so by providing more precise models of knowledge acquisition which will help teachers to design appropriate, practicable curricula and formative assessment systems.

THE EFFECT OF CONTEXT ON LEARNING

The above theories have focused on covert intellectual processes considered to be involved in learning. In each of the theories, learning is viewed as involving a singular mind, that of the learner, in the organisation and retention of experience. In the last analysis this, of course, is a truism: all retention is idiosyncratic. That being said, it is now recognised that the social setting of experience is critically influential in regard to the nature of that experience and the manner of its subsequent organisation in memory.

Studies of the mathematical competence of young Brazilian street traders show them to be ruthlessly competent at the mathematics of commerce, including the calculation of multiple unit price, discount, pricing, inflation and change. The same children, exposed to school tests involving similar operations and quantities, fail dismally. By the same token, children competent at school mathematics are readily defeated by real world problems. There appears to be something about the setting in which learning proceeds and which shapes, to a very considerable degree, what is learned. In particular, the culture of the social setting of learners is now considered to be a major determinant of the manner, quality and quantity of learning.

For example, school learning has been perceived to be different from workplace learning on at least three dimensions. In the workplace, learning predominantly takes place in teams; a large number of people are involved and must interact productively if effective learning is to ensue. In schools, such team work in learning is the exception. Ostensible group work in learning usually turns out to involve little more than sharing material rather than intellectual resources. In the main, pupils are expected to work in isolation and especially so in preparation for assessment.

A second difference between workplace and school learning involves the use of cognitive tools. In the workplace a large number of cognitive tools (e.g. computers, checklists, standard tables) are the norm. These tools are intended to provide intellectual support for workers and to free attention for more important matters such as monitoring progress. Schools, in contrast, show resistance to the use of such devices. Pupils are expected to understand the cognitive fundamentals and to work things out for themselves. There is still strong resistance in schools to calculators on the grounds that they make pupils lazy and incompetent. One immediate effect of this is that pupils spend a great deal of mental energy focusing on details of intellectual processes and have little spare attention to focus on the broader problem. Schools then demand individual, pure cognition whilst the workplace demands a sharing of cognitive resources supported by the use of cognitive tools.

A third difference between classroom learning and workplace learning lies in the mode of representation of a problem. Schools require the manipulation of abstract symbols whilst out-of-school learners use the whole physical context of a problem to support reasoning. An example from research involves the use of fractions. A recipe for four people had to be converted to make a meal for three people. The recipe for four demanded two-thirds of a cup of cottage cheese. How to get three-quarters of two-thirds? In school, esoteric processes for multiplying fractions are taught. In the kitchen, two-thirds of a real cup of cottage cheese may be made into a pancake which can then be divided into quarters. The cheese, in practice, becomes part of the solution. Out-of-school people are continuously engaged with objects and situations which make sense: action is grounded in the immediate purpose of the setting. Such is the power of settings that educating people to be good learners in schools or, more generally, classrooms, may not be sufficient to help them become good out-of-school learners. These differences between two learning cultures pose serious challenges to the prospects of transfer from one culture to another – challenges striking at the heart of schooling's major purpose.

Classrooms have been shown to have a particular learning culture. They have been characterised as information environments. Sources of information include books, posters, displays, work cards and vast amounts of verbal and non-verbal behaviour. Humans can only process a limited amount of information at any one time. In order to adapt to the classroom culture, pupils must learn to make fruitful selections amongst available information.

Teachers engage pupils in learning through setting work. Classroom work is the vehicle for school learning. Teachers set work, pupils complete it and teachers reward their efforts. Assessment is the key to this process. In this perspective there is an exchange of performance for grades. In selecting information for classroom adaptation, assessment information is central. This view of classrooms is not an account of how pupils learn. Rather, it emphasises that classroom learning takes place in the work setting established in classrooms, and that the classroom assessment system plays a central role in the management of classroom work.

Since there is an intimate relationship between classroom work and classroom order – busy classrooms being well-ordered classrooms in the culture of schooling – classroom assessment tends to reward lower-order processes such as tidiness and work completion. Classroom assessment has tended to narrow curriculum experience to that which is concrete and easily measurable. A great deal of classroom work is precisely that: work. Very frequently, teachers and pupils pass learning by in the management of low-order, production-line work. Teachers manage learners rather than learning.

Teachers and children alike adopt the language of the production line to characterise classroom life. Work intended to foster learning becomes an end in itself. Teachers assume that if children are working, then they are learning. By the same token, people in classrooms are, effectively, learning to do classroom work. As we shall see, this creates barriers to the effective utilisation of lessons learned in school in out-of-school contexts.

KNOWLEDGE UTILISATION AND THE THEORY OF SITUATED LEARNING

The issue of knowledge utilisation or knowledge transfer has been a persistent theme in the above discussion. Every theory of learning is expected to be able to explain how knowledge acquired in one setting may be used in a novel setting. We have seen how, conceptually, associationism, constructivism and connectionism handle this matter and how the 'learning as problem-solving' approach dismisses it in theoretical terms as based on a false dichotomy between knowing and doing.

educational agenda by the life's work of John Dewey. No one before him had so persistently argued for the need for educational practice to be grounded in sound philosophical principles (and, of equal importance to him, but often neglected by commentators, the corresponding need for philosophical reflection to be informed by educational practice). Certainly no philosopher writing about education has ever, before or since, been so prolific (over 40 books and 800 articles: Phillips, 1985). Dewey, through his voluminous publications and his many talks and articles as a public intellectual, had a singular effect on the theory and practice of education. His approach, broadly termed 'progressive education', but often conflated with the wider movement of progressivism in the USA after the turn of the century, emphasised the independent motivations of the learner, the need for schools to be small-scale laboratories for experiments in democratic social reform, and the basis of authentic learning in enquiry and experience. Yet the lasting legacy of Dewey must be traced, not only in terms of the shifting fortunes of progressivism as an educational philosophy (about which even Dewey voiced scepticism as it took various shapes in US schools), but in the establishment of the idea that practitioners must have an educational philosophy, and the relentless promotion of a particular one as the potential basis of *all* educational thought and practice.

It is during this period that we see the first codified account of the phrase 'philosophy of education' in Paul Monroe's *Cyclopedia of Education* in 1911–1913 (Chambliss, 1996). We see the beginnings of the argument for requiring courses in the preparation of educators that seek to promote the systematic, grounded formulation and justification of educational aims. And we see, significantly, the first professional organisation dedicated to philosophical reflection on education, the John Dewey Society (JDS), in 1935.

The emergence of professional organisations is crucial for a variety of reasons. As these took shape across a range of academic disciplines in the USA just after the turn of the century, they were not simply the institutionalised embodiment of fields of intellectual practice, nor simply convocations of like-minded scholars seeking an opportunity to share their ideas. They had consistent effects in reshaping the fields they represented (Furner, 1975; Haskell, 1977). As we shall see, this is strikingly true in the case of philosophy of education. For this reason, it is not an exaggeration to consider 'the possibility that the origins of educational philosophy were better attached to the organizations of its embodiment than to their annotated bibliographies' (Kaminsky, 1993, p. vii). This claim becomes even more plausible when one considers the shifting fortunes of the publications sponsored by these organisations – the publications that, by accepting and rejecting certain articles, determine what *can* be included on 'annotated bibliographies' (see Kaminsky, 1993, 1996; Nelson, 1996; Smeyers and Marshall, 1995).

In the case of the John Dewey Society, as with other professional organisations in the social sciences and humanities, debates often centred around the degree and forms of social activism and advocacy that were appropriate to a professional organisation, as such. Inspired by Dewey's own role as a public intellectual and his involvement across a range of political issues throughout his career, the members of JDS saw a close connection between their teaching, writing and social commitments. Yet within this shared understanding, there were strong disagreements over the substance of political issues and over the kinds of activism that were appropriate. Many of these debates revolved around the journal *The Social Frontier*, which, under the editorship of George S. Counts, expressed positions that rested

In practical terms, however, it is a very real problem. There is extensive evidence that whilst students remember significant amounts of school knowledge, they are very poor indeed at using or applying it. Once institutions such as schools, universities or commercial training colleges are set up and dedicated to promoting learning, it behoves professional educators to ensure that such learning is usable. This, after all, is the *raison d'être* of formal educators at all ages and stages.

The problem is particularly daunting when viewed in the perspective of the theory of situated cognition. In the associationist, constructivist, connectionist and problem-solving approaches to learning there is a common assumption that there is something called 'knowledge' which can be abstracted from a situation or experience, stored in mind or body, and used in a novel situation given appropriate circumstances. In the case of associationism, for example, knowledge takes the form of a link between significant events. The connection is stored in the nervous system and something in the new situation evokes the 'old' knowledge.

Some psychologists have refuted this 'abstraction' theory of knowledge. It is argued that knowledge cannot be separated from the context in which it is experienced. This is a massive conceptual step beyond the recognition, described earlier, that the setting or context of experience is significant in determining the quantity and quality of the learning which may take place. Learning in this view is a fundamentally social activity, a social practice which is defined, rather than merely influenced, by the context of the learning setting. This perspective explains forcefully the lack of learning transfer from one setting to another. For example, with reference to the Brazilian street traders, in this perspective of situated learning, practising maths on the street needs all the clues and cues of the street including the goods to hand, customers and, crucially, the immediacy of the customer/vendor relationship. The street mathematicians have not learned mathematics, they have learned vending.

In this view of situated learning, we do not acquire associations nor do we create theories. Rather, we learn the working practices of the setting in which we operate. Students in schools or universities or on courses learn the working practices of the classroom. By definition, working practices do not transfer from one culture of activity to another. In this theory a lack of knowledge transfer from one setting to another would be expected. Transfer and not the lack of it, would be the problem to be explained.

Knowledge, in the situated learning perspective, consists of the working practices of a culture of learning. Science in this view is, literally, what scientists do. Experts, in this perspective, are polished exponents of the working practices of a particular subject culture. They are deeply familiar with the ways of working of their discipline.

Novices must be inducted into the working practices of the domain in question through a form of apprenticeship. Pupils and students will not learn to use and apply their knowledge met in classrooms if it is experienced in the form of ordinary classroom work or college lectures structured by textbooks and standard assessment tasks. If pupils are to master a discipline or a domain, then they must learn through the authentic experiences of that domain. Learning science involves doing what scientists do. If pupils are to learn mathematics then they must proceed as an apprentice mathematician. The teacher's task is to arrange these forms of intellectual apprenticeship. A central principle in this approach is that the class must be actively involved in the work. Students must be encouraged to utilise the practices of the discipline or domain on relevant problems. The fundamental difference between this approach and the problem-solving approach is that whilst in the latter, students are challenged to work on the 'big ideas' of a subject, in the situated learning perspective the focus is on the working practices of the subject.

In respect to education, the four central claims of situated learning theory are:

- that learning is grounded in the practical situation in which it occurs;
- that knowledge does not transfer between situations;
- that training for abstraction is a conceptual nonsense; and,
- that teaching should proceed in settings authentic to the domain in question.

The challenge to contemporary educational practice is profound. The gulf between the culture of classrooms and cultures of learning authentic to academic subjects seems unbridgeable. The demands on teachers' knowledge and experience are staggering. For example, it would be rare that a science teacher were or ever had been a working, researching scientist. The challenge for teachers' professional development is revolutionary. Needless to say, there have been forays into the development of teachers' skills consistent with the theory of situated learning but it is too soon to evaluate these.

THE STUDENTS' ROLE IN LEARNING

In any group of students there are wide differences in aptitudes, abilities, propensities and background knowledge (general and specific) relevant to the curriculum in hand. These differences, so-called 'individual differences' and their interactions with learning settings have been the subject of massive research interest. Very little of any value has been generated. The general contribution of this field to understanding learning and improving the management of learning is not worthy of attention here.

Amongst the vast array of individual difference studies there are some, however, which conceptually at least are more proximal to the practice of learning than others. Whatever the origins of these factors, it is broadly agreed that the theories and beliefs a student holds about knowledge and learning are bound to have a profound influence on their approach to learning. Unfortunately, very little is known about these fundamentals and little fruitful research seems likely until clearer definitions of these processes can be agreed and testable models for their operation can be developed.

Setting aside the fundamentals of beliefs, something is known about students' approaches to learning in practice. It turns out that students' behaviour and attitudes in the academic context are much better predictors of learning outcomes than are more general psychological variables such as personality.

These 'approaches to learning' have been identified amongst university students. Some take a so-called 'deep' approach to study, seeking an active engagement with the curriculum in a search for meaning. Others take a 'surface' approach. These are occupied with memorising and reproducing the curriculum, paying close attention to the course requirements and being driven, in the main, by a fear of failure. A third approach, the 'strategic' approach, is exhibited by students with high need for achievement as a form of intellectual competition rather than as a route to understanding. These approaches are in part dispositional, i.e. they are enduring properties of the individual, and they are in part situational in that different forms of curriculum arrangement and management are associated with different reactive adjustments of approach. For example, departments demanding heavy workloads and disallowing student choice over content and methods seem to encourage a surface approach to learning, whilst departments allowing choice amongst content, support for learning, and encouraging a wide range of study methods are perceived to evoke deep approaches. Clearly there are interactions between the characteristic dispositions of students and the provision and management of learning experience by departments. Unfortunately, not enough is known about these interactions as they themselves interact with academic content. The discipline matters. For example, there are well-established learning culture differences between science departments on the one hand and arts departments on the other. The degree to which these differences are manipulated in pursuit of enhanced learning outcomes is not known.

What *is* generally agreed is that in the long term the most effective learners become self-regulating, i.e. they adopt an approach to engaging with learning involving goal setting, strategic choice of methods and sustained monitoring, evaluation and review of progress. To progress in this way requires on the part of the learner high levels of metacognitive awareness, i.e. powerful knowledge about the process of learning *per se*. Whether this be explicit and rule governed (q.v. associationism, constructivism) or implicit and enculturated (q.v. connectionism, problem-solving) depends on one's theoretical stance. A self-regulating, metacognitive approach to learning is a valued output for all persuasions.

It follows logically that feedback is a necessity for all self-regulated activity. Feedback is generated by the monitoring process. Feedback may come from external sources (teachers and peers) or internally (from self-reflection). It might be about the learning process (cost/benefit analysis), the goal (should this be redefined), or progress towards success. Unfortunately, very little is known about how feedback is integrated into self-regulated approaches or about how the sources, nature and timing of feedback interact with one another. Certainly formal assessment as feedback is associated with rather bleak adjustments to learning. The issue of feedback and self-regulation seems close to the heart of the learning process and central to a highly desired learning output – i.e. self-regulating learning. Research here is only just beginning to develop models reflecting the complexity of the process. Sadly, the models are data- rather than theory-driven and, as a consequence, we can expect little if any progress in this crucial field.

It is sad to conclude that whilst the learner is central to the business of education and whilst rhetoric abounds on 'how to do it' for learners, very little indeed is known about how learning may be made successful from the learner's perspective. Much of the advice given to learners is generated directly from assumptions about the nature of knowledge rather than from sound empirical studies of what works. The advice in general is akin to teaching students that a useful note-taking strategy is to underline the key idea in each paragraph of a task. This is all very well if you know the key idea. What to do if you do not?

What is needed here is a programme of theory-driven research into successful learners where success means that the learners have had to overcome difficulties in learning. More generally what is needed to organise this and other fields of research relevant to education is a powerful theory of learning which poses educational rather than purely psychological issues. Riding on the back of psychological work, it is possible to discover the emergence of such a theory.

AN EDUCATIONAL LEARNING THEORY

The business of education is not short of theories of instruction, that is to say, theories that prescribe how best to promote learning. Some but not all of these theories have at their core a psychological theory of learning and several such theories have been reviewed above. It is clear that educational systems have not been well served by these theories. In practice, educational systems fall well short of expectation in promoting learning and self-regulating learners.

What is needed is a descriptive theory of education, that is to say, a theory with the goal of explaining institutional learning as it operates in practice. If schooling (at all ages and stages) were better understood, it might more efficiently and effectively be improved. At heart, such a theory would explain how learners bring their resources (intellectual, social and material) to bear on the acquisition of expertise. An educational theory would focus on the acquisition of higher-level learning such as self-regulating expertise, there being very little need for a theory of how easier learning is attained. Extensive foundational work in specifying such a theory has been conducted by Carl Bereiter and the following account draws heavily on his efforts.

Research has shown that the human mind is capable of functioning in a wide range of ways and on an infinite number of levels of analysis. At a descriptive level, every one of the psychological theories set out earlier is consistent with aspects of human mental functioning. We do learn by making associations, developing theories, solving problems and so on. These different kinds of processing are evident in, for example, the art of reading. Particular words may have been learned by association; we have a general theory about the meaning of the whole text and should we become confused or lose the thread of meaning, we indulge in problem-solving – at a variety of levels – to clarify the sense. How are these intellectual resources brought to bear on learning?

Bereiter suggests that it is useful to conceive of the mind as organised on a modular basis. A module is an autonomous cognitive unit characterised by speed, effortlessness, reliability and inaccessibility to consciousness and to conscious modification, i.e. modules operate automatically. These properties are consistent with the intellectual residues anticipated to be the products of the immersion approach to problem-solving. It is suggested that some modules may be innate (a language acquisition module for example) but to an educational theory, acquired modularity is more interesting. Bereiter invents the hypothetical construct of the 'contextual module'. This is a cognitive unit, operating on representations of experience and acquired in particular contexts to make for effective intellectual operation in such a context. The learner does not simply learn a body of knowledge and/or skills in a context, there is a more general and multi-faceted adaptation to learning settings involving, according to Bereiter, the acquisition of relevant knowledge, goal structures, problem models and code of conduct. This specification is consistent with all the learning theories discussed earlier whilst at the same time not being merely eclectic. The contextual module represents the entire complex of knowledge, skills, goals, values, actions and feelings of the learner's adjustment to a particular setting or context. It embodies the person's whole relationship to that context. The contextual module has properties of real human significance.

By way of example, school itself may be seen as a context requiring considerable and rapid adaptation on the part of learners. There is evidence that most children adapt quickly to school as a job. They organise their resources – intellectual, social and material – to do their work. Bereiter describes this adaptation in terms of the development of a school-work module. The school-work module is highly adapted to identifying the procedural needs of school tasks and to delivering a product that meets the teacher's assessment criteria. By way of example, a teacher might set a maths task ostensibly to practise addition. From the learner's point of view, as accommodated in the classroom, the task is a production-line piece of work merely to be completed.

The general theory of contextual modularity and the specific concept of the school-work module go a very long way to describing most of the findings of research on classroom learning at all levels of education, and especially its limited applicability and the relatively low order of achievement. The worst effects of the school-work module are hidden by established assessment processes, since students may perform well enough on these precisely through the reproduction of low-level school-work.

What is the response of the school-work module to meeting difficulties in learning? This, it will be recalled, is the central question for an educational learning theory. It is hypothesised that this is not perceived as learning difficulty at all but rather as work that is too hard. The response is to pressure the teacher to reduce the workload or work challenge. If students in this case try harder, they do not try harder to learn, since learning is not an issue for the school-work module. Rather, they will try harder to complete the work or try harder to have the challenge in the work diminished. From this theoretical perspective, many if not most students do not see themselves as learners at all (even amongst university students) – an image that is reinforced by parents and others asking, 'What did you *do* at school today?'

The goal of schooling is to produce intentional learners, to establish in students the determination and capacity to learn as an important part of the self concept. Such learners do exist and some settings are known to promote intentional learning more than others. How this is achieved is not at all understood.

The concept of the 'intentional learning module' is important here. A student with an intentional learning module is oriented to extending their knowledge and understanding to mastery rather than performance. Important research questions are:

- How do intentional learners operate?
- How do they become intentional learners?
- What factors promote and which inhibit intentional learning and the acquisition of an intentional learning module?

A considerable amount is known about how political factors (such as national assessment systems) and institutional factors (such as school policies, classroom management) constrain learning and foster the development of the school-work module. Surprisingly, almost nothing is known about how intentional learning is promoted and sustained in everyday classrooms.

SELECT BIBLIOGRAPHY

Bereiter, C. (1991) 'Implications of connectionism for thinking about rules'. *Educational Researcher*, 20, 3, 10–16.

Desforges, C. (ed.) (1995) *An Introduction to Teaching: Psychological Perspectives*, Oxford: Blackwell.

Ranson, S. (ed.) (1998) *Inside the Learning Society*, London: Cassell.

Valsiner, J. and Voss, H. G. (eds) (1996) *The Structure of Learning Processes*, Norwood, NJ: Ablex.

6

HAS CLASSROOM TEACHING
SERVED ITS DAY?

Donald McIntyre

INTRODUCTION: WHAT IS TEACHING?

Teaching is a relatively easy concept to define: teaching is acting so as deliberately and directly to facilitate learning. While *what* is done to achieve the purpose of teaching may be almost infinitely diverse, it is the purpose of these activities, not the activities themselves, which is definitive. Similarly, teaching of important kinds is undertaken in many different contexts and by many people in diverse roles. The concept of teaching has no implications for *where* or *by whom* teaching is done. It is only the purpose of the activity, that of facilitating learning, that is crucial to the definition.

This definition of teaching is of course a crude one, which might properly be the subject of various elaborations and qualifications. Yet the central truth that it offers is of much more than semantic importance, since it emphasises the point that, in a world where the importance of learning is beyond debate, nothing can be taken for granted about the importance of any kind of teaching, except its purpose of facilitating learning. Answers to the question of what kind of teaching is needed or is useful must always be contingent on answers to other questions, primarily about what will best facilitate the kinds of learning that we most want.

We have become accustomed to having various institutions designed for the facilitation of learning, and it is a matter of judgement as to whether it will be helpful to go back to first principles to question the value of any of these institutions. Two such institutions which each have a history of at least two or three millennia are those of *professional teaching* and *schools*. Arguments have certainly been offered, some decades ago, for questioning the usefulness of these institutions for the twenty-first century (Illich, 1976; Reimer, 1971). Yet the scale of the learning in which everyone needs to engage for twenty-first century living makes the idea of doing without schools look increasingly like a romantic dream. For the purposes of this essay it will be assumed that schooling is necessary, and that professional teaching is necessary to make it work. But it will not be assumed that schooling needs to be organised as it has been in the twentieth century. On the contrary, this essay argues that a more significant issue concerns the dominant way in which professional teaching in schools has been structured during the last century or two, and it asks how well suited that way of structuring professional teaching is for the contentious and problematic tasks which school-teachers currently face. That dominant way of structuring professional teaching in schools is taken to be classroom teaching.

In raising this issue, the essay seeks quite explicitly to challenge current suggestions that the central issues facing schooling are to be construed primarily in terms of *teachers'* skills:

> Expectations of politicians, parents and employers of what schools should accomplish in terms of student achievement, broadly conceived, have been rising for over twenty years. And they will continue to accelerate as we take further steps into the information age or the knowledge society. . . . It is plain that if teachers do not acquire and display the capacity to redefine their skills for the task of teaching, and if they do not model in their own conduct the very qualities – flexibility, networking, creativity – that are now key outcomes for students, then the challenge of schooling in the next millennium will not be met.
>
> (Hargreaves, 1999, pp. 122–123)

While David Hargreaves' above diagnosis of the situation must be very largely correct, the argument here is that he, together with the British government, its Teacher Training Agency and many others, is wrong to suggest that the solution can be found simply through the further development of teachers' expertise. The general thesis of this essay is instead that, however hard teachers work, however sensitive they are to what is needed, however skilled they become, there are limits to what is possible through the classroom teaching system that we have inherited. Furthermore, we may be approaching these limits now, at a time when much more is being expected of schools; and so it is unlikely that expectations can be met except by going beyond the classroom teaching system.

THE SYSTEM OF CLASSROOM TEACHING

During the last two centuries, and therefore during the entire history of public systems of schooling in most countries, classroom teaching has been the dominant form of schoolteaching. The most fundamental characteristics of classroom teaching are that a teacher is located in one enclosed room with a group – a class – of pupils for whose teaching he or she is directly responsible. Schools, on this model, are little more than organised collections of classrooms, with virtually all the organised teaching and learning being classroom based. Gradually, during the history of classroom teaching, there has been a trend towards classroom specialisation, with differentiation according to the subjects being taught in them: gymnasia, laboratories, art and music rooms, technical workshops of various kinds and latterly computer rooms. In general, however, these specialist spaces have been types of classroom, with the fundamental characteristics identified above, rather than alternative ways of organising teaching and learning. Libraries, and sometimes resource centres of a broader character, have tended to be the only places in schools other than classrooms designed for learning, but even these have rarely been designed for alternative ways of organising teaching.

Classroom teaching became the dominant pattern of schoolteaching in England after a long period of competition, in the first half of the nineteenth century, with the monitorial system, in which one teacher was responsible for the teaching of all pupils in the school, but only indirectly for most of them. Only the senior pupils were taught by the teacher, and they in turn were responsible for teaching their juniors. Reminiscent of Bentham's *Panopticon*, planned as a rational, economical and civilised approach to incarceration, the monitorial system had, as its inventor Andrew Bell claimed, 'excellent mechanical advantages' (Bell, 1807, quoted by Hartley, 1997). That classroom teaching none the less emerged as the unrivalled basis for the mass elementary education for which the English government took responsibility in the second half of the nineteenth century says much for its merits as a flexible and balanced system, impressive in terms of pedagogical, managerial and economic criteria.

The dominance of classroom teaching has been such that, throughout the twentieth century, it has very widely been taken for granted as the 'natural' way of organising teaching and schooling. It clearly has very considerable merits as a way of organising schooling, from both managerial and pedagogical perspectives. Managerially, it makes the individual teacher unambiguously responsible for the teaching and learning in his or her classroom; it allows pupils to be categorised tidily and allocated to teachers according to whatever variables are deemed appropriate: age, prior attainments, general or subject-specific ability, and/or course; and it allows teachers and/or classes to be matched with appropriate rooms.

Pedagogically, Hamilton (1986) informs us, it was attractive to early advocates of classroom teaching such as Adam Smith because it allowed direct two-way communication between the teacher and the pupils (currently known as whole-class interactive teaching) and because it allowed pupils to observe each other's performances easily and so encouraged emulation of the most successful. In some respects, it has also proved to offer a highly flexible framework for teaching, adaptable to group and individualised working, and to various kinds of practical as well as language-based activities.

Perhaps the key feature of classroom teaching as a system for schooling is that all responsibility for facilitating pupils' learning is concentrated on the individual teacher. Whatever has been decided or demanded by government, parents, headteacher, head of department or others has to be 'delivered' by the classroom teacher, who is unambiguously accountable for everything that happens in the classroom. This simple truth is, furthermore, not lost on the other inhabitants of the classroom: the pupils too learn quickly that it is the teacher who has total authority over their classroom activities and is responsible for facilitating their learning, which militates strongly against the development of learning activities not planned by the teacher (cf. Holt, 1969, 1971). As school effectiveness scholars are gradually coming to understand, the effectiveness of schooling under this system depends overwhelmingly on what the individual teacher, alone in the classroom with his or her pupils, is able to do.

Having been developed and adapted over two centuries, unquestioned as the appropriate way of delivering schooling on a mass scale, classroom teaching must be assumed to be the pattern for schooling in the future unless there are very persuasive arguments to the contrary. Here I shall aim first to understand something of what classroom teaching involves from the perspective of teachers themselves. Next, I shall consider some of the demands for development which schools are currently being asked to meet; and I shall explore the relationship of these demands to the nature of teachers' classroom expertise. We can then consider some of the possible implications for the future.

LIFE IN CLASSROOMS

The above subheading is borrowed from the title of a book by Philip Jackson, published in 1968. It was one of the first and most influential of the many studies which, in the last 30 years, have sought very usefully to stand back from the question 'What ought teachers to be doing?' to ask the prior question 'How can we best understand what teachers do?'

One of the features of classrooms that Jackson noted was that they are busy and crowded places, which led to 'four unpublicised features of school life: delay, denial, interruption, and social distraction' (Jackson, 1968, p. 17) and imposed severe constraints upon how teachers and pupils could work. Later investigators have picked up this theme of the complexity of classroom life. It has perhaps been most fully articulated by Doyle in terms of 'six intrinsic features of the classroom environment [which] create constant pressures that shape the task of teaching' (Doyle, 1986, pp. 394–395). These he identified as:

1 *Multidimensionality* There are not only many different people in any classroom, with different preferences, needs and abilities, but also many different tasks to which the teacher has to attend. A restricted range of resources must be used for different purposes. Many different events must be planned and implemented in mutually complementary ways, taking account of differences among people and constantly changing circumstances. 'Records must be kept, schedules met, supplies organised and stored, and student work collected and evaluated.' Furthermore, each event has multiple possible repercussions, especially in terms of the implications of the teacher's interactions with one pupil for the work of others. Choices, therefore, are never simple.

2 *Simultaneity* Many things happen at once in classrooms. Most simply, whatever type of activity is going on, the teacher has to attend to what all the pupils are doing: Are they engaged in appropriate activities? Are they understanding what they are doing? Are they interested? Do they need help or guidance of one sort or another? At the same time, whatever the type of activity, the teacher needs to be concerned with the passage of time, the standard of work being done, the needs of all pupils and appropriate ways of taking the learning forward. The teacher must monitor and regulate several different activities at once.

3 *Immediacy* This refers to the rapid pace of classroom events. Teachers in practice are constantly engaged in successive, quick interactions with pupils, giving directions and explanations, questioning or answering questions, commenting, praising or reprimanding, and all the time deciding whether to intervene in an individual or group's activities or not, whether to interrupt one conversation or activity in order to engage in another more urgent one, and with the constant need to maintain the momentum and flow of events. In most instances, therefore, teachers have little time to reflect before acting.

4 *Unpredictability* It is difficult to predict how any activity will go on a particular day with a particular group of pupils. In addition, individual pupils have unexpected needs, and interruptions and distractions are frequent. Detailed long-term planning is counter-productive and even short-term plans need to be very flexible.

5 *Transparency* (or 'publicness' to use Doyle's term) 'Teachers act in fishbowls; each child normally can see how the others are treated' (Lortie, 1975, p. 70, quoted by Doyle 1986). Whatever teachers do in classrooms is observed by all the pupils, who thus learn important

information about the teachers' skills and attitudes. What teachers do on any occasion can have important future repercussions.

6 *History* When the same class meets with a teacher several times each week over many months, it establishes shared experiences, understandings and norms which inform its future activities. For example, early meetings of classes with their teachers can often shape events for the rest of the year. Planning and decision-making needs to take account of a class's history.

There are of course many other complexities which teachers in specific circumstances face. For example, the tension between 'covering' a set curriculum and preparing pupils for external assessments on one hand, and trying to teach for understanding or the development of autonomy on the other, can be a major complicating factor in teachers' work. Similarly, trying to ensure thorough learning while at the same time trying to 'sell' the subject can add to the complexity. And the ever-widening range of responsibilities given to teachers, for example for identifying pupils' special needs or possible symptoms of child abuse, or checking immediately on unexplained absences, makes classroom teaching an extraordinarily complex job.

HOW DO TEACHERS COPE WITH THIS COMPLEXITY?

It seems that, very rationally, teachers prioritise and develop sophisticated skills for dealing with priority aspects of their task. The priorities are determined by the nature of the task, as outlined, for example, by Doyle's six facets of classroom complexity. Teachers must, to survive with any degree of satisfaction, be able to deal with the unpredictable, immediate, public, simultaneous, multidimensional demands of classroom life in ways that win and maintain some respect from their pupils, their colleagues, their managers and themselves. What precisely that means will vary according to the particular context, including for example the age of the pupils and whether they have come willingly to school. None the less, it is the ways in which teachers deal with life in the classroom, rather than wider concerns, that have to be priorities for all classroom teachers.

The sophisticated skills that teachers develop for dealing with classroom life are far from adequately understood. This is partly due to the inherent isolation of traditional classroom life: the teacher, alone in the classroom, has to make things happen and has to deal with what happens. Unlike the doctor, the lawyer, the engineer or the architect, the teacher cannot discuss with colleagues most of the priority decisions that need to be made before making them; and, to judge from teachers' practice, there seems little point in discussing them afterwards. Since there is no apparent point in talking about their classroom expertise, the inherently tacit nature of that expertise is compounded by the lack of need to articulate it. Many commentators have remarked on teachers' lack of any specialist language for discussing their work. Jackson, for example, noted that 'when teachers talk together, almost any reasonably intelligent adult can listen in and comprehend what is being said' (Jackson, 1968, p. 143). It is only in recent years, therefore, that researchers have begun to find out, through purposeful investigation, something of the nature of teachers' expertise.

One way in which researchers have studied the nature of teachers' classroom expertise is by comparing experienced teachers with novices. Berliner, for example, concluded from his studies of this kind that:

> experienced teachers differ from less experienced or inexperienced teachers in profound ways. Their experience has given them mental representations of typical students . . . they have fully developed student schemata, by means of which they operate. . . . Novices and postulants have facts, concepts and principles, a kind of propositional knowledge. . . . The experienced teachers use their rich base of personal knowledge to instantiate concepts (labels) such as 'shy' or 'emotionally handicapped'. . . . Like experienced/expert individuals in other fields, our experienced teachers show memory for information that is different from the memory of less experienced teachers. Their perception is different, thus they remember different things. And their memory is organised differently. What they remember seems to be more functional. They focus primarily on instructional events and issues.
>
> (Berliner, 1987, pp. 75–76)

As Berliner indicates, these findings show similarities with work contrasting experts and novices in some other professions. For example, Hubert and Stuart Dreyfus's (1986) model of the development of complex forms of human expertise emphasises that increased expertise is related centrally to *the degree of intuition involved* in overall awareness of a situation, recognising key relevant features of it, sensing what is important, and deciding what to do. It is a model that seems to fit quite well the evidence about expertise in classroom teaching.

Expert teaching seems then to involve the use of complex schemata of diverse kinds, developed through experience, through which teachers intuitively recognise typical situations or pupils and relate these to what they themselves want to achieve and to the ways they have learned to achieve these goals. Through the use of these schemata they are able, from the vast amount of information constantly available, both to filter out irrelevant information and to use the relevant information in highly efficient ways. It is not of course simply a matter of teaching various *types* of lessons to different *types* of pupils, using appropriate *types* of activities and making appropriate *types* of reaction to whatever *types* of situation arise: each lesson, each pupil, each activity, each situation and each reaction is unique. Part of the importance of thinking intuitively rather than in terms of propositional concepts and principles seems to be that instead of recognising examples of formally defined categories and then responding to 'the type', experienced teachers generally appear to recognise situations or pupils as being 'like' others that they have encountered in the past. They seem to be guided by their past experience both in being able to tune in to the general nature of the situation and also in knowing which distinctive features of the unique new situation need to be taken into account.

Studies of teachers' thinking while engaged in interactive teaching (e.g. Brown and McIntyre, 1993; Cooper and McIntyre, 1996) consistently suggest that teachers take account of a very large number of situational and pupil factors in making classroom choices about how to go about achieving their purposes, and also in judging what standards are appropriate in assessing how well things go. For each of the many 'decisions' that teachers appear to make almost instantaneously in the course of most lessons, there are likely to be several factors involved. Many of these factors are elements of teachers' knowledge about their pupils, both individually and as groups: for example, how able, attentive, confident, tenacious or mature they are. Other factors relate to the current state of pupils, as observed by the teacher: for example, whether they are excited, tired, bored, bewildered or enthusiastic. In addition, there are a wide variety of other conditions of which teachers take account, including their own stable or temporary characteristics (e.g. expertise, tiredness), the availability of accommodation, equipment, materials and time, characteristics of the content of the lesson, the weather, and other things going on. Nobody who is knowledgeable about teaching could complain that teachers do not take account of a very great deal of relevant information in their classroom teaching.

Teachers are not, of course, engaged in interactive teaching all the time. They also spend a good deal of time planning for their teaching, making and recording assessments of students' work, and preparing materials. One might expect their thinking to be very different in these quite different circumstances, when they are away from their pupils. That does indeed seem to be the case, but experienced teachers' planning does not contrast with the intuitive nature of their classroom decision-making to the extent that it approximates to the widely prescribed 'rational planning model'. Far from focusing first on desired outcomes and then planning how to attain them, experienced (and novice) teachers' planning seems generally to focus first and most on teaching content and on pupil activities, to involve a cyclical process through which initial ideas are gradually developed, and to be heavily dependent on visualisation of the intended teaching activity in the specific context of their own classrooms (Clark and Peterson, 1986): a feel for the situation is apparently very important in preactive teacher thinking also. Significant too is the consistent research finding that, among the many kinds of planning in which teachers regularly engage, 'lesson planning is rarely claimed as an important part of the repertoire of experienced teachers' (ibid., p. 262). Presumably, given that one has a general idea of how the lesson will fit into longer-term plans, the unpredictability of classroom life makes dependence on one's interactive skills a more fruitful and flexible way of dealing with detailed aspects of a lesson than planning in advance; this is another way of prioritising what is important.

SIMPLIFYING THE WORK OF CLASSROOM TEACHING

A central proposition of this essay is that the expertise of experienced classroom teachers is well and sophisticatedly geared to the realities of classroom life. One important element of that sophisticated realism is teachers' simplification of those aspects of their task which do not require priority attention. Where large amounts of information can be reduced to simple information that is easier to store and to use, and where this does not interfere with dealing effectively with their priority classroom tasks, teachers seem to be very efficient in engaging in such simplification. Some of the most pervasive ways in which this is done merit attention.

Short-term perspectives

While engaged in classroom teaching, teachers seem generally to focus their attention on short-term goals. It seems that thinking about longer-term goals, and in particular about how classroom activities will contribute to the attainment of the learning goals that are implicit or explicit in the curriculum, does not help to deal with the complexities of the classroom. Not thinking in any kind of sustained way beyond the short-term is apparently one very important way in which teachers are able to simplify their task of classroom teaching. (As noted above, lesson planning too seems generally to be focused on lesson content and classroom activities and not on learning goals. While it is true that such short-term planning is typically nested within longer-term planning, the latter seems typically to be concerned with the content to be covered, not with the teaching.)

Jackson was one of the first researchers to highlight this feature of classroom teaching. He wrote of *immediacy*, not as Doyle was later to do in referring to the reality that faced teachers, but as a striking characteristic of teachers' ways of thinking about, and especially of evaluating, their teaching. He contrasted what seemed to him a reasonable expectation with the reality he found:

> In the most global terms, the goal of the schools is to promote learning. Thus, ideally we might expect teachers to derive a major source of their satisfactions from observing growth in achievement among their students. Further, the students' performance on tests of achievement (commercial or teacher-made) would seem to provide objective and readily obtainable evidence of this growth. Logically at least, the conscientious teacher ought to point with pride or disappointment to the gains or losses of students as measured by test performance.
>
> (Jackson, 1968, p. 123)

In practice, he found that the expert US elementary school teachers he was studying (as nominated by superintendents) treated such evidence of learning outcomes as of minor importance. Instead, they reported that their evidence for knowing whether they were doing a good job came from 'looking at their faces . . . they look alert; they look interested; they look questioning'; from 'the way they sound: there is a sound that you can tell, and you can tell when they're really working'; from whether or not 'they bring things to you like articles out of magazines or pictures they have drawn'; from 'asking a few questions to know whether they're learning or not . . . if they [first-grade children] don't *understand* what you're doing, they usually won't express it verbally . . . They will climb on the desk or under the chair or make some quiet attempt to escape'; from 'the degree to which the kids feel part of the activities of the room and participate in them with pleasure'; from 'their attitudes and by their notebooks'. Jackson concluded that

> how well the outstanding elementary teacher is doing seems to be answered by the continual flow of information from the students during the teaching session. Spontaneous expressions of interest and enthusiasm are among the most highly valued indicators of good teaching, although the quality of the students' contributions to daily sessions is also mentioned frequently.
>
> (Ibid., p. 126)

Later studies of teachers' classroom thinking have reached very similar conclusions. Brown and McIntyre (1993), for example, studied Scottish 'good teachers', as identified by their pupils, and mostly working at secondary school level. Having observed teachers teaching lessons, and also units of work made up of several lessons, they asked the individual teachers what they were pleased with about these lessons and units. While without exception the teachers focused not on their own activities but on those of their pupils, they rarely made any claims, or referred to any evidence of, outcomes of their pupils' curriculum learning. Instead, they used what the researchers saw as two main types of criteria for judging success. The more common of these were *normal desirable states of pupil activity*. Each teacher tended to have distinctive criteria of this sort, relating to each of the different phases of units or lessons, or the different modes of classroom working, which that teacher distinguished, but all relating to some conception of 'working well'. The other type of criterion, *progress*, was more internally diverse, and included various ways in which teachers perceived pupils to be making progress. These included, for example, progress towards normal desirable states, i.e. learning to work appropriately, progress in the production of written or other artefacts, progress through the work to be covered, and progress in pupils' cognitive or affective developments. Even these progress criteria, then, were in the great majority of cases quite short-term.

While these short-term indicators of success, and the goals which they seem to reflect, no doubt reveal in large measure implicit theories of how pupils can best be helped to attain longer-term learning goals, the lack of spontaneous mention of such rationales suggests that they are quite far from the surface of teachers' conscious thinking about their teaching. In the classroom, the short-term is totally dominant: in order to cope with its immediate complexities, it seems, longer-term concerns are very firmly suspended from consideration.

Although such patterns seem to be common, it should not, however, be inferred that they are either necessary or universal. In what was in many respects a very similar later study, in the context of the introduction of a new National Curriculum in England, Cooper and McIntyre (1996) found that teachers did sometimes spontaneously relate their teaching to longer-term learning goals. The researchers tentatively concluded that this difference from earlier findings resulted in part from teachers' concern at that time to think out how to modify their practices so as to maximise their pupils' attainment of National Curriculum targets, and in part from their own explicit focus as researchers on teaching for effective learning. Teachers, it is clear, are perfectly capable of fluent and sophisticated thinking that relates classroom teaching to long-term learning goals; but it seems that such thinking is not in normal circumstances well geared to dealing with the realities of classroom life.

Consideration of the relationship between the findings of educational research and the prescriptions of educational policy-makers reveals a quite remarkable discrepancy in this respect. In recent decades, the rational planning model, according to which teaching should be very deliberately structured in order to achieve carefully chosen and clearly formulated curriculum learning objectives, has been frequently and consistently demonstrated to bear very little relationship to the ways in which able and experienced classroom teachers normally set about their work. Yet policy-makers during the same period have become increasingly assertive in their demands that schools and teachers should approach their work as that model prescribes, shaping and evaluating their teaching in relation to specified targets of educational achievement.

Within classroom walls

Classroom teachers also appear generally to limit the range of information which needs to be incorporated into their thinking by taking little account of the lives and learning of their pupils outside their classrooms. It is, however, with less certainty that one can attribute this to the needs of classroom teaching, because there seems to be an even more total neglect of extra-classroom learning in the ways in which most curricula that teachers are asked to implement are formulated: at best, such curriculum frameworks give little help to any efforts which teachers might make to relate their teaching to children's lives outside of the classroom. Furthermore, there seem to be substantial variations in teachers' practices in this respect, variations related to the ages and academic success levels of pupils: it is with the 'academic' sets in secondary schools that this tendency appears to be most consistent and most extreme (e.g. Keddie, 1971).

None the less, there can be no doubt that classroom teaching is made much simpler and more viable by teachers' neglect of such extra-classroom information. In so far as the task of teaching can be contained within classroom walls, it is one over which teachers have much greater control and which is therefore likely to be much more manageable. Externally prescribed curricula and 'standards', and related systems of assessment and qualification may plausibly be understood as structures that support this kind of simplification of classroom teaching.

This feature of classroom teaching is the more remarkable given widely accepted educational arguments against such isolation of classroom learning. Traditional 'progressive' educational thinking emphasises the indivisibility of the whole child, and over the years increasingly informed and persuasive arguments have been sustained for the importance of continuity of learning across the home–school divide (e.g. Tett and Crowther, 1998); but even teachers of the youngest children at schools appear generally to pay little attention to the content or the processes of children's learning in their home contexts. Second, it is difficult to contest the claim that school-based learning is useful only in so far as it has value in contexts other than the school. That is no small challenge and it is clearly one that schools have repeatedly failed to meet adequately. And third, research from several traditions, including for example on the public understanding of science (e.g. Richards, 1996), has demonstrated very clearly the powerful influence of learning in other contexts and that schoolteaching which neglects this tends not to be very effective. There must be a real need for this kind of simplification that leads schooling in general, and classroom teaching in particular, to sustain it against the force of such arguments.

Simplification of differences among pupils

Jackson (1968) is one of many observers who have been struck by the extent to which the joys of teaching for schoolteachers, especially elementary school teachers, are in watching the development of *individual* children. Research consistently shows that teachers are interested in the individual characteristics of their students and take account of many of these characteristics in their teaching. Yet it is also the case that teachers' practice seems to depend on considerable simplification in the ways in which differences among pupils are taken into account. What teachers most need to know in order to take account of the differences among their pupils is how they can each be expected to respond to different classroom situations and tasks. The more predictable the pupils' behaviour, the more manageable will situations be for teachers. Teachers therefore seem to structure their perceptions of different pupils in ways that emphasise predictable differences among pupils in the extent to which they will do what teachers would like them to do.

What this means in practice varies according to context. For example, 'maturity' seems frequently to be a central organising concept in teachers' perceptions of children in the earlier years of primary school teaching. However, as Hargreaves (1972, pp. 155–156) suggests, the likelihood that teachers will perceive and evaluate their pupils on the basis of the two main dimensions of their own role, those of maintaining order and facilitating learning is supported by a good deal of evidence. These two dimensions seem to be quite dominant, although their precise nature and relationship to each other vary according to teachers' views and contexts (e.g. McIntyre *et al.*, 1966). A teacher who can confidently place each pupil on each of these two dimensions seems to be in a good position to know what to expect from each pupil in the classroom, in relation to those matters which are of major concern. It is therefore of the greatest importance for teachers to get to know pupils as quickly as possible in relation to these two priority dimensions. Yet it seems that an important distinction has to be made in this respect even between these two dimensions. Hargreaves *et al.* (1975) describe in detail the ways in which teachers' perceptions of pupils' behaviour gradually developed in the early stages of secondary schooling, with the firm labelling of some as 'troublemakers' not happening until their third year. In contrast, Cooper and McIntyre (1996), for example, found pupils being very firmly placed by their teachers as more or less able long before the end of their first year in secondary school.

Despite 30 years' experience of comprehensive schooling; despite persuasive arguments from psychologists that cognitive differences are best understood in terms of 'multiple intelligences' (Gardner, 1993); despite the equally compelling argument from Benjamin Bloom (1977) that differences in school achievements can more validly and constructively be understood as the effects of 'alterable variables' such as prior knowledge, motivation and quality of teaching than as the consequences of differences in general ability; and despite evidence that confronts all teachers frequently of wide variations in individual pupils' achievements between and within subjects (e.g. Denton and Postlethwaite, 1985; McIntyre and Brown, 1978), the simplifying notion of 'general ability' continues to be very widely used by teachers as a way of reducing the complexity of classroom life.

Practicality

Doyle and Ponder (1977) coined the term 'the practicality ethic' to capture the moral imperative felt by classroom teachers about 'keeping one's feet on the ground' in thinking about the work of classroom teaching. It is in the contexts of initial teacher education and of proposed curriculum or pedagogical innovations that teachers' concern with 'practicality' is most apparent. Teachers are often in these contexts reported as showing little concern for wider educational ideals, for theoretical or research-based arguments or for generalised principles. Instead, they are reported as being concerned with pragmatic considerations about what is feasible, realistic and effective within their own contexts. Two examples of this widely reported tendency may suffice to indicate its nature.

In the context of an attempt to introduce into the early years of secondary schooling in Scotland a national programme of integrated science teaching with a number of innovative features, the national working party's arguments for these innovations were compared with those offered for and against the innovations in meetings of science staff in each of 50 secondary schools (Brown *et al.*, 1976). Whereas the working party's arguments focused on the nature of science, the needs of society and theories of learning, the teachers' arguments (whether for or against the innovations) focused on the availability of necessary resources, the adequacy of their own expertise and practical implications for classroom activities, school timetabling and organisation. Both groups were concerned with implications for pupils, but with that exception the lack of common concerns was almost total. Especially important for the interpretation of these findings was the fact that a large proportion of the national working party's members were practising teachers, while most of the remainder were ex-teachers. Differences of emphases seemed to arise not from the kinds of people involved but from the roles they were occupying.

A second example may be taken from the work of an initial teacher education partnership in England (Davies, 1997). The university lecturer responsible for the training of graduate secondary school English teachers was concerned with the wide diversity of versions of 'English' to which the trainees had been exposed as undergraduates, and wanted them to understand both this diversity and the implications for secondary school teaching of these diverse versions. The trainees themselves responded very positively to this agenda, but they found in the English departments of partner schools a pervasive resistance from their mentors and heads of department to engaging with such a 'theoretical' agenda. It was not that the experienced teachers were unaware of their own commitment in their practice to distinctive versions of English. It seemed rather that learning *how* to teach the department's distinctive version of English was for them the practical task on which the trainees should obviously be concentrating, instead of asking challenging questions about *why* or *with what consequences* – which were not immediately relevant to getting on with that department's conception of its job.

It is all too easy for academic commentators to complain about the restricted vision of practising teachers, and unfortunately the teacher education literature is replete with such complaints. It is more fruitful to understand 'the practicality ethic' as reflecting in an especially clear way the need for classroom teachers to concentrate their energies on those things that are inescapably of high priority for them, and therefore their need to neglect or simplify other things.

SUMMARY OF THE ARGUMENT

Research on the nature of expert classroom teaching suggests that expert classroom teachers are highly impressive in the complexity of the information that they constructively take into account in order to achieve their purposes. Their expertise seems exceptionally well tuned to the realities of classroom teaching. It involves:

1 very sophisticated, experience-based schemata;
2 highly intuitive judgements and decision-making;
3 largely tacit, individual and quite private expert knowledge;
4 prioritisation and simplification geared to teaching purposes, for example, through

- short-term perspectives
- working within classroom walls
- simplification of differences among pupils
- practicality.

SOME LIMITATIONS OF CURRENT CLASSROOM TEACHING

Having developed as a very distinctive type of expertise over the last two centuries, class-room teaching is at its best very good at doing certain kinds of things, less good at others. Of course, not all good classroom teaching is the same: most strikingly, classrooms for different age-groups tend to be very different. The early years classroom, in which the teacher is not only with the same class throughout the school day, but also aspires to concern himself with the multifaceted development of each 'whole child', is very different from the narrowly focused A-level classroom, memorably described by Stevens (1960), in which the teacher's expertise may be directed solely towards her pupils' examination success. But these are, it is claimed, variations on a central theme: classroom teaching, with one adult figure responsible for the learning of a substantial number of young people within one large room for substantial periods of time, has its distinctive strengths and limitations.

Its strengths, as already argued, are reflected in its total and virtually unchallenged dominance of schooling throughout the twentieth century. It has allowed mass schooling on an unprecedented scale not only to be possible but also to achieve enormous success: it has kept millions of young people of ever-increasing ages off the labour market and generally peaceful and law-abiding; and it has enabled most of them to be literate, numerate and to acquire diverse qualifications and knowledge which have allowed them more or less to thrive in societies that have been changing at an accelerating rate.

None the less, it is the limitations of this classroom teaching system which are most frequently commented upon. These frequent complaints are of course rarely focused on the system, but instead upon those who inhabit the system: most frequently teachers, but also teacher educators, educational researchers, school managers, parents and young people. It would be as wrong to assume that the system is inherently flawed as it is to assume that any of these different groups of people are generically incompetent or irresponsible; but it is useful to look at the nature of some of the complaints that are frequently made and to relate these to what has already been said about the nature of classroom teaching expertise.

The general thesis of this section of the argument is that many of the complaints made about the inadequacies of schoolteaching in recent years can best be understood as com-plaints about teachers' failure to take account in their teaching of various kinds of informa-tion or evidence. These complaints are therefore seen as fundamental challenges to the sophisticated kind of classroom expertise upon which teachers have learned to depend, with its emphasis on the intuitive and the tacit, on prioritisation and on simplification. It is not suggested that it is impossible for classroom teachers to respond to any such demands: there is plenty of evidence that classroom teaching is, within limits, quite flexible, and that classroom teachers can, when motivated by strong convictions or pressures, adapt their teaching to take account of new kinds of information. It is suggested, however, that class-room teaching is not at all well suited as a system to meeting the demand that all these multiple kinds of information should be used by teachers. It is further suggested, therefore, that it is this unsuitability of classroom teaching as a system that has led teachers to be generally unresponsive to these demands and complaints, even though the use of each of these kinds of information can plausibly be argued to contribute to increased teaching effectiveness.

Four ways have already been discussed in which classroom teachers characteristically make their task more manageable by prioritising, and simplifying, the information available to them. Each of these has brought with it complaints and demands for change from critics who believe that pupils' learning could be more effectively facilitated if such prioritisation and simplification were avoided. On the other hand, informed observers might reasonably argue that, unfortunate as it is that teachers do not make fuller use of the wider range of information potentially available to them, neglect of that information is a reasonable price to pay for the benefits of skilled classroom teaching. However, if it is the case that mounting complaints of diverse kinds are all to be understood as consequences of the complexity of classroom life and of teachers' best efforts to cope with it, then it might seem that the balance of the argument has swung against the classroom system, and that the costs to be paid for continuing to rely upon it are too great. The focus of the essay now turns to five major areas of concern:

1 differentiation;
2 formative assessment;
3 home–school partnership;
4 students' own perspectives;
5 teaching as an evidence-based profession.

These will be examined in turn below.

Differentiation

It has already been noted that teachers widely depend on notions of 'general ability' in their classroom teaching. They do so in varying the materials they use, the tasks they set, the questions they ask, the explanations they offer and the standards they set, according to the perceived needs of pupils of differing abilities. Although strongly opposed by many commentators because of its oversimplifying dependence on 'general ability' (e.g. Hart, 1996, 1998), such differentiation tends to be officially encouraged in the UK, both by politicians and by Her Majesty's Inspectorate, as a realistic way of taking account of differences among pupils. Alongside such encouragement, however, come repeated complaints that teachers do not differentiate adequately among their pupils.

Both inspectors and researchers have sought to judge the adequacy with which teachers vary tasks to take account of differences in ability (HMI, 1978; Bennett *et al.*, 1984; Simpson, 1989), and have with some consistency concluded that, both for more able and for less able pupils, tasks are often poorly matched to student needs. Teachers, it appears from these studies, tend in practice to overestimate the capabilities of children whom they see as 'less able' and to underestimate the capabilities of pupils whom they see as 'more able'.

Why does this happen? The researcher who was conducting one of these studies (Simpson, 1989) fed her findings back to the primary school teachers involved and asked them to comment. The teachers agreed that the tasks they set probably did over- and underestimate pupils' capabilities as the research report suggested, and commented as follows.

1 There were limits to the number of different groups or distinctive individuals with which they could cope at any one time.

2 Having a wide spread of ability in their classes was greatly preferable for both teachers and children to grouping children into classes according to ability.

3 Whereas the study had been concerned only with children's 'academic' needs, it was also important to cater for their diverse social and emotional needs.

4 They deliberately gave special attention and extra resources to the lower ability pupils, because their need for teaching help was greater.

5 More able children in the classroom were a valuable resource in that they offered models of effective learning and problem-solving which could help the learning of the other children.

6 It was more useful for children's education to be broadened than for them to 'shoot ahead' of their peers; however, the provision of breadth depended on the availability of appropriate resources and time.

7 While the research had concentrated on number and language tasks, it was necessary to provide a wide curriculum.

8 If able children appeared to be over-practising, it was almost certainly related to the teachers' concern to ensure that the basic skills had been thoroughly mastered; the teachers had to be mindful of the prerequisites for the children's learning with the next teacher, the next stage of the curriculum, or the next school to which they were going.

The problem, these teachers suggest, is not with teachers' knowledge of the different learning needs of different children, nor even with finding ways of catering for these needs. The problem is that the careful professional prioritisation which is necessary in dealing with the complexity of classroom teaching involves the simplification or neglect of much available information, with the inevitable consequence that interested parties whose priorities are different from those of the teachers will, to some extent, be disappointed. We must recognise, they are telling us, the limits of what is possible through classroom teaching.

Formative assessment

In the last few years, the concept of differentiation seems to some extent to have been replaced as a solution to the problems of classroom teaching, as offered for example in inspection reports, by that of formative assessment. Here the focus is less on stable differences among children and more on the use of information about their current individual achievements and problems, as discovered through their teachers' assessments, to guide their future learning. Unlike assessment for other purposes, for this purpose 'the aspiration is that assessment should become fully integrated with teaching and learning, and therefore part of the educational process rather than a "bolt-on" activity' (James, 1998, p. 172).

Formative assessment is a much less contentious idea than differentiation by ability, and indeed it is difficult to find any cases of people arguing against it. It is such an obviously sensible idea that academic commentators have been queuing up for around 30 years to commend it to teachers (e.g. McIntyre, 1970; Scriven, 1967). It has recently been given new impetus and importance by an authoritative review of research in the field by Black and Wiliam (1998), whose main conclusion is 'The research reported here shows conclusively that formative assessment does improve learning. The gains in achievement appear to be quite considerable . . . among the largest ever reported for educational interventions.' They also report, however, that there is 'extensive evidence to show that present levels of practice in this aspect of teaching are low' (ibid.).

Why is it that, despite 30 years of propaganda, teachers appear to make little use of formative assessment in their classroom practice? Is it, as Black and Wiliam suggest, because there has not been sufficient external encouragement and support for such good practice? That may be the case but a more plausible hypothesis, derived from their own and others' conclusions, might be that regular effective formative assessment so adds to the complexity of classroom teaching as to make it an impracticable option for teachers. Black and Wiliam found from their review of classroom research that feedback or formative assessment is unlikely to have beneficial effects on performance or learning unless it meets a number of quite demanding conditions. On one hand, they conclude that the more summary kinds of feedback widely used by teachers, such as marks, grades, corrections, praise or criticism, tend to be counter-productive. On the other hand, they suggest that feedback practices guided by the following precepts are likely to promote learning (James, 1998, pp. 98–99):

- Feedback is most effective when it stimulates correction of errors through a thoughtful approach.
- Feedback should concentrate on specific errors and poor strategy and make suggestions about how to improve.
- Suggestions for improvement should act as 'scaffolding', i.e. students should be given as much help as they need to use their knowledge but they should not be given a complete solution as soon as they get stuck or they will not think things through for themselves.
- Students should be helped to find alternative solutions if a simple repetition of an explanation on the part of the teacher continues to fail.
- A focus on process goals is often more effective than a focus on product goals; and feedback on progress over a number of attempts is more effective than performance treated as isolated events.
- The quality of the dialogue in feedback is important and some research indicates that oral feedback is more effective than written feedback.
- Students need to have skills to ask for assistance and to help others.

Another recently published study of formative assessment, by Torrance and Pryor (1998, p. 151), concludes that the impact of formative assessment is 'complex, multifaceted, and is not necessarily always as positive as might be intended by teachers and as some advocates of formative assessment would have us believe'. They go on to describe two ideal types of classroom assessment. *Convergent assessment*, which is 'routinely accomplished', is characterised by 'analysis of the interaction of the child and the curriculum from the point of view of the curriculum' and is close to what is done in much current classroom assessment practice. *Divergent assessment*, which 'emphasises the learner's understanding rather than the agenda of the assessor', is 'aimed at prompting pupils to reflect on their own thinking (or) focusing on . . . aspects of learners' work which yield insights into their current understanding' and 'accepts the complexity of formative assessment'. Developed instances of divergent assessment were found to be rare, to derive from 'ideological commitments to a "child-centred approach" and [to be] not necessarily as well structured as they could and (we would argue) should be'. While Torrance and Pryor consider that both types of classroom assessment have their place, they suggest that 'divergent assessment is the more interesting approach, and the one that seems to offer more scope for positively affecting children's learning' (ibid., p. 154); and they go on to make more detailed suggestions about how the quality of formative assessment may be improved.

Increasingly, then, researchers seem to be able to provide teachers with detailed guidance – about how they can use formative assessment in ways that will contribute significantly to their students' effective learning. There is, however, a problem: all this advice offered by Black and Wiliam and by Torrance and Pryor to teachers seems to involve sustained, high-quality, non-routine interaction – either orally or in writing – between the teacher and either individual students or small groups. How far does this advice take account of the complexity of classroom life, and of the sophisticated ways in which expert teachers have learned to work effectively in classrooms through rigorous prioritisation, simplification and intuitive decision-making? We can have a good deal of confidence in the validity of these researchers' conclusions that it is feedback from, and interaction with, teachers of the kinds they suggest which can best facilitate pupils' learning. What may well be doubted is that the current lack of frequency of such practices in classrooms is a consequence of teachers' ignorance or lack of understanding of what would be valuable, or the lack of external encouragement. On the contrary, it would seem much more likely that, sensing that effective formative assessment depends on such unrealistic, high-quality engagement with individual pupils, teachers do not attempt widely to build such assessment into their classroom teaching. Current efforts to encourage and support teachers in the fuller and more effective use of formative assessment may prove this wrong, and show instead that the researchers' insights into good classroom practice are far ahead of the insights of most teachers. However, a more plausible expectation would be that the researchers' guidance will founder on their failure to take account of the real constraints imposed by classroom teaching as a system.

The point of the argument is not, of course, that we must resign ourselves to the present levels of effectiveness achieved by classroom teaching. It is instead that, if our schooling system is to become substantially more effective, through for example taking account of new insights into the effective use of formative assessment, this improvement may depend on a questioning of the system of classroom teaching which we have learned to take for granted. It would be wrong to leave this section without noting that James, Black and Wiliam and Torrance and Pryor offer some seeds of ideas about what such questioning might lead to, ideas to which I shall return.

Home–school partnership

British traditions of schooling have involved very limited levels of collaboration between the school and the home. Throughout the twentieth century, however, there has been a sustained critique of these traditions from progressive educational thinkers, including increasing numbers of teachers, especially in primary schools. They argue that 'meaningful' education of 'the whole child' depends, among other things, on children's experience of continuity across the home–school divide. The most important assault on the separation of schooling from home life came in the 1960s when successive studies, culminating in the Plowden Report (1967), demonstrated very clearly that children's progress and success throughout schooling were closely related to the nature of their home background. Although initially these research findings were often interpreted rather naïvely as showing a simple causal relationship between home characteristics and educational success, even this led to calls for closer home–school relationships aimed at encouraging parents to take greater interest in their children's school learning and to become more involved in the work of the school. Subsequent thinking, much influenced by the powerful theoretical contributions of Bourdieu (especially Bourdieu and Passeron, 1977) and of Bernstein (1970, 1975) and by research such as that of Tizard and Hughes (1984), has increasingly construed the problem not in terms of the deficiencies of working-class homes but as resulting from the gap between the home lives of many children and their school experiences. Accordingly it has emphasised the need for schools to work in partnership with parents, the primary educators of their children, in order to bridge that gap.

What is most needed, it has been argued, most forcibly by Atkins and Bastiani (1988), is for teachers to listen to parents. Teachers' classroom practice, it is suggested, can be made much more effective if they have the benefit of parents' authoritative insights into their children's lives away from school: their interests, their talents, their achievements, their aspirations and their learning needs. The argument is surely persuasive, since parents have much more opportunity, and generally more motivation, to understand their own children than teachers can have, especially secondary school teachers who are weekly teaching over a hundred students. Yet there is very little evidence of teachers being motivated to listen to such valuable information. The opportunities created for such sharing of information tend, again especially in secondary schools, to be rare and brief, and most of the talking seems generally to be done by the teachers. On the whole, parents do not complain. They have for the most part accepted the ideology of professionalism and are ready to accept that teachers know best; and so they learn not to offer their insights about their children to a system that clearly does not want to hear them.

It is very tempting to be critical of teachers because of their apparent unwillingness to work in genuine partnership with parents, and especially because of their lack of readiness to take advantage of the information that parents could provide. But classroom teachers have to select and to use the information that they find most conducive to the management of many pupils' learning activities in a classroom. The information that parents can provide, based as it is on a completely different perspective, may not be easily usable by teachers. Randell (1998), in a study of different perspectives on students' progress in their first year at secondary school, found that teachers talked about the individual students in a largely judgemental way – the two dimensions of ability and hard work/good behaviour suggested earlier – whereas parents talked predominantly about their needs. Teachers, it seemed, found it difficult, and also perhaps of questionable value, to adapt their classroom practice to take account of the distinctive needs that parents perceived their children to have.

It may thus be the case that the information which parents think they can usefully offer teachers to facilitate their children's learning cannot generally be effectively used to inform classroom teaching. The problem remains that the progress made by school systems in recent decades in serving the more socially and economically disadvantaged half of the population has been very slow; and it seems highly improbable that better progress can be made in future unless schools develop more genuine and effective ways of working in partnership with disadvantaged communities and families. It is probably unreasonable and unproductive to continue to place the major responsibility for engaging effectively in such partnerships on individual teachers working within the constraining framework of class-room teaching.

Students' own perspectives

> While teachers are for the most part supportive, stimulating and selfless in the hours they put in to help young people, the *conditions of learning* that are common across secondary schools do not adequately take account of the social maturity of young people, nor of the tensions and pressures they feel as they struggle to reconcile the demands of their social and personal lives with the development of their identity as learners.
>
> (Rudduck *et al.*, 1996, p. 1)

That is how Rudduck and her colleagues summarise what they learned from secondary school pupils in their extensive study of pupils' own perspectives on their schooling. In introducing their book, they also quote Silberman and agree with his dictum that 'we should affirm the right of students to negotiate our purposes and demands so that the activities we undertake with them have greatest possible meaning to all' (Silberman, 1971, p. 364). Teachers are under increasing pressure not only to take responsibility for students' attain-ment of learning targets but also to listen to students' voices and to take fuller account of their perspectives on their schooling. This seems to be partly in response to a view that students' rights need to be more widely respected in schools, but perhaps even more because of a recognition that improved school effectiveness will depend in large measure on the creation of conditions of learning which take fuller account of what students feel and think.

One of the major themes in the research reports from Rudduck and her colleagues concerns the significance of pupils' sense of having some control over their own learning:

> It was noticeable that when pupils spoke about work that they had designed themselves and that they felt was very much their own – whether project work in technology or work in art – they had a strong sense of purpose, strategy and goal. . . . Clearly, the meaningfulness of particular tasks is greater when pupils have a degree of control over the planning and execution of the work: they have a greater sense of ownership.
>
> (Rudduck *et al.*, 1996, p. 48)

However, pupils did not *expect* to have control over their learning:

> [I]t seemed that pupils did not feel that it was necessary to know, or that they had the right to know, where lessons were heading or how they fitted together. The pupils we interviewed were, in the main, prepared to live in the present and to take lessons as they came without much concern for overall sequencing in learning.
>
> (Ibid., p. 47)

The researchers describe too 'pupils who *wanted* to learn but felt that they had little control over their own learning' (ibid., p. 46). Sometimes blame was attached to teachers, sometimes to their own past behaviour or absences, sometimes to other (disruptive) pupils, but rarely did the pupils feel that they themselves were in a position to overcome any learning problems they had.

In classroom teaching, it is the teacher who has responsibility for determining the activ-ities to be engaged in and the learning tasks to be undertaken. The teacher can, of course, share this responsibility with pupils or take account of pupils' interests and felt needs in deciding what to do. Cooper and McIntyre (1996) found that the teachers whom they studied always took some account of their pupils' perspectives. They characterised the teaching they observed as varying from *interactive* teaching, in which pupils' contributions would be taken into account within the framework of teachers' predetermined plans, to *reactive* teaching, in which teachers were willing to take more fundamental account of pupils' concerns in deciding what to do. They found reactive teaching less common, and apparently more complex, since the teacher's plans depended on finding out and using information about the different perspectives of the pupils in a class as well as about the set curriculum.

Arguments that secondary school students are not sufficiently treated as partners in their own learning are highly persuasive, both in terms of their rights to have their perspectives taken into account and also instrumentally in terms of their commitment to learning. The lack of control which students generally have over their own lives in institutions that would claim to be serving their interests can indeed be seen as quite remarkable. Within the context of classroom teaching, however, the task for the teacher of treating students as partners while continuing to take responsibility for classroom activities and outcomes cannot but be seen as adding to the complexity of the teacher's task.

Teaching as an evidence-based profession

There has been vigorous debate over recent years about the usefulness of educational research. Although the obvious target of most of the criticism has been educational researchers, a much more fundamental challenge implicit in this debate has been in relation to classroom teachers. The aspiration of the powerful groups who have been promoting this debate – that teaching should be directly informed by research evidence about the relative effectiveness of different practices – gives research an importance hitherto undreamed of, but asks teachers to transform their ways of working. It asks that teachers should somehow integrate into their subtle, complex, tacit and intuitive decision-making the very different propositional kind of knowledge offered by research results. Teaching would therefore become a less idiosyncratic craft, and instead one informed by a standard but constantly developing set of validated generalisations about the consequences of using clearly specified practices in specified types of context. The Teacher Training Agency outlines this conception of teaching and research:

> Good teachers relish the opportunity to draw upon the most up to date knowledge. They continually challenge their own practice in order to do the best for their pupils. They want to be able to examine what they do in the light of important new knowledge, scientific investigation and evaluation, disciplined enquiry and rigorous comparison of practice in this country and in others – provided such resources are relevant to their field and accessible. Many of the resources they need to do this are, or ought to be precisely those provided by good research.
>
> (Teacher Training Agency, 1996, p. 2)

As yet there is a relatively modest corpus of such knowledge, especially in relation to the British context. However – and this is the complaint against educational researchers – this can in very large measure be explained by the neglect over the last 20 years by British researchers of the kinds of research which could have generated such knowledge. Although comparisons with engineering and medicine have to be treated with some scepticism, there is no reason to believe that a useful body of such knowledge could not be generated. Nor can one deny that, if the body of knowledge were sufficiently substantial and wide-ranging, as well as rigorously validated, a teaching profession guaranteed to be working consistently in accordance with such knowledge would be likely to command greater confidence from the public. Much more problematic, however, is the idea that such knowledge, if available, would be used by classroom teachers. The authors of the review of educational research commissioned in England by the Department for Education and Employment had some sense, on the basis of their assessment of current practice, that this could not be taken for granted:

> Whatever the relevance and the quality of the research and the user-friendliness of the output, its eventual impact will depend on the willingness and the capacity of policy-makers and practitioners to take research into account in their decision-making and their actions. This relies on a commitment to the principle, an understanding of what research can offer, and the practical capacity to interpret research.
>
> (Hillage *et al.*, 1998, p. 53)

It depends on all that, but in relation to classroom teaching it depends much more on how such research-based knowledge can be integrated into the kind of classroom expertise on which teachers currently rely: the two kinds of knowledge are so different that this seems highly problematic.

The idea of evidence-based teaching is not, of course, limited to the proposal that the profession should be research-based. Increasingly, teachers are being asked to analyse and to plan their teaching in the light of evidence of various other kinds, such as how their pupils (and subgroups of their pupils) have performed in external examinations, in comparison to others with comparable prior attainments. The relationship of all such evidence and its use to teachers' developed classroom expertise is equally uncertain.

SUMMARY OF THE ARGUMENT

Having first sought to outline the nature of the expertise which teachers have successfully developed for the distinctive task of classroom teaching, with its considerable strengths but also with some limitations, my aim in this section has been to exemplify the mounting pressure on the classroom teaching system. I have outlined five major kinds of information to which teachers are increasingly being urged to become more responsive, but there is as yet little sign of this happening. In each case, I have argued that it is not realistic to ask teachers to take account of the additional information while maintaining the kind of expertise which has made classroom teaching a viable and indeed very successful system. I have emphasised that classroom teaching has been quite flexible as a system, and that classroom teachers have shown themselves to be highly adaptable; so it may be quite possible for highly motivated teachers to incorporate any one of these five demands into their classroom expertise, or to go a little way towards absorbing all of them. None the less, I am persuaded that the classroom teaching system is near to its limits, and that it will not be able to respond adequately to the accelerating 'expectations ... of what schools should accomplish' (Hargreaves, 1999, p. 122).

The argument here has been focused on the classroom teacher's position as solely responsible for what happens in his or her classroom, on the complexity of classroom life, on the teacher's need to find special ways of handling very large amounts and diverse kinds of information, and finally on the lack of realism in asking teachers to attend carefully to an accumulation of new kinds of information traditionally neglected. That is one kind of argument for believing that classroom teaching may have served its day. But we should note briefly that there are other very good arguments which could lead us to the same conclusion. One of these is that classroom teaching seems peculiarly ill-suited to most of the more exciting possibilities for using information technology to enhance the quality of learning in schools, as seems to be reflected in the very limited impact it has had on schooling in the last quarter century. Another might be that the very strong boundary which we have noted between classroom learning and learning in other contexts has been accepted for long enough, and that schools must, to enhance their effectiveness and usefulness, find ways of organising learning activities so that these *normally*, not just exceptionally, relate to pupils' learning in other contexts. More pragmatic arguments might emphasise the escalating costs of provision for 'lifelong learning' and consequent pressures for greater efficiency in schooling, or the likelihood that the shortage of well-qualified subject teachers in secondary schools will be endemic. The pressures on the viability of the classroom teaching system are of many kinds.

THE WAY AHEAD

To offer a clear vision of how schooling might be more effectively organised than on the classroom teaching system would be as foolhardy as it is unnecessary. There seems little doubt that change via a new system will come, but – we must hope and seek to ensure – only gradually over the next 20 years. New approaches will need to be developed, tested, modified and perfected, preferably with the help of careful research. A major constraint will be the architecture of schools, very obviously designed for classroom teaching and very badly designed for anything else. So, as new approaches are tried and found useful, they will be built into the architecture of new schools and then, one hopes, found even more useful. The change should properly be piecemeal, but it may come about in relatively efficient, rational and well-researched ways under the control of professional educators, or chaotically and through a series of reluctant and unhappy compromises to cope with external economic and political pressures. If we are clear about why change is necessary and about the principles by which the changes should be guided, the benefits can be maximised and the pain of change minimised.

What should we be seeking in a new system? Some elements of what is needed are obvious and are already apparent on a small scale in changing patterns of teachers' work. The problems of the classroom teaching system may properly be viewed as resulting from an over-dependence on certain elements which in themselves have considerable merits. The aim must be not to abandon these valuable elements, but to achieve a new balance in which dependence on their strengths does not automatically lead to problems because of their limitations. There are at least four ways in which a proper balance will require radical change:

● *Especially in secondary schools, a very different balance must be achieved between students and teachers in terms of responsibilities for generating and using information about students' achievements and needs in making decisions about their learning objectives and activities.* The research on formative assessment discussed earlier (Black and Wiliam, 1998) strongly suggests that the improved learning which can come from formative assessment is most likely through students themselves gaining a thorough understanding of the criteria for effective learning, through them assessing themselves, individually and as peers, and through them having opportunities, encouragement and responsibilities for using the information from such assessment in order to improve their understanding and skills (cf. James, 1998, chapter 9). Students, of course, have to learn how to do these things and how to take these responsibilities, and facilitating that learning must be an important task for schools; but while this move towards greater student responsibility is no doubt possible to some degree in classrooms, it seems much more likely to happen where the social settings more obviously reflect this shift in responsibilities.

● *A very different balance must be achieved between reliance on intuitive, tacit and private decision-making and on collaborative, explicit and evidence-based decision-making.* In all complex professional activities, as Dreyfus and Dreyfus (1986) and Schon (1983), for example, have argued, there is necessarily a heavy dependence on tacit and intuitive understanding and decision-making, just as in teaching. Classroom teaching is distinctive, however, in the scale of its dependence on such decision-making, with very little use being made traditionally of attempts to evaluate and synthesise available evidence, explicitly or rationally or collaboratively, as a basis for decision-making. The astonishingly wide acceptance of Schon's idea of reflective practice as an ideal for classroom teaching might reasonably be interpreted as a recognition of the rarity and difficulty of such explicit consideration of the evidence and of the choices to be made for important classroom decisions. The need for a change springs both from the inherent merits of rational thinking and use of evidence for the most important decisions, and also from the current state of affairs where – as has been demonstrated – even expert, intuitive, classroom decision-making cannot take account of much of the evidence which could be highly relevant for facilitating learning. Already in recent years, a greater proportion of the time and professional energy of teachers has been spent on gathering information, explicitly analysing it, sharing it and discussing its implications with colleagues, and planning collaboratively for pupils' learning. The work of schoolteachers should move increasingly in this direction, with more and more decision-making being explicit, rationally justified and corporate, and with such decision-making being a larger part of teachers' work, while face-to-face teaching, though still important, will occupy less of teachers' time. As in other professions, teachers' capacities for expert intuitive decision-making must continue to be of great importance, but it should cease to be all-important. How it can best be used to complement more explicit decision-making is a matter that will require extensive research and learning from experience.

● *A very different balance must be achieved between exclusive decision-making by professional schoolteachers and shared decision-making with adults who are not professional teachers.* Schoolteachers have, and will continue to have, a crucial and distinctive kind of expertise for facilitating learning. However, partly because they have been fully occupied with

105

classroom teaching, and partly in order to simplify their classroom teaching work, teachers have denied themselves a great deal of valuable information and insights, and have failed to develop vital shared understandings with others. A slightly greater proportion of teachers' time and professional energies seems currently to be being spent on collaborative planning with other adults who are not fellow-teachers. The work of schoolteachers should move much more in this direction, with increased consultation and joint decision-making with learning support staff, with parents, with community members, with employers and with other specialist professional workers: again, this will be possible only in so far as less time is spent in face-to-face teaching.

- *A very different balance must be achieved between the amount of pupils' learning done in classroom teaching groups and the amount done in other kinds of social groups and settings.* Individual work in resource centres, on work experience and other contexts has increased and should increase further, as should small-group work on joint projects and investigations in different contexts. Much of this work in contexts other than classrooms is likely to be related to diverse uses of computers and other modern technology. Teachers should spend much more of their time in planning and evaluating and in negotiating, with other teachers, with students and with others. However, they should continue to spend much of their time in face-to-face contact with students, individually and with groups of different sizes. Teaching – deliberately and directly facilitating learning – must continue to be their overriding responsibility.

The problem inevitably seems a good deal clearer than the solution. This essay has aspired only to offer a tentative formulation of the problem and some very preliminary ideas towards a solution. It seems likely that the changes needed will be of different kinds and different degrees in different contexts and for different groups of pupils, for example perhaps being much more fundamental at secondary school level than at primary. Much of the school-based research and development work of the next 20 years should be directed towards formulating and investigating possible solutions.

REFERENCES

Atkins, J. and Bastiani, J. (1988) *Listening to Parents: An Approach to the Improvement of Home–School Relations*. London: Croom Helm.

Bell, A. (1807) 'Extract of a sermon on the education of the poor under an appropriate system'. Preached at St Mary's, Lambeth, 28 June, 1807. London: Cadell & Davies.

Bennett, N., Desforges, C., Cockburn, A. and Wilkinson, B. (1984) *The Quality of Pupil Learning Experiences*. London: Lawrence Erlbaum Associates.

Berliner, D. C. (1987) 'Ways of thinking about students and classrooms by more and less experienced teachers'. In J. Calderhead (ed.), *Teachers' Thinking*. London: Cassell, 60–83.

Bernstein, B. (1970) 'Education cannot compensate for society'. In D. Rubinstein and C. Stoneman (eds), *Education for Democracy*. Harmondsworth: Penguin, 104–116.

Bernstein, B. (1975) *Class, Codes and Control, vol. 3*. London: Routledge & Kegan Paul.

Black, P. and Wiliam, D. (1998) 'Assessment and Classroom Learning', *Assessment in Education*, 5 (1).

Bloom, B. S. (1977) *Human Characteristics and Student Learning*. New York: McGraw-Hill.

Bourdieu, P. and Passeron, J. C. (1977) *Reproduction in Education, Society and Culture*. London-Beverly Hills: Sage.

Brown, S. and McIntyre, D. (1993) *Making Sense of Teaching*. Buckingham: Open University Press.

Brown, S., McIntyre, D., Drever, E. and Davies, J. K. (1976) *Innovations: Teachers' Views*. Stirling Educational Monographs, no. 2. Stirling: Department of Education, University of Stirling.

Clark, C. M. and Peterson, P. L. (1986) 'Teachers' thought processes'. In M. C. Wittrock (ed.) *Handbook of Research on Teaching, Third Edition*. New York: Macmillan, 255–296.

Cooper, P. and McIntyre, D. (1996) *Effective Teaching and Learning: Teachers' and Pupils' Perspectives*. Buckingham: Open University Press.

Davies, C. W. R. (1997) 'Problems about achievement of shared understandings about ITE between schools and university'. In D. McIntyre (ed.) *Teacher Education Research in a New Context*. New BERA Dialogues. London: Paul Chapman Publishing, 16–41.

Denton, C. and Postlethwaite, K. (1985) *Able Children*. Slough: NFER-Nelson.

Doyle, W. (1986) 'Classroom organisation and management'. In M. C. Wittrock (ed.) *Handbook of Research on Teaching, 3rd edn*. New York: Macmillan, 392–431.

Doyle, W. and Ponder, G. (1977) 'The practicality ethic in teacher decision-making'. *Interchange*, 8 (3), 1–12.

Dreyfus, H. L. and Dreyfus, S. E. (1986) *Mind over Machine: The Power of Human Intuition and Expertise in the Era of the Computer*. New York: Macmillan.

Gardner, H. (1993) *Frames of Mind: The Theory of Multiple Intelligences*. London: Fontana Press.

Hamilton, D. (1986) 'Adam Smith and the moral economy of the classroom system'. In P. H. Taylor (ed.) *Recent Developments in Curriculum Studies*. Windsor: NFER-Nelson, 84–111.

Hargreaves, D. H. (1972) *Interpersonal Relations and Education*. London: Routledge & Kegan Paul.

Hargreaves, D. H. (1999) 'The knowledge-creating school', *British Journal of Educational Studies*, 47 (2), 122–144.

Hargreaves, D. H., Hester, S. K. and Mellor, F. J. (1975) *Deviance in Classrooms*. London: Routledge & Kegan Paul.

Hart, S. (ed.) (1996) *Differentiation and the Secondary Curriculum: Debates and Dilemmas*. London: Routledge.

Hart, S. (1998) 'A sorry tail: ability, pedagogy and educational reform'. In *British Journal of Educational Studies*, 46 (2), 153–168.

Hartley, D. (1997) *Re-schooling Society*. London: Falmer Press.

Hillage, J., Pearson, R., Anderson, A. and Tamkin, P. (1998) *Excellence in Research on Schools*. Research Report RR74. London: Department for Education and Employment.

HMI (Her Majesty's Inspectorate) (1978) *Mixed Ability Work in Comprehensive Schools*. London: HMSO.

Holt, J. (1969) *How Children Fail*. Harmondsworth: Penguin.

Holt, J. (1971) *The Underachieving School*. Harmondsworth: Penguin.

Illich, I. (1976) *Deschooling Society*. Harmondsworth: Penguin.

Jackson, P. W. (1968) *Life in Classrooms*. New York: Holt, Rinehart & Winston.

James, M. (1998) *Using Assessment for School Improvement*. Oxford: Heinemann.

Keddie, N. (1971) 'Classroom knowledge'. In M. F. D. Young (ed.), *Knowledge and Control*. London: Collier-Macmillan, 133–160.

Lortie, D. C. (1975) *Schoolteacher*. Chicago: University of Chicago Press.

McIntyre, D. (1970) 'Assessment for teaching'. In D. Rubinstein and C. Stoneman (eds), *Education for Democracy*. Harmondsworth: Penguin, 164–171.

McIntyre, D. and Brown, S. (1978) 'The conceptualisation of attainment'. *British Educational Research Journal*, 4 (2). 41–50.

McIntyre, D., Morrison, A. and Sutherland. J. (1966) 'Social and educational variables relating to teachers' assessments of primary school pupils', *British Journal of Educational Psychology*, 36, 272–279.

Plowden Report (1967) *Children and Their Primary Schools*. London: HMSO.

Randell, S. (1998) 'Parents, teachers, pupils: Different contributions to understanding pupils' needs?' unpublished D. Phil diss., University of Oxford.

Reimer, E. (1971) *School Is Dead*. Harmondsworth: Penguin.

Richards, M. (1996) 'Lay and professional knowledge of genetics and inheritance', *Public Understanding of Science*, 5, 217–230.

Rudduck, J., Chaplain, R. and Wallace, G. (eds) 1996. *School Improvement: What Can Pupils Tell Us?* London: David Fulton.

Schon, D. A. (1983) *The Reflective Practitioner*. London: Temple Smith.

Scriven, M. (1967) *The Methodology of Evaluation*. American Educational Research Association.

Silberman, M. L. (1971) 'Discussion' in M. L. Silberman, *The Experience of Schooling*. New York: Holt, Rinehart & Winston.

Simpson, M. (1989) *A Study of Differentiation and Learning in Schools*. Aberdeen: Northern College.

Stevens, F. (1960) *The Living Tradition*. London: n. p.

Teacher Training Agency (1996) *Teaching as a Research-based Profession*. London: Teacher Training Agency.

Tett, L. and Crowther, J. (1998) 'Families at a disadvantage: Class, culture and literacies', *British Educational Research Journal*, 24 (4), 449–460.

Tizard, B. and Hughes, M. (1984) *Young Children Learning: Talking and Thinking at Home and at School*. London: Fontana.

Torrance, H. and Pryor, J. (1998) *Investigating Formative Assessment*. Buckingham: Open University Press.

7

HOW IS LANGUAGE USED AS A MEDIUM FOR CLASSROOM EDUCATION?

Neil Mercer

INTRODUCTION

This chapter is about language as a medium for education in school. Most of its content is about spoken language, with a discussion of some aspects of written language in the later part.

Classrooms generate some typical structures of language use, patterns that reflect the nature of teaching and learning as a social, communicative process which takes place in the distinctive institutional settings of school. Some features of classroom language, described below, have been found in classrooms across the world; and to some extent at least this reflects the fact that language has a similar function in schools the world over. There are also some local, regional and national characteristics in the ways that language is used in the classroom, and different expectations are made of students in different cultures and even by different teachers within one country's education system which may also be reflected in language. Moreover, according to their out-of-school experience, students may find the language of classroom life more or less intelligible or compatible with their out-of-school life. On entering school, every student will have to engage some learning about how to use the language of the classroom. Even for students who have the classroom language as their native or first language, this will involve grasping the conventions of how spoken and written language is normally used in school, taking up the specialised vocabularies of curriculum subjects and becoming able to present ideas within the constraints of the accepted genres or discourses of spoken and written language.

Teachers have responsibility for guiding students' use of language as a social mode of thinking, and to express their understanding in the appropriate language genres or discourses. Where teachers and students are using a second or other language as the medium of classroom education, distinctive patterns of language use in the classroom are also apparent. Teachers and students may 'code-switch' between languages in class, and the content of the talk may reveal teachers' concern with the learning of a second language as well as the learning of the curriculum subject, or a teacher's concern with the enforcement of the norms of the standard, official variety of language used in school.

FUNCTION

Schools are special kinds of places, social institutions with particular purposes, conventions and traditions. There are some interesting differences in how teachers' and learners' interests interact in classrooms in different countries. But schools the world over also have much in common in how they function, and this functional similarity is reflected in the ways language is used in their classrooms.

The patterns of language use established by teachers have important consequences for how their students use language. One of the most obvious functions of spoken language in a classroom is for teachers to tell students what they are to do, how they are to do it, when to start and when to stop. Unless they resort to corporal punishment, language is the main tool of teachers' control of events in the classroom. They also assess students' learning through talk, in the familiar question-and-answer sequences of classroom life. Talk also is the means by which teachers can provide children with information, much of which it would be very hard to communicate in any other way. They tell students stories, read texts to them and describe objects, events and processes (sometimes introducing new descriptive vocabulary as they do so).

An essential element of formal education is dialogue between a teacher and a learner, an exchange of ideas which enables the learner to gain knowledge and understanding and the teacher to provide relevant guidance and evaluation. It is because we can use language to share and create knowledge and understanding that we have been able to transform the world and organise our lives in ways that are so qualitatively different from those of any other species. The prime justification for setting up education systems is to enable the process of *the guided construction of knowledge* (Mercer, 1995) to be carried out effectively.

Guiding students' construction of knowledge depends on the creation of shared experience and joint understanding. Day by day, in various activities and interactions, teachers and their classes generate shared experience which they use as the basis for further activity. They can talk about what they have done, what they are doing and what they will do next, so that experiences shared over long periods of time can become woven together. Each day's talk in a classroom forms part of what Janet Maybin (1994) has called the 'long conversation' between teachers and learners, a series of related dialogues that constitute the time that teachers and students spend together in school.

Throughout the process of classroom education, wherever in the world it is carried out, teachers have a special, professional responsibility for helping students achieve an understanding of a specific body of knowledge represented by 'the curriculum'. They are expected to help students understand a specific body of knowledge, and to help them acquire 'educated' ways of analysing and solving problems. They also need to help students learn to talk and write about their knowledge in appropriate varieties of language. Life in classrooms generates and sustains some distinctive ways of using language (discussed in more detail below), though this is often not well recognised by teachers because they are immersed in it, and because they take these features for granted. Even children whose mother tongue is the language used in the classroom have much to learn about how that language is used as an educational medium.

STRUCTURE

Much of the classroom talk between teachers and students is usually recognisably 'educational' in its form and content. This can be illustrated through the consideration of a particular transcribed sequence of classroom talk. Sequence 1 (below) was recorded in a secondary school in England. As part of their English curriculum, a class of 14 year olds had taken part in an extended computer-based communication with children in a nearby primary school. Working in groups of three, the secondary students acted out the role of characters stranded in time and space. By e-mail, they explained their predicament to the primary school children, who responded with suggestions about what to do; and so the dialogue continued. In Sequence 1, the teacher is questioning one group of girls (with the whole class present) about their most recent e-mail interactions and their future plans.

Sequence 1

Teacher: What about the word 'dimension', because you were going to include that in your message, weren't you?

Anne: Yeh. And there's going to be – if they go in the right room, then they'll find a letter in the floor and that'll spell 'dimension'.

Teacher: What happens if they do go in the wrong room?

Emma: Well, there's no letter in the bottom, in the floor.

Teacher: Oh God! So they've got to get it right, or that's it! [*everyone laughs*] The adventurers are stuck there for ever. And Cath can't get back to her own time. What do you mean the letters are in the room, I don't quite follow that?

Emma: On the floor, like a tile or something.

Teacher: Oh I see. Why did you choose the word 'dimension'?

Anne: Don't know. [*the three students speak together, looking to each other, seeming uncertain*]

Emma: It just came up. Just said, you know, 'dimension' and everyone agreed.

Sharon: Don't know.

Teacher: Right, because it seemed to fit in with, what, the fantasy flow, flavour?

Sharon: Yeh.

Teacher: OK. Why do they go through the maze rather than go back? I mean what motivation do they have for going through it in the first place?

Sharon: Um, I think that it was the king told them that Joe would be in the maze or at the end of the maze, and they didn't go back because of Joe, think it was. I'm not sure about that.

Teacher: You've really got to sort that out. It's got to be very, very clear.

(Mercer, 1995, pp. 30–31)

One noticeable feature of Sequence 1 is that all the questions were asked by the teacher. This is a common, almost universal feature of classroom talk. Teachers have good reasons for asking so many questions: they have to learn what the students have been doing, so that they can evaluate activity and provide further guidance. The questions and answers are also typical in their structural pattern. Repeatedly, the teacher elicits information from one or more students and then comments on the pupil's response. So a teacher's question is followed by a student's response, followed in turn by some feedback or evaluation from the teacher. This pattern of classroom talk was first described by the British linguists Sinclair and Coulthard (1975) and is usually known as an Initiation–Response–Feedback (IRF) exchange. IRF exchanges are sometimes also called IRE sequences, where the 'E' stands for 'Evaluation'. We can separate the parts of each exchange, technically known as 'moves', as follows:

	Move
Teacher: Why do they go through the maze rather than go back? I mean what motivation do they have for going through it in the first place?	Initiation
Sharon: Um, I think that it was the king told them that Joe would be in the maze or at the end of the maze, and they didn't go back because of Joe, think it was. I'm not sure about that.	Response
Teacher: You've really go to sort that out. It's got to be very, very clear.	Feedback or evaluation

Of course, other patterns of exchanges (e.g. in which students ask questions) also happen in classrooms. But although they were originally identified in the talk of rather formal British secondary classrooms, IRF exchanges are elements of the structure of classroom talk which have since been found occurring frequently in classrooms all over the world. They can be thought of as the archetypal form of interaction between a teacher and a pupil. Thus Ian Malcolm (an Australian researcher who has studied language use in Aboriginal schools) has claimed: 'This [IRF] pattern is near-universal (at least in the Western world) where teachers are interacting with a class of children as a whole. It is a discourse pattern which is entailed in the social situation' (Malcolm, 1982, p. 121).

In Sequence 1 we can also see IRF exchanges occurring as slightly more complex, linked structures. So in the following example, the teacher obtains three 'responses' to her 'initiation', and her second 'feedback' comment also functions as a further 'initiation':

	Move
Teacher: Why did you choose the word 'dimension'?	I
Anne: Don't know.	R
Emma: It just came up. Just said, you know, 'dimension' and everyone agreed.	R
Sharon: Don't know.	R
Teacher: Right, because it seemed to fit in with, what, the fantasy flow, flavour?	F/I
Sharon: Yeh.	R
Teacher: OK.	F

QUESTIONS

Teachers' heavy reliance on questions has been criticised by educational researchers. For example, Dillon (1988) and Wood (1992) claim that because most teachers' questions are designed to elicit just one brief 'right answer' (which often amounts to a reiteration of information provided earlier by the teacher) this unduly limits and suppresses students' contributions to the dialogic process of teaching-and-learning. When a pupil fails to provide the only possible right answer, a teacher ignores the wrong answer which has been offered and goes on to accept a second 'bid' for an answer from a second pupil. This particular kind of use of question-and-answer by a teacher – asking 'closed' questions to which the teacher knows the answer – is the most common function of IRF exchanges in classrooms. Sequence 2 below illustrates very well how this does indeed narrowly constrain the scope that students have for making an active contribution to talk in the classroom.

Sequence 2

Teacher: Argentina, what is the capital of Argentina?
Pupil 1: Argentina city. [*some students laugh, others say 'Sir, sir' and raise their hands*]
Teacher: [*to a pupil who has hand raised*] Brian?
Pupil 2: Buenos Aires.
Teacher: Yes, good Buenos [*writing on board*] Aires.

Wood comments:

> If the aim of a lesson or teacher–pupil interaction is simply to establish whether or not facts have been learned and committed to memory, then talk which is rich in teacher questions and high in control will probably achieve the result intended. If, however, the aim is to discover what students think, what they want to know, or what they are prepared to share with their peers, then such lessons will prove self-defeating. If you wish to know 'where the learner is at' or where they would like to go next, then avoid frequent questions.
>
> (Wood, 1992, p. 209)

Wood goes on to suggest that, constrained in this way, students get little opportunity to formulate knowledge and make coherent sense of what they are being taught, or to practise their own ways of using language to reason, argue and explain. There are therefore some good reasons for agreeing with such criticisms of teachers' heavy dependence on the use of IRF exchanges in which the 'I' components consist of closed questions.

However, if we look back to Sequence 1, we can see that the teacher there is not using IRFs in this way. Rather, she is asking questions to find out what the students have done and why they have done it – things that she does not know. Her questions are 'open' in that only the students know the answers. The teacher is asking students clearly to describe what they have done and to account for it, encouraging them to review their actions and plan future activities accordingly. She is using her enquiries not only to assess her students' learning, but also to guide it. Through questions like 'Why did you choose the word "dimension"?' and 'Why do they go through the maze rather than go back?' she directs their attention to matters requiring more thought and clarification when they return to their work. In this way, she is not only focusing their attention on how best to communicate by e-mail with the primary school children, but also shaping their own awareness and understanding of what they are doing.

The educational content and function of the teacher's questions and students' responses in Sequence 1 are therefore very different to those in Sequence 2. So while Dillon's and Wood's critical analysis of how teachers use questions has some force, we must beware of equating language structures with language functions. An accepted principle of discourse analysis is that particular language structures – in this case IRF exchanges – can be used for more than one purpose and function. From an educational perspective, this means that we can only understand, and evaluate, the ways in which language is used in classrooms by taking account of the *content* and *context* of any particular interaction.

We should also note that the use of IRF exchanges in classrooms depends on all the participants being familiar with the conventions of this kind of question-and-answer routine, and being willing to abide by those conventions. Research in classrooms in Britain and the USA encourages the belief that most children in those countries rapidly become familiar with the IRF structure of classroom talk, and so are able and willing to participate in it fairly readily. However, now consider Sequence 3 (below) which was recorded in an infant classroom in Western Australia. The children (aged 5–6) were all Aboriginal Australians, and at the point the sequence begins, the teacher had read them a story in which a child finds a kitten.

Sequence 3

Teacher: How do we know she liked the kitten? How do we know she liked the kitten? [*no responses from children*] No, you think about it, now. She got the kitten, I mean she found the kitten . . . an' then she said to Mum and Dad she wanted to?

Child 1: Keep it.

Child 2: Keep it.

Teacher: Keep it. So if she didn't want the kitten she wouldn't have kept it, would she? What do you think, Brenda?

Brenda: [*silence*]

Teacher: Well, you listen carefully.

(Adapted from Malcolm, 1982, p. 129)

The researcher who recorded this sequence (Ian Malcolm) describes it as typical of interactions in Aboriginal classrooms. It appears that Aboriginal children are extremely reluctant to engage in IRF exchanges, not because of any lack of fluency in English but rather because such interactions are at odds with the conversational practices of their home culture. That is, in Aboriginal society overt interrogations and demonstrations of understanding are not considered polite.

Classroom researchers elsewhere – for example in Hawaii, and amongst Native Americans in the USA and Mexico – also have reported that children from some cultural backgrounds find IRF patterns of question-and-answer alien and discomforting. But that research also shows that teachers usually persist in their normal practice despite such reluctance or incomprehension. It is also reported that schools rarely make efforts to admit or incorporate the language practices which children experience in home communities if these are not part of the 'mainstream', middle class of their societies, whether they be the story-telling of Irish travellers in Britain, the 'rapping' of Afro-Caribbean teenagers, or the imaginative story-poems heard amongst young children in working-class black American communities. This problem is well elaborated by Stephen Boggs (1985), who spent more than ten years observing language use in Hawaiian communities and classrooms. He describes some of the 'oral arts' which were an important part of Hawaiian children's informal social lives and yet were completely ignored by their schools:

> The children showed very close attention to the exact pronunciation of lyrics and rhythm when learning new songs . . . I observed children in the third and fourth grades pronounce the lyrics of songs in Tahitian, Samoan, Maori – and even Standard English! Particular Standard English phonemes not pronounced in everyday speech would be pronounced in songs, as in names. . . . This . . . shows the close relationship between verbal learning and socially valued communication. Singing is a highly valued social activity.
>
> (Boggs, 1985, p. 125)

Other researchers have described such divergences between the language practices children encounter in and out of school, in many parts of the English-speaking world (e.g. Heath, 1983; Wells, 1986), and often suggest that this is a source of educational problems. But one should perhaps be cautious in drawing the obvious conclusion that if teachers made great efforts to incorporate children's out-of-school informal language practices into the life of the classroom, this would necessarily either be welcomed by the children or be successful as a strategy for promoting educational success. One of the vital and attractive qualities of informal language practices, from a child's perspective, is that they are an integral part of life outside the classroom and are not harnessed pragmatically to the institutional purposes of school.

CUES

If a teacher asks a question and a student is unable to provide the required answer, the teacher will typically ask another student in the class, and perhaps then another, until a 'right' answer is found. If no such answer emerges, one might expect teachers simply to provide the required information. But providing answers to their own questions is one thing that teachers seem at great pains to avoid. Instead, they commonly resort to what Edwards and Mercer (1987) call *cued elicitation*. This is a way of drawing out from learners the information a teacher is seeking – the 'right' answers to their questions – by providing strong visual clues and verbal hints as to what answer is required. An example is provided by Sequence 4 below, recorded in a British primary school on an occasion when children were being taught about the science topic of 'pendulums'. The teacher introduced the topic to the children by describing Galileo sitting in church, 'very bored', when his attention was taken by a swinging incense burner:

115

Sequence 4

Teacher: . . . and he wanted to time it, just for inter-   *Teacher begins to swing her hand*
est's sake, just to see how long it took to make a   *back and forward in rhythm, as*
complete swing. Now he didn't have a watch, but   *she talks.*
he had on him something that was a very good
timekeeper that he could use to hand straight away.

  Teacher snaps her fingers on
  'straight away' and looks invit-
  ingly at students as if posing a
  question or inviting a response.

Teacher: You've got it. I've got it. What is it? What   *Teacher points on 'You've' and*
could we use to count beats?   *'I've'. She beats her hand on the*
  table slowly, looking around the
What have you got? You've got it. I've got it.   *group of students who smile and*
What is it? What could we use to count beats?   *shrug.*
What have you got?
Teacher: You can feel it here.   *Teacher puts her fingers on her*
  wrist.

Students: Pulse   *Speaking in near unison.*
Teacher: A pulse. Everybody see if you can find it.   *All copy her, feeling their wrists.*
  (Mercer, 1995, pp. 26–27)

The use of cues as a teaching technique can be traced back to the Socratic dialogues constructed by the Ancient Greek philosopher Plato. Why do teachers use cues so much? One
likely reason is because they want learners to take an active part, however small, in the dialogue.

Sequence 4 also illustrates how the use of cues, gestures and other signs can be an
important component of classroom teaching. However, the non-verbal signs used by
teachers vary, sometimes considerably, between cultures. So Zukow-Goldring *et al.* (1994)
observed that teachers in south California who were native Spanish speakers tended to use
more gestures and physical demonstrations in their interactions with students than their
Anglo (native English-speaking) colleagues, regardless of whether English or Spanish was
being used at the time.

VOCABULARY

As students progress through their years of schooling, they encounter an increasing number
of specialised technical terms. Used effectively, the technical vocabularies of science, mathematics, art or any other subject provide clear and economical ways of describing and discussing complex and abstract issues. A shared understanding of musical vocabulary, for instance
– 'octave', 'bar', 'key' and so on – makes it possible for two people to discuss, in the abstract,
phenomena that otherwise would have to be concretely demonstrated. However, the discourse of educated people talking about their specialism is clear only to the initiated.

Becoming familiar with the language of a subject is therefore both an important require-ment for educational success, and also an important goal if students wish to enter an intellectual community of scientists, mathematicians, artists or whatever.

An important part of a teacher's job is to help students learn and understand the special-ised vocabulary of curriculum subjects. Research has shown that technical language is a common source of confusion and misunderstanding amongst students. However, teachers seem often to assume that the meaning of a word will become obvious as students hear or read it repeatedly, while students are usually reluctant to reveal their ignorance by asking questions. Some technical words may be used only rarely in the wider world, but they may represent ideas that are not difficult for students to grasp, because they can easily be explained or exemplified. (A good example is 'alliteration'.) Others may be impossible to explain through a concrete set of instances. This applies to many scientific concepts describ-ing properties of matter (like 'density') and processes (like 'evolution' and 'photosynthesis'). A consequence may be that many technical words remain for students mere jargon, and as such represent an obstacle to their developing understanding.

Many teachers and educational researchers can recount bizarre and salutary examples of how technical vocabulary has been misunderstood by students. Two such examples are of a 12 year old who thought that 'quandary' meant a four-sided figure, and a 16 year old who, after saying that he had never understood 'subtractions', later commented that he could do 'take-aways'. Robert Hull (1985) a British secondary teacher and researcher, discovered that some of his 14 year old students believed that 'Animals harbour insects' meant that they ate them; and that 'The lowest bridge-town' was a 'slum on a bridge'. He concluded that even terms like 'molten iron', 'physical feature', 'factor' and 'western leader' were often insuperable obstacles to students' comprehension.

For children who are learning English as a second or other language, the vocabulary and style of technical English may pose even greater problems. And if teachers themselves are not confident users of technical English, good explanations may not be available. For example, Cleghorn *et al.* (1989) found that Kenyan teachers who were teaching science through the medium of English were often unable to explain in English the meanings of terms they were using (such as 'parasite'). They comment: 'When teachers have to search for English equiva-lents of what is familiar but often not conceptually the same in the local language, the actual meaning of what is being taught can be altered' (Cleghorn *et al.*, 1989, p. 21).

ORACY

As mentioned above (see section on 'Questions') some educational researchers have argued that too much 'instructional' teacher talk in class will not achieve the important goal of encouraging students to become educated users of language. Instead it is suggested that children must have opportunities to develop and practise using language in situations that are not continuously dominated by the presence of the teacher. One outcome of such arguments was the emergence of what is sometimes called the 'oracy movement', referring to an explicit concern amongst educationalists in the UK, Australia and some other coun-tries, with the development of children's skills in oral language use. (The term 'oracy' was coined by the British educational researcher Andrew Wilkinson in the 1960s.) In countries where such ideas have been given some support, it has become increasingly common to set up activities in which students work and talk together without the continual presence of a teacher. There is no doubt that organising students to work on their own in groups or pairs generates quite different patterns of talk from those that typify teacher–pupil interactions (Barnes and Todd, 1995; Mercer, 1995; Norman, 1992).

Sequence 5 (below) is taken from a discussion between a group of 13 year olds in a classroom in a secondary school on the edge of a large city in northern England. Their teacher had divided the class into groups of four students. Each group had some information about the setting up of the Lake District National Park in the UK and were asked to address together a set of questions about how the conservation of an area of natural beauty might be reconciled with the needs of different users of the park, such as farmers, ramblers and tourists. The sequence is the first minute or so of the discussion of one group (two girls and two boys). In the right-hand column are analytic comments about the function of the talk provided by the researchers (Barnes and Todd) who recorded the talk.

Sequence 5

Alan: Do you think that this is a good idea for big National Parks?

Initiates discussion of the usefulness of National Parks, an issue not set on the task card.

I think it is an excellent idea because, erm, people like us have the erm countryside around us, but other people in the, erm, centre of Leeds are less fortunate, and do not have, erm, centre – countryside that they can go out to within easy reach.

Bill: Yes.

Provides encouragement.

Alan: Without being polluted and, erm, chimney stacks all over the place.

Makes the antithesis more explicit.

Pauline: This is all right as long as there aren't going to be too many buildings around the place, because it's going to spoil it completely I think. It's all right for a few like cafes or, er, camping sites, a few camping sites. That's all right, but nothing else.

Qualifies Alan's contributions, thus turning the discussion towards the set questions. She reinforces part of what Alan said, but suggests that limits need to be drawn.

Alan: I think this is one of the best ideas of the, erm, National Parks because they, erm, do not, don't allow buildings to be built without permissions and planning special, you know, so it blends with the countryside and not stuck out like a sore thumb.

Accepts the qualification which leads to his extending the concept of National Parks to include the regulation of building.

Jeannette: Yes, but it just depends on what the ground's like, doesn't it?

Qualifies that part of Alan's statement that refers to blending with the countryside.

(Barnes and Todd, 1995, pp. 24–25)

118

Even though the students in Sequence 5 are responding to a question set by their teacher, it is apparent that the quality of their talk is quite different from that of class discussions led by a teacher. Many of the participants make quite extended contributions. They expand on each other's comments. They are willing to express uncertainty to each other, and to offer each other explanations. Talk is being used to share knowledge and construct joint understandings in ways that reflect the fact that they all have similar status in the discussion, as learners who can contribute to the discussion from the wealth of their individual experiences.

Discussion activities of this kind are only educationally valuable if they encourage students to use language as a way of thinking rationally together. The thinking and the talking in these circumstances must become inseparable, so that language is used as a *social mode of thinking* (Mercer, 1995). The organisation and requirements of the task should be such that students have to talk about what they are doing to collaborate successfully. The quality of students' talk is an important educational issue. Even when talking and working without a teacher, students are expected to use language in ways that are educationally appropriate. That is, when a teacher asks students to 'discuss' a topic, the teacher is usually expecting something quite specific of them – to make explicit descriptions, formulate reasons and explanations, and to agree on possible solutions to problems. One important part of becoming educated is learning how to use such 'educated' styles of language, the kinds of discursive practices which are used in cultural activities like science, law, politics and business negotiation. Research suggests that students' engagement with language-based activities can be motivated and improved by making such aims and expectations clear. But one other clear finding of classroom research is that teachers rarely do so. Similar issues arise in relation to the use of written language in school (see 'Genre' below).

LEARNING

Earlier parts of this chapter (see 'Structure' and 'Questions') described ways in which teachers use language to try to direct and constrain the contributions that students make to the process of teaching and learning. The broader demands that participation in the 'official' talk of the classroom makes on students are worth careful consideration. Imagine a child, any child, starting the first day at a school. There are three kinds of learning task which that child can face, and which are crucial to their educational progress:

1 Students have to learn the special ways of using their native language that apply in school, because they are unfamiliar with educational conventions and the technical language of curriculum subjects.
2 Students have to learn to speak and write in a language that is different from the language of their home environment.
3 Students have to learn to use the standard form of their native language, because they have grown up speaking a 'non-standard' variety outside school.

In reality, the task facing any particular pupil may not neatly fit any of these three descriptions (e.g. they may be fluent speakers of a language, but not be literate in it); but this three-part distinction can nevertheless be helpful for making sense of reality in all its complexity. (See also 'Code-switching' and 'Standard' below.)

A useful and commonly encountered case for consideration is of classrooms where English is the official language of teaching-and-learning but not the native or first language of the students. This situation arises in two main forms. The first occurs in countries where English-medium education goes on, even though the mother tongue of most of the children is not English. The second is where students whose mother tongue is not English enter schools in a predominantly English-speaking country.

In any situation where English is used as a classroom language but is not the main language of children's home or community, teachers may have the multiple task of teaching (a) the English language, (b) the educational ground rules for using it in the classroom, and (c) any specific subject content. An illustration is provided by research carried out by Arthur (1992) in primary school classrooms in Botswana. English was used as the medium of education, but it was not the main language of the students' local community. Arthur observed that when teachers were teaching mathematics, they commonly used question-and-answer sessions as opportunities for schooling children in the use of appropriate 'classroom English' as well as maths. For example, one primary teacher commonly insisted that students reply to questions 'in full sentences', as shown below:

Sequence 6

Teacher: How many parts are left here [*first pupil's name*]?
First pupil: Seven parts.
Teacher: Answer fully. How many parts are there?
Pupil: There are . . . there are seven parts.
Teacher: How many parts are left? Sit down my boy. You have tried. Yes [*second pupil's name*]?
Second pupil: We are left with seven parts.
Teacher: We are left with seven parts. Say that [*second pupil's name*].
Second pupil: We are left with seven parts.
Teacher: Good boy. We are left with seven parts.

(Arthur, 1992, p. 7)

To make proper sense of the demands of the task they face, the Botswanan students needed to understand that their teacher was using these exchanges not only to evaluate their mathematical understanding, but also to test their fluency in spoken English and their ability to conform to a 'ground rule' that she enforced in her classroom, viz. to 'answer in full sentences'. For students in this kind of bilingual situation, the demands of classroom communication are complicated because their teacher is attempting to get them to focus on both the medium (in this case English) and the message (mathematics).

CODE-SWITCHING

In circumstances where the classroom language is not the students' first language, a teacher who is bilingual may 'code-switch' to the first language if problems of comprehension arise. Sometimes the first language may be used only for asides, for control purposes or to make personal comments. However, when code-switching amounts to translation by the teacher of the curriculum content being taught, its use as an explanatory teaching strategy is somewhat controversial. On the one hand, there are those who argue that it is a sensible, common-sense response by a teacher to the specific kind of teaching and learning situation. Thus in studying its use in English-medium classrooms in China, Lin explains a teacher's use of translation as follows: 'The teacher was anxious that her students might not understand the point clearly; she therefore sought to ensure thorough comprehension through presenting the message again in Cantonese which is the students' dominant language' (Lin, 1988, p. 78).

Researchers of bilingual code-switching have often concluded that it is of dubious value as a teaching strategy, if one of the aims of the teaching is to improve students' competence in English. Thus Jacobson comments: '[T]he translation into the child's vernacular of everything that is being taught may prevent him/her from ever developing the kind of English language proficiency that must be one of the objectives of a sound bilingual programme' (Jacobson, 1990, p. 6).

It seems, however, that teachers often use code-switching in more complex ways than simply translating content directly into another language. On observing classrooms in Hong Kong, Johnson and Lee (1987) observed that the switching strategy most commonly employed by teachers had a three-part structure as follows:

1 'key statement' of topic in English;
2 expansion, clarification or explanation in Cantonese;
3 restatement in English.

They comment that 'direct translation was comparatively rare; the general effect was of a spiralling and apparently haphazard recycling of content, which on closer examination proved to be more organised than it appeared' (ibid., p. 106). The implication is that teachers in those bilingual settings were pursuing the familiar task of guiding children's understanding of curriculum content through language, but using special bilingual techniques to do so. Observing teachers in Malta, Antoinette Camilleri (1994) found that code-switching was used as a teaching technique by teachers in a variety of ways. Below are two short sequences of talk of a teacher in a Maltese secondary school, during a lesson about the production and use of wool which was based on a textbook written in English. The teacher begins by reading part of the text. (Talk in Maltese is italicised and the English translation is given in the right-hand column.)

Camilleri notes that the first speech passage in Sequence 7 shows the teacher using the switch from English to Maltese to amplify the point being made, rather than simply repeating it in translation. In the second extract the teacher explains the English statement in Maltese, again avoiding direct translation. Camilleri comments that the lesson therefore is a particular kind of language event, in which there are 'two parallel discourses – the written one in English, the spoken one in Maltese' (ibid., p. 12).

121

Sequence 7

Teacher: England, Australia, New Zealand and Argentina are the best producers of wool. *Dawk l-aktar li għandom* farms *li jrabbu n-nagħag għassuf* . . .

They have the largest number of farms and the largest number of sheep for wool . . .

Teacher: Wool *issa* it does not crease but it has to be washed with care *issa din importanti ma għidtil komx illi jek ikolli nara xagħra jew sufa waħda* under the microscope *ghandha qisha ħafna* scales . . . *tal ħuta issa jek ma nahslux sewwa dawk l-i* scales *jitgħaqqdu* . . .

now this is important didn't I tell you that if I had to look at a single hair or fibre . . .

. . . it has many scales which if not washed properly get entangled . . .

(Adapted from Camilleri, 1994)

Studies of code-switching in classrooms have revealed a variety of patterns of bilingual use. For example, Zentella (1981) observed and recorded events in two bilingual classes in New York schools, one first-grade class (in which the children were about 6 years old) and the other a sixth grade (in which the average age would be about 12). The students and teachers were all native Spanish speakers, of Puerto Rican origin, but the official medium for classroom education was English. One of the focuses of her analysis of teacher–pupil interactions was IRF sequences. Both Spanish and English were actually used by teachers and students in the classes, and Zentella was able to show that there were three recurring patterns of language-switching in IRF sequences, which seemed to represent the use of certain 'ground rules' governing language choice. These are summarised below:

Table 7.1 Teachers' language choices in bilingual classrooms

Rules governing language choice	Teacher initiation	Student reply	Teacher feedback
1 Teacher and student: 'follow the leader'	English Spanish	English Spanish	English Spanish
2 Teacher: 'follow the child'	English Spanish	Spanish English	Spanish English
3 Teacher: 'include the child's choice and yours'	English Spanish	Spanish English	both languages both languages

Source: Adapted from Zentella, 1981

Distinctive patterns of language use emerge in bilingual classrooms, overlaying the familiar patterns of teacher-led IRF exchanges. The extent to which features such as 'code-switching' between English and other languages occur in any particular classroom will depend on a whole range of factors, including the degree of fluency in English that members of a particular class have achieved, the bilingual competence of teachers, the specific teaching goals of teachers, and the attitudes of both children and teachers to the other languages involved.

POLICY

The use of any particular language by teachers and students in a state school system is likely to reflect, though not necessarily conform to, official educational language policy of the relevant country or region. Policy and practice in schools is often influenced by political imperatives and allegiances, as well as ideas about the supposed cognitive and social effects on children of growing up bilingual. For example, the enforcement of a severe prohibition policy on the use of a mother tongue in school was well documented in nineteenth-century Wales, where any child heard speaking Welsh on the school premises was reprimanded and made to wear round their necks a rope called the 'Welsh knot' to show that they were in disgrace. By the late 1980s, however, both Welsh and English had become officially recognised as classroom languages in Wales.

Some countries, such as Canada and various states in India, have long-standing policies of recognising English alongside other community languages in schools. On the other hand, at the point of writing in the late 1990s, established policies of tolerance towards the use of Spanish and other languages in many state schools in the USA seem in danger of being overturned in response to a strong 'English first' campaign to establish English constitutionally as the only recognised language in schools, workplaces and public life. A specific and controversial language issue in educational policy in many parts of the world in the latter part of the twentieth century has been the choice between English (as a 'world language') and other local languages as a medium for education. English is only the obvious choice in situations where it is the only official language of a country or state and where it is spoken by the vast majority of people. Yet English has been chosen as the medium for classroom education in many countries where these conditions do not apply. Examples would be many states in India, where students receive their education in English although it is their second language. In officially bilingual countries like Canada, choices have to be made at the level of state and city about whether French or English should be used as the main language in class. In such countries, educational policy may be framed to allow parents some degree of choice of classroom language for their children. Thus in Wales, the balance of Welsh- and English-medium schools is officially monitored and is supposed to be adjusted to suit demand.

Sometimes it may seem that there is not really much choice about which language to use as a medium for education, because one language is already the dominant language in a community. However, economic and cultural factors may make such assumptions dangerous – as exemplified by the serious consideration given by the government of The Netherlands in the early 1990s to a proposal to conduct all Dutch higher education in English. If a policy choice has to be made about whether one or other language should be used as the classroom medium in a country's schools, the decision may be a matter of political controversy. As Mazrui and Mazrui (1992) put it, when discussing the use of English in African schools and other state institutions:

Africa . . . is a great battleground between Western languages and non-Western languages. English, French and Portuguese have had particularly wide-ranging influences. . . . Africa's ethnic heterogeneity finds its diverse differentiation in language. *Per capita* there is a wider range of languages in Africa than in any other region of the world. By a strange twist of destiny, there are also more French-speaking, English-speaking and Portuguese-speaking countries in Africa than anywhere else in the world.

(Mazrui and Mazrui, 1992, p. 84)

STANDARD FORMS

In most countries it is normally expected that in their written work students should conform to the requirements of the standard form or variety of the official language of that country. (Standard conventions applied in schools even for one language often vary between countries, so that the Standard Englishes of the UK, USA, India and Australia show some variation, as do the standard forms of Portuguese in Portugal and Brazil.) It is also a fairly common expectation that students should use standard vocabulary and grammar in their spoken language in the formal business of the classroom – that is, when replying to teachers' questions, or making oral reports or formal presentations to an audience. In public examinations, marks may be lost if students express themselves in regional non-standard varieties. So as mentioned above (see 'Learning' and 'Policy'), students may have to learn to use Standard English, because they have grown up speaking a regional or non-British variety of English. As even the great majority of native-speakers of English use regional varieties of English – which are by definition non-standard – in their out-of-school lives, this kind of learning is faced by the majority of such students entering English-medium classrooms.

An insistence on the use of, say, the official, standard variety of English in the schools of an English-speaking country may seem unsurprising, easy to justify and, at first consideration, uncontroversial. But this may become a heated and complex political issue, as has certainly been the case for many years in Britain. The more vociferous advocates of a policy which insists on the use of Standard English as a classroom language in Britain have sometimes argued that the issue is not simply one of a choice between which variety or dialect of English is most appropriate for use in the classroom, but one of maintaining standards of correctness which reflect established cultural values. Debate about these matters in the popular mass media is usually depressingly ill-informed. For example, in the British press the use by children of non-standard grammar in speech or a strong regional accent in school is often treated as part and parcel of a larger educational issue, in which perceived changes in standards of spelling, functional writing and oral communication skills amongst young people are taken to embody the moral and economic decline of society. People on both sides of this debate may take a variety of positions, but most opposition to populist enforcement of standards seems to stem from concern about the effects that any official denigration and devaluation of the local languages or non-standard varieties of communities may have on the self-esteem of students who are members of those communities.

As well as tackling the issue of the use of a standard form of a language or a particular language as a medium for classroom education, educational language policy commonly has also to deal with the issue of whether or not students should be expressly taught about other languages or varieties of a language as part of the school curriculum.

GENRE

Just as one of the tasks facing all students who are being educated in English is that of learning certain educational 'ground rules' or conventions for using spoken English in the classroom (see 'Learning' above), educational success also depends on students learning to use the conventions that are used by educated writers. However, research has shown that these 'ground rules' are rarely taught explicitly by teachers. Instead, as the research of Sheeran and Barnes (1991) has shown, students are expected to infer them from whatever instructions and feedback teachers provide on the students' work. This kind of realisation stimulated a group of Australian language researchers (Christie and Martin, 1997) to devise a new approach to the study and teaching of writing in the classroom, based on the work of the linguist Michael Halliday, and now generally known as the 'genre approach'. One of the aims of this approach has been to focus the attention of teachers and students on how written texts in English are expected to vary according to their nature and function. The task of writing a text in any particular genre – a business letter, a report of a scientific experiment, a poem, or a short story – can be analysed in terms of the conventional expectations in any society about what such a text should look like, and what assumptions an author can reasonably make about the knowledge a reader will bring to the text. Although the genre theorists have mainly concentrated on the learning of styles of writing, their approach is also applicable to the learning of spoken genres.

One strength of the genre approach is that it offers teachers and students an analysis of how English or any other language is used in specific social contexts, and attempts to make explicit the 'ground rules' for producing socially appropriate ways of writing. The essence of most criticisms of the genre approach are set out below:

- It tends to encourage the teaching of narrowly defined models for specific kinds of texts, when 'educated' writing involves the development of a much more flexible and creative ability;
- It tends to support an uncritical view of how established, powerful groups in a society use English (or any other language);
- Learning 'powerful' ways of using a language does not necessarily gain the user access to power.

Considering the use of language in education across countries and cultures, it is apparent that the genre requirements that students encounter may vary significantly. That is, the conventional expectations amongst teachers about what constitutes a good essay, story or scientific report may be different even in countries that share the same language as a medium of education (as, say, India, Australia, the USA and the UK). It was suggested above that when children enter an English-medium classroom (having grown up speaking another language and having been educated in a country with very different cultural tradi-tions) it may be difficult for both teachers and children to distinguish between the first two 'learning tasks' listed earlier – acquiring a basic fluency in English and learning the conven-tions of particular genres of English which are used in school. This variation can become a problem for students who move from one country to another. Moreover it can be difficult for a teacher to tell whether a new pupil (especially one who is not fluent in English) who appears to be having difficulties with the language demands of education, is struggling with general aspects of using English, or with the 'local' ground rules for using written or spoken language in the classroom.

REFERENCES

Arthur, J. (1992) 'Talking like teachers: teacher and pupil discourse in standard six Botswana class-rooms'. Working Paper no. 25, Centre for Language in Social Life, Lancaster University.

Barnes, D. and Todd, F. (1995) *Communication and Learning Revisited*, Portsmouth, NH: Heinemann.

Boggs, S. (1985) *Speaking, Relating and Learning: a Study of Hawaiian Children at Home and in School*, Norwood, NJ: Ablex Publishing.

Camilleri, A. (1994) 'Talking bilingually, writing monolingually'. Paper presented at the Sociolinguistics Symposium, Lancaster University, March 1994.

Christie, F. and Martin, J. (1997) *Genre and Institutions: Social Processes in the Workplace and School*, London: Cassell.

Cleghorn, A., Merritt, M. and Obagi, J. O. (1989) 'Language policy and science instruction in Kenyan primary schools'. *Comparative Education Review* 33 (1) 2–39.

Dillon, J. J. (1988) (ed.) *Questioning and Discussion: a Multidisciplinary Study*, London: Croom Helm.

Edwards, D. and Mercer, N. (1987) *Common Knowledge: the Development of Understanding in the Classroom*, London: Methuen/Routledge.

Heath, S. B. (1983) *Ways with Words: Language, Life and Work in Communities and Classrooms*, Cambridge: Cambridge University Press.

Hull, R. (1985) *The Language Gap*, London: Methuen.

Jacobson, R. (1990) 'Allocating two languages as a key feature of a bilingual methodology'. In R. Jacobson and C. Faltis (eds) *Language Distribution Issues in Bilingual Schooling*, Clevedon: Multilingual Matters.

Johnson, R. K. and Lee, P. L. M. (1987) 'Modes of instruction: Teaching strategies and students responses'. In R. Lord and H. Cheng (eds) *Language Education in Hong Kong*, Hong Kong: The Chinese University Press.

Lin, A. (1988) 'Pedagogical and para-pedagogical levels of interaction in the classroom: a social interactional approach to the analysis of the code-switching behaviour of a bilingual teacher in an English language lesson'. *Working Papers in Linguistics and Language Teaching No.11*. University of Hong Kong Language Centre.

Malcolm, I. (1982) 'Speech events of the Aboriginal classroom'. *International Journal of the Sociology of Language* 36, 115–134.

Maybin, J. (1994) 'Children's voices: talk, knowledge and identity'. In D. Graddol, J. Maybin, and B. Stierer (eds) *Researching Language and Literacy in Social Context*, Clevedon: Multilingual Matters.

Mazrui, A. M. and Mazrui, A. A. (1992) 'Language in a multicultural context: the African Experi-ence', *Language and Education*, 6 (2, 3 & 4), 83–98.

Mercer, N. (1995) *The Guided Construction of Knowledge: Talk amongst Teachers and Learners*, Clevedon: Multilingual Matters.

Norman, K. (ed.) (1992) *Thinking Voices: the Work of the National Oracy Project*, London: Hodder & Stoughton.

Sheeran, Y. and Barnes, D. (1991) *School Writing: Discovering the Ground Rules*, Milton Keynes: Open University Press.

Sinclair, J. and Coulthard, M. (1975) *Towards an Analysis of Discourse: the English Used by Teachers and Students*, London: Oxford University Press.

Wells, G. (1986) *The Meaning Makers*, London: Hodder & Stoughton.

Wood, D. (1992) 'Teaching talk'. In K. Norman, (ed.) *Thinking Voices: the Work of the National Oracy Project*, London: Hodder & Stoughton.

Zentella, A. C. (1981) '*Ta bien*, you could answer me in *cualquier idioma*: Puerto Rican code-switching in bilingual classrooms'. In R. Duran (ed.) *Latino Language and Communicative Behavior*, Norwood, NJ: Ablex Publishing Corporation.

Zukow-Goldring, P., Romo, L. and Duncan, K. R. (1994) 'Gestures speak louder than words: achieving consensus in latino classrooms'. In A. Alvarez and P. del Rio (eds) *Education as Cultural Construction* (Explorations in Socio-Cultural Studies, vol. 4.), Madrid: Infancia y Aprendizaje.

8

THE ECONOMICS AND RESOURCING OF EDUCATION

Mun C. Tsang

SCOPE OF THE FIELD

The economics of education is dedicated to seeking the most efficient use of scarce resources by studying the consequences of their mobilisation, allocation, and utilisation in the production of education. One convenient way to understand the scope of this field is to see the production of education as a process consisting of input, process, output and outcome components. In this conceptualisation, scarce inputs (such as teachers' and students' time, school facilities and instructional materials) are mobilised, allocated and transformed through a process (encompassing organisation, evaluation, instructional technology, etc.) to yield output (such as student learning) which is subsequently utilised to generate desired outcome (economic outcome such as higher earnings and more employment opportunities).

In this chapter, the survey of the literature on the economics of education is organised according to a number of themes. Themes on education-outcome are focused on the economic outcomes of education; they include the economic effects of education and the impact of education on the labour market and the world economy. Themes concerned with the economic analysis of educational process and educational output include educational production and the economics of educational technology. Economic analysis of educational inputs is covered by themes on the costs and economic evalution of education, and educational financing. While most of the analyses on the economics of education fall neatly into one of the components of the educational process, some analyses pertain to one or more of the components. In this survey, these latter analyses are first discussed under a theme for one component but their relationship to other education components is subsequently indicated.

This survey is aimed at summarising concisely the status of knowledge of the field, highlighting major unresolved issues or controversies, and indicating prominent directions for future research. However, because of space limitations, it cannot cover all the themes or topics in the literature, so some selective emphases and omissions are necessary.

The next two sections review respectively the historical development, and theoretical and methodological aspects of the field that apply generally to the different components of educational production. The rest of the chapter deals with themes on the educational components.

HISTORICAL DEVELOPMENT

The birth of the economics of education as a field could be traced to the keen interest in research on the determinants of economic growth after the Second World War. With a strong push through the works of T. W. Schultz and E. Denison and others in the late 1950s and early 1960s, the economics of education quickly established itself as an interdisciplinary field of study of education and the economy. In the past four decades, a primary impetus for the development of the field has been derived from public and private interest in the economic outcomes of education.

In the 1950s, a key concern in national development for many countries was national reconstruction through economic growth. Policy-makers and researchers alike were interested in understanding the determinants of economic growth, including the role of education in economic growth. Human capital theory, first introduced by T. W. Schultz around 1960 and further developed by J. Mincer, G. Becker and others, highlights the concept of human capital and the positive linkages between education, individual productivity and increased individual earnings and national output. In explaining how investment in education can be an effective policy instrument for promoting individual welfare and national economic growth, the theory became widely accepted by academics and policy-makers and has remained the mainstream perspective in the field to date. Since the 1960s, a significant amount of research in this field has been devoted to the estimation of the rate of return to public and private investment in education.

However, human capital theory is not without its detractors. The experience of national development in the 1960s and the early 1970s among developed countries showed that, despite increased national investment and greater equality in the provision of education, economic growth did not result in a significant reduction in social inequality and many developing countries had stagnant economies, soaring unemployment rates and widening social inequality. The oil crises and economic recession in the early 1970s added to the pressure for a review of national development goals, with a resultant call for the dual goals of economic growth and social equality. In this new context, alternative perspectives on the economic outcome of education emerged, including the screening hypothesis, credentialism, labour market segmentation theory, and differential (or radical) socialisation theory. These perspectives are different from human capital theory in important ways, including the focus of analysis and research methodology. For example, they emphasise research on the relationship between education, employment and labour market structure, as well as on the reproduction of socio-economic inequality. Instead of using the individual as the unit of analysis, some of the alternative perspectives tend to use institutional or class-based frameworks. The 1970s marked a new page in the development of the field.

Although the field did not experience epochal development in the 1980s, there were nevertheless some new initiatives besides analyses based on previous perspectives and research focus. For example, there were new theoretical interpretations of the relationship between education and work which highlighted the contradictory nature of schooling within the larger context of a capitalist democracy. New areas of empirical research include the study of the economic impact of overeducation, the implication of high technology for education, and the economic return to investment in education quality.

Since the early 1990s, there has been increasing interest in a number of emerging issues, such as education policies and the globalisation of economic production, the impact of information technology on education production, and the links between education and a fast-changing, information-based economy. The changing external contexts have significant implications for the contents, pedagogy and mode of learning. To be productive in today's and tomorrow's workplace, individuals have to acquire good problem-solving, communication and social skills. Advances in education technology are increasing the demand for non-traditional delivery of education contents. Recurrent or lifelong learning is a necessity and out-of-school (especially in the workplace) learning is increasing in importance. Nevertheless, the challenge for education's contribution to the dual goals of economic growth and equitable income distribution remains.

In short, the field has witnessed its most significant theoretical and methodological advances in the analyses of the economic outcomes of education. The interest in the 'external' outcome of education has also prompted interest in applying economic theory to the study of the 'internal' process and output of education, especially since the 1970s. Seeing education as an industry and comparing educational production to economic production, researchers have developed the construct of the educational production function to relate student achievement (as a measure of education output) to variables measuring school process and inputs. Other researchers have examined the impact of market mechanisms on school choice, the unionisation of the teachers' market, the 'micro-economics' of school production, and the economics of educational technology. These economic studies of educational production have certainly enriched the field; they also have narrowed the disciplinary gap between economists and educators.

Studies of the costs and financing of education deal with analyses of the amount, mobilisation, allocation and utilisation of resources in educational production. While they are obviously concerned with the education-input component, they also involve cross-component analyses (such as cost-effectiveness evaluation of education costs and education output). While the interest in education expenditure and revenue predated the birth of the field, the economic analyses of education costs added to the development of this field by introducing the concept of economic costs or opportunity costs. In addition to education expenditure, this concept calls attention to foregone opportunities of students' time and to parental spending on education and its impact on education. Studies of education financing are not only economic enquiries, they are often related to the larger education reforms and the political mood of the time.

While most of the earlier studies in the economics of education tended to confine themselves to one country, over time cross-national and comparative studies have become more common. With the globalisation of economic production and the shortening of physical space through communication advances, cross-national concerns and analyses are likely to increase in importance.

Studies on the economics of education can be found in many academic journals, including *Economics of Education Review*, *Journal of Human Resources* and *Educational Economics*. More recent reviews and collections of studies can be found in Blaug (1985), Cohn and Geske (1990) and Carnoy (1995b).

THEORIES AND METHODOLOGIES

Human capital theory

Human capital refers to the skills and values that an individual acquires in or out of school that are related to the productive capacity of the individual. Education enhances the human capital of an individual and, thus, his or her productive capacity. In a competitive labour market (an assumption in the mainstream neoclassical economic theory) a more productive individual is paid a higher wage. Thus there is a positive correlation between the education and earnings of an individual and this correlation has been verified empirically. From both private and societal perspectives, spending on additional education can be regarded as a form of investment which leads to higher individual earnings and more aggregate national output. Private and social rates of return to education can be computed by comparing private costs to private benefits and by comparing social costs to social benefits. This theory is based on methodological individualism or reductionism. According to this methodology, complex social phenomena can be better understood by analysing individual behaviour. A key assumption is that individuals are rational with forward-looking behaviour: individuals are willing to make present sacrifices in order to reap higher returns in the future: and they will choose to invest their resources in those activities with the highest rates of return, other things being equal (Becker, 1975; Schultz, 1971). In research on economic outcomes of education, this theory has stimulated numerous studies on the relationships between individual education and individual earnings, national economic growth and personal income distribution. In the study of education process and output, much attention has been focused on the analysis of the acquisition of cognitive skills by the individual learner. The individual learner is assumed to join the education process with an *a priori* set of personal characteristics.

Screening hypothesis

Like human capital theory, screening hypothesis accepts the empirical evidence on the positive relationship between education and earnings, but it provides an alternative explanation of the correlation. The screening hypothesis assumes that persons of higher productive ability obtain more education but education itself may not raise individual productivity. In a labour market with imperfect information, employers have to rely on some characteristics or signals about the ability of potential employees to assist in their hiring decision. To the extent that education is a reliable signal about individual ability (and thus productivity), employers are willing to pay more educated individuals with higher pay (Arrow, 1973; Spence, 1973). Thus, individuals with more education have higher earnings because of the signalling function of education. However, if the ability-enhancing role of education is minimal or non-existent, additional spending on education can be a wasteful public investment because it does not result in higher individual productivity and additional national output, even though it can be very profitable from the perspective of an individual. The screening hypothesis is also based on methodological individualism. It has stimulated empirical studies on screening in the workplace (Hartog, 1981), but not studies on education process and output. To date, it remains controversial among researchers in this field with regard to the explanation for the education–earnings relationship; the extent of the productivity/ability-enhancing versus information role of education is yet to be resolved. The screening hypothesis presented a significant challenge to the human capital theory in the 1970s, but interest in this perspective began to decline in the 1980s.

Segmented labour market theories

These try to explain the education–earnings relationship by drawing attention to the structure of labour markets. In contrast to human capital theory, which assumes one competitive labour market, the earlier theories of labour market segmentation (Doeringer and Piore, 1971; Reich *et al.*, 1973) point out that the labour market is divided into two or more segments with little or no labour mobility between them. In the 'low-skill' labour market segment, for example, employment is seasonal or temporary, and the pay and education qualifications of workers are lower. In the 'high-skill' labour market segment, in contrast, employment is more stable, and the pay and education qualifications are higher. While there is an overall relationship between education and earnings for workers across the labour market segments and in the 'high-skill' segment, there may not be such a relationship in the 'low-skill' segment. In addition to explaining the education–earnings relationship, these alternative perspectives also highlight job mobility within a firm (the 'internal' labour market) and why there is persistent unemployment and low earnings among disadvantaged groups of society (DeFreitas *et al.*, 1991; Hartmann, 1987). However, these perspectives are not homogeneous in their theoretical and methodological underpinnings. Some perspectives draw from institutional economics and emphasise the influences of government regulations, employer and labour organisations, and market structure. Other perspectives draw from more radical or Marxist tradition and examine the historical development of labour market segmentation within the larger context of a capitalist economy; they are based on holistic analyses of a class-based society. Analyses of labour market segmentation since 1980, however, have questioned the rigid dualism of the earlier theories (Berger and Piore, 1980; Ryan, 1981). Instead, segmentation has increasingly been seen as a dynamic labour market process characterised by discontinuity rather than dualism and by compartmentalisation of workers in diverse forms. Both the earlier and more recent studies of segmentation are focused on the economic outcomes of education; they have little or no analysis on education process and output. The expansion of studies on the structure of labour markets through historical and multidisciplinary analyses in more national settings has kept this research area lively.

Radical socialisation theory

While proponents of human capital theory point to the importance of cognitive skills in raising individual productivity, radical socialisation theorists shift attention to the productive role of non-cognitive skills and the important socialisation process in schooling for acquiring such skills (Bowles and Gintis, 1976). Differentiation and fragmentation in the capitalist workplace lead to different kinds of jobs which require different worker traits.

Some jobs need workers who are independent, creative and inquisitive, while other jobs are suitable for workers who are docile and receptive to authority, and who follow instructions from superiors without question. The school serves the needs of the capitalist economy through the inculcation of students from different social classes with different sets of traits or non-cognitive skills required by the capitalist workplace. In this way, schools are very functional in supporting capitalist production and in the reproduction of social classes. This perspective draws from the Marxist tradition with a focus on the role of education in the reproduction of the social relation of production. It is also characterised by economic determinism, in which the function of school is determined by the economy and has little autonomy relative to the economy. This perspective highlights the interrelationship between social class, the stratified education process and unequal economic outcomes of education.

Schooling in democratic capitalism

According to this perspective, schooling in the United States is part of a democratic state associated with a capitalist mode of production. As such, schooling in the United States is subject to the influences of two forces: (a) the force of capitalist production, which places demand on schooling to undertake differential socialisation of students for an unequal and undemocratic capitalist workplace and (b) the force for democracy and equality, which seeks to promote democracy and equality in school and in the society at large. The development of schooling in the past two centuries in the USA could be interpreted as responding to the varying extent of influences of the two forces. These two forces being opposite to each other, schooling has often been regarded as problematic and with contradictory roles (Carnoy and Levin, 1985). Being part of a democratic state, schooling has some autonomy relative to the economy and its development could depart from the requirement of the economy and exacerbate contradictions within the economy. This perspective highlights the inter-relationship between social class, a stratified but contested education process within a democratic state, and an unequal and undemocratic workplace with its own internal contradictions.

THE ECONOMIC EFFECTS OF EDUCATION

Education and productivity

Education and productivity is a core relationship in the economic argument for investment in education. It is generally assumed that education contributes to higher individual productivity. Theoretically, several arguments have been proposed to explain how education may raise an individual's performance:

1 The individual acquires literacy and computational skills in school which are important for good performance in the workplace.
2 The individual makes better allocative decisions of resources in a changing environment.

3 The individual makes better use of more advanced machines and equipment (that is, human capital and physical capital are complementary).
4 Education socialises the individuals in the skills, values and dispositions necessary for the modern workplace.

However, because of the complexity of the factors affecting productivity and the difficulty of measuring productivity across production activities, proving the relationship empirically has been a challenging and somewhat elusive task. Studies of education and productivity in agriculture in Asia, Latin America, North America and Africa have found that education, beyond a certain threshold level, can have a significant, positive impact on productivity and that such an impact is stronger in a modernising environment (Moock and Addou, 1995). Direct evidence for such a relationship is rather weak in industry, particularly because of the difficulty of making productivity comparison among jobs. By assuming the existence of a competitive labour market, some analysts have used earnings differentials as a proxy for productivity differentials and have found a significant positive relationship between education and earnings. Even though there is some supportive evidence that earnings may be a good proxy for productivity for unskilled workers (Hellerstein and Neumark, 1995), earnings may generally not be a valid proxy when the labour market is not competitive. Also, as screening theorists have pointed out, education may not have an impact on individual productivity at all (see section above on 'Theories and Methodologies').

Recent studies of the economic effect of over-education have argued that the education–productivity relationship is not necessarily linear and positive (Rumberger, 1981; Tsang and Levin, 1985). Productivity in the workplace depends on a worker's education, the educational requirement of his/her job, and the match or mismatch between the worker's education and educational requirement. Over-education (or under-utilisation of education) may lead to lower work effort and thus lower productivity. This implies that, as the education of the labour force increases over time, higher worker productivity can be realised by pursuing changes in the workplace that provide more opportunities for the workers more fully to utilise their education skills. To date, the economic impact of over-education is not yet settled.

Education and earnings

While the education–productivity relationship is important from the perspective of public investment in education, an individual is generally more concerned with the education–earnings relationship. The positive relationship between schooling and earnings has been well established in empirical studies across many countries. In economic analysis, this relationship is represented by the age-earning profiles, which show how earnings vary with age by level of educational attainment. Based on cross-sectional data, the stylised age-earnings profiles show that: (a) the profiles are higher for higher levels of schooling; (b) the profiles are concave in age; and (c) the slope of a profile increases with the level of schooling (Mincer, 1974). Thus individual spending to acquire additional education can result in economic benefits measured in terms of additional lifetime earnings. The profitability of private investment in education can be measured by comparing the present value of additional lifetime earnings with the present value of the private costs of education; empirical studies in both developed and less developed countries have found private investment in schooling to be profitable (see section below, 'Cost Analysis in Education').

However, individuals with the same level of schooling do have different earnings, depending on their gender, race and other factors. For example, studies of the male–female earnings gap in developed countries have consistently shown that females earn less than males after controlling for schooling level, and that the gap has been declining at a varying pace and at different time periods during the second half of the twentieth century (Ferber, 1995). In the United States, African-Americans and Latinos have lower educational attainment and lower earnings than whites. The economic return to education has historically been lower for non-whites than for whites. However, racial/ethnic earnings differentials vary by gender. In particular, the earnings gap between African-American females and white females is smaller than that between African-American males and white males (Chiswick, 1987). Analysts of the determinants of earnings generally agree on the importance of education as a factor, but they disagree on how education contributes to higher earnings and on the importance of other factors. The earnings impact of education may be due to the productivity-enhancing effect of human capital or to a screening effect. While some analysts emphasise human-capital variables, other analysts draw attention to discrimination and structural conditions of the labour market.

Studies of vocational training in less developed countries have found that vocational training can have a significant positive impact on earnings and a high rate of return (Middleton et al., 1993). The earnings impact, however, can differ by gender; for example, in Peru vocational training raises the earnings of males but not of females (Arriagada, 1990). In the United States, a review of the Comprehensive Employment and Training Act programmes has found a substantial earnings impact for some training programmes and negligible impact for other programmes; the earnings impact also differs by gender and ethnic groups (Barnow, 1987).

Education and economic growth

The contribution of education to economic growth is presumed to occur through increased individual productivity at the micro level and increased aggregate human-capital input at the macro level. Implicitly based on human capital theory, most of the studies on education and economic growth to date use the theoretical construct of an aggregate economic production function. Among these studies, some employ the growth-accounting approach (which relates the growth rate in aggregate output to growth rates in inputs) to determine the magnitude of education's contribution to national growth rate. Education is found to have a substantial contribution in some countries and a small contribution in other countries (Denison, 1979; Psacharopoulos, 1984); but there is uncertainty as to the exact magnitude of education's contribution. Other studies use econometric methods to relate some education variables to economic growth rates, and they find a significant relationship. For example, a study of 75 less developed countries for the period 1960–1977 found that real per capita GNP was significantly correlated with adult literacy rates (Hicks, 1980). A study by the World Bank argues that investment in human capital is an important factor in the high growth rates of East Asian countries, and that in these countries economic growth has been accompanied by more equal income distribution (World Bank, 1993). However, another World Bank study found that growth in human capital was significantly and negatively related to the rate of growth of output per worker (Pritchett, 1996). The aggregate production function remains a controversial analytical tool. Proponents recognise the need for better model specification and better data. Critics find such analyses irrelevant for understanding education's role in capitalist production.

Education and income distribution

Most of the recent studies of income distribution concentrate on an analysis of personal distribution of earnings and on whether education can promote a more equal distribution of personal earnings. According to human capital theory, given the relationship between education, productivity and earnings, the distribution of education is related to the distribution of earnings. Thus, theoretically, a more equal distribution of education can lead to a more equal distribution of earnings. In some countries, strong state education policies have been found to be associated with more equal education attainment among gender and ethnic groups (Lillard and Willis, 1994). Empirical testing of the human-capital model on earnings distribution has yielded mixed results; and the findings can differ substantially between developed countries and less developed countries (Park, 1996; Ram, 1990). The unsettled debate about model specification and empirical findings among proponents of human capital theory is paralleled by critics who argue that education has minimal or no influence on earnings distribution. A recent study in the United States argues that the pattern of wage inequality over time can better be explained by changes in market demand and economic structure rather than changes in the supply of personal characteristics such as education (Blueston, 1990). Politico-economic analysis indicates that no simple relationship exists between education and earnings distribution. Education's effect on the earnings distribution is dependent on contested state policies (Carnoy and Levin, 1985).

EDUCATION, LABOUR MARKET AND THE NEW WORLD ECONOMY

Education and the labour market in developed countries

The topic of education and the labour market deals with the relationship between the educational qualifications of individuals and the characteristics of the jobs they hold. A large number of empirical studies in developed countries have consistently found two empirical relationships: that educational qualifications are a major criterion used by employers to hire new employees, and that there is a close correlation between the educational attainment and expected lifetime earnings of individuals. There are three major perspectives providing alternative explanations of the same empirical relationship between education and labour market in these countries:

1 the 'wage competition' model based on human capital theory and mainstream economic theory;

2 screening theory;
3 labour market segementation theory.

The controversy among these theoretical explanations (previously examined in the section on 'Theories and Methodologies') has gone on for about two decades and has yet to be resolved.

Education and the labour market in less developed countries

The theoretical perspectives put forward by analysts in developed countries have also been used to explain education and labour markets in less developed countries. Labour markets in less developed countries do differ from those in developed countries in at least two major respects. First, labour markets in less developed countries are often dualistic in structure, consisting of the formal/modern sector and the informal sector. In terms of the proportion of employment, the formal sector is much smaller in less developed countries than in developed countries. Second, within the formal sector, public employment is more substantial in less developed countries than in developed countries. Thus more attention should be given to the analysis of informal labour markets and public employment in less developed countries. It was found that in some African and Latin American countries, formal education had a significant positive effect on earnings in the informal sector but the effect was smaller than that for the formal sector. The impact of training on earnings was negligible in the informal sector but significantly positive in the formal sector (Tueros, 1995). In countries where public employment is substantial, wages are set administratively and are rather inflexible; analysis based on screening theory may be more appropriate than the wage competition model (Hinchliffe, 1995). A study of Peru found that, for males, training has an earnings impact in the private sector but not the public sector; and training improves employment prospects in the public sector but not the private or self-employed sectors. For females, training improves employment prospect in all sectors, though it has no impact on earnings (Arriagada, 1990).

The economics of the brain drain

The brain drain is technically concerned with unrecorded international human-capital flow associated with permanent migration. In the public policy arena, it is most frequently discussed in terms of the migration of highly skilled individuals who are trained in one country and then live and work in another country. Previous studies have identified a number of factors influencing the migration decisions of such individuals, including expected real income, professional opportunities, working conditions, political considerations, and sociological and cultural aspects of life (Bratsberg, 1995; Grubel and Scott, 1977). Although existing data are deficient for determining the magnitude of this human capital flow, the brain drain has been a political and often emotional issue in national and international forums because of its negative economic impact on the country of emigration (generally a less developed country) and the gain of the country of immigration (generally an industrialised country). Alternative strategies for reducing brain drain have been proposed, but widely accepted strategies are few. The increased globalisation of economic production will likely maintain public interest in this issue. There is a need for more informed and less emotional discussion of this issue through the collection of better data and a more comprehensive analysis of the effects of brain drain in a global context.

Education and the information-based world economy

A recent review has examined the characteristics of the new world economy, its impact on the labour market, and implications for education policy (Carnoy, 1995a). According to this review, the globalisation of economic production in the past two decades has several major features:

- more intensive use of new knowledge and information in production activities;
- shift from production of material goods to information-processing activities in industrialised countries;
- move of production organisation from mass-standardised production to flexible customised production;
- increased cross-national scope of all production decision;
- a mutually supporting relationship between information technologies and global economic and organisational changes.

These global economic changes are associated with observable changes in the labour market. An increasing proportion of jobs are located in the high-technology sector, requiring more flexible responses from managers and workers. Traditional stable jobs in large firms are being replaced with more temporary and less secure jobs, resulting in more changes in employment over the working life. Across countries, there is increased participation of women in the labour market, and the informal segment of the labour market has developed. To meet the challenges of the new world economy, education institutions have to promote critical thinking and problem-solving skills, and to focus more on general flexible skills instead of specific vocational skills. Quality education programmes should be accessible to all children. Lifelong learning is becoming more necessary over time (Rumberger and Levin, 1989).

High technology and the demand for education

With the advent of high technology, such as computer technology, a key concern for both the policy and research communities since the 1980s is the demand of such technology for educated workers in the labour market. An unsettled debate has emerged on whether high technology will raise skill requirements for jobs in the national economy. There are three views: (a) that high technology will raise skill requirements, (b) that high technology will lower skill requirements, and (c) that the skill impact of high technology cannot be predetermined. A literature consisting of aggregate analyses and case studies on the United States exists which examines the impact of high technology on the composition of jobs in the national economy and on the contents of jobs (Spenner, 1988). Aggregate analyses (which generally focus on the composition shift in the national economy) have found skills upgrading over time, especially in terms of the skill level and complexity. On the other hand, case studies (which generally focus on content shift in jobs) have found skills down-grading in some jobs and upgrading in other jobs, especially in terms of the loss in workers' job autonomy. The net effect of both shifts has been some slight increase in the overall skills requirements of jobs in the national economy, a change much slower and smaller than that anticipated by proponents of skills upgrading. Models of skills demand tend to highlight the changing and contingent nature of the skills impact of high technology (Flynn, 1988; Spenner, 1988) and how firms are organised can affect the use of technology and skills requirements (Levin 1987). Further research is needed to examine cross-national dynamics of high technology because of the important role of high technology in the globalisation of economic production.

EDUCATIONAL PRODUCTION

Economic studies of the education process generally liken educational production to economic production and apply economic concepts and methods to the analyses of the operation of education institutions and education systems. Common applications are discussed in this section. A central concern of these studies is the identification of factors that contribute to higher student learning.

Educational production functions

These functions relate education output (such as student achievement) to education input and process variables with the objective to determine, statistically, the determinants of education output. Based on the works of Coleman *et al.* (1966) and others, reviews of education–production–function studies in the early 1970s concluded that the most important determinants of student achievement were family background and socio-economic factors and that school variables had little impact on student achievement (Averch *et al.*, 1974). This negative assessment, however, was challenged by subsequent studies in the United States and elsewhere. They found that teachers and school factors could make a difference in student achievement (Purkey and Smith, 1983) and that school variables had stronger effects on achievement in poor countries than rich ones (Heyneman and Loxley, 1983). Also, dissatisfaction with previous production function studies based on aggregate data has driven some analysts to undertake more micro-oriented, production function studies using measures of actual inputs supplied to individual students (Brown and Saks, 1987). While some interest in education production functions continues in the 1990s, so does the dis-agreement on the relationship between school variables and student achievement, particu-larly the impact of school resources on student achievement (Hedges *et al.*, 1994; Hanushek, 1989).

Micro-economics of school production

A literature has emerged since the 1980s on the micro-economics of school production. Instead of using education production functions empirically to relate education output to its determinants, some recent studies have conducted micro-economic analysis of the education process itself. These studies tend to be more conceptually oriented and have applied micro-economics principles such as the law of diminishing marginal productivity, and the substitutability of inputs. For example, the analysis of grouped instruction shows that there is a tradeoff between the gains of those students who receive the attention of an instructor and the loss of the remaining students who are less proximate to the instructor (Arnott and Rowse, 1987). The application of game theory to the analysis of co-operation in education production shows that it is possible for both teachers and students to gain from co-operation in education but that there are structural difficulties to promote such co-operation (Correa and Gruver, 1987). The literature is rather technical in nature and has yet to be widely read within the educational policy community.

Economic analysis of teacher supply

Teachers are a key ingredient of educational production and an adequate supply of skilled teachers is a prominent policy concern in many countries. The economic factors affecting teacher supply are teachers' salaries and working conditions relative to those in other occupations, and the costs of teacher preparation relative to those for other occupations. Empirical studies in developed and less developed countries have shown that incentives matter; teacher supply increases when salaries and working conditions for teachers improve relative to other occupations. And more stringent training and licensing requirements can restrict teacher supply. For example, in the United Kingdon, higher relative salaries for teachers increase the size of the pool of college graduates who enter teaching, reduce teacher turnover, and increase ex-teachers' return to teaching (see review in Dolton, 1996). Relative salaries also affect the attrition rates of novice teachers in the United States (Murnane et al., 1991). In less developed countries, the harsh working conditions in rural areas often lead to a shortage of skilled teachers in these areas (Ankhara-Dove, 1982). In the United States, the proportion of black college graduates in the pool of newly licensed teachers is adversely affected by test-score requirements for licensing (Murnane et al., 1991). Besides these economic factors, teacher supply is also strongly influenced by demographics (Kirby et al., 1991). A limitation of existing research on teacher supply is the lack of studies on the impact of economic factors on the quality of the teaching force. The scarcity of published studies on developing countries indicates a need for more research on such countries.

Economics of teacher unionisation

Teacher unions are commonly found in developed countries. Their major task is to perform collective bargaining for their members and the structure and scope of the collective bargaining process vary substantially across these countries (Blackmore and Spaull, 1987; Duclaud-Williams, 1985; Freeman and Medoff, 1984). Through collective bargaining, teacher unions have become a force that affects the costs, operation and effectiveness of state schools. Studies in the United States have found that, compared to non-unionised teachers, unionised teachers have higher salaries and influence on instructional policies (such as teacher–student ratio and teachers' instruction time). The net effect of unionisation on student achievement seems to vary with the achievement level of students: compared to non-unionised districts, unionised districts do better with the average student but less well with students well below or well above the average (Ebert and Stone, 1984). Unionisation does not appear to be a cost-effective way of raising student achievement.

Market choice in school

The debate on market choice in school has gone on for a while in developed countries like the United States. The movement for more market choice in school has increased in strength in the 1990s. This trend is largely a reaction to a combination of concerns about US public schools (such as poor student performance, inefficient operation, insufficient capacity to meet enrolment demand) and a belief in the superiority of market mechanisms and reduced government involvement (Clune and Witte, 1990; Friedman, 1962; James, 1987). Opponents of this movement in the US emphasise the role of public schooling in promoting and sustaining democracy; they argue that market mechanisms can lead to increased socio-economic fragmentation and thus undermine this important role of public schooling (Levin, 1991).

Politico-economic perspective of schooling production

Most of the economic analyses of educational production reviewed above are based implicitly on the mainstream neoclassical economic framework and assume that education institutions function like private firms. Critics argue that such a framework and assumptions are not useful for understanding educational production. They point out that most educational institutions operate in the public domain and are public sector organisations. As such, these education institutions are subject to the competing political and economic demands of the larger society, and to the bureaucratic demand of educational organisations at various levels. Thus education institutions will not function like private firms. In the United States, for example, formal schooling is part of a democratic state and is thus subject to competing demands from major societal forces. The historical development of education in the US in the past two centuries cannot be adequately explained by seeing education institutions as private firms responding to economic interests only (Carnoy and Levin, 1985).

Production of training

A significant part of human capital is produced outside the school through a variety of training programmes, such as on-the-job training, off-the-job training, apprenticeship and non-formal education programmes. These training programmes may have different providers (including the employer, the government and non-governmental community organisations) and different training objectives. A large literature has emerged on the economic analysis of these diverse training programmes, examining issues such as the type of skill training, optimal level of provision of training, costs and financing, training effectiveness, and the organisation of training (Becker, 1975; Coombs and Ahmed, 1974; Groot, 1995; Hamilton, 1990; Middleton *et al.*, 1993; Stern and Ritzen, 1991). These studies find that unit costs of training vary substantially across training mode; and employer-provided training is generally cost-effective.

THE ECONOMICS OF EDUCATIONAL TECHNOLOGY

Uses of educational technology

The technology of education refers to the techniques and methods by which education inputs are transformed into education output. Educational technology may involve different mixes of labour (such as teachers) and capital (such as school buildings, computers and other equipment). One type of educational technology that has historically aroused the interest and reaction of educators and non-educators alike concerns the use of capital-intensive media such as radio, television, computer and multimedia distance education in educational production. Historically, new educational media were used to achieve a number of educational objectives, such as providing educational opportunity to previously excluded groups, reducing the unit costs of education services (to meet tight budgetary constraints or to expand access), improving student learning, and raising the cost-effectiveness of educational spending. But economic evaluation has produced mixed findings on the costs, effectiveness and cost-effectiveness of different educational media.

Economic evaluation of educational technology

The findings of reviews of economic evaluation of new educational media across countries (Klees, 1995; Tsang, 1988) can be summarised as follows. Conventional analyses of radio generally find this 'little' medium to be inexpensive, effective (with respect to student achievement) and cost-effective. A prominent example is the interactive radio instruction (IRI) approach piloted in the Nicaragua Radio Mathematics Project (Anzalone, 1991). But critics caution that these analyses have underestimated the costs of IRI, have overestimated the achievement gains of IRI, and have generally failed to persuade countries who have piloted this approach to implement it on a national scale (see Klees, 1995, p. 401).

Educational television hardly has any impact in school in developed countries like the United States (Cuban, 1986), though it has managed to be a component of open university systems. In less developed countries, educational television has been an expensive add-on to the traditional school and it has not provided sustainable achievement gains over time. Little media like radio have generally been found to be less costly and more cost-effective than big media like television. The generally negative experience with this big medium has been partly due to logistical or mechanical problems. But critics also point out that educational television has been strongly resisted by teachers who see it as a threat to their professional development and career. And to the extent that inappropriate curricula from a donor country are transmitted through educational television in an assisted country, educational television is also criticised as a tool of cultural indoctrination.

Several media, including radio and television, have been used in a variety of distance education programmes, such as primary education programmes for children in remote areas, school equivalency programmes at various levels, open university programmes and teacher training (Eicher *et al.*, 1982; Jamison and Orivel, 1982; Nettleton, 1991). Their primary objectives are to expand education access and to serve as a less expensive alternative to conventional schooling. Cost analysis indicates that these education media demonstrate economics of scale and since they involve large start-up costs, these programmes have to have large enrolments and a long period of operation in order to be comparable to traditional schooling in terms of unit costs. But distance education programmes are not comparable to traditional education programmes in terms of education output or outcome because of their narrow academic focus. Evidence on the effectiveness of such programmes is fragmentary and since there is no systematic evaluation of the cost-effectiveness of distance teaching, firm conclusions are not warranted.

Computers and information-based technology are the new educational technology of our day. In contrast to previous generations of educational media such as film, radio and television, proponents argue that computer technologies are more likely to have a discernible impact on education because of their wide adoption in the workplace, their acceptance by key stakeholders of education, and their symbolic association with national progress. Studies on computer technology in education have focused on one application to date, namely, computer-assisted instruction (CAI). The findings on the effectiveness of CAI are mixed and there is not enough evidence to support the claim of superior cost-effectiveness relative to conventional school interventions (Levin, 1995). More research is necessary on this application. But in developed countries, a new area of application with fast-growing public interest is the educational uses of the Internet. This application is in its early stages of experimentation and economic evaluation is certainly necessary now and in the future. Despite its declining cost over time, computers are still expensive for most of the households in developing countries, especially low-income ones. As computer literacy and skills are increasingly required in the workplace, the failure to teach these skills as basic competencies in school will exacerbate existing inequalities within and among countries.

A key to understanding much of the disagreement or debate in the economic analysis of new educational techology in general and new educational media in particular is the role of new technology in education production. If new educational technology is seen as a neutral instrument for achieving given educational objectives, then much of the challenge in the application of such technology lies in proper design, careful experimentation and implementation, and other technical solutions. If new educational technology is used as a non-neutral instrument for advancing the educational and other objectives of some groups over those of other groups, then the challenges are more politico-economic in nature. The effects of new technology in education and their evaluation are intimately related to the conception of new educational technology and its intended uses (Eraut, 1989).

COST ANALYSIS IN EDUCATION

There is a large body of literature on education costs in both less developed countries and developed countries that demonstrates the important applications of cost analysis in education. Cost analysis can reveal the cost implication of an education policy, assess the financial feasibility and sustainability of an education reform, provide diagnosis of past and current resource utilisation in education, project future cost requirements, and evaluate the relative efficiency of alternative education policies or interventions. Cost studies can contribute significantly to decision-making, planning and monitoring in education (Tsang, 1988). Cost studies can be grouped into three categories: costing and feasibility-testing studies; behavioural studies of educational costs; and cost-benefit and cost-effectiveness studies.

Costing and feasibility-testing studies

These studies are concerned with education inputs only. Their major tasks consist in identifying and measuring the costs of various inputs to education and they are often conducted to estimate resource requirements and to test the financial feasibility and sustainability of an educational intervention. A significant contribution of economic analysis of education costs is the application of the concept of economic costs, which are defined to be the economic value of inputs in their best alternative use (also known as opportunity costs). This concept implies that education costs are concerned not only with education expenditure, but also with parental spending on education, donated inputs to education institutions and the economic value of students' time.

Educational costing is one of the earliest and most common applications of educational cost analysis. Previous studies range from the costing of an educational intervention in the classroom, an education project, or an education programme, to the costing of the reform in a subsector of education, or a five-year plan for the entire education system. Earlier studies tended to focus on education costs for the government, but more recent research has demonstrated the importance of private education costs. Studies on a number of countries in Asia, Africa and South America have found that private costs have a number of positive and negative consequences:

- they constitute a significant part of the total cost of education;
- they are a source of funding for important education inputs (such as textbooks) that promote education quality;
- they contribute to inequality and inequity in education;
- they affect the relative efficiency between state schools and private schools (Tsang, 1995).

The resource mobilisation and inequality/inequity impacts of private costs can be a source of dilemma for education policy-makers considering a shift towards private financing of education.

Behavioural studies of education costs

These studies are concerned with the relationship among education inputs and the utilisation of education inputs in the education production process, with the purpose of ascertaining the behavioural patterns of education costs and the extent of under-utilisation of scarce education resources. They include studies on education expenditures and unit costs, surveys of utilisation rates of education resources and studies of economies of scale in education. Previous studies have found that, in both less developed countries and developed countries, public investment in education had been phenomenal in the 1960s and 1970s but has slowed down or levelled off since the late 1970s. The slowdown could be attributed to three factors: slower rates of economic growth; a relative decrease in the demand for education; and a change in government attitude towards education. Per student expenditure has some common patterns across education systems:

- it rises with the level of schooling;
- it is dominated by personnel costs;
- it is higher for boarding schools than day schools at the secondary level;
- it is generally higher for vocational/technical education than general/academic education;
- it is higher for engineering and sciences subjects than for arts and humanity at the tertiary level;
- it has a built-in tendency to rise over time.

Low rates of utilisation were reported for secondary schools and universities in a number of studies of less developed countries. Econometric studies of developed countries such as Canada, United States and United Kingdom have found that there are economies of scale in primary, secondary and higher education. Economies of scale have also been reported for China and other less developed countries.

Cost-benefit and cost-effectiveness studies in education

Cost-benefit studies in education are studies which compare the benefits of education (such as increased productivity and earnings) with the costs of education and cost-effectiveness studies are studies which compare the effects of education (such as student learning) with the costs of education. Both are conducted for choosing among alternative education investments so that scarce education resources can be allocated more efficiently. A large literature exists on cost-benefit studies in education in less developed countries and developed countries. The stylised findings across countries are:

- investment in education is profitable, with rates generally above the 10 per cent benchmark rate:
- primary education has the highest rates of return among all education levels;
- private rates of return are higher than social rates of return;
- at a given level, the rate of return is higher for less developed countries than for developed countries;
- female education has higher rates than education for males;

- at the secondary level, the rate of return is higher for academic education than for vocational/technical education (Psacharopoulos, 1994).

However, other analysts point out that the above cost-benefit studies focus on the quantity of education and fail to take account of the quality of schooling, thus resulting in biased findings. The social rate of return to quality of schooling could exceed the social rate of return to quantity of schooling (Behrman and Birdsall, 1985). Thus it may be more profitable to invest in the quality of education than in the quantity of education. Moreover, in countries with rapid industrialisation and rapid educational expansion, the rate of return to schooling can increase with the level of schooling (Ryoo *et al.*, 1993). A recent review has documented the methodological and conceptual difficulties of these studies (Hough, 1994).

Compared to cost-benefit studies, the applications of cost-effectiveness analysis to traditional education are relatively few, especially in less developed countries. Among the few applications are studies on textbooks, teacher training, mathematics curricula and computer-assisted instruction (Levin, 1995). A prominent application in non-traditional education is in the area of new educational media (see section on the 'Economics of Educational Technology' for more detail).

Looking ahead, there should be continued and even increased interest in cost studies in education, in the light of the need to improve education quality and expand education access under tightening budgetary constraint. These cost studies may include, in particular, analysis of quality basic education for marginalised populations, analysis of new educational technology (e.g. computers and communication through the Internet) and analysis of life-long learning for adults in various settings. To facilitate the use of cost analysis in education decision-making, there is a need to strengthen the informational base for cost studies, to encourage more research on education costs, and to increase the awareness of education policy-makers about the usefulness of educational cost analysis.

FINANCING OF EDUCATION

Principles and recurrent debates in education finance

Financing of education refers to the mechanisms or processes by which resources are obtained and allocated to support desired education activities. Countries differ substantially on how on their education resources are obtained and allocated. There is no one best system for education financing; financing practices are closely bound to the specific historical and politico-economic conditions of a country. Nevertheless, there are three common principles or criteria for judging the soundness of education finance: adequacy of funding; efficiency in how resources are obtained and allocated; and equity in how resources are obtained and allocated (Benson, 1995). A key issue in education finance is the proper division of financial responsibility between the government and the individual. According to the principle of benefits received, the various constituencies of society should bear the costs of schooling in relation to the benefits they receive. A distinction can be made between private benefits that accrue to individuals and social benefits that accrue to society. Presumably, individuals (or society) should pay more for education when there are more private (or social) benefits.

However, the challenge in operationalising this principle lies in determining precisely the social and private benefits of schooling. In addition, there are several recurrent debates or controversies over financing that cut across countries and levels of education. They include debates concerning the appropriate form of control (as reflected in the debate on centralised financing versus decentralised financing; see Benson, 1995), parental choice and the democratic role of schooling (Levin, 1991), as well as the proper allocation of resources by level of education (as in the emphasis on compulsory versus post-compulsory education; see World Bank, 1995) and by type of curriculum (as in the emphasis on vocational/technical versus academic curriculum at the secondary level; see Middleton *et al.*, 1993).

School finance

Traditionally, there is a distinction between school finance (dealing with primary and secondary schooling) and higher education finance, because of differences in the mechanisms (such as revenue sources, locus of control and allocation methods) for resource mobilisation and allocation. Economic analysis can be applied to many traditional issues in school finance (Monk, 1990). In recent years three issues have dominated school finance across countries:

1 *Choice and market mechanisms in the financing of education.* For example, the call for the increased use of vouchers and more choice in state schools has gathered momentum in the United States since the early 1990s. The debate on the strengths and weaknesses of market mechanisms versus public-choice approaches to expand choice in education is still very much alive (Goldhaber, 1996; Levin, 1991; Odden and Kotowski, 1992).

2 *Access to quality basic education for children from all backgrounds* (as defined by the specific context of a country). At the international level, this concern is represented by the 'Education-for-All' movement with an initial declaration in Jomtien, Thailand in 1990 (Inter-Agency Commission, 1990). In some countries, it is reflected by efforts to improve education for disadvantaged populations by utilising existing resources and restructuring the education process in schools (Levin, 1993).

3 *Proper mix of private and government involvement for mobilising additional resources to basic schooling.* Increasing parental and community financing of schools (Bray and Lillis, 1988) is a strategy being promoted by some international agencies. However, studies in a number of developing countries have shown that this strategy often exacerbates existing inequalities in education and should be complemented by intergovernmental grants targeted at the disadvantaged populations and areas (Tsang, 1995). To achieve quality basic education for all, there should be increased government financial commitment to the most disadvantaged groups and areas.

Higher education finance

Several policy concerns permeate studies of higher education finance: the use of student aid to facilitate access to higher education; reduced public subsidisation and increased cost recovery for mobilising resources for higher education; the inequality or redistributional impact of higher education; and the use of alternative modes of delivery to make higher education more accessible and less costly. Studies of student grants in the United States have found mixed results on access: a study of the 1970s found a decrease in participation rate for low-income students despite increases in student aid (Hansen, 1983); but a more recent review and analysis concludes that student aid does increase access (Leslie and Brinkman, 1988). Studies in Denmark, Sweden and the United States have concluded that loan schemes have performed reasonably well in these developed countries and there are efficiency and equity arguments for introducing or increasing their use in less developed countries (Woodhall, 1988). Much of the ongoing debate about student loans as a strategy for financing higher education centres around issues of implementation: the extent and pace of cost recovery; the methods and cost of administration; and the means for reducing default. No definitive findings have emerged from studies of the redistribution effects of higher education. The review by Blaug (1982) suggests that higher education may possibly be more advantageous to the poor than to the rich in the United States, and more advantageous to the rich than to the poor in the United Kingdom, Europe and other parts of the world. The open university, with the use of the new education technology, has been adopted as a model to expand access to higher education and reduce the unit costs of higher education (Klees, 1995). Tightening budgetary constraint has increased the demand for higher faculty productivity and more accountability in the utilisation of public funds for higher education. These policy concerns will no doubt continue to occupy the attention of research on higher education finance in the near future.

Financing adult and continuing education

This is an area which traditionally has received much less attention than formal schooling. However, its importance will probably increase in the future as there will be increased demand for adult education and training from several sources:

- the need for basic literacy programmes for adults as part of the overall effort in achieving quality basic education for all;
- the need for adults continually to upgrade their skills as a result of rapid production changes in the workplace;
- the need for adults to acquire new skills on their own as industries restructure and traditional employment yields to more temporary employment or self-employment.

A combination of financing sources can be considered, including the individual, the government and the employer (Timmermann, 1983). As with formal schooling programmes, issues in the financing of adult and continuing education are concerned with the adequacy of funding, the relevance of programmes, efficiency in programme delivery, and accessibility to adults from all backgrounds.

International education financing

International education assistance, in grants and/or loans, and from bilateral and/or multilateral sources, can be an important means for financing education in some countries. Changing national priorities and international relationships in recent years have combined to create uncertainties and a demand for change in the educational relationship between developed countries (generally the donors) and less developed countries (generally the recipients, especially poor ones). A recent review has identified four critical concerns in international education assistance: the negative effects of international debt burden on recipients; the fungibility of assistance; the conditions imposed by donors on recipients; and increased competition among recipient countries along with declining political support in donor countries (Windham, 1995). Several strategies may be considered to address these concerns in the coming years: increasing the participation of non-governmental organisations; promoting a more equal partnership between donors and recipients; promoting regional co-operation and educational structures; employing more broadly based programmatic approaches; raising the efficiency of the utilisation of international education assistance; and, in particular, strengthening the political willingness of donors to contribute to international education assistance.

ACKNOWLEDGEMENTS

The author would like to acknowledge the helpful comments of Henry Levin and the assistance of Jessica Trotter.

REFERENCES

Ankhara-Dove, L. (1982) 'The development and training of teachers for remote rural schools in less-developed countries'. *International Review of Education*, 28 (1), 3–27.

Anzalone, S. (1991) 'Educational technology and the improvement of education in developing countries'. In M. Lockheed, J. Middleton and G. Nettleton (eds) *Education Technology: Sustainable and Effective Use*. Washington, DC: World Bank.

Arnott, R. and Rowse, J. (1987) 'Peer group effects and educational attainment'. *Journal of Public Economics*, 32, 287–305.

Arriagada, A. (1990) 'Labor market outcomes of non-formal training for male and female workers in Peru'. *Economics of Education Review*, 9 (4), 331–342.

Arrow, K. (1973) 'Higher education as a filter'. *Journal of Public Economics*, 2 (3), 193–216.

Averch, H., Carroll, S., Donaldson, T., Kiesing, H. and Pincus, J. (1974). *How Effective is Schooling? A Critical Review of Research*. Englewood Cliffs, NJ: Educational Technology Publications.

Barnow, B. (1987) 'The impact of CETA programs on earnings: A review of the literature'. *Journal of Human Resources*, 22, 157–193.

Becker, G. (1975) *Human Capital*. Chicago: University of Chicago Press.

Behrman, J., and Birdsall, N. (1985) 'The quality of schooling: Quantity alone is misleading'. *American Economic Review*, 73 (December), 928–946.

Benson, C. (1995) 'Educational financing'. In M. Carnoy (ed.) *The International Encyclopedia of Economics of Education*. Oxford: Pergamon Press, 408–412.

Berger, S. and Piore, M. (1980) *Dualism and Discontinuity in Industrial Societies*. Cambridge: Cambridge University Press.

Blackmore, J. and Spaull, A. (1987) 'Australian teacher unionism: New directions'. In W. Boyd and D. Smart (eds) *Educational Policy in Australia and America: Comparative Perspectives*. New York: Falmer Press.

Blaug, M. (1982) 'The distributional effects of higher education subsidies'. *Economics of Education Review*, 2 (3), 209–231.

Blaug, M. (1985) 'Where are we now in the economics of education?' *Economics of Education Review*, 4 (1), 17–28.

Blueston, B. (1990) 'The impact of schooling and industrial restructuring on recent trends in wage inequality in the United States'. *American Economic Review*, 80 (2), 303–307.

Bowles, S. and Gintis, H. (1976) *Schooling in Capitalist America*. New York: Basic Books.

Bratsberg, B. (1995) 'The incidence of non-return among foreign students in the United States'. *Economics of Education Review*, 14 (4), 373–384.

Bray, M. and Lillis, K. (eds) (1988) *Community Financing of Education: Issues and Policy Implications in Less Developed Countries*. Oxford: Pergamon Press.

Brown, B. and Saks, D. (1987) 'The microeconomics of the allocation of teachers: Time and student learning'. *Economics of Education Review*, 6 (4), 319–332.

Carnoy, M. (1995a) 'Education and the international division of labour'. In M. Carnoy (ed.) *The International Encyclopedia of Economics of Education*. Oxford: Pergamon, 211–217.

Carnoy, M. (ed.) (1995b) *The International Encyclopedia of Economics of Education*. Oxford: Pergamon Press.

Carnoy, M. and Levin, H. (1985) *Schooling and Work in the Democratic State*. Stanford, CA: Stanford University Press.

Chiswick, B. (1987) 'Race earnings differentials'. In G. Psacharopoulos (ed.) *Economics of Education: Research and Studies*. Oxford: Pergamon Press, 232–237.

Clune, W. and Witte, J. (1990) *Choice and Control in American Education*. London: Falmer Press.

Cohn, E. and Geske, T. (1990) *Economics of Education*. Oxford: Pergamon.

Coleman, J., Campbell, E., Hobson, C., McPartland, J., Mood, A., Weinfall, F. and York, R. (1966) *Equality of Educational Opportunity*. Washington, DC: US Government Printing Press.

Coombs, P. and Ahmed, M. (1974) *Attacking Rural Poverty: How Nonformal Education Can Help*. Baltimore: Johns Hopkins University Press.

Correa, H. and Gruver, G. (1987) 'Teacher–student interaction: A game theoretic extension of the economic theory of education'. *Mathematical Social Sciences*, 13, 19–47.

Cuban, L. (1986) *Teachers and Machines: The Classroom Uses of Technology since 1920*. New York: Teachers College Press.

DeFreitas, G., Marsden, D. and Ryan, P. (1991) 'Youth employment patterns in segmented labor markets in the US and Europe'. *Eastern Economic Journal*, 17 (2), 223–236.

Denison, E. (1979) *Accounting for Slower Economic Growth: The United States in the 1970s*. Washington, DC: The Brookings Institution.

Doeringer, P. and Piore, M. (1971) *Internal Labour Market and Manpower Analysis*. Lexington, MA: D.C. Heath.

Dolton, P. (1996) 'Modelling the labour market for teachers: Some lessons from the UK'. *Education Economics*, 4 (2), 187–205.

Duclaud-Williams, R. (1985) 'Teacher unions and educational policy in France'. In M. Lawn (ed.) *The Politics of Teacher Unionism: International Perspectives*. London: Croom Helm.

Ebert, R. and Stone, J. (1984) *Unions and Public Schools: The Effect of Collective Bargaining on American Education*. Lexington, MA: Lexington Books.

Eicher, J., Hawkridge, D., McAnany, E., Mariet, F. and Orivel, F. (eds) (1982) *The Economics of New Educational Media*. Paris: UNESCO.

Eraut, M. (1989) 'Specifying and using objectives'. In M. Eraut (ed.) *The International Encyclopedia of Educational Technology*. Oxford: Pergamon Press.

Ferber, M. (1995) 'Gender differences in earnings'. In M. Carnoy (ed.) (1995). *The International Encyclopedia of Economics of Education*. Oxford: Pergamon Press.

Flynn, P. (1988) *Facilitating Technological Change: The Human Resource Challenge*. Cambridge, MA: Ballinger.

Freeman, R. and Medoff, J. (1984). *What Do Unions Do?* New York: Basic Books.

Friedman, M. (1962) 'The role of government in education'. In M. Friedman, *Capitalism and Freedom*. Chicago, IL: University of Chicago Press.

Goldhaber, D. (1996) 'Public and private high schools: Is school choice an answer to the productivity problem?' *Economics of Education Review*, 15 (2), 93–109.

Groot, W. (1995) 'Type-specific returns to enterprise-related training'. *Economics of Education Review*, 14 (4), 323–333.

Grubel, H. and Scott, A. (1977) *The Brain Drain: Determinants, Measurement, and Welfare Effects*. Waterloo: Wilfred Laurier University Press.

Hamilton, S. (1990) *Apprenticeship for Adulthood: Preparing Youth for the Future*. New York: Free Press.

Hansen, L. (1983) 'Impact of financial aid and access'. In J. Froomkin (ed.) *The Crisis in Higher Education*. New York: Political Academic of Science.

Hanushek, E. (1989) 'The impact of differential expenditures on school performance'. *Educational Researcher*, 18 (4), 45–52, 62.

Hartmann, H. (1987) 'Internal labor markets and gender: A case study of promotion'. In C. Brown and J. Pechman (eds) *Gender in the Workplace*. Washington, DC: Brookings Institution.

Hartog, J. (1981) 'Wages and allocation under imperfection information'. *De Economist*, 129, 311–323.

Hedges, L., Laine, R. and Greenwald, R. (1994) 'Does money matter? A meta-analysis of studies of the effects of differential school inputs on student outcomes'. *Educational Researcher*, 23 (3), 5–14.

Hellerstein, J. and Neumark, D. (1995) 'Are earnings profiles steeper than productivity profiles? Evidence from Israeli firm-level data'. *Journal of Human Resources*, XXX (1), 89–109.

Heyneman, S. and Loxley, W. (1983) 'The effect of school quality on academic achievement across 29 high- and low-income countries'. *American Journal of Sociology*, 88 (6), 1162–1194.

Hicks, N. (1980) 'Is there a tradeoff between growth and basic needs?' *Finance and Development*, 17 (2), 17–20.

Hinchliffe, K. (1995) 'Education and the labor market'. In M. Carnoy (ed.). *The International Encyclopedia of Economics of Education*. Oxford: Pergamon, 20–24.

Hough, J. (1994) 'Educational cost-benefit analysis'. *Education Economics*, 2 (2), 93–128.

Inter-Agency Commission (1990) *Education for All*. New York: Inter-Agency Commission.

James, E. (1987) 'The public/private division of responsibility for education: An international comparison'. *Economics of Education Review*, 6 (1), 1–14.

Jamison, D. and Orivel, F. (1982) 'The cost-effectiveness of distance education for school equivalency'. In H. Peraton (ed.) *Alternative Routes to Formal Education: Distance Education for School Equivalency*. Baltimore, MD: Johns Hopkins University Press.

Kirby, S., Grissmer, D. and Hudson, L. (1991) *New and Returning Teachers in Indiana: Sources of Supply*. Santa Monica, CA: The Rand Corporation.

Klees, S. (1995) 'Economics of educational technology'. In M. Carnoy (ed.) *The International Encyclopedia of Economics of Education*. Oxford: Pergamon, 398–406.

Leslie, L. and Brinkman, P. (1988) *The Economic Values of Higher Education*. New York: Macmillan.

Levin, H. (1987) 'Improving productivity through education and technology'. In G. Burke and R. Rumberger (eds) *The Future Impact of Technology on Work and Education*. London: The Falmer Press, 194–214.

Levin, H. (1991) 'The economics of education choice'. *Economics of Education Review*, 10 (2), 137–158.

Levin, H. (1993) 'The economics of education for at-risk students'. In E. Hoffman (ed.) *Essays on the Economics of Education*. Kalamazoo, MI: W. E. Upjohn Institute for Employment Research, 11–33.

Levin, H. (1995) 'Cost-effectiveness analysis'. In M. Carnoy (ed.) *The International Encyclopedia of Economics of Education*. Oxford: Pergamon, 381–386.

Lillard, L. and Willis, R. (1994) 'Intergenerational educational mobility: Effects of family and state in Malaysia'. *Journal of Human Resources*, XXIX (4), 1126–1166.

Middleton, J., Ziderman, A. and Van Adams, A. (1993) *Skills for Productivity: Vocational Education and Training in Developing Countries*. Oxford: Oxford University Press.

Mincer, J. (1974) *Schooling, Experience, and Earnings*. New York: Columbia University Press.

Monk, D. (1990) *Educational Finance: An Economic Approach*. New York: McGraw-Hill.

Moock, P. and Addou, P. (1995) 'Agriculture productivity and education'. In M. Carnoy (ed.). *The*

International Encyclopedia of Economics of Education. Oxford: Pergamon, 130–140.

Murnane, R., Singer, J. Willett, J., Kemple, J. and Olsen, R. (1991) *Who Will Teach: Policies that Matter*. Cambridge, MA: Harvard University Press.

Nettleton, G. (1991) 'Uses and costs of educational technology for distance education in developing countries'. In M. Lockheed, J. Middleton and G. Nettleton (eds) *Education Technology: Sustainable and Effective Use*. Washington, DC: World Bank.

Odden, A. and Kotowski, N. (1992) 'Financing public school choice: Policy issues and options'. In A. Odden (ed.) *Rethinking School Finance*. San Francisco, CA: Jossey-Bass, 225–259.

Park, K. (1996) 'Educational expansion and educational inequality on income distribution'. *Economics of Education Review*, 15 (1), 51–58.

Pritchett, L. (1996) 'Where has all the education gone?' Washington, DC: Policy Research Working Paper 1581, Poverty and Human Resource Division, the World Bank.

Psacharopoulos, G. (1984) 'The contribution of education to economic growth'. In J. Kendrick (ed.) *International Comparisons of Productivity and Causes of the Slowdown*. Cambridge, MA: Ballinger, 335–355.

Psacharopoulos, G. (1994) 'Returns to investment in education: A global update'. *World Development*, 22 (9), 1325–43.

Purkey, S. and Smith, M. (1983) 'Effective schools: A review'. *Elementary School Journal*, 83, 427–452.

Ram, R. (1990) 'Educational expansion and schooling inequality: International evidence and some implications'. *Review of Economics and Statistics*, 62, 266–274.

Reich, M., Gordon, D. and Edwards, R. (1973) 'Dual labor market: A theory of labor market segmentation'. *American Economic Review*, 50 (May), 359–365.

Rumberger, R. (1981) *Overeducation in the US Labor Market*. New York: Praeger.

Rumberger, R. and Levin, H. (1989) 'Schooling for the modern workplace'. In Commission on Workplace Quality and Labor Market Efficiency. *Investing in People: A Strategy for Addressing America's Workforce Crisis* (Background papers, vol. 1). Washington, DC: US Department of Labor.

Ryan, P. (1981) 'Segmentation duality, and the internal labour market'. In F. Wilkinson (ed.) *The Dynamics of Labour Market Segmentation*. Cambridge: Cambridge University Press.

Ryoo, J., Nam, Y. and Carnoy M. (1993) 'Changing rates of return to education over time. A Korean case study'. *Economics of Education Review*, 12 (1), 71–80.

Schultz, T. (1971) *Investment in Human Capital*. New York: The Free Press.

Spence, M. (1973) 'Job market signaling'. *Quarterly Journal of Economics*, 87 (3), 355–374.

Spenner, K. (1988) 'Technological change, skill requirements and education: The case for uncertainty'. In R. Cyert and D. Mowery (eds) *The Impact of Technological Change on Employment and Economic Growth*. Cambridge, MA: Ballinger.

Stern, D. and Ritzen, M. (1991) (eds) *Market Failure in Training? New Economic Analysis and Evidence on Training of Adult Employees*. Berlin: Springer-Verlag.

Timmermann, D. (1983) 'Financing mechanisms: Their impact on postcompulsory education'. In H. Levin and H. Schutze (eds) *Financing Recurrent Education*. Beverly Hills, CA: Sage.

Tsang, M. (1988) 'Cost analysis for policymaking in education: A review of cost studies in education in developing countries'. *Review of Educational Research*, 58 (2), 181–230.

Tsang, M. (1995) 'Public and private costs of schooling in developing countries'. In M. Carnoy (ed.) *The International Encyclopedia of Economics of Education*. Oxford: Pergamon, 393–398.

Tsang, M. and Levin, H. (1985) 'The economics of overeducation'. *Economics of Education Review*, 4 (2), 93–104.

Tueros, M. (1995) 'Education and informal labor markets'. In M. Carnoy (ed.) (1995). *The International Encyclopedia of Economics of Education*. Oxford: Pergamon.

Windham, D. (1995) 'International financing of education'. In M. Carnoy (ed.) *The International Encyclopedia of Economics of Education*. Oxford: Pergamon, 433–438.

Woodhall, M. (1988) 'Designing a student-loan scheme for a developing country: The relevance of international experience'. *Economics of Education Review*, 7 (1), 153–161.

World Bank (1993) *The East Asian Miracle*. Oxford: Oxford University Press.

World Bank (1995) *Priorities and Strategies for Education: A World Bank Review*. Washington, DC: World Bank.

9

ARE WE POST-MODERN YET?

Historical and theoretical explorations in
comparative education

Esther E. Gottlieb

INTRODUCTION

Comparative education (CE), a relatively young field in the 'sciences' of education, strongly tied to modernisation projects in colonies and non-Westernised countries, has recently experienced attempts to take on a more post-modern posture. Such attempts follow over 50 years of knowledge production under the domination of functionalism, with modernisation theory in sociology and human capital theory in economics being the main theoretical underpinning of comparative education. The calls for 'new ways of knowing' dating from the late 1980s have only become more insistent as this century nears its end, while the political and economic interests in education continue as strong as ever. In this chapter I hope not only to review the intellectual history of comparative education but also to show that we comparativists are not yet fully post-modern.

Comparative education has always been an interdisciplinary field of study like comparative religion, comparative economics, comparative government and comparative law. It applies historical, philosophical and social theories and methods from a wide variety of disciplines to the study of education worldwide. From the study of similarities and differences of school systems in several countries, comparative education moved to an attempt to be an objective, analytic, scientific field. This approach was stimulated by a practical consideration: the increasing demand for using education as an instrument of social, economic and political development, especially in the new nations formed after the Second World War.

From a theoretical perspective, comparative education sought to challenge the traditional study of education by using concepts and techniques from the social sciences, especially anthropology, sociology, political science and economics as they were shaping up at the end of the nineteenth century. To advocate the use of such social science methods and techniques implies conceiving of scientific comparative education as dealing with objective, measurable and concrete levels of reality which, in principle at least, existed independently of the observer. The comparative researcher's objective is to reveal all the relationships preferences or ideologies (Anderson, 1961, p. 2). 'To study education well is to study it comparatively' became the motto of comparative education (Adams, 1966, p. 1).

Comparative research tends to involve the study of patterns and processes where characteristics of an elementary part are compared across two or more research situations (i.e. countries). The question is whether the characteristics of two or more elementary parts, two or more relationships, or two or more patterns can be said to differ or to be the same. The emphasis in enquiry is on the study of the interrelationships between the elementary parts, which are assumed to be interdependent within the whole. This amounts to two different strategies: either the emphasis falls on providing an account of wholes and the need to describe holistic qualities, or it falls on the decomposition into parts and a comparison and further examination of the characteristics of a part in two or more situations.

Looking back from the vantage-point of the present, over nearly 50 years of comparative studies, we can observe, on one hand, fragmented and heterogeneous theorising, and on the other, an overwhelming functionalist orthodoxy in theory and practice alike. Like other fields of research in education, comparative education is overridden with arguments over different research paradigms and tensions between theory building and the training of the next cadre of researchers, professors, and education planners at universities, with international agencies, major foundations and bilateral donors all promoting 'human resources development' and calling on research to serve practice, policy formation and implementation.

Starting with a history of comparative education, this chapter will next outline major theories and studies in CE within dominant paradigms, then review examples of international large studies in CE and finally conclude with a view ahead, asking what issues the field is facing at the turn of the century.

HISTORY: THE CREATION OF A FIELD

Building an alliance with social sciences

Marc-Antoine Jullien is credited with originating comparative education when in 1816 and 1817 he published five articles outlining a method of investigating education in different countries. Standardised questionnaires were to be used to collect data, and findings were to be analysed into comprehensive tables so that differences and similarities would be apparent (Fraser, 1964). Jullien's ambition for this new field to be 'an almost science' that took into account factors outside the school in order to understand education was vigorously embraced after the Second World War.

The growing importance of foreign markets, along with improved transportation and communication systems, led to a new view of the interdependent and complex nature of social problems. Simplistic explanations and causal relationships for observed phenomena were no longer acceptable. The response of professional practices such as education was to apply the theory and methods of social sciences to educational concerns. In the 1950s, new texts appeared from early twentieth-century pioneers of comparative education, such as the third edition of Hans' *Comparative Education: A Study of Educational Factors and Traditions* (1958), and Kandel's *The New Era in Education: A Comparative Study* (1955). While Hans (1959) and Kandel (1959), set the example of using derivative conceptual frameworks in the effort to legitimise comparative enquiry, the conclusions they deduced – that the national system of education embodied the historical roots and philosophical wisdom of their own society – were simplistic, subjective and totalistic. The newly emerging scholars in North America (at Columbia and New York Universities, at the time) embraced the dominant social paradigm of the late 1950s and early 1960s, structural functionalism, along with a positivist view of the possibility of conducting empirical comparative research on educational questions. It was these scholars who established comparative education as a 'scientific' field of study (Bereday, 1958, 1964; Brickman 1956, 1960; Eckstein and Noah, 1969). In Britain, Brian Holmes published 'The problem approach in comparative education' (1958), using John Dewey's method of reflective thinking and Popper's critical dualism. Aligning himself with the practice of educational policy-making, Holmes had reached the conclusion that positivism was not a framework within which he wished to develop research methods in comparative education (Holmes, 1981, p. 13). In spite of the coherence of Holmes's 'problem-solving approach' to comparative education, researchers such as Edmund King in his classic study, *Other Schools and Ours: A Comparative Study for Today* (1958), objected to the narrow scope of Holmes's perspective. This search to secure a knowledge base that would legitimise the authority and hence the prestige of the educational professional units within the academy, moved comparative educators to continue to develop an objective theory of education by combining the study of societal education relations with the scientific method. Structural functionalism and its variants, modernisation theory and human capital theory, hold out the promise of putting the field on an objective footing.

The growth of comparative education centres at a few research universities provided, for the first time, international visibility for the schools of education that housed them. Most notable amongst these was the Comparative Education Center at the University of Chicago, founded in 1958. The new Director, C. Arnold (a sociologist), Mary Jean Bowman (an economist), and Philip Foster (Anderson's PhD student at the time, who had studied economics, sociology and anthropology at the London School of Economics), together with their new students (who took classes in all the social sciences but worked on graduate degrees in comparative education), established a prominent new presence in the field. They and their students produced and are still producing one of the most significant bodies of research in CE emphasising social scientific applications, in particular the role of education in economic and social development (Anderson, 1961, 1977; Anderson and Bowman, 1965, 1968; Bowman, 1966; Foster, 1960, 1965a, 1965b).

Other major university centres followed Teachers College and Chicago: Syracuse University's Center for Development Education, and Stanford University's Stanford International Development Education Committee (SIDEC). The University of Pittsburgh's International and Development Education Program (IDEP) and centres at other mid-west public institutions such as Kent State University, University of Michigan, the University of Wisconsin, SUNY Buffalo and later at Albany. In the 1970s programmes were developed at Harvard University (Harvard Institute for International Development), the University of California at Los Angeles and Florida State.[1]

This proliferation of programmes was a consequence of CE becoming strongly connected to the project of development and the Cold War agenda. At a conference on 'Education and the Development of Nations' held in 1963 at Syracuse, Don Adams (a graduate of the University of Connecticut, who had worked with the Parsonian sociologist Robert

Bjork; see Adams and Bjork, 1971) coined the term 'Development Education'. It focused on institutional and sector change in less developed countries, and subsequently came to refer to 'studies and policies of relationships between education and external process of development' (Adams, 1977, p. 296).

Institutional building

While the above description has centred on the development of CE as an intellectual field at universities and research institutions, after the Second World War, two other institutional developments contributed to shaping the field:

1 the organisation of the discipline through the establishment of professional societies; and
2 the interest of international agencies, major foundations activities and bilateral donor organisations in actively participating in educational planning, reform and implementation in relation to economic development and nation-building.

Both professional organisations and international agencies established formal channels in the form of conferences, journals and proceedings, to accumulate, document, exchange and distribute comparative education's theoretical and practical knowledge. Among these professional developments were the following:

- *The Year Book of Education*, published annually by The University of London, Institute of Education, took on a new dimension in 1954 by being jointly edited with Teachers College, Columbia. This volume, which was devoted to Education and Technology Development, addressed the role, successes and failures of bilateral and multilateral aid assistance programmes in education. As Holmes noted: 'Undoubtedly this was a pioneering comparative study, the quality of which has rarely been surpassed in the subsequent literature dealing with educational planning in what we choose to call developing countries or countries of the Third World' (Holmes, 1981, p. 7).
- In 1954 William Brickman began annual conferences at New York University on various aspects of comparative education (Brickman, 1956). Two years later, in 1956, the Comparative and International Education Society (CIES) was established.[2]
- The journal *Comparative Education Review* (CER) was established in 1957 as the official journal of the CIES under the editorship of George Z. F. Bereday of Teachers College, Columbia University. A peer-reviewed journal, CER is published quarterly by the University of Chicago.[3] The Journal is distributed to 1,327 institutional subscribers (735 US and 592 from other countries) and to 974 individuals (707 from the US and 267 from other countries) (Epstein, 1992).
- The Comparative Education Society in Europe (CESE) was founded in 1961 during a meeting organised by Joseph Lauwerys at the University of London School of Education. The general assembly of the CESE meets once every two years. First published in the autumn of 1964, the British-based journal *Comparative Education* was an idea of Bill Halls and Edmund King. Published by Carfax, it has an all-British editorial board.
- The World Council of Comparative Education Societies (WCCES) was conceived by Joseph Katz, in conjunction with the International Education Year which was declared

by UNESCO as 1970. WCCES comprises 28 national Comparative Societies from every continent. Nevertheless, countries of the southern hemisphere participate less than those of the northern, a factor that is beginning to be addressed by holding the 1998 congress in South Africa.

• The British Comparative and International Education Society became independent of the European society in the 1970. *Compare* is the official journal of the British society.

In 1977 the third World Congress of Comparative Education Societies met in London and the field's status and development was on the agenda. Both *Comparative Education* and *Comparative Education Review* (CER) published special issues, the *Comparative Education* issue being devoted to 'Comparative Education – its Present and Future Prospects,' celebrating 13 years of publishing, while CER published a double issue 'The State of the Art: Twenty Years of Comparative Education' with an image on the cover of Humpty Dumpty sitting on a perch of building blocks labelled 'structural functionalism', 'pedagogy', 'production' and 'development'. As Ross *et al.* (1992) observed, this picture suited the field on its twentieth anniversary, when 'comparative educators stood on shifting ground with thinkers from virtually every social science discipline' intensely debating the nature, purpose and consequences of CE. The brilliant metaphor of a worried-looking Humpty Dumpty on the CER cover of the special issue reveals the precarious circumstances in which comparative education found itself at that time. Those circumstances would become increasingly precarious over the next ten years.

In addition to comparative education's academic institutionalisation, its growth has been stimulated by the many organisations whose existence or acts do not depend on the will of the nation state. The interest of such organisations in education is not new; religious organisations (such as the Roman Catholic Church) have had their own vested interest in education on a global scale for many years. However, new organisations were formed after the Second World War specifically to deal with the decolonised and the newly established nations, to maintain the peace efforts, and preserve the arrangements of the geographic divisions between the Eastern and the Western blocs. These new international composites, in exchange for influence on policy, offer the following to public education systems:

1 general funding for education;
2 funding for specific studies or projects;
3 building of physical facilities;
4 conferences and travel for teachers;
5 donation of books and equipment;
6 technical expertise in educational planning and implementation (Reiffers, 1982).

A few of the best-known agencies operating in education on a global scale are:

• *United Nations Educational, Scientific and Cultural Organisation* (UNESCO) which was created at the founding conference held in London in 1946. The members are states who share the belief in 'full and equal opportunities of education for all'. The organisation is charged with the task of advancing and diffusing knowledge and mutual understanding. In 1949 UNESCO formally adopted the concept of development and launched a technical assistance programme devoted to education. National authorities decide on educational action, while UNESCO undertakes fund-raising and sponsors research and information exchange among member countries with respect to innovation and planned change. UNESCO is involved in the efforts to develop international educational indicators; its *Statistical Yearbook* and *World Education Report* are widely distributed, and its data are used as a basis for comparison in many research studies and in decision-making on international aid and loans. UNESCO publishes two journals which often feature comparative studies: *International Review of Education* and *Prospects*.

- *Organisation for Economic Co-operation and Development* (OECD), founded in 1961 as an instrument for international co-operation among 24 industrialised member countries. Its activities are geared to assist in promoting economic growth, employment, and the sound and harmonious development of world economy (OECD, 1971). Most OECD work is prepared in over 200 committees, including an education committee and a Centre for Educational Research and Innovation (CERI). The educational programmes of the OECD reflect changing educational concerns since the 1960s. Early work was directed at the relationship between education and manpower planning. From equality and questions of access and social demand for education in the 1970s, issues have moved to quality of education and post-secondary education in the 1980s. OECD is involved, along with UNESCO and other international testing agencies, in the efforts to develop international educational indicators (Bottani *et al.*, 1992). Projects produced a considerable body of publications distributed from Paris and announced via an OECD newsletter, called *Innovations in Education*.

- *Carnegie, Ford, Rockefeller and other major US foundations*   These were among the first non-religious organisations to be involved in spreading Western schooling to nations of Africa, Asia and Latin America. Foundation officers viewed the extension of democratically grounded education as crucial to the stability, prosperity and orderly development of these nations (Arnove, 1982). Foundations made donations to invest in education and sponsored research studies that demonstrated the powerful linkages between education, economic growth and national development. For example, early on, the Carnegie Corporation worked with the British Ministry of Overseas Development in the former British colonies, focusing on African teacher education and linking up African institutions with Columbia University's Teachers College in Africa (Berman, 1983). Columbia was given broad latitude in administrative and programmatic aspects of the programme (see above Teachers College, Columbia's contribution to the establishment of comparative education). The Ford Foundation funds educational projects nowadays in a great many conflict-ridden regions around the world; for example, they have funded educational peace activities in Israel, a few large educational programmes in South Africa, and teacher training and reconstruction in Bosnia. Although programmes have changed in the course of the past 50 years, the direction of Foundation funding has shared comparative education's faith in the ability of social sciences to help the nations in Africa, Asia and Latin America hasten societal development through the expansion of mass education.

- *National and multinational aid agencies*   The highly visible role of foundations should not overshadow the involvement of both national and multinational aid agencies, which have increasingly advocated similar policies while simultaneously underwriting research studies to show the relationship that education programmes have to economic and social development. Multinationals involved in educational funding include the

World Bank, the Asian Development Bank and the United Nations Development Program. Such undertakings are not part of the past. An Asian Development Bank (ADB) technical working paper of April 1998 on 'Education and national development in Asia', directly addressed education and economic growth; education and poverty reduction; education, social change and social cohesion, using UNESCO, World Bank and ADB data. The report concludes with recommendations on how the Bank can develop more effective assistance to national systems of education. The Asian Development Bank, mostly controlled by Japan, is used for regional diffusion of primarily Japanese ideas about education and development (Cummings, 1997).

Bilateral groups, such as the United States Aid for International Development (USAID) and the British Ministry of Overseas Development, pursue their own educational programmes in view of national policy in the US and Britain, respectively. Such agencies work directly with ministries of education in the host countries, while employing a host of consultants who bid on these projects and the work overseas. The shifts of focus in grant-giving mirror the shift in CE research projects.[4] Thus we can observe educational programmes and funding expanding from infrastructure projects in the 1950s to early 1960s to include school construction in the late 1960s; teacher education, textbook printing, distance education, non-formal education and rural development in the mid-1970s; and improving the efficiency of education systems, the effectiveness of education systems and educational quality in the 1980s.

The World Bank and other international assistance agencies directly affect policy and practice in education in a few ways:

- by providing loans only for bank-specified programmes;
- by establishing conditions that must be met before loans can be implemented;
- by hiring the foreign consultants to help plan and implement the project;
- by providing overseas training and education at institutions approved by the Bank;
- by organising exchange among policy-makers in various countries;
- by using research to justify recommendations for specific programmes (Samoff, 1993).

Such institutional arrangements and activities are directly relevant to the history of comparative education. Comparative educators act as policy-makers and consultants for international agencies, foundations and donor agencies, as well as academics and practitioners. Their backgrounds reflect not just the historical development of international agencies and foundations that fund research and educational developments, but also the tensions that have characterised the social studies in their attempt to become scientific.

The next section describes comparative education's theoretical frameworks, competing methodologies and some of the claims that research studies have made.

THEORETICAL EXPLORATIONS IN COMPARATIVE EDUCATION

University programmes in comparative education as well as significant research in the sociology and economic aspects of education have their origins in theories of development. This postwar discourse of the social and political scientists who played such a significant role in the Cold War, introduced the concepts of 'development' and 'underdevelopment'. The social scientists were guided by the conviction that the US and the 'West' stood at a crossroads, their future determined by competition with the Soviet Union in the Third World, and this conviction had a direct impact on the analysis of development (Gendzier, 1985). The fear of a 'socialist development' shaped the thinking and the language of planning strategies of education for the 'uncommitted areas of the world'. The 'new nations' drew the attention of US policy-makers concerned with the claim that Marxism presented a better and logical road to incorporation into the modern world. 'They also captured the attention and imagination of US scholars who, in pursuit of knowledge as well as the desire to influence appropriate governmental policy, began to produce a vast body of literature on the "developing" nations' (Valenzuela and Valenzuela, 1979, p. 31).

The question of comparative education as a field of study has been widely documented (e.g. Burns and Welch, 1992; Eckstein and Noah, 1969; Fagerlind and Saha, 1983; Paulston, 1977, 1992; Schriewer and Holmes, 1988). Researchers (including myself) in the International Development Education Project (IDEP, 1985–1987) at the University of Pittsburgh, led by Professors Don Adams, Rolland Paulston and John Singleton, identified four broad intellectual paradigms within which knowledge CE was produced. These paradigms – functionalist, radical structuralist, radical humanist and interpretive – each represents a separate socio-scientific reality with regard to the nature of science and of society; therefore educational planning, policy and implementation in each is differently elaborated. 'By analyzing the four paradigms in which knowledge of comparative education had been constructed, we can provide a map for a retrospective account (an intellectual history) of theoretical studies in comparative education' (Gottlieb, 1988). Of the four paradigms, functionalism has dominated most of the production of knowledge over the past 50 years of comparative education.

The intellectual 'imperialism' of functionalism in comparative education

Kuhn's assertion that science begins with the emergence of a dominant paradigm describes the situation of comparative education. The functionalist paradigm dominated the social sciences at the time when comparative education was articulated in the 1950s and 1960s. Any articulation of competing worldviews within the field had to face the hegemony of the functionalist paradigm and its intellectual 'imperialism'. Functionalism's capacity to incorporate other perspectives through strategies of co-optation have contributed to its lasting vigour. Modernisation theory in sociology and human capital theory in economics have provided the main functionalist theoretical frameworks for comparative education.

Modernisation

Sociologists have defined modernisation variously, but always within the framework of an evolutionary perspective which involves a multilinear transition of developing societies from tradition to modernity. Hoselitz, founder and editor of *Economic Development and Cultural Change*, conceptualised the problem by asking whether modernisation is only the acquisition of new skills and the exercise of new forms of productivity, or also 'accompanied by or contingent upon more basic changes in social relations, and even the structure of values and beliefs of a culture' (Hoselitz, 1952, p. 8). Education as an agent of social change thus becomes an obvious focus of attention, and the way was opened to such constructs as 'individual modernity' (Inkeles, 1969; Lerner, 1958). Individual modernity is the process by which individuals supposedly change from a traditional way of life to a rapidly changing, urban, technological way of life. Alex Inkeles and his Harvard project, 'Making men modern: On the causes and consequences of individual change in six developing countries', produced a scale on which to measure modernity in terms of a number of psychological variables supposedly constituting the typical modern man. All the original studies of individual modernity (Inkeles, 1969; Inkeles and Smith, 1974; Lerner, 1958) took education into account as one of the influences on individual modernity; the Harvard study found education to be the most powerful factor in making 'man modern'.

Human capital theory

Drawn from economics, and given impetus by the urgent search for capital formation and means of economic development in developing countries, human capital theory, more than any other theoretical construct, had a profound influence on concepts of the place of education in Third World modernisation and development. 'The human investment revolution in economic thought, ' as Mary Jean Bowman (1966, p. 111) called it, took over the study of the economics of education with surprising rapidity. Although it was already known that resources devoted to the human component of capital could be considered investments, just how to measure human capital was an open question of economic analysis. The view of education as an investment in future income was elaborated during the 1960s with formulae and calculations. The major methodological procedure in estimating the educational stock of human capital remains that of Schultz's *The Economic Value of Education* (1963). Education was conceived of as both an indicator of modernisation (as in studies of individual modernity, and as a parameter of 'nation-building') and as an initiator of further social change.

Methods

By perpetually preoccupying themselves with methodological questions, development specialists have allowed their agenda to be determined by the agenda of functionalism, which tends to reduce the issues in the social science disciplines to methodological ones (data-gathering and data-analysis). An example is the debate over how to calculate rate of return to investment in education. This 20 year old debate has focused on the accuracy of data from Third World countries, or on what should count as indicators of the impact of education on economic growth (Psacharopoulos, 1973, 1985, 1994). By focusing on such methodological questions, the participants in the debate are distracted from the substantive question of whether there is, after all, a causal relation between schooling and the higher productivity of labour (Carnoy, 1985, p. 161).

A large proportion of empirical research in comparative education (e.g. costs and/or benefits measures, measuring individual modernity, manpower planning techniques) incorporates methods and techniques taken directly from neoclassical economics using quasi-experimental statistical methods.

> In education, most quantitative studies of the effects of educational inputs on outputs – or of educational attainment on outcomes like income, unemployment, job satisfaction, or productivity – are now using regression analysis techniques. There are both theoretical and empirical reasons to argue that such methods provide no useful information.
>
> (Klees, 1986, p. 599)

The functionalist distinctions between macro and micro theories, and between relating to society, the organisation, the institution, the group and the individual, tended to obscure much more important assumptions about what model of society theorists use to underwrite their analyses, let alone assumptions about ontology and epistemology. A field like comparative education, which sought to align itself with the social sciences, could not escape the paradigm wars that have erupted in the disciplines of sociology, economics and later in anthropology (Brown, 1977; McCloskey, 1985; Marcus and Cushman, 1982). The elaboration of conflict theory and dependency theory as an alternative to functionalism, and the promotion of ethnographic methods and other forms of qualitative research as an alternative to the positivism and scientism of mainstream comparative research, defined the terms for much of the paradigmatic conflicts that dominated the field in the 1980s (Epstein, 1983; Kelly and Altbach, 1986; Masemann, 1982).

Radical theories of comparative education

Contrary to the claims of liberal theorists and historians that education offers possibilities for individual cognitive development, social mobility and political and economic opportunities, radical theorists have argued that the main functions of schools in capitalist societies are (a) the reproduction of the dominant patterns of wealth and power and their forms of knowledge and (b) the transfer of skills needed to reproduce the social division of labour (see Bowles, 1972; Bowles and Gintis, 1976). In the radical structuralist perspective, schools as institutions can only be understood through an analysis of their relation to the state and the economy at large (see Carnoy, 1972, 1985). Marxist and neo-communists, sociologists and philosophers have made the state a primary focus of the analysis of education's economic relations. In their discussions, attention to the capitalist economy and state apparatuses reveals how schools 'functioned as agencies of social and cultural reproduction – that is, how they legitimated capitalist rationality and sustained dominant social practices' (Aronowitz and Giroux, 1985, p. 69). International dependence as part of a world system has implications well beyond economic structures, as Wallerstein (1974) has argued. Martin Carnoy presented one of the first major efforts at describing formal education within the context of international imperialism.

Carnoy argued that knowledge itself has been 'colonized', and that 'colonized knowledge perpetuates the hierarchical structure of society' (Carnoy, 1974). Bowles (1972), Levin (1974), Altbach (1977) and Arnove (1980) began to look at how educational systems serve societal groups differentially and how social inequalities are played out at the international level. They emphasised the relationship between education and the development of capitalist relations, and argued that the nature of economic systems and of state control make a difference in what schools teach and the outcomes of education. Thus, within international dependency theories, education was seen as part of the structure of dominance. Formal and informal linkages kept educational systems in the periphery tied to those in the centre. Legitimation of education objectives, curriculum and academic standards was given by the metropolitan centres. Imperialism, colonialism and a world economic system spread capitalism and its supporting form of education around the world.

In spite of significant differences among Marxists, neo-Marxists and dependency theorists regarding the historical and potential role of education and development, they have all shared two general views of education:

1 First, these scholars have rejected the traditional view in Western educational history, accepted by modernisation and human capital theorists, that education is a liberating and empowering experience. Radical structuralists have argued that, to the contrary, educational systems, primarily through 'screening' and allocation, assist in the development of a disciplined and compliant workforce for the modern economic sector which is controlled by the local bourgeoisie and, ultimately, by the world capitalist system. The educational system reproduces social inequality rather than offering opportunities for social mobility (see Weis, 1979, on Ghana). Legitimating societal roles, rather than education's cognitive teachings (as human capital theorists assume), constitutes the major linkage between schooling and the economy.

2 A second set of claims bears on education as an integral component of international capitalism. Western education is seen as a means explicitly used by the centre to control the periphery. Within the underdeveloped nations, educational systems are validated and legitimated by political authorities at local and national levels as appropriate for socialisation and certification purposes within a structure of international dependency (Berman, 1983).

Educational reforms initiated in the periphery could be expected to have little impact on economic development, since they would not affect the international division of labour (Arnove, 1980). Moreover, dependent education has specific negative economic and political consequences. Education helps to form markets in peripheral areas for economic and cultural products of the centre, since modernisation contributes to the formation of a consumer-goods orientation.

Education itself could be viewed as a commodity which the countries in the centre sell for profit. Furthermore, educational systems, through language, knowledge and values, open up markets for other commodities (Altbach and Kelly, 1978, pp. 301–330).

Comparative education within the radical structuralist paradigm accepts neither the functionalist construction of the real state of affairs nor the functionalist discourse in which it is constructed. Therefore the radical structuralist social educators recontextualise the familiar terms 'schooling' and 'education', integrating them into a new discursive context where their meaning is changed. In effect, to recontextualise a term is to create a metaphor, and the creation of new underlying metaphors has the potential of creating new knowledge. Carnoy's metaphor of 'education as cultural imperialism' is a powerful discursive tool for effecting a paradigm shift away from functionalism and for opening up new ways of thinking about education in non-Western settings (Gottlieb, 1989).

Radical humanism and the interpretive paradigms

The radical humanist paradigm is shaped by its positioning of a state of 'full humanity', which provides a universal point of departure from which to mount a critique of the present state of education and development. The discursive structure of the knowledge which this paradigm makes available for comparative educators is constructed by showing the gap between full humanity and the present state of alienation, as well as knowledge of the means by which this gap can be closed. Paolo Freire (1973), whose pedagogical philosophy involves consciousness-raising, helped comparative educators see the oppressive conditions to which the poor with whom he worked were subjected. By exposing and deconstructing the underlying metaphors of the oppressors' discourse (e.g. 'cultural invasion', 'education as banking' and 'people as things') and substituting them with liberating metaphors (e.g. 'revolution as dialogue'), Freire helped shape a new discourse of liberation whose ultimate reference is the posited state of 'full humanity' (Gottlieb and LaBelle, 1990). Freirean consciousness-raising is a timeless and non-linear process. This is why it was widely used both in Latin America and Africa for formal and non-formal education, and by the revolutionary movement in Nicaragua (LaBelle, 1987). Within this paradigm, educators and teachers have a different role in affecting social change, considering the learner as a political actor capable of transforming oppression.

The interpretive paradigm

Strictly speaking, there is neither theorising nor research in comparative education within the interpretive paradigm. This is because 'development', 'comparative' and 'education', as constructed in the functionalist, radical structuralist, and even in the radical humanist paradigms, are transcultural categories applicable throughout the world. Furthermore, these categories are backed up by the authority of 'grand theories' (Gendzier, 1985), whether modernisation theory, dependency theory or world economic system theory. By contrast, the interpretivist seeks to understand how the actors in a culture experience and understand their own social world, including those phenomena of that social world which a Westerner might describe under the categories of 'development' or 'development education'. The interpretivist, however, would resist using those Western categories, preferring to describe the cultural situation in terms of the actors' own categories and points of view. Thus, an interpretivist's research might well cover aspects of a culture which researchers in other paradigms would regard as belonging to comparative education, and his or her research might be of great interest and value to developmentalists, but he or she would not be likely either to conduct research or to theorise in terms of a transcultural category such as 'Development'. Anthropologists have challenged the validity of conventional depictions of 'cultural flow' in the light of examinations of the ways in which global processes have affected particular localities. Education too could readdress the status of 'global' and 'local' as organising terms of comparative knowledge (Fardon, 1995).

If we are to speculate about what an interpretive comparative education would be like, this can be done most conveniently by constructing a hypothetical agenda of issues which interpretivists working in an area of education in another country would be likely to address.

The first issue on such an agenda would be that of understanding education phenomena from the actor's point of view. This has implications especially for research methodology. Where researchers within other paradigms bring their own pre-established categories (e.g. 'individual modernity', 'social mobility', 'cultural imperialism') to the field and construct procedures that will yield data about those categories, researchers in the interpretive paradigm would attempt to observe the categories through which members of the observed culture give meaning to their own behaviour. Such categories are not imported from the West and imposed upon the non-Western culture, but 'negotiated' between the observer and the observed.

Thus, the interpretivist will not study education in the sense of linkages between education and processes of economic, social and political change, since these Western categories may be non-commensurable with those of the observed culture; rather he will attempt to grasp the meanings and interpretations that the 'actors' attach to phenomena which, in Western terms, might be assigned to the categories of 'education', 'economic change', etc.

In Paolo Freire's discourse, as we have seen, the peasant is allowed to express his own reality in his own words, yet here his voice is deprived of all historical and cultural specificity: he or she speaks with the voice of oppressed peoples in general, expressing a universal humanism and not a particular social and cultural reality. The interpretivist, by contrast, would attempt to open up the discourse to the voices of the actors themselves, expressing their own specific cultural realities authoritatively. Willis (1981), for example, in his account of working-class school-leavers in Britain, incorporates the discourse of his informants alongside his own ethnographic and theorising discourses in a collage of voices. Whether this involves sharing the authority of the text with the informants is an open question. Marcus and Cushman (1982, p. 44) see such 'experimental ethnography' as tending to give up interpretive authority, such as we find in traditional authoritative ethnography, and to become instead a 'mix of multiple negotiated realities . . . of dispersed authority'. This is a recognition of the authenticity of the subjective voice.

Interpretive methods offered comparative education quite a few new 'ways of knowing' (see Masemann, 1994). Nevertheless, so far very few have framed their research within such a theory. Feminist critique and post-modern knowledge have not informed research and practice in comparative education. Val Rust in his presidential address at the CIES annual conference in 1990 argued that post-modernism should be a central concept in comparative education (Rust, 1991). Both Rust's presidential address of 1990 and Paulston's 'invitation to post-modern social cartography' in his edited 1996 volume have had at best a slow trickle-down effect on the field. One of the problems with such calls for change is that they rarely involve analysis of cases, or educational planning using any of the research tools from post-modernism's toolkits. They only talk about the need to 'deconstruct meta-narratives' (Paulston, 1996, pp. 7–28), but who among the comparativists knows how to deconstruct? Or who would advise ministries of education and donor agencies on the idea and practice of 'development education' without modernisation and human capital theories or 'rates of return' to investment in education? The field is increasingly making gestures towards renovation of functionalism and showing symptoms of withdrawal from modernisation's meta-narratives, as can be seen in some of the 1999 CIES annual conference programme titles and symposia (see, http://www.ied.edu.hk/cric/cies99/draftp.htm). At that 1999 conference Paulston's work was again debated by students, younger and older colleagues alike, and he was honoured for his lifelong contribution to comparative education. Harold Noah and Max Eckstein, the founding fathers, and their many students (Paulston, among them) were honoured at the Columbia Teachers College Centennial Reception celebrating a hundred years' involvement in comparative and international education and marking the renaming of their programme as 'International and Transcultural Studies'. Such moves are not just ritualistic; they may in the long run effect a discursive turn.

Conclusion

What the paradigms of comparative education all share (or three out of four of them, at any rate; the case of the interpretive paradigm is problematic in this respect) is the category 'education' itself, and this permits educators from different paradigms to continue the conversation. Nevertheless implicitly, if not explicitly, each paradigm embodies incompatible answers to the question of the influence, role and values of Western education in the developing world. Within the functionalist paradigm, education is seen as a liberating and empowering experience, contributing to individual modernisation and national social change. Within the radical structuralist paradigm, by contrast, education is seen as assisting, through screening and allocation, in the preparation of a compliant workforce for the modern economic sectors, leaving the 'uneducated' in the non-modernised sectors. Here education reproduces social inequality rather than affording the opportunity for individual social mobility. Within the radical humanist paradigm, education in the developing countries is seen as part of the alienating institutions which drive a wedge between people and their true consciousness. A 'pedagogy of the oppressed' would seek to rehumanise education through dialogue and consciousness-raising.

It would be simplistic to conclude that lack of firm academic institutional structures led to the field's fragmentation with competing goals, theories, methodologies, claims and role ambiguity inherent in practice: scholar versus policy-maker, practitioner versus social scientist. The question is whether this fragmentation made it impossible for comparative educators to work or exchange information with one another given the different worldviews they embraced as an initial point of dialogue (Epstein, 1983), or whether this fragmentation indicated a commitment to diversity and openness to competing framing and research methodologies (Kelly and Altbach, 1986).

COMPARATIVE STUDIES

There are a few large comparative studies spanning almost 20 years that have remained outside the paradigm wars, mostly safely nested within positivistic research methods, applying statistical analysis to large, cross-national data sets. Two such groups of studies will be reviewed: one using the 'system' as the unit of analysis, the other using the individual students as the basic unit of enquiry. In addition some multi-country, US-funded projects will be mentioned in order to get a flavour of current issues in North American comparative research.

The expansion of mass education

One line of research on 'the world educational revolution' that seeks to explain the origins and expansion of mass education, has occupied comparativists at Stanford and their students for 20 years (Benavot and Riddle, 1988; Boli, 1989; Boli and Ramirez, 1992; Meyer *at al.*, 1977; Ramirez and Boli, 1987). According to Ramirez, mass schooling did not arise to meet a systematic need for better integrated populations as the social order theorists have asserted. Nor did the need for a disciplined labour force trigger mass schooling expansion throughout the newly decolonialised nations, as Bowles and Gintis have asserted (1976). Instead the many studies produced by this group used an institutional perspective to show how mass schooling as a national state project was not just part of the 'world capitalist economy' and 'inter-state system', but involved concomitant transformations in culture blueprints that led to a proliferation of the 'Western model of national society' (Ramirez and Boli, 1987).

Most functionalist arguments about the spread of Western schooling rely on naturalistic and mechanistic analogies to view such activities as a convergent technical adjustment to solve a common problem (i.e. underdevelopment) in some natural environment (i.e. the state public schools). By contrast, Meyer *et al.* (1977) depart from functionalism by viewing the expansion of Western-style mass education as a symbolic affirmation that makes sense within a cultural model. They found that industrialisation, urbanisation, state power or any other measure of internal structure did not support the rate of growth in primary enrolment between 1870 and 1940 (from 1930 on, data was available for 115 countries). Instead mass schooling expansion is better understood if we assume that different societies were sampling from a common world recipe for national progress, in which growth of mass schooling was a critical ingredient. This thesis is further supported by the finding that countries that were politically organised to look like nation-state candidates were more likely to establish earlier mass enrolments.

This group studied not only compulsory education and expansion of primary enrolments but also the standardisation of primary curriculum and curriculum content, educational expansion and economic growth (Benavot, 1992). There is still little systematic cross-national research that has evaluated the assumption that more unified and integrated national curricular frameworks will result in higher science and mathematics achievements which, in turn, will increase the quality of the labour force, and hence generate economic growth. This argument tends to determine how the international achievement comparisons by the International Association for the Evaluation of Educational Achievement (IEA) are handled in the media. The national significance of the science and mathematics achievement scores of school-goers is internationally recognised (hence the continued support for such statistical analysis as the IEA) because it follows a model of society and progress that originated in the West (i.e. modernisation and human capital theory) and is now globally validated.

The IEA studies

The International Association for the Evaluation of Educational Achievement (IEA) was established in 1959 in Stockholm and since has become perhaps the most influential non-governmental international association in education. It is an 'institution' that engages in comparative studies of different aspects of educational achievements in different countries. Since the 1960s countries (about 60 by 1997) by their own choice fund and participate in the collection of a vast amount of comparative data about students' achievement, attitudes and background factors through the large-scale IEA survey studies (Husen, 1967). These international studies of achievements in mathematics and science, civic education and reading, among others, have been repeated, consequently longitudinal studies have been carried out and reports are available. In addition the studies have provided opportunities for theory building; such theories as curriculum implementation and causal models of learning have been able to be tested empirically (Keeves, 1992).

Complex statistical multivariate and multilevel analyses, in addition to considerable effort in planning collection and analysis of data, have resulted in the drawing of comparisons between national systems and the advancement of an input–output utilisation model of education (Postlethwaite and Wiley, 1992). Other innovative methods are used in the preparation of the surveys and data collection via observation and interview. For example, the IEA Preprimary Project with 15 countries participating is the first international pre-school study (see Chapter 33 by Patricia Olmsted in this volume).

Not all IEA studies claim complete comparability of target population and national samples. This was the case with the IEA Classroom Environment Study; yet the data and analysis from observational sessions in many classrooms over several months produced one of the more interesting comparative studies of the process of teaching and interaction (Anderson *et al.*, 1989). During the 1994 mathematics international study, the US had funded and constructed an experimental data collection of over 70 hours of videotaping in classrooms in the US, Germany and Japan to study classroom interaction and student/teacher learning processes not accessible through questionnaires and observations. The choice of countries has an obvious motive: the US is comparing itself to the countries with which it is in direct economic competition. The IEA is currently planning the next phase of international testing, and the organisation is growing stronger as new countries join the association.

Recent USAID-funded projects

BRIDGES

Basic Research and Implementation in Developing Educational Systems (BRIDGES) was a USAID long-term, multi-country project of the Harvard Institute for International Development and the Harvard Graduate School, with subcontracts at the Institute for International Research at Michigan State University, the Research Triangle Institute in North Carolina and Texas Southern University. BRIDGES' commission was to 'identify policy options that will increase children's access to schooling, reduce the frequency of early school-leaving and repetition, improve the amount and quality of what is learned, and optimise the use of fiscal and educational resources' in participating countries as diverse as Egypt, Indonesia, North Yemen, Pakistan, Thailand, Sri Lanka and Burundi. This project of the mid-1980s signals a shift from direct educational aid allotted to various developing countries to a more restricted funding of efforts to strengthen the research and evaluation capacities of those involved in education planning and implementation. This project produced a large volume of research papers, reports and even a software tool, an educational simulation planning game to train for 'decision-makers concerned with Third World education' (Healey and Crouch, n.d.).[5]

IEES

Another USAID-supported project, to Improve the Efficiency of Education Systems (IEES) was a long-term intervention deployed in ten nations in Africa, the Caribbean and Asia from 1984 to 1994. It applied the systems approach to policy informed educational reform. Florida State University Learning Systems Institute was the contractor of this project with subcontracts to professors at such universities as SUNY–Albany (Chapman and Windham, 1986; Windham, 1988) and at the University of Pittsburgh (Adams *et al.*, 1991) and other consultants such as Claffey (1990), who all published reports and research papers. For this project the concept of efficiency provided a broad perspective from which to analyse an education system, one in which the cost of education inputs and processes can be related to benefits such as improved effectiveness. This concept has meaning only if outputs and outcomes are correctly specified and measured. Here we are again asking the classic comparative method questions since inputs, outputs and outcomes may vary significantly from one country, region or community to another: How are these terms defined? How are they measured and why compare the systems to one another? In educational planning and economics of education, it is customary to distinguish internal efficiency from external efficiency. Internal efficiency is in many World Bank studies equated with effectiveness measures of output expressed in non-monetary terms and with measures of input expressed in monetary terms.

This may explain how the 'school effectiveness' movement disappeared from the educational research in North America and the 'effective school movement' was short-lived in the US while prevailing among comparative researchers working on studies in developing countries where donor agencies have continued to be interested in measures of effectiveness. This project lasted for ten years and produced studies such as *Improving Educational Quality: A Global Perspective* (Chapman and Carrier, 1990).

IEQ

Improving Educational Quality (IEQ) refers both to a multi-country, five-year (1990–1995) USAID project and to a movement in CE research which replaced earlier attention to educational expansion and effectiveness (Heyneman and Loxley, 1983). The Washington DC-based contractor Institute for International Research (IIR) led this project with Jaurez and Associates, Inc. and the University of Pittsburgh (Professors Don Adams and Mark Ginsburg). The attention to 'quality' had replaced issues of equity and access in the 1980s. 'Improving educational quality' became one of the highest national priorities for the next decade in face of 'severe challenges facing the education system in most countries today'. In those countries where IEQ activities had been carried out (Ghana, Guatemala and Mali), IEQ staff collaborated to operationalise educational quality. Educational quality may refer to inputs (number of teachers, amount of teacher training, number of textbooks), processes (amount of direct instructional time, extent of active learning), outputs (test scores, graduation rates) and outcomes (performance in subsequent employment) (Adams, 1993).

CONCLUDING NOTE

The past ten years have been devoted to 'educational reform'. This movement took hold of education systems in the industrialised countries as well as in developing countries, so we could refer to it as a global movement to fix or repair what has been built by the modern schooling institutions. Improving and reforming the existing system is the way comparative researchers would like to handle the 'crisis' in education. In doing just that, comparativists are no different from many other groups with a long-standing investment in education. Yet many predict that the next 20 years may be devoted to revolutionising modern education, not just to reforming it. The last time that Illich (1970) predicted the 'deschooling' of society it did not happen. This time the 'deschooling' idea comes from comparative educators working in the former Soviet Union, where state support systems are collapsing. Nor is the former Soviet Union alone in this respect; outside Russia we are witnessing the abandonment of state responsibilities in public sectors such as health-care in the US and education in Japan and Korea. In the latter case, the state has steadily shifted many of the costs to parents, though schooling is still considered 'free public education' (Adams and Gottlieb, 1993).

The literature documents well some of the relevant changes expected at the start of the twenty-first century, such as a change-over from industry-dominated society to cybernetics-dominated society, and a shift in the scientific basis of innovation from big science (chemistry and physics) to small science (biology), mathematics and computers. Instant and unlimited information will change how we think and communicate. Work may come increasingly to be performed alone or with network collaborators 'working together alone' in far-flung locations. Responsibility may come to be placed not on the state but rather on individual citizens to prepare themselves for their futures. Such preparation will certainly include an educational foundation, but what kind we cannot be sure. School, as we know it, tends to shut out external developments and not to allow itself to be influenced by them. Young people today do not learn only in school, yet for the most part they receive their formal education in conventional schools. Adults no longer in school seek continuing education in order to get the education they think they need to join or advance in the workforce. Thus the population of those wanting education may change. Major constraints on learning may come to be attributed to the educational process and not to the learner, which may move us to customised curricula. Such predictions of change are fraught with uncertainty for the educational system on a global scale. If educators have not ventured predictions about what such a future might be, nevertheless questions are in the air. Who will pay for education? Who will take responsibility for education if the state will not? If work changes, will education too, and, if so, in what ways? Finally, who will teach? While the requirements for teaching have increased, the rewards have tended to remain modest, and the challenges for the future teacher will multiply.

Will the connection between education and societal and economic development change, or will they continue to be linked as they have been in theories of education and development? Some of these theories arose at a time when the rhythm of the modern school, with its break-up of the day into carefully defined shifts, imitated the clock-determined work at the factory and office. With a workforce that will have control over its own schedules, working alone or in independent teams, school attainment might not be found to be correlating with productivity or preparing for lifelong earnings. The intellectual field of comparative education may not be able to continue getting away with the production of academic capital that is so formalised and removed from daily social practice that its usefulness can be seriously questioned. Given the changes in the institutional arrangements of many comparative education programmes in the US (some of them having been absorbed into other programmes, others losing their independent degree programmes, together with cuts in funding for education by international donor agencies), no wonder that the type of research Western-educated comparative educators produce tends to be safe, predictable and easily accessible for an audience in search of common ground.

If the field is to grow in the face of some of these changes and their unpredictable consequences, it will have to explore in a more sophisticated way the social practices of its own culture, in addition to those of other cultures. It will have to admit that comparative research in education cannot continue to be based at a few major Western universities. Other educational systems and cultures are complex and ambiguous in ways different to our own. When the imbalances in conducting comparative research change and a shift occurs in who studies whom and where, we may find like-minded scholars in unexpected places.

Irving Epstein concludes that the most important choice comparative researchers can make today is to pursue the 'other':

> to investigate phenomena grounded in contexts demonstrably different from those with which we are most familiar, and in so doing, [to] play the role of outsider. Given the inherently personal nature of educational endeavors, the courage required to extend oneself and expose oneself to cultural difference, or simply to conceive of educational issues and policies in cross-cultural terms, is not insignificant. But because the pursuit of 'other' is inextricably linked with questions of identity and sense of self that fail to be fully resolved, it is my contention that the limited understanding of self restricts scope and possibility within the comparative field.
>
> (Epstein, 1995, p. 8)

This is very much in line with the interpretive worldview discussed above. The 'post-modern turn' in comparative education, if and when it takes place, will most likely result in a construction of knowledge different from that in theories of modernization and human capital. The destabilisation of the dominant modernist genres of discourse and the opening up of space for the actors' voices and authority will introduce indigenous knowledge and new categories into the semantic universe of comparative education, through the typical interpretive underlying metaphors of culture as text, dialogue and game.

NOTES

1 Social foundation subdisciplines such as comparative education have suffered as a result of general trends in US academic institutions to increased disciplinary specialisation and the downsizing at public universities with shrinking enrolments. This has resulted in programme reduction, e.g. the

IDEP at Pittsburgh was incorporated in 1988 as part of Administration and Policy Studies, and even elimination, e.g. the programme at Stanford University SIDEC was closed in 1993, and the programme at Florida State in 1997.

2 The CIES meets every year with about half of the 1000 members (70 per cent of members are US scholars) in attendance. The conference is organised in various locations, mostly in North America by the president elect and takes the form of parallel sessions on a great variety of topics.

3 Harold Noah, also of Teachers College, succeeded Bereday the founding editor. For the next 25 years the journal was influenced by University of Chicago school of thought: Andreas Kazamias worked for a while at Chicago before moving to University of Wisconsin, Madison. Philip Altbach and Erwin Epstein, both graduates of the University of Chicago, edited CER for ten years each. This gave the journal its University of Chicago economistic flavour with a bias toward qualitative analysis and a conservative outlook in search for rigour in comparative research, with little contribution from developing countries. In 1999 editorship is moving to the West Coast university, to UCLA, with four editors working as a team, whose educational and professional experience is quite diverse. The first woman editor is on this team (Hawkins, Rust, Stomquist and Torres, 1998).

4 According to Heyneman (1998) there have been many small shifts in the purpose and rationale behind the Bank's international aid to education, 'but in my experience these can be categorized into three overall stages: a first when the dominant rationale was that of manpower planning (1963–1980); a second (1980–1996), when the rationale included earning functions and empirical relationships with other benefits, health and family planning behavior and the like; and a third in which the rationale may diverge from education's effects on individuals towards its effects on the society at large and, in particular, on social cohesion' (Heyneman, 1998).

5 This use of the term 'Third World' in such context as this BRIDGES project user's guide (written in the late 1980s) must be one of the reasons Mathew Zachariah wrote in a letter to the editor of *Comparative Education Review*: 'It is time to stop using the phrase "The Third World"' (1992).

REFERENCES

Adams, D. K. (ed.) (1966) *Introduction to Education: A Comparative Analysis*. Belmont, CA: Wadsworth Publishing Co.

Adams, D. K. (1977) 'Developmental education', *Comparative Education Review*, 21 (2/3), 296–310.

Adams, D. K. (1993) *Defining Educational Quality*, IEQ Publication no. 1, Arlington, VA: Institute for International Research.

Adams, D. K. and Bjork, R. M. (1971) *Education in Developing Areas*. New York: David McKay.

Adams, D. K. and Gottlieb, E. E. (1993) *Education and Social Change in Korea*. New York and London: Garland Publishing.

Adams, D., Cigana, C., Gottlieb, E. E., Gunduz, K., Karip, E., Richard, M. and Sylvester, J. (1991) *A Global Analysis of Education, Social and Economic Change in Rapidly Industrializing Societies*. Pittsburgh, PA: The University of Pittsburgh, Administration and Policy Studies.

Almond, G. and Coleman, J. (eds) (1960) *The Politics of Developing Areas*. Princeton, NJ: Princeton University Press.

Altbach, P. G. (1977) 'Servitude of the mind: Education, dependency and neocolonialism', *Teachers College Record*, 79, 187–204.

Altbach, P. G. and Kelly, G. P. (eds) (1978) *Education and Colonialism*, New York: Longman.

Anderson, C. A. (1961) 'Methodology in comparative education', *International Review of Education*, 7 (1), 1–23.

Anderson, C. A. (1977) 'A quarter century of comparative education', *Comparative Education Review*, 21 (2/3), 405–416.

Anderson, C. A. and Bowman, M. J. (eds) (1965) *Education and Economic Development*. Chicago: Aldin.

Anderson, C. A. and Bowman, M. J. (1968) 'Theoretical considerations in educational planning'. In

Mark Blaug (ed.), *The Economics of Education: Selected Readings*. London and Baltimore: Penguin, 351–383

Anderson, L. W., Ryan, D. W. and Shapiro, B. J. (eds) (1989) *The IEA Classroom Study*. Oxford: Pergamon Press.

Arnove, R. F. (1980) 'Comparative education and world systems analysis', *Comparative Education Review*, 24 (1) 48–62.

Arnove, R. F. (1982) *Philanthropy and Cultural Imperialism*, Bloomington, IND: University of Indiana Press.

Aronowitz, S. and Giroux, H. (1985) *Education under Siege*. Hadley, MA: Bergin & Garvey.

Benavot, A. (1992) 'Curricular content, educational expansion, and economic growth', *Comparative Education Review*, 36 (2), 150–174.

Benavot, A. and Riddle, P. (1988) 'National estimates of expansion of mass education, 1870–1940', *Sociology of Education*, 61, 191–210.

Bereday, G. Z. F. (1958) 'Some methods of teaching comparative education', *Comparative Education Review*, 1 (3), 4–9.

Bereday, G. Z. F. (1964) *Comparative Methods in Education*. New York: Holt, Rinehart & Winston.

Berman, E. H. (1983) *The Ideology of Philanthropy*. Albany: State University of New York Press.

Boli, J. (1989) *New Citizenship for a New Society: The Institutional Origins of Mass Schooling in Sweden*. Oxford: Pergamon.

Boli, J. and Ramirez, F. O. (1992) 'Compulsory schooling in the Western cultural context'. In R. Arnove, P. Altbach, and G. Kelly (eds) *Emergent Issues in Education: Comparative Perspectives*. Westport, CT: Greenwood Press, 65–92.

Bottani W. N., Duchence, C. and Tuijnman, A. (1992) *1992 Education at a Glance: OECD Indicators*. Paris: OECD.

Bowles, S. (1972) 'Schooling and inequality from generation to generation', *Journal of Political Economy*, 80 (3), 217–251.

Bowles, S. and Gintis, H. (1976) *Schooling in Capitalist America*. New York: Basic Books.

Bowman, M. J. (1966) 'The human investment revolution in economic thought', *Sociology of Education*, 9 (2), 111–137.

Bowman, M. J. (1976) 'Review of M. Carnoy, *Education as Cultural Imperialism*', *Economic Development and Cultural Change*, 24, 833–840.

Brickman, W. W. (1956) 'Report on New York University Third Annual Conference on Comparative Education', *Journal of Educational Sociology*, 30, 113.

Brickman, W. W. (1960) 'A historical introduction to comparative education', *Comparative Education Review*, 3 (3), 6–13.

Brown, R. H. (1977) *A Poetic for Sociology: Toward a Logic of Discovery for the Human Sciences*. Cambridge, UK: Cambridge University Press.

Burns, R. J. and Welch, A. R. (eds) (1992) *Contemporary Perspectives in Comparative Education*. New York and London: Garland Publishing.

Carnoy, M. (1972) 'The political economy of education'. In T. J. LaBelle (ed.), *Education and Development in Latin America and the Caribbean*. Los Angeles: UCLA Latin American Center.

Carnoy, M. (1974) *Education as Cultural Imperialism*. New York: David McKay.

Carnoy, M. (1985) 'The political economy of education', *International Social Science*, 37, 157–171.

Chapman, D. W. and Carrier, C. A. (eds) (1990) *Improving Educational Quality: A Global Perspective*. New York: Greenwood Press.

Chapman D. W. and Windham, D. M. (1986) 'The evaluation of efficiency in educational development activities'. Tallahassee: Florida State University, IEES project.

Claffey, J. M. (1990) 'The donor role in instructional improvement'. In D. W. Chapman and C. A. Carrier (eds), *Improving the Educational Quality: A Global Perspective*. New York: Greenwood Press, 87–108.

Cumming, W. K. (1997) 'Human resource development: The Japan model'. In W. K. Cumming and P. G. Altbach (eds), *The Challenge of Eastern Asian Education*. Albany: State University of New York Press.

173

Eckstein, A. and Noah, H. J. (1969) *Scientific Investigations in Comparative Education*. London: Macmillan.

Epstein, E. H. (1983) 'Ideology in comparative education', *Comparative Education Review*, 27 (1), 3–29.

Epstein E. H. (1992) *Comparative Education Review Annual Report for 1992*, CIES Annual Meeting.

Epstein, Irving (1995) 'Comparative education in North America: The search for other through the escape from self?', *Compare*, 25 (1), 5–16.

Fagerlind, I. and Saha, S. J. (1983) *Education and National Development: A Comparative Perspective*. Oxford: Pergamon Press.

Fardon, R. (1995) *Counterworks: Managing the Diversity of Knowledge*. London and New York: Routledge.

Foster, P. (1960) 'Comparative methodology and the study of African education', *Comparative Education Review*, 4 (2), 110–117.

Foster, P. (1965a) *Education and Social Change in Ghana*. Chicago: University of Chicago Press.

Foster, P. J. (1965b) 'Vocational fallacy in development planning'. In C. A. Anderson and M. J. Bowman (eds) *Education and Economic Development*. Chicago: Aldine Publishing Company, 142–167.

Fraser, S. E. (1964) *Jullien's Plan for Comparative Education, 1816–1817*. New York: Teachers College, Columbia University.

Freire, P. (1973) *Education for Critical Consciousness*. New York: Seabury.

Gendzier, I. (1985) *Managing Political Change: Social Scientists and the Third World*. Boulder, CO: Westview Press.

Gottlieb, E. E. (1988) 'Development education: How knowledge is constructed by and through discourse in intellectual paradigms'. Paper presented at the CIES Annual Conference, Atlanta, Georgia.

Gottlieb, E. E. (1989) 'The discursive construction of knowledge: The case of radical education discourse', *Quantitative Studies in Education*, 2 (2), 131–144.

Gottlieb, E. E. and LaBelle, T. J. (1990) 'Ethnographic contextualisation of Freire's discourse: Consciousness-raising, theory and practice', *Anthropology and Education Quarterly*, 21 (1), 3–18.

Grant, N. (1977) 'Comparative education – its present and future prospects', Editorial, *Comparative Education*, 13 (2), 75–76.

Halls, W. D. (1989) *Comparative Education: Contemporary Issues and Trends*. London: Jessica Kingsley.

Hans, N. (1958) *Comparative Education: A Study of Educational Factors and Traditions*. 3rd edn. London: Routledge and Kegan Paul.

Hans, N. (1959) 'The historical approach to comparative education', *International Review of Education*, 5, 299–309.

Hawkins, J., Rust, V., Stomquist, N. and Torres, C. A. (1998) 'Comparative Education Review editorship changes hands after ten years', *CIES Newsletter*, 118, 1–4.

Healey, F. H. and Crouch L. A. (n.d.) *Optimising Policies for Education Systems (OPES) Users' Guide and Technical Description*. North Carolina: Center for International Development, Research Triangle Institute. USAID Contract no. 5824–A–5076 BRIDGES project.

Heyneman, S. P. (1986) 'Investing in education: A quarter century of World Bank experience', Washington, DC: World Bank, Economic Development Institute, Seminar Paper No. 30.

Heyneman, S. P. (1998) 'Development Aid in Education: A Personal View'. Sent on line on Wed. 24 June 1998 15:59:58 –0400 (EDT) Multiple recipients of list <wbedpol@lists.fsu.edu> World Bank Education Policy Discussion Group, Florida State University. To appear in Lene Buchert and Kenneth King (eds) *Changing International Aid To Education: Global Patterns and National Contexts*. Paris: UNESCO.

Heyneman, S. P. and Loxley, W. (1983) 'The effect of primary school quality on academic achievement across 29 high and low-income countries', *American Journal of Sociology*, 88 (6), 1162–94.

Holmes, B. (1958) 'The problem approach in comparative education', *Comparative Education Review*, 2 (1), 4–19.

Holmes, B. (1981) *Comparative Education: Some Considerations of Method*. London: George Allen & Unwin.

Hoselitz, B. (1952) 'Non-economic barriers to economic development', *Economic Development and Cultural Change*, I, 8–21.

Husen, T. (ed.) (1967) *International Study of Achievement in Mathematics; A Comparison of 12 Countries*, Vol 1 (2). New York: John Wiley & Son.

IDEP Project (1985–1987) 'Theories of development and education 1950–1986'. Unpublished manuscript, International and Development Education Program, University of Pittsburgh.

Illich, I. (1970) *Deschooling Society*. New York: Harper & Row.

Inkeles, A. (1969) 'Making men modern: On the causes and consequences of individual change in six developing countries', *American Journal of Sociology*, 75, 208–225.

Inkeles, A. (1983) *Exploring Individual Modernity*. New York: Columbia University Press.

Inkeles, A. and Smith, D. H. (1974). *Becoming Modern*. Cambridge, MA: Harvard University Press.

Kandel, I. L. (1955) *The New Era in Education: A Comparative Study*. Cambridge, MA: Houghton Mifflin.

Kandel, I. L. (1959) 'The methodology of comparative education', *International Review of Education*. 5, 270–280.

Keeves, J. P. (ed.) (1992) *The IEA Study of Science III: Changes in Science Education and Achievements: 1970 to 1984*. Oxford: Pergamon Press.

Kelly, G. P. and Altbach, P. G. (1986) 'Comparative education: Challenge and response', *Comparative Education Review*, 30 (1), 89–109.

King, E. J. (1958) *Other Schools and Ours: A Comparative Study for Today*. New York: Holt, Rinehart, & Winston.

Klees, S. J. (1986) 'Planning and policy analysis in education: What can economics tell us?', *Comparative Education Review*, 30 (4), 577–607.

LaBelle, T. J. (1987) 'From consciousness-raising to popular education in Latin America and the Caribbean', *Comparative Education Review*, 31 (2), 201–217.

Lerner, D. (1958) *The Passing of Traditional Society*. Glencoe, IL: Free Press.

Levin, H. M. (1974) 'Educational reform and social change', *Journal of Applied Behavioral Science*, 4, 314–325.

Lockheed, M. and Verspoor, A. (1991) *Improving Primary Education in Developing Countries*. Oxford: Pergamon Press.

Loxley, W. (1994) 'Comparative education and international education: Organisations and institutions'. In T. Husen and T. N. Postlethwaite (eds). *International Encyclopedia of Education*, London: Pergamon, 933–942.

McCloskey, D. N. (1985) *The Rhetoric of Economics*. Madison: University of Wisconsin Press.

Marcus, G. E. and Cushman, D. (1982) 'Ethnographies as texts', *Annual Review of Anthropology*, 11, 25–70.

Masemann, V. L. (1982) 'Critical ethnography in the study of comparative education', *Comparative Education Review*, 21 (3), 1–15.

Masemann, V. (1994) 'Ways of knowing: Implications for comparative education', *Comparative Education Review*, 34 (3), 465–473.

Meyer, J., Ramirez, F. O., Robinson, R. and Boli-Bennett, J. (1977) 'The world educational revolution, 1950–1970', *Sociology of Education*, 50, 242–258.

Noah, H. J. and Eckstein, A. (1969) *Toward a Science of Comparative Education*. New York: Macmillan.

Noah, H. J. and Eckstein, M. A. (1988) 'Dependency theory in comparative education: Twelve lessons from the literature'. In J. Schriewer and B. Holmes (eds), *Theories and Methods in Comparative Education*. Frankfurt: Verlag Peter Lang, 165–196.

Paulston, R. G. (1977) 'Social and educational change: Conceptual frameworks', *Comparative Education Review*, 21 (2/3), 370–395.

Paulston, R. G. (1992) 'Comparative and international education: Paradigms and theories'. In T. Husen and T. N. Postlethwaite (eds). *International Encyclopedia of Education*, 2nd edn, London: Pergamon.

Paulston, R. G. (ed.) (1996) *Social Cartography: Mapping Ways of Seeing Social and Educational Change*. New York and London: Garland Publishing.

175

Postlethwaite, T. N. and Wiley, D. (1992) *The IEA Study of Science Achievement in Twenty Three Countries*. Oxford: Pergamon Press.

Psacharopoulos, G. (1973) *Returns to Education: An International Comparison*. San Francisco: Jossey-Bass.

Psacharopoulos, G. (1985) 'Return to education: A further international update and implications', *Journal of Human Resources*, 20 (4), 583–597.

Psacharopoulos, G. (1994) 'Returns to investments in education: A global update', *World Development*, 22 (9), 340–356.

Organisation for Economic Co-operation and Development (OECD) (1971) *Educational Policies for the 1970s*. Paris: OECD.

Ramirez, F. O. and Boli, J. (1987) 'The political construction of mass schooling: European origins and worldwide institutionalization', *Sociology of Education*, 60, 2–17.

Reiffers, J. (1982) *Transnational Corporations and Endogenous Development*. Paris: UNESCO.

Ross, H., To, C., Cave, W. and Bair, D. E. (1992) 'On shifting ground: The post-paradigm identity of US comparative education, 1979–88', *Compare*, 22 (2), 113–131.

Rust, V. (1991) 'Post-modernisation and its comparative education implications', *Comparative Education Review*, 35 (4), 610–626.

Samoff, J. (1993) 'The reconstruction of schooling in Africa', *Comparative Education Review*, 37 (2), 81–122.

Schriewer, J. and Holmes, B. (eds) (1988) *Theories and Methods in Comparative Education*. Frankfurt: Verlag Peter Lang.

Schultz, T. W. (1963) *The Economic Value of Education*. New York: Columbia University Press.

Valenzuela, J. S. and Valenzuela, A. (1979) 'Latin American underdevelopment'. In J. J. Villamil (ed.). *Transnational Capitalism and National Development*. New Jersey: Humanities Press.

Wallerstein, I. (1974) *The Modern World System*. New York: Academic Press.

Weis, L. (1979) 'Education and the reproduction of inequality: The case of Ghana', *Comparative Education Review*, 23 (1), 41–51.

Willis, P. (1981)[1977] *Learning to Labor*. New York: Columbia University Press.

Windham, D. M. (1988) 'Effectiveness indicators in economic analysis of educational activities', *International Journal of Educational Research*, 12 (6), 575–665.

Zachariah, M. (1992) Letter to the editor: 'It is time to stop using the phrase "The Third World"', *Comparative Education Review*, 36 (4), 551–554.

Part II

PROCESSES

10

THE CONDUCT AND APPRAISAL
OF EDUCATIONAL RESEARCH

Robert E. Floden

Research is, as the word suggests, an investigation or search. Research is distinguished from other investigations by being, as the *Oxford English Dictionary* puts it, 'careful'. Educational researchers belong to one or more research communities (sometimes referred to as scientific communities or scholarly communities), each of which has developed its own conception of what it means to be 'careful'. The communities are concerned both about epistemological care (i.e. does the way the search was conducted give good reasons to trust its results?) and about moral care (has the research been conducted ethically, especially in the way it treated those studied?).

This companion entry describes several prominent educational research communities, together with their conceptions of 'care'. It also discusses major activities of research (e.g. conceptualisation, interpretation, communication) that cut across communities. The entry ends by considering how these communities have developed, how they maintain themselves, and how they relate to other social groups, especially communities of practice.

TRUSTWORTHINESS OF RESEARCH

Researchers are 'careful' in their investigations because they want to have good reasons for trusting what they find out or what they conclude. The particular care with which research investigations are carried out gives the investigators confidence in the results, and also gives others good reason to trust the conclusions.

Various terms are used to label trustworthiness: validity, objectivity, reliability, generalisability. Articles explicating these concepts associate particular aspects of trustworthiness with one term rather than another, but their usages are overlapping. To say that a research conclusion is 'valid', 'objective', 'reliable' or 'generalisable' is to say that it is entitled to be trusted in some way. Note that the terms typically are applied to a conclusion or to a conclusion and its supporting arguments and evidence, rather than to a research study as a whole. Saying that a study is valid is a loose way of saying that the conclusions of the study are valid because of the way the investigation was conducted.

The meaning or value of these concepts is sometimes attacked by claiming that objectivity is impossible. Some of these attacks rest on a confusion between, on the one hand, 'trustworthy' or 'warranted' (to use Dewey's adjective) and, on the other hand, 'true'. Such attacks move from the generally accepted principle that a researcher can never be certain that a conclusion is true to the dubious claim that a researcher can never know whether a conclusion is warranted, to the anarchistic conclusion that all conclusions are equally worthy of being trusted. The fallacy comes in jumping from 'I might be wrong' to 'I don't care whether or not I'm wrong' (Phillips, 1992, ch. 5). Even though one can never achieve certainty, a research conclusion can be judged according to whether the evidence and argument supporting the conclusion meet the standards held within the research community. Sometimes the standards are met by following accepted procedures; in other cases, innovative procedures can be judged by members of the community (Shulman, 1988).

Validity

Some scholars argue that 'validity' is the most encompassing of these terms, incorporating all the others. To say that a conclusion is valid is to say that it is well supported by evidence and argument. Measurement theorists distinguish among four types of validity: construct validity, criterion validity, content validity and consequential validity (Messick, 1989; Shepard, 1993).

Judgements about construct validity are made by assessing a range of evidence to evaluate whether all aspects of an argument fit with available evidence. Criterion validity is assessed by looking at a narrower range of information, specifically the correlations between scores on the test and the scores on another instrument thought to measure the same characteristic. Content validity uses an expert review of the measuring instrument itself, rather than considering scores obtained. Consequential validity resembles construct validity in drawing on a wide range of evidence, but addresses claims about the effects of actions based on test scores, rather than on the meaning of the test scores themselves. In each case, saying that an interpretation of test scores has a particular degree of validity means that the relevant evidence supports that interpretation.

Judgements of validity can be made about research claims other than test scores and their interpretations. For claims about cause and effect relationships, judgements about *internal* validity address the evidence for the particular circumstances (people involved, measures used, historical context) of the study. Did, for example, that new reading programme lead to more learning in this particular case? Judgements about *external* validity address the evidence in support of extending conclusions to different circumstances – a different sample of students, a related curriculum, a different measurement instrument. Would this reading programme have similar effects with older students in a different city?

The trustworthiness of interpretations can also be considered an issue of validity (Maxwell, 1992). In a report about how students interpreted a poetry lesson, for example, a judgement of *descriptive* validity evaluates whether the investigator accurately reported the events that occurred in the lesson. *Interpretive* validity relates to whether the investigator's reports of student interpretations of events is accurate. *Theoretical* validity relates to whether the investigator's explanations of the events make appropriate use of theoretical constructs and accurately represent relationships among those constructs.

All judgements of validity are matters of degree. An interpretation of a test score is not flatly valid or invalid, but rather valid to a greater or lesser extent. Because validity is based on supporting evidence and argument, the degree of validity will change as more evidence becomes available or as weaknesses in an argument are uncovered. The validity of a causal claim may be strengthened by evidence refuting alternative explanations of change, or weakened by the discovery of a possible confounding factor.

Objectivity

Judgements of objectivity resemble those about validity, but focus particularly on concerns about bias arising from the situation, beliefs or values of those making the claim. Claims made by publishers about the efficacy of their proprietary curriculum materials, for example, might raise worries about the possibility of bias stemming from self-interest. The worry is that, intentionally or not, the publishers might make design decisions or data interpretations favouring their materials. Such bias would constitute a reduction in objectivity, hence a reduction in the validity of the claim.

As with claims about validity, objectivity is judged by assessing the evidence and the argument that supports the claims. Use of procedures that can be critically scrutinised by others, especially those with other situations and interests, is a way of strengthening the argument for objectivity (assuming that those scrutinising the evidence reach similar conclusions).

Recent feminist scholarship has stressed the value of reports that include personal comments about the researcher. For example, they applaud inclusion of information about why the investigator has grown interested in a line of work, how the work is connected to the scholar's personal and professional life history, and more generally what the work means to the investigator as a person. Attention to the investigator as a person is sometimes viewed as a move away from objectivity, because it identifies the work with a particular person, who has a particular point of view. If objectivity is pursued by laying the grounds for conclusions open to critical scrutiny, however, personal information about the investigator is a support for objectivity, rather than an impediment. The additional information about the motivation and history of the research project gives members of the investigator's research community clues about where the argument might be challenged. When objectivity is associated with an approach that encourages others to examine key inferences, subjectivity and objectivity can be mutually supportive, rather than standing in opposition.

Reliability

For educational research, judgements of reliability evaluate the extent to which measurements taken will be similar despite differences in conditions of measurement considered irrelevant to the characteristic of interest. Thus a measurement procedure is reliable to the extent that it yields similar measurements across changes in the sample of test items chosen (from a pool of items all taken to measure the characteristic), across different raters used to score the test, across testing occasions (assuming that the characteristic itself has not changed between test administrations), and so on. Studies of test reliability may use a variety of designs and methods of computing a numerical indicator, depending on what sources of error are addressed. 'Generalisability theory' is an extension of classical approaches that allows for the simultaneous consideration of multiple sources of error (Brennan, 1983). For example, a student taking a performance assessment may get a higher score from one rater than from another, or may score higher or lower depending on the particular task that must be performed. Using generalisability theory, an investigator can determine the relative size in score variations from each source. Do students' scores vary more because different raters would assign different scores to the same performance, or because different students find particular tasks easy or hard? By knowing which factor contributes more variation, the investigator can design an assessment process that more efficiently yields stable scores. If scores vary more across tasks than across raters, for example, it is more efficient to have a student do several tasks with a single rater than to have the student do a single task that is scored by several raters.

Like objectivity, reliability can be considered a particular case of validity. Where objectivity focuses on worries about bias, reliability attends to random variation in measurements. Although explicit attention to reliability is most common in studies that feature numerical measurements, random variation is a more general concern. An ethnographer watching the way a teacher begins a class must worry about which features of the event will be a regular part of the class segment and which are incidental. Just as the test developer wishes to know how many test items must be included to give an acceptably reliable total score, the ethnographer wishes to know how many times a type of event must be observed to be able reliably to identify typical features.

Generalisation

Researchers and readers of research have a pressing interest in whether insights or results from a study will hold up under other circumstances. Even investigators who focus most of their attention on understanding particular occasions in depth probably hope the understanding achieved for one occasion supports insights in other instances.

In surveys based on a statistically representative sample, probability theory can be used to estimate results for groups other than the respondents themselves and to describe the likelihood of error. In most other situations, the arguments supporting generalisation draw on a range of evidence in building a plausible argument. Because many educational phenomena depend on a host of factors, support for generalisations is usually strengthened by having detailed descriptions of contexts, people and events. Although it is most common to see the researcher as responsible for making and supporting generalisations, readers can also assume responsibility for making and defending generalisations to other circumstances (Firestone, 1993).

COMMUNITIES OF EDUCATIONAL RESEARCH

Judgements about the trustworthiness of research conclusions are based on standards shared within a community of researchers. In his seminal, though still controversial, *Structure of*

Scientific Revolutions (1962), Kuhn argued that a complex of key ideas – what he called a 'paradigm', defines a scientific community and that, in turn, a scientific community is defined by the paradigm its members share. Although some scholars question whether social science is 'mature' enough to have paradigms in Kuhn's sense, subgroups within educational research can be readily distinguished. Moreover these communities explicitly discuss how their key assumptions differ from other groups of educational researchers, maintain their own sets of publications, and meet with those of similar persuasions. The boundaries among groups are, however, fuzzy and permeable. In some circumstances researchers from supposedly different communities manage to collaborate or even to operate within the assumptions of communities other than their own. Thus any list of communities is bound to be criticised, with good reason. Without some sketch of the territory, however, variations in methods and evaluative standards can lead to an unwarranted belief that all research is idiosyncratic.

Some writers cast the central distinctions between educational research communities as quantitative versus qualitative, or as positivistic versus interpretivist. In the first case, the quantitative research community is portrayed as studying the relationships among variables, each of which is measured according to some numerical scale. As E. L. Thorndike put it, 'Everything that exists, exists in some degree, and can be measured.' The qualitative researchers, on the other hand, seek to describe educational phenomena in written narratives, including characteristics that do not lend themselves to numerical measurement.

The positivist/interpretivist distinction draws a similar line between communities, but emphasises the difference in what constitutes the proper subject of study, rather than the difference between description with and description without numbers. Positivists, under this description, see research as the study of what can be directly observed, building complex descriptions and explanations out of many focused observations. Interpretivists, in contrast, seek to record the meanings that human actors make of or attach to their experiences. These interpretivists study meanings both by asking those they study to explain how events should be understood, and by longer-term participation in the social group under investigation (Hammersley and Atkinson, 1983).

Both of these distinctions are crude. Some writers have argued that these ways of casting core debates is unprofitable (Howe, 1992). Others have pointed out that 'positivist' is often used as a general term of criticism, with little connection to the historical development of the positivist approach to science (Phillips, 1983).

For much empirical research in education, connections to social science disciplines offer more insight into assumptions and standards. Educational psychologists, for example, were for decades the dominant group in educational research. They drew models for research from their colleagues in psychology departments. Just as psychologists themselves have affiliated with behaviourist, information-processing, ecological and cognitive science traditions, educational psychologists have worked within the corresponding communities, each of which has changed over the decades. Other empirical researchers in education have worked within traditions from sociology, anthropology, history and so on. These disciplinary affiliations are often maintained by publication patterns or even joint membership or academic appointment. Using these as the points of reference helps to explain why some researchers discuss both variables and meanings (as their colleagues in cognitive science do, for example). The links to the disciplines also help to explain some of the differences within the cruder groupings.

Explicit discussions of the characteristics of and differences among individual research communities give some insight into their separate traditions. The accounts one community gives of another (e.g. an anthropologist describing how psychologists conduct research) must understandably be treated with caution. Descriptions of that 'other' tradition may be exaggerated to highlight differences or may simply include misunderstandings. One starting-point for examining differences is a volume (Jaeger, 1997) produced by the American Educational Research Association, with sections on various research traditions. Each section contains both an article describing the tradition written by a scholar in the field and a previously published report representative of the tradition. Other comparisons can be found in recent handbooks and edited volumes designed to give introductions to the various traditions (e.g. Denzin and Lincoln, 1994; Eisner and Peshkin, 1990; Keeves, 1988).

Three traditions of research are often omitted from these comparisons: philosophical research, evaluation studies and feminist research. Philosophical research may be omitted from comparisons among traditions because it lacks the central attention to empirical investigation often associated with research. Like other research traditions, however, philosophical research is distinguished from everyday investigations by the care taken in making arguments, examining evidence and drawing conclusions (Floden and Buchmann, 1990).

Evaluation studies can be thought of both as following a more encompassing tradition (e.g. survey research) and as being a tradition apart. Evaluation studies are distinguished by the emphasis given to judging *particular* educational programmes, policies, or curricula and by an emphasis on informing decision-makers, rather than members of the scholarly community. In the United States, evaluators maintain their own professional society, publish journals specialising in evaluation, establish standards for their studies (Joint Committee on Standards for Educational Evaluation, 1994). Individual evaluators often also maintain affiliations with other research communities.

Feminist research

Although education was once one of the few areas of employment for college-educated women, feminist research is a relative newcomer to educational research. Feminist studies sometimes are distinguished by the topics addressed and sometimes are set apart by the conventions for gathering and assessing evidence. Like many other traditions, the proper definition of the area is currently under debate. The discussion within feminist research seems more heated, perhaps owing in part to its recent emergence and in part to its interplay with the evolving broader discussions about gender issues.

A central premise in feminist research is that most earlier research has been flawed by its reliance on a male perspective. Whether or not the prior research was done exclusively by males, the contention is that the research suffered because of the dominance of males in the research community. In studies of moral development, for example, initial studies were carried out using male subjects. On the basis of the initial empirical and theoretical analysis, a progression of stages of moral development was described. When female subjects were then studied, their degree of moral development was measured using these stages.

In an influential series of studies, Gilligan (1982) showed that the empirical progression of stages was different for women than for men. More significantly, she argued that the value attached to the stages was based on a view of ethics that placed detachment and objectivity above relationship. Gilligan noted that this ordering paralleled the difference between the psychological development of men, for whom individuation *from* the mother is a primary issue, and the development of women, for whom identification *with* the mother is a continuing value. Thus Gilligan suggested that the progression of moral stages women move through is as praiseworthy as that men undergo. The initial focus on males led to an incomplete, distorted conclusion.

Some feminist researchers believe that the problem with prior research is that some facts were neglected or samples skewed because of an overemphasis on males. They believe that when these omisions are identified, the problem will be corrected, using the existing methods of research.

Other feminist researchers assert that the socio-political position of the investigator affects the interpretations drawn from any study. Building on the arguments that all inter-pretations are shaped by what the investigator brings to a study, these feminist standpoint theorists hold that male investigators will see some things differently from females because of the differences in their experiences and in their current societal positions. In the study of teaching careers, for example, men may see teachers leaving the profession to raise children as lack of career commitment, while women may see it as part of a broader commitment to the well-being of children.

Some feminist researchers acknowledge the differences produced by varying standpoint, yet still believe that investigators can make judgements about which claims are better supported or more likely to be accurate. These researchers continue to measure work according to some standards of trustworthiness that keep the spirit of prior analyses of validity, objectivity and reliability. Others see these ways of judging research as a product of male-dominated research tradition, hence suspect. Harding (1986) has written a thorough and informative discussion of these contrasting feminist perspectives.

Attention to the influence of standpoint on interpretation has led feminist researchers to incorporate personal descriptions of their lives and interests into their research reports. If the reader knows more about the standpoint of the researcher, the reader may be able to imagine what interpretations are likely and where the researcher is likely to make omissions or to draw a different conclusion than others might. Writing about connections between the individual researcher and the studies themselves may dispel some of the illusion that the investigator has no stake in the work. It does not, however, absolve the investigator of working to make the study trustworthy. Nor can the researcher's account of personal history and interest be simply taken at face value, for that account itself is bound to be shaped by the researcher's standpoint.

The perceived importance of the personal lives of researchers has led to increased atten-tion to personal biographies of educational researchers, both men and women. Joining the biographies and autobiographies of scholars at their career's end are now mid-career accounts, such as those assembled in a recent volume on educational researchers (Neumann and Peterson, 1986).

PROCESSES OF RESEARCH

When people speak of doing research, they often have in mind the collection and analysis of data. Those are important components of research, but thinking only of these processes obscures aspects of an investigator's activities that significantly influence what is learned from the investigation, both by the investigator and by others in the educational community. By thinking about research as including processes of conceptualisation, design, interpretation and communication, as well as data collection and analysis, the range of decisions the investigator must make becomes clearer. Moreover, this broader conception highlights the range of literature that can inform research.

Conceptualisation

The way a research topic is conceptualised shapes the questions that will be asked and the range of possible answers. Attempts to understand how to improve student achievement will take one form if the problem is framed as one of improving classroom instruction, and will take quite a different form if family circumstances and community norms are considered as possible influences on what children learn.

In choosing a general area for research and formulating specific questions, a researcher may attend to related scholarship, to problems of educational practice, and to current social and political forces. For a study of bilingual education, for example, an investigator can consider how the processes of second-language learning have been viewed by prior research and what researchers have concluded about the factors that influence language learning, learning of other subjects, and long-term patterns of school success. The investigator may also take into account the problems teachers and school administrators have expressed about the operations and effects of competing models of bilingual education. Such considerations might lead the investigator to give more attention to difficulties of managing transitions from one language to another during the school day. Attention to social and political forces might lead the investigator to see effects on cultural pride as an outcome that should be considered alongside test performance.

An especially dramatic (in more than one sense) description of the importance of research conceptualisation is Gusfield's (1981) analysis of research on drunken driving. Drawing on a framework for literary analysis, Gusfield shows how the interpretations depend on whether the problem is viewed as one of individual responsibility for driving or collective responsibility for building safe cars and roads, and on whether the driver who has been drinking is seen as a drunk or as a social drinker.

No conceptualisation of a research problem is 'best' in any absolute sense, but different conceptualisations highlight different features and will be more or less likely to lead to improvements in theory or in practice. At the very least, researchers do well to consider alternatives in conceptualising a study, and to think about those conceptualisations in the light of prior research, information about practice and the social context. A study of teacher quality might highlight the curriculum of teacher preparation, the family backgrounds of those entering teaching or the incentives for teachers to continue learning. How the situation is viewed will affect what information is collected and where the locus of problems or successes is placed.

In the past two decades much attention has been given to approaches to summarising prior research. Statistical procedures for meta-analysis have grown sophisticated and attention has also been given to approaches to more interpretive reviews (Cooper and Hedges, 1994).

Design

The parameters of research design vary according to the research tradition. Surveys, for example, require decisions about sampling procedures, selection and sequence of items, and method of administration. Ethnographic studies on the other hand, require decisions about how to stay in the field, how to identify and approach key informants, how much to remain an outsider. Some decisions can be made in advance of data collection; others will be made in process.

In making design decisions, the investigator will typically choose trade-offs among cost, precision, efficiency and chance of significant error. Although no design will be best in all respects, some designs will be better than others (e.g. some sampling designs have smaller sampling error at the same cost). Many books on research methods compare the advantages of competing designs (Jaeger, 1984).

Analysis

The amount of information collected is virtually always more than can be reported, or even surveyed by an individual investigator. The task of analysis is to summarise what has come out of the investigation in a way that captures as many important features as possible with minimal distortion. To keep the work open to critique from other members of the research community, the analysis should also use an approach that can be described well enough to allow others to appreciate the risks of error it introduces. For some procedures (e.g. some statistical analyses) the description may allow others to replicate the analysis (i.e. to get the same results from the same initial data); for other procedures (e.g. some approaches to extracting themes from field notes), the description merely allows others to understand what processes were used to guard against likely error (e.g. searching for disconfirming evidence).

Statistics textbooks outline commonly used procedures for analysing numerical data, including the limitations of these methods and the likelihood that they will lead to erroneous conclusions (Glass and Hopkins, 1995; Shavelson, 1996). Some texts describing methods of analysing interview and narrative observation data are also available (Bogdan and Biklen, 1997; Lecompte *et al.*, 1993; Miles and Huberman, 1984). In neither case is data analysis a mechanical process. Investigators' choices about analytic approaches influence what aspects of a study are seen in sharp focus and which are relegated to the background. Concerns about different types of errors (e.g. missing an important connection versus mistaking random variation for a substantive link) are connected to analytic decisions.

Analysis often evolves, rather than strictly following a pre-set plan. As initial analysis uncovers hints of unexpected results, new analyses are conducted, often displacing those originally projected. Surprises prompt attention, so that they are neither overlooked nor too quickly accepted.

Communication

Conduct of research includes communicating its results. The communication can be seen as concluding with the publication of results in a scholarly journal or presentation at a professional conference. Some researchers view such communication as straightforwardly reporting what was done, with what result.

This simple view of research communication is constructed around an important grain of truth. The care that sets research apart from other investigations depends crucially on laying the work open to criticism from other members of the research community. Without a clear sense of the events in an enquiry, informed criticism is impossible. Systematic, detailed presentation of research events is thus essential.

At the same time, the desire for clarity ironically obscures the inevitable, yet consequential, choices that researchers make in their writing and speaking. The formal prose and structure of many research reports typically hide the slips and false starts that accompany most research work. The report is usually a rational reconstruction of the argument behind the conclusions, rather than an account of the adjustments or even radical revisions of the envisioned study as it proceeded. Studies of laboratory work in natural science reveal the mix of clear reason and practical accommodation that lies behind the myth of the scientist in a white lab coat; accounts of studies in education suggest a similar editing for a simpler story line in publication. The simplification of research procedures and results is more pronounced in publications for practitioner and policy audiences.

Researchers evidently do make choices in communicating their work. Acknowledging that published accounts omit some aspects of the work does not, however, lead to the conclusion that research reports are 'fictions' in the sense that they bear no connection to reality. The point to note is rather that researcher judgement enters into reporting, just as it does in other aspects of the work. Research is a human activity, in which investigators build a plan of work, design activities and make interpretations. As such, tools for examining human constructions (e.g. concepts of rhetorical analysis) can give insight into research activities and bases of research conclusions in reason and argument.

CONNECTIONS TO POLICY AND PRACTICE

Although scholars disagree on what mixture of basic and applied research will be most beneficial, they agree that educational research should have a connection to policy and practice. Some have argued for a chain in which researchers conduct investigations, then give the results to practitioners, who implement them. This so-called research-development-dissemination (RD&D) model was the basis for a system of national research funding in the United States in the 1960s and 1970s.

Although the RD&D model still has adherents, it is now generally believed to oversimplify the connections between research, policy and practice and to suggest too sharp a role division between researchers and those doing the practical work of education. Studies of the connections, informed by broader investigations of knowledge use, have shown that the important consequences of research come indirectly. A set of studies, for example, may influence the climate of opinion, altering the ways educational problems are perceived rather than dictating some single solution. The idea that policy-makers and practitioners would simply follow researchers' advice has also been found to be naïve. Actors draw on many sources of information, often valuing the views of those working in similar situations over the pronouncements of researchers working at a distance (Lindblom and Cohen, 1979; Weiss, 1979). Practitioners also contribute to knowledge, rather than merely consuming it. Researchers now often draw valuable insights from those in the field, making the connection run in two directions.

RESEARCH ETHICS

The meaning of 'care' that distinguishes research from other enquiries is primarily care about the grounds for believing claims, the 'trustworthiness' discussed above. Increasingly, educational researchers have also stressed the care with which those involved in research, particularly those whose thoughts and actions are described, should be treated. Research in US universities is now scrutinised by institutional review boards, mandated by the federal government. Scholars also discuss how rights and interests should be considered and protected in the course of research.

Institutional review boards were created in the United States in reaction to medical research studies that examined effects of treatment by subjecting patients to dangerous treatments or by denying them treatment without their consent, or even without their knowledge. The investigators conducted such studies with the thought that the overall benefits to society outweighed the risks to individuals, but the general public and the research community itself placed a higher value on the rights of individuals to make such decisions for themselves.

Institutional review boards focus most of their attention on procedures for 'informed consent'. A general principle is that participants in research have the right to know what risks they run through participation, including risks resulting from public descriptions of their actions. Investigators must describe these risks and give potential participants the opportunity to refuse their participation, or to withdraw from the study at a later time. Although many studies can conform to the principle with little difficulty, some cases pose practical problems or ethical dilemmas. In long-term collaborative work with teachers, for example, does the personal relationship that often develops between investigator and practitioner make it inappropriately difficult for the practitioner to withdraw from a study that seems likely to reveal something embarrassing or damaging to her reputation? Does the evaluative role teachers have over students allow them (or their parents) the freedom to refuse to participate (Howe and Dougherty, 1993)?

Other ethical issues revolve around conflicting interests of various stakeholders in a situation. What if, for example, an investigator studying a school administration uncovers evidence of fiscal mismanagement or malfeasance? How should the investigator weigh commitments made to maintain confidentiality against public interests or legal obligations? Analysis of such ethical issues has as yet received little attention in the research community and seldom receives much attention in research training.

The standards developed by professional associations do, however, include guidelines for some of the ethical issues arising in research. One set of standards addresses issues surrounding testing; another addresses issues in programme evaluation (American Psychological Association, 1986; Joint Committee on Standards for Educational Evaluation, 1994).

RESEARCH AS AN EVOLVING INSTITUTION

The standards and methods of research are based in research communities or traditions of research. At any point in time individual investigators are making decisions in their studies, drawing on their understandings of the norms in their community. Two processes of change aid in understanding the decisions at such single points in time: processes by which investigators learn the norms of their communities and processes by which those norms themselves change.

Historical studies of educational research give some sense of the changes in research over the past century and why those changes came about. Few studies encompass educational research as a whole, even for the United States. (One recent exception is Lagemann, 1996.) Ideas about the evolution of particular communities can be gleaned from many narrative research reviews, as well as from biographical and autobiographical accounts of leading scholars.

University- and research-organisation-based educational researchers typically learn the norms of their research community initially through completion of a doctoral degree at a college of education. Reputational studies report on the differences in status and external funding of colleges of education with graduate programmes, but reveal little about what the colleges do to prepare students to carry out research. The curricula across these doctoral programmes undoubtedly vary, but little systematic information is available to compare what students study and learn. After completing their degrees, researchers strengthen connections to their communities by participation in professional organisations, and by reading and contributing to scholarly journals. Some attention has been given to the status and citation influence of leading journals.

Teacher research has gained increased attention in the United States. Many authors have written to advocate such teacher involvement, but little has been written about the evolution of communities of teacher research that embody and pass on standards for evidence and argument. The greater number of opportunities for teachers to learn about research and the smaller number of opportunities (e.g. professional meetings and journals) to open teacher research to critical comment suggest that the community may exert less influence on this work.

REFERENCES

American Psychological Association (1986) *Standards for Educational and Psychological Testing*. Hyattsville, MD: American Psychological Association.

Bogdan, R. C. and Biklen, S. K. (1997) *Qualitative Research for Education: An Introduction to Theory and Methods* (3rd edn). Needham Heights, MA: Allyn & Bacon.

Brennan, R. (1983) *Elements of Generalizability Theory*. Iowa City, IA: American College Testing Service.

Cooper, H. and Hedges, L. V. (1994) *The Handbook of Research Synthesis*. New York: Russell Sage Foundation.

Denzin, N. K. and Lincoln, Y. S. (eds) (1994) *Handbook of Qualitative Research*. Thousand Oaks, CA: Sage Publications.

Eisner, E. and Peshkin, A. (eds) (1990) *Qualitative Inquiry in Education: The Continuing Debate*. New York: Teachers College Press.

Firestone, W. (1993) 'Alternative arguments for generalizing from data as applied to qualitative research'. *Educational Researcher* 22 (4), 16–23.

Floden, R. E. and Buchmann, M. (1990) 'Philosophical inquiry in teacher education'. In R. Houston (ed.) *Handbook of Research on Teacher Education*. New York: Macmillan.

Gilligan, C. (1982) *In a Different Voice: Psychological Theory and Women's Development*. Cambridge, MA: Harvard University Press.

Glass, G. V. and Hopkins, K. D. (1995) *Statistical Methods in Education and Psychology* (3rd edn). Needham Heights, MA: Allyn & Bacon.

Gusfield, J. R. (1981) *The Culture of Public Problems: Drinking-Driving and the Symbolic Order*. Chicago: University of Chicago Press.

Hammersley, M. and Atkinson, P. (1983) 'What is ethnography?' In M. Hammersley and P. Atkinson (eds) *Ethnography: Principles in Practice*. London: Tavistock, 1–22.

Harding, S. (1986) *The Science Question in Feminism*. Ithaca, NY: Cornell University Press.

Howe, K. R. (1992) 'Getting over the quantitative–qualitative debate'. *American Journal of Education* 100 (2), 236–256.

Howe, K. R. and Dougherty, K. C. (1993) 'Ethics, institutional review boards, and the changing face of educational research'. *Educational Researcher*, 22 (9), 16–21.

Jaeger, R. (1984) *Sampling in Education and the Social Sciences*. New York: Longman.

Jaeger, R. M. (ed.) (1997) *Complementary Methods for Research in Education* (2nd edn). Washington, DC: American Educational Research Association. 1st edition 1988.

Joint Committee on Standards for Educational Evaluation (1994) *The Program Evaluation Standards: How to Assess Evaluations of Educational Programs*. Thousand Oaks, CA: Sage Publications.

Keeves, J. P. (ed.) (1988) *Educational Research, Methodology and Measurement: An International Handbook*. New York: Pergamon Press.

Kuhn, T. (1962) *The Structure of Scientific Revolutions*. Chicago: University of Chicago Press.

Lagemann, E. C. (1996) 'Contested terrain: A history of education research in the United States, 1890–1990'. *Educational Researcher*, 26 (9), 5–17.

Lecompte, M. D., Preissle, J. and Tesch, R. (1993) *Ethnography and Qualitative Design in Educational Research*. New York: Academic Press.

Lindblom, C. E. and Cohen, D. K. (1979) *Usable Knowledge*. New Haven, CT: Yale University Press.

Maxwell, J. (1992) 'Understanding and validity in qualitative research'. *Harvard Educational Review*, 62, 279–301.

Messick, S. (1989) 'Validity'. In R. L. Linn (ed.) *Educational Measurement* (3rd edn). New York: American Council on Education and Macmillan, 13–103.

Miles, M. B. and Huberman, M. (1984) *Qualitative Data Analysis: A Sourcebook of New Methods*. Beverly Hills, CA: Sage.

Neumann, A. and Peterson, P. (eds) (1986) *Research and Everyday Life: The Personal Origins of Educational Inquiry*. New York: Teachers College Press.

191

Phillips, D. C. (1983) 'After the wake: Postpositivist educational thought'. *Educational Researcher* 12 (5), 4–12.

Phillips, D. C. (1992) *The Social Scientist's Bestiary: A Guide to Fabled Threats to, and Defenses of, Naturalistic Social Science*. New York: Pergamon Press.

Shavelson, R. J. (1996) *Statistical Reasoning for the Behavioral Sciences* (3rd edn). Needham Heights, MA: Allyn & Bacon.

Shepard, L. A. (1993) 'Evaluating test validity'. *Review of Research in Education*, 19, 405–450.

Shulman, L. S. (1988) 'Disciplines of inquiry in education: An overview'. In R. M. Jaeger (ed.) *Complementary Methods for Research in Education*. Washington, DC: American Educational Research Association: 3–17.

Weiss, C. H. (1979) 'The many meanings of research utilization'. *Public Administration Review* 39 (5), 426–431.

11

EDUCATIONAL POLICY-MAKING AND ANALYSIS

Diverse viewpoints

Rosemary Deem and Kevin J. Brehony

Our intention here is to provide an overview of major debates and conceptual analyses in the field of educational policy. This is not a straightforward task. First, there is no consensus about what the term policy means for educational researchers even within a single country. Second, but just as important, there is also no clear agreement about what constitutes educational research, with a continuum of views ranging from the claim that education is a discipline in its own right to the contention that research carried out in educational settings draws on a range of disciplines, mostly located within the social sciences (Deem, 1996a). Since no commonality in perspective or disciplinary background can be assumed, even for researchers working on similar concerns within the same or similar settings, it would indeed be surprising if there were significant agreement about what constitutes educational policy.

Educational policy is a term used to refer to almost any analysis of changes, reforms or developments in education, whether these occur at the macro (national or supra-national), meso (middle) or micro (local) level, and irrespective of whether the focus is on contemporary or historical events and processes. Thus those who see themselves as educational policy analysts, or as conducting research on educational policy-making, range from researchers conducting macro analyses of national or international policy on education to those studying policy-making and implementation that is confined to an individual institution.

Despite this diversity, we would suggest that educational policy analysis worthy of the name involves taking into account the role of states and governments (whether these exist at the global, national, regional or local level) in the formulation, implementation and monitoring of educational policies. Such a definition does not exclude meso and micro level policy analyses, nor does it suggest that states or governments will always lie at the very centre of researchers' concerns. However, taking cognisance of the crucial role of local and nation states in educational policy-making does remind us that in much of the world, education, regardless of the extent to which educational provision at different levels is privately or publicly funded, remains within the purview of regional, national and, to an increasing extent, transnational state forms (e.g. the European Union). Furthermore, educational provision is normally subject to regulation emanating from one or more of these states. This being so, it is difficult to conceive of informed educational policy analysis which completely ignores the state (Ozga, 1990). It is probably unrealistic to expect all educational policy researchers to be aware of the complexities of theories of states and governments. Nevertheless it is important that educational researchers are aware of and pay some attention to the macro-level debates about policies and states if their analyses are not to remain parochial and atheoretical.

POLICY-MAKING AND POLICY IMPLEMENTATION

It is important for those interested in the academic study of educational policy to understand the complex relationships that exist between educational policy-making and educational policy implementation. Though some researchers make a clear distinction between policy-making and implementation (which implies that implementation is largely a question of routine procedure), such a separation is, in practice, hard to sustain. First, it is rarely the case that policy itself, however clearly outlined, has no unintended consequences. So the processes by which policies are interpreted will almost always have uncertain outcomes, even if it were possible to predict the intentions of policy-makers, which is notoriously difficult. Second, it is unusual to find examples of clearly bounded policy innovations or developments. A well-informed historical awareness of the situated nature of educational policy frequently reveals that legislation itself either simply puts a regulatory framework around developments that are already in place or continues a trend or change already considered for some time beforehand.

Third, it is often the case that what Lipsky calls 'street-level bureaucrats' play a key role in how a policy actually operates. This in turn is affected by the extent to which discretion is available to those expected to put policies into practice (Lipsky, 1980). In order to take account of this micro-level reinterpretation of policy, Bowe and Ball have developed a concept known as the policy cycle (Ball, 1994; Bowe et al., 1992) which, they claim, overcomes some of the problems of separating out policy-making from policy implementation. The concept attributes to those in educational institutions the capacity to interpret or 'recontextualise' policies: an activity over which policy writers have little control. A policy cycle approach thus removes the state from centre-stage in the policy process, whilst acknowledging its existence as an initiator of policy change. Policy cycle approaches also place considerable emphasis on policies as texts and how those texts are 'read' by practitioners. However, there are some texts in centralised education reform processes (e.g. standard assessment tasks [SATs] as used in English, Welsh and Northern Ireland national assessment policies) where the interpretation of practitioners or their resistance to what is proposed does no more than delay the implementation of the practices required (Hatcher and Troyna, 1994). Thus the notion of policy texts which can be significantly reinterpreted by practitioners is not quite as persuasive as it might first appear. Nor does the policy cycle model dissolve the vexed problem of the connections between institutional structures (as in government) and agents (in this case, educational practitioners). Finally, it does not remove the need to ensure that the role of the state is always acknowledged in any exploration of educational policy.

SOCIAL POLICY AND EDUCATIONAL POLICY

Though it might be thought from the discussion so far that educational policy analysis has a wide remit, the parameters of that analysis are sometimes rather narrow. Educational policy, unlike other areas of policy, is not always considered in its wider context and it is still relatively rare for educational researchers to pay much attention to other aspects of social policy that might have some relationship to education. By contrast, social policy researchers often include education in their remit (Hill, 1996). Though there is a not inconsiderable literature on educational policy, much of it is less theoretically based than the literature on social policy, an area often closely associated with an analysis of issues related to social welfare and (recently) with explanations about why Western societies are tending to reduce spending on social welfare services.

A number of theoretical debates relevant to educational policy analysis are also found in political science. These are particularly concerned with the examination of public policy, whether this takes the form of analysing decision-making structures and processes, the content of policies, or the policy networks that give rise to new policies. In both social and public policy, considerable attention is paid to the importance of economies and the central and local state. Furthermore, there is also a focus on the phenomena loosely grouped under the heading of globalisation, and on the possible effects of worldwide economic, social and cultural changes on the policies of nation states (Held, 1995).

Though some researchers working in education have recognised the significance of these wider parameters of policy (Ball, 1994; Kogan *et al.*, 1984), the tracing of the kinds of connections between social policy, educational policy and political science which we have emphasised in our research on citizenship and school governance (Deem *et al.*, 1995) is still rare in a field dominated by empiricism. The latter implies an excessive emphasis on the collection of data from the so-called real world, with reportage of events and processes having little or no regard to questions about the nature of social reality and social science knowledge. This has meant that educational researchers are not always aware of important debates about policy as a field of study. Thus, though Ham and Hill's distinction between analysis *of* policy and analysis *for* policy (Ham and Hill, 1984) is helpful in enabling some differentiation to be made in respect of the purposes of and audiences for research, such a separation is rarely recognised or utilised in the field of education. Yet it is important to be able to differentiate between those investigations of educational policy that are directed towards critiques and the development of new or existing theoretical debates (analysis *of* policy) and those that are intended to lead to formulation of new policy and are thus fairly applied in their outlook (analysis *for* policy).

The notion of policy-relevant research (as opposed to analysis for the purposes of policy formation) is also an important subcategory of analysis *of* policy. It implies that whilst the research is of a basic rather than applied kind, the researchers concerned are cognisant of the possibility that it can also be used by others to inform future policy. Within edu-cational policy research itself, the closest analogy to Ham and Hill's analysis *of* policy is that of policy sociology, defined as a field of analysis which seeks to establish the intersoci-etal, intrasocietal and collective aspects of educational policy-making (Ozga, 1990). Policy sociology seeks to establish whether there is a difference between a largely descriptive analysis of educational policy at the micro level, and a critical analysis of national and international policy at the macro and meso levels which is informed by a sociological perspective.

EDUCATION REFORM AND EDUCATIONAL POLICY ANALYSIS

It is clear that there is a symbiotic relationship between reform movements in education, policy formulation and implementation processes and the kinds of analyses that social scientists make of those reforms and the processes involved. When the reform of education is at the centre of political debate and activity, it is reasonable to assume that there will be a concomitant rise in the number of researchers working on and research investigations into, educational policy processes. This can be conceptualised as a 'policy turn' (Deem, 1996b). Though this is in itself no more than a restatement of the link between social theory and the prevailing social/economic/political conditions, nevertheless it is worth reflecting on this linkage. It can help to explain why the field of educational policy is dominated by descriptive accounts of particular policy developments. Of course, description of the effects of policy is a necessary part of policy analysis, but good description is always conducted through the lens of theoretical explanation and interpretation.

The study of particular educational changes or reforms also raises another issue: whether such reforms are unique to the society in which they occur. The likelihood that, in the late twentieth century, any particular education reform will be utilised in part or full by others in different national settings (sometimes termed policy borrowing [Halpin and Troyna, 1995]) underlines how important it is for educational policy analysts to pay attention to cross-cultural research as well as monocultural research. There is also a clear need for educational policy analysts to understand how, where and why educational policy innovations are lifted out of context and transferred to another setting. Furthermore, any study of how policy changes are translated from one context to another needs to take into account not only national but also international policy networks, as one means by which details of particular policy developments are made known in contexts other than those where they originated. This is particularly important since policy transfer from one country to another may involve active co-operation, and political consensus over educational objectives, as well as mere borrowing of policy ideas.

CURRENT THEORETICAL DEBATES IN POLICY ANALYSIS

There are a good many theoretical debates in the field of policy analysis and the relative salience of these will vary among countries. However, the various positions crystallise under four main headings: pluralist theories; Marxist theories; post-structuralist theories; and feminist theories. As with any categorisation, these are not watertight compartments and there are elements that are common to more than one theoretical debate. Thus it is possible to see elements of Marxism in some feminist analyses and post-structuralist accounts sometimes make pluralist assumptions about power.

Pluralist theories

Pluralist theories about education policy-making and implementation abound. Pluralist theories recognise the importance of the state in educational policy but also emphasise the role of other groups and agencies, including municipal authorities and teacher organisations. In some countries, including the UK, such analyses have included the idea that policy emerges from a partnership between the central state, local state and teacher unions. Underlying this is an assumption that power is distributed more or less equally between the partners or centres of decision-making. Furthermore it is assumed that each partner or centre exercises some autonomy over policy and related resource deployment. Thus much of the research rooted in this tradition has concentrated on examination of the administrative structure within which policy operates, and on the individuals who play key roles in such structures, as well as examining the nature of the policies themselves.

The pluralist perspective assumes that educational policy proceeds largely on the basis of consensus. It thus has some characteristics in common with Habermas's notion of an ideal speech community (Habermas, 1987). There is, on occasion, a tendency to mask the extent to which struggles and conflicts arise in the policy process. The theorisation of power in pluralist accounts often relies heavily on what Ranson terms 'exchange theory', in which it is assumed that policy proceeds by means of a bargaining process between the main contenders in relation to resources and policy options (Ranson, 1995). Analytic emphasis is often placed on the internal consistency or contradictions found within policies, the extent to which specific policies are administered in a rational way, and the appropriateness of the mechanisms by which policies are implemented. When properly conducted, pluralist research can be very useful both as analysis *for* policy and analysis *of* policy, as the work of Kogan shows (Cordingley and Kogan, 1993; Kogan, 1988). However, not all pluralist work on education policy is as successful; though the political nature of policy is emphasised, the notion of policies as policies is often understated. In addition, although pluralist accounts are not necessarily descriptive, the importance of contemporary events and processes may be overemphasised. Furthermore, though there is acceptance of the existence of different interests, the inequalities between policy interest groups are often minimised and there is sometimes too little attention paid to cultural values and the material conditions underlying these.

Marxist perspectives

Marxist perspectives see the role of the state and the interaction between capital and the state as pivotal to an understanding of educational policy. Theories of power in Marxist accounts suggest that it is based on economic and political control, such as ownership of or control over the means of production. Power inequalities mean that the policy process is not just one in which more or less equal contenders decide on the allocation and exchange of resources. Rather, those with economic and political power bases have a considerable advantage over those who merely sell their labour power. In Marxist and neo-Marxist accounts, the state is omnipresent in policy processes. Educational policies often display evidence of struggles between owners of capital and sellers of labour power over the content and emphasis of educational policy. This might, for example, involve debates over the amount of public money to be invested in education. Just as pluralist theories often critique Marxist accounts, so too Marxist accounts often take as their starting-point critiques of pluralist theories of educational policy. Marxist and neo-Marxist theories (the latter is a term sometimes used by those theorists who wish to distance themselves from what they see as rather crude forms of Marxist theory which place considerable emphasis on economic determinism) often use historically grounded accounts of the relative roles of capital and state and the struggles between social class groupings over education as a starting-point for their analysis (Simon, 1991).

Another Marxist approach is to examine education policy in order to determine the extent to which it helps the state to secure the conditions of its own existence and subsequently those of the capitalist mode of production (Dale, 1989). Marxists also explore the role of a particular state or states in the formation of educational and social policy over a particular time period. Though neo-Marxist analysis of educational policy does pay attention to the meso and micro levels of policy, much of the emphasis is on the macro level (Ozga, 1994), and thus there is sometimes a tendency to pay more attention to structure than to agency. However those adopting post-Fordist analyses, by concentrating on the educational consequences of the rejection of state-managed economies and the introduction of flexible systems of capital accumulation and labour processes, have tried to overcome this problem by focusing on educational institutions.

Post-structuralism and post-modernism

Post-structuralist accounts of educational policy attempt to remedy the deficiencies of both descriptive, pluralist accounts of educational policy (in which power flows between different partners) and those of Marxist accounts (which emphasise the macro-level role of the state and the generation of policy as a result of zero-sum power struggles between economic and political agents). Post-structuralists regard agency as crucial to an understanding of policy, and they place much emphasis on the fluidity of power and its possession by all agents. They also draw attention to the importance of policies as texts, which are then subject to a range of interpretations. The most notable theorist here has been Stephen Ball (Ball, 1994; Bowe et al., 1992). Following the trend set by social theorists who have made the 'linguistic turn' (the tendency to argue that everything is a text which may be read like a language), Ball proposes that education policy be treated as a text and that some policy texts are writerly and others readerly. Readerly texts are those that do not permit the production of many meanings by virtue of their structure. Writerly texts, on the other hand, do permit this. Authorial intentions, or what policy-makers intended, can be ignored, as according to prominent theorists in the formulations of structuralism and post-structuralism, the author is dead. This claim is linked to the view that the source of all meaning lies in discourses and not in individual, knowing, human subjects.

What theoretical advantages are claimed by the textualisation of education policy? It certainly breaks with any rationalist notion of a policy cycle with discernible stages of formulation and implementation. Reading of texts takes place constantly and as no meanings are fixed, multiple and even conflictual meanings may be produced by readers of policies. This view assumes that the readers or implementers are permitted quite a large amount of discretion in order to pursue their particular reading and not that of others.

A second adaptation of a post-structuralist category that Ball has attempted is Foucault's notion of discourse (Ball, 1994). From a discourse perspective, policies become 'regimes of truth' which set limits to their interpretation and enactment. The textualist approach emphasises the indeterminacy and openness of policy outcomes and the impossibility of reading off outcomes from statements of intent. Theories of discourse do, however, argue that people or subjects are constituted by the language in which they speak. Thus discourses produce subjects who are subjected to power and domination from which it is difficult to escape. This is because there is no obvious point from which that domination may be contested and overthrown. Moreover, because discourse involves the operation of circuits of power that do not emanate from the state, the state's role in educational policy is diminished. This view comes close to some of the assumptions of pluralist theories; however, the dominance of discourses over agents implies a monolith closer to crude Marxist theories, albeit from a different source. Post-structuralism attempts to address some of the criticisms of Marxist and pluralist accounts of educational policy, notably concerns about over-determined views of policy and the absence of agency but thus far it may not have succeeded in superseding earlier theoretical formulations.

Feminist theories

Feminist theories about educational policy differ from other theories in that they highlight the importance of gender, that is, culturally and socially constructed notions about how women and men and girls and boys should act and think, and socially/culturally constructed ideas about sexual identities and sexuality. They also address the importance of gender power relations in the construction and interpretation of educational policy and the shaping of the policy process. Gender is frequently ignored by other education policy theorists, although histories of the struggles for girls and women to gain access to and acceptance of their place in all levels of education are well documented for almost all countries. Feminist theories themselves are not all of a piece. They range from liberal theories about the impact of socialisation into gender-typed roles on educational policy and provision (such as the argument that girls should take cookery and history rather than physics or computing), to post-structuralist accounts of the formation of internally contradictory gender identities within discourses of education and the difficulties of dealing with this within the confines of equal opportunities policies which assume a more deterministic process of gender identity formation.

It is not possible to speak of a single feminist approach to educational policy. However, the distinctive element of feminist approaches to educational policy lies in the emphasis on gender and sexuality as part of the policy process and context. It also relates to an awareness of how gender relations and culturally shaped gender identities may affect policy and the policy process, whether at the macro level of the state or states or at the micro level of individual educational institutions or practitioners. Though it is not the case that feminist analyses always take gender as the sole or main determining factor in educational policy analysis, this remains a risk. Indeed, it is important that other major dimensions of social exclusion and inclusion such as ethnicity, disability and social class are also taken seriously.

Gender analysis of policy is not confined to recent developments. Some feminist accounts of policy are historically grounded, whilst others are more focused on contemporary events. Thus a number of recent studies examine processes of education reform (Arnot *et al.*, 1996; Blackmore *et al.*, 1994). Gendered analyses of education may be popularly associated with issues related to women's schooling. However, an analysis informed by awareness of the power struggles by gays and lesbians in education is also beginning to emerge (Epstein, 1994). In addition, the increased popularity of the study of masculine cultures in educational settings (Mac an Ghaill, 1994) suggests that it will not be long before policy studies include as much attention to masculinity as to femininity.

GLOBALISATION THEORIES

We have already drawn attention to the extent to which modern communications and international or transnational policy networks permit and even encourage the transmission of ideas about educational policy from one country to another. We have also noted the tendency of educational policy analysis to lag behind important debates in the social sciences, including new developments in social and political theory. One important conceptual debate which has yet to have a significant effect on educational policy analysis is that of globalisation. Globalisation is not just an academic issue. Politicians and journalists are also very exercised by it. One form that this more popular thinking takes is to suggest that the idea of independent nation states is outmoded and has been superseded by transnational bodies such as G7 (a group consisting of the seven leading industrialised countries) and the Organisation for Economic Co-operation and Development (OECD). It is claimed that this shift has been powered by the development of a global economy facilitated by financial deregulation (e.g. the removal of restrictions on the amounts of foreign currencies allowed to circulate in particular countries) and the deregulation of labour (as, for example, in the abolition of minimum wage agreements and the loss of protection of workers against unfair dismissal). As the global economy has grown, it is argued that nation states have become relatively powerless and are forced to pursue policies that facilitate the operation of the global market. This includes governments vying with one another to produce low-wage economies and so attract whatever investment is available. However, both proponents of globalisation theories (Held, 1995), as well as those more sceptical of the claims made (Hirst and Thompson, 1996), have pointed out that this is a rather simplistic analysis. Moreover, divisions exist between those who see economic forces as the determining instance and those who argue that the economic, the political and the cultural levels are structurally independent (Waters, 1995).

What follows are some examples of how current educational policies that are global in scope may be linked to each of these three levels. First, at the *economic level*, policies such as privatisation and marketisation are clearly not motivated just by national concerns. Sometimes these policies involve wholesale movement of educational provision from public to private funding but more typically they involve the introduction of quasi-markets to publicly funded education. For these to exist, no money changes hands but parents and students are encouraged to make a choice among state-funded schools rather than simply letting children go to the nearest school; school performance indicators such as exam pass and truancy rates are used to encourage competition between schools. A further example of semi-privatisation would be where educational institutions such as universities are encouraged to seek private rather than public funding for an increasing proportion of their activities. Another example of global and economically driven policies relates to the educational impact of migration. Big movements of populations across the world have occurred in the postwar period on an unprecedented scale. This is related to various causes, including war, poverty and the demand for labour. Population movements of this kind have had considerable consequences for education policy, including issues related to the teaching of mother tongue languages and the adoption of multicultural approaches to schooling.

At the *political level*, the spread of democracy across the world raises questions of how to educate for democracy and citizenship, as well as issues about the democratisation of the governance of schooling by lay people. Though education is itself a basic entitlement or citizenship right enshrined in many postwar welfare states (Marshall, 1965), it is also a means by which the qualities required for participative citizenship can be fostered (Ranson and Stewart, 1994).

Finally, at the *socio-cultural level*, policies regarding curriculum content (which mark out highly and less valued knowledge) are becoming affected by global processes. Global consumer culture (e.g. the spread of international markets in music and clothing) tends to remove or de-differentiate bourgeois culture from mass culture and it disrupts categories of knowledge previously considered worthwhile. Hence policies have been adopted explicitly to do the work of cultural restoration. For example, the National Curriculum in England is seen by some proponents as a way of reviving interest in English culture, including literature and history, amongst school students.

Despite global developments, the nation state has by no means been superseded by global organisations when it comes to education policies. However, what Giddens calls 'time-space compression' (Giddens, 1990), or the shrinkage of the globe, permits the broader dispersal of policies and their much quicker adoption than was possible in the past. Bodies like the World Bank and the OECD are important vectors of education policies which governments often find hard to resist. In concluding this section, we want to emphasise that the study of education policy needs to take more account of the theorisation of globalisation. However, the theories of globalisation adopted do have consequences for the analysis undertaken. For those who accept the primacy of the economic, education policy on a global scale is seen to be driven by changes in the forces and relations of production. Followers of Giddens focus more on the nation state and its capacity to wage war as an agent of change (Giddens, 1985). Those preferring Robertson's analysis pay most attention to changes in culture, consumerism and cultural cleavages (Robertson, 1992).

EDUCATIONAL POLICY ANALYSES IN WIDER PERSPECTIVE

What we have attempted here is but a brief sketch of some of the current debates and major concepts in use in the field of educational policy. However, as noted earlier, the context in which educational policy is studied is never a neutral or static one and the actual policies and policy processes studied will inevitably affect the kinds of debates, theories and concepts utilised. So too will the values of researchers and the societies in which they research. Theoretically, the exploration of educational policy is one in which a range of positions may be invoked. Nevertheless, we would like to repeat our earlier plea that whatever the location of policy analysis, it is helpful if educational policy can be seen as part of a wider study of social and public policy in which the role of states as well as individuals and institutions is seen to be significant. Furthermore the theorisation of educational policy will be strengthened by a fuller awareness of current debates and developments in the social sciences as a whole.

REFERENCES

Arnot, M. (1996) *Educational Reforms and Gender Equality in Schools*. Manchester: Equal Opportunities Commission.

Ball, S. (1994) *Education Reform: A Critical and Post-structuralist Approach*. Buckingham: Open University Press.

Blackmore, G., Kenway, J. Willis, S. and Rennie, L. (1994) 'What's working for girls? The reception of gender equity policy in two Australian schools'. in C. Marshall (ed.) *The New Politics of Race and Gender*. London: Falmer, 183–202.

Bowe, R., Ball, S. and Gold, Anne (1992) *Reforming Education and Changing Schools*. London: Routledge.

Cordingley, P. and Kogan, M. (1993) *In Support of Education: Governing the Reformed System*. London: Jessica Kingsley.

Dale, R. (1989) *The State and Educational Policy*. Milton Keynes: Open University Press.

Deem, R. (1996a) 'Educational research in the context of the social sciences: A special case?' *British Journal of Educational Studies*, XXXXIV (2), 141–158.

Deem, R. (1996b) 'Border territories: A journey through sociology, education and women's studies'. *British Journal of Sociology of Education*, 17 (1), 5–19.

Deem, R., Brehony, K. J. and Heath, S. J. (1995) *Active Citizenship and the Governing of Schools*. Buckingham: Open University Press.

Epstein, D. (ed.) (1994) *Challenging Lesbian and Gay Inequalities in Education*. Buckingham: Open University Press.

Giddens, A. (1985) *The Nation State and Violence*. Cambridge: Polity Press.

Giddens, A. (1990) *The Consequences of Modernity*. Cambridge: Polity Press.

Habermas, J. (1987) *The Theory of Communicative Action: Lifeworld and System: a Critique of Functionalist Reason*. Cambridge: Polity Press.

Halpin, D. and Troyna, B. (1995) 'The politics of educational policy borrowing'. *Comparative Education* 31 (3), 303–310.

Ham, C. and Hill, M. (1984) *The Policy Process in the Modern Capitalist State*. London: Harvester Wheatsheaf.

Hatcher, R. and Troyna, B. (1994) 'The "policy cycle": a Ball by Ball account'. *Journal of Education Policy* 9 (2), 155–170.

Held, D. (1995) *Democracy and the Global Order*. Cambridge: Polity Press.

Hill, M. (1996) *Social Policy – A Comparative Analysis*. Hemel Hempstead: Prentice-Hall/Harvester Wheatsheaf.

Hirst, P. and Thompson, G. (1996) *Globalisation in Question*. Cambridge: Polity Press.

Kogan, M. (1988) *Education Accountability*. London: Hutchinson.

Kogan, M., Johnson, D., Packwood, T. and Whitaker, T. (1984) *School Governing Bodies*. London: Heinemann.

Lipsky, M. (1980) *Street Level Bureaucracy*. New York: Russell Sage.

Mac an Ghaill, M. (1994) *The Making of Men*. Buckingham: Open University Press.

Marshall, T. H. (1965) *Social Policy*. London: Hutchinson.

Ozga, J. (1990) 'Policy research and policy theory: A comment on Fitz and Halpin'. *Journal of Education Policy* 5 (4), 359–362.

Ozga, J. (1994) 'Framework for policy analysis in education'. In D. Kallos and S. Lindblad (eds) *New Policy Contexts for Education: Sweden and the United Kingdom*. Umea, Sweden: Umea Universitet, 205–235.

Ranson, S. (1995) 'Theorising educational policy'. *Journal of Educational Policy* 10 (4), 427–448.

Ranson, S. and Stewart, J. (1994) *Management for the Public Domain – Enabling the Learning Society*. London: Macmillan.

Robertson, R. (1992) *Globalization*. London: Sage.

Simon, B. (1991) *Education and the Social Order 1940–1990*. London: Lawrence & Wishart.

Waters, M. (1995) *Globalization*. London: Routledge.

12

CURRICULUM

The case for a focus on learning

Robert McCormick and Patricia Murphy

INTRODUCTION

'Curriculum' is understood in many ways and has been the subject of study from a number of perspectives. Three levels of analysis have become evident over the years, namely that of the *specified*, the *enacted*, and the *experienced* curricula. Early perspectives focused on the aims and content of what was to be taught; the *specified curriculum*. This focus on the specified curriculum led to analyses that sought to establish the relationships between educational knowledge and the social and economic interests of a society. These analyses have since been expanded to consider the socio–historical influences on the production and validation of the knowledge specified in curricula. More recently this has focused attention on how knowledge is selected, organised, transmitted and evaluated (Bernstein, 1971); and the extent to which worldwide processes are at play in this, in terms of the emergence of standardised models of society and of education (Benavot *et al.*, 1992). These developments had a twofold effect; they extended the context of the curriculum debate in relation to the mediating influences that were identified. They also, and importantly, extended the levels of study of curriculum to include the arena of the 'classroom', i.e. the *enacted curriculum*. In this sense curriculum and instruction were seen as inseparable, reflecting Goodson's concept of curriculum as 'constructed, negotiated, and re-negotiated at a number of levels and in a number of arenas' (Goodson, 1994, p. 111).

Implicated in this shift of perspective were changing views of pedagogy, and of teachers' roles within it, based on developments in understanding about the nature of human action and learning, which led to a focus on a further level of curriculum definition: that of the learners and the curriculum they experience. The *experienced* curriculum has largely been ignored in curriculum debates and it is our contention that this reflects the limited understanding about learning of those involved. If learners are the passive receivers of the enacted curriculum, then the received and the enacted curriculum correspond. What distinguishes these levels is the ability of the learners to learn or receive. If, however, learning is a social process and if learners' agency, like teachers' agency, is recognised, then what is experienced is determined by the participants and the nature of their participation in the arenas in which curricula are enacted; for example, the learning activities and associated assessment. Furthermore, as Murphy (1990) argued, theories of how students learn and develop help determine: *what* is selected for inclusion in the curriculum; *how* it is taught, including which classroom resources, organisation and pedagogical strategies are judged to be appropriate; and the *nature* of the teacher's role and relationship with learners (Murphy, 1990, p. 35), i.e. all three levels of curriculum definition.

To understand curriculum then, it is necessary to consider the mediating influences and their effects at all three levels of curriculum negotiation; the specified, enacted and experienced.[1] Furthermore, central to these influences are views of learning and associated views of knowledge.

There has been an international trend towards legislating for curricula in schools (Skilbeck, 1990), though this is not universal; with some countries such as France going in the opposite direction (i.e. allowing more local control of the curriculum). The focus in the early 1990s, in those countries where legislation existed, was therefore on the specified curriculum. However, these curricula were invariably accompanied by assessment systems that *enacted* national proposals. This appeared to leave curriculum considerations at the level of policy-makers, with the job of teachers only to follow prescriptions. Work on curriculum change has, however, made it clear, even at policy level, that there is no mere transmission from proposals to classroom activities. Teachers' agency is reflected in their views about the curriculum, about learning, knowledge and pedagogy, and these all affect the way curricular proposals and assessment systems are implemented and valued. The enacted curriculum is consequently unlikely to correspond to the specified curriculum. Some policy-makers may see this situation as one that can be 'rectified' through teacher training, though they seldom make the resources available to carry this out. However, this view is but one concerning the nature of change and one that still leaves much at stake in terms of what goes on in classrooms.

Governments have become increasingly concerned with raising the performance of students by all manner of mechanisms, few of which involve the teachers or learners in the development of these mechanisms. These include prescriptions about teaching methods, such as has occurred in England with respect to the literacy hour; a period when the learning activities are laid down in detail in a handbook given to all primary schoolteachers (DfEE, 1998). National tests also reflect prescriptions of what knowledge is valued and how that knowledge is judged to be accessed and made explicit by learners. Often teacher development is perceived as learning the government script, while achievement is seen as learning the teacher's script. Nevertheless, governments recognise that it is in the various 'classroom' arenas across the phases of education that the battle for standards must be fought. These prescriptions are specifications that have to be enacted and experienced, and the government can have little control over these latter levels of curriculum; certainly not without a more profound understanding of learning than they currently exhibit.

We therefore have something of a dilemma. Where national curricula and assessment systems are being imposed, teachers have on the face of it less reason to be involved in curriculum issues. Yet it is increasingly evident that creating a specified curriculum is merely one element of development and that it is the curriculum at all three levels that needs to be the focus of concern. This therefore involves those arenas that teachers and learners occupy and policy-makers are least able to affect. New understandings about learning have made possible a more profound analysis of the curriculum than hitherto. We shall argue that this understanding affects all levels and elements of curriculum considerations and, paradoxically, emphasises the enacted and experienced curriculum to an extent that the specified curriculum is less important; teaching and learning take centre-stage. This serves as the justification for the involvement of teachers in curriculum discussions at a time when it appears they have least say. It also implies that policy-makers need to have a more explicit and justified view of learning than is usually evident in their pronouncements on curriculum issues. Furthermore, assessment systems need to reflect these views of learning and learners, and the systems' limitations as a consequence made explicit.

Of course, even from the earliest times of the study of curriculum considerations, learning was seen to be important. Early views of the curriculum focused on the curriculum development process, and Hilda Taba's classic text is an illustration of that approach (Taba, 1962). In describing her approach to curriculum development, Taba sees 'analyses of society and culture, studies of the learner and learning process, and analyses of the nature of knowledge' as being at the heart of rational curriculum planning (Taba, 1962, p. 10). The situation is no different today (though we would argue about the ideas of rational planning), but our understanding of how learning interrelates these four sources of curriculum considerations changes the nature of the analyses that Taba envisaged. Her enlightened accounts of each of these areas at the time followed a discipline-based approach to the study of the curriculum:

- 'society' reflected a sociological analysis;
- 'culture' an anthropological analysis;
- 'learning' a psychological analysis;
- 'knowledge' a philosophical analysis.

These sources are seen as inputs to curriculum design, with important interactions. Thus different cultures require different kinds of knowledge and, hence, the objectives of education, the selection of content, and the stress on particular learning activities could be derived from a cultural analysis. Likewise ideas on learning determine what objectives are possible under what conditions, and how content can be organised for effective learning. Knowledge is seen in terms of (subject) disciplines, with their different structures and contributions; philosophical considerations allow an analysis of these disciplines and of the goals of education.

Teaching methods interacted with this view of curriculum. Taba saw the definition of the curriculum as somewhere between what we have characterised the *specified* curriculum and the *experienced* curriculum, and she was reluctant just to incorporate issues of teaching and learning activities into the idea of 'teaching methods'. Pedagogy does not feature in this view of curriculum, except perhaps as a continental European version of 'teaching methods'. Similarly assessment (or 'evaluation' as Taba called it) was seen as determining only that (or if) the ends of education had been achieved. In general this approach to thinking about the curriculum, as a progression from the specified, through the enacted to the experienced curriculum, is limited.

We shall argue that, since Taba's time, our understanding of learning has transformed how we should consider the curriculum. This transformation links learning, culture, knowledge, assessment and pedagogy in a way that requires us to rethink our views of the

206

curriculum. This does not mean that interactions among the sources of curriculum development have not been recognised previously. For example, the impact of the sociology of knowledge in the 1970s was witness to the way knowledge was seen to be socially constructed with implications for different groups and types of knowledge manifesting themselves in differential access to the curriculum (Young, 1971).[2] However, we shall argue that we need to explore these interrelationships, and to do so with views of learning as an important feature of the exploration. Whatever view we take of learning, it must be at the centre of our concerns for the curriculum. It is, after all, the main point of creating and enacting any curriculum. Further, it is this focus that in our view enables the three levels of curriculum analysis to be most clearly linked. This does not mean simply reversing the progression, such that the analysis starts with the experienced and ends with the specified curriculum, but that learning has something to say at each level and in a way that adds some coherence to the analysis.

The study of the curriculum has lost its way in recent years. Picking almost randomly two recent texts that aim to represent the contemporary field of curriculum studies, we find that they pay scant attention to learning; even seeing it as much less central than those in the 1960s and 1970s. For example, Marsh (1997) surveys a number of texts across the world to arrive at key concepts in curriculum and, although these concepts include student and teacher perspectives, there is little explicit concern for learning, and no discussion of theories or views of learning.[3] Likewise, a recent curriculum studies reader (Flinders and Thornton, 1997) fails to include any account of learning, with only two entries in the index; one relating to behaviourism and the other to Dewey. Likewise, Eisner with a book entitled *Cognition and Curriculum Reconsidered*, makes only a passing reference to the developing theories of learning, concluding that they are a 'promising development' to 'replace behaviourism' (Eisner, 1996, p. 28). Even the Open University team (Open University, 1976), writing over 20 years ago, had picked up the implications of learning and drawn on the most significant theorists of the time (Bruner and Piaget). Yet there have been significant developments in our understanding of learning, not just since the days of Dewey or early twentieth-century behaviourism, but since the 1960s and 1970s, when issues of learning were being explored for their implications for the curriculum. Our current understandings have, in our view, great significance for contemporary views of the curriculum.

To examine this significance we shall consider:

- contemporary views of learning and some of the important aspects that have a bearing on curriculum analyses;
- how these views of learning relate to views of the nature and types of knowledge;
- the three major curriculum considerations of knowledge (in ways that take us beyond the specified curriculum alone), assessment and pedagogy;
- three enduring curriculum issues (problem-solving, transfer of learning and group work) to see how they can be considered in a way that allows all three levels of analysis to be brought together.

When we examine the curriculum considerations and issues, we shall try to show how the interrelationship of the specified, the enacted and the experienced curriculum is achieved through a focus on learning.

CONTEMPORARY VIEWS OF LEARNING: TWO APPROACHES TO MIND

Bruner's views have developed since he was drawn on by the likes of Taba (1962) and Open University (1976). His latest book sets the scene of his consideration of learning by sketching out two views of mind; computational and the cultural (Bruner, 1996). Others have characterised these as *symbol-processing* and *situated* views of the mind (Bredo, 1994). The symbol-processing view, as the name suggests, sees the mind as a manipulator of symbols. These symbols are learned and stored in memory; when confronted with a problem, a person searches the memory for symbols to represent the problem and then manipulates them to solve the problem. There are, of course, different views of how these symbols are learned, i.e. of what constitutes the learning process. At one end of the spectrum is the information-processing view, where the learner is a passive processor of information. But the most widely held view sees learning as a knowledge construction process, i.e. learners make meaning from experiences. This places learners in an active role and problem-solving as a central process in knowledge construction. Bredo (1994) characterises symbol-processing in terms of three dualisms: language and reality; mind and body; and individual and society. Under the first (language and reality), symbol-processing sees the symbols as mirrors of reality and, as such, these representations are transmitted to, or at least acquired by, learners. The mind–body dualism from a symbol-processing approach sees thinking as separate from the actions the body takes, while the individual–society dualism sees thinking as an individual process. There are, however, variations between the different theorists in how the knowledge construction process is understood and what are its ends.

Through the latter part of the twentieth century, there were those theorists who focused increasingly on the social aspects of knowledge construction and the social nature of knowledge, and hence minimised the individual–society dualism. These led to a group of theories labelled as social constructivist, a label which itself has many variations. What is common to this view of learning is the role of others in creating and sharing meaning. All constructivist approaches have some social element in the construction process. Thus Piaget, although focused upon individual internalisation of knowledge, saw a role for peer interaction to produce cognitive conflict that would result in a change in the thinking of the individual, leading to the internalisation of a concept or idea.[4] By challenging the role of others in the construction of knowledge, social constructivists to varying degrees challenged views of the nature of knowledge and of culture. (Bruner [1986, p. 65] describes culture as the 'implicit semi-connected knowledge of the world, from which through negotiation people arrive at satisfactory ways of acting in given contexts'.)

A more radical challenge to constructivism has emerged in the last two decades from theorists who view learning as a process of participation in cultural activity. This approach to learning has been labelled as 'situated', and is contrasted with a symbol-processing view by Bredo (1994), although he includes all social constructivists under this label.[5] However, those who take a situated approach see a different role for the interactions with others, where 'participation' is a central process. This approach stems in part from Vygotsky and action theory (Bredo, 1997; Lave, 1996). Meaning is created through participating in social activity. In this sense there is no individual notion of an idea or concept, but a distributed one. Rather than seeing learning as a process of transfer of knowledge from the knowledgeable to the less knowledgeable, we have engagement in culturally authentic activity. Such activity is part of a 'community of practice'. To learn to be a doctor is not just to learn the requisite physiology, anatomy, etc., but to enter into the community of practice of doctors. A novice starts on the outside of the community and, as understanding increases, moves towards a more central participation in that community of practice, eventually taking part in its transformation; what Lave and Wenger (1991) rather inelegantly termed a movement from 'legitimate peripheral participation' to central participation. Mutual understanding, or 'intersubjectivity' comes through this participation (Rogoff, 1990), and with it a transformation of identity. A situated approach to learning also brings with it a particular view of how to analyse learning. Just as we have argued that curriculum needs to be understood at different levels of negotiation and definition, so too does learning from a situated approach.

Participation can therefore be understood in different ways, depending upon the level of analysis. Rogoff (1995) identifies three interrelated perspectives on learning associated with three planes of analysis. The three planes are 'community', 'interpersonal' and 'personal'; the view of the learning process associated with each of these is *apprenticeship, guided participation* and *participatory appropriation*. Lave and Wenger (1991) focus on the community level and hence the idea of the community of practice, with apprentices 'learning the trade'. At the interpersonal level, the process of guided participation focuses attention on the interpersonal activities that are 'managed collaboratively by individuals and their social partners' (Rogoff, 1995, p. 146). For both levels the role of the 'expert' is important in the collaboration that takes place, with the learner and the expert involved in joint problem-solving. Nevertheless, at the interpersonal level all participants in communal activity are significant. Participatory appropriation is the process 'by which individuals transform their understanding of, and responsibility for, activities through their own participation' (Rogoff, 1995, p. 150). Rogoff uses this term, rather than the symbol-processing idea of 'internalisation' (i.e. the individual construction of knowledge), to emphasise the interrelationship of the person and the social context. What is central to a situated view of learning is that all three planes of analysis have to be considered in developing understanding of any one plane.

To view learning as a transformation of identity and enculturation into communities of practice also requires a quite different conception of knowledge to that held by cognitivist or symbol-processing views of mind. In symbol-processing, 'concepts' are objects to be internalised (stored in memory); in situated learning 'the activity in which knowledge is developed and deployed is not separable from or ancillary to learning and cognition' (Brown *et al.*, 1989, p. 32). (We shall take up the issue of knowledge in the next section.)

From this view of situated learning comes a central focus on collaboration (between peers and others) and problem-solving. Unlike the symbol-processing view, problem-solving in a situated view is a shared activity, even when it is undertaken with an expert; expert and novices jointly solve problems. Problems emerge from activity. Thus they are not given (the assumption in most teaching situations) but experienced. Likewise the solutions to problems emerge from actions in resolving experienced dilemmas. The idea of a dilemma is important: 'a problem is a dilemma with which the problem solver is emotionally engaged' (Lave, 1988, p. 175). A dilemma has no unique or stable resolution and there may be no entirely satisfactory solution (Lave, 1988, p. 139). It is these dilemmas that become the *emergent problems* as the activity progresses. Collaboration is at the heart of this situated view, and the development of intersubjectivity. Intersubjectivity between participants arises from the 'shared understanding based on a common focus of attention and some shared pre-suppositions that form the ground for communication' (Rogoff, 1990, p. 71). (We shall return to some of these ideas when we consider 'group work'.)

In summary, to reflect on the situated view, we see that in taking such an approach, all three of Bredo's dualisms (Bredo, 1994) lose their distinctions: there is no mind–body dualism, nor is there a simple separation of individual and society, nor of language and reality.

This leaves one important idea of learning, namely, *metacognition*. This is seen as including knowledge about cognitive resources (which would include concepts) and self-regulatory mechanisms (Duell, 1986). Knowledge about cognitive resources is seen as a form of reflection on learning. How metacognitive knowledge is understood is determined also by the view of learning that obtains. In a symbol-processing approach, planning precedes action. Metacognition is an element of this planning through self-regulation. (Self-regulation involves planning what to do next, checking outcomes of strategies, and evaluating and revising strategies.) In a situated approach to learning, planning is a dynamic process that both precedes and is a consequence of action. Central to this view of planning is a view of reflection that von Glasersfeld (1989) refers to as 'operative knowledge'. 'Operative knowledge is not associative retrieval of a particular answer [as in symbol-processing views of mind], but rather knowledge of what to do in order to produce an answer [a solution]' (von Glasersfeld, 1989, p. 12). If an individual is to be able to reflect on her cognition, then this requires further knowledge than she apparently has; you can't know what you don't know. In the situated approach to learning collaboration and the need for intersubjectivity provide the means by which operative or metacognitive knowledge can be both deployed and developed. We are, however, straying into a discussion of the nature of knowledge.

VIEWS OF KNOWLEDGE AND VIEWS OF LEARNING

Different views of learning assume distinctly different views of the nature of knowledge (and of achievement). Therefore, how we view learning is central to how we:

- define knowledge in the *specified* curriculum;
- select activities and establish characteristics of pedagogies to develop that knowledge in the *enacted* curriculum;
- choose the mechanisms both of teaching and assessment that are employed to gain access to the *experienced* curriculum.

Here we shall examine the implications for views of knowledge that arise from these contrasting views of learning (symbol-processing and situated). In particular we shall examine the different views of the nature of knowledge and how we talk about knowledge and different types of knowledge.

The nature of knowledge

The two dominant views of learning we have been considering take different views of knowledge. Table 12.1 takes the two views of mind and compares them on the three dualisms identified by Bredo (1994).

210

Table 12.1 Ideas about knowledge as depicted by symbol-processing and situated cognition

Dualism	Symbol-processing	Situated cognition
Language and reality	Objective reality	Knowledge is not a mirror of reality
Mind and body	Knowledge in the head	Knowledge related to action
Individual and society	Knowledge as individual property	Knowledge as social

From this comparison it is possible to see how they each view the properties of knowledge: views about objective knowledge, truth, the match of knowledge and reality, and the extent to which knowledge is individual or social.

Participation, in the situated approach, is more than just a social affair: activity takes place in a social *and* physical world. In contrast to the symbol-processing view, knowledge guides action, and action guides knowledge. Knowledge is integrated with activity, along with the tools, sign systems and skills associated with the activity. A classic study illustrating the interrelationship of knowledge and activity was of dairy workers (Scribner, 1985). One part of the study looked at how what they did in their various jobs (clerical, delivery or warehouse) affected how they thought about the dairy products, compared for example with consumers. Most consumers thought of the products in terms of 'kinds' (e.g. milk and cheese), whereas drivers thought about 'kind' and 'size' (e.g. quart), and warehouse workers in terms of 'kind', 'size' and 'location'. Each of the groups of dairy workers had their thinking organised by the kinds of activity in which they engaged. But their knowledge also guided action. When warehouse workers made up an order from an order form, they would group the items on the list to be brought for central loading in ways that reduced journey distance. They used the accumulated social knowledge that went into the layout of the warehouse, and individual knowledge that reflected the current stacking arrangement. Observations showed that they would take very efficient travel distances, and would group items on the order form in ways that aided this efficiency. Looking at this from the point of view of learning (i.e. to be a dairy worker), Scribner concludes that 'What you learn is bound up with what you have to do' (1985, p. 203).

An increasing sense of identity is what it means to become a part of a community of practice, but not as an 'explicit objective of change' (Lave and Wenger, 1991, p. 112). Lave and Wenger claim that 'the development of identity is central to the careers of newcomers in communities of practice' (ibid., p. 115). They equate the outcome of learning (knowledge) with the process of learning (participation), because they state that 'learning and a sense of identity are inseparable', i.e. they equate learning and identity. The formation of a sense of identity is learning, and the identity itself is knowledge.

Identity and self-esteem are seen by Bruner as one of the nine tenets of what he calls a psycho-cultural approach to education (Bruner, 1996). These tenets reflect a situated view of the nature of mind and of the nature of culture. For him cultural learning lies at the intersection of these two. He considers identity and self-esteem as two elements, with agency leading to 'the construction of a conceptual system that organises . . . a "record" of agentive encounters in the world' (ibid., p. 36). In the formation of identity, the agency of an individual builds up skills and know-how based upon successes and failures. For a young person, school will be an important institution that defines criteria for these successes and failures, through, for example, assessment. The second element, self-esteem, stems from such evaluations, and if schools do not nurture this self-esteem, other parts of life will, as various forms of disaffection with schooling show (for example, groups of truants, street gangs and drug users). These kinds of issues are not just applicable to the education of young people, although it is evident that the early years are formative in the creation of identities. Nurses (or doctors) will be forming an identity as 'carers', 'efficient professionals', 'upholders of life' or whatever may be the ethos that is part of the profession. (At the same time they may have and be forming other identities as student, wife, father or 'responsible adult'.) When individuals move into a new situation where they join a company or group, they may (or may not) want to become part of that and share the identity of those who belong. Developing an identity is thus the subject matter of all learning, and is therefore on the face of it 'knowledge'.

The identities that individual learners bring to learning activities will position them, and they will be positioned by them, in ways that will influence their participation and hence the experienced curriculum. A situated view of learning makes identity central to the study of curriculum, including the assessment of its outcomes.

Metaphors

Sfard (1998) argues that two metaphors underlie theories of learning that relate to how we understand the nature of knowledge and achievement:

- the acquisition metaphor;
- the participation metaphor.

The acquisition metaphor (AM) is evident when we think about knowledge as a commodity (an object), that can be developed (e.g. we talk of 'concept development' with the concept as a basic unit of knowledge), or constructed. Whether knowledge acquisition is seen as either a transmission process or as a construction process, the individual accumulates it, like some kind of material. Typical words used that display this metaphor are: knowledge, concept, conception, idea, notion, misconception, meaning, sense, schema, fact, representation, material and contents. There are a number of processes (the mechanisms of learning) that we use to describe how learners make knowledge their own: reception, acquisition, construction, internalisation, appropriation, transmission, attainment, development, accumulation and grasp. These processes may, of course, be different, but in the end the knowledge becomes individual property that, once acquired, can be applied, transferred and shared.

The participation metaphor (PM) avoids referring to knowledge as an entity and replaces 'knowledge' with 'knowing', and replaces 'having knowledge' with 'doing'. Through the use of ideas of participation and discourse it is 'participation in activities' that is important, not 'possession of knowledge'; 'becoming a member' replaces 'learning a subject'. The curriculum at each level will be radically different, depending on which metaphor or mix of metaphors underpins the perspectives of those participants involved in the arenas at the various levels of curriculum definition and negotiation.

Types of knowledge

Different views of learning also determine what types of knowledge are specified in the curriculum, which in turn influences the enacted and experienced curriculum. The language of 'traditional' philosophers of knowledge in the curriculum area (e.g. Hirst and Peters, 1970) is to talk of concepts and methodological processes. These they derive from an analysis of subject disciplines. These disciplines they took to be the refinement of human achievements in the creation of knowledge. This kind of analysis, by its nature, favours a particular kind of knowledge, as contemporary critiques make clear (Lewis, 1993); in particular theoretical knowledge rather than practical knowledge. Taking a view of knowledge through views of mind and learning provides new insights into such distinctions, as we hope to illustrate.

Discussions of types of knowledge are treated differently in the two different approaches to learning we have been considering. From the symbol-processing approach two types of knowledge are distinguished, namely conceptual and procedural knowledge.

Procedural knowledge is simply 'know how to do it' knowledge. Part of the complexity of procedural knowledge comes in trying to link it to terms such as 'process', 'problem-solving', 'strategic thinking' and the like, which in turn requires us to distinguish different levels of procedure. This gives the idea of a hierarchy of knowledge, and in particular of procedural knowledge. Stevenson (1994, pp. 13–14), writing from the vocational education perspective, proposes three levels of procedures:

- *First order*: these are directed to known goals and are automatic, fluid, algorithmic (i.e. follow a fixed sequence of steps), and include specific skills such as hammering in a nail.
- *Second order*: these achieve unfamiliar goals, and operate on specific procedures and include strategic skills such as problem-solving.
- *Third order*: this switches cognition between the other two levels and hence it has a controlling function (i.e. metacognition).

Conceptual knowledge, on the other hand, is concerned with relationships among 'items' of knowledge, so that when students can identify these links we talk of them having 'conceptual understanding'. Thus, in the area of 'gearing' in the subject technology, we hope that students will see the relationship among 'direction of rotation', 'change of speed' and 'torque'. In geography the relationships for a concept like 'sustainability' might be made up of ideas on 'energy consumption', 'material consumption' and 'economic growth' (each of which have subconcepts associated with them).

The situated approach is likely to avoid the distinction of conceptual and procedural knowledge. More important, those who support this view (Lave and Wenger, 1991) reject the distinction of abstract and practical knowledge; the former was elevated by the philosophers of knowledge as the main point of education. The rejection of these distinctions is founded on two premises:

1 Such distinctions separate knowledge and action; concepts are the 'knowledge' and procedures the 'action'.
2 The acquisition metaphor, which underlies the symbol-processing approach, separates knowledge from context.

213

The Harvard researchers from the Smithsonian Institute for Astrophysics, featured in the BBC television programme *Simple Minds*, showed how knowledge is linked to context for learners in their work in high school science lessons, just as much as it is for experts in the context of their use of knowledge. The programme showed a girl who had done some work on simple electric circuits using standard science lesson equipment (battery, bulb, bulb-holder and wires). Prior to this work in science she was able to connect up a battery to light the bulb using only wires. When, in an interview, she was given the materials she had used in the science, she drew a circuit diagram that would get full marks in a test, but, as she connected up the circuit, she insisted that the circuit needed the bulb-holder. Even when pressed by the interviewer, she said the circuit would not work without it, and she was astounded when it did. Thus, when this girl learned about electric circuits she associated bulb-holders as a necessary part of the circuit. This issue of context is at the heart of understanding about the process of knowledge construction and the notion of 'transfer' of knowledge, to which we shall return when we consider the implications of views of learning and knowledge for such curriculum issues.

We have tried to illustrate that views of learning and views of knowledge are intimately connected, and therefore that the experienced and specified curriculum need to be considered together. In doing so it will have become evident that, although there are problems with a situated view, it provides for us a more convincing explanation of learning that allows the curriculum to be seen in a new light. However, even for those who might not share this view of learning (e.g. those from the symbol-processing tradition), the general argument about the importance of a focus on learning still holds. We shall illustrate this importance by examining central elements of curriculum considerations.

IMPLICATIONS FOR VIEWS OF THE CURRICULUM

The discussion of learning and knowledge in the previous sections gives rise to some implications on how we should approach central curriculum considerations. We shall therefore examine these considerations through knowledge, assessment and pedagogy. For each of the considerations we shall show how learning addresses and interrelates the specified, enacted and experienced curricula.

Knowledge

We have already argued that a focus on learning gives a different approach to the analyses that are necessary to view knowledge in the curriculum, either as an 'input' to the (specified) curriculum or as a consideration in the enacted and experienced curricula. The 'disciplines of knowledge' are superseded by the idea of communities of practice in the situated approach. Philosophical analyses have always tried to reflect knowledge that is culturally valued, but took a narrow view of what represented culture in terms of educational goals.[6] The idea of *cultural authenticity* remains important; a critical idea in engaging in a community of practice is that activity is authentic. This means it is coherent, meaningful and purposeful within a social framework – the ordinary practices of the culture. Thus learning activities must allow students to engage in this authentic activity. However, there is a second sense in which authenticity needs to be considered, that of *personal* authenticity; i.e. that is personally meaningful. Without this second element no construction of knowledge or participation, which will lead to learning, can take place. These two aspects of authenticity are interrelated but they can be thought of distinctly. They are distinct in that personal authenticity relates to the view of the learners and not to the view of knowledge, which is what cultural authenticity refers to. This means that the experienced curriculum is bound to decisions about the specified curriculum through the enacted curriculum. In making a task that is set as a 'problem' personally meaningful, students must be involved in the context of the problem. They must also be given significant decisions to make, which allow them to create solutions. Thus, in making bridges between school learning and everyday experience, it is not essential that the situations in which school activities are set are 'real'. The central requirement is that they afford the students authentic dilemmas that, in Lave's words, 'furnish opportunities [to the students] to improvise new practice [i.e. to learn]' (Lave, 1992, p. 85).

We therefore have the two kinds of authenticity coming together to provide a focus for the specified curriculum (communities of practice representing cultural authenticity) as a selection from culture, linked to the experienced curriculum (learners engaged with dilemmas that have both personal and cultural authenticity). The enacted curriculum must in some sense mediate the other two levels. This can be done for particular elements of the enacted curriculum, such as a set of learning activities or more holistically through a complete pedagogic strategy, for example, by adopting a 'community of learners' approach (we shall return to this in the consideration of pedagogy).

A movement away from disciplines as the source of knowledge for education (i.e. as an input to the specified curriculum), requires a more universal term than the 'subject' that is so often the focus of knowledge issues in the curriculum. Using a philosophical analysis of disciplines, a domain will be seen in terms of concepts, procedures, skills, etc., that relate together in a way that can be characterised as having some identity. Yet a community of practice is also a domain. Terms that might be used to characterise a domain, such as 'bodies of knowledge', 'practices' and 'ways of organising our experience', encapsulate views of the nature of learning and knowledge. Whatever way we think about the idea of a domain, we must be clear that it has many guises. Glaser, taking a symbol-processing (AM) approach, has a vision of a domain that is not just a subject. He talked of 'chess configurations, functional interpretations of circuit diagrams or representations of anatomical abnormalities in x-rays' (Glaser, 1992, pp. 64–65), and said that the structure and organisation are 'tied to the goal structure' of the problems that experts meet (ibid., p. 67). In this sense we are seeing the domain knowledge as situated, and hence it must be related to action and hence to practices, which of course takes us to the participation metaphor. When we think of a domain as a subject, we also tend to think of it only in cognitive terms, i.e. devoid of affect. Greeno et al. (1997) indicate that it is not as straightforward as this. In the cognitive (or symbol-processing) approach there are 'beliefs', and in the situated approach there seems to be no separation of cognitive and affective aspects of knowledge (e.g. identity is made up of both).

The specified curriculum is therefore affected, not just by a philosophical or cultural analysis, but by a consideration of learning and associated views of mind. Again we are simultaneously engaging with the specified and the experienced curriculum, with the former not just being an 'input' to the latter. Philosophical analyses of the nature of knowledge, or even anthropological ones of how knowledge is produced by say scientists (e.g. Latour and Woolgar, 1979), provide but one element of analysis at the global level (parallel to Rogoff's community level noted earlier). We also need to see the interrelationships of the discussion at the interactional and the individual level, to see how this knowledge is constructed through participatory appropriation or internalisation (depending upon the view of learning). Although the acquisition metaphor does allow for philosophical analyses of the specified curriculum, the participation metaphor requires a more complex view and one that has to enable us to see the three levels of specified, enacted and experienced curricula together.

There are implications of the discussion of kinds of knowledge in the last section, that lead us to view important distinctions made between 'content and process' and the role of practical knowledge in the curriculum. In many areas of the curriculum there are discussions of the distinction between content and process (or concepts and process). In science and in technology education there are such discussions (e.g. Murphy and McCormick, 1997; Wellington, 1989), where each is seen as important yet inseparable from the other. The 'scientific method' or 'design', as the respective processes of science and technology, are taken as important goals for education; students are to learn how to use the scientific method and to design. These complex methods are often idealised incorrectly in the educational setting (as we shall explore in the next section in relation to problem-solving), so that they no longer reflect the way they are used by those who are part of the communities of practice. For example, biologists, chemists and physicists might all use different methods of proceeding in practical investigations, yet they are characterised as carrying out the same methods.[7] Similarly, in various branches of technology, design may be carried out in a variety of ways, none of which conforms to the staged process that is represented as part of the school curriculum (as in national curricular statements such as DfE/WO, 1995). In addition to the problem of whether the school curriculum represents such processes authentically, there is the issue of whether they are indeed separate from conceptual knowledge. Research in areas such as science and mathematics education has established that conceptual and procedural knowledge is, as we indicated above, inseparable (Gott and Murphy, 1987; Hiebert and Lefevre, 1986). This is supported by the fact that research on problem-solving (i.e. strategic procedural knowledge) indicates that experts do not operate procedurally without (conceptual) knowledge (Glaser, 1984).

This discussion of conceptual and procedural knowledge leads on to the role of practical knowledge, which as indicated earlier, is not usually the stuff of education, and hence does not feature much in the curriculum. Where it does, for example in craft subjects, then it is usually of a lower status than those subjects that are more theoretical; for example, science and mathematics. Putting aside the status issues that Lewis (1993) discusses, there is an assumption that we teach academic or theoretical knowledge because it is applicable in all situations, unlike practical knowledge which is limited to particular situations. We assume that theoretical knowledge is decontextualised, and therefore that it can be transferred from the classroom and used in practical situations outside schools and colleges. As noted earlier, the situated approach to learning disputes this and this has important implications for the idea of transfer of learning, a curriculum issue we shall examine in the next section. The link of knowledge with context, illustrated in the previous example of the girl and the bulb-holder taken from *Simple Minds*, is a feature of expert knowledge as much as it is with novices. Furthermore, expert knowledge is indicated by its qualitative nature (McCormick, 1999). This qualitative knowledge leads to qualitative reasoning, which is also procedural in nature and can be seen as a form of narrative; it shows a causal link in a set of events that do not require the complete logical scientific thinking (Bruner, 1996, p. 39).

In distinguishing between a computational (symbol-processing) approach to learning and a cultural (situated) approach, Bruner (1996) draws attention to the role of narrative as a process of making meaning, i.e. knowledge construction. Bruner describes narrative as a mode of thinking and feeling that will create a personal world. Narrative looks for interpret-ation, understanding not explanation, and is a way of organising and contextualising pro-positions that cannot be completely verified in a disciplined way. This contrasts with how we think of scientific explanations, i.e. as stripped down and devoid of a personal perspec-tive. A situated view of learning requires us to take more account of narrative as a form of knowledge, and Lave and Wenger (1991) take this up through the idea of 'Discourse and Practice'. They examined the nature of talk *within* and *about* a practice and it was clear that 'stories', i.e. narratives, were an important element of this process. Bruner's argument for narratives in an American Educational Research Association (AERA) conference lecture was directed at developing certain areas of the school curriculum with an equal rigour to that of science. In fact a narrative approach to science is common in much science school teaching and in higher education, as part of the history and philosophy of science (to which some science students may be exposed). Recounting how famous scientists went about discovering or developing a scientific idea is not just a motivational device to relieve the teaching of heavy conceptual ideas, but a way of conveying the nature of scientific activity, i.e. the practice of science. It is intended to show how scientific knowledge is created and verified. Evans's (1996) defence of history was made in terms of an examination of stories about historians such as Elton and Carr, and he did this to examine the nature of historical knowledge, in particular its objectivity. This idea is not only applicable to academic subjects (and school ones at that), as Lave and Wenger (1991) refer to 'war stories' by technicians learning to repair photocopying machines.[8]

Thus we have a level of analysis relating to the experienced curriculum (of practical knowledge and narrative) that has profound implications for how we consider the specified curriculum (particularly 'domains') and the enacted curriculum (how these domains are treated in the classroom).

Assessment

In spite of attention to the role of assessment in the development of curriculum, only rarely have assessment systems been analysed from a perspective on learning. Increasingly the specified curriculum is enacted to a degree in national assessment systems, yet seldom are the educational purposes and values of such systems considered in conjunction. It is common, for example, for constructivist rhetoric to underpin the specified curriculum, but to be noticeably absent from assessment of the curriculum (Murphy, 1996). The tensions that this creates are then manifest at the levels of the enacted and experienced curricula.

217

In recent debates the view of knowledge and of learning underpinning most assessment practice has been challenged (Black and Wiliam, 1998; Gardner, 1992; Gipps, 1994; Murphy, 1995). Typically, assessment systems reflect the psychometric tradition that had its roots in views of mind that saw ability as an innate trait that could be measured. At its most extreme, this led to unidimensional views of ability encapsulated in notions of general intelligence. The 'measurement' approach tried to distinguish students according to ability, usually to match a 'normal' statistical distribution of such ability that was supposed to exist in the population. Thus the task was to separate students, so they could be selected for curricula that would suit them, or for jobs that they would be able to perform. Challenges to assessment, derived from a Vygotskian perspective, have emerged through the 1980s and 1990s, but have tended to focus on the assessment of learning *in situ*, rather than on national systems; for example Brown and Ferrara (1985), Newman *et al.* (1989) and Lunt (1993). Analyses of national, large-scale assessment based on situated views of knowledge have been rare and have tended to focus on equity in relation to gender (Murphy, 1995) and on social class (Cooper, 1992). It is only recently that more general critiques have emerged, but these have typically been associated with subject perspectives, rather than assessment perspectives *per se*; for example, mathematics (Boaler, 1997) and science (Roth, 1997).

Within the field of assessment it is the case that, although a symbol-processing view of mind or a behaviourist view was rejected, no alternative views of mind are offered to counter them. Rather the critiques were against the unhelpful purposes of assessment that this spawned (Gipps, 1994). Even eloquent and authoritative accounts of the formative function of assessment (e.g. Black, 1998), to allow a close relationship between assessment and learning, were not driven by a clear alternative view of mind or theory of the learning processes that derives from that alternative view. Writers such as Black recognise that a theory of learning underlies assessment (e.g. Black, 1999),[9] but feel no obligation to articulate these views in any coherent fashion. Where theories of learning do appear to have a profound message for assessment (e.g. the role of metacognition in justifying self-assessment; Black, 1998, pp. 132–133), then the theoretical basis is articulated. Inevitably this is a partial exposition and, it appears, not applied consistently across the various assessment issues identified. Thus group assessment is viewed as a technical issue of assigning grades to individuals within the group, or as an issue of validity (ensuring that if the aim is 'learning to collaborate' then the contribution to the group process is the aspect to be assessed). This is not to belittle the importance of these issues, but a situated view of learning requires a radical rethink of assessment that would encompass, for example, shared understanding. At the very least it would make group assessment a central issue, rather than an issue of continual conflict with national assessment systems that overwhelmingly reward individual, rather than group, achievement (despite the apparent calls from those outside education for the opposite approach).

We shall examine three assessment issues in terms of how the views of learning and knowledge illuminate them. These issues are:

- the nature of tasks and the teacher's interpretation of the performance of students that result from how these tasks are conceived by the student;
- the role of self-assessment; and
- notions of validity.

Nature of tasks

If we take a symbol-processing view of learning, then an assessment task will have a stability that allows responses to be evaluated against an accepted 'answer'. The response will show an understanding of a concept or procedure that can be matched against an accepted view. A constructivist version of this sees learners on their way to understanding, and various responses could exemplify misconceptions that they have and indicate how future learning could be adjusted to confront these misconceptions and arrive at an accepted one. From a situated view, then, the stability of the task is an issue. Newman *et al.* (1989) refer to a task as a 'strategic fiction'. When a teacher sets a 'problem', then what is actually problematic is at issue. Also, what the student sees as salient in the information given can vary, not just depending upon their 'level of understanding' (what the task is trying to assess), but depending upon the qualitative differences in the communities in which they participate. For example, gender and race locate learners in different communities, and their interpretations of tasks reflect the qualitative differences between these communities (e.g. for gender see Murphy, 1991; Gipps and Murphy, 1994). Thus, a girl working with boys on a task of a scientific investigation involving the dissolving of sugar may interpret the task differently from that intended by the teacher or perceived by the boys, because she takes the context of the task (tea cooling in a cup) seriously, whereas they ignore it (Murphy and McCormick, 1997). Numerous examples of these differences in views of salience, and the consequences for what tasks students perceive and the solutions they judge to be appropriate, have been demonstrated in assessment situations (Boaler, 1994; Cooper, 1992; Murphy, 1991). That these same effects obtain in learning situations has also been demonstrated (Murphy and McCormick, 1997).

The dynamic nature of tasks means that interpretations of responses are made problematic, i.e. the central issue of validity in assessment. Furthermore, such a view leads one to anticipate variation in response from an individual to demands in assessment tasks, irrespective of the theoretical construct assumed. Consequently the traditional notion of reliability is under threat in a situated approach to assessment. The implications of this for assessment methods are demanding, and beyond the scope of this chapter, but it will be evident that we must be more modest in what we think assessment is able to achieve, and at the same time more creative in the practices we implement. The need to expand the kinds of evidence that are used in assessment is obvious, to accompany the move to authentic assessments (such as work-based assessment). Thus interpreting student responses to tasks can be seen in the context of the community of practice; it may imply more interrogation of the student to establish the context of response, along with the kind of evidence gained from such things as process-folios ('instruments of learning . . . [that] contain full process-tracing records of a student's involvement in one or more . . . works' [Gardner, 1992, p. 103]). The broader the range of assessment used to illuminate a complex achievement or performance, the better will be the understanding of the student. However, assessment information provides only an understanding of achievement, or an indicator of it, not actual achievement. Thus, how we use assessment to monitor progress in the experienced curriculum, or to determine the outcomes of the specified and enacted curriculum, depends crucially on how we understand learning and learners.

Self-assessment

As with many curriculum initiatives, the advocates of self-assessment may be driven by an ideology such as child- or student-centred approaches. Thus self-assessment is seen in terms of empowering and valuing the students' view and the criteria they may bring to their learning. Our discussion of views of learning gives another and more powerful rationale. Metacognition, with its operative and self-regulatory elements, requires students to develop an awareness of learning, and to achieve this they need an involvement in reflecting upon their learning. Without some element of self-assessment this awareness cannot be developed. Self-assessment, present in for example peer assessment (where students assess each other), is central to the development of a strategic approach to their learning. This is the constructive aspect of operative knowledge that is best demonstrated, according to von Glasersfeld (1989, p. 12) 'where something new is generated, something that was not already available to the operator'. Thus, learning to solve problems requires knowing when to solve them, or recognising particular kinds of problems, and when it is appropriate to use particular solutions. Children may be taught how to carry out a 'fair test' as a form of scientific investigation but, if they are unaware of when a fair test should be carried out, they will be unable to use this test without a teacher to tell them (Murphy *et al.*, 1996).

Self-assessment is also a prerequisite for students learning the norms of a community of practice. Schoenfeld (1996) advocates conducting undergraduate mathematics classes in a way that is true to what he and other mathematicians do (Lave *et al.*, 1988; Schoenfeld, 1996). Students, for example, have to convince each other about what constitutes a solution to a mathematical problem (as mathematicians do), not just produce 'right answers' (that is 'right' according to the teacher's judgement). In a similar vein, in critical literacy approaches, students are encouraged to examine texts to understand how identities are constructed in various discourses (Moss, 1996). Whether this constitutes a good model for other areas of the curriculum is of course a point for debate.

Validity

Finally we turn to the notions of validity of assessment that might flow from different views of learning. These different notions give different views of knowledge and hence of domains, as we have already argued. But such views of knowledge also imply that validity cannot come directly from how we see subjects or domains. Face and content validity are derived from teachers' or experts' views of a subject; for example, an assessment is judged valid if it reflects the content of a subject. If we are to take seriously the ideas on interpretations of tasks by students, and hence some caution in interpreting their responses, then we cannot judge validity only in terms of content. Messick (1989) argued strongly for the overarching importance of construct validity. This requires both a view of the theoretical construct (what is the model of achievement in the domain) and the empirical data of performance on the assessment instrument, upon which to judge the construct validity. Messick did not argue this in terms of views of learning, as we would, but nevertheless his stance is an accepted one among assessment theorists. What is less evident, however, is the operationalisation of the theoretical constructs that are sensitive to different views of learning. Greeno and his colleagues (1997) laid out such theoretical constructs to reflect both the symbol-processing (what they called the 'cognitive') approach and the situated approach. Further, they outlined these for both literacy and mathematics. This we see as ground-breaking work, particularly with respect to the situated approach, and we hope that other domains could be elaborated, and assessment procedures implemented, that tried to assess achievement against these constructs.

Each of these three issues (nature of tasks, self-assessment and validity) reflects the different levels of analysis of the curriculum:

- Validity draws on the specified curriculum through its articulation of the theoretical construct, and the experienced curriculum through the empirical data of students' responses to the assessment based upon the construct.
- The nature of tasks is central to the determination of the enacted curriculum, yet requires a view of learning drawing together the specified level of communities of practice and experienced curriculum in the interpretation of tasks.
- The discussion of self-assessment started with the experienced curriculum in terms of its role in student learning, yet with the example of encouraging students to participate in a community of practice (of mathematicians) we have this level feeding through to the other two levels.

Pedagogy

We have argued that changing views about the nature of learning and of knowledge have focused attention on the experienced curriculum. We have shown how, in many ways, the agency of learners and of teachers can lead to a diversity of meanings being constructed within any one curriculum level. We have also argued that, as a consequence, a situated view of learning creates new roles for assessment to enable the progression and diversity of these meanings to be monitored in order to support students' learning. What we consider here is how the teaching and learning process is understood in a situated view and the implications of this for understanding the curriculum.

We have already noted that Taba wanted to go beyond teaching methods but did not use the term 'pedagogy', so why have we chosen to use it? The term 'teaching methods' carries with it a view that a teacher does things to learners (teaches them), and hence may have a connotation that these methods exist outside a view of learning and of learners. It is not just that particular teaching methods may only suit particular learners, but that they encapsulate particular views of learning. If we think that giving lectures is a way of teaching, then we must have some kind of view of learning as information-processing if the learner is not allowed an active role. On the other hand, the lecture might achieve such an active role in learners through controversial statements and tasks to be followed up with other kinds of activities. This starts to broaden to a consideration of a number of issues, including the role of the learner and the teacher, the kinds of learning activities that are provided, and the nature of the assessment of the learning. If we then put together these features with that of views of learning and knowledge, we have a pedagogic *approach*, or a pedagogic *strategy*. For governments to focus on teaching methods in isolation, as in the UK government's concern to increase 'whole-class teaching' (Reynolds and Farrell, 1996), is to ignore the other peda-gogic dimensions that mediate the implementation of this method. A teacher who sees the learner as agentive (Bruner, 1996) would use such whole-class methods to engage students in interactions with one another and herself, to reflect the view of learning associated with the method. A teacher adopting a symbol-processing approach to learning may find the implementation more difficult, as the notion of the sharing of understanding is less import-ant than the individual internalisation. Indeed, such a teacher may ironically (given the association of whole-class teaching with 'traditional' views of learning) have more difficulty with this approach!

The crucial notion of a pedagogic approach, then, is the coherence and consistency that exist among the dimensions of the pedagogy that constitutes the 'pedagogic arena' (Lave, 1988, pp. 148–152):

1 goals of learning;
2 knowledge that is the focus of learning;
3 learning and assessment activities;
4 the teacher–student roles and relationships;
5 'classroom' discourse.

Thus, if we are to see the use of group work as part of a pedagogic approach reflecting a situated view of learning, it would demonstrate the following characteristics (Brown and Campione, 1990):

● the learning activities would focus on collaboration;
● students would share ideas with a teacher and each other;
● the teacher would model activity that reflects the community of practice that is the focus of learning;
● this would, in turn, create a community of learners.

Learning would be assessed through the acknowledgement of the way the learners partici-pate in the community. No pedagogic approach is likely to achieve coherence, not least because there are conflicting goals in education and conflicting views of learning and know-ledge between the specified curriculum and those involved in the educational process (including the learners).

The pedagogic dimensions that constitute a pedagogic arena serve to frame a learner's activity; but each learner will negotiate and experience this arena in different ways, creating a *setting*. Thus a setting is an individual's experience of an arena. The arena is then the enacted curriculum and the setting is the experienced curriculum in a situated view. This reflects the distinction that Lave and Wenger (1991, p. 97) make between the teaching and the learning curricula, as we discuss in the final section of the chapter.

Along with the idea that pedagogies will reflect the dimensions of the arena, is that the teachers who construct this pedagogy will have a variety of views of these dimensions, i.e. goals, knowledge, learners, teachers, learning activities and assessment, and associated dis-courses. Grossman and Stodolsky (1995) were able empirically to relate views on such issues to the particular subject to which teachers belong. Thus, we have subcultures of teachers reflecting their subjects. This is not of course new, but such subcultures have traditionally emerged from sociological studies of subjects (e.g. Goodson *et al.*, 1998; Paechter, 1995).

What is new is to understand that teachers and their views just as much reflect their perceptions of their core task of teaching and learning, as they are the outcome of the mediating influences of the macro-politics of subjects at national and school level.[10]

IMPLICATIONS FOR CURRICULUM ISSUES

In this penultimate section we examine the implications for curricular issues that have existed in the literature for some time, but which we believe are given new insights by a concern for the contemporary views of learning we have discussed. The enduring issues we examine are: problem-solving, transfer and group work. In each case it should be evident how views of learning bind together the analyses at the three levels of curriculum definitions. For example, we shall show that for the issue of transfer, views of learning have implications for the aims of education, and upon how we choose to organise the curriculum. In that sense views of learning are not just concerned with teaching and learning methods.

Problem-solving

This, as an issue in the curriculum, has a history stemming from Dewey's advocacy of reflective enquiry. Thus, in the 1960s, the enquiry-based curriculum had its adherents (e.g. James, 1968) who focused on the curriculum organisation necessary to support inter-disciplinary approaches. More extreme 'child-centred' approaches, claiming to be based on Dewey, saw the child as choosing the problems. This reflected a particular view of knowledge, i.e. that the organisation of the child's mind led to a different organisation of knowledge related to his or her needs and desires. Philosophers of knowledge of the time mounted defences against this view, reasserting the place of the disciplines as the basis for any curriculum organisation (e.g. Pring, 1971). These child-centred approaches diverted attention from the agentive view of mind that Dewey was in effect advocating, and which we have indicated sees problem-solving as a central feature of learning.

Many curricular statements see problem-solving as a central goal of education; for example, in England the subject of Design and Technology specifies 'being able to solve problems' as the ultimate aim (DES/WO, 1989). The rationale for this is not always clear. A recent examination of problem-solving based on a view of learning helps to clarify the various rationales that can be given (Hiebert *et al.*, 1996). Hiebert and his colleagues argue that most problem-solving is seen as a demonstration of understanding, what they call the 'application' of knowledge, whereas Dewey, for example, was concerned with the acquisition of knowledge (the learner as agentive). We have already indicated the importance of the latter, and Hiebert *et al.*, similarly argue for it to be a central instructional principle; subjects need to be problematised for learning to occur. This is an issue for each level of curriculum definition, for it is necessary to consider two perspectives in understanding subjects (in the case Hiebert *et al.*, argue, the subject is mathematics):

- *functional perspective*: where the concern is to learn to participate in the community of practice, in which confronting and solving problems is a central activity;

223

- *structural perspective*: where there are a number of residues of problem-solving activity (conceptual understanding; strategic procedural understanding, i.e. being able to solve problems; dispositions towards the subject).

Whichever of these perspectives dominates, it is important that problems should have both cultural and personal authenticity. The child-centred approach placed reliance only on personal authenticity. In professional education, such as in medicine, problem-based approaches have succeeded in combining both structural and functional perspectives, with students taking on the kinds of problems faced by doctors, yet still being able to learn the conventional subjects (anatomy, physiology, etc.) as they tackle the problems (Oates, 1992). In addition to these issues, which in part are about the specified curriculum, there are numerous issues related to problem-solving that affect the enacted and experienced curriculum. We have already indicated the importance of problems being meaningful to learners, and there are other issues: the pedagogic approaches necessary to prevent problem-solving becoming ritualistic and to support student problem-solving (see, for example, McCormick, 1997; Murphy and McCormick, 1997).

These kinds of consideration take us away from the rhetoric of old and give us a basis for the inclusion of problem-solving in the curriculum that is better grounded in learning theory. This grounding is available to be used as a rationale for its inclusion as an educational goal and as a means for other kinds of learning, thus unifying considerations of all three levels of curriculum definition.

Transfer

The assumption of transfer of knowledge underlies much of schooling and indeed all education associated with educational institutions, at whatever level. The specified curriculum typically assumes that general-purpose knowledge is learned for use at another time and in another context. This assumption permeates many aspects of how we view curriculum. For example, we assume that students who learn mathematics in the mathematics lesson can use this in the geography lesson; that is, we make the assumption that knowledge learned in one part of the curriculum is available for use in any other part. This implies a particular organisation and enactment of the specified curriculum. Yet teachers and researchers will testify to the continual failing of this assumption, and our own investigations of classrooms have provided empirical evidence of this for some areas of the curriculum (Davidson *et al.*, 1998; Evens and McCormick, 1997; McCormick *et al.*, 1998). To take the view of 'transfer of learning' is to adopt a symbol-processing view of mind; symbols stored in memory are abstracted knowledge that can then be used when confronted with a problem in any context. We have already indicated that those who hold a situated view of mind reject this view, and in particular reject the idea of abstract knowledge devoid of context (Lave and Wenger, 1991); they hold a quite distinctly different view of generalised knowledge. Indeed, transfer lies at the heart of the dispute between the symbol-processing and the situated views. For those who support the idea of transfer, there is a certainty about the process, while others harbour doubts about the empirical evidence. For example, Lave (1988) reviews many of the studies of transfer and concludes that the evidence fails to show that the concept of transfer is a helpful one. Those who believe that we store in our minds symbol representations that we recall for use in particular situations dismiss this kind of argument and claim that there are many examples of transfer established in the literature (Anderson *et al.*, 1996). The arguments between the two sides are extensive and continuing: a recent book (Detterman and Sternberg, 1993) has as its first chapter 'The case for the prosecution: transfer as an epiphenomenon'; *Cognitive Science* gave over the whole of volume 17 in 1993 to an argument between those who supported situated cognition and those who wanted to take a symbolic cognition view; the argument in the 1996 issue of *Educational Researcher* was taken up by the combatants again in 1998 (Greeno, 1998; Anderson *et al.*, 1998). The argument is less about whether or not transfer can occur, than about whether the mechanism envisaged by the symbol process theorists is the correct one, and the nature of the knowledge that is generated.

Ultimately the argument comes down to which view of learning is supported. However, there are two important points that come out of this argument. The first is that the conditions under which transfer will take place depend on a match between the situation where the learning took place and the situation where the knowledge is used. This doesn't look much like transfer ('transportation' might be a better word). The second point Anderson *et al.* (1996) make is that we need to pay more attention to the cues that signal the relevance of skill (or knowledge), i.e. the crucial issues are where and what the cues are. Typically students learn some mathematical or scientific idea and then move on to problems that require them to use it. The idea is for the students to strip out the context and 'see' the science.[11] The salience lies in the equations, etc. What learners, like the girl who attributed salience to the bulb-holder, need to come to understand, is where the salience lies. In the science lesson it is in the stripped away situation; in the real world it is embedded in the context. Under these circumstances learning the salience or the 'cues', as Anderson *et al.* (1996) describe it (or 'affordances' as Clancey [1993] puts it), is what should be the focus and not, in our view, transfer.

This argument is not merely academic, but it reveals some common elements about how transfer can be supported (Murphy *et al.*, 1999, pp. 94–95):

- providing a bridge between novel and new contexts;
- enabling tacit and explicit communication using experts and peers who serve as resources in collaborative settings;
- using analogies to identify similarities between situations;
- explicit treatment of the features in a situation to point up alternative views of salience;
- teachers act as partners, coaches, modelling practices;
- self-monitoring of learning processes (i.e. develop metacognitive awareness).

But underlying the common strategies is the argument of whether the mechanism sees the transfer of the same knowledge between situations or an engagement in new learning.

The curriculum implications of this argument we have discussed are (a) that the teaching of abstract knowledge for later use may be flawed and (b) that the use of knowledge across the curriculum and hence the curriculum organisation may similarly be based upon an incorrect premise about the nature of that knowledge. These kinds of issues come to the fore in the argument about the teaching of *core* or *key skills*. They are discussed at all levels of education from schools to universities and, although the formulation varies according to that level, they are usually of the following kind (Wolf, 1999):

- problem-solving;
- communication;
- personal skills ('learning to learn' and 'working with others');
- numeracy (application of number);
- information technology.

Sometimes these skills have overlapping categories, such as thinking skills, critical skills and creative skills.

Those who take a situated view will find problems with these skills seen out of any context of their use. But even those who might take a symbol-processing view will find it problematic, because the evidence is that experts draw heavily on domain-specific knowledge, not these general-purpose skills (Glaser, 1992). But there is a long history of such courses, especially in general thinking skills, and they have many adherents; for example de Bono's *CoRT Thinking Lessons* (de Bono, 1974), and Feuerstein's *Instrumental Enrichment* (Feuerstein *et al.*, 1980). The various reviews of curricular programmes based on such skills have not been generally supportive of them (Ennis, 1989; Glaser, 1984). A recent review of work by an advocate of thinking skills (Adey, 1997) could find convincing evidence for only the one with which he was connected, namely *Cognitive Acceleration through Science Education* (CASE). Besides these specific courses, Ennis (1989) examined three further ways in which such skills could be developed:

1 infused through a domain-specific course, in such a way that the skills are made explicit;
2 immersed within a domain-specific course, and not made explicit;
3 the mixed model, with a combination of separate core skills courses and domain courses.

Those who do not believe that such general skills exist advocate the immersion model, and this is the kind of argument made by universities for what constitutes graduateness (good problem-solvers, communicators, etc.). More commonly, courses are based on the infusion model. For example, Blagg and his colleagues developed thinking-skills modules related to work. Such courses were mainly aimed at enhancing 'metacognitive skills associated with task and contingency management, i.e. the development of higher order skills concerned with understanding, planning, executing and reviewing work-related tasks'. (Blagg *et al.*, 1994, p. 7), but also enhancing self-esteem, promoting personal autonomy, developing oral communication skills and fostering interpersonal skills, especially those associated with group work.

Examples of the activities, and the support they give, seem to reflect the mechanisms that would ensure the effective learning we considered earlier, rather than being a specific course in itself geared to producing core thinking skills. Not surprisingly then, the thinking-skills modules Blagg and his colleagues designed were more successful in improving learning on the specifics of the module, than in showing transfer to problem-solving tasks far removed from those in the module (though there was some evidence of the latter). More success in 'far' transfer is claimed for the CASE course mentioned above (Adey and Shayer, 1994). In the original work, and in more recent reports, the course claims not only to improve science learning, but also that in tests of science and English a year later, and at public examinations some years later than the period of the course, students perform better than control groups (Shayer, 1996). On the face of it the reasoning patterns they discuss look like domain-specific knowledge, though the proponents of the course would argue that the far transfer is evidence that these skills are general. This is a claim that is hard to disentangle from the effect of the other elements of the programme. Making students better learners (e.g. through teaching metacognitive strategies) would inevitably lead to a general all-round improvement in learning. The CASE approach highlights a strategic approach to student learning and, it could be argued, encourages students to search for salience across contexts. Adey (1997), however, denies any role for context in learning.

Once again, we are convinced that a view of learning has central implications for a significant curriculum issue, and one that can be viewed through each curriculum level. Without a clear view of learning and related ideas on knowledge, any discussion of such issues becomes empty rhetoric. These views reflect on the aims of education (e.g. to provide general-purpose skills that transcend initial learning), and upon how we choose to organise the curriculum (e.g. around problems or core skills). In that sense they are not just concerned with teaching and learning methods.

Group work

This final issue is often seen as a question of which teaching method to adopt, perhaps for reasons only associated with classroom management (e.g. the amount of teaching resources available). We have chosen to use the term 'group work' because this is often how it is dealt with in the curriculum. However, we see underlying this the central issue of *collaboration*, which depends on intersubjectivity. This term stems from views of learning, both as a *means* and as an *end* of learning. As a means, i.e. collaborating to learn, it stems from the views we discussed earlier, where the development of intersubjectivity was central, at least in the situated view. Even Piagetian approaches see symmetrical collaboration among peers as a prerequisite for knowledge construction through cognitive conflict and hence change. Collaboration is thus a central part of learning mechanisms. What a situated view brings to this is, however, the need for collaboration to be seen not only among peers, but also between experts (e.g. teachers) and learners. The collaboration from this approach is not just about purely cognitive issues (in the terms Piaget might have seen it), but also about relations among people, as the participation metaphor emphasises.

That, of course, relates to our second curriculum view of collaboration, namely as an end in itself. Here it is important for students to learn how to collaborate so that they will be able to identify and share common reference points and models of the situation. For collaboration to take place, students must engage in each other's thinking. But it also means that the tasks should enable this. The idea in the use of the term 'group work' is that it is a way of carrying out a classroom task, without there necessarily being any implication for the nature of this task. We would dispute this; tasks must give students the opportunity to share. Students inevitably reformulate tasks, and alternative perceptions of purposes and salience emerge. Collaboration is often gendered territory, and there is evidence that girls and boys not only bring different views of salience to activities, but collaborate differently (Murphy, 1999a). Some argue that central to all collaborative activity is exploratory talk (Mercer,

1995). Thus, tasks must give opportunities for talk, including the sharing of information, joint planning, presenting of ideas to the group, joint reasoning, evaluation and decision-taking. If collaboration is also learning to participate, this talk cannot be separated from what is being talked about; the community of practice will have a language that reflects the domain of the practice. This kind of view of collaboration, with the need to learn skills (including collaborative talk), places great demands on teachers and learners, and is more complex than the mere arrangement of students into groups. Murphy (1999a) provides a summary of the factors necessary for effective collaboration:

- a 'true' group task;
- a requirement to plan, record, act and communicate as a group;
- teacher support for both skills for collaboration as well as collaboration for learning;
- teacher provision of tools for making thinking explicit, including forms of the representation of tools, equipment, etc.;
- student autonomy;
- monitoring by the teacher of the dialectic between the students, and students and tasks;
- encouragement of reflective discourse between students;
- students' explicit awareness of the agenda in relation to the subject and to collaboration.

However, any changes to the way collaboration is supported through the nature of tasks and other features of pedagogy listed above, need to be accompanied by changes to all elements of a pedagogic approach, particularly assessment. Many of the developments in national curricula that have included assessment systems, have focused almost exclusively upon individual assessment. This means that the focus of tasks that include an element of assessment will detract from any collaborative effort. Further, there still seems to be a lack of routine assessment techniques that allow assessment of participation (and hence collaboration), despite the development of models of achievement for the situated approach indicated earlier (Greeno et al., 1997). A renewed focus on learning in relation to both assessment and collaboration may spur this development.

Looking back over the three curriculum issues, each is a central feature of contemporary views of learning and hence provides a focus for the experienced curriculum. Yet each has different reflections at the other two levels: problem-solving in specifications about the aims of its use, organisation of the curriculum and the types of knowledge specified, and about the tasks and learning activities planned (the structural and functional perspectives of Hiebert et al., 1996), i.e. the enacted curriculum. Transfer leads to arguments about whether the curriculum should be organised around key skills either as a goal for education or as a structural feature of its organisation. This also has implications for assessment methods that try to record achievement in these key skills, whatever view is ultimately taken of their existence or role. Group work is, on the face of it, a classroom organisational issue, yet in as much as participation in communities of practice is important, it reflects a view of knowledge as it is specified. Equally, as a means or an end, it requires task definition, the enacted curriculum.

LIFELONG LEARNING AND A MORE RADICAL VIEW OF CURRICULUM

We have argued that putting learning at the heart of curriculum considerations will throw new light on some lasting issues, and return the focus to what is, after all, the central concern of the curriculum: student learning. We would extend this argument to take a more radical view of the nature of the curriculum, at least as a subject of study. To do this we shall build on the situated approach. As will have been evident in the earlier discussion, we tend to this view of learning, and it offers a potentially more radical view of the curriculum than we currently have.

Much of our thinking about the curriculum focuses upon educational institutions and, more commonly, upon schools. Thus models and considerations tend to be bounded by the concerns of these institutions. What of the curriculum of the home or the workplace? Few would dispute that learning takes place in each of these situations, and the curriculum considerations need not only be concerned with studying 'courses' (through distance learning or otherwise). Nor does the term 'informal learning' do justice to the significance for such learning. Lave and Wenger (1991) note that this kind of learning is associated with the observation and imitation characteristic of apprenticeship in the trades, where skill development is the focus, and does not do justice to the idea of participation that they advocate. Learning to participate through apprenticeship is not just following the tasks of work, but these can be sequenced in a way that allows participation to be increased to match the understanding of the learners. Apprenticeship therefore need not only be associated with skill learning, where observation is possible, but should be seen as a metaphor for all learning in the way Collins *et al.* (1991) advocated in their phrase 'making thinking visible'.[12]

More important is how Lave and Wenger contrast the teaching and the learning curriculum, noted earlier. They define a learning curriculum as consisting of 'situated opportunities . . . for the improvisational development of new practice' (Lave and Wenger, 1991, p. 97). A teaching curriculum, on the other hand, is constructed for newcomers and mediates the meaning of what is learned through the external view of the teacher. They argue that the learning curriculum views the learning resources from the perspective of the learner. We take this idea to match against the rhetoric of lifelong learning, which is often no more than 'lifelong courses', and as such typifies a teaching rather than a learning curriculum. Young (1998) also mounts a critique of such approaches to post-compulsory education, and advocates a connective model of the learning society, building on the work of those who share the situated approach. This model seeks a connection between learning and production (in the industrial context). Thus it sees the working environment in terms of its learning opportunities. This is pointing towards the views of those in the situated approach, but still does not articulate the need to consider the workplace as one of learning, where there are 'opportunities to improvise new practice' as we noted earlier. With this view of learning we envisage workplaces, for example, in terms of how they enable workers to solve problems, to collaborate and to share thinking: what resources can be provided to allow opportunities and support for these activities?[13] This would lead us to curriculum considerations for learning at work – considerations that are likely to be more radical than work-based learning (Duckenfield, 1992).

Thoughts and investigations such as these could give us a radical view of the curriculum, as radical as Freire gave us some 30 years ago (Freire, 1970).

NOTES

1 These three levels of analysis we refer to also as levels of 'definition' and/or 'negotiation', reflecting both our definition of these levels and the negotiation that takes place at each level.

2 Young has updated his original work and extended the whole analysis, to meet the developing ideas in learning, in his recent book (Young, 1998).

3 Marsh has, in an earlier text, written more about learning, but still it did not reflect the mainstream accounts of learning even of this earlier time (Marsh, 1991).

4 See Rogoff (1990) for an account of how Piaget and Vygotsky differ on their consideration of the social dimension.

5 Roth has distinguished between social constructivist theories and theories labelled as situated because of his interest in looking at views of knowledge. In looking at learning as Bredo did, the terms 'situated' embraced both. This is because for all the different theories, context was crucial to learning. However, what was understood by 'context' varied between the theories, and so how learning occurs and how to understand it varied.

6 Lest the reader think that this view, represented originally by Hirst and Peters (1970), has long since disappeared, its adherents still exist (e.g. Pring, 1995).

7 This puts aside other complexities that exist in the discussions of the nature of science. See Driver *et al.* (1996, chapter 1) for a succinct account of the history of this debate.

8 This is where technicians would return from repairing machines and tell of the horrors they had encountered. These 'war stories' as they were called, are narratives that have a function in the learning of other technicans.

9 However, his views are based on those of Piaget and Vygotsky and do not include an examination of the implications for situated views of learning.

10 Paradoxically, Goodson (1998) refers to such an approach as 'The Micropolitics of Curriculum Change'!

11 Patricia Murphy has shown how gendered this is (Murphy, 1991).

12 Collins *et al.* (1991) have a clear model that enacts this view of learning.

13 This kind of view represented the agenda of the Institute for Research on Learning (1993a, 1993b).

ACKNOWLEDGEMENTS

We would like to acknowledge our indebtedness to those involved in the Open University course *E836, Curriculum, Learning and Assessment*, in which context we developed some of the ideas for this contribution. The readers associated with this course contain many of the sources we draw upon (see McCormick and Paechter, 1999; Moon and Leach, 1999; Moon and Murphy, 1999; Murphy, 1999b). We would also like to thank Mary James, who offered helpful comments on a draft of the chapter.

REFERENCES

Adey, P. S. (1997) 'It all depends on context, doesn't it? Searching for general, educable dragons'. *Studies in Science Education*, 29, 45–92.

Adey, P. S. and Shayer, M. (1994) *Really Raising Standards: Cognitive Intervention and Academic Achievement*. London: Routledge.

Anderson, J. R., Reder, L. M. and Simon, H. A. (1996) 'Situated learning and education'. *Educational Researcher*, 25 (4), 5–11.

Anderson, J. R., Reder, L. M. and Simon, H. A. (1998) 'Situative versus cognitive perspectives: Form versus substance'. *Educational Researcher*, 26 (1), 18–21.

Benavot, A., Cha, Y.-K., Kamens, D. H., Meyer, J. and Wong, S.-Y. (1992) 'Knowledge for the masses: world models and national curricula, 1920–1986'. In J. Meyer, D. Kamens, A. Benavot, Y.-K. Cha and S. Wong (eds) *School Knowledge for the Masses. World Models and National Primary Curricular Categories in the Twentieth Century.* London: Falmer.

Bernstein, B. (1971) 'On classification and framing of educational knowledge'. In M. F. D. Young (ed.) *Knowledge and Control.* London: Collier-Macmillan, 47–69.

Black, P. (1998) *Testing: Friend or Foe? Theory and Practice of Assessment and Testing.* London: Falmer.

Black, P. (1999) 'Assessment, learning theories and testing systems'. In P. Murphy (ed.) *Learners, Learning and Assessment.* London: Paul Chapman.

Black, P. and Wiliam, D. (1998) 'Assessment and classroom learning'. *Assessment in Education,* 5 (1), 1–75.

Blagg, N., Lewis, R. and Ballinger, M. (1994) *Thinking and Learning at Work. A Report on the Development and Evaluation of the Thinking Skills at Work Modules.* Sheffield: Employment Department.

Boaler, J. (1994) 'When do girls prefer football to fashion? An analysis of female underachievement in relation to realistic mathematics contexts'. *British Educational Research Journal,* 20 (5), 551–564.

Boaler, J. (1997) 'Alternative approaches to teaching, learning and assessing mathematics'. Paper presented at the 7th Conference of the European Association for Research in Learning and Instruction held in Athens, Greece in August.

Bredo, E. (1994) 'Reconstructing educational psychology: Situated cognition and Deweyian pragmatism'. *Educational Psychologist,* 29 (1), 23–35.

Bredo, E. (1997) 'The social construction of learning'. In G. D. Phye (ed.) *Handbook of Academic Learning: Construction of Knowledge.* San Diego: Academic Press.

Brown, A. L. and Campione, J. C. (1990) 'Communities of learning and thinking, or a context by any other name'. In D. Kuhn (ed.) *Developmental Perspectives on Teaching and Learning Thinking Skills. Contributions to Human Development.* Basle: Karger, 108–126.

Brown, A. L., and Ferrara, R. A. (1985). 'Diagnosing zones of proximal development'. In J. Wertsch (ed.) *Culture, Communication, and Cognition: Vygotskian Perspectives.* New York: Cambridge University Press.

Brown, J. S., Collins, A. and Duguid, P. (1989) 'Situated cognition and the culture of learning'. *Educational Researcher,* 18 (1), 32–41.

Bruner, J. (1986) *Actual Minds, Possible Worlds.* Cambridge, MA: Harvard University Press.

Bruner, J. (1996) *The Culture of Education.* Cambridge, MA: Harvard University Press.

Clancey, W. J. (1993) 'Situated action: A neuropsychological interpretation response to Vera and Simon'. *Cognitive Science,* 17, 87–116.

Collins, A., Brown, J. S. and Holum, A. (1991) 'Cognitive apprenticeship: Making thinking visible'. *American Educator* (Winter), 6–11, 38–46.

Cooper, B. (1992) 'Testing National Curriculum mathematics: Some critical comments on the treatment of "real" contexts for mathematics'. *Curriculum Journal,* 3, 231–243.

Davidson, M., Evens, H. and McCormick, R. (1998) 'Bridging the gap. The use of concepts from science and mathematics in design and technology at KS3'. In J. S. Smith and E. W. L. Norman (eds) *IDATER 98 – International Conference on Design and Technology Educational Research and Curriculum Development.* Loughborough: University of Loughborough, 48–53.

de Bono, E. (1974) *CoRT Thinking Lessons.* Blandford Forum, Dorset: Direct Educational Services.

Department of Education and Science and the Welsh Office (DES/WO) (1989) *Design and Technology for Ages 5 to 16.* London: HMSO.

Department for Education and Employment (DfEE) (1998) *National Literacy Strategy. Framework for Teaching.* London: HMSO.

Department for Education and the Welsh Office (DfE/WO) (1995) *Design and Technology in the National Curriculum.* London: HMSO.

Detterman, D. K. and Sternberg, R. J. (1993) *Transfer on Trial: Intelligence, Cognition and Instruction.* Norwood, NJ: Ablex Publishing Corporation.

Driver, R., Leach. J., Millar, R. and Scott, P. (1996) *Young People's Images of Science.* Milton Keynes: Open University Press.

Duckenfield, M. (1992) *Learning Through Work*. Sheffield: Employment Department, Higher Education Branch.

Duell, O. K. (1986) 'Metacognitive skills'. In G. D. Phye and T. Andre (eds) *Cognitive Classroom Learning: Understanding, Thinking, and Problem-Solving*. Orlando: Academic Press, 205–242.

Eisner, E. W. (1996) *Cognition and Curriculum Reconsidered* (2nd edn). London: Paul Chapman.

Ennis, R. H. (1989) 'Critical thinking and subject specificity: Clarification and needed research'. *Educational Researcher*, 18 (3), 4–10.

Evans, R. J. (1996) *In Defence of History*. London: Granta Books.

Evens, H. and McCormick, R. (1997) *Mathematics by Design: An Investigation at Key Stage 3* (Final Report for the Design Council). Milton Keynes: School of Education, The Open University.

Feuerstein, R., Rand, Y., Hoffman, M. and Millar, R. (1980) *Instrumental Enrichment*. Baltimore, MD: University Park Press.

Flinders, D. J. and Thornton, S. J. (eds) (1997) *The Curriculum Studies Reader*. New York: Routledge.

Freire, P. (1970) *Pedagogy of the Oppressed*. Harmondsworth: Penguin.

Gardner, H. (1992) 'Assessment in context: The alternative to standardized testing'. In B. R. Gifford and M. C. O'Connor (eds) *Changing Assessment: Alternative Views of Aptitude, Achievement and Instruction*. London: Kluwer.

Gipps, C. V. (1994) *Beyond Testing: Towards a Theory of Educational Assessment*. London: Falmer.

Gipps, C. and Murphy, P. (1994) *A Fair Test? Assessment, Achievement and Equity*. Buckingham: Open University Press.

Glaser, R. (1984) 'Education and thinking: The role of knowledge'. *American Psychologist*, 39 (2), 93–104.

Glaser, R. (1992) 'Expert knowledge and processes of thinking'. In D. F. Halpern (ed.) *Enhancing Thinking Skills in the Sciences and Mathematics*. Hillsdale, NJ: Erlbaum, 63–75.

Goodson, I. F. (1994) *Studying the Curriculum*. Buckingham: Open University Press.

Goodson, I. F. (1998) 'The micro politics of curriculum change: European Studies'. In Goodson *et al.*, *Subject Knowledge*. London: Falmer, 38–50.

Goodson, I. F., Anstead, C. J. and Mangan, J. M. (1998) *Subject Knowledge: Readings for the Study of School Subjects*. London: Falmer.

Gott, R. and Murphy, P. (1987) *Assessing Investigations at Ages 13 and 15*. Hatfield: Association for Science Education.

Greeno, J. G. (1998) 'On claims that answer the wrong question'. *Educational Researcher*, 26 (1), 5–17.

Greeno, J. G., Pearson, P. D. and Schoenfeld, A. H. (1997) 'Implications for national assessment of educational progress of research and cognition'. In R. Glaser and R. Linn (eds) *Assessment in Transition: Monitoring the Nation's Educational Progress. Background Studies*. Stanford, CA: National Academy of Education, Stanford University.

Grossman, P. L. and Stodolsky, S. S. (1995) 'Content as context: The role of school subjects in secondary school teaching'. *Educational Researcher*, 24 (8), 5–11, 23.

Hiebert, J. and Lefevre, P. (1986) 'Conceptual and procedural knowledge in mathematics: An introductory analysis'. In J. Hiebert (ed.) *Procedural and Conceptual Knowledge: The Case of Mathematics*. London: Lawrence Erlbaum Associates, 1–27.

Hiebert, J., Carpenter, T. P., Fennema, E., Fuson, K., Human, P., Murray, H., Olivier, A. and Wearne, D. (1996) 'Problem-solving as a basis for reform in curriculum and instruction: The case of mathematics'. *Educational Researcher*, 25 (4), 12–21.

Hirst, P. H. and Peters, R. S. (1970) *The Logic of Education*. London: Routledge and Kegan Paul.

Institute for Research on Learning (IRL) (1993a) *A New Learning Agenda 'Putting People First'*. Palo Alto, CA: IRL.

Institute for Research on Learning (IRL) (1993b) *Annual Report 1993*. Palo Alto, CA: IRL.

James, C. (1968) *Young Lives at Stake: A Reappraisal of Secondary Schools*. London: Collins.

Latour, B. and Woolgar, S. (1979) *Laboratory Life: The Construction of Scientific Facts*. Princeton, NJ: Princeton University Press.

Lave, J. (1988) *Cognition in Practice: Mind, Mathematics and Culture in Everyday Life*. New York: Cambridge University Press.

Lave, J. (1992) 'Word problems: A microcosm of theories of learning'. In P. Light and G. Butterworth (eds) *Context and Cognition: Ways of Learning and Knowing*. London: Harvester Wheatsheaf, 74–92.

Lave, J. (1996) 'The practice of learning'. In S. Chaiklin and J. Lave (eds) *Understanding Practice: Perspectives on Activity and Context*. Cambridge: Cambridge University Press, 3–32.

Lave, J. and Wenger, E. (1991) *Situated Learning: Legitimate Peripheral Participation*. Cambridge: Cambridge University Press.

Lave, J., Greeno, J. G., Schoenfeld, A., Smith, S. and Butler, M. (eds) (1988) *Learning Mathematical Problem Solving*. (Report No. IRL88–0006) Palo Alto, CA: Institute for Research on Learning.

Lewis, T. (1993) 'Valid knowledge and the problem of the practical arts curricula'. *Curriculum Inquiry*, 23 (2), 175–202.

Lunt, I. (1993) 'The practice of assessment'. In H. Daniels (ed.) *Charting the Agenda: Educational Activity after Vygotsky*. London: Routledge, 145–170.

McCormick, R. (1997) 'Conceptual and procedural knowledge'. *International Journal of Technology and Design Education*, 7 (1–2), 141–159.

McCormick, R. (1999) 'Practical knowledge: A view from the snooker table'. In McCormick and Paechter (eds) *Learning and Knowledge*. London: Paul Chapman, 112–135.

McCormick, R. and Paechter, C. (eds) (1999) *Learning and Knowledge*. London: Paul Chapman.

McCormick, R., Murphy, P., Davidson, M., Evens, H. and Spence, M. (1998) *The Use of Mathematics in Science and Technology Education*. Symposium at the British Educational Research Association annual conference, September, Queen's University, Belfast.

Marsh, C. (1991) 'Curriculum approaches'. In C. Marsh and P. Morris (eds) *Curriculum Development in East Asia*. London: Falmer Press, 3–21.

Marsh, C. (1997) *Perspectives: Key Concepts for Understanding Curriculum*. London: Falmer Press.

Mercer, N. (1995) *The Guided Construction of Knowledge: Talk amongst Teachers and Learners*. Clevedon, UK: Multilingual Matters.

Messick, S. (1989) 'Meaning and values in test validation: The science and ethics of assessment'. *Educational Researcher*, 18 (2), 5–11.

Moon, R. and Leach, J. (eds) (1999) *Learners and Pedagogy*. London: Paul Chapman.

Moon, R. and Murphy, P. (eds) (1999) *Curriculum in Context*. London: Paul Chapman.

Moss, G. (1996) 'Negotiated literacies: How children enact what counts as reading in a different social setting'. Unpublished PhD thesis. Milton Keynes: Open University.

Murphy, P. (1990) 'Learning and the curriculum'. In M. Lawn, B. Moon and P. Murphy (eds) *Curriculum, Learning and Assessment (E819). Study Guide*. Milton Keynes: Open University Press, 35–36.

Murphy, P. (1991) 'Gender and practical work'. In B. Woolnough (ed.) *Practical Work in Science*. Milton Keynes: Open University Press.

Murphy, P. (1995) 'Sources of inequity: Understanding students' responses to assessment'. *Assessment in Education: Principles, Policy and Practice*, 2 (3), 249–270.

Murphy, P. (1996) 'Integrating learning and assessment – the role of learning theories'. In P. Woods (ed.) *Contemporary Issues in Teaching and Learning*. London: Routledge, 173–193.

Murphy, P. (1999a) 'Supporting collaborative learning: A gender dimension'. In P. Murphy (ed.) *Learners, Learning and Assessment*. London: Paul Chapman, 258–276.

Murphy, P. (ed.) (1999b) *Learners, Learning and Assessment*. London: Paul Chapman.

Murphy, P. and McCormick, R. (1997) 'Problem solving in science and technology education'. *Research in Science and Education*, 27 (3), 461–481.

Murphy, P., Scanlon, E. and Issroff, K. with Hodgson, B. and Whitelegg, E. (1996) 'Group work in Primary Science – emerging issues for learning and teaching'. In K. Schnack (ed.) *Studies in Educational Theory and Curriculum*, vol. 14. Copenhagen: Danish School of Educational Studies.

Murphy, P., Moon, B., McCormick, R. and Leach, J. (1999) *Learning, Curriculum and Assessment* (E836 Study Guide). Milton Keynes: Open University Press.

Newman, D., Griffin, P. and Cole, M. (1989) *The Construction Zone: Working for Cognitive Change in Schools*. Cambridge: Cambridge University Press.

Oates, T. (1992) 'Core skills and transfer: aiming high'. *Education and Training Technology International*, 29 (3), 227–239.

Open University (1976) *The Child, the School and Society* (E203, Curriculum Design and Development, Units 5, 6, 7 and 8). Milton Keynes: Open University Press.

Paechter, C. (1995) *Crossing Subject Boundaries: The Micropolitics of Curriculum Innovation*. London: HMSO/King's College, School of Education.

Pring, R. A. (1971) 'Curriculum integration'. In R. Hooper (ed.) *The Curriculum: Context, Design and Development*. Edinburgh: Oliver and Boyd, 265–272.

Pring, R. A. (1995) *Closing the Gap: Liberal Education and Vocational Preparation*. London: Hodder & Stoughton.

Reynolds, D. and Farrell, S. (1996) *Worlds Apart? A Review of International Surveys of Educational Achievement Involving England*. (Ofsted reviews of research.) London: HMSO.

Rogoff, B. (1990) *Apprenticeship in Thinking: Cognitive Development in a Social Context*. New York: Oxford University Press.

Rogoff, B. (1995) 'Observing sociocultural activity on three planes: Participatory appropriation, guided participation and apprenticeship'. In J. V. Wertsch, P. del Río, and A. Alverez (eds) *Sociocultural Studies of Mind*. Cambridge: Cambridge University Press, 139–164.

Roth, W. M. (1997) 'Situated cognition and assessment of competence in science'. Paper presented at the 7th Conference of the European Association for Research in Learning and Instruction. Athens, Greece.

Schoenfeld, A. (1996) 'In fostering communities of inquiry, must it matter that the teacher knows the answer?' *For the Learning of Mathematics*, 14 (1), 44–55.

Scribner, S. (1985) 'Knowledge at work'. *Anthropology and Education Quarterly*, 16 (3), 199–206.

Sfard, A. (1998) 'On two metaphors for learning and the dangers of choosing just one. *Educational Researcher*, 27 (2), 4–13.

Shayer, M. (1996) *Long-term Effects of Cognitive Acceleration through Science Education on Achievement*. London: King's College, Centre for the Advancement of Thinking.

Skilbeck, M. (1990) *Curriculum Reform: An Overview of Trends*. Paris: OECD.

Stevenson, J. (1994) 'Vocational expertise'. In J. Stevenson (ed.) *Cognition at Work*. Leabrook, South Australia: National Centre for Vocational Education Research, 7–35.

Taba, H. (1962) *Curriculum Development: Theory and Practice*. New York: Harcourt, Brace and World.

Von Glasersfeld, E. (1989) 'Learning as constructive activity'. In P. Murphy and B. Moon (eds) *Developments in Learning and Assessment*. London: Hodder & Stoughton, 5–18.

Wellington, J. (ed.) (1989) *Skills and Processes in Science Education: A Critical Analysis*. London: Routledge.

Wolf, A. (1999) 'Outcomes, competencies and trainee-centred learning: the gap between theoretic and reality'. In P. Murphy (ed.) *Learners, Learning and Assessment*. London: Paul Chapman, 191–213.

Young, M. F. D. (ed.) (1971) *Knowledge and Control*. London: Collier-Macmillan.

Young, M. F. D. (1998) *Curriculum of the Future: From the 'New Sociology of Education' to a Critical Theory of Learning*. London: Falmer.

13

UNDERSTANDING EUROPEAN
DIDACTICS

Bjørg B. Gundem

INTRODUCTION: DEFINITIONS AND APPROACHES TO THE FIELD

'Didactic' as a word used in English has a rather negative connotation. It is, for example, found as an adjective meaning 'behaving like a teacher' (*Concise Oxford Dictionary of Current English*, 1959) or 'teaching or intending to teach a moral lesson' (*Webster's Encyclopedic Unabridged Dictionary*, 1994). The term 'didactics', generally avoided in Anglo-Saxon educational contexts, refers when used, to practical and methodological problems of mediation and does not claim to be an independent educational discipline let alone a scientific or research programme.

In this article the word 'didactics' will be used to convey the meaning of *Didaktik* (German-speaking countries), *didaktik(k)* (the Nordic countries) and *didactique* (France). In these countries the word is used only to a limited degree in common language, while it is in educational contexts one of the most central ones, and is used extensively. It has, however, when applied professionally, a variety of meanings. A uniform or unambiguous understanding of the subject matter, scope, methodology and system of didactics as part of education as a scientific discipline does not exist. Differing schools, traditions and models may be clearly discerned. There exists consequently a variety of definitions which all claim to be legitimate both historically and in contemporary contexts. Some definitions focusing on the field and scope of didactics are:

1 *Didactics as a science and theory about teaching and learning in all circumstances and in all forms.* This is the most comprehensive and widest definition (e.g. Dolch, 1965).
2 *Didactics as the science or theory of teaching.* Didactics defined in this way comprises the broad sphere of reality consisting of socially legitimated and organised teaching and learning processes accomplished on a professional foundation (e.g. Heimann *et al.*, 1965).
3 *Didactics as the theory of the contents of formation [Bildung] and of its structure and selection* (Weniger, 1965, 1994). This understanding of didactics focuses on formation [*Bildung*] and the formation potential of subject matter (Klafki, 1958; Weniger, 1965).
4 *Didactics as theory about the steering and controlling of the learning process.* In this

235

understanding, teaching and learning processes are regarded as analogues to cyberneti-cally controlled technical systems (von Cube, 1972; König and Riedel, 1972).

5 *Didactics as the application of psychological teaching and learning theories.* Within this understanding the research aspect is predominant. The leading research interest is the bettering of all factors related to teaching and learning (Marton, 1983; Roth, 1962). One way to illustrate these different definitions focusing on the scope or object of didactics is shown in Figure 13.1.

6 *Didactics = the theory and practice of teaching and learning.* Today in both a German and Scandinavian educational context there is a marked tendency to include educational practice as part of the concept of didactics (Jank and Meyer, 1991).

Related to each of these definitons are, as indicated, specific people and specific schools of didactics. Simplified we may say that the concerns of didactics are:

- what should be taught and learnt (the content aspect);
- how to teach and learn (the aspects of transmitting and learning);
- to what purpose or intention something should be taught and learnt (the goal/aims aspect) (Künzli, 1994).

To put it another way, as a *real phenomenon* in the educational contexts of Scandinavia and German-speaking countries, didactics exists:

- as theory and as prescription – and consequently as reflection and action – underlining differing theories and models of didactics with their different foci and views of its scope and function;
- at different levels of abstraction, e.g. 'general didactics', 'special didactics' and 'school subject didactics';
- as a scientific discipline, as a research area and as courses of study – that is the institutionalised aspect.

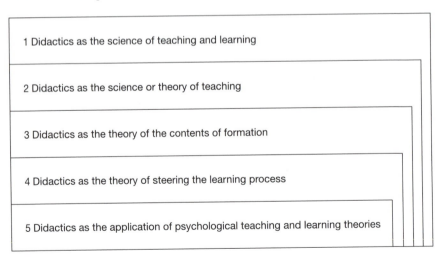

Figure 13.1 Classification of didactics according to subject area.
Source: Kron 1994, p. 43 (my translation)

These are, however, analytic categories: as real phenomena they overlap.

Still another way to put it is to say that one can at least identify three levels as core areas of didactics:

1 *a theoretical or research level*, where the expression denotes a field of study;
2 *a practical level*, where didactics is exercised, comprising among other fields, the fields of teaching, curriculum-making and the planning of teaching and learning;
3 *a discursive level*, where didactics implies a 'frame of reference' for professional dialogues between teachers and between teachers and other interest groups discussing school matters (Hopmann and Riquarts, 1995).

Institutions naming the core of their activities 'didactics' may be found in the fields of educational research (e.g. institute for the didactics of mathematics), teacher education (departments of general didactics and subject matter didactics), school administration, curriculum-making and textbook production, as well as in-service training contexts, just to mention a few.

Didactics is consequently neither an equivalent of curriculum studies, nor just a habit or a practical approach, but is embedded in almost all professional activities dealing with teaching and schooling. The professional knowledge of teachers is called 'didactics' (*Didaktik*, *didaktikk*). Most of teacher training deals with it. Researchers studying teaching and learning processes in classrooms would call their research didactic. 'Didactics' may be characterised as having a language of its own, with a vocabulary of its own and a group of 'native' speakers, who have a certain kind of professional education and/or a certain field of professional work in common. It is further worth noticing that didactics subsumes 'curriculum' as one issue besides or interwoven with other issues like teaching and learning, schooling, school administration, etc. (cf. Hopmann and Riquarts, 1995; Hopmann and Gundem, 1998).

The relevance of the topic of didactics today is linked to a growing international co-operation and rapprochement within the educational field, making necessary a growing understanding, especially with regard to differing traditions of planning in teaching and learning. One may say that there exist two main traditions: the Anglo-Saxon tradition of curriculum studies and the Continental and North European tradition of didactics. While the curriculum studies tradition is internationally acknowledged, adopted and adapted, the tradition of didactics is still relatively unknown in Anglo-Saxon educational contexts and settings.

However, the centrality of didactics in the past and present of the educational life of the Germanic and Scandinavian countries makes it imperative that all people who want to grasp the realities of this life also gain insights into the area of didactics. Further, the important role being attributed to didactics in current policy decisions, research and debate within the educational area in all the Nordic and Germanic countries, indicates values embedded in this tradition that are worth exporting into an international arena. And it is worth noticing that a certain degree of rapprochement already exists in the international use of concepts and expressions within the area, not least due to an international project 'Didaktik meets Curriculum' which has instigated a continuing international dialogue across these traditions (see *Journal of Curriculum Studies*, vol. 27, no. 1; Gundem and Hopmann, 1998).

ETYMOLOGY, ROOTS AND HISTORY

The word *didactics* originates from the Greek *didaskein*, which meant 'to be a teacher, to educate'. Some derivatives are:

didaktikos: apt at teaching; instructive
didaskaleion: school, classroom, class
didaskalia: teach, information, enlightenment, advice; correction
didaskalikos: belonging to teaching; instructive
didaskalion: knowledge, science; school fees
didaskalos: teacher
didasko: to be a teacher, teach; be instructed and taught; learn, learn by one self, acquire; give somebody a lesson, let somebody be educated
didachae: lesson, precept, warning, doctrine, dogma, theory science.

There are in the Greek words, a great range of basic meanings which have been kept alive, for example:

1 *the ability* to teach, to instruct and inform
2 *the people* who have this ability
3 *the content* that should be learnt
4 *the teaching aids*, including methods and media
5 *the school* and the class where the learning takes place
6 *the learning* as the main activity of pupils (Kron, 1993).

The Greek root of the didactic is cognate with '*deik*' and means the action of showing and indicating. Didactics would thus be the art of showing, of pointing and drawing attention to, of allowing something that does not simply demonstrate itself, or cannot be understood, to be perceived and recognised. In keeping with this original meaning of the word, didactics can be used to mean the science of instruction and the embodiment of knowledge about instruction (Kron, 1993).

On the other hand, it can also be used to refer to the more or less binding set of rules governing skilled teaching and reflecting the professional ability of the teacher. No strict delineation is made between the two meanings, that is between the *science of instruction* and *the art of instruction*. An inclination to synthesise the theory and the craft of teaching has been a marked characteristic of didactics from the early days until today, where an increasing importance is put on this aspect (Jank and Meyer, 1991; Künzli, 1998).

Another characteristic of didactics that can be traced through the original meanings of the word, is the opening up for a normative, prescriptive aspect. *Didactics exists both as theory and as prescription.*

It was in seventeenth-century Europe that the concepts of 'curriculum' and 'didactics' were first used to denote educational phenomena. Didactics was linked to Wolfgang Ratke's (1571–1635) *methodus didactica* and to Johann Amos Comenius's (1592–1670) *Didactica Magna*. The use of the term 'curriculum' may be linked to Daniel Georgius Morhof (1639–1691), professor in Rostock from 1660. From this time traditions developed in which the expression 'didactics' became the prevalent one on the Continent, while the term 'curriculum' was the one used in the English-speaking Western world.

238

In Comenius's shortest definition, given in his *Didactica Magna*, didactics contains three elements, *omnis omnia docere*, i.e. 'teaching everything to everyone'. To teach everything meant relating the microcosmos of instruction to the macrocosmos of the world. Didactically translated, such teaching required knowing what the content of instruction should be like, where it came from, how it was used: to have a representation of content which followed its natural or social appearance. Furthermore, teaching is only possible if instruction takes care of the progress of learning and the development of the learner. Comenius supplied a theory of the learner based on natural stages of development. Finally teaching had to be aware of both the content and the learner. Research efforts to reassess the didactic heritage of Comenius in the light of his Pansophy and specifically his *General Considerations Concerning Human Affairs* have come from the Comenius Institute of Education in Prague. This reassessment of Comenius is tied not only to the criticism of *Didactica Magna* but also to the many misinterpretations of Comenius which make *Didactica Magna* his educational heritage without including and integrating his pansophy and the message of *Pampaedia* and other parts of the *General Considerations Concerning Human Affairs*. As a result of this reassessment:

1 There is ample evidence that Comenius dissociated himself with his initial didactical concept and revised it.
2 The revision of his didactical concept was content related: to teach those things that serve human improvement.
3 What emerged was not only a theory of instruction, but a theory of education where the content aspect was included and his pansophical and threefold understanding of knowledge integrated. It was *bildungstheoretisch* and *geisteswissenschaftlich* (Schaller 1992, 1995).

The rise of mass schooling linked to the Lutheran reformation brought about a situation in which didactics became the common approach for planning lessons and legitimising schooling in Central and Northern Europe. Two factors were especially influential: the curriculum guidelines issued by governments and other state institutions, and the expansion of teacher education creating a market for a supporting literature where the methodological aspect of didactics, the *how*, became predominant. However, method was not understood in the limited fashion predominant today. In fact, the search for the best method implied that there exists a natural way of teaching and learning that is in accord with the nature of content. The most developed historical example of this approach is Johann Friedrich Herbart's (1776–1814) linking of his didactic thinking to theories of learning, thus combining classical rhetoric with modern psychology.

Herbart distinguished three layers of education: government, discipline and instruction. *Government* means sustaining order by leadership and command. *Discipline* or *character* is the general compliance to order inside and outside school that teachers try to implant. Whereas government is based on direct intervention and discipline on the self-control of the learner, *instruction* mediates between both, by content, i.e., it educates by developing the learner's knowledge of obligations, opportunities and choices. In Herbart's view, instruction is education by content, and he created the model of educating instruction, ['*erziender Unterricht*'], as the core of schooling. The most important contribution of Herbart, and to some degree the Herbartians, was to extract didactics from general educational theory, turning it into a discipline of its own, dealing with instruction under the conditions of schooling as distinct from other instructional settings. But in doing so, the Herbartians changed Herbart's analytical tools into schematic sequences pre-forming any hour and minute of teaching.

To sum up (Kron 1994, p. 73):

1 Interest and range of thinking [*Gedankenkreis*] are classified as basic phenomena of didactical deliberation. By this is meant that an outline of the first draft or plan of cultural conveyance, or a first didactical theory, is formed.
2 The articulation of teaching is seen by analogy with the development of the interests and range of thinking of the learners. This leads to the development of a first modern time concept of instructional planning. It led to reformulation of the planning aspect of teaching. A new planning model appeared.
3 Through the so-called *Formalstufen* a formalisation of didactical thinking and practice took place, didactical reflection and practice became formalised.

The didactics of Herbart became successful because of state curriculum-making, and because of the gap between legislation and the local needs of teachers and students. However, it was not Herbart's sophisticated arguments which gradually permeated teacher education and schooling, but the simplifications developed by his followers, the so-called Herbartians like Tuiskon Ziller (1817–1882) and Wilhelm Rein (1847–1929).

The tendency towards a rigid, schematic approach to teaching was challenged by a theory of education and teaching, the *bildungstheoretische Didaktik*, rooted in a specific branch of 'reform pedagogy', which built on the philosophy of life and pedagogy of Wilhelm Dilthey (1833–1911).

THE INFLUENCE ON DIDACTICS OF HUMAN SCIENCES AND THE DEVELOPMENT OF A HUMAN SCIENCE DIDACTICS

The expression *geisteswissenschaftlich* relates to the distinction made by the German philosopher Wilhelm Dilthey between the exact sciences (*Naturwissenschaften*) and the human sciences (*Geisteswissenschaften*); the former dealing with measurable and predictable areas of reality, the latter with all that has to do with human beings. This had, argued Dilthey, consequences for the way to proceed with an examination of these different realities: 'Die Naturen erklären wir, das Seelenleben verstehen wir' [We explain nature, but understand human life] (Dilthey, 1924). The hermeneutic approach advocated by Dilthey as the essential core of the human sciences stressed the need for a holistic and comprehensive context, an examination of the researcher's preconceived ideas as well as adherence to philological rules of text interpretation.

The way human science education [*geisteswissenschaftliche Pädagogik*] developed after Dilthey through the contributions of Edward Spranger (1882–1963), Theodor Litt (1880–1962), Hermann Nohl (1879–1969), Wilhelm Flitner (1898–1989) and Erich Weniger (1894–1960) was also heavily influenced by the writings of Friedrich Schleiermacher (1768–1834), especially concerning the hermeneutical approach and the practice–theory relationship. And in this process of development, the autonomy of education as a genuine field with its specific problems and concepts – detached from related disciplines like philosophy – emerged.

240

In analysing the impact on didactics from this human science perspective, certain characteristics may be identified:

1 *Der Primat der Praxis*: educational practice is given priority;
2 Concept formation and theory development start in practice;
3 Historicity, taking into account the past, the present and the future;
4 An awareness of the complexities embedded in all relations related to schooling, teaching and learning.

What is meant by *Der Primat der Praxis* and the claim that concept formation, and consequently theory development, must have educational practice as a point of departure? A central idea embedded in the thinking of Dilthey is that an understanding of life may only be gained by lived experience. When applied to the educational arena understood as practice, this implies that real understanding of the nature, problems and tasks of practice will only be attained by experiencing practice directly. It follows that the only legitimate approach to theory building is to examine the educational phenomena as they exist in the practice of teaching and schooling. Wolfgang Klafki explained this theory–practice relationship by arguing that in education, theory and practice are not clearly separated entities: theory-like assumptions, beliefs and convictions are embedded in educational practice, though mostly unreflected. The role of educational research is to develop these influxes of theory into a research-based knowledge in a methodologically stringent way (Klafki, 1971).

The third characteristic underlines the context-dependent aspect of educational practice and theory, especially taking into account the past, the present and the future aspects.

As a consequence of the fourth characteristic, deduction from overall principles and aims as well as easy ends–means relations are unwanted in the educational planning process. (This may be discerned also in the curriculum 'theory' or models pertaining to didactic theories influenced by the behavioural sciences from the 1960s – a general contribution to the development of curriculum theory, as it were.)

It was Erich Weniger who developed, from the 1930s, a specific curriculum theory of hermeneutic didactics taking into consideration the characteristics of the human science or *geisteswissenschaftliche* tradition. From the 1950s onwards Wolfgang Klafki (1927–) is regarded as the most prominent and influential representative of this tradition.

GERMAN THEORIES AND SCHOOLS OF DIDACTICS FROM THE 1950s ONWARDS: THE CONCEPTION OF *BILDUNG*

In his book *Theorien und Modelle der Didaktik*, Herwig Blankertz (1975) describes the range of didactic theories along a continuum from human science didactics [*geisteswissenschaftliche Didaktik*] to cybernetic didactics [*kybernetische Didaktik*] at the other end. It is of interest to ask what makes it possible to distinguish theories of didactics in this way. Thus we can distinguish:

● differing scientific and sometimes ideological affiliations;
● differing views of man and society;

- differing understandings of what constitutes *Bildung* [formation], knowledge and learning, and consequently
- differing assumptions as to the aims and content of schooling.

It is thus important to note that didactic theories are legitimated by social and scientific context as well as by their relationship to theories of learning and instruction. This has, as we shall see, consequences for the scope and the foci of particular didactic theories, their specific didactic categories and didactic functions, and the criteria chosen for the selection of the content of teaching and learning – all leading to variations in their subordinate curriculum theories and strategies for curriculum development. The line from theory to model and to prescription is manifest, and to a certain degree, self-evident, as are the didactic competences and skills a teacher should attain and exercise.

As indicated, we may locate didactic theories on a continuum, from a human science-formative-theoretical approach at one end, through theories influenced by the behavioural sciences to the exact sciences at the other end. Thus the now 'classical' division or categorisation by Blankertz (1975) included *bildungstheoretische Modelle* [educational formative models], *lern/lehrtheoretische Modelle* [models based on learning/teaching theories] and *informationstheoretische Modelle* [models based on informatics and cybernetic theories of didactics]. In other words, there is not one 'didactics', but several.

The 'tradition': human science didactics

In spite of the fact that there is not one trend of didactics but several, the expression 'the didactic tradition' is often used to refer solely to the specific human science didactics [*geisteswissenschaftliche Didaktik*] (Frey, 1986, pp. 11–16). Of course, this has been the main tradition of didactics and has had the longest and most profound impact.

The focus of this curricular thinking as well as of the overarching didactic theory is *Bildung*, formation. *Bildung* refers to the process and product of personal development, guided by reason. The concept of *Bildung* is rooted in the multifaceted understanding of the concept which developed in the period around 1770–1830. It was elaborated particularly in German-speaking areas of Europe, but had from the beginning a worldwide perspective. The conception absorbed stimuli from the European Enlightenment: Lessing, Kant, Herder, Goethe, Schiller, Pestalozzi and Herbart, Schleiermacher, Fichte, Hegel, Froebel and Diesterweg all contributed to its development. However, in spite of differences, and sometimes even contradictory notions, a few fundamental yet common points emerged, especially the idea of the responsible and socially aware person contributing to his or her own destiny and capable of knowing, feeling and acting.

Didactic theory as *Bildungstheorie*, or theory of formation, was gradually firmly established, and further developed, among others, by Wolfgang Klafki (1975). He developed the idea of *kategoriale Bildung*. An underlying assumption is the dialectic relation between dichotomies like self-realisation and solidarity, and that societal power relations define, influence and steer the learning processes aimed at mediating formation. The individual person will always find herself or himself in a state of tension between demands from the outer world and the right to follow one's own path. We get a dialectic tension between what

Klafki calls *Weltbewältigung* [to master the world] and *Personwertung* [valuing the 'personal']. According to Klafki, 'formation' constitutes a mediating category within this field of tension.

The focus on *Bildung* had consequences for the applied or prescriptive aspects. An overarching aim has been to identify the formative elements of the disciplines as well as the values and norms embedded in the cultural heritage and secure their transmission into the curriculum via the school subjects. The content of schooling, or what to teach, was focused on stressing what was worth teaching. Methods of teaching were of minor concern and were consequently neglected in teacher training, as was pointed out by the growing critiques of the 1960s.

The critique from learning and teaching theory-based didactics

The critique of human science didactics came, as already indicated, from two very different educational trends. First and foremost from the didactics influenced by the behavioural sciences, first learning theories and then theories about the teaching process. 'A realistic turn' in educational research and didactics emerged as the theory of the teaching process and not of the content of schooling. The focus was now on teaching methods, or *how to do it*. Educational technology entered the didactic scene. Objectivity in the planning process and the notion of teachers acting in accordance with theory seemed plausible and attainable, if difficult. A new didactic era dawned. A title illustrates the situation: *Geisteswissenschaftliche Pädagogik am Ausgang ihrer Epoche* [The End of the Era of Human Science Education] (Dahmer and Klafki, 1968).

The didactic analyses tried to encompass the anthropological and socio-cultural preconditions as well as the areas of decision for the teacher: intentions or aims, themes, methods and teaching material (see Figure 13.3).

The understanding of formation [*Bildung*] also underwent changes:

1 *Bildung* is to be obtainable for all, through public schooling.
2 Individual persons are to decide on the degree of compliance/adaptation.
3 *Bildung* may be expressed through behaviour.
4 *Bildung* is part of a lifelong process.
5 Progress must be measurable.

The critique from critical didactics: the influence of the Frankfurt School

This new position, as well as the traditional *Didaktik*, came under attack from a critical or radical didactics inspired mainly by the social science theories of the Frankfurt School, which argued that the important questions of didactics are the *why* questions and not the *what* and *how* ones. In building its frame of reference, critical didactics relied heavily on many of the key concepts of human science education, [*geisteswissenschaftliche Pädagogik*], like autonomy, emancipation, self-reflection and *Mündigkeit* [coming of age]. But the dogmatism and lack of social and educational realism in the tradition, as well as the technological dependence of its critics, were criticised under the slogan of 'ideology-critique', 'self-reflection' and 'knowledge-critique'. The ideology-critique was linked to the uncovering of 'false consciousness' and understanding because of a lack of consciousness related to societal issues, resulting in societal emancipation. Self-reflection was related to personal emancipation, and the knowledge-critique to epistemological, historical and social aspects of knowledge.

Consequently, the idea of formation [*Bildung*] within this tradition emphasised the inner and outer man – emancipated in relation to himself/herself and to societal forces and circumstances. The aim was not responsible acting, as in human science didactics, nor functioning adequately, as in teaching-theory based didactics, but the ability to shape a personal future as well as to shape a better society.

An emphasis on social interaction and communication enhanced the development of critical communicative didactics (e.g. Schäfer and Schaller, 1972), which in turn influenced the field of didactics more broadly.

Synthesis and critical-constructive didactics

The development of didactics in Europe after the 1970s saw a rapprochement of different positions. Self-reflection and self-criticism seem to have taken place. In 1971 Wolfgang Klafki wrote the now famous essay 'Erziehungswissenschaft als kritisch-konstruktive Theorie: Hermeneutik – Empirie – Ideologiekritik', [The science of education as critical-constructive theory: Hermeneutics – empirics – ideology critique]. This title clearly indicated that established positions had been criss-crossed – signalling a synthesis in didactics as theory and practice, and in didactic research. The more analytical and theory-based didactics of the Berlin School (Heimann and Schulz) emerged as the Hamburg School of didactics (see Figure 13.4).

Thus Wolfgang Klafki developed a revision of traditional German didactics, the so-called 'critical-constructive didactics'. The development of critical-constructive didactics is linked to a general influence on human science education and didactics, and consequently on the concept of *Bildung* from critical theory and especially from the approaches of people like Theodor W. Adorno, Max Horkheimer, Jürgen Habermas, Herwig Blankertz and Dietrich Benner. In this context 'critical' is to be understood in the sense of 'social criticism', implying a constant reflection between schooling and instruction – aims, content, methods, forms of organisation, on the one hand, and between schooling and social conditions and social processes on the other hand. The term 'constructive' indicates an emphasis on practice: initially it implied reform, and is intrinsically linked to the shaping of schooling, teaching and learning in keeping with the principles of self-determination, participation in decision-making and solidarity (Klafki, 1998).

DIDACTIC ANALYSIS AND MODELS OF DIDACTICS

A changing understanding of the concept: the didactics–methods relation

In order to grasp the nature of the didactical analyses and the foci and categories of the models of different schools of didactics, the meanings attributed to the term 'didactics' *within these schools* must be understood. The focus and content of general didactics have been a matter of dispute and have shifted with changing educational winds. So, also, have the meanings attributed to the term itself. As indicated, human science didactics [*geisteswissenschaftliche Didaktik*] promoted a narrow conception of didactics, leaving the methodological aspects aside. The technological and behavioural sciences' impact that dominated the problem area of didactics in Germany and the Scandinavian countries from the 1950s led, however, to a broadening in the scope of didactics. 'Methods' and 'evaluation' came to be included, as was the problem area of justification and legitimation regarding didactic decision-making process and the social and societal contexts. After 1968, under the influence of critical didactics, two aspects predominated: the linkage of didactics to politics and society and the emphasis on a problem-oriented and participant-based didactics. Some proponents of critical didactics shifted their focus to the notion of 'didactic rationality' understood as 'goal rationality' and stressed the rational relation between content and form in education.

Thus the understanding of the implications of didactics has changed over the years. It has been transformed from an unreflective concept that may or may not imply instructional methods as well as curricular matters, to an explicitly narrow concept including only the aims and themes and only methodological consequences of aims and subject matter, to a wider concept which includes aims, themes, methods, teaching aids, evaluation and the preconditions of teaching, and to a still broader one to include the school–society relationship, often seen in a critical perspective (ideology-critique). Simply stated, this progression has moved from a narrow concept that included only the *Whats*, to a widened understanding that also includes the *Hows* and to an expanded concept which includes the *Whats*, *Hows* and the *Whys*. How then does this general development and the conception of what constitutes didactics affect the nature of didactic analyses and the categories of didactic models?

Didactic analysis

Didactic analysis has been and still is the core element of didactics:

> It deals with questions related to the content of schooling and the teaching of this content – and all past and prevailing determining and forming influences on the content as well as on the teaching, and consequently influencing the contexts of teachers and pupils.
>
> (Arfwedson and Arfwedson, 1991, p. 27. My translation)

Didactic analysis is today closely related to decision-making at different levels:

1 *An ideological-normative level*: school politics encompassing the decisions taken at national, regional and local levels.
2 *A descriptive-analytical level* represented by didactic research in its varying forms.

245

3 *A concrete-pragmatic level* encompassing teacher and pupil interests (ibid., p. 25).

Historically, didactic analysis was mainly linked, as a tool, to the preparation and planning of classroom teaching as part of a teacher's task. Didactic analysis was what the teachers were supposed to do when preparing or evaluating a lesson or a course of study. It dealt with the questions of how to instruct a given content. In German teacher education – and to a certain degree in Scandinavian teacher education – it still does.

The best known and now classic example of didactical analysis (still in use in German teacher education) is Wolfgang Klafki's 'Didaktische Analyse als Kern der Unterrichtsvorbereitung' [Didactical analysis as the core of preparation of instruction] of 1958. The leading questions of the 'didactic analyses' are closely related to the content of the school subjects, examining:

- the exemplary value of the content;
- the fundamental value of the content for mental development and in view of future life;
- the elementary structure of the content (in order to make that content teachable through a transformation process from academic discipline to school subject)

An inherent aspect of the didactic analysis is the division between reflection and engagement. In a teaching-theory oriented didactics, like Heimann–Schulz's, the objective and detached aspect of reflection would be stressed in relation to the subjective engagement involved in the teaching process.

There is also a tradition, particularly in recent Norwegian and Danish didactics, to include meta-analysis as part of the didactic analysis. In doing so didactic analysis is linked to the professional development of teachers and the teaching–learning milieu as well as to the role of the teacher in the theory-building of didactics. One origin may be found in Erich Weniger's different levels of deliberation and in the *Bedingungsprüfung* [testing of preconditions] of the learning-theory oriented didactics or most probably in the philosophical base of human science didactics [*geisteswissenschaftliche Pädagogik*]. Didactic reflection thus concerns practice conceived of as existing at three levels. The first level constitutes the teaching situation itself: interactive teaching. The second level entails the pre-and post-activities connected with the teaching situation. The third level of practice, being ethical in nature, constitutes reflection and deliberation about the two 'lower' levels of practice (Løvlie, 1972). The expression 'didactic rationality' may be used to denote the internal consistency that ought to exist between these levels, implying the necessity of a critique being involved at the third level of reflection and the need of deliberation and open discussion related to an analysis of legitimisation and selection procedures at both national, local and instructional levels (Dale, 1989).

Models of didactics

Didactic analysis is in practice closely linked to models of didactics, and must be considered in this context. Graphic portrayals of concepts or ideas in the form of models have always been part of didactics, and they have, due to their explanatory value, been well accepted. Models in this sense are tools – forms, heuristics, rules, schemata, classification patterns and interpretational views – for the design and planning as well as for the analyses of instruction. Their instrumentality varies, as does the level of instructional planning at which they aim. Models range from theorisation of a general kind to the structuring of curricula and teaching tasks, to the daily preparation of the teacher (Künzli, 1994).

The didactic triangle

Perhaps the best-known model is the Didactic Triangle.

It is an explanatory and classificatory arrangement and co-relates the rather general elements of any teaching – the teacher, the subject matter and the student. In all teaching there is first of all a subject to be taught and learnt. Second there is a learner to whom the subject is offered. Third, teaching requires a teacher, a person or agent who serves as a bridge between the learner and the subject. Teachers need to have a good knowledge of the subjects they teach. This constitutive dimension of teaching may be called *doctrinaire*. Teaching also presupposes insight as to the knowledge, skills, interests, needs and abilities of the students concerned. This may be called the *maieutic* dimension of teaching. Finally,

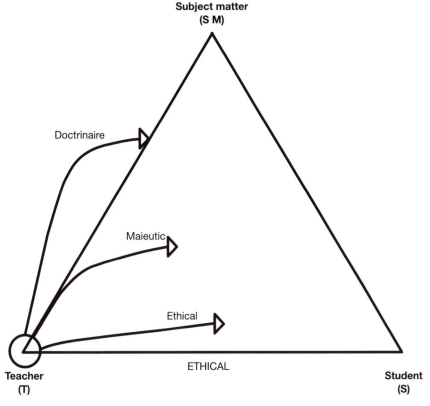

Figure 13.2 The Didactic Triangle.
Source: Künzli 1998, p. 35

247

teaching requires the teacher's full awareness of her intentions and interactions with her pupils. This may be called the *ethical* dimension of teaching (Künzli, 1998, pp. 34–36).

A Danish model

A classical comprehensive model in general didactics is Carl Aage Larsen's model of *the structure and elements of the instructional task*, representing the didactic climate of the Royal Danish School of Education, where from the 1960s a narrow conception of didactics prevailed (Gundem, 1980, pp. 21–24). It was introduced in Scandinavia as part of an effort to break and replace the then prevailing tradition in colleges of education of a recipe-like instruction in teaching methods. This model restricts the scope of didactics to the aims of

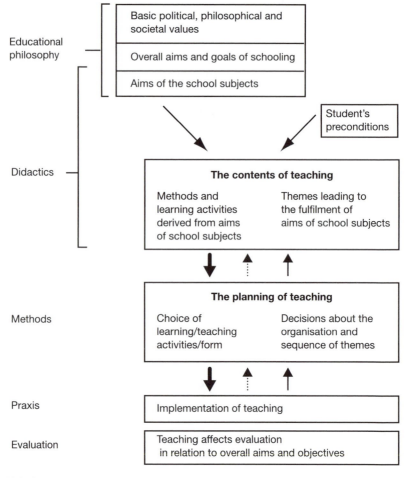

Figure 13.3 Carl Aage Larsen's model of the structure and elements of the instructional task.
Source: Larsen 1969 (my translation)

schooling, the objectives and content of school subjects, and the methods derived from these aims and objectives.

A widened scope of didactic analysis was strengthened by a change in German didactics. The Schulz–Heimann model (Heimann, 1972; Schulz 1965, 1972) of didactic analysis (see Figure 13.4) was recognised as a revitalisation of didactic analysis and was adopted in teacher training, and used extensively in the graduate courses of didactics.

The Schulz–Heimann model

A number of important points about this model are worth mentioning:

1 Compared to the last model (see Figure 13.3), this analysis presents a considerably wider scope. It includes at the first level of reflection the area of teacher decisions

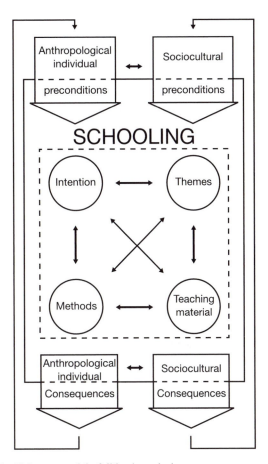

Figure 13.4 The Schulz–Heimann model of didactic analysis.
Source: Schulz, 1972, p. 414 (my translation)

[*Entscheidungsfelder des Lehrers*], that is what the teacher has to decide upon: intentions or aims, themes, methods and teaching material.

2 The interrelatedness and interaction between components (as emphasised by the lines in Figure 13.5) indicate that the didactic analysis may begin at any point, thereby breaking the hegenomy of the aims–means model.

3 The preconditions of teaching, that are 'anthropological' and 'socio–cultural' in nature, constitute the teaching antecedents [*Bedingungsfelder des Unterrichts*], and are part of the analysis at a second level of reflection. The model also stipulates analysis of consequences.

4 The Schulz–Heimann model, when it appeared in the middle of the 1960s, represented an explicit critique of the prevailing tradition in German and Danish didactics. The inherent didactic analysis of the Schulz–Heimann model is influenced by *geisteswis-senschaftliche Didaktik* [human science didactics] and is built upon an awareness of the complexity of teaching and learning. The place of theory differs, however, in teacher education and in research. The learning/teaching didactic theory of Paul Heimann and Wolfgang Schulz implied a theory-governed teacher behaviour and suggested that this theory, based on objective didactical research, would provide the foundation for curriculum reform.

In this respect, the dichotomy between theory-based and experienced-based reflection must be grasped. In the first phase of reflection, the teacher is considered to be emotion-ally neutral and distanced, as well as objectively confronting the knowledge-base for reflection. In the second one, which is the teaching situation, the teacher is personally involved and constructive in decision-making.

5 Finally it is acknowledged that the *Bedingungsfelder des Unterrichts*, that is the precondi-tions of teaching, are subject to an evaluation guided by a critique of societal and cultural norms, of forms of pedagogy and relevant facts (*Ideology Critique – didaktische Strukturfilter*) (Blankertz, 1974, p. 106).

Inherent is a potential for a development of a critical didactical analysis influenced by the Frankfurt School of sociology. Both ideology critique and the formulation of *didactische Strukturfilter* became during the 1970s important as part of the didactic analysis. This was the case perhaps not so much in teacher preparation as in the preparation of state and local curricula: for instance, the curricula formulated and implemented by the Blankertz group at Münster in the early 1970s (Blankertz, 1974a, 1974b). This may be seen as a further development of the initially rather neutral and objective general scrutiny of influencing ideologies formulated by Heimann, but gradually radicalised by Schulz.

This German model has proved influential in the formation of Scandinavian teachers and of the professional didacticians as part of the syllabus in general didactics in teacher educa-tion and as part of the university graduate courses of study in education (Gundem, 1995). And, no less important, the underlying ideas and rationale have been among the most influencing forces of the development of the most used model of didactic analysis today in Norway: The model of didactic relational deliberation.

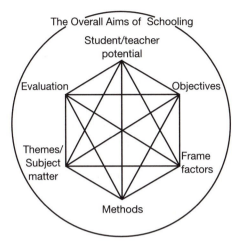

Figure 13.5 An interactive model for didactic analysis: the model of didactic relational deliberation.
Source: Norwegian Royal Ministry for Education and Church Affairs, 1989, p. 8.

The model of didactic relational deliberation

Certain points are worth underlining:

1 In relation to the Schulz–Heimann model it represents a further development, combining the two levels of reflection into one level, thus integrating all the categories of didactical analysis in one model.
2 The model stresses the interplay of the didactic categories implied by instructional planning: pupil and teacher potential, subject matter, objectives, learning activities, learning media, frame factors and evaluation.
3 The model allows for professional planning of lessons by the individual teacher and in decentralised and local or school-based curriculum development by groups of teachers within the overall national framework of superordinate goals and the national curriculum guidelines.
4 The success of the model has been ascribed to the fact that it seemingly corresponds to the way teachers reason when planning lessons and courses for study. They very seldom start with objectives, but plan taking into consideration a series of interacting factors being mutually implied.

The Hamburg Model for analyses and planning of teaching

During the 1980s Schulz redeveloped this model into what is now called the Hamburg Model for Analyses and Planning of Teaching (Schulz, 1986). It consists of five steps:

1. *Criteria for planning* – Some keywords are life orientation; science/discipline or subject matter/didactical orientation; action/performance orientation; methods and media

orientation; orientation towards organisation of teaching and towards control of results, including assessment.

2. *Structure of the components of the didactic action/performance* – These components postulate/create the criteria of planning: mutual understanding between teacher and student/pupil; defining/deciding on instructional objectives, determination of starting-points and the variables of mediation; decisions about and statements regarding outcome/ evaluation of outcome; working out of the institutional conditions; and cognisance of societal conflicts. Based on an understanding of the complexity of the didactic field, the interrelated-ness and interaction between components are implied, and any analysis and understanding of one of the components is only possible in the context of the whole (see Figure 13.6).

3. *Skills and functions of didactical action* – According to Schulz these are: advising, assess-ing, analysing, planning, realising, managing/administering, and co-operative action (see Figure 13.7)

4. *Fundamental deliberation inherent in the planning* – This point stresses the structural connection between experience and intentions. The theme or the content comes to the foreground of the planning interest with its different goal aspects:

- *the content aspect*, securing competence linked to societal and scientific tasks;
- *the personal aspect*, linked to becoming an integrated person;
- *the societal aspect*, linked to solidarity and responsible group participation.

This presupposes school experiences linked to subject matter as well as to emotional and social realities. This point is strongly related to an emancipatory interest bearing on the individual and society, and to an attitude of critique related to science and the content of schooling [*Erkentnisskritik*].

5. *Levels of planning* – The Hamburg Model distinguishes different levels of planning:

- *planning in perspective* for a longer period of time related to the whole curriculum or groups of school subjects or a specific school subject [*Die Perspektiveplanung*];
- *planning for teaching units* [*Die Umrissplanung*];
- *process planning*, that is planning for decisions to be taken at the proper point of time [*Die Prozessplanung*];
- *planning revision*, planning decisions taken during the process when unexpected points of view make it necessary [*Die Planungskorrektur*].

SCHOOL SUBJECT/SUBJECT MATTER DIDACTICS

Didactics at different levels of concretisation

In Germany and all the Nordic countries from the last century onwards, questions relating to the aims and goals of schooling, to the selection and transmission of the content of schooling, to the curriculum, as well as to teaching and learning theories have been treated

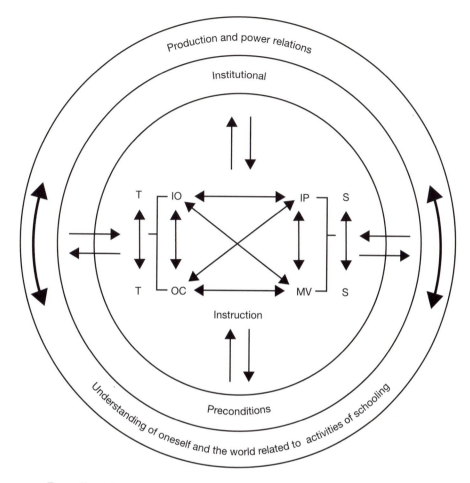

T = Teacher
S = Student as a partner in the planning of teaching
IO = Instructional objectives: Intentions and themes
IP = Initial position of teacher and students
MV = Mediation variables like methods, media and school organisation support
OC = Outcome control of oneself by the student and the teacher respectively

Figure 13.6 The structure of the interrelationship between the components of the didactical action/performance.
Source: Schulz, 1996, p. 32 after Kron, 1994, p. 146) (my translation)

under the heading of 'general didactics' [*Allgemeine Didaktik; almenn didaktikk*], except in Sweden where the use of the term disappeared at the beginning of this century to reappear in the 1980s. In certain countries, especially Finland and Germany, the more recent term 'school didactics' is used to indicate a wide conception of didactics implying general didactics. The term is institutionalised, implying that a professor in a German university may have school didactics as one of his teaching and research areas.

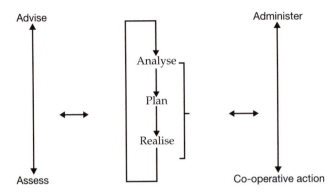

Figure 13.7 Skills and functions of didactical action.
Source: Schulz 1986, p. 35 after Kron 1994, p. 147 (my translation)

One recent phenomenon has been the effort to adapt general didactics to specific levels of schooling like pre-school education, university teaching, etc. In Germany this is called *Speziell Didaktik* [special didactics]. In the Nordic countries this is not formally insti-tutionalised, but coursebooks frequently appear with such titles as 'Didactics for Vocational Schooling' and 'Pre-school Didactics'.

School subject didactics

What really, however, created a new wave of interest in didactics during the 1980s, especially in the Nordic countries and in France, was the notion of a didactics linked to the disciplines, that is to the courses of study and school subjects. It stems from *geisteswissenschaftliche Didaktik* (Derbolav, 1960; Klafki, 1973; Weniger, 1965), as further developed and established, among others, by proponents of social science-influenced critical didactics (Blankertz, 1974a, 1974b).

In Germany a marked development may be noticed away from general didactics to stressing school subject didactics, as manifested by the establishment of chairs in school subject didactics in higher teacher education institutions (universities). A similar process is taking place in the 1990s in the Nordic countries, without, however, minimising the influ-ence of general didactics. In France, however, didactics is, first and foremost, linked to school subjects or to vocational training.

In other words, school subject didactics gathers all efforts from different disciplines as well as neighbour and part-disciplines of didactics in order to transmit and convey disciplinary organised cultural content.

The traditional model

In an early publication (Sveidahl, 1973), meant as an introduction to the field of school subject didactics, the scope is outlined in a list of topics to be examined and reflected upon, ranging from the large and fundamental issues to questions related to practical teaching in the classroom. This follows closely the line of thought outlined in Wolfgang Klafki's (1963) 'Didactic analysis as the core of preparation of instruction' in its scope:

- the historical background of the discipline and school subject;
- the changes undergone as to the content, structure and scope of the school subject;
- the contemporary value of the school subject;
- the role of the school subject in the overall programme of schooling;
- the nature and structure of the discipline related to the transformation process from scientific discipline to school subject, including phenomena like representation, selection and adaptation;
- issues concerned with instruction and evaluation.

The French model

According to Eric Plaisance and Gérard Vergnaud didactics [*la didactique*] may be defined as:

> a study of the processes of instruction and teaching related to a particular knowledge area: a discipline or an occupation/trade. It is supported by pedagogy, psychology and of course the bulk of knowledge of the apprenticeship in question. It may not, however, be reduced to it.
>
> (Plaisance and Vergnaud, 1993, p. 56)

In France didactics is based on psychology, pedagogy and epistemology. Even so, a specific frame of reference or theory of its own has been developed. Three basic concepts may be identified:

- the didactic situation [*le concept de situation didactique*],
- the transposition [*le concept de transposition*],
- the contract [*le concept de contrat didactique*].

The concept of the didactic situation is developed by Brousseau (1986). His analysis has made it possible to extract [*dégager*] certain principles of 'didactic engineering', that is the elaboration techniques of the decision-making situation of the problem – appealing to the most basic aspects of a certain domain.

The concept of transposition was introduced by Yves Chevallard (1985). It refers to the transformations, deformations and reductions submitted by the expert [*savoir savant*] when he is introduced to the study, material and the practice of teaching.

The concept of the contract was introduced by Brousseau (1990) to illustrate the reciprocal student–teacher system of expectations related to a given knowledge area. If this contract is broken by one or both of the parties involved, unwanted phenomena will be created/produced (Plaisance and Vergnaud, 1993, p. 57).

The theoretic reference related to the different school subjects may vary substantially. However, there are in France signs of the development of an integrative theory of the didactics of school subjects (Plaisance and Vergnaud, 1993, pp. 57–61).

In a way the French understanding of didactics may be linked to a certain Swedish understanding represented by the Marton Group at the Educational Institute of the University of Gothenburg. Their concern is not general didactics, but what they call particular didactics [*fackdidaktik*], and their special interest is the teaching and learning of concepts related to school subjects as well as, in a more general way, a branch of didactics they call 'phenomenographic' (Marton, 1983).

Some problematic issues

It follows from these points that the discipline or course of study in question will influence the content of didactics linked to it: the subject didactics of foreign languages will differ from the subject didactics of a history course. This is a fact that makes an integrative theory of school subject didactics difficult to develop. Thus representatives from the disciplines argue that a common theory of school subject didactics is inherently impossible.

This leads to the question of institutionalising – a question just hinted at so far. The institutionalising of school subject didactics meant, in fact, an invasion from pedagogy into the area of the knowledge of the disciplines where the representatives of the disciplines are the main actors. In Norway today subject didactics is formally established as part of undergraduate university courses, and every professor teaching a course of study relevant for teaching as a school subject has to include elements of didactics in the course. Still the question as to who is the most competent to teach such a course remains unresolved: the general didactician or, to take an example, the historian. The question will often arise – especially in the case of vacancies to be filled or when new chairs are established. The dilemma seems most acute within the social studies, while the tradition of appointing science people for positions within the didactics of science is more firmly established.

RESEARCH IN DIDACTICS

There are several approaches to the question of research in didactics. One approach focuses on concepts and function, another one on research trends or the object of the research, and a third on research methods.

Concepts and function of research

Three aspects of research in didactics will be touched upon in this section: the relation to theory, to practice, and the use of research findings.

Research in didactics may be said to be related to practice as well as to relevant educational theories like learning theories, curriculum theories, anthropological theories, theories related to media, and social theories in general. This double binding on the one hand to practice and on the other to theory is characteristic of research in didactics.

The praxis of education is a complex reality, a more or less permanent experiment between interacting people, contexts and circumstances characterised by constant unrest and crisis. In this praxis, experience-based 'practical theories' develop and are applied. Research in didactics may also turn to those kind of 'theories' (Kron, 1994, p. 195).

When research findings are applied, it seldom means that they are applied in an instrumental way, that is directly applied in practical situations. This may, however, happen – as when teachers implemented process–oriented writing after learning from promising results from research. Research findings may also be used to put matters on the political agenda. It is then very often a question of impending and long-felt problems, where the research serves as a catalyst for action.

Applied use of didactical research may be said to be generally of a conceptual, elucidatory kind. The aim is to give the users concepts for describing and understanding problems, relations and contingencies. By providing, however, more than a bare description, the results help to give a clearer picture of a situation. The aim is to penetrate, explain and articulate alternative paths to take. Without providing direct advice about what action to take or what policy decision to make, the results show that different choices have different consequences. The critical and unveiling aspect is therefore often present in didactical research – as in illuminating conflicting motives behind curriculum reform.

To summarise the main points of the argument:

- Research in didactics may be understood as a bridge between theory and praxis.
- Didactic research has to take theory into consideration: theories represent the collective results from research. Theories serve as a systematic knowledge 'reservoir', and at the same time research is necessary for theory production.
- Didactical research is always dependent on praxis for defining the research objects – the problems of praxis – and as an applied science (Kron 1994, pp. 194–195).

Research lines/trends: levels and phenomena

One way to organise research in didactics is according to the represented phenomena at different levels: a macro social level, a micro social level, and an individual level:

- *Educational research [Bildungsforschung; utdanningsforskning]* representing research of the total area of the school system at the macro social level.
- *Research of schooling* at the micro social level as a clarification/explanation of the realities of schooling and teaching in praxis, and at the macro social level tied to all institutions where teaching and learning are taking place (e.g. pre-school education, vocational training, further education, adult education), implying the societal preconditions and functional implications.
- *Research on teaching*, focusing on the central factors in all areas of organised teaching and learning at the micro social level. This line of research may be said to be the classical one within didactical research, and is more and more linked to different school subjects.

There is, however, a growing awareness that research linked to school subjects must be related to other components or parts of what constitutes the didactic system. There is today a significant development within didactic research, for example, in the following areas:

- *Curriculum research* as research on the cultural content, its selection, administration and form in historical, contemporary and comparative perspectives. This is one of the most central fields within didactic research (Hopmann, 1988).
- *Research on teaching and learning* as research on teaching/learning situations at micro or

individual levels. Examples might include research on teacher thinking and classroom research.

- *Research on learning linked to individual learning processes* like concept formation. An example: The students' subjective experiences of the teaching and learning situation according to their personal predispositions and background constitute the research point of departure, focusing on the so-called phenomenographic interview by which the pupils' conceptions and understandings of the subject matter are elucidated (Kroksmark, 1987; Kroksmark and Marton, 1987).
- *Media research* as research on teaching and learning technologies, information and mediation strategies, including the process and its consequences on all levels (Kron, 1994, pp. 197–199).

A tentative overview of lines in didactic research is shown in Figure 13.8.

Research methods

The concept of research methods in didactics is, in empirically orientated didactics, understood as methods from the field of social research. But as a result of didactics as comprehending (understanding) and explaining, the classical methods of the human science tradition appear besides the empirical methodologies. The 'bow' of modern didactic research stretches over both these basic methodological approaches (Kron, 1994, p. 201).

In the following – without being able to elucidate further – some groups of methods that seem to be most usual in didactic research will be mentioned like (a) historical-hermeneutical and (b) phenomenological research methods (which both have their roots in the human science tradition of thinking), (c) quantitative, (d) qualitative empirical research methods (Kron, 1994, pp. 201–204). Methods of dialectics are usually implied by the first

	Didactic Research
Macro social level	Educational research Research on schooling Curriculum research Media research
Micro social level	Research on schooling Research on teaching Research on teaching and learning Curriculum research Media research
Individual level	Research on teaching and learning Research on learning Curriculum research Media research

Figure 13.8 A visual representation of a tentative categorisation of lines in didactic research
Source: Kron 1994, p. 198 (my translation)

two groups. Today methods of dialectics are especially associated with (e) social analysis and ideology critique (Klafki, 1971, 1993, 1998).

There is on the part of the many who work in didactics a strong conviction that a synthesis of different methodological approaches will often be necessary; in Klafki's words:

> If any of these groups of methods is applied to questions of *Didaktik*, then consistent scientific reflection will inevitably confront the researcher with preconditions or limits that can only be overcome with the help of the other approaches. In other words, when the knowledge which can be gained using any one of these method groups has reached its limits, it becomes apparent that the epistemic process can only be advanced with the help of one of the other approaches. When this happens, constructive method synthesis is necessary.
>
> (Klafki, 1998, pp. 318–319)

Historical-hermeneutic methods aim to clarify meaningful phenomena in a scientific way – being tools to comprehension in the interpretation of different kinds of documents, didactical decisions, actions and processes. Didactics in a historical-hermeneutic perspective aspires to clarify the sense of decisions, developments, discussions and mechanisms in didactics, including phenomena like hidden historical conditions with their philosophical implications (Klafki, 1998, pp. 319–320).

As Klafki also points out, where historical studies refer directly to current problems of teaching and learning, the inclusion of empirical research processes is imperative. It cannot be ascertained by historical-hermeneutic methods whether the instruction taking place in schools corresponds to the stated objectives and aims of the school subject and teaching in question. Questions of this kind require empirical research – even though empirical research has its hermeneutic aspects, e.g. 'pre-understanding' related to choice of research object, in data collecting and in data analysis (Klafki, 1993, pp. 320–324).

THE DIDACTICS OF TOMORROW: TOWARDS A NEW AGENDA

Looking towards the future, three points will be made. The first concerns the relevance of some of the key processes of didactics; the second the relevance of didactics to practice; and the third concerns emerging tendencies within the field.

The key processes of European Continental didactics may be said to be formation [*Bildung*], didactical analyses and reflection/deliberation. The analytical framework inherent in these processes has until now remained a European Continental tradition. There are signs that this situation is changing owing to a growing awareness among Anglo-Saxon educational researchers of the relevance of *Bildung*, didactic analyses and deliberation linked to decisions about content selection and teaching, as well as teacher professionalisation. We may be on our way to a new era of interchange and understanding regarding teaching and learning inherent within the different traditions of *Didaktik* and curriculum.

Linked to a growing awareness among researchers of a need for understanding across different traditions is the question of the relevance of didactics to practice – to the realities of curriculum work and development, and to the practice of classrooms. It concerns the relationship between academic research and practice – a relationship that has developed very differently in different countries (see Hopmann and Gundem, 1998, pp. 341–343). None the less, it may be said that educational thinking in most countries has lost its anticipatory and guiding force outside its own academic environment. It seems that didactics has a lot to offer in order to remedy this situation – not least since the practitioners themselves look upon didactics as their domain.

There is strong evidence that didactics linked to the school subjects and to classroom practice is gaining ground in Scandinavia and Continental Europe. In France this is the very essence of didactics. Indeed these are the aspects of didactics that seem to be creating the most interest across the Atlantic. This is the challenge confronting didactics as theory, as prescription and as research at the dawn of the new century.

ACKNOWLEDGEMENTS

It would not have been possible for me to write this essay were it not for the generosity of a number of colleagues and friends: first and foremost, Professor Friedrich W. Kron from Universität-Mainz, Germany, who let me draw freely from his book *Grundwissen Didaktik*. I am very grateful. I also want to thank Professor Stefan Hopmann of Trondheim and Oslo University, Norway, and Professor Rudolf Künzli from Didaktikum Aarau, Zurich University, Switzerland, who both gave me valuable access to their insights and writings. Last but not least I am grateful to Professor Ian Westbury from the University of Illinois at Urbana-Champaign, USA, for his valuable comments and help with the English.

REFERENCES

Arfwedson, Gerd and Arfwedson, Gerhard (1991) *Didaktik för lärare*. [Didactics for Teachers]. Didactica 1 Stockholm: HLS förlag.

Bjørndal, Bjarne and Lieberg, Sigmund (1974) *Innføring i Økopedagogikk* [Introduction to the Pedagogy of Ecology], Oslo: Aschehoug.

Blankertz, Herwig (ed.) (1974a) *Curriculumforschung – Strategien, Strukturierung, Konstruktion* [Curriculum Research – Strategies, Structures, Construction], Essen: Neue Deutsche Schule Verlagsgesellschaft MBH.

Blankertz, Herwig (ed.) (1974b) *Fachdidaktische Curriculumforschung – Strukturansätze für Geschichte, Deutsch, Biologi*, [School Subject Curriculum Research – a Tentative Structure for History, German, Biology], Essen: Neue Deutsche Schule Verlagsgesellschaft MBH.

Blankertz, Herwig (1975) *Theorien und Modelle der Didaktik* [Theories and Models of Didactics], Munich: Juventa Verlag.

Brousseau, Guy (1986) 'Théorisation des phénomènes de la didactique des mathématiques'. Unpublished thesis. Bordeaux: University of Bordeaux.

Chevallard, Yves (1985) *La Transposition didactique: du savoir savant au savoir enseigné*, Grenoble: La Pensée Sauvage.

Concise Oxford Dictionary of Current English (1959) Oxford: Oxford University Press.

Cube, Felix von (1972) 'Der kybernetische Ansatz in der Didaktik'. In: Kochan, D.C. (ed.) *Allgemeine Didaktik, Fachdidaktik, Fachwissenschaft*, Darmstadt: Wissenschaftliche Buchgesellschaft, 140–170.

Dahmer, Ilse and Klafki, Wolfgang (eds) (1968) *Geisteswissenschaftliche Pädagogik am Ausgang ihrer Epoche*, Weinheim: Verlag Julius Beltz.

Dale, Erling Lars (1989) *Pedagogisk profesjonalitet* [Educational Professionalism], Oslo: Gyldendal.

Derbolav, Joseph (1960) 'Versuch einer wissenschaftlichen Grundlegen der Didaktik'. *Zeitschrift für Pädagogik*, 6 (2), 17–45.

Dilthey, Wilhelm (1924) *Abhandlungen zur Grundlegung der Geisteswissenschaften: Die Geistige Welt: Einleitung in die Philosophie des Lebens.* vol. 5, *Einleitung in die Geisteswissenschaften,* Leipzig and Berlin: Verlag von G. B. Teubner.

Dolch, Joseph (1965) *Grundbegriffe der pädagogischen Fachsprache,* Munich: Ehrenwirth Verlag.

Frey, Karl (1986) 'European traditions of curriculum research', In: Hameyer *et al.* (eds) *Curriculum Research in Europe,* Berwyn: Swets North America Inc. 11–16.

Gundem, Bjørg Brandtzæg (1980) *Tradisjon – Kritikk – Syntese En analyse av hovedtrekk ved samtidig tysk didaktikk – med en relatering til aktuelle spørsmål i nordisk sammenheng.* [Tradition – Critique – Synthesis: Trends in German Didactic Theory with Reference to Nordic Curricular Issues] Institute for Educational Research, University of Oslo Report no. 7. Institute for Educational Research.

Gundem, Bjørg B. (1995) 'The role of Didactics in curriculum in Scandinavia', *Journal of Curriculum and Supervision,* 10. (4), Summer.

Gundem, Bjørg B. and Hopmann, S. (eds) (1998) *Didaktik and/or Curriculum: An International Dialogue.* New York: Peter Lang Publishing.

Heimann, Paul (1972) [1962] 'Didaktik als Theorie und Lehre'. In: Kochan, D.C. (ed.) *Allgemeine Didaktik, Fachdidaktik, Fachwissenschaft,* Darmstadt: Wissenschaftliche Buchgesellschaft, 110–142.

Heimann, Paul, Otto, Gunther and Schulz, Wolfgang (1965) *Unterricht: Analyse und Planung,* Hanover: Hermann Schroedel Verlag.

Hopmann, Stefan (1988) *Lehrplanarbeit als Verwaltungshandeln* [Curriculum Work as Administration] Kiel: IPN.

Hopmann, Stefan and Gundem Bjørg B. (1998) 'Didaktik meets Curriculum: Towards a new agenda. In: Gundem, Bjørg B. and Hopmann, Stefan (eds) *Didaktik and/or Curriculum – an International Dialogue,* New York: Peter Lang Publishing, 331–351.

Hopmann, Stefan and Riquarts Kurt (eds) (1995) *Didaktik and/or Curriculum,* Kiel, Universität-Karl-Albrechts: IPN.

Jank, Werner and Meyer, Hilbert (1991) *Didaktische Modelle.* Berlin: Cornelsen Verlag.

Klafki, Wolfgang (1975) [1963] 'Didaktische Analyse als Kern der Unterrichtsvorbereitung'. In: Wolfgang Klafki, *Studien zur Bildungstheorie und Didaktik,* Weinheim: Beltz Verlag, 127–150.

Klafki, Wolfgang (1971) 'Erziehungswissenschaft als kritischkonstruktive Theorie: Hermeneutik – Empirie – Ideologikritik', *Zeitschrift für Pädagogik,* 17 (3), 351–385.

Klafki, Wolfgang (1973) [1963] *Studien zur Bildungstheorie und Didaktik,* Weinheim and Basle: Beltz Verlag.

Klafki, Wolfgang (1993) *Neue Studien zur Bildungstheorie und Didaktik,* Weinheim and Basle: Beltz Verlag

Klafki, Wolfgang (1995) 'On the problem of teaching and learning contents from the standpoint of critical-constructive Didaktik'. In: Hopmann, Stefan and Riquarts, Kurt (eds) *Didaktik and/or Curriculum,* Kiel: Universität-Karl-Albrechts: IPN, 187–200

Klafki, Wolfgang (1995) [1958] 'Didactic analysis as the core of preparation of instruction', *Journal of Curriculum Studies* 27 (1) 13–30.

Klafki, Wolfgang (1998) 'Characteristics of critical-constructive Didaktik'. In: Gundem, Bjørg B. and Hopmann, Stefan (eds) *Didaktik and/or Curriculum – an International Dialogue,* New York: Peter Lang Publishing, 307–330.

König E. and Riegel, H. (1972) *Unterrichtsplanung als Konstruktion,* Weinheim: Julius Beltz Verlag.

Kroksmark, Tomas (1987) *Fenomenografisk didaktik* [Phenomengraphic didactics], Gothenburg Studies in Educational Sciences, 63.

Kroksmark, Tomas and Marton, Ference (1987) 'Läran om undervisning' [The theory of teaching] *Forskning om utbildning* [Research on Teaching] 14 (3), 14–26.

Kron, Friedrich W. (1994) *Grundwissen Didaktik* (2nd edn), Munich: Ernst Reinhardt Verlag.

Künzli, Rudolf (1994) *Didaktik: Modelle der Darstellung, des Umgangs und der Erfahrung,* Zurich: Zurich University, Didaktikum Aarau.

Künzli, Rudolf (1998) 'Common frame and places of didaktik'. In: Bjørg B. Gundem and Hopmann, Stefan (eds) *Didaktik and/or Curriculum – an International Dialogue.* New York: Peter Lang Publishing, 29–46.

Larsen, Carl Aage (1969) 'Didaktik', *Pædagogik og fag* 1969–1970, (1), 9–25.

Løvlie, Lars (1972) 'Universitetspedagogikk eller debatten som ble vekk' [The pedagogics of university education – or the loss of a debate]. In: Mediaas, Nils *et al.*, *Etablert pedagogikk – makt eller avmakt*, Oslo: Gyldendal 29–35.

Lundgren, Ulf P. (1972) *Frame Factors and the Teaching Process*, Stockholm: Almquist och Wiksell.

Marton Ference (1983) *Från utbildningsmetodisk till fackdidaktisk forskning*. Report no. 100, Institute of Education, University of Linköping.

Norwegian Royal Ministry for Education and Church Affairs (KUD) (1989) *Guidelines for the Development of Curricula for School Subjects in Upper Secondary Education*, The National Council for Upper Secondary Education.

Otto, Gunter (1983) 'Zur Etablierung der Didaktiken als Wissenschaften. Erinnerungen, Beobachtungen, Anmerkungen. Versuch einer Zwischenbilanz 1983' *Zeitschrift für Pädagogik* 29 (4) 519–543.

Plaisance, Eric and Vergnaud, Gérard (1993) *Les Sciences de l'education*, Paris: Éditions La Découverte.

Roth, Heinrich (1962) *Pädagogische Psychologie des Lehrens und Lernens*, Darmstadt/Berlin/Hanover: Hermann Schrödel Verlag.

Schäfer, K.-H. and Schaller, Klaus (1972) *Kritische Erziehungswissenschaft und Kommunikative Didaktik*, Heidelberg: Quelle and Meyer.

Schaller, Klaus (1992) 'Didaktik und Pädagogik in Werke des Johann Amos Comenius', *Der Evangelische Erzieher* 92 (2), 20–28.

Schaller, Klaus (1995) 'Die Didaktik des Johann Amos Comenius zwischen Unterrrichtstechnologie und Bildungstheorie' [The didactics of J. A. Comenius between instructional technology and formation theory]. *Zeitschrift für Pädagogik. Beiheft 33 Didaktik und/oder Curriculum: Grundprobleme einer internationaler vergleichenden Didaktik*, Weinheim: Beltz Verlag, 47–60.

Schulz, Wolfgang (1965) 'Unterricht – Analyse und Planung'. In: Heimann, Paul, Otto, Gunter and Schulz, Wolfgang (eds), *Unterricht: Analyse und Planung*, Hanover: Hermann Schroedel Verlag, 13–47.

Schulz, Wolfgang (1972) 'Aufgaben der Didaktik'. In: Kochan D.C. (ed.) *Allgemeine Didaktik, Fachdidaktik, Fachwissenschaft*, Darmstadt: Wissenschaftliche Buchgesellschaft, 405–440.

Schulz, Wolfgang (1986) 'Die lehrtheoretische Didaktik'. In: Gudjons, H. *et al.* (eds) *Didaktische Theorien*, Hamburg: n.p., 29–45.

Sveidahl, Eric (1973) 'Fagdidaktikk' [Subject Didactics]. In *Praksisopplæringen i lærerskolen* [The Practical Instruction of The Colleges of Education], Royal Ministry of Education and Church Affairs (KUD), The Council for Innovation in Schools, 46–58.

Weniger, Erich (1965) [1926] *Didaktik als Bildungslehre. Teil 1. Die Theorie der Bildungsinhalte und des Lehrplans*, Weinheim: Julius Beltz Verlag.

Weniger, Erich (1994) [1952] 'Didaktik as theory of education'. In: Ian Westbury *et al.* (eds) *The German Didaktik Tradition: Implications for Pedagogical Research*, Urbana: College of Education, University of Illinois, 67–82..

Westbury, Ian (1995) 'Didaktik and curriculum theory: Are they the two sides of the same coin?. In: Hopmann, Stefan and Riquarts, Kurt (eds) *Didaktik and/or Curriculum*. Kiel: Universität-Karl-Albrechts: IPN, 233–264.

Westbury, Ian (1998) 'Didaktik and curriculum studies'. In: Gundem, Bjørg B. and Hopmann, Stefan (eds) *Didaktik and/or Curriculum – an International Dialogue*, New York: Peter Lang Publishing, 47–78.

14

FROM TESTING TO ASSESSMENT

Current issues and future prospects

Harry Torrance

Any review of assessment and testing must recognise from the outset that the two terms imply quite different approaches to the identification and reporting of educational achievement. Thus educational assessment can be carried out by a variety of means, including the collection of evidence of routine student performance produced under ordinary classroom conditions; and it can be reported descriptively, in narrative form, rather than simply as a numerical score or grade. It is generally considered to involve a more holistic and rounded set of activities than simply sitting one-off, paper-and-pencil tests or final examination papers. In this respect assessment might be considered a generic term which can include testing (though more commonly 'educational assessment' is thought of as antithetical to 'testing'), and in most contexts of debate the terms represent opposite ends of a continuum of approaches to identifying and describing educational achievement.

Also while broad trends in approaches to assessment can be discerned across national education systems, these trends are played out in quite specific ways in particular national contexts. Thus general assumptions about, and approaches to, assessment may change over time, with similar developments in methods of assessment taking place in different countries. However, the ways in which these are implemented (e.g. in all examined subjects, only certain 'core curriculum' subjects, etc.) and the age and stage of education at which these methods are employed (e.g. school leaving, entry to higher education, etc.) may vary considerably, and thus serve different purposes and carry rather different consequences for different national systems.

So it is apparent that there is no single definition or easily demarcated set of functions that one can identify with 'assessment'. The assessment of student performance serves many different and sometimes conflicting purposes in educational systems, and can often produce unintended consequences. Assessment carries consequences for the individual student, with respect to progression within the system and eventual certification of achievement; for teachers and schools, with respect to the overall evaluation of their performance; and for the social system as a whole, with respect to the development and certification of the knowledge, skills and attitudes required of new generations of citizens. However, all of these consequences can be adversely affected as well as intentionally pursued by assessment, depending on the methods of assessment employed and the ways in which these methods are deployed.

To take each in turn, at the level of the individual pupil, assessment can provide an incentive and a source of motivation for individuals and cohorts; and it can provide an important source of feedback on progress, to aid learning, though the more truncated this is (i.e. marks and grades rather than descriptive guidance), the less effective it is likely to be. Assessment can also provide a source of evidence for certification and qualification, which in turn can aid social mobility (and this increasingly includes international mobility). However, any system which too crudely categorises successes and failures, and at too young an age, can also generate anxiety and inhibit learning, leading to the self-fulfilling prophecy of early labelling, overall educational failure and social exclusion.

With respect to teachers and teaching, assessment procedures and methods can provide an important source of syllabus guidance – focusing teacher attention (particularly that of novice teachers, or inadequately trained teachers) on what curriculum planners believe to be the most important goals of any particular educational programme. In turn assessment can provide evidence for teachers' own informal curriculum evaluation – indicating what pupils have and have not learned and understood, and where revision (of material and/or teaching methods) might be appropriate. Also the motivating effect on pupils can bring benefits to teachers in terms of classroom control – there is no denying that for large numbers of relatively uninterested adolescents, assessment provides teachers with a very powerful carrot and stick. And with this observation we are alerted to another facet of assessment – that its pursuit is by no means as uniformly benign and beneficial as many politicians and indeed educationalists would have us believe. Poor teachers probably benefit far more from poor approaches to assessment than do poor students. Good teachers, on the other hand, can be inhibited by poor assessment methods. Narrow approaches to assessment can lead to narrow and/or instrumental approaches to teaching – teaching to the test, to raise scores, rather than to educate pupils. Similarly assessment can bring pressures of curriculum 'coverage' for teachers – always having to move on to the next examinable topic – and restrict innovative approaches to subject matter and teaching methods. Likewise, too much pressure on pupils can lead to demotivation and disaffection, especially, though not exclusively, if the pressure is associated with failure. The traditional way that teachers and schools have dealt with this problem, of course, is by overt and covert selection – those motivated by assessment are taught, those not motivated are not taught; being left to drift and drop out if they do not cause too much disruption, being deliberately excluded from school if they do cause disruption. However this is hardly an effective solution for society as a whole.

Moving on to the level of the social system, that which is assessed in school crystallises and expresses the essential core of legitimate values, knowledge, skills and attitudes that a society wishes to inculcate in the next generation. Taking control of the school examination system has been a major feature of the educational programmes of newly independent developing countries, and is increasingly a feature of educational change in advanced industrial and post-industrial economies as governments seek to render their education systems more effective in the face of international economic and cultural competition. In turn the results of key assessments can provide important data for monitoring the effectiveness of the system and guiding decisions about how best to intervene to improve it. Assessment also plays a very significant role in identifying competent individuals for positions of economic and social leadership and in turn regulating social competition for such positions and their attendant rewards. However, such benefits depend on the assessment system working very effectively both to provide accurate and relevant data for system management and to iden- tify the right individuals for further study and employment. Unfortunately the history of compulsory schooling and associated tests and examinations suggests this is far from the case. Thus assessment can also stifle creativity, inhibit social change, and lead to enormous wastage of human resources. Assessment systems and procedures are also very expensive to design and administer, and while it is fashionable to question whether or not schools are delivering value for money, the same could be asked of current methods of assessment.

A major reason for the complexities and contradictions inherent in contemporary assess- ment systems is that they have been developed largely in response to demands at the level of the social system, rather than to enhance teaching and learning, though this balance is changing, thereby contributing to the multiplicity of issues to be addressed. Historians of educational assessment, particularly examinations, usually trace the origins of such prac- tices back to Imperial China (*c.* eighth century BC) when various tests of practical and academic skills (archery, calligraphy) were introduced to combat nepotism in relation to selection for state employment. Similar reasoning underpinned the introduction of examin- ations into Europe, and particularly Britain, in the nineteenth century; as economic devel- opment led to social mobility and indeed social uncertainty, it was increasingly seen as necessary to provide the basis for a fairer and more effective (i.e. meritocratic) selection system for entry to higher education and the rapidly expanding Imperial and domestic Civil Service. In turn, the school system itself introduced various forms of assessment in order to allocate students to particular pathways. Mental testing began with attempts to identify more precisely those children requiring special educational provision (in France) and developed rapidly in Britain in the context of 11+ selection for secondary (grammar) school. Thus assessment in the latter half of the nineteenth century and the first half of the twentieth century was largely concerned with devising apparently fairer ways of discrimin- ating between individuals when distributing access to different forms of education and subsequent life-chances. Business and commerce eventually followed suit, increasingly employing academic qualifications as appropriate selection devices, and the tensions engendered by such practices have been with us ever since; tensions, that is, caused by the social and political trade-off between the inequalities created by assessment practices whose validity and reliability can never be perfect (and are often very questionable indeed), and the inequality which they seek to replace – if not assessment, then what?

Thus educational assessment has come to play a crucial legitimating role in the ideology of modern societies, providing a mechanism by which judgements about merit (however rough-and-ready) can be made, while at the same time helping to define the very concept of merit in modern societies. Academic achievement is assumed to indicate abilities that will allow the individual to progress and succeed in modern society, while at the same time allowing society to select those who will be able to contribute most to society in terms of economic and social leadership.

It can be argued therefore, that educational assessment has developed to facilitate the social and economic process of selection, rather than the educational purpose of teaching and learning, with the many negative 'backwash' effects on teaching being either ignored or considered a necessary evil. Some have even argued that since society in general comprises winners and losers, so too must education systems: the sooner children learn about the harsh realities of competition and their place in the pecking order, the better.

More recently however, attention has been paid to the many potentially negative effects of assessment on the school system and on individual student motivation, and on the best means by which to develop assessment practices to underpin, rather than undermine, the process of learning. As noted above, it is argued that too narrow an approach to assessment can lead to a very restricted and overly academic curriculum. The need for easily administered, paper-and-pencil testing of large numbers of candidates is said to have led to a focus on assessing (and thus teaching) that which is most easily tested through such procedures – recall of knowledge – rather than practical skills, intellectual understanding and more general personal and social development. Such criticisms have overlapped with others concerning the relationship of assessment to learning, and it has also been argued that an overly competitive system, which produces far more losers than winners, can carry very negative consequences for individual motivation and self-esteem, leading to wastage of individual talent and the creation of anti-school 'subcultures' of disaffected students. In turn psychologists have begun to turn their attention away from the measurement of supposedly fixed and innate individual differences to focus on how assessment can assist the process of learning by identifying individual learning needs and problems, and producing evidence of students' strengths and weaknesses, so that students (and their teachers) can use such evidence – such 'formative feedback' – to improve their performance and level of achievement.

A number of key social and scientific determinants of this change in emphasis can be discerned; perhaps the most important of which in the industrialised economies of Western Europe is the increasingly perceived need to develop the skills and knowledge of all young people to as high a level as possible, rather than only to identify, select and educate a few leaders to a high level. In an increasingly competitive global environment, the terms of traditional manufacturing trade have turned decisively against the now aging economies of Western Europe. To continue to compete, they can no longer rely on hierarchical economic and social organisation, with elite groups educated to take decisions, design systems and issue orders which others must then simply carry out; rather the skills and talents of the majority must be developed to provide a much larger pool of educated and flexible workers for the knowledge-based and innovation-driven industries of the future. In the shorthand of contemporary economic analysis, this is the move from 'Fordist' to 'Post-Fordist' modes of production and consumption, and assessment must therefore be developed to play its part in the changing social and educational agenda of inclusion and human resource development, rather than exclusion and reconciliation to one's fate. However, while one might discern such a trend, whether or not it is desirable is still highly contested, as well as whether or not it is possible to bring it about. Such contestation is the stuff of contemporary educational politics, with governments such as the United Kingdom's seeking to educate all (with the introduction of a National Curriculum, along with other developments such as the expansion of higher education) while also harking back to the old 'verities' of traditional academic standards and selection for certain schools or streams within schools.

Linked to these developments – though again, not in a uniformly coherent fashion – is an increasing emphasis in curriculum on the understanding and application of knowledge, and the development and attestation of competence. In turn, therefore, assessment practices

266

must be developed which can capture these practical competences *in situ*, rather than just measure traditional academic achievements. Such developments are manifest in the introduction of the technical and vocational options in the French *Baccalauréat* and the German *Abitur*, as well as in the British General Certificate of Secondary Education (GCSE) examination at 16+ and the National Certificate of Vocational Qualification (NCVQ) in further and higher education. There is considerable ambiguity however, particularly in the United Kingdom, as to whether or not all students can and should pursue a broader curriculum to a higher standard. Hence we see the development of different academic and vocational tracks, leading to different qualifications which, while ostensibly equivalent, will inevitably have a different status, at least in the short term. (Interestingly enough, the Japanese have not yet gone down this route, preferring to persevere with a programme of academic education dominated by the 'examination hell' of a highly competitive system, as the platform for subsequent vocational training in the workplace. Whether this survives the recent downturn in their relative productivity remains to be seen.)

In parallel with this specifically educational debate about the need for a broader curriculum assessed by more flexible means, there is also a more general level of intellectual debate about the nature, purpose and methods of scientific enquiry which have had their impact on how we think about assessment. Thus traditionally, assessment has been conceived of as a process of measurement, with research and development focused on technical issues of the validity and reliability of the measuring instrument, i.e. the improvement of the technology. Examinations and tests were akin to a quasi-experimental situation, whereby the task was to hold all extraneous variables constant (by holding the examination under strictly controlled conditions) in order to isolate and measure the variable in which the test designers were interested – be it general ability (IQ) or achievement in a specific subject area. The underpinning assumption was that abilities and achievements did indeed inhere in individuals, and could indeed be isolated and measured. Latterly such views have come to be significantly modified with the purpose of scientific enquiry (certainly in the social sciences) being seen in more anthropological terms with respect to the exploration and generation of meaning and understanding in context, rather than the discovery of universally applicable knowledge; in turn human achievements and their identification and description are seen to be a function of context and task. Furthermore, the variety of performance that is likely to be observed as the context of performance differs, can now be seen as additional evidence on which to base a decision (albeit a complicated decision) about a candidate's overall competence, rather than a source of error which should be controlled and if possible eliminated.

Where then does this leave the field of educational assessment? On the positive side we can see that assessment is no longer treated as an isolated technology which can be developed and implemented within education systems without regard to its wider effects on those systems. On the other hand it is precisely the recognition of those wider interaction effects that has led to assessment being seized upon as a key focus for educational reform and a key mechanism with which to bring such reform about, such that the demands on assessment procedures and methods far outweigh what can reasonably be accomplished.

On the educational side, change is pursued in order to underpin curriculum development and promote learning. Thus it is argued that the school curriculum must become more practically and technologically oriented, and more vocationally relevant. New subject matter must be introduced, along with new approaches to teaching more traditional subject matter:

for example more practical work and oral work focusing on the development of understanding rather than just the recall of knowledge. In turn higher-order skills should be pursued, such as applying previously acquired knowledge in new contexts, gathering and interpreting data, and writing reports. For such new elements of the curriculum to be validly assessed, new forms of assessment must be developed and employed – extended tasks that require planning and perseverance, and produce evidence of the process of their accomplishment, as well as the eventual product. Some proponents of such arguments would go further, suggesting not just that assessment methods should change in order validly to assess such new curricular goals, but that new forms of assessment could actually underpin and even 'drive' the curriculum in desirable directions; the argument being that if you broaden the scope of the assessment system and increase the complexity and the demands of the tasks involved, you will broaden the curriculum and raise the standards of teaching. Educational reform has never been so mechanistic however. Such a strategy begs many questions about the capability of test developers to design demanding tasks which can nevertheless also be implemented on a large scale. Likewise it begs questions with regard to teachers' understanding of the purposes of changes in assessment and their preparedness both to respond to the new assessment tasks and teach to higher standards. Thus just because poor tests can inhibit good teaching, it does not necessarily follow that better tests will produce better teaching: they are a necessary but not sufficient condition. And with regard to scale of implementation, the experience of National Assessment in England and Wales is instructive: the more complex the tests, the more difficult they were to implement on a large scale; and the imperatives of large-scale implementation led to the tests becoming narrower and narrower in design.

Arguments about learning tend to focus more on the classroom and the quality of teacher–pupil interaction – on pedagogy in fact, rather than curriculum goals and content. Diagnostic assessment has a long history, especially in the medically influenced field of special education; that is using tests, usually in a one-to-one situation, and often orally, to identify particular learning difficulties. Also of course, as noted already, assessment can have a *negative* impact on learning. However, the argument about the potentially beneficial impact of a more pedagogically integrated approach to assessment – formative assessment – moves beyond the clinical genesis of diagnostic assessment. Rather, with formative assessment the basic proposition is that if pupils have a clear understanding of the goals of the programme and are provided with detailed feedback on their strengths and weaknesses, they will be better able to monitor the quality of their own work and to improve. In turn teachers will also be better able to judge the appropriateness of the task set and be better able to modify it and/or intervene at relevant points to support learning. However, such a strategy could yet look very similar to diagnostic assessment in practice, becoming decoupled from classroom teaching and implemented in a periodic and incremental way that may not have as positive an impact on learning as intended. A more dynamic and forward-looking approach still, deriving in part from the interest of cognitive scientists in Vygotskian approaches to teaching and learning and attempts to identify the nature and extent of children's 'zone of proximal development', is one which attempts to integrate fully the relationship between assessment, teaching and learning. Here the interest is not so much in what has or has not been learned, but what *might* be learned, in the immediate future, with the collaborative help ('scaffolding') of a teacher or peer. Once again then, the imperative is to develop and use a range of relatively informal assessment techniques *in situ* – observing children at work in the classroom and questioning them about what they are doing and why.

The social and political functions of assessment have also come to be better understood over recent years. Thus governments around the world have alighted on assessment as a key mechanism with which to intervene in and attempt to manipulate the education system *as a system*, rather than simply accepting the cumulative social and economic consequences of the ad hoc pursuit of extant qualifications by myriad individual students. However, the motive for intervention has tended to stem from two rather different perspectives on current economic and political problems, and the new roles proposed for assessment can be rather contradictory. Thus, as we have seen above, there has been extensive political as well as educational interest in developing a more technically and vocationally relevant curriculum and attendant assessment and certification procedures. Running in parallel with this agenda however, and in some ways overtaking it, has been an increasing concern with educational standards defined in fairly traditional terms, along with measuring and monitoring school effectiveness and accountability.

The interest in developing technical and vocational education is manifest in changes taking place in the content of traditionally high status academic examinations (e.g. the *Bac*, *Abitur* and GCSE cited above) and also in the much wider debate surrounding the development and accreditation of competence in vocational training *per se*. This debate derives from a fundamental critique of academic education, arguing that it is at best irrelevant to the ways in which most children learn about and understand the world around them, and to the economic needs of society (we should be interested in what people can do, rather than what they know) – and at worst positively harmful to individual development and economic performance. The critique carries enormous resonance for governments and business leaders worried by relative economic decline, and for this reason has probably had most impact in the United Kingdom, though it has also had considerable influence in the United States, Australia, New Zealand and South Africa. The implication of the critique once again drives the discussion of assessment methods down the road of assessing practical tasks by direct observation.

Here, however, arguments about developing more vocationally relevant curriculum and assessment methods come into direct conflict with a quite different analysis and solution to the 'problem' of the relationship of education to economic performance. Governments around the world have also become increasingly alarmed at what they perceive to be falling (academic) standards of education combined with the escalating cost of education, particularly schooling. A key part of the problem is perceived to be poor standards of teaching. Therefore, far from placing more influence in the hands of teachers by further developing extended practical tasks which would have to be conducted and assessed by teachers in classrooms and school laboratories, the imperative is to lay down standards centrally and to develop externally set and marked testing programmes with which to measure their accomplishment. Once again these ideas have had most impact in the United Kingdom, with its programme of National Curriculum and Assessment, but have also been influential elsewhere. Such developments, of course, run all the risks outlined above of narrowing the curriculum to that which is most easily tested; thus it might come to be the case that even as test scores rise (because teachers coach for the tests), educational standards fall.

Part of the problem here is that in the UK one overarching system of National

Assessment is expected to achieve everything: educational quality is claimed to be inherent in the goals of the National Curriculum, and the attendant tests are claimed to motivate pupils and teachers, certify standards, and provide overall measures of local and national performance at four different ages (7, 11, 14 and 16). Other countries do it differently. Thus in France and Germany the *Baccalauréat* and *Abitur* are primarily academic examinations, success in which guarantees entry to higher education, though both now have technical tracks. However, in France the *Bac* is very much a traditionally set and marked external examination, while in Germany's federal system, curriculum is decided at the level of the *Länder* (states), albeit within commonly understood goals and overlapping practices, including selection for different forms of schooling, with assessment for the *Abitur* being school based – i.e. conducted by teachers. Thus teacher competence, overall standards and comparability of grades do not seem to be questioned in Germany. In other European countries there is more concern with comparability and standards, but these concerns tend to be addressed by specific developments such as centrally devised but locally administered and marked tests in core subjects (e.g. Sweden) or sample national monitoring of standards, conducted separately from national examinations (e.g. Holland; France also has national monitoring of standards in French and maths at ages 9 and 14).

Noting these variations of practice brings us back to the point made right at the beginning of this chapter – that broad trends can be discerned in the development of assessment, but that they are played out in different ways in different countries. Thus it is clear that the emphasis in debates about assessment has shifted from fair selection to the promotion of learning; from exclusion to inclusion; from trying to find out what students know to finding out what they understand and can do; from one-off measures capable of predicting (generalising about) future performance to situated demonstrations of particular competences. In this, assessment is reflecting a more general pattern of recognising complexity and diversity while exercising caution in judgement, which is pervading the social sciences. At one and the same time however, the social and political imperatives for assessment are also changing. Governments are seeking to control and manage education systems in novel ways and have alighted upon assessment practices and procedures – what is assessed and how it is assessed – as a key mechanism for intervention. However, control and management in a context of debate about standards and effectiveness implies the development of simple procedures easily implemented, and yielding readily understandable (and unambiguous) results. These broad trends are manifest in different national systems which start from different current practices and place differing emphases on the various elements of the overall debate. Thus German practice seems largely untouched, while in the UK successive reforms have placed more and more contradictory demands on a single national system. Better political sense seems to have been displayed in countries such as France and Holland where national examinations and more formative in-school guidance have developed to reflect some of the educational trends, while sample national monitoring of standards has been implemented to provide at least some of the politically important managerial data.

For the future, the agenda is to design and implement large-scale systems of performance-based assessments which encapsulate high-quality educational goals and both contribute to the development of, and attest to the acquisition of, analytic skills and practical competences. The challenge will be to pursue such an agenda while also responding to the legitimate demands of governments and individual students for comparable results which recognise issues of equity and can provide data on overall system performance. The challenge is likely to be best confronted by developing different forms of assessment for different purposes, but of course, as has been apparent throughout this essay, what one might construe as the 'best' solution in terms of assessment practices and their impact on educational processes, cannot take place in a social and political vacuum. Trade-offs are inevitable, though we can perhaps hope that the more self-conscious the trade-offs, the more likely they are to maximise the positive impact of assessment and minimise the negative.

SELECT BIBLIOGRAPHY

Broadfoot, P. (1996) *Education, Assessment and Society*. Milton Keynes: Open University Press.

Eckstein, M. and Noah, H. (eds) (1992) *Examinations: Comparative and International Studies*. Oxford, Pergamon Press.

Gifford, B. and O'Connor, M. (eds) (1992) *Future Assessments: Changing Views of Aptitude, Achievement and Instruction*. Boston: Kluwer.

Kellaghan, T. and Greaney, V. (1992) *Using Examinations to Improve Education*. Washington, DC: World Bank.

Nisbet, J. (ed.) (1993) *Curriculum Reform: Assessment in Question*. Paris: OECD.

Office of Technology Assessment (Congress of the United States) (1992) *Testing in American Schools: Asking the Right Questions* (summary report). Washington, DC: OTA.

Stake, R. E. (ed.) (1991) *Advances in Program Evaluation. Using Assessment Policy to Reform Education*. Greenwich: JAI Press.

Torrance, H. (ed.) (1995) *Evaluating Authentic Assessment*. Milton Keynes: Open University Press.

Weston, P. (ed.) (1991) *Assessment of Pupil Achievement: Motivation and School Success*. Amsterdam: Swets and Zeitlinger.

Wolf, A. (1995) *Competence Based Assessment*. Milton Keynes: Open University Press.

15

ADMINISTRATION AND MANAGEMENT IN EDUCATION

Theory and practice

Tony Bush

ORIGINS, DEVELOPMENT AND CURRENT STATUS

The origins and development of educational management as a distinct discipline have been chronicled by Bone (1982), Bush (1995), Culbertson (1980) and Hughes and Bush (1991). It began in the United States as a variant of general management. The work of Taylor (1947) was particularly influential and his 'scientific management movement' is still subject to vigorous debate, particularly by those who oppose a 'managerial' approach to education. Another important contributor to management theory was the French writer Fayol (1916), whose 'general principles of management' are still significant. Weber's (1989) work on bureaucracy, developed in the nineteenth century, remains a powerful conception of educational management. All these theories emerged outside education and were subsequently applied to schools and colleges, with mixed results.

The establishment of educational management as a field of study and practice in the United Kingdom came as recently as the 1960s. There were similar developments in other Commonwealth countries, leading to the foundation of the Commonwealth Council for Educational Administration, now the Commonwealth Council for Educational Administration and Management (CCEAM), in 1970. There has been rapid expansion of the subject since then as governments and practitioners have come to appreciate that, just as education underpins economic growth, so effective management is a prerequisite for educational improvement.

The clumsy title of this chapter requires an explanation and justification. The term 'educational administration' is used in the United States and has been adopted widely in the Commonwealth. In the UK, this notation was employed in the early stages of the subject and the national professional body was titled 'British Educational Administration Society'. By the late 1970s, however, 'educational management' was increasingly used, notably in the pioneering courses developed by the Open University, and this term became the norm in the UK and much of Europe.

One emerging trend in the late 1990s seems likely to be significant in the new millennium. This concerns a new emphasis on *strategic management* in schools and colleges. This approach involves consideration of all aspects of the organisation and linking them together to ensure coherence and consistency. It also requires a long-term perspective. A significant manifestation of strategic management in the UK is development planning in schools (Hargreaves and Hopkins, 1991) which aims to connect curriculum planning to staff and financial management.

The shift towards strategic management is linked to, and been given added urgency by, the widespread introduction of self-management.

SELF-MANAGEMENT

In many countries, the traditional model of management was pluralist with responsibilities shared between the professionals, in teacher unions and in institutions, central government and, in most cases, a local agency. This was lauded in the UK as a 'partnership' but this view, always utopian, became untenable during the 1980s with conflict replacing the previous consensual norms. The influence of professionals on policy and practice has declined following the claim by former Secretary of State Kenneth Baker that education was 'producer dominated', a charge echoed in other countries. There was also an ideological schism between a Conservative central government and 'loony left' local authorities, leading to 'a new, uncompromising hostility between the centre and the periphery in British politics' (Maclure, 1988, p. xi).

This political conflict provided the context for the UK variant of the international movement towards self-management in education. In Australia, New Zealand and parts of the USA, as well as the UK, the management of schools has been largely devolved to principals and governing boards. The Australian writers Caldwell and Spinks have been amongst the foremost exponents of self-management which they define as follows: 'A self-managing school is a school in a system of education where there has been significant and consistent decentralisation to the school level of authority to make decisions related to the allocation of resources' (Caldwell and Spinks, 1992, p. 4)

The main advantage of self-management is that leaders are able to determine spending on the basis of their own priorities rather than having to operate in accordance with a budget determined by an external agency. The assumption is that decisions about the needs of pupils and students should be made by those who are closest to them rather than those who, however well intentioned, are determining policies on a local, regional or national basis: 'A single school in possession of its own decision-making must provide better quality education than a school run by a centralised bureaucracy' (Levacic, 1995, p. 1)

The New Zealand version of self-management has seen the intermediate tier of local government removed completely. There is now a direct relationship between the state and the school board:

> In addition to national requirements, boards of trustees are required to develop a Charter, which forms the legal basis of the relationship between the State, as the purchaser of services, and the school Board of Trustees, as the provider of those services
>
> (Minister of Education, 1995, p. 15)

The main manifestation of self-management in England and Wales, affecting 95 per cent of schools, is Local Management of Schools (LMS). The remaining state schools (*c.* 1,100) chose to 'opt out' of Local Education Authority (LEA) control and become Grant Maintained (GM). The principals and governors of these schools were responsible for managing all their resources; a process which may be regarded as a 'pure' form of LMS. Research with the first 100 GM schools shows that opting out is perceived as successful (Bush et al., 1993). GM schools were abolished in 1999 as part of a restructuring of provision, but all schools will retain substantial control over finance and staffing. The shift to self-management also applies to further education colleges, which are now 'incorporated' institutions run by their principals and governing bodies.

Self-management is underpinned by notions of competition. Funding formulas in England and Wales, and in New Zealand, are based largely on student numbers, encouraging institutions to compete for enrolments. Popular schools and colleges attract more students, leading to increased income, more staff and materials and the potential for higher standards. The market also has 'losers' which fail to attract clients, leading to a fall in income and the possibility of closure. Success in recruiting students is an important test of leadership in the educational market engendered by the legislative changes of the 1980s and 1990s.

Self-management provides a searching examination of the capability of educational leaders. Principals are responsible for almost all aspects of management instead of sharing that responsibility with central or local government officials. The 'buck' stops with the head in a process which clarifies accountability but reduces or removes professional support. This 'new model' management has proved to be highly motivating for entrepreneurial heads (Bush et al., 1993) but damaging for those principals who prefer to work within a climate of partnership.

The high levels of stress-related retirements in England and Wales (Crawford, 1997) may be attributable to the anxieties experienced by principals and staff unable to adjust to this competitive climate. Staff have less protection from the decisions of principals and governing bodies because of the absence or weakness of an intermediate tier. Some heads, in turn, are uncomfortable with the enhanced position of lay governors which has proved to be problematic, not least because of a weak definition of the respective roles of governing bodies and senior professionals.

Even educational systems that have been centrally controlled are moving towards greater autonomy for their schools. In Singapore, for example, government control has been loosened for certain schools in order to gain the perceived benefits of self-management, as Prime Minister Goh Chok Tong explains: 'I believe that where a school has capable leadership, giving it more autonomy has the potential of raising its quality'. (PEC, 1996) The shift towards self-management is predicated on the assumption that it will lead to school improvement (Bush, 1996).

SCHOOL IMPROVEMENT

School improvement has become an international movement designed to raise standards in schools by disseminating research findings of good practice (Hopkins et al., 1994). It is underpinned by the notion that all educational organisations are capable of improvement and that all children and students are entitled to the best education that schools can provide. Linked to this view is the tenet that youngsters should not be handicapped by the low expectations that sometimes exist amongst the staff of schools in less favoured areas, for example in inner cities. This stance, encapsulated in the phrase, 'that's the best we can expect from children around here', is regarded as defeatist and likely to institutionalise inequality.

In their report of the International School Improvement Project (ISIP), Blum and Butler define the term as follows: 'School improvement means systematic, sustained change to accomplish educational goals more effectively. . . . School improvement is a long-term, incremental, evolving and painstaking process' (Blum and Butler, 1989, pp. 18–19). Blum and Butler emphasise the importance of effective management in achieving school improvement and recommend setting a long-term mission or vision for the school and developing and implementing goals consistent with this vision. It is evident from the research that improving any school does not involve a 'quick fix' but requires a sustained programme of change managed effectively by committed leaders.

The UK government's emphasis on 'league tables' of examination and test results, coupled with a nationally controlled inspection regime, has intensified the pressure on principals and teachers to improve their performance. However, there is some concern that the focus on measurable academic outcomes may lead to the neglect of more elusive but still important aspects of education, including student and staff welfare. The use of raw data, taking no account of socio-economic variables, is also problematic, leading researchers and some politicians to advocate 'value added' approaches to measurement.

THE EDUCATIONAL MANAGEMENT CURRICULUM

Educational management, or administration, is a popular subject for teachers seeking post-graduate qualifications in many countries. The success of specialist bodies such as the CCEAM and the European Forum, together with a growth in the number of international journals and conferences, has facilitated the development of a 'core curriculum' which transcends national boundaries. This core, which is supplemented by components linked to the local political and educational context, comprises the following elements:

- strategic management
- leadership
- curriculum management
- human resource management
- financial management
- accountability and external relations.

This curriculum has evolved over the last 30 years of the twentieth century in response to policy change and insights from an emerging body of research on theory and practice. The shift to self-management in many countries has led to a greater emphasis on finance and external relations as well as underpinning the emergence of strategic planning. The research on school effectiveness in the 1990s (Scheerens, 1992) has prompted a renewed interest in teaching and learning within curriculum management programmes. Significantly, most of these 'core' topics also appear in general MBA programmes offered by business schools, although the contexts and exemplars are very different.

The international curriculum of educational management has evolved largely on the basis of literature prepared by academics in the United States, Britain and Australia, where the subject is well established and the market is large enough to interest publishers. In many other countries, including much of the Commonwealth, dependence on imported books and journals may be inhibiting the development of a more relevant indigenous literature based firmly on local research and practice.

While educational management is increasingly international, and there are clear benefits to be gained from sharing ideas and experience, it is important to avoid academic 'colonialism' where ideas developed in one context are transplanted uncritically to another country. Dadey and Harber (1991) point to the weakness of transferring models from Europe and the USA to the African context, while former CCEA President, Meredyth Hughes, takes a similar view: 'The uncritical transportation of theories and methodologies across the world, without regard to the qualities and circumstances of different communities, can no longer be regarded as acceptable' (Hughes, 1990, p. 3).

In those countries where educational management is more firmly established, there is a developing literature, some of it based on research, to underpin the many courses now available in universities. As a 'live' subject based on practice in schools, colleges and universities that are themselves changing, the educational management curriculum will continue to evolve in the new millennium. A significant element of this curriculum relates to the theory of educational management.

THEORY DEVELOPMENT

Educational management is a relatively new discipline. When the CCEA was founded in 1970, theory was located primarily within the bureaucratic perspective. Derived from the work of the German sociologist Max Weber, this was thought to provide the most appropriate framework for the management of schools. Bureaucracy gives prominence to the official, usually hierarchical, structure of the organisation. Decision-making is thought to be a rational process. Bureaucracy emphasises the positional authority of leaders and stresses their accountability to sponsoring bodies (Bush, 1995).

Weber argued that bureaucracy is the most efficient form of management:

> The purely bureaucratic type of administrative organization . . . is, from a technical point of view, capable of attaining the highest degree of efficiency and is in this sense formally the most rational means of carrying out imperative control over human beings. It is superior to any other form in precision, in stability, in the stringency of its discipline, and in its reliability.

> (Weber, 1989, p. 16)

Schools and colleges have many bureaucratic features but there are difficulties in applying the concept too enthusiastically to schools:

> The dominance of the hierarchy is compromised by the expertise possessed by professional staff. The supposed rationality of the decision-making process requires modification to allow for the pace and complexity of change. The concept of organisational goals is challenged by those who point to the existence of multiple objectives in education and the possible conflict between goals held at individual, departmental and institutional levels.

> (Bush, 1995, p. 48)

Owens and Shakeshaft (1992) refer to a reduction of confidence in bureaucratic models and a 'paradigm shift' to a more sophisticated analysis. There are now many alternative theories jostling for supremacy. In some countries, the preferred perspective is that of *collegiality*, promoted in England and Wales as 'the official model of good practice' (Wallace, 1989, p. 182). In South Africa, for example, collegiality is regarded as wholly consistent with the democratic ideals underpinning the post-apartheid education system.

Collegiality is a normative model which emphasises teachers' authority of expertise and their right to share in decision-making processes. It assumes a common set of values held by members of the organisation which are thought to facilitate decision-making by consensus. Collegiality works more effectively in small groups and this may lead to representative democracy in large schools and colleges while primary schools, for example, may operate whole-school collegiality (Bush, 1995).

Collegiality has become increasingly popular in the literature on educational management but its advocates have not dealt adequately with its limitations, including the slow pace of decision-making, the likelihood that consensus will give way to conflict, and the problem of sustaining accountability where leaders have ceded power to staff. Hargreaves (1994) makes a more fundamental criticism, arguing that collegiality is being 'contrived' by governments and principals in order to secure the implementation of national or school policies. For all these reasons, those who aspire to collegiality often find that it cannot be operated effectively. Little (1990, p. 187), following substantial research in the United States, concludes that collegiality 'turns out to be rare'.

During the 1970s, several new theories were advanced to challenge the hegemony of bureaucracy. Political models, or *micropolitics*, were claimed to be a more realistic representation of management than either collegiality or bureaucracy (Baldridge *et al.*, 1978). The focus on interests and interest groups, the notion of conflict, bargaining and negotiation amongst groups, and the belief that power is the ultimate determinant of outcomes, appears highly plausible to those who understand how schools operate (Ball, 1987; Hoyle, 1986).

The Canadian writer Thomas Greenfield produced a powerful critique of bureaucracy and advanced an alternative model based on *subjective*, phenomenological and interactionist approaches. This theory gives primacy to individual interpretations of events which are likely to differ according to participants' values, experience and background. Structure is regarded as a fiction and goals are perceived as individual rather than organisational: 'What is an organisation that it can have such a thing as a goal?' (Greenfield, 1973, p. 553).

The American researchers Cohen and March challenged the assumed clarity of bureaucracy and advocated an alternative conception based on ambiguity. Their '*garbage can*' model emphasises the lack of clarity about goals, the problematic technology of school learning processes and the fluid participation of members in decision-making. Their analysis produces an imagery far removed from the orderly assumptions of bureaucracy: 'A key to understanding the processes within organisations is to view a choice opportunity as a garbage can into which various problems and solutions are dumped by participants' (Cohen and March, 1986, p. 81).

The concept of organisational *culture* provides a relatively new approach to educational management theory. It was not included in the author's first book on this subject (Bush, 1986) but merits a separate chapter in the second edition (Bush, 1995). The concept of culture focuses on the values and beliefs of participants and assumes that they will coalesce into shared norms and meanings. Schools develop distinctive features, 'the way we do things around here', which are expressed through rituals and ceremonies and celebrated through anointing heroes and heroines. Culture emphasises the informal dimension of organisations, a valuable counterpoint to the formal assumptions of bureaucracy.

Conventional theories of educational management are criticised by feminists and others who claim that they fail to acknowledge the different values of women. Theory is thought to be largely rooted in a male perspective while feminine traits, such as collaborative and co-operative behaviours and humanist values, are undervalued or overlooked (Al Khalifa, 1992). Shakeshaft (1987, p. 12) shows that 'in a synthesis of hundreds of studies . . . women were found to do as well or better than men', while Coleman (1994) points to the link between 'feminine' styles and effective management.

There is some overlap between 'feminine' characteristics of management and those associated with collegiality. Concepts of participation and consensual decision-making feature in both approaches but Nias *et al.* (1989, p. 71), on the basis of research in English primary schools, conclude that 'to argue that a collaborative culture is gender-specific is simplistic'. However, feminist and other gender-related approaches to theory are gaining ground and are likely to be increasingly significant in the new millennium.

There is no generally accepted theory of educational management. Rather, a clutch of models vie for supremacy and their relative significance depends on the specific context and the macro-educational environment. Collegiality is the normatively preferred model in much of the literature but there is also evidence of a return to 'top-down' bureaucratic approaches in some self-managing institutions (Elliott and Hall, 1994; Thompson, 1992). There have been a few attempts to develop integrative models (Davies and Morgan, 1983; Ellstrom, 1983) but these have been plausible rather than convincing. Research to produce a new synthesis applicable to self-managing schools is urgently required.

MANAGEMENT DEVELOPMENT: PRODUCING EDUCATIONAL LEADERS

The importance of effective management in contributing to excellence in education has been widely acknowledged. The major research projects on school effectiveness identify high-quality leadership as a significant factor in delineating successful schools (Mortimore *et al.*, 1986; Rutter *et al.*, 1979; Scheerens, 1992). However, in many countries there has been no requirement for aspiring principals to train as managers. Many teachers do take master's degrees in educational management (there are more than 1,000 participants in 39 countries on Leicester University's specialist MBA programme) but this has not been a prerequisite for appointment to senior posts in the UK.

There are examples of a more structured approach to management development. In parts of the United States, training for principals is licensed to universities (Cooper and Shute, 1988). In Singapore, widely admired for its exceptional economic growth, there has been a training programme for aspiring principals since 1984. The Diploma in Educational Administration (DEA) is a one-year, full-time course for staff identified by the Ministry of Education as potential principals (Bush and Chew, 1999). Participants attend courses at the National Institute of Education and are attached for eight weeks to a school led by a mentor principal. Here the aspirants become associate heads, undertaking tasks on behalf of the principal and gaining experience in several aspects of the new role. The mentoring dimension is very significant and many DEA graduates identify the placement as the most important aspect of their training (Coleman *et al.* 1996). Full-time training for one year is very expensive but illustrates the importance attached to developing the next generation of educational leaders.

In England and Wales, the Teacher Training Agency's (TTA's) National Professional Qualification for Headship (NPQH), introduced in 1997, is a more modest attempt to develop potential heads. The TTA has defined National Standards for headship and aspirants have to undertake training or demonstrate prior capability through a regional assessment centre. The standards are competence-based and are founded firmly on the notion that the requirements for headship can be specified and measured, as the TTA's Chief Executive, Anthea Millett, suggests:

> The central issue we need to tackle is leadership, in particular how the qualities of leadership can be identified and fostered . . . we should make explicit all of the key characteristics of those most likely to succeed in establishing and maintaining excellence as the headteacher of a school.
>
> (Millett, 1996)

This hard-edged stance is philosophically different from the mentoring approach recommended by the School Management Task Force and implemented in 1991. This latter model is predicated on the assumption that new heads will benefit from the advice and support of established school leaders who will pass on their experience to the new generation of principals. It is an intriguing mixture of apprenticeship and peer support (Bush *et al.*, 1996; Southworth, 1995) but eschews the notion of measurable criteria to distinguish between good leaders and those who are less successful. Arguably, a headship training programme which combines competencies and summative assessment with mentoring, as in Singapore, is likely to be more effective than a process based solely on competence.

CONCLUSION: EDUCATIONAL MANAGEMENT IN THE TWENTY-FIRST CENTURY

Because educational management is a relatively new discipline it is still evolving rapidly and has few established orthodoxies. The subject has become increasingly international but the many differences in educational systems require the application of generic concepts to be tailored to national contexts. It is difficult, and perhaps dangerous, to speculate about such a diverse and rapidly changing landscape but two broad themes are worth further discussion and analysis in this concluding section. Both topics suggest fundamental contradictions which seem likely to influence the management of education well into the new century.

The international trend to self-management is well established and seems likely to embrace, in a modified form, some of those countries that have hitherto preferred a nationally controlled system of education. The tentative steps towards institutional autonomy in Singapore and South Africa, for example, suggest that the evidence linking self-management to school effectiveness (Beare *et al.*, 1992; Bush, 1996; Finn, 1984) is becoming increasingly persuasive. Where self-managing schools have been subject to empirical research, as in the UK, the findings confirm the normative view that locating decisions at the institutional level is likely to promote school improvement (Bush *et al.*, 1993; Levacic, 1995). This is partly because their leaders are able to adopt a strategic approach to management, as we noted earlier. Where systems remain tightly controlled, as in China, this reflects political ideology, and a relative weakness in management development for school leaders, rather than an explicit rejection of the international research evidence.

Political considerations remain important in developed capitalist countries as well as developing communist societies and lead to a dichotomy between autonomy and control. In New Zealand the devolution of power to boards of trustees has been counterbalanced by the introduction of an Education Review Office (ERO) to audit the quality of services and review student achievement. The shift to self-government in England and Wales has also been accompanied by a tough inspection regime as well as increasing curriculum control. The belief that self-management and competition between schools serve to raise standards jostles with the contrary view that tight central controls are required to secure school improvement. In both countries the outcome is an apparent paradox of more powers for the centre and more autonomy for individual institutions but this 'belt and braces' strategy may be essential, as Maclure argues: 'It is only possible to take the risks inherent in setting schools free . . . if there were established conventions, reinforced if need be by ministerial authority, within which their independence could be exercised' (Maclure, 1988, p. xiii).

The second broad theme relates to the internal management of schools where there is a contradiction analogous to that found in the wider educational system. There is a normative preference for collegial approaches to management which empower teachers as professionals and lead to 'ownership' and enthusiastic implementation of school policies agreed through a participative process. According to Caldwell and Spinks (1992), devolution of authority to schools should be matched by power-sharing within them to engage staff commitment to change. Self-management provides the potential for the greater involvement of staff because the major decisions are located within schools rather than being imposed upon them.

In practice, however, the evidence for genuine collegiality is scarce (Little, 1990), and Hargreaves's (1994) assertion that it is 'contrived' to legitimate imposed change seems to ring true. There is a genuine dilemma for school leaders. Many believe in democratic processes and professional involvement in decision-making, but the increasing pressures for accountability to external agencies often serve to limit the extent of collegiality, for example in English further education (Lumby, 1996). Collegiality is unproblematic if it produces the principal's preferred outcome but if the decision is 'wrong', the head is faced with a stark choice: accept the decision and defend it to external bodies or overrule it and damage the participative process. Many principals respond to this uncomfortable position by allowing only conditional democracy, where certain major decisions are not open to debate (Bush, 1995; Hoyle, 1986,).

The study and practice of educational management and administration in the twenty-first century are likely to take place in the context of stronger links between educational outcomes and economic development. Governments will expect schools, colleges and universities to help their countries to compete in the global economy. 'Performance' may become the watchword for successful education. Individuals and institutions that perform well against measurable criteria are likely to thrive but there will be increasing pressure on those people and schools whose performance is deemed to be inadequate. A major test for educational managers will be to 'deliver' high quality. Teacher professionalism and collegiality may be sacrificed to the imperative of higher educational standards.

ACKNOWLEDGEMENT

I am grateful for the advice of Professor Mike Thurlow of the University of Natal, John O'Neill of Massey University, New Zealand, Joy Chew of the National Institute of Education, Singapore and my University of Leicester colleagues Marianne Coleman, Keith Foreman, Jacky Lumby and David Middlewood who all gave valuable comments on a draft of this text.

REFERENCES

Al Khalifa, E. (1992) 'Management by halves: Women and school management', in Bennett, N., Crawford, M. and Riches, C. (eds), *Managing Change in Education*, London: Paul Chapman,

Baldridge, J. V., Curtis, D. V., Ecker, G. and Riley, G. L. (1978) *Policy Making and Effective Leadership*, San Francisco: Jossey Bass.

Ball, S. (1987) *The Micropolitics of the School: Towards a Theory of School Organization*, London: Methuen.

Beare, H., Caldwell, B. and Millikan, R. (1992) 'A model for managing an excellent school', in Bennett, N., Crawford, M. and Riches, C. (eds), *Managing Change in Education*, London: Paul Chapman.

Blum, R. E. and Butler, J. A. (1989) 'The role of school leaders in school improvement', in Blum, R. E. and Butler, J. A. (eds), *School Leader Development for School Improvement*, Leuven: Acco.

Bone, T. (1982) 'Educational administration', *British Journal of Educational Studies*, 30, 32–42.

Bush, T. (1986) *Theories of Educational Management*, London: Paul Chapman.

Bush, T. (1995) *Theories of Educational Management* (2nd edn), London: Paul Chapman.

Bush, T. (1996) 'School autonomy and school improvement', in Gray, J., Reynolds, D., Fitz-Gibbon, C. and Jesson, D. (eds), *Merging Traditions: The Future of Research on School Effectiveness and School Improvement*, London: Cassell.

Bush, T. and Chew, J. (1999) 'Developing human capital: training and mentoring for principals', *Compare*, 29 (1), 41–52.

Bush, T., Coleman, M. and Glover, D. (1993) *Managing Autonomous Schools: The Grant Maintained Experience*, London: Paul Chapman.

Bush, T., Coleman, M., Wall, D. and West-Burnham, J. (1996) 'Mentoring and continuing professional development', in McIntyre, D. and Hagger, H. (eds), *Mentoring in Schools: Developing the Profession of Teaching*, London: David Fulton.

Caldwell, B. and Spinks, J. (1992) *Leading the Self-Managing School*, London: Falmer Press.

Cohen, M. D. and March, J. G. (1986) *Leadership and Ambiguity: the American College President*, Boston, MA: Harvard Business School Press.

Coleman, M. (1994) 'Women in educational management', in Bush, T. and West-Burnham, J. (eds), *The Principles of Educational Management*, Harlow: Longman.

Coleman, M., Low, G. T., Bush, T. and Chew, J. (1996) 'Re-thinking Training for Principals'. The Role of Mentoring', Paper presented at the AERA Conference, New York, April.

Cooper, B. S., and Shute, R. W. (1988) *Training for School Management: Lessons from the American Experience*, Bedford Way Papers, no. 33. London: Institute of Education, University of London.

Crawford, M. (1997) 'Managing stress in education', in Bush, T. and Middlewood, D. (eds), *Managing People in Education*, London: Paul Chapman.

Culbertson, J. (1980) 'Educational Administration: Where we are and where we are going'. Paper presented at the 4th International Intervisitation Program in Educational Administration, Vancouver.

Dadey, A. and Harber, C. (1991) *Training and Professional Support for Headship in Africa*, London: Commonwealth Secretariat.

Davies, J. L. and Morgan, A. W. (1983) 'Management of higher education in a period of contraction and uncertainty', in Boyd-Barrett, O., Bush, T., Goodey, J., McNay, I. and Preedy, M. (eds), *Approaches to Post School Management*, London: Harper & Row.

Elliott, G. and Hall, V. (1994) 'FE Inc.: Business orientation in further education and the introduction of human resource management', *School Organisation*, 14, (1), 3–10.

Ellstrom, P. E. (1983) 'Four faces of educational organisations', *Higher Education*, 12, 231–241.

Fayol, H. (1916) *General and Industrial Management*, London: Pitman.

Finn, C. E. (1984) 'Towards strategic independence: Nine commandments for enhancing school effectiveness', *Phi Delta Kappan*, February, 518–524.

Greenfield, T. B. (1973) 'Organisations as social inventions: Rethinking assumptions about change', *Journal of Applied Behavioural Science*, 9 (5), 551–574.

Hargreaves, A. (1994) *Changing Teachers, Changing Times: Teachers' Work and Culture in the Postmodern Age*, London: Cassell.

Hargreaves, D. and Hopkins, D. (1991) *The Empowered School*, London: Cassell.

Hopkins, D., Ainscow, M. and West, M. (1994) *School Improvement in an Era of Change*, London: Cassell.

Hoyle, E. (1986) *The Politics of School Management*, London: Hodder & Stoughton.

Hughes, M. (1990) 'Improving education and training for educational administrators and managers: Urgent needs'. Paper presented to UNESCO International Congress, Planning and Management of Educational Development, Mexico.

Hughes, M. and Bush, T. (1991) 'Theory and research as catalysts for change', in Walker, W., Farquhar, R. and Hughes, M. (eds), *Advancing Education: School Leadership in Action*, London: Falmer Press.

Levacic, R. (1995) *Local Management of Schools: Analysis and Practice*, Milton Keynes: Open University Press.

Little, J. (1990) 'Teachers as colleagues', in Lieberman, A. (ed.), *Schools as Collaborative Cultures: Creating the Future Now*, London: Falmer Press.

Lumby, J. (1996) 'Curriculum change in further education', *Journal of Vocational Education and Training*, 48 (4) 333–348.

Maclure, S. (1988) *Education Reformed*, Sevenoaks: Hodder & Stoughton.

Millett, A. (1996) 'A head is more than a manager', *Times Educational Supplement*, 15 July.

Minister of Education (1995), *New Zealand Schools 1994*, Wellington: Learning Medi Limited.

Mortimore, P., Sammons, P., Stoll, L., Lewis, D. and Ecob, R. (1986) *The Junior School Project: A Summary of the Main Report*, London: Inner London Education Authority.

Nias, J., Southworth, G. and Yeomans, R. (1989) *Staff Relationships in the Primary School*, London: Cassell.

Owens, R. and Shakeshaft, C. (1992) 'The new "revolution" in administrative theory', *Journal of Educational Management*, 30 (9), 4–17.

Principals' Executive Centre (PEC) (1996) *Brochure*, PEC, Singapore.

Rutter, M., Maughan, B., Mortimore, P. and Ouston, J. (1979), *Fifteen Thousand Hours – Secondary Schools and their Effects on Children*, London: Open Books.

Scheerens, J. (1992) *Effective Schooling: Research, Theory and Practice*, London: Cassell.

Shakeshaft, C. (1987) *Women in Educational Administration*, Newbury Park: Sage.

Southworth, G. (1995) 'Reflections on mentoring for new school leaders', *Journal of Educational Administration*, 33 (5), 17–28.

Taylor, F. (1947) *Principles of Scientific Management*, New York: Harper & Row.

Thompson, M. (1992) 'The experience of going grant-maintained: The perceptions of AMMA teacher representatives', *Journal of Teacher Development*, 1 (3), 133–140.

Wallace, M. (1989) 'Towards a collegiate approach to curriculum management in primary and middle schools', in Preedy, M. (ed.), *Approaches to Curriculum Management*, Milton Keynes: Open University Press.

Weber, M. (1989) 'Legal authority in a bureaucracy', in Bush, T. (ed.), *Managing Education: Theory and Practice*, Milton Keynes: Open University Press.

16

FUNDAMENTAL SHIFTS IN SCHOOLING
Implications for principal leadership

Charles Hausman and Joseph Murphy

INTRODUCTION

Given the widely held belief that public schooling is suspended in a state of mediocrity, many reformers have turned their attention to the pivotal role played by principals in school improvement. Recent reforms of a radical nature have caused the roles and responsibilities of these school leaders vastly to increase in number and complexity (Murphy, 1994). After noting how wholesale changes in their roles may afford Australian principals unprecedented opportunities for self-fulfilment, Caldwell cautions, 'A welter of requirements on industrial matters and expectations for accountability may make the whole a thankless and overwhelming nightmare' (Caldwell, 1992, p. 18). Similarly, from his study of school heads in England and Wales, Weindling (1992, p. 75) concludes, 'But it is not just a change of emphasis; it is also a change of intensity. . . . There was even a danger that eventually, "many or all heads will reach saturation point and schools will collapse with exhaustion".' To complicate matters further, these added tasks have resulted in a great deal of role ambiguity (Bredeson, 1989; Murphy, 1990).

In this chapter, we describe the evolving picture of school management that is taking shape in response to educational reform initiatives. Elsewhere, we have chronicled the nature of these measures (Murphy, 1990; 1991; 1994; 1996; Murphy and Beck, 1995). When viewed collectively, they reveal three fundamental shifts in our thinking about schooling. First, they suggest a movement from public and monopolistic conceptions of schooling to more market-flavoured views of education. Second, they expose a struggle to redefine the organisational infrastructure of schooling – a struggle to move from a hierarchical to a community-centred foundation. And third, they reveal an attempt to infuse social constructivist perspectives of learning and teaching into schooling while de-emphasising the more established behavioural underpinnings of education. These are the basic alterations in our understanding of education that define the changing nature of school management described below.

FACILITATIVE LEADERSHIP

With the involvement of new groups of stakeholders in the decision-making process, the need for participative leaders with well-developed interpersonal skills has become critical. Conley and Goldman (1994, p. 237) use the term *'facilitative leadership'* to describe how 'principals come to lead without dominating'. This type of leadership has also been referred to as *enabling* (Prestine, 1991) and *indirect leadership* (Peterson, 1989). Empirical evidence has shed light on ways principals can 'become less prominent and play primarily a support-ing role' (Shields and Newton, 1992, p. 5). They can diminish micro-management (Chris-tensen, 1992); 'encourage participation, acknowledge individual contributions and ensure effective implementation of Committee decisions' (Chapman, 1990, p. 23); and model col-laborative behaviour (Conley, 1991). In their study of restructuring schools, Leithwood *et al.* (1992, p. 30) identified 'delegating authentic leadership responsibilities [and instituting] collaborative decision-making processes in the school' as prerequisites for successful reform. This conclusion has consistently been reaffirmed (Christensen, 1992; Prestine, 1991).

Tightly coupled to facilitative leadership, principals who lead schools that utilise a formal process of collaborative decision-making must rely increasingly upon well-developed human resource orientations. Pivotal human resource roles include: mediator, motivator, and builder-of-trust. As different constituencies are receiving a voice in the decision-making process, tensions between these groups are intensifying. One recurring conflict tends to be between parents who want to be empowered in core technology decisions and teachers who view themselves as the experts in curriculum and instruction (Hallinger *et al.*, 1993). Given discrepant viewpoints and turf battles, principals of restructuring schools must be effective mediators and team builders.

Because principals are dependent upon teachers to implement all types of education – contemporary and reformed – the relationship between the principal and the teacher is particularly salient. Teachers are agents of change, and one of the primary duties of the principal is to motivate and ensure teacher commitment. In contexts where radical reform is being implemented, motivation is even more crucial because so many changes are taking place and time is a precious commodity. Research has provided evidence that principals must view teachers' time as a scarce resource. Restructuring does not succeed in a climate of 'projectitis', the practice of implementing too many innovations simultaneously (Hill and Bonan, 1991).

Finally, school administrators in shared decision-making contexts must establish a cli-mate of trust (Chapman, 1990). Every decision is a test, and parents and teachers will not participate if they perceive their influence as unauthentic. The work of Smylie (1992) confirms the importance of teachers perceiving their relationship with the principal as open and facilitative, as opposed to controlling.

Although there is evidence that altering the traditional influence patterns in schools is leading to enhanced teacher involvement, creating new roles for parents and teachers and improving relations among staff, the outcomes of this change are not always positive (Mur-phy and Beck, 1995). The primary apprehension is the lack of a clear connection between restructuring initiatives and teaching and learning outcomes (Murphy, 1991). This missing linkage is ironic in light of the central reform element noted above – the transformation of the learning and teaching process into a sociologically and cognitively grounded model. In order to correct this flaw, reformers are calling for change measures to be more tightly coupled to the core technology of schools (Dimmock, 1993; Murphy, 1991). One suggested method of achieving this aim is 'backward mapping' from the student (Elmore, 1979–1980). In other words, in-depth understandings of students and learning and teaching should drive structural reforms rather than the assumption that structural changes in adult roles will lead to improved outcomes for students.

MIDDLE MANAGEMENT

To date, reductions in the hierarchy of school systems have not accompanied increases in parent and teacher empowerment brought on by restructuring initiatives. Consequently, 'the principalship is becoming more a middle manager position than in the past; principals are in the middle of a triadic relationship with parents and superiors at the central office' (Goldring, 1993, p. 94). Hallinger and Hausman drew the same conclusion after observing that principals of restructuring schools are:

> sandwiched between local pressures exerted by school-based management and centralizing forces exerted by external mandates and central office personnel who are reluctant to relinquish their authority. The principals are under constant pressure to remain responsive to parents and staff, while simultaneously meeting the expectations of centrally imposed guidelines.
>
> (Hallinger and Hausman, 1994, p. 163)

INSTRUCTIONAL LEADERSHIP

Research has repeatedly identified instructional leadership as a characteristic of effective schools (Bossert *et al.*, 1982; Hallinger and Murphy, 1985). However, operationalisation and measurement of this role have been ambiguous (Murphy, 1988). In spite of this ambiguity, more current research has confirmed the influence of context on the enactment of instructional leadership by principals (Hallinger and Murphy, 1987; Heck and Marcoulides, 1993).

With the implementation of more radical reform strategies, the popularity of and interest in the instructional leadership role of the principal has diminished – this despite the fact that the principal remains the central authority of the school site, the primary business of which is teaching and learning. As the following quote indicates, many believe that instructional leadership is an obsolete concept:

> 'Instructional leadership' is an idea that has served many schools well throughout the 1980s and 1990s. But in the light of current restructuring initiatives designed to take schools into the twenty-first century, 'instructional leadership' no longer appears to capture the heart of what school administration will have to become. 'Transformational leadership' evokes a more appropriate range of practice.
>
> (Leithwood, 1992, p. 8)

The assumption of this contention is that principals will function as leaders of leaders. Although the evidence is mixed, some empirical data lend credibility to this belief

(Leithwood, 1994). In contrast, in their single case study of a restructuring school, Hallinger and Hausman concluded:

> While responsibility for instructional leadership is clearly more diffuse . . . than in the past, this has not diminished the need for the principal's instructional leadership. With more people involved in educational decision-making, it has been our observation that there is an even greater need for the principal to understand the nature of educational processes and their impact on teachers and students.
>
> (Hallinger and Hausman, 1993, p. 140)

Irrespective of the appropriateness of the role, researchers around the globe are reporting that new administrative functions required by restructuring are reducing school heads' time available for instructional leadership (Bennett *et al.*, 1992; Earley and Baker, 1989). For example, in New Zealand:

> Principals who formerly had time for direct classroom support of teachers and their students, and were involved in demonstration teaching, special programmes or coaching, now found the demands of restructuring had shifted the emphasis of their actions, time and commitment. They felt that a management emphasis had taken over from instructional leadership.
>
> (McConnell and Jeffries, 1991, p. 24)

ENTREPRENEURIAL LEADERSHIP

As predicted by the theoretical frameworks of Crow (1991) and Kerchner (1988), experimental data have affirmed the premium placed on entrepreneurial leadership in the market environment of education (Murphy, 1994). Hallinger and Hausman (1993) report that American principals in schools of choice spend increased time marketing the school's programme and services. Specifically, the principals in their study allocated additional time to parent tours, informational meetings and creation of marketing tools such as brochures. This finding has held true in other countries, including Israel (Goldring, 1992). Likewise, in Great Britain, Earley *et al.* (1990, p. 13) have observed, 'The public image of schools has become increasingly a matter of attention by heads', while Davies and his colleagues (1993, p. 2) have highlighted the renewed emphasis on 'the importance of client perceptions of schools'.

ENVIRONMENTAL LEADERSHIP

School choice and restructuring strategies, by expanding external boundaries, alter the relationships between schools and their constituencies. Schools are no longer assigned students from a defined neighbourhood catchment area. On the contrary, they are part of a more open system and must interact more frequently with their external environments. Chapman describes the impact of this extension of the school community:

> Increased school management . . . dramatically alters the nature of the principal's professional life. Principals are forced to assume a more public role, interacting with people in the wider community, forging links with the school and its environment.
>
> (Chapman, 1990, p. 229)

A large body of evidence demonstrates that environmental management functions of the principal are enlarged as a consequence of school restructuring initiatives, particularly those affording parents greater voice (Earley and Baker, 1989; Goldring, 1992; Murphy, 1994). Specifically, school principals are being urged to expand parent outreach efforts, empower parents in the decision-making process, and garner additional community resources. These responsibilities have been labelled *boundary management* (Earley *et al.*, 1990, p. 8) and *environmental leadership* (Hallinger and Hausman, 1993, p. 137).

In their investigation of the principal's role as environmental leader, Goldring and Rallis (1993) identified organisational design and strategic manoeuvring as the two strategies that effective principals used to enable their schools to adapt to their external environments. Organisational design entails changing the school's design features to create the best fit with its environment. Research has indicated that mechanistic structures are appropriate for organisations with simple, stable and predictable environments, while more organic structures are necessary for institutions with complex, uncertain and volatile surroundings (Burns and Stalks, 1961).

MORAL LEADERSHIP

The notion that schools should function as communities is becoming increasingly widespread in the educational literature:

> From a communitarian perspective, a school is perceived as a 'small society', where emphasis is given to informal and enduring social relationships and a strong attachment to a common ethos. An operational consequence of this view is a diffuse adult role and a minimal division of labor.
>
> (Bryk *et al.*, 1990, p. 137)

The connection between restructuring and community has broadened the discussion of schools as communities. In a study comparing public and private schools, Coleman and Hoffer (1987) assess the effect of community on the extent of social integration between schools and the families they serve. Coleman and Hoffer allege that the type and magnitude of community influence social ties between schools and families. These researchers distinguish between two types of communities: functional and value. 'Functional communities are characterised by structural consistency between generations in which social norms and sanctions arise out of the social structure itself, and both reinforce and perpetuate that structure' (Goldring *et al.*, 1993, p. 28). With regard to education, value communities are a group of individuals with congruent beliefs about schooling, but they are not linked to a specific neighbourhood and are, therefore, not functional communities.

School choice advocates claim that choice creates value communities within schools by fostering shared values among parents and school personnel. In an extensive study of magnet schools, Smrekar (1991) reported that organisational structures and processes embedded in these schools foster qualities of value communities among diverse groups of parents. Further, those communal qualities mediate the impact of differences in cultural capital that influence school–family interactions. In a separate study comparing a Catholic, a magnet, and a traditional publicly funded school, Smrekar argues that 'choice is a powerful engine for creating the constituent elements of community' (Smrekar, 1993, p. 21).

In a bureaucratic model of schooling, the authority of principals is the result of their position in the hierarchy and of the rules and regulations. On the contrary, the communitarian viewpoint suggests that the authority of principals arises from their professional knowledge and moral beliefs. The principal becomes a moral leader – the individual primarily responsible for communicating the values and beliefs that define the school as a community (Murphy, 1991, 1992).

In a context of school choice, if parents make rational, value-based decisions when exercising their options and if those decisions lead to the formation of value communities, then principals must make the school's values explicit throughout the larger school environment. Similarly, in restructuring schools characterised by shared decision-making, principals must promote a climate of collegiality and provide for professional development consistent with the school's values.

CO-ORDINATION OF INTEGRATED SERVICES

The social fabric of many nations is undergoing rapid change. Among these changes are demographic shifts resulting in a significantly larger number of students whom the publicly funded school system has been unable to serve successfully (Murphy, 1991, 1992). Pivotal indicators of social well-being continue to worsen. As a result of these social changes, the schools have been assigned several new responsibilities – dealing with diversity, drug education, violence prevention, character education and so forth. Despite this heightened attention, numerous societal problems continue to show their resilience.

The extent to which the schools serve the needs of disadvantaged youth will be largely contingent on the school's leadership. Alterations in the social and moral fabric of society place a premium on principals' ability to serve as builders of *civic capacity*: 'the ability to build and maintain an effective alliance among institutional representatives in the public, private, and independent sectors to work toward a common community goal' (Henig, 1994, p. 220). This metaphor is consistent with an oft-cited, African proverb: 'It takes the whole village to educate a child.'

The importance of interagency collaboration for schools has only recently been emphasised (Crowson and Boyd, 1993). It seems likely that the principal will serve at the nexus of this partnership and activate services for many students (Murphy, 1992). Although sufficient time has not passed for empirical studies to provide large-scale data on the outcomes of interagency collaboration, some evidence has been collected. In an investigation in the United States, Wechsler reports that:

> the working style of a collaborative – the extent to which it shared leadership, made decisions jointly, and had members who trusted each other and felt ownership of their local initiative – was not related to the effectiveness of the services it delivered. . . . However, these governance level factors were important in terms of keeping agencies committed to an interagency, school-linked, and consumer-oriented service approach to service reform.
>
> (Wechsler, 1996, p. 11)

In addition, enhanced support from principals, teachers and students was found among those initiatives that were well integrated into the local schools. Principal support was higher for and a crucial element of those services that were provided beyond the routine school day.

CONCLUSIONS

Fundamental shifts in schooling have collectively created a new context for principal leadership. These changes include the introduction of market forces in education, a focus on the communal organisation of schools, and the implementation of a social and cognitive model of learning and teaching. 'Although some of these reforms are highly controversial, they are being implemented with major consequences for school management' (Bolam *et al.*, 1992, p. 1). These reforms have generated turbulent and uncertain environments for schools and have added new and often ambiguous role demands for school principals. This chapter has described responsibilities for principal leadership that have arisen in response to this new landscape. We hope that it will help school heads make sense of their emerging roles.

REFERENCES

Bennett, A. L., Bryk, A. S., Easton, J. Y., Kerbow, D., Luppescu, S. and Sebring, P. A. (1992) *Charting Reform: The Principals' Perspective*. Chicago: Consortium on Chicago School Research.

Bolam, R., McMahon, A., Pocklington, K. and Weindling, D. (1992) 'Teachers' and headteachers' perceptions of effective management in British primary schools'. Paper presented at the annual meeting of the American Educational Research Association, San Francisco.

Bossert, S. T., Dwyer, D. C., Rowan, B. and Lee, G. V. (1982) 'The instructional management role of the principal'. *Educational Administration Quarterly*, 18 (3), 34–64.

Bredeson, P. V. (1989) 'Redefining leadership and the roles of school principals: Responses to changes in the professional worklife of teachers'. Paper presented at the annual meeting of the American Educational Research Association, San Francisco.

Burns, T. and Stalks, G. M. (1961) *The Management of Innovation*. London: Tavistock.

Bryk, A., Lee, V. and Smith, J. (1990) 'High school organization and its effects on teachers and students'. In W. Clune and I. Witte (eds), *Choice and Control in American Education, vol. 1.: The theory of choice and control in American Education*. Bristol, PA: Falmer Press, 135–226.

Caldwell, B. J. (1992) 'The principal as leader of the self-managing school in Australia'. *Journal of Educational Administration*, 30 (3), 6–19.

Chapman, J. (1990) 'School-based decision-making and management: Implications for school personnel'. In C. Chapman (ed.), *School-based Decision-making and Management*. London: Falmer, 221–224.

Christensen, G. (1992). 'The changing role of the administrator in an accelerated school'. Paper presented at the annual meeting of the American Educational Research Association, San Francisco.

Coleman, J. and Hoffer, T. (1987) *Public and Private High Schools: The Impact of Communities*. New York: Basic Books.

Conley, D. T. (1991) 'Lessons from laboratories in school restructuring and site-based decision making'. *Oregon School Study Bulletin*, 34 (7), 1–61.

Conley, D. T. and Goldman, P. (1994) 'Ten propositions of facilitative leadership'. In J. Murphy and K. S. Louis (eds), *Reshaping the Principalship: Insights from Transformational Reform Efforts*. Thousand Oaks, CA: Corwin Press, 237–262.

Crow, G. (1991) 'The principal in schools of choice: Middle manager, entrepreneur, and symbol manager'. Paper presented at the Annual Meeting of the American Educational Research Association, Chicago.

Crowson, R. I. and Boyd, W. L. (1993) 'Coordinated services for children: Designing arks for storms and seas unknown'. *American Journal of Education*, 101 (2), 140–179.

Davies, B., Ellison, L., Thompson, N. and Vann, B. (1993) 'Internal and external markets: Client perceptions and school management responses'. Paper presented at the Annual Meeting of the American Educational Research Association, Atlanta.

Dimmock, C. (1993) 'School-based management and linkage with the curriculum'. In C. Dimmock (ed.), *School-based Management and School Effectiveness*. London: Routledge, 1–21.

Earley, P. and Baker, L. (1989) *The Recruitment, Retention, Motivation and Morale of Senior Staff in Schools*. London: National Foundation for Educational Research in England and Wales.

Earley, P., Baker, L. and Weindling, D. (1990) *'Keeping the raft afloat': Secondary Headship Five Years On*. London: National Foundation for Educational Research in England and Wales.

Elmore, R. F. (1979–1980) 'Backward mapping: Implementation research and policy decisions'. *Political Science Quarterly*, 94 (4), 601–616.

Goldring, E. B. (1992) 'System-wide diversity in Israel: Principals as transformational and environmental leaders'. *Journal of Educational Administration*, 30 (3), 49–62.

Goldring, E. B. (1993) 'Principals, parents, and administrative superiors'. *Educational Administration Quarterly*, 29 (1), 93–117.

Goldring, E. B. and Rallis, S. (1993) 'Principals as environmental leaders: The external link for facilitating change'. Paper presented at the Annual Meeting of the American Educational Research Association, Atlanta.

Goldring, E., Hawley, W., Saffold, R. and Smrekar, C. (1993) 'Parental choice: Consequences for students, families, and schools'. Paper presented at the International Conference, Theory and Practice in School Autonomy: Bringing the Community Back In, Tel Aviv University, June 14–17.

Hallinger, P. and Hausman, C. (1993) 'The changing role of the principal in a school of choice'. In J. Murphy and P. Hallinger (eds), *Restructuring Schooling: Learning from Ongoing Efforts*. Newbury Park, CA: Corwin Press, 114–142.

Hallinger, P. and Hausman, C. (1994) 'From Attila the Hun to Mary Had a Little Lamb: Principal role ambiguity in restructured schools'. In J. Murphy and K. S. Louis (eds), *Reshaping the Principalship: Insights from Transformational Reform Efforts*. Thousand Oaks, CA: Corwin Press, 154–176.

Hallinger, P. and Murphy, J. (1985) 'Assessing the instructional management behavior of principals'. *The Elementary School Journal*, 86 (2), 217–247.

Hallinger, P. and Murphy, J. (1987) 'Organizational and social context and the instructional leadership role of the principal'. Paper presented at the annual meeting of the American Educational Research Association, Washington, DC.

Hallinger, P., Murphy, J. and Hausman, C. (1993) 'Conceptualizing school restructuring: Principals' and teachers' perceptions'. In C. Dimmock (ed.), *School-based Management and School Effectiveness*. London: Routledge, 22–40.

Heck, R. H. and Marcoulides, G. A. (1993) 'Principal assessment: conceptual problem, methodological problem, or both?' *Peabody Journal of Education*, 69, 124–144.

Henig, J. R. (1994) *Rethinking School Choice: Limits of the Market Metaphor*. Princeton, NJ: Princeton University Press.

Hill, P. and Bonan, J. (1991) *Decentralization and Accountability in Public Education*. Santa Monica, CA: Rand Corporation, Institute for Education and Training.

Kerchner, C. (1988). 'Bureaucratic entrepreneurship: The implications of choice for school administration'. *Educational Administration Quarterly*, 24 (4), 381–392.

Leithwood, K. A. (1992) 'Images of future school administration: Moving on from "instructional leadership" to "transformational leadership"'. *Educational Leadership*, 49 (5), 8–12.

Leithwood, K. A. (1994) 'Leadership for school restructuring'. *Educational Administration Quarterly*, 30 (4), 498–518.

Leithwood, K. A., Jantzi, D., Silins, H. and Dart, B. (1992) 'Transformational leadership and school restructuring'. Paper presented at the International Congress for School Effectiveness and School Improvement, Victoria, BC, Canada.

McConnell, R. and Jeffries, R. (1991) *Monitoring Today's Schools: The First Year*. Hamilton, New Zealand: University of Waikato Press.

Murphy, J. (1988) 'Methodological, measurement, and conceptual problems in the study of instructional leadership'. *Educational Evaluation and Policy Analysis*, 10, 106–116.

Murphy, J. (1990) 'The educational reform movement of the 1980s: A comprehensive analysis'. In J. Murphy (ed.), *The Reform of American Public Education in the 1980s: Perspectives and Cases*. Berkeley, CA: McCutchan, 3–55.

Murphy, J. (1991) *Restructuring Schools: Capturing and Assessing the Phenomenon*. New York: Teachers College Press.

Murphy, J. (1992) *The Landscape of Leadership Preparation: Reframing the Education of School Administrators*. Newbury Park, CA: Corwin.

Murphy, J. (1994) 'Transformational change and the evolving role of the principalship: Early empirical evidence'. In J. Murphy and K. S. Louis (eds), *Reshaping the Principalship: Insights from Transformational Reform Efforts*. Thousand Oaks, CA: Corwin, 20–53.

Murphy, J. (1996) *The Privatization of Schooling: Problems and Possibilities*. Thousand Oaks, CA: Corwin.

Murphy, J. and Beck, L. G. (1995) *School-based Management as School Reform: Taking Stock*. Thousand Oaks, CA: Corwin.

Peterson, K. D. (1989) *Secondary Principals and Instructional Leadership: Complexities in a Diverse Role*. Madison, WI: Center for Educational Research.

Prestine, N. (1991) 'Completing the essential schools metaphor: Principal as enabler'. Paper presented at the annual meeting of the American Educational Research Association, Chicago.

Shields, C. and Newton, E. (1992) 'Empowered leadership: Realizing the good news'. Paper presented at the annual meeting of the American Educational Research Association, San Francisco.

Smrekar, C. (1991) 'Building community: The influence of school organization on family–school interactions'. Unpublished doctoral dissertation, Stanford University, School of Education, Palo Alto.

Smrekar, C. (1993) 'Building community: The influence of school organization and management'. *Advances in Research and Theories of School Management and Educational Policy*, 2, 1–24.

Smylie, M. A. (1992) 'Teacher participation in school decision-making: Assessing willingness to participate'. *Educational Evaluation and Policy Analysis*, 14 (1), 53–67.

Wechsler, M. E. (1996) 'Interagency collaboration: Hard work but worth it'. Paper presented at the annual meeting of the American Educational Research Association, New York.

Weindling, D. (1992) 'Marathon running on a sand dune: The changing role of the headteacher in England and Wales'. *Journal of Educational Administration*, 30 (3), 63–76.

17

SCHOOL GOVERNANCE
Educational excellence as shared aspiration

Jon Nixon

The last 20 years have been characterised by far-reaching reform of the public sector. No public institution has been left intact and the relation between institutions, local government and central government has shifted significantly, with the consequent erosion of local government influence in certain key areas and a sharp increase overall in the privatisation of publicly owned institutions. These changes have had a profound effect on the way in which public institutions are managed and governed and the way in which managers and governors perceive their responsibilities. 'Governance' is one of the keywords associated with these changes in structure and perception. The shift from 'government' to 'governance' is significant: current usage does not treat the two words as synonymous. Indeed, governance highlights a significant shift in the meaning of government: what governance refers to is a new approach to government; a new method of ordered rule; a new conception, even, of who governs whom.

This chapter is concerned with the impact of that shift upon schools and with the way in which schools, through their particular institutional practices and educational purposes, are interpreting that shift. Two underlying assumptions guide the analysis. First, while recent reforms imply a clear distinction between the responsibilities of those who manage and those who govern, they have in practice been associated with corresponding shifts in the style of educational management: shifts denoted by the term 'new managerialism' or 'new public management'. So interrelated are these two sets of developments that any serious consideration of governance must come to terms with its ideological underpinning in the new public management of education. Second, one of the major themes implicit in the reforms that have shaped the governance of education over the last 15 years is the need to achieve a notion of 'quality' that balances educational excellence and equality of provision. There remains considerable difference of opinion among professional educators, social commentators and educational researchers as to how that balance might be achieved. However, the various shifts which this chapter seeks to track suggest an increasing emphasis on equity as the prerequisite of educational excellence.

THE MAIN THEMES

Governance is best characterised as a reaction against an earlier set of assumptions and institutional practices; a reaction against what the critics of those assumptions and practices see as an overreliance on professional monopolies, bureaucratic hierarchies and external regulation. The notion of governance holds out the promise of increased public choice and participation, greater permeability and flexibility of organisational structure, and an increased emphasis on decentralisation through institutional self-organisation. Whether these aspirations represent a genuine break with the past remains an open question. Have the monopolies been eradicated or merely diverted to different professional groups? Have the hierarchies been flattened or just reconstructed around different interest groups? Has the regulatory function been transformed or simply shunted to different external agencies? Important though these critical questions are (we shall return to them later), the idea of 'governing without Government' remains a unifying theme in the commentary on school governance.

Public choice, the new managerialism and decentralisation remain central themes in trying to make sense of school governance in the late twentieth century and in trying to envisage what school governance might look like in the early twenty-first century. It is worth reminding ourselves, briefly, of how these themes emerged. Since the mid-1970s social and economic conditions in Western industrial societies have changed to the extent that the Keynesian postwar settlement has now virtually disintegrated. The changed conditions are in part a result of heightened global competition and in part a consequence of the particular policies adopted in response to that challenge. Those policies were driven by the ascendancy of the New Right between the mid-1970s and the end of the 1980s and affected a radical reorganisation not only of the economy but of the whole civil society and its constituent elements. The New Right 'project' was directed at institutions and at the way in which institutions are managed and governed.

It is important to emphasise that the ideology underlying this 'project' appealed, in different ways and in different places, to both left and right. The neo-liberal and neo-conservative policies that it incorporated and promoted had wide currency and assumed a different political complexion within different societies. While within the UK the central themes were defined and prioritised by a popularist conservative administration, in other societies such as New Zealand they were promoted by Labourist administrations. The emphasis on choice, managerialism and decentralisation crossed, and to some extent redrew, the old political boundaries. We cannot, in other words, assume a single point of political origin for the ideological apparatus underpinning the arrangements by which schools and other public institutions are currently governed.

Nor can we assume a single point of destination. Within the public debate on school governance many different ends and purposes are evoked. One of the central issues in the debate is how schools can best be governed so as to ensure both educational excellence and social equity. For some, these two sets of priorities are seen as being in deep tension, such that the latter inevitably loses out if too great an emphasis is placed on the former. From this perspective the process of governance involves setting limits to public participation in state education with a view to protecting excellence. For others, however, academic excellence is itself seen as the prime means by which social equality and justice are promoted. From this alternative perspective, governance is the process whereby public participation is encouraged through the development of inclusive policies that seek to integrate previously excluded constituencies and to extend and enhance educational opportunity.

This shift in perspective enables us to elaborate the central themes of the debate in a way that recognises the educational reforms of previous decades while looking forward to new possibilities and challenges. The terms of the debate on school governance are shifting from an exclusive and ideologically driven concern with choice, managerialism and decentralisation to an emphasis on new forms of participation and partnership at both the institutional and local levels. Those forms are as yet still emergent and fragmentary. Their presence, however, suggests that school governance is still very much in a process of transition. Indeed, the notion of 'governance' (as distinct from 'government') may itself denote a transitional phase; in which case an important task is to locate and seek to understand if not the endpoints of change, then the prevailing tendencies. The following three sections take on that task, while the final section explores some of the implications of the complex dynamics occurring within and around the field of school governance.

FROM PARENTAL 'CHOICE' TO PUBLIC PARTICIPATION

One of the ways in which the state has sought to preserve excellence without resorting to increased central government control is by exposing schools to the rigours of the market. Governance conceived as 'government without Government' has utilised 'choice' as a key mechanism in the institution of local markets, which (it is argued) allow educational excellence to win over educational mediocrity and force 'failing' schools to close through lack of parental support. The free exercise of parental choice, it is claimed, enables the best schools to become better and improves standards throughout the education system as a whole. Parental choice is thus one of the main means whereby central government has sought to control the quality of educational provision through the unmediated impact of market forces.

Choice, however, is not a fixed, evenly distributed category. Some individuals, families and groups have more 'choice' than others. The key factors affecting choice constitute a bundle of variables that can be usefully analysed in terms of social class. If, for example, you or your partner is employed, owns the house you and your family live in, and has the benefit of a university education, you are likely to enjoy the geographical and social mobility necessary to exercise considerable choice in respect of your children's schooling. If on the other hand, you and your partner are unemployed, are not home owners, and left school with few academic qualifications, the choice open to you in respect of your children's schooling is likely to be determined by what is locally available. If to these two scenarios are added gender and ethnicity as key determinants, then the uneven distribution of 'choice' becomes even more apparent. 'Choice' is loaded in respect of social and cultural origins and their attendant aspirations.

If the emphasis on 'choice' can in hindsight be seen to have sought excellence at the expense of equity, recent changes to the constitution and remit of school governing bodies (variously termed 'boards', 'trusts' or 'councils') have aimed to balance both sets of priorities. Almost all school governing bodies include a small number of professional educators (including, usually, the headteacher) who work in the school concerned. Increasingly, however, they also include a larger group of lay people who may or may not have direct connections with the school concerned. In New Zealand and Spain this lay group is entirely made up of parents, but in most countries (including the countries of the UK) other lay groups are also included. Overall, there is undoubtedly a stronger parental presence on school governing boards and a greater emphasis on governors appointed from the business community.

These changes are clearly intended to engage consumerist accountability: governing bodies no longer have vaguely defined powers of oversight; instead, they have specific powers relating to the monitoring and regulation of professional educators. This clarification of powers and responsibilities involves an explicit distinction between the management and governance of schooling, with the role of the headteacher (or principal) defined in terms of managerial responsibilities. While headteachers might be expected to advise the governing body, their task is to manage the school not govern it. The line of accountability from those who manage to those who govern is unequivocal.

Changes to the constitution and remit of governing bodies may, therefore, be seen as a significant shift in the balance of power between professional educators and the public. However, critics still point to the under-representation of certain groups on school governing bodies and to the lack of educational and political know-how among many of those who serve as governors. Governors, in other words, are likely to be drawn from a fairly narrow social spectrum and (in spite of the growth of training and induction programmes) to lack the detailed knowledge that might help them to withstand steers from either professional bodies, central government agencies or local pressure groups. These problems are compounded by the fact that governors 'represent' consumers only in a very broad and undifferentiated sense. For example, the system of representation operating in respect of school governance rarely takes account of the fact that consumers are differently positioned in respect of gender, ethnicity and social class. Where more sophisticated notions of representation are brought into play (for example, in New Zealand where minority ethnic groups are reflected in the composition of the boards of trustees), the different constituencies can be fully recognised and governing bodies be seen to have a vital role in democratising education.

The crucial question for those concerned with that democratic quest is the extent to which governors can, in the public interest, participate in the process of school governance. A recent study of school governance within the UK offered a somewhat gloomy response to that question:

> School governors do not fit neatly into any of the theories of citizenship. . . . There are vestiges to be found of the nineteenth century citizen; generally a man of property engaged in good work. . . . Chronologically this image of a school governor was superseded by one drawn from notions of participatory democracy. In the new managerialist perspective, self-development through political action is relegated in the pursuit of efficiency, economy and excellence, so that governing bodies are seen purely as conduits through which consumers can express their views and sanction professionals if they're seen to be failing.
>
> (Deem *et al.*, 1995, p. 62)

In order to judge the relevance of this chronology we need to explore more fully what exactly is involved in 'the new managerialist perspective'.

FROM 'MANAGERIALISM' TO PARTICIPATIVE MANAGEMENT

Although recent educational reforms have tended to sharpen the distinction between the management of schools and their governance, the latter has relied heavily on the reorientation of school management towards the goals of cost-effectiveness, increased efficiency and internal review. The shorthand for this reorientation is 'managerialism' or 'new public management'; terms that carry heavily pejorative overtones. In order to understand how the ideology of managerialism influences, and is influenced by, the procedures of school governance we need to understand both the positive and negative aspects of that ideology. 'Managerialism' is by no means as simple a construct as some of its critics would suggest.

School governance reforms require a shift in the culture of schooling. It is the task of management to effect that shift. Educational reform of school governance has, therefore, been complemented by reforms at the institutional level relating to the management of schools. A crucial element in these reforms is the introduction of new forms of accountability. Internal accountability involves institutional target-setting (with often rigorous taxonomies of process and outcome measures), together with monitoring procedures to ensure that specified targets are met. External accountability procedures include systems of school inspection that hold the promise (largely unfulfilled) of national and even international comparison in respect of learning outcomes and of objective judgements of school effectiveness.

The vocabulary of managerialism is rich with reference to 'customers', 'producers', 'consumers', 'empowerment', 'charters', 'excellence' and 'performance indicators'. Some of these keywords are simply reductive (students and parents, for example, are more than 'customers' and not simply 'consumers'); but others seem to offer new possibilities (parents and students, for example, might welcome a greater degree of 'empowerment' or the kind of public statement of rights and responsibilities that is suggested by the term 'charter'). The language of managerialism faces more than one way; one of the faces it presents looks towards increased participation as a condition of educational excellence.

Nevertheless, certain aspects of managerialism represent a significant loss in terms of the community dimension of schooling and in terms of close links with traditional catchment areas attached to schools. The emphasis on managerial efficiency and cost-effectiveness has had the paradoxical effect of forcing schools to be more inward-looking in respect of organisational structure and more outward-looking in respect of market forces. What can be lost from this equation is any sense of a privileged relationship between the school and the particular cultures and community interests from which the school students are drawn. Thus, efficiency, cost-effectiveness and competitive edge may be gained at the expense of community participation and involvement. The issue at stake is again that of excellence in relation to equity. To what extent does managerialism insist upon a view of educational excellence that excludes the full recognition of community interests, thereby reducing learning to a form of 'consumption' and parents and students to the status of 'customers'?

In addressing that question it should be acknowledged that, notwithstanding the emphasis on parent choice and increased participation, many parents feel they are not sufficiently involved in their children's formal education and that parental involvement in school governance is to be welcomed. A recent survey of over one thousand parents of secondary school pupils across the national regions of the UK found that an overwhelming majority agreed or strongly agreed with the statement 'Parents should be more involved in making decisions about what schools do' (50% agreed; 39% strongly agreed) and that an even stronger majority agreed or strongly agreed with the statement 'It is a good thing that parents are on school governing bodies' (55% agreed; 39% strongly agreed). Reflecting upon the relation between professional interest, parent participation and school management, the authors of the paper reporting the survey concluded that

> The issue of parental participation in particular must be regarded in the context of a generally, although not universally, passive public culture. The threat to the traditional professional in negotiating and mediating with parents is real. Nevertheless, the movement towards an increasingly assertive citizenship within society cannot be reversed. Rather, it needs to be reinforced. In the contexts we describe, a response to the conditions of civil society will need to be learnt. Not least because, for some, the lesson of civility in the face of cultural differences will be a difficult one. The task of managing difference will be complex . . . [and] will require an acknowledgement of the need for individuals within society to work with and through others.
>
> (Martin *et al.*, 1996, p. 226)

FROM INSTITUTIONAL SELF-ORGANISATION TO LOCAL PARTNERSHIP

The point at which the new governance of education and the new managerialism most closely converge is in their shared assumption that institutions work best when they are allowed to take responsibility for their own affairs. In some countries (notably England and New Zealand) this assumption has led to governing bodies (boards of trustees in New Zealand) being given almost sole responsibility for schools at the local level with virtually no intermediate tier between schools and central government. (States in Australia and the USA have also adopted systems of institutional self-organisation, although in the USA school districts retain nominal control.) Ironically, in those countries where decentralisation of this kind has been most enthusiastically pursued, there has been a correspondingly strong drive towards developing centrally controlled curriculum frameworks.

The devolved school budget is an important strand within this contradictory combination of elements and provides a significant interface between those with responsibility for governing schools and those with responsibility for managing them. Each has had to assume new and important responsibilities in relation to the setting of budgetary targets and the monitoring of expenditure. Typically, headteachers (or principals) are now responsible for the overall financial management of their schools, while governing bodies are publicly accountable in respect of the fulfilment of those responsibilities. In effect this means that governing bodies are likely to spend a considerable amount of time discussing budgets. Since the resource allocation to schools is dependent upon levels of intake (the more students there are in a school, the more that school has to spend), governors of most schools are also likely to be discussing these budgetary concerns in relation to student recruitment. For some schools with falling rolls such discussions and their outcomes may be a matter of institutional survival.

Two consequences follow from this preoccupation with financial viability and effectiveness. First, it is likely to leave less time for the serious discussion by school governors of educational ends and purposes and of matters relating to the school curriculum and teaching programmes. Since governors are in the main lay persons who may have little knowledge or experience of financial management, discussion on this topic may be particularly time-consuming and is likely to rely heavily on whatever expertise is available (including that of the headteacher). This not only calls into question the independence of school governing bodies on matters relating to financial management. It also highlights the irony whereby lay governors may, because of the pressure of other priorities, be failing to contribute in the one area where they are supremely qualified to do so: the continuing discussion regarding the ends and purposes of education as these relate to local circumstance and need. On the other hand, of course, there is a logic to minimising the discussion of educational ends and purposes when these are already fixed within a centrally controlled curriculum framework.

Second, the preoccupation with financial viability and effectiveness is likely to minimise the opportunities for discussion between governors of different schools. Indeed, since in many cases schools are competing for student placements in order to ensure their institutional viability, such discussions might be judged by the schools themselves to be counter-productive. The effect is to isolate school governing bodies and to accentuate the lack of any planning of educational provision across schools. The possibility of a concerted approach by schools to locally shared problems and needs is thereby greatly reduced. Financial strategies are developed at the institutional level rather than regionally.

This lack of regional planning may be offset by the creation of regionally elected boards. From the free-marketeer's perspective, this return to an intermediate level of government may be seen as a betrayal. Increasingly, however, the need for some mediating influence between institutional autonomy and market forces is being recognised. Regional boards provide such an influence in that they allow, and indeed encourage, institutions to plan with each other's needs in mind and with a clear sense of the overall needs of the localities involved. Excellence, from this perspective, relates to very different sets of needs and aptitudes; and equity denotes, not a bland 'sameness' of provision, but a differentiated response based upon a clear recognition of these differences.

Institutional self-organisation need not imply self-interested autonomy. It can imply an openness to other institutional trajectories, a willingness to seek collaborative solutions to shared problems, a determination to argue beyond the point of disagreement. Governance, under these changed circumstances, would require a cross-institutional perspective: a strong sense of how schools might complement one another. Some intermediate or regional forum located as a key element within the process of governance is therefore highly desirable.

The stronger, more self-confident and self-directing school is to be welcomed. It satisfies both the political aspirations of the period and the professional view, hard won from research and curriculum development, that to be effective schools need a good deal of autonomy. But that is not to argue that they can function effectively in isolation, still less in an isolated but competitive milieu. . . . Seen in this wide context of the nature of human learning, the place of families and professional teachers, and the social and economic imperatives now at work, there must be a strong argument in favour of providing services and support for schools on an area basis. . . . The local body should be democratically accountable because that would both sharpen and help to discharge some of its deeper purposes. Whether it is a single-purpose authority or part of a multipurpose authority, whether it is directly elected or appointed by those elected locally (issues which have seemed of primary importance in the past) are now much less important than that an intermediate tier of educational government should exist so that our future does not come to depend on the monolithic and distant control of government on the one hand and the unavoidably narrow and self-concerned institution of the school on the other.

(Tomlinson, 1994, p. 18)

In at least some of the countries that have embraced institutional self-organisation as a democratic ideal, this projected turn to an intermediate tier of governance may be seen as a return to some of the structures of local government that were dismantled in the heady days of New Right ascendancy.

THE KEY PLAYERS

Governance, to return to an earlier point, may be just a transitional phase of a complex process, the ends and purposes of which cannot be fully determined. This chapter has, nevertheless, sought to uncover some of the main tendencies within this process: the tendency towards increased public participation; towards more participative and integrative forms of educational management; towards new partnerships which allow for planned provision across institutions. If these are the dominant tendencies, then their impact on *professional educators, school governors* and *parents* is likely to be considerable. This final section focuses on each of these groups in turn with a view to exploring the implications of local government reform for some of the key players involved.

Professional educators will need to become increasingly outward-looking in their relationships with parents, the wider public and other professional groups. They will need to work closely with their governors, informing them when necessary (on technical and specialist matters) and recognising the importance of their experience and background (on matters relating to local needs and priorities). Headteachers (principals), in particular, will need to be sensitive to the crucial distinction between management and governance and the importance of supporting governing bodies while recognising and respecting their powers. Implicit in this professional reorientation is a new kind of professional ethic based upon accountability, openness and reciprocity. Professionalism will no longer aspire to the status of a self-regulating club (based, for example, on the principles of professional autonomy and professional loyalty), but will denote a principled association (based, for example, on the practice of community partnership and public service). Professional educators will see their *educational* role as complementary to that of parents and, potentially, to a wide range of community-based developments.

School governors (trustees) will require training and support together with a recognition of their public role as civic leaders. For their own part they will need to take seriously both the responsibilities associated with their office and the conditions necessary for the fulfilment of those responsibilities. Those conditions include an informed understanding of relevant educational issues, the opportunity for open dialogue with professional educators and school managers, and the development of a special and formalised (in its consultative procedures) relationship with parents. Again, the implicit ethic is one of accountability, openness and reciprocity. Governors will be accountable to the public through their strong links with parents and other interested parties in the local community. They will work with professional educators within their own schools and liaise closely with governors in neighbouring schools to ensure excellence and equity of educational provision.

Parents will have an increasingly important role to play in the education of their children. That role will be recognised through close links with boards of governors and, in particular, with their elected representatives on those boards. In their relationship with professional educators, parents will be seen as complementary educators working in partnership with their children's teachers; in their relationship with their board of governors, they will be seen as key constituents to be consulted and involved as fully as possible in discussions regarding educational priorities, local needs, and the ends and purposes of education. This level of parental involvement will be seen not as a middle-class phenomenon (a characteristic, that is, of schools with a critical mass of aspiring, relatively affluent parents), but as a necessary condition of educational excellence in all schools (including those located in economically depressed areas with high levels of unemployment and where existing employment is limited in the main to working-class occupations or to casual labour).

CONCLUSION

The conjectures outlined above are based on the assumption of a shift away from educational excellence, perceived as a scarce resource for which schools must compete, towards a view of educational excellence as a shared aspiration which becomes achievable through increased participation and partnership. Governance denotes a complex set of practices and priorities which are often in tension and sometimes at odds with one another. A dominant trend, nevertheless, is towards patterns of school governance that recognise local needs, in respect of educational excellence, and that recognise, also, the extent to which an adequate response to these needs requires, as a necessary condition of excellence, a middle tier of planned resource allocation based upon equitable principles.

SELECT BIBLIOGRAPHY

Arnott, M. and Raab, C (eds) (2000) *The Governance of Schools: Comparative Studies of Devolved Management*. London: Routledge.

Ball, S. (1994) *Education Reform: A Critical and Post-Structuralist Approach*. Buckingham: Open University Press.

Cusack, B. (1994) 'Future shock: prospects from New Zealand'. In A. Thody (ed.) *School Governors – Leaders or Followers?* London: Longman, 99–113.

Deem, R., Brehoy, K. and Heath, S. (1995) *Active Citizenship and the Governing of Schools*. Buckingham: Open University Press.

Gamage, D. (1994) 'School governance: Australian perspectives'. In A. Thody (ed.) *School Governors – Leaders or Followers?* London: Longman, 114–127.

Martin, J., Ranson, R., McKeown, P. and Nixon, J. (1996) 'School governance for the civil society: Redefining the boundary between schools and parents', *Local Government Studies*, 22, 4 (Winter), 210–228.

Nixon, J., Martin, J., McKeown, P. and Ranson, S. 'Towards a learning profession: changing codes of occupational practice within the "new management" of education', *British Journal of Sociology of Education*, 21, 1, 5–28.

Radnor, H. A., Ball, S. J. and Vincent, C. (1997) 'Whither democratic accountability in education? An investigation into headteachers' perspectives on accountability in the 1990s with reference to their relationships with their LEAs and governors', *Research Papers in Education*, 12 (2), 205–222.

Ranson, S., Martin, J. and Nixon, J. (1997) 'A learning democracy for co-operative action', *Oxford Review of Education*, 23 (1), 117–131.

Tomlinson, J. (1994) 'The case for an intermediate tier'. In S. Ranson and J. Tomlinson (eds) *School Co-operation: New Forms of Local Governance*. London: Longman, 1–18.

18

SCHOOL EFFECTIVENESS AND SCHOOL IMPROVEMENT
Past, present and future

David Reynolds and Charles Teddlie

INTRODUCTION

School Effectiveness Research (SER) has emerged from virtual total obscurity to a now central position in the educational discourse that is taking place within many countries. From the position 30 years ago that 'schools make no difference' that was assumed to be the conclusions of the Coleman *et al.* (1966) and Jencks *et al.* (1972) studies, there is now a widespread assumption internationally that schools affect children's development, that there are observable regularities in the schools that 'add value', and that the task of educational policies is to improve all schools in general and the more ineffective schools in particular by transmission of this knowledge to educational practitioners.

Overall, there have been three major strands of SER:

- *School Effects Research*, which is studies of the scientific properties of school effects evolving from input–output studies to current research utilising multilevel models;
- *Effective Schools Research* which is research concerned with the processes of effective schooling, evolving from case studies of outlier schools through to contemporary studies merging qualitative and quantitative methods in the simultaneous study of the class and the school;
- *School Improvement Research*, which examines the processes whereby schools can be changed, utilising increasingly sophisticated models that have gone beyond simple applications of school effectiveness knowledge to sophisticated 'multiple-lever' models.

In this chapter we aim to outline the historical development of these three areas of the field over the past 30 years, looking at the developments in the United States where the field originated and then moving on to look at the United Kingdom, The Netherlands and Australia, where growth in SER began later but has been rapid. We also attempt to conduct an analysis of the ways in which the various phases of development of the field are internationally linked with the changing perceptions of the educational system that have been evident within advanced industrial societies over these last 30 years. We then attempt to conduct an 'intellectual audit' of the school effectiveness and improvement knowledge base and its various strengths and weaknesses within various countries, as a prelude to outlining in our final section what are likely to be the cutting-edge areas for the development of the field over the next decade.

SER IN THE UNITED STATES

There are four overlapping stages that SER has been through in the USA. Stage 1 was the period in which economically driven input–output studies predominated. These studies focused on inputs such as school resource variables (e.g. per pupil expenditure) and student background characteristics (student socio-economic status or SES) to predict school outputs. In these studies, school outcomes were limited to student achievement on standardised tests. The results of these studies in the USA (Coleman *et al.*, 1966; Jencks *et al.*, 1972) indicated that differences in children's achievement were more strongly associated with societally determined family SES than with potentially malleable, school-based resource variables. As noted by many reviewers (e.g. Averch *et al.*, 1971; Brookover *et al.*, 1979; Miller, 1983), these early economic and sociological studies of school effects did not include adequate measures of school socio-psychological climate and other classroom/school process variables, and their exclusion contributed to the underestimation of the magnitude of school effects.

Stage 2 of SER in the USA involved studies that were conducted to dispute the results of Coleman and Jencks. Some researchers studied schools that were doing exceptional jobs of educating students from very poor backgrounds and sought to describe the processes ongoing in those schools. In a classic study from this period, Weber (1971) conducted extensive case studies of four low-SES inner-city schools characterised by high achievement at the third-grade level. His research emphasised the importance of the actual processes ongoing at schools (e.g. strong leadership, high expectations, good atmosphere and a careful evaluation of pupil progress). Several methodological advances occurred in the American research during this decade of the 1970s, such as the inclusion of more sensitive measures of classroom input, the development of socio-psychological scales to measure school processes, and the utilisation of more sensitive outcome measures.

The foremost proponent of the equity ideal during the next Stage 3 of SER in the USA (the late 1970s through the mid-1980s) was Ron Edmonds, who took the results of his own research (Edmonds 1978, 1979a, 1979b) and that of others (e.g. Lezotte and Bancroft, 1985; Weber, 1971) to make a powerful case for the creation of 'effective schools for the urban poor'. Edmonds and his colleagues were no longer interested in just describing effective schools: they also wished to create effective schools, especially for the urban poor. The five-factor model generated through the effective schools research had included the following factors:

- strong instructional leadership from the principal;
- a pervasive and broadly understood instructional focus;
- a safe and orderly school learning environment or 'climate';
- high expectations for achievement from all students;
- the use of student achievement test data for evaluating programme and school success.

The aim was to incorporate these effectiveness characteristics into improvement programmes, but this equity orientation, with its emphasis on school improvement and its sampling biases towards the study of low-SES schools, led to predictable responses from the educational research community in the early to mid-1980s. The hailstorm of criticism (e.g. Cuban, 1983, 1984; Firestone and Herriot, 1982; Good and Brophy, 1986; Purkey and Smith, 1983; Rowan, 1984; Rowan *et al.*, 1983) aimed at the reform orientation of those pursuing the equity ideal in SER had the effect of paving the way for the more sophisticated studies of SER, which used more defensible sampling and analysis strategies.

The new, more methodologically sophisticated Stage 4 of SER began with the first context studies (Hallinger and Murphy, 1986; Teddlie *et al.*, 1985, 1990) which explored the factors that were producing greater effectiveness in middle-class schools, in suburban schools and in secondary schools. These studies explicitly explored the differences in school effects that occurred across different school contexts, instead of focusing on one particular context. The new value-base was inclusive, since it involved the study of schools serving all types of students in all types of contexts, and emphasised school improvement across all of those contexts.

SER IN THE UNITED KINGDOM

Early work came mostly from a medical and medico-social environment, with Power (1967; Power *et al.*, 1972) showing differences in delinquency rates between schools and Gath (1977) showing differences in child guidance referral rates. Early work by Reynolds (1976, 1982) into the characteristics of the learning environments of apparently differentially effective secondary schools, using group-based, cross-sectional data on intakes and outcomes, was followed by work by Rutter *et al.* (1979) on differences between schools measured on the outcomes of academic achievement, delinquency, attendance and levels of behavioural problems, utilising this time a cohort design that involved the matching of individual pupil data at intake to school and at age 16.

Subsequent work in the 1980s included:

1 'Value-added' comparisons of educational authorities on their academic outcomes (Department of Education and Science, 1983, 1984; Gray and Jesson, 1987; Gray *et al.*, 1984; Woodhouse and Goldstein, 1988; Willms, 1987)
2 Comparisons of 'selective' school systems with comprehensive or 'all ability' systems (Gray *et al.*, 1983; Reynolds *et al.*, 1987; Steedman, 1980, 1983)
3 Work into the scientific properties of school effects, such as size (Gray, 1981, 1982; Gray *et al.*, 1986), the differential effectiveness of different academic subunits or departments (Fitz-Gibbon, 1985; Fitz-Gibbon *et al.*, 1989; Willms and Cuttance, 1985), contextual or 'balance' effects (Willms, 1985, 1986) and the differential effectiveness of schools upon pupils of different characteristics (Aitken and Longford, 1986; Nuttall *et al.*, 1989)
4 Small-scale studies that focused upon usually one outcome and attempted to relate this to various intra-school processes. This was particularly interesting in the cases of disruptive behaviour (Galloway, 1983) and some Scottish studies of disciplinary problems (McLean, 1987; McManus, 1987; Maxwell, 1987).

Towards the end of the 1980s, two landmark studies appeared, concerning school effectiveness in primary schools (Mortimore *et al.*, 1988) and in secondary schools (Smith and Tomlinson, 1989). The Mortimore study was notable for the wide range of outcomes on which schools were assessed (including mathematics, reading, writing, attendance, behaviour and attitudes to school), for the collection of a wide range of data upon school processes and, for the first time in British school effectiveness research, for a focus upon classroom processes. The Smith and Tomlinson (1989) study was notable for the large differences shown in academic effectiveness between schools, with for certain groups of pupils the variation in examination results between similar individuals in different schools amounting to up to a quarter of the total variation in examination results.

Work in the United Kingdom in the 1990s remained only partially situated within the same intellectual traditions and at the same intellectual cutting edge as in the 1980s. Contemporary areas of importance include research on:

1 Stability over time of school effects (Goldstein *et al.*, 1993; Gray *et al.*, 1995; Thomas *et al.*, 1997)
2 Consistency of school effects on different outcomes – for example, in terms of different subjects or different outcome domains such as cognitive/affective (Goldstein *et al.*, 1993; Sammons *et al.*, 1993)
3 Differential effects of schools for different groups of students, for example, of different ethnic or socio-economic backgrounds or with different levels of prior attainment (Goldstein *et al.*, 1993; Jesson and Gray, 1991; Sammons *et al.*, 1993)
4 The relative continuity of the effect of school sectors over time (Goldstein, 1995; Sammons *et al.*, 1995a)
5 The existence or size of school effects (Daly, 1991; Gray *et al.*, 1990; Thomas *et al.*, 1997), where there are strong suggestions that the size of primary school effects may be greater than those of secondary schools (Sammons *et al.*, 1993, 1995b)
6 Departmental differences in educational effectiveness (Fitz-Gibbon, 1992). The ALIS (A Level Information System) method of performance monitoring of Fitz-Gibbon and her colleagues has been expanded to include public examinations at age 16, a scheme known as YELLIS (Year Eleven Information System), and has been also expanded into the primary school sector with PIPS (Performance Indicators in Primary Schools).

Additional recent foci of interest have included:

1 Work at the school effectiveness/special educational needs interface, studying how schools vary in their definitions, labelling practices and teacher/pupil interactions with such children (Brown *et al.*, 1996)
2 Work on the potential 'context specificity' of effective schools' characteristics internationally, as in the International School Effectiveness Research Project (ISERP), a nine nation study that involves schools in the United Kingdom, the United States, The Netherlands, Canada, Taiwan, Hong Kong, Norway, Australia and the Republic of Ireland (Reynolds *et al.*, 1994, 1995; Creemers *et al.*, 1996). Reviews of cross-national studies have also been conducted (Reynolds and Farrell, 1996) and indeed the entire issue of international country effects is a particularly live one in the United Kingdom currently
3 The 'site' of ineffective schools, the exploration of their characteristics and the policy

implications that flow from these (Barber, 1995; Reynolds, 1996; Stoll and Myers, 1997)

4 The possibility of routinely assessing the 'value-added' of schools using already available data (Fitz-Gibbon and Tymms, 1996), rather than by utilisation of specially collected data

5 The characteristics of 'improving' schools and those factors that are associated with successful change over time, especially important at the policy level since existing school effectiveness research gives only the characteristics of schools that have *become* effective (this work is being undertaken by Gray, Hopkins and Reynolds)

6 The description of the characteristics of effective departments (Harris *et al.*, 1995; Sammons *et al.*, 1997).

Further reviews of the British literature are available in Gray and Wilcox (1995), Mortimore (1991), Reynolds *et al.* (1989, 1994), Reynolds and Cuttance (1992), Rutter (1983) and Sammons *et al.* (1995a).

SER IN THE NETHERLANDS

Although instructionally based educational research has been a well-established speciality in The Netherlands since the late 1970s, SER did not begin in volume until the mid-1980s, although research on teacher effectiveness, school organisation and the educational careers of students from the very varied selective educational systems of The Netherlands had all been a focus of past interest (historical reviews are available in Creemers and Knuver [1989] and Scheerens [1992]).

Table 18.1 presents an overview of existing Dutch school effectiveness studies in primary and secondary education, and shows the total number of positive and negative significant correlations between educational processes and educational attainment.

When considering the factors that 'work' in Dutch education, the conclusion from Table 18.1 must be that the conventional effective schools model is not confirmed by the data. The two conditions from the American 'five-factor' theory thought to be effectiveness-enhancing that are found to have a significant positive association with the effectiveness criteria in primary education (structured teaching and evaluation practices), are found in no more than 5 out of 29 studies. Moreover, 'other' factors predominate both in primary and secondary education as being associated with effectiveness. It is also striking that if an effect of instructional leadership and differentiation is found, it is often negative.

SER IN AUSTRALIA

Australians were initially reluctant to become involved in SER largely because of concern about standardised testing procedures. The emphasis upon student performance on standardised achievement tests as the key measurement of an 'effective' school, as proposed by Edmonds (1979a, 1979b) was met with various levels of scepticism and there were a number of Australian researchers such as Angus (1986a, 1986b), Ashenden (1987) and Banks (1988)

Table 18.1 Number of Dutch studies in which certain school and instructional conditions correlated significantly with outcome variables, after control for pupils' background characteristics

	Primary level		Secondary level	
	Positive association	Negative association	Positive association	Negative association
Structured teaching/feedback	5		1	
Teacher experience	3	1		1
Instructional leadership		2	1	
Orderly climate	2		3	1
Student evaluation	5		0	
Differentiation		2	0	
Whole-class teaching	3		0	
Achievement orientation	4		4	
Team stability/co-operation		3		3
Time/homework	4		4	
Other variables	16		8	
Average between school variance	9		13.5	
Number of studies	29		13	

Note: Not all variables mentioned in the rows were measured in each and every study

who clearly indicated their concern that a concentration on effectiveness as it had been originally defined by Edmonds meant a diminution of concern about other equally relevant educational issues such as equality, participation and social justice.

There was some early research that considered issues of school effectiveness. Caldwell and Misko (1983), Caldwell and Spinks (1986), Mellor and Chapman (1984), Hyde and Werner (1984), and Silver and Moyle (1985) all identified characteristics of school effectiveness, but it could be argued that these studies were related more to school improvement issues than to school effectiveness research.

A number of SER studies have occurred in the last few years. These have considered a variety of issues including the concept of school effectiveness (Banks, 1992; Townsend, 1994), the concept of school quality, factors affecting student reading achievement (Rowe, 1991; Rowe and Rowe, 1992), the characteristics of schools in which students perform well in both mathematics and reading and in which there are positive student attitudes and high levels of parent participation (Rowe et al., 1994), the relationship between school development planning and effectiveness (Davis and Caust, 1994), effectiveness and school self-management (Caldwell and Spinks, 1988, 1992), a consideration of the relationship between classroom effectiveness and school effectiveness (Rowe et al., 1993, 1994, 1995), the effect of restructuring on school effectiveness (Townsend, 1995a, 1995b) and a longitudinal study of the unique role of principals in the restructuring activity (Caldwell et al., 1994; Thomas et al., 1995a, 1995b).

SER AND INTERNATIONAL EDUCATIONAL CHANGE

Our survey of different countries so far in this chapter shows clear trends across time, both for the individual countries surveyed and for the SER enterprise across countries. The early SER studies in the United States and the United Kingdom reflected, in their concentration upon physical and material inputs, the existence of a paradigm which saw access to the 'material', financially determined world of schooling as the key to improving both equality of education opportunity and the overall 'excellence' of school outcomes. This 'liberal' belief in the value of education was also linked with an essentially positivistic, quantitatively orientated methodology that was utilised to generate 'truths' about education, which were then used to generate curriculum and organisational reforms that were implemented in a 'top-down' manner in schools.

The failure of this liberal dream to generate much progress in both excellence and equity terms generated a major intellectual reaction, with the next phase of school effectiveness research reinforcing a powerful belief that 'schools make no difference'. Instead of a search for quantitative positivistic truths, educational research (now doubting the validity of the truths that had failed to deliver improved outcomes and systemic reform) in the 1970s celebrated with rich, detailed, qualitatively orientated case studies of schools and classrooms. SER too, as we have noted above, increasingly involved qualitative case studies of effective schools, and school improvement both in the United States and in Europe entered a phase that gave primacy to practitioner beliefs as the levers to generate school change.

From the late 1980s onwards, the changing economic and social contexts within advanced industrial societies such as the USA, the United Kingdom, Australia and The Netherlands all combined to shift educational reform, and the SER paradigm, to centre-stage. The economic pressures from emerging Pacific Rim economies, the need again to address issues of equity that had been brought into sharp focus by the emerging 'underclass' that appeared to be differentiating itself from mainstream society, and the revival of interest in educational policy matters that came with the arrival of a new generation of educational researchers who had not been intellectually and personally 'burnt' by the failure of the 1960s liberal dream, all combined to increase governmental and educational system interest in SER.

SER itself by the late 1980s and early 1990s had additionally found high levels of professional self-confidence. Groups of persons who were marginal to their national educational research communities organised their own professional association and their own journal, and rapidly developed their own widely accepted definition of 'normal science'. In the United Kingdom, school effectiveness researchers advise government, while the British Labour Party education programme for the 1997 election reflected similar involvement. The Australian Federal Government initiated a major national enquiry on 'What makes schools effective?' in 1991, and ongoing research into teacher and school effectiveness is central to educational policies in many Australian states (e.g. Hill [1997] in Victoria). In The Netherlands, school effectiveness researchers began directly to contribute to national education policy, as in the case of the National Commission on Special Education. Even in the USA, where SER had intellectually, practically and politically 'boomed and busted' in the mid-1980s as we noted earlier, the growth of contextually sensitive SER and of closer links between the SER and the school improvement communities, resulted in a renaissance of SER by the mid-1990s, symbolised by the meeting of the International Congress for School Effectiveness and Improvement in Memphis in 1997.

It will be obvious from the content of this chapter that SER has changed, evolved and markedly improved in both quality and quantity over the last 30 years. As it moved intellectually in the USA from the early, simplistic focus upon input–output analysis to more recent, contextually specific formulations, and as it moved geographically from its original homeland in the USA to the present situation where perhaps ten times more studies are being conducted outside the USA than inside it, it is clear that there are culturally or country-specific contributions that are distinctive.

Australia shows evidence of:

- close links between school effectiveness and school improvement;
- work on the conceptual basis of school effectiveness and school quality;
- a close relationship between effectiveness/improvement and educational policy, with national policies that clearly relate to and draw on these knowledge bases.

By contrast, The Netherlands shows a flourishing, quantitatively sophisticated research base which strangely seems to be relatively unused within practice. It also shows:

- continued context specificity, with many of the most validated school effectiveness factors from outside The Netherlands failing to be replicated within;
- sophisticated theoretical formulation, and multiple-level research on classrooms and schools;
- continued progress in conceptualising and linking theoretically the instructional *and* school levels, together with recognition of the need for the adoption of contingency models that might explain the failure of many school effectiveness factors to 'travel' in Dutch contexts.

The United Kingdom shows:

- considerable methodological sophistication, with now axiomatic use of multilevel modelling, cohort studies and multiple-intake measures including that of student achievement. Britain has also been at the forefront of the development of multilevel statistical modelling (Goldstein, 1995);
- limited attempts to analyse instructional processes combined with sophisticated work at the school level, building upon the earlier sociology of education;
- use of multiple measures of outcomes;
- a historic 'split' between effectiveness researchers and improvement practitioners, only recently fading with the arrival of 'blended' programmes which utilise the knowledge bases of both school effectiveness and school improvement in carefully evaluated 'experiments of nature';
- a historic inability to investigate the possible context specificity of effective schools' characteristics because of sample selection being mostly from disadvantaged communities.

Finally, the USA shows:

- contextually sensitive effectiveness research, small in quantity, but increasingly conducted within a 'mixed methods' tradition;

- considerable progress in describing and analysing both teacher and school effects together;
- an emergence of a large number of school improvement orientated programmes which incorporate rigorous evaluation of effects;
- the existence of a wide variety of fields which are school effects related.

THE FUTURE OF SCHOOL EFFECTIVENESS RESEARCH

Several authors have speculated upon the future of school effectiveness research (e.g. Good and Brophy, 1986; Mortimore, 1991; Reynolds, 1992; Scheerens and Bosker, 1997; Teddlie and Stringfield, 1993) over the past decade. However, owing to rapid developments in the field, both in terms of methodology and substantive findings, the areas identified in need of further research ten years ago or even five years ago are either no longer relevant, or have been significantly reconceptualised. We outline here a number of areas where 'cutting-edge' advances may be made over the next decade.

THE USE OF MULTIPLE OUTCOME MEASURES

This issue has been discussed by many since the 1970s (e.g. Good and Brophy, 1986; Levine and Lezotte, 1990; Rutter, 1983; Rutter et al., 1979; Sammons et al., 1996), with most commenting that multiple criteria for school effectiveness are needed. Critics have noted that schools may not have consistent effects across different criteria, and that to use one criterion (typically academic achievement) is not adequate for ascertaining the true effectiveness status of a school. It is also now widely recognised that multiple outcomes force the development of more sensitive explorations than are likely with restricted measures, since the pattern of why school and teacher factors are associated with some outcomes but not others (as in Mortimore et al. [1988] for example) is exactly the kind of scientific dissonance that is needed for creative theorising.

Within the past decade, researchers have been making progress in this area and studies from the UK have continued to compare different criteria for school effectiveness beyond academic achievement scores. These comparisons have included academic versus affective/social, different measures of attitudes, different measures of behaviour and different measures of self-concept (Sammons et al., 1996). These results and studies point the way towards research that utilises multiple criteria in the determination of school effectiveness status. Guidelines as to 'good practice' should include the following:

- The use of varied measures of the effectiveness of schooling, including academic achievement, attitudes (towards self, and towards others), and behaviour.
- The use of measures that are sensitive to the mission of schools in the twenty-first century. For instance, measures of perceived racism may be important indicators of the effectiveness of schooling in some contexts (e.g. Fitz-Gibbon, 1996). Equal opportunities concerns are important in schools in many countries, yet equal opportunities-orientated behaviours and attitudes are rarely used to assess school effectiveness. 'Learning to learn'

or 'knowledge acquisition' skills are widely argued to be essential in the information age, yet the achievement tests that are utilised continue to emphasise student ability to recapitulate existing knowledge.

STUDYING THE THIRD DIMENSION OF SCHOOLING (RELATIONSHIP PATTERNS)

A new area of study has emerged in SER over the past few years: the relationship patterns that exist within staff and within student groups. This relational component constitutes the third dimension of schooling, joining the more frequently studied organisational and cultural components (Reynolds, 1992). There are three reasons why the relational component of schooling has not been featured much in SER until now. First, relational patterns of teachers and students are difficult to measure, since questionnaires and interviews regarding school relationships may constitute 'reactive' instruments susceptible to socially desirable responses (e.g. Webb *et al.*, 1981). Second, the interpersonal relations of teachers and of students have been difficult to conceptualise and analyse due to the complexity of interactions within such social groups. Third, there is a common perception that interpersonal relations within a school, especially among staff members, are very difficult to change, so researchers in the school improvement area have not been particularly interested in studying these patterns of relationships until recently.

The recent realisation of the importance of the relational dimension, especially in the case of interpersonal relations among staff members (Reynolds, 1991, 1996), has been due to three factors. First, empirical work in the USA (e.g. Durland, 1996; Durland and Teddlie, 1996; Teddlie and Kochan, 1991) that has successfully linked the effectiveness levels of schools with their different patterns of interpersonal relations among staff members. Second, more speculative work done both in the school effectiveness and school improvement traditions in the UK and the USA that has linked ineffective schools with the presence of dysfunctional relations among staff members (e.g. Reynolds, 1992, 1996; Myers, 1995; Stoll, 1995; Stoll and Fink, 1996; Stoll *et al.*, 1996; Teddlie and Stringfield, 1993). Reynolds (1996, p. 154) has characterised these 'grossly dysfunctional relationships' in such schools thus: 'The presence of numerous personality clashes, feuds, personal agendas and fractured interpersonal relationships within the staff group, which operate . . . to make rational decision-making a very difficult process'. These dysfunctional relationships arise through the unique socio-psychological history of the school (Teddlie and Stringfield, 1993) and have a tendency to continue unless drastic changes (planned or not) occur. Often these relationships manifest themselves in the generation of sharply delineated subcultures (Stoll and Fink, 1996) or cliques within the school.

Third, some of those in the school improvement tradition have recently found that the existence of relational 'shadows' or 'ghosts' of the past has had a considerable influence on attempts at staff professional development (Hopkins *et al.*, 1994).

Further research in this area could develop in several ways. More work needs to be done on more refined descriptions of effective and ineffective schools in terms of sociometric indices and sociograms. It is to be hoped that this work will lead us to sets of prototypical sociometric indices and sociograms for differentially effective schools. Longitudinal studies of sociometric indices and sociograms could prove useful in describing how social relations change over time (e.g. setting the sociograms 'in motion' over time) and in showing whether or not those changes are associated with changes in effectiveness status. Sociometric indices and sociograms should also be developed for students within classrooms. These data may be considered as additional school effectiveness indicators, if one assumes that effective schools should be fostering positive relationships among students. It may also be that there are different student relational patterns in more effective classes and schools than in less effective.

EXPANDING THE STUDY OF CONTEXT VARIABLES

The introduction of context variables into SER has had a large impact on all three strands within the field (school effects, effective schools and school improvement). The consideration of contextual variation in SER has also led to increased sophistication in theory development (e.g. Creemers and Scheerens, 1994; Scheerens, 1992; Scheerens and Creemers, 1989; Slater and Teddlie, 1992) as theorists have explicitly taken into account the impact that different levels of a context variable can have on school effects and processes associated with them. These 'contextually sensitive' theories of school effectiveness have incorporated tenets of contingency theory (e.g. Mintzberg, 1979; Owens, 1987) as a framework from which to interpret results from SER. Contingency theory purports to explain why certain school effectiveness variables 'travel' across levels of context, while others do not. For instance, the failure of the well-known principal leadership effect on student achievement in The Netherlands (e.g. van de Grift, 1989, 1990) is a good illustration of a school effectiveness variable that did not 'travel' from one country to another due to the differences in country contexts.

The study of context in SER is also beginning to have an impact on theories of school improvement, because school improvers realise now that there aren't 'silver bullets' that always lead to school improvement. Instead, contextually sensitive models for school improvement with 'multiple levers' have emerged as studies have demonstrated that what works to change school processes can vary to a large degree by context factors such as SES of catchment area, school effectiveness level or schools improvement 'trend line'. Several context variables (i.e. SES of student body, community type, grade phase and governance structure) are now established to have a 'main effect' upon school effects and the processes that accompany them.

While the impact of context variables in SER is now well established, there are several research areas where additional work would be useful. First, the variation in context could be expanded by the enhanced use of 'nation' as a context variable. However, the enhanced range of educational factors and cultural contexts that this produces may be potentially damaging if study leads to the simplistic, direct import of 'what works' without analysis of cultural differences. The study of the interaction between educational and context variables is clearly of considerable importance.

Second, researchers should enhance the variation in context factors where possible. Considering international studies, it would be very beneficial to have more developing societies in comparative studies of SER. It would be interesting to determine the magnitude of school effects for these countries compared to 'First World' countries using a common methodology, and it would be also interesting to expand further our knowledge of their 'context specificity' in effectiveness factors which was mentioned earlier.

Third, other new context variables should be added to SER designs. For instance, the region of a country could have a large impact in some countries. In the USA, for instance, it could be argued that school effects and the processes associated with them may be quite different in the Northeast, the Midwest, the South, and the West. In the UK, there are considerable historical differences and cultural differences between regions (Reynolds, 1992), such as the tradition of sons following their fathers into mining or industrial employment in the Northeast, compared with the Welsh tradition of encouraging the 'escape' of children from the prospects of such employment, both of which differential contextual responses to disadvantage could be argued to have considerable implications for 'what works' within schools. Another example concerns grade level: pre-school and university could be added as additional levels of this context variable.

ANALYSING RANGE WITHIN SCHOOLS AND CLASSROOMS

There are some interesting hints in the recent literature that the range or variation in school and teacher factors may be important determinants of outcomes and effectiveness additionally to the average levels scored on the factors themselves. The Louisiana School Effectiveness Studies (see Table 18.2) mentioned earlier noted the reduced range evident in effective schools and in their teachers within lesson behaviours (Teddlie and Stringfield, 1993). The International School Effectiveness Research Project (ISERP) of Creemers *et al.* (1996) also found that successful and educationally effective countries possessed a more homogeneous set of teachers and schools, and that effective schools in all of the nine countries participating evidenced predictability and consistency in their organisational processes both over time and between organisational members at a point in time. Interesting speculations about consistency, constancy and cohesion, and the power of these factors to control young people socially, have been offered by Creemers (1994) and Reynolds (1996). In a similar way, Murphy (1992) has talked about the symbolic, cultural and organisational 'tightness' of effective school organisations and, by implication, the looseness and range of ineffective organisations.

From school improvement has come a recognition that reliability or fidelity of implementation (i.e. lack of range) is necessary to ensure improved educational outcomes from school improvement programmes. Indeed, the growing recognition that school improvement can generate enhanced range (and lower its potential effectiveness) because the educational ceiling of competent persons/schools improves much faster than the floor of less competent persons/schools, seems to be a powerful face valid explanation for the consistently disappointing effects of historic school improvement that has been unconcerned with 'range', viewing it as a necessary part of teacher professional development.

It is arguable, though, that the influence of the range of school and teacher factors may have become more important of late, since many of the more historically consistent influences upon child development such as the family, the community, the mass media and the wider society have all become more heterogeneous and varied. The past possibility that

Table 18.2 Comparison of variance in scores on teacher behaviour for effective versus ineffective schools

| Variable | Teachers in effective schools (n = 30) | | | |
	Lowest score	Highest score	Range	Coefficient of variation
Time-on-task (interactive)	0.15	0.85	0.71	31.22
Time-on-task (overall)	0.55	0.90	0.36	10.39
Management	2.37	5.00	2.64	11.78
Instruction 1	2.74	4.61	1.88	12.28
Instruction 2	2.75	4.88	2.14	12.42
Climate 1	2.60	4.90	2.31	12.71
Climate 2	2.33	5.00	2.68	17.88
Variable	Teachers in ineffective schools (n = 27)			
	Lowest score	Highest score	Range	Coefficient of variation
Time-on-task (interactive)	0.08	0.75	0.68	34.45
Time-on-task (overall)	0.48	0.96	0.49	19.01
Management	2.10	4.60	2.51	18.86
Instruction 1	1.28	4.30	3.03	23.74
Instruction 2	1.38	4.38	3.01	22.04
Climate 1	2.30	4.80	2.51	16.97
Climate 2	1.50	4.67	3.18	22.07

Note: The coefficient of variation is computed by dividing the standard deviation by the mean and multiplying by 100.

inconsistent schooling, with a wide range in goals and means, might have been outweighed in any possible negative influences by the consistency emanating from non-educational sources seems to have been reduced by social changes of the last 30 years.

All this suggests that we need further research to establish the importance of 'range', 'variance' and variation in such areas as:

- teacher behaviour in lessons, looking at differences between teachers at a point in time, and at individual teacher consistency over time;
- the goals of education as perceived and practised by school members;
- consistency in the relationship between classroom factors, school factors, district level factors and societal factors.

THE NEED TO EXPLORE THE INTERFACE BETWEEN LEVELS OF SCHOOLING

The recent popularity of multilevel methodology in SER has clearly created a need for reconceptualisation of the process data that have historically been collected, since the use of individual, class, school and potentially outside school factors (such as district or even possibly country) has clearly created multiple levels where formerly in the early years of SER there was only one (a group of pupils generating a school mean).

At present, we have very little understanding of the 'interactions' or 'transactions' between levels, either at the more commonly used focus of classrooms nested in schools (class/school) or the more rarely used focus of schools nested in districts (school/district), although Bosker and Scheerens (1997) have begun to explore this issue. The growing recognition of the importance of 'range' or variation noted also above propels us urgently in this direction, given that the management interface between school and classroom generates enormous variation in classroom effectiveness in some settings, but not in others (e.g. Teddlie and Stringfield, 1993).

What might the focus of investigation be, for example, of the classroom/school interface? Possible areas of interest might include:

- the selection of teachers;
- monitoring of the teachers' performance by the principal (at the school level);
- the school's use of mechanisms to ensure homogeneity of teachers' goal orientation;
- the use made of performance data to detect 'unusual' or 'outlier' teacher performance;
- the constancy of personnel at the two levels, and the relational patterns between them.

Other interactions take place at other levels, with perhaps the interaction between the school and the LEA/district level being of considerable importance. Areas of interest here include:

- school variation in what is evoked from LEA/district level advisers, inspectors and personnel;
- district differential allocation of staff to different schools (in the case of schools in the USA where this is a possibility).

The pupil/class interface would also be an intriguing one to explore further, with interesting areas here including:

- the extent to which there are well-managed transitions between teachers across grades/ years;
- the co-ordination of various distinctive pupil-level programmes for children with special needs perhaps, or for children of high ability.

THE NEED TO EXPAND VARIATION AT THE SCHOOL LEVEL

The literature in the field at present is strongly suggestive of the view that the 'class' level or 'learning' level is a more powerful influence over children's levels of development and their rate of development than the 'school' level, which is, in turn, a more powerful level than that of the District or Local Education Authority. Until the development of various forms of multilevel methodology, variance at the classroom level was 'hidden' by the exclusive use of school level 'averages'. Now the classroom variance within schools is clearly exposed. As Stringfield (1994) rather nicely puts it, 'Children don't learn at the principal's knee – they learn in classrooms', although if one examined SER historically, one would see much greater concentration upon the principal's knee than the classroom context. The teacher and classroom are the 'proximal variables'.

However, part of the reason for the inability of researchers to show much 'strength' or 'power' at school level has been that we have been operating with highly constricted variance in the 'school' factor itself, since samples have been taken from within countries and cultures that already possess schools that are quite similar because of the influence of national traditions. As an example, British schools for the primary age range vary from a smallest of perhaps 15 pupils to a largest of perhaps 750 pupils, so within Britain sampling will generate a certain range. However, in Taiwan the smallest schools (in the rural areas) are of a restricted size of perhaps 60, whilst the largest is perhaps of 8,000 pupils. Sampling cross-culturally and across national boundaries would therefore be likely to generate much greater variation than sampling within country.

Of course, classroom variation in other factors is unlikely to increase by as much as school variation if sampling were to be cross-national. To take size as a factor, class sizes within the United Kingdom perhaps range from 17–18 up to a maximum of 40. Sampling across the globe would probably only increase this variation in class size to 12–13 at the lower end and 60–70 in some developing societies at the top end.

The hugely enhanced range, and therefore likely enhanced explanatory power of the school, if one deliberately seeks to maximise its range rather than minimise it by within nation sampling, is also likely to be found in terms of school *quality* factors, not just *quantity* factors. As an example, within Britain there would be a degree of variation in the leadership styles of headteachers, ranging from the moderately lateral and involving/participatory, to the moderately centralised and dominating. Looking outside the United Kingdom context, one could see apparently totally autocratic, non-participatory leadership in Pacific Rim societies such as Taiwan, and also apparently virtually totally 'lateral' decision-making within the primary schools of Denmark, where school policy is generated by teachers themselves.

We would argue, then, that our existing estimates as to the size of school effects are an artefact of researchers' unwillingness to explore the full range of variation on the 'school variable'. Cross-national research would expand variation on the school level by much more than on the classroom level – since classrooms are more alike internationally than are schools – and is essential if a more valid picture of school/classroom influence is to be generated.

THE NEED TO STUDY SCHOOL FAILURE/DYSFUNCTIONALITY

SER has historically taken a very different disciplinary route to that of many other 'applied' disciplines such as medicine and dentistry, in that it has studied schools that are 'well' or effective, rather than those that are 'sick' or ineffective. Indeed, with notable exceptions in SER (Reynolds, 1996; Stoll and Myers, 1997), the dominant paradigm has been to study those already effective or well and simply to propose the adoption of the characteristics of the former organisations as the goal for the less effective.

In medicine by contrast, research and study focus upon the sick person and on their symptoms, the causes of their sickness and on the needed interventions that may be appropriate to generate health. The study of medicine does not attempt to combat illness through the study of good health, as does school effectiveness: it studies illness to combat illness.

It is, of course, easy to see why school effectiveness has studied the already 'well' or effective schools. The failure of the experiments of social engineering in the 1970s (Reynolds *et al.*, 1987), combined with the research and advocacy that suggested that schools make no difference (Coleman *et al.*, 1966; Jencks *et al.*, 1972) led to a defensiveness within the field of school effectiveness and to an unwillingness to explore the 'trailing edge' of 'sick' schools for fear of giving the educational system an even poorer public image. Access to 'sick' schools additionally has always been more difficult than to 'well' or effective schools, given the well-known tendency of such ineffective schools to isolate themselves from potential sources of criticism from the world outside. The routine involvements of professional life in education have also tended to be between the good schools and the researchers (who generally prefer to involve themselves in the successful schools, rather than to put up with the toxicity, problems and organisational trauma that is often the day-to-day life of the ineffective school).

The problems for SER because it has concentrated upon the effective rather than the ineffective schools are numerous. Because the effective schools have already become effective, we do not know what factors *made* them effective over time. There may be whole areas of schooling that are central to educational life in non-effective schools that simply cannot be seen in effective schools, such as staff groups that possess 'cliques' or interpersonal conflict between staff members, for example. Dropping into the context of the ineffective school those factors that exist in the effective school may be to generate simply unreachable goals for the ineffective school, since the distance between the practice of one setting and the practice of the other may be too great to be easily eradicated.

If SER were to reorientate itself towards the study of the sick, then a number of likely events would follow. Given that these schools are increasingly likely to become the site for numerous interventions to improve them, then there will be naturally occurring experiments going on that are much more rare in the 'steady state' effective schools. The study of sickness usually necessitates a clinical audit to see which aspects of the patient are abnormal – an educational audit can perform the same function, which of course is not necessary in an effective school because there is no concern about organisational functioning.

We believe that SER has been fundamentally misguided in its belief that the way to understand and combat sickness is through the study of the already well. The sooner that the discipline reorientates itself to the study of sickness, ineffectiveness, dysfunctionality and failure the better.

CONCLUSIONS

We have outlined in this chapter a large volume of research on school effectiveness and school improvement, emanating from a wide range of countries. The problem, though, that besets all countries is to ensure that the effectiveness knowledge base is routinely used to improve school and teacher practice, which often has not been the case historically. There have, of course, been the American 'direct transplant' models that brought effectiveness knowledge to practitioners and there have been attempts in the United Kingdom to gener-ate 'merged models' (Reynolds *et al.*, 1993) of both effectiveness and improvement know-ledge that might be expected to 'root' better in schools than some of the earlier 'pure' effectiveness knowledge did (see survey in Reynolds *et al.*, 1996).

However, the problems of combining effectiveness and improvement insights and prac-tices have been hindered by the very different epistemological and philosophical back-grounds of the people in the 'improvement' community and those in the 'effectiveness' community, particularly in Britain, which is still to be seen in recent exchanges about effectiveness research (Elliott, 1996; Sammons and Reynolds, 1997). Where researchers and practitioners in the two fields have suspended hostilities and simply sought for agreement as to 'what works', there is evidence of an interesting synergy of perspectives and indeed for a new, more integrated paradigm that represents a blend of approaches. This is in evidence in some of the writing from members of the new paradigm (Gray *et al.*, 1996; Reynolds *et al.*, 1993; Stoll and Fink, 1996).

It is sincerely to be hoped that adherents to the new paradigm can further develop both the understanding of effectiveness and improvement and the practical policies that can follow from them.

SELECT BIBLIOGRAPHY

Gray, J., Reynolds, D., Fitz-Gibbon, C. and Jesson, D. (1996) *Merging Traditions: The Future of Research on School Effectiveness and School Improvement.* London: Cassell.

Hopkins, D., Ainscow, M. and West, M. (1994) *School Improvement in an Era of Change.* London: Cassell.

Reynolds, D., Creemers, B. P. M., Hopkins, D., Stoll, L. and Bollen, R. (1996) *Making Good Schools.* London: Routledge.

Scheerens, J. and Bosker, R. (1997) *The Foundations of School Effectiveness.* Oxford: Pergamon Press.

Stoll, L. and Fink, D. (1996) *Changing Our Schools.* Buckingham: Open University Press.

Teddlie, C. and Reynolds, D. (1999) *The International Handbook of School Effectiveness Research.* Lewes: Falmer Press.

REFERENCES

Aitkin, M. and Longford, N. (1986) 'Statistical modeling issues in school effectiveness studies'. *Journal of the Royal Statistical Society, Series A,* 149 (1), 1–43.

Angus, L. B. (1986a) *Schooling, the School Effectiveness Movement and Educational Reform.* Geelong: Deakin University Press.

Angus, L. B. (1986b) 'The risk of school effectiveness: A comment on recent education reports'. *The Australian Administrator, 7,* 1–4.

Ashenden, D. (1987) 'An odd couple? Social justice. Performance Indicators'. Public lecture sponsored by the Victorian State Board of Education. Melbourne, Australia.

Averch, H. A., Carroll, S. J., Donaldson, T. S., Kiesling, H. J. and Pincus, J. (1971) *How Effective Is Schooling? A Critical Review and Synthesis of Research Findings.* Santa Monica, CA: Rand Corporation.

Banks, D. (1988) 'Effective schools research and educational policy making in Australia'. Paper presented at the First International Congress for School Effectiveness. London, England.

Banks, D. (1992) 'Effective schools research: A multilevel analysis of the conceptual framework'. Unpublished doctoral thesis, Melbourne University.

Barber, M. (1995) 'Shedding light on the dark side of the moon'. *Times Education Supplement*, 12 May, 3–4.

Brookover, W. B., Beady, C., Flood, P., Schweitzer, J. and Wisenbaker, J. (1979) *Schools, Social Systems and Student Achievement: Schools Can Make a Difference*. New York: Praeger.

Brown, S., Riddell, S. and Duffield, J. (1996) 'Possibilities and problems of small-scale studies to unpack the findings of large-scale studies of school effectiveness'. In J. Gray, D. Reynolds, C. Fitz-Gibbon and D. Jesson (eds) *Merging Traditions: The Future of Research on School Effectiveness and School Improvement*, London: Cassell, 93–120.

Caldwell, B. and Misko, J. (1983) *The Report of the Effective Resource Allocation in Schools Project*. Hobart: Centre for Education, University of Tasmania.

Caldwell, B. and Spinks, J. (1986) *Policy Making and Planning for School Effectiveness*. Hobart: Department of Education.

Caldwell, B. and Spinks, J. (1988) *The Self-managing School*. Lewes: Falmer Press.

Caldwell, B. and Spinks, J. (1992) *Leading the Self-managing School*. Lewes: Falmer Press.

Caldwell, B., Lawrence, A., Peck, F. and Thomas, F. (1994) 'Leading Victoria's schools of the future: Baseline survey in 1993'. Paper presented at the 7th Annual Conference of the International Congress for School Effectiveness and Improvement, Melbourne, Australia.

Coleman, J. S., Campbell, E., Hobson, C., McPartland, J., Mood, A., Weinfeld, R. and York, R. (1966) *Equality of Educational Opportunity*. Washington, DC: Government Printing Office.

Creemers, B. P. M. (1994) *The Effective School*. London: Cassell.

Creemers, B. P. M. and Knuver, A. W. M. (1989) 'The Netherlands'. In B. P. M. Creemers, T. Peters and D. Reynolds (eds) *School Effectiveness and School Improvement. Proceedings of the 2nd International Congress, Rotterdam*, 79– 82. Lisse: Swets and Zeitlinger.

Creemers, B. P. M. and Scheerens, J. (1994) 'Developments in the educational effectiveness research programme'. In R. J. Bosker, B. P. M. Creemers and J. Scheerens (eds) *Conceptual and Methodological Advances in Educational Effectiveness Research. Special issue of International Journal of Educational Research*, 21 (2), 125–140.

Creemers, B. P. M., Reynolds, D., Stringfield, S. and Teddlie, C. (1996) 'World class schools: Some further findings'. Paper presented at the annual meeting of the American Educational Research Association, New York.

Cuban, L. (1983) 'Effective schools: A friendly but cautionary note'. *Phi Delta Kappan*, 64, 695–696.

Cuban, L. (1984) 'Transforming the frog into a prince: Effective schools research, policy, and practice at the district level'. *Harvard Educational Review*, 54, 129–151.

Daly, P. (1991) 'How large are secondary school effects in Northern Ireland?' *School Effectiveness and School Improvement*, 2 (4), 305–323.

Davis, E. and Caust, M. (1994) 'How effective are South Australian schools? Development of and results from effective practice instruments'. Paper presented at the 7th Annual Conference of the International Congress for School Effectiveness and Improvement, Melbourne, Australia.

Department of Education and Science (DES) (1983) *School Standards and Spending: Statistical Analysis*. London: DES.

Department of Education and Science (DES) (1984) *School Standards and Spending Statistical Analysis: A Further Appreciation*. London: DES.

Durland, M. M. (1996) 'The application of network analysis to the study of differentially effective schools'. Unpublished doctoral dissertation, Louisiana State University, Baton Rouge, LA.

Durland, M. and Teddlie, C. (1996) 'A network analysis of the structural dimensions of principal leadership in differentially effective schools'. Paper presented at the annual meeting of the American Educational Research Association, New York, NY.

Edmonds, R. R. (1978) 'A discussion of the literature and issues related to effective schooling'. Paper prepared for the National Conference on Urban Education, St Louis, MO.

Edmonds, R. R. (1979a) 'Effective schools for the urban poor'. *Educational Leadership*, 37 (10), 15–24.

Edmonds, R. R. (1979b) 'Some schools work and more can'. *Social Policy*, 9 (2), 28–32.

Elliott, J. (1996) 'School effectiveness research and its critics: Alternative visions of schooling'. *Cambridge Journal of Education*, 26 (2), 199–223.

Firestone, W. A. and Herriott, R. (1982) 'Prescriptions for effective elementary schools don't fit secondary schools'. *Educational Leadership*, 40 (12), 51–52.

Fitz-Gibbon, C. T. (1985) 'A-level results in comprehensive schools: The Combse project, year 1'. *Oxford Review of Education*, 11 (1), 43–58.

Fitz-Gibbon, C. T. (1992) 'School effects at A level: Genesis of an information system'. In D. Reynolds and P. Cuttance (eds) *School Effectiveness: Research, Policy and Practice*, London: Cassell.

Fitz-Gibbon, C. T. (1996) *Monitoring Education: Indicators, Quality and Effectiveness*. London and New York: Cassell.

Fitz-Gibbon, C. T. and Tymms, P. B. (1996) *The Value Added National Project: First Report*. London: School Curriculum and Assessment Authority.

Fitz-Gibbon, C. T., Tymms, P. B. and Hazlewood, R. D. (1989) 'Performance indicators and information systems'. In D. Reynolds, B. P. M. Creemers and T. Peters (eds), *School Effectiveness and Improvement: Selected Proceedings of the First International Congress for School Effectiveness*. Groningen, The Netherlands: RION, 141–152.

Galloway, D. (1983) 'Disruptive pupils and effective pastoral care'. *School Organisation*, 13, 245–254.

Gath, D. (1977) *Child Guidance and Delinquency in a London Borough*. London: Oxford University Press.

Goldstein, H. (1995) *Multilevel Models in Educational and Social Research: A Revised Edition*. London: Edward Arnold.

Goldstein, H., Rasbash, J., Yang, M., Woodhouse, G., Pan, H., Nuttall, D. and Thomas, S. (1993) 'A multilevel analysis of school examination results'. *Oxford Review of Education*, 19 (4), 425–433.

Good, T. L. and Brophy, J. E. (1986) 'School effects'. In M. Wittrock (ed.), *Third Handbook of Research on Teaching*. New York: Macmillan.

Gray, J. (1981) 'A competitive edge: Examination results and the probable limits of secondary school effectiveness'. *Educational Review*, 33 (1), 25–35.

Gray, J. (1982) 'Towards effective schools: Problems and progress in British research'. *British Educational Research Journal*, 7 (1), 59–79.

Gray, J. and Jesson, D. (1987) 'Exam results and local authority league tables'. *Education and Training UK 1987*, 33–41.

Gray, J. and Wilcox, B. (1995) *Good School, Bad School*. Buckingham: Open University Press.

Gray, J., McPherson, A. F. and Raffe, D. (1983) *Reconstructions of Secondary Education: Theory, Myth and Practice since the War*. London: Routledge & Kegan Paul.

Gray, J. and Jesson, D. and Jones, B. (1984) 'Predicting differences in examination results between local education authorities: Does school organisation matter? *Oxford Review of Education*, 10 (1), 45–68.

Gray, J., Jesson, D. and Jones, B. (1986) 'The search for a fairer way of comparing schools' examination results'. *Research Reports in Education*, 1 (2), 91–122.

Gray, J., Jesson, D. and Sime, N. (1990) 'Estimating differences in the examination performance of secondary schools in six LEAs – a multilevel approach to school effectiveness'. *Oxford Review of Education*, 16 (2), 137–158.

Gray, J., Jesson, D., Goldstein, H., Hedger, K. and Rasbash, J. (1995) 'A multi-level analysis of school improvement: Changes in schools' performance over time'. *School Effectiveness and School Improvement*, 6 (2), 97–114.

Gray, J., Reynolds, D., Fitz-Gibbon, C. and Jesson, D. (1996) *Merging Traditions: The Future of Research on School Effectiveness and School Improvement*. London: Cassell.

Hallinger, P. and Murphy, J. (1986) 'The social context of effective schools'. *American Journal of Education*, 94, 328–355.

Harris, A., Jamieson, I. and Russ, J. (1995) 'A study of effective departments in secondary schools'. *School Organisation*, 15 (3), 283–299.

Hill, P. (1997) 'Shaking the foundations: Research-driven school reform'. Plenary address to International Congress for School Effectiveness and Improvement, Memphis.

Hopkins, D., Ainscow, M. and West, M. (1994) *School Improvement in an Era of Change*. London: Cassell.

Hyde, N. and Werner, T. (1984) *The Context for School Improvement in Western Australian Primary Schools*. Paris: OECD/CERI Report for the International School Improvement Project.

Jencks, C. S., Smith, M., Ackland, H., Bane, M. J., Cohen, D., Ginter, H., Heyns, B. and Michelson, S. (1972) *Inequality: A Reassessment of the Effect of the Family and Schooling in America*. New York: Basic Books.

Jesson, D. and Gray, J. (1991) 'Slants on slopes: Using multi-level models to investigate differential school effectiveness and its impact on pupils' examination results'. *School Effectiveness and School Improvement*, 2 (3), 230–247.

Levine, D. U. and Lezotte, L. W. (1990) *Unusually Effective Schools: A Review and Analysis of Research and Practice*. Madison, WI: The National Center for Effective Schools Research and Development.

Lezotte, L. W. and Bancroft, B. (1985) 'Growing use of effective schools model for school improvement'. *Educational Leadership*, 42 (3), 23–27.

McLean, A. (1987) 'After the belt: school processes in low exclusion schools'. *School Organisation*, 7 (3), 303–310.

McManus, M. (1987) 'Suspension and exclusion from high school – the association with catchment and school variables'. *School Organisation*, 7 (3), 261–271.

Maxwell, W. S. (1987) 'Teachers' attitudes towards disruptive behaviour in secondary schools'. *Educational Review*, 39 (3), 203–216.

Mellor, W. and Chapman, J. (1984) 'Organisational effectiveness in schools'. *Educational Administration Review*, 2, 25–36.

Miller, S. K. (1983) *The History of Effective Schools Research: A Critical Overview*. Annual Meeting of the American Educational Research Association, Montreal, Canada. ERIC Document no. ED 231818.

Mintzberg, H. (1979) *The Structuring of Organisations*. Englewood Cliffs, NJ: Prentice Hall.

Mortimore, P. (1991) 'School effectiveness research: Which way at the crossroads?' *School Effectiveness and School Improvement*, 2 (3), 213–229.

Mortimore, P., Sammons, P., Stoll, L., Lewis, D. and Ecob, R. (1988) *School Matters*. Wells, Somerset: Open Books.

Murphy, J. (1992) 'School effectiveness and school restructuring: Contributions to educational improvement'. *School Effectiveness and School Improvement*, 3 (2), 90–109.

Myers, K. (1995) *School Improvement in Practice: Schools Make a Difference Project*. London: Falmer Press.

Nuttall, D. L., Goldstein, H., Prosser, R. and Rasbash, J. (1989) 'Differential school effectiveness'. In B. P. M. Creemers and J. Scheerens (eds) *Developments in School Effectiveness Research*. Special Issue of *International Journal of Educational Research*, 13 (7), 769–776.

Owens, R. G. (1987) *Organisational behavior in education* (3rd. edn). Englewood Cliffs, NJ: Prentice Hall.

Power, M. J. and Morris J. N. (1967) 'Delinquent Schools?' *New Society*, 10, 542–543.

Power, M. J., Benn, R. T. and Morris, J. N. (1972) 'Neighbourhood, school and juveniles before the courts'. *British Journal of Criminology*, 12, 111–132.

Purkey, S. and Smith, M. (1983) 'Effective schools'. *The Elementary School Journal*, 83, 427–452.

Reynolds, D. (1976) 'The delinquent school'. In P. Woods, (ed.) *The Process of Schooling*. London: Routledge & Kegan Paul.

Reynolds, D. (1982) 'The search for effective schools'. *School Organisation*, 2 (3), 215–237.

Reynolds, D. (1991) 'Changing ineffective schools'. In M. Ainscow (ed.), *Effective Schools for All*. London: David Fulton.

Reynolds, D. (1992) 'School effectiveness and school improvement: An updated review of the British literature'. In D. Reynolds and P. Cuttance (eds) *School Effectiveness: Research, Policy and Practice*. London: Cassell, 1–24.

Reynolds, D. (1996) 'Turning around ineffective schools: Some evidence and some speculations'. In J. Gray, D. Reynolds, C. Fitz-Gibbon and D. Jesson, (eds) *Merging Traditions: The Future of Research on School Effectiveness and School Improvement*. London: Cassell.

Reynolds, D. and Cuttance, P. (1992) *School Effectiveness: Research, Policy and Practice*. London: Cassell.

Reynolds, D. and Farrell, S. (1996) *Worlds Apart? – A Review of International Studies of Educational Achievement Involving England*. London: HMSO for OFSTED.

Reynolds, D., Sullivan, M. and Murgatroyd, S. J. (1987) *The Comprehensive Experiment*. Lewes: Falmer Press.

Reynolds, D., Davie, R. and Phillips, D. (1989) 'The Cardiff programme – an effective school improvement programme based on school effectiveness research'. *Developments in School Effectiveness Research*. Special issue of the *International Journal of Educational Research*, 13 (7), 800–814.

Reynolds, D., Hopkins, D. and Stoll, L. (1993) 'Linking school effectiveness knowledge and school improvement practice: Towards a synergy'. *School Effectiveness and School Improvement*, 4 (1), 37–58.

Reynolds, D., Creemers, B., Nesselrodt, P., Schaffer, E., Stringfield, S. and Teddlie, C. (1994) *Advances in School Effectiveness Research and Practice*. Oxford: Pergamon, Press.

Reynolds, D., Teddlie, C., Creemers, B. P. M. and Stringfield, S. (1995) 'World class schools: A review of data from the International School Effectiveness Research Programme'. Paper presented at the British Educational Research Association, Bath, United Kingdom.

Reynolds, D., Creemers, B. P. M., Hopkins, D., Stoll, L. and Bollen, R. (1996) *Making Good Schools*. London: Routledge.

Rowan, B. (1984) 'Shamanistic rituals in effective schools'. *Issues in Education*, 2, 76–87.

Rowan, B., Bossert, S. T. and Dwyer, D. C. (1983) 'Research on effective schools: A cautionary note'. *Educational Researcher*, 12 (4), 24–31.

Rowe, K. (1991) *Students, Parents, Teachers and Schools Make a Difference: A Summary Report of Major Findings from the 100 schools Project – Literacy programs Study*. Melbourne: School Programs Division, Ministry of Education.

Rowe, K. J. and Rowe, K. S. (1992) 'Impact of antisocial, inattentive and restless behaviours on reading'. In J. Elkins and J. Izzard (eds) *Student Behaviour Problems: Context Initiatives and Programs*. Hawthorn, Vic.: The Australian Council for Educational Research.

Rowe, K., Holmes-Smith, P. and Hill, P. (1993) 'The link between school effectiveness research, policy and school improvement'. Paper presented at the 1993 annual conference of the Australian Association for Research in Education, Fremantle, Western Australia, November 22–25.

Rowe, K. J., Hill, P. W. and Holmes-Smith, P. (1994) 'The Victorian Quality Schools Project: A report on the first stage of a longitudinal study of school and teacher effectiveness'. Symposium paper presented at the 7th International Congress for School Effectiveness and Improvement, The World Congress Centre, Melbourne.

Rowe, K. J., Hill, P. W. and Holmes-Smith, P. (1995) 'Methodological issues in educational performance and school effectiveness research: A discussion with worked examples'. *Australian Journal of Education*, 39, 217–248.

Rutter, M. (1983) 'School effects on pupil progress – findings and policy implications'. *Child Development*, 54 (1), 1–29.

Rutter, M., Maughan, B., Mortimore, P. and Ouston, J. with Smith, A. (1979) *Fifteen Thousand Hours: Secondary Schools and Their Effects on Children*. London: Open Books and Boston, MA: Harvard University Press.

Sammons, P. and Reynolds, D. (1997) 'A partisan evaluation – John Elliott on school effectiveness'. *Cambridge Journal of Education*, 27 (1), 123–126.

Sammons, P., Nuttall, D. and Cuttance, P. (1993) 'Differential school effectiveness: Results from a reanalysis of the Inner London Education Authority's junior school project data'. *British Educational Research Journal*, 19 (4), 381–405.

Sammons, P., Hillman, J. and Mortimore, P. (1995a) *Key Characteristics of Effective Schools: A Review of School Effectiveness Research*. London: OFSTED.

Sammons, P., Nuttall, D., Cuttance, P. and Thomas, S. (1995b) 'Continuity of school effects: A longitudinal analysis of primary and secondary school effects on GCSE performance'. *School Effectiveness and School Improvement*, 6 (4), 285–307.

Sammons, P., Mortimore, P. and Thomas, S. (1996) 'Do schools perform consistently across outcomes and areas?' In J. Gray, D. Reynolds, C. Fitz-Gibbon, and D. Jesson (eds) *Merging Traditions: The Future of Research on School Effectiveness and School Improvement*. London: Cassell, 3–29.

Sammons, P., Thomas, S. and Mortimore, P. (1997) *Forging Links: Effective Schools and Effective Departments*. London: Paul Chapman.

Scheerens, J. (1992) *Effective Schooling: Research, Theory and Practice*. London Cassell.

Scheerens, J. and Creemers, B. P. M. (1989) 'Conceptualising school effectiveness'. *International Journal of Educational Research*, 13, 689–706.

Scheerens, J. and Bosker, R. (1997) *The Foundations of School Effectiveness*. Oxford: Pergamon Press.

Silver, P. and Moyle, C. (1985) 'The impact of school leadership on school effectiveness'. *Educational Magazine*, 42, 42–45.

Slater, R. O. and Teddlie, C. (1992) 'Toward a theory of school effectiveness and leadership'. *School Effectiveness and School Improvement*, 3 (4), 247–257.

Smith, D. J. and Tomlinson, S. (1989) *The School Effect. A Study of Multi-racial Comprehensives*. London: Policy Studies Institute.

Steedman, J. (1980) *Progress in Secondary Schools*. London: National Children's Bureau.

Steedman, J. (1983) *Examination Results in Selective and Non-Selective Schools*. London: National Children's Bureau.

Stoll, L. (1995) 'The complexity and challenge of ineffective schools'. Paper presented at the European Conference on Educational Research Association, Bath, UK.

Stoll, L. and Fink, D. (1996) *Changing Our Schools*. Buckingham: Open University Press.

Stoll, L. and Myers, K. (1997) *No Quick Fixes: Perspectives on Schools in Difficulty*. Lewes: Falmer Press.

Stoll, L., Myers, K. and Reynolds, D. (1996) *Understanding Ineffectiveness*. Paper presented at the annual meeting of the American Educational Research Association, New York.

Stringfield, S. (1994) 'A model of elementary school effects'. In D. Reynolds, B. P. M. Creemers, P.S. Nesselrodt, E. C. Schaffer, S. Stringfield and C. Teddlie (eds) *Advances in School Effectiveness Research and Practice*. London: Pergamon Press, 153–188.

Teddlie, C. and Kochan, S. (1991) 'Evaluation of a troubled high school: Methods, results, and implications'. Paper presented at the annual meeting of the American Education Research Association, Chicago, IL.

Teddlie, C. and Stringfield, S. (1993) *Schools Make a Difference: Lessons Learned from a 10-Year Study of School Effects*. York: Teachers College Press.

Teddlie, C., Stringfield, S. and Desselle, S. (1985) 'Methods, history, selected findings, and recommendations from the Louisiana School Effectiveness Study: 1980-85'. *Journal of Classroom Interaction*, 20 (2), 22–30.

Teddlie, C., Virgilio, I. and Oescher, J. (1990) 'Development and validation of the Virgilio Teacher Behavior Inventory'. *Educational and Psychological Measurement*, 50 (2), 421–430.

Thomas, F., Beare, H., Bishop, P., Caldwell, B., Lawrence, A., Liddicoat, T., Peck, F. and Wardlaw, C. (1995a) *One Year Later: Co-operative Research Project Leading Victoria's Schools of the Future*. Melbourne, Vic.: Directorate of School Education.

Thomas, F., Beare, H., Bishop, P., Caldwell, B., Lawrence, A., Liddicoat, T., Peck, F. and Wardlaw, C. (1995b) *Taking Stock: Co-operative Research Project Leading Victoria's Schools of the Future*. Melbourne, Vic.: Directorate of School Education.

Thomas, S., Sammons, P. and Mortimore, P. (1997) 'Stability and consistency in secondary schools' effects on students' GCSE outcomes over 3 years'. *School Effectiveness and Improvement*, 8.

Townsend, A. C. (1995a) 'Matching the goals of schools of the future with the demographic characteristics of their local communities'. An ongoing research project funded by the *Australian Research Council*.

Townsend, A. C. (1995b) 'Community perceptions of the schools of the future'. An ongoing research project funded by the Research Committee of the Faculty of Education, Monash University.

Townsend, T. (1994) 'Goals for effective schools: The view from the field'. *School Effectiveness and School Improvement*, 5 (2), 127–148.

Van de Grift, W. (1989) 'Self perceptions of educational leadership and mean pupil achievements'. In D. Reynolds, B. P. M. Creemers and T. Peters (eds) *School Effectiveness and Improvement: Selected Proceedings of the First International Congress for School Effectiveness*. Groningen, The Netherlands: RION, 227–242..

322

Van de Grift; W. (1990) 'Educational leadership and academic achievement in secondary education'. *School Effectiveness and School Improvement*, 1 (1), 26–40.

Webb, E. J., Campbell, D. T., Schwartz, R. D., Sechrest, L. and Grove, J. B. (1981) *Nonreactive Measures in the Social Sciences*. Boston, MA: Houghton Mifflin.

Weber, G. (1971) *Inner-city Children Can Be Taught to Read: Four Successful Schools*. Washington, DC: Council for Basic Education.

Willms, J. D. (1985) 'The balance thesis – contextual effects of ability on pupils "O" grade examination results'. *Oxford Review of Education*, 11 (1), 33–41.

Willms, J. D. (1986) 'Social class segregation and its relationship to pupils' examination results in Scotland'. *American Sociological Review*, 51 (2), 224–241.

Willms, J. D. and Cuttance, P. (1985) 'School effects in Scottish secondary schools'. *British Journal of Sociology of Education*, 6 (3), 289–305.

19

COMMUNITY EDUCATION THROUGH THE TWENTIETH CENTURY

Colin Fletcher

INTRODUCTION

The linking of 'community' with 'education' at the very least implies a readiness to negotiate – perhaps even to reverse – some of the traditional role relationships between the 'us' and 'them' of the educational process e.g. teacher and student parent, professional and lay person, producer and consumer. In this sense 'community' represents the changing world outside the institutional cocoon of the professional worker and 'community education' is about evolving more open, participatory and democratic relationships between educators (of all kinds) and their constituencies.

(Martin, 1987a, p. 17)

Raising the school leaving age to 90.

(Rée quoted in Gregory, 1991, p. 23)

The commitment to community education . . . rests on a moral foundation which is the same as that for comprehensive education. This is the democratic ideal, best summarised by the three dimensions of Liberty, Equality and Fraternity.

(O'Hagan, 1988, p. 2)

Two main questions are considered: 'How has community education developed and what form will it take in the twenty-first century?' Throughout the twentieth century, community education was pushed forward by a minority of professionals, politicians and administrators and it was encouraged by some big charities. Few charities were concerned with supporting community education as such. Their purpose was to help with the realisation of social reforms: to reduce rural depopulation; to reduce urban unemployment; to reduce women's dependency upon men's exploitation; to reduce the isolation and exclusion of the aged. Generally speaking, charities have sponsored community education projects and local governments have supported community education services.

Community Education in China has developed rapidly in Beijing, Shanghai, Tianjin, Shenyoung . . . and in many rural areas. But in the whole country, community education is very unbalanced.

(Li Yixian, 1995, p. 2)

In the Cook Islands there are a number of on-going community education programmes targeted at different audiences. These are handled by a number of different government departments and non-government organizations. Some have been operating for many years and some are new. Some are high-tech while others are basic. Some require and offer examinations and certificates while others require a minimum of involvement. No doubt this is the same as elsewhere in the Pacific but the whole framework makes up the complex mosaic that is community education.

(Hagan, 1996, p. 4)

Only in Scotland is there a national policy for community education.

(Alexander *et al.*, 1984, p. 8)

In all other countries, community education sits alongside school education, adult education, youth work and community development. From this position, community education is also a challenge to the purposes and practices of contemporary education.

The problems for community education are massive and the odds on overcoming them are poor. Community education is generally chosen when other approaches have failed or would quickly fail. Community education is set against circumstances which make any gain difficult. Its practitioners are made to feel like fire-fighters.

From the perspective of practice, community education is a varied set of initiatives and real achievements of committed people which seldom have been studied by academics. From the perspective of theory, community education is an idea, an ideal from which more orthodox education can be criticised. Practice defines what community education is currently; theory defines what community education might be and how different it could be from an education which is solely concerned with the individual and the economy:

[A]ll efforts should be made to enhance participation of local people in educational provision, and consequently help the local community to promote occupational skills, preserve resources and environment and strengthen their capacities for problem-solving, for the improvement of the quality of life for all people and in all countries.

(Sirindhorn, 1995, p. 2)

The attitude to learning is central to community education. Freire (1975, 1977, 1979) is often quoted to contrast empowerment with domestication. His work and writings show a link between two 'parts' of education which are often in ignorance of each other: compulsory school education and voluntary adult education. The latter has long held to the belief that many schools waste most of their pupils' talents. Adult illiteracy the world over is testimony to how often when school provision is made, those formal schools and their instructional schooling fail. Writing about Pakistan, Inayatullah says:

There is no clear indication as to how the horrid mess in primary education will be cleared up, what steps will be taken to arrest high (more than 50 per cent) drop-out rate? . . . How will the widespread absenteeism of teachers be controlled?

(Inayatullah, 1994, p. 3)

Community education, then, is a reform movement in each country which has:

- its own concrete forms in projects and in services;
- its own concepts;
- its critical commentary on formal education;
- its connections with other positive forces for social well-being.

Community education is conditioned by culture. It has its local history, heroes and heroines but does not seek to reproduce the dominant culture or hegemony. It is often in opposition: in opposition to disparities of power and the ravages of injustice. Its vision

325

excludes the nation state and its ambitions; rather it engages with awareness and with empowerment to stimulate and support social change. It is the local governments who have comprehensive community education policies whilst the nation states have selective meanings and measures of community education (Devon County Council, 1994).

Heroes and heroines remain important. In every country there are founders and true disciples of community education. These men and women have redefined their professions and have been criticised for it. Thus working with families has been criticised as being social work, working with pupils out of school as being youth work, and working with other professionals as playing politics. The broad, all-inclusive concept sets high ambitions, it is said – ambitions which cannot possibly be fulfilled. The ideological battle over community education takes the form of a good idea up against the wrong time and unprofessional behaviour.

When a more *inclusive* definition of community education is in favour and is politically supported, locally community schools are designated; headteachers have additional responsibilities and salaries; schools are more intensively and extensively used by local people who are regarded as members. When a more *exclusive* definition is used, there are target groups of people at risk; for example from AIDS; from domestic violence; from sexual abuse; people trapped in poverty. In both schools and projects, programmes are formed that are intended to encourage participation and self-reliance and to become self-financing.

At its most basic, community education is part of a wider social policy (Martin, 1987a) in the same way as is, for example, special education or adult literacy. They, too, are long-term pursuits of democratic rights which often depend upon the funding of short-term projects for their examples of good practice.

The greatest part of this chapter is devoted to the concrete forms of good practice and to the global pattern. The second largest part is looking forward to 2100. Predictions and prophecies are made. Between these two come the debates upon ideas and, in particular, difficulties associated with the term 'community'. At this point, too, come the questions of national differences. For essentially, until virtually the close of the twentieth century, every country had its own version of community education both as an idea and as cherished initiatives. The unifying aspect is the appropriateness of community education as a challenge to powerlessness and to poverty. Community education stands for common sense and common wealth. It is philosophically inclined to see the individual as an inseparable part of the social, the person within the group.

From England and Wales comes the definition:

> that community education is primarily about lifelong education. The 'cradle to grave' concept is usually associated with community education. . . . [I]t is a developmental concept . . . and its practice has to match the needs of the community which it serves.
>
> (AMA 1991, p. 8)

In the USA one authoritative definition is as follows:

> Community education extends the concept of public education known as 'schooling'. It is not limited by traditional school schedules and roles. It focuses on community needs. Do the community's children need health and nutrition services? Do their families need support from community agencies? Do adults in the community need literacy training or new job skills? Community education uses all available community resources – including the resources of the school – to meet the needs of community members.

At the heart of community education is a simple idea: schools are not just places to teach children, but centres for the entire community because learning is lifelong.

(Decker and Boo, 1995, p. 7)

Community education refers essentially to a radical reform of public education in developed countries and a radical commitment to community development in developing countries: in both visions schools need to be shared and learners to be fit for citizenship.

COMMUNITY EDUCATION THROUGH THE TWENTIETH CENTURY

The advance of community education has been gradual in every country. It starts with outstanding innovation and practice which leads to liberal and socialist interest. There are periods of major initiatives followed by rapid retreats from further commitments. It begins as marginal and remains marginal despite intense periods. On the geographical and social edges it may thrive more continuously whilst affecting relatively few. The ambiguity of challenging the mainstream and of creating alternatives does not remain unclear for long.

The keyword is local and is often used in the environmentalist slogan, 'Think locally, act globally'. Community is used to refer to neighbourhoods in affluent Western suburbs right across the spectrum to remote fishing villages in the Western Pacific (Baird, 1996). Community, too, is locally defined. It can mean one distinct place or one set of distinct interests; a town for example or the interests of young people.

Communities are more or less tight networks of families, residents and interest groups. They are characterised by loyalties, special languages, respect for the very young and very old, open conflicts and yet an ultimate tolerance of individual differences within. The term and ideas are emotionally charged. Very few would deny that 'community' is important and valuable, at least in principle. There are few people in whom there is no longing for community of any sort. Family patterns change as do recreational, vocational and political interests, as do homes and their locations. Adults find their bearings by banding together and being in contact by telephone, fax and e-mail as much as by being face to face. Those for whom networks of interest and of residence are fused are teenagers. Young people are usually the most intensely locally loyal. They are insistently local dialect users. Such territorial identity as develops in the teenage years seems remarkably resilient in later life.

These generalisations are as obvious to some as they are contentious to others. They have to do with where people feel safe and can have a good time, with mutual support and hilarious moments, with making things happen and sharing hopes.

Community is the configuration of people we live next to, as well as of people with whom we share deep common bonds: work, love, an ideology, artistic talent, a religion, a culture, a sexual preference, a struggle, a movement, a history and so on. Community can be difficult to define uniformly in terms of where people live; for within the same geographical area there can exist different communities, and it is not uncommon for their interests to clash.

(Munoz and Garcia-Blanco, 1989, p. 5).

This attempt to capture a meaning for community succeeds well until the end. It seeks to define community uniformly in spatial terms – as it applies to any distinct community – and then moves to arguing that, in effect, people cannot have multiple community identities between which there are also degrees of conflict. But it is this second point which has

327

become increasingly significant in the twentieth century. The initial imagery of community does come from 'common' and 'commune' and does derive from descriptions of villages and nineteenth-century urban neighbourhoods. The understanding, then, was one of an area of residence being also a social stratum, a language or dialect, a set of values and a profound emotional identity.

As the twentieth century developed, community was also applied to communities of interest; generations, hobbies, sexual orientations and so on. By the late twentieth century all communities of residence had been cross-cut by communities of interest in that any individual can feel both at home and at odds with aspects of where they live and how they spend their time. Each person is a mix of community identifications of place, of purpose and of prime interests. It is possible to feel both belonging and belittling at the same time, to support and oppose aspects of communities of residence and communities of interest simultaneously.

> Although the word 'community' can be used apparently to encompass everyone, the concept does not imply a majority of people thinking, believing and behaving in unison. Rather it implies a multiplicity of interests. When not used synonymously with 'society', the word 'community' usually refers to minorities – lots of them bundled together and intersecting and interrelating in myriad ways but minorities nevertheless.
>
> (Newman, 1979, p. 209)

However, throughout the twentieth century, the term community was often used in an unproblematic way. Williams (1976) warned against its warm glow and thought that there should be suspicion of any such term which has no opposite. Jackson (1980) argued that the community can be attributed powers for good and ill which it simply does not possess. Deep societal problems can be laid at the door of some community education initiative: problems which it has little, if any, capacity to resolve.

By reflecting on these initiatives, one can identify three models of community education which are apparent in professionals' work. These three models were defined by Martin (1987a) as being either universal, reformist or radical. In the same decade O'Hagan (1991) developed his comparable models of efficiency, enrichment and empowerment. Thorpe (1985) in Australia similarly related community education to social change as being that of consensus (based on co-operation), pluralist (based on social planning), or structuralist (based on direct action). Professional purposes differ between the models. There are contrasting and conflicting images of community (Fletcher, 1987).

In community education, participants are asked to be aware of the professional's meaning for community. They are also asked to be aware of how far their learning is likely to go. It could be back into their current understandings of community, or onwards to wider reforms or further still to confrontation and transformation. The closer that community education practice moves towards radical change, the more precise the understanding of the immediate community becomes and the more clearly the pattern of competing definitions is perceived. Who the community is may not seem to be a problem – simplistically it is 'all of us who are not them' (Fletcher, 1984b). The more there is conflict, the more the exact meanings of 'us' and 'them' are troublesome and in tension.

In the late 1970s and 1980s, the idea of community was overtaken by the idea of market. For a time community appeared to have disappeared altogether. In the 1990s there was a return to coexistence: to the community challenging the market and vice versa. Having been contrasted with each other absolutely, they now offer useful commentaries on each other's prime concerns. Community education has been a quiet challenge to market education; it has survived and may now be revived.

For example, in Thailand, Bangkok Petroleum Co. encourages farmers to form co-operatives to own and manage small petroleum stations. In 1995 there were about 400 such co-operatives, involving 700,000 farmer families with about 3.5 million people. As Wasi pointed out, 'Once possessing management skill, the farmer co-operatives can expand their activities in many ways such as other businesses, sub-contracting etc. The role of business in strengthening community organization can have significant and rapid impact' (Wasi 1995, p. 6).

For many lifelong community educators, there have been defining moments, both events and writings which have had great significance for the identification of their own practice. In the USA this could be said of Minzey and Latarte's (1972) text on Community Education. In the UK, Ian Martin's 1987b article could be similarly described. Two events were the Melbourne Conference of 1979 (with its six unique volumes of papers) and the formation of Peuple et Culture in France immediately after the Second World War. These moments have all 'globalised' theory for practitioners.

CASE STUDY 1: COMMUNITY SCHOOLS IN THE USA

There have been both community education and community schools throughout the twentieth century. In the USA it could be claimed that community education started in Wisconsin in 1911 with the lighted school house concept in Milwaukee. In 1935 in Flint, Michigan, Frank Manley advocated the 'lighted school house' as he struggled to establish the principle of community ownership of schools. Samuel Everett's 'The Community School' was published soon afterwards, in 1938.

> The USA is still the only country in the world to have enacted legislation – the Community School Development Act of 1974 – to secure the national implementation of a community education programme (for schools).
>
> (Poster and Krüger, 1990, p. 19)

Community schools are part of the US system of free and public education. 'There is renewed interest in the concept of community schools – that is communities and schools that form partnerships to enhance the educational environment for children as well as the quality of life for the community' (Edwards and Biocchi, 1996, p. iii). These authors identify 135 US schools and districts as having 'outstanding characteristics':

- a community centre during and after normal school hours and on weekends and in the summer;
- activities beyond the regular curriculum which build self-esteem;
- collaborate with other agencies to use community members to identify their own needs and so bring accessible support services;
- educate community citizens;
- encourage extended families to take a role in a child's learning;
- have open governance structures;

- view their students in a holistic manner;
- practise co-operative learning;
- have administrators and board members who understand education as a lifelong process;
- promote public policy development which supports children and families at risk.

No single school or district has all of these characteristics and this fact implies that there could be types of community schools and districts in the USA. I analysed these 135 schools and districts to look for patterns. The analysis began by considering how old the school or district was in relation to the prevalence of poverty (which is indicated when there is a higher percentage of free school meals).

The founding of community schools with high incidences of poverty (80 per cent and above) occurred between 1943 and 1950 and did not happen again until 1960 (see Table 19.1).

From the Second World War until the end of the century, community schools were likely to be part of combatting poverty, especially at the beginning and end of the fifty-year period. The 1970s and 1980s were periods when community schools were designated in relatively affluent suburbs. By simple projection in the year 2000 there were to be old and new community schools whose purpose was to reduce the effects of poverty. There were also mature community schools in prosperous neighbourhoods.

A further analysis was made of the characteristics of the 135 entries and four broad types emerged (see Table 19.2).

The four types are broadly recognisable:

1 Mixed-raced urban and suburban districts with high average poverty concentrating on their elementary schools and their full-time staff (Type 1)
2 White schools at any level with half their students having free school meals, balanced school funding and programme funding, full-time and part-time staff (Type 2)
3 Hispanic-African elementary and middle urban schools employing a large part-time staff with programme funding (Type 3)
4 White urban high schools, with some poverty, mostly school-funded supplemented by small programmes (Type 4).

Community education school districts are generally at least 20 years old; other types have been founded later. All four types do have programmes in common, particularly those concerned with health, criminal justice, employment and social services. The differences between the types are:

Table 19.1 The founding of US community schools and districts: average percentage levels of poverty (FSM's) per decade

	Free School Meals	Rank
1960–1969	52%	2
1970–1979	46%	3
1980–1989	34%	4
1990–1994	59%	1

330

Table 19.2 Types of school and district in 135 exemplars: USA 1995

	Type 1	*Type 2*	*Type 3*	*Type 4*
Setting	Urban/Suburban	Rural/Small City	Urban	Urban
Scale	District	School	School	School
Staffing	Large mostly full-time staff	Balance full-time and part-time staff	Large part-time staff	Small schemes staffing
Funding	Mixed funded school, grant. Other agencies	Mixed school, grant, programme-funded.	Programme funded.	School funded.
Average free school meals	56%	41%	72%	44%
Mode free school meals	24%	45%	44%	10%
School	Mostly elementary	Mixed elementary, middle, high	Mixed elementary, middle	Mostly high
Ethnicity of district	White with African and Hispanic	White	Hispanic/African	White

- no university links or neighbourhood groups for Hispanic schools but business and leisure services instead and
- stronger church links with mixed districts (Type 1).

The method used was hierarchical linkage analysis – Ward's method (Nornsis, 1993, p. 270) – and for each of the variables there were very large standard deviations. The identification of four types is inexact; each contains much variation. In precise particulars each district and school is unique whilst more generally there are common emphases. The document from which these data were taken was not a survey. If it were, Type 3s are very rare and Type 4s are rare too. Furthermore, there is a great contrast between the sizes and structures of the types (see Table 19.3).

Community education in US community schools is in addition to ordinary schooling and is intended to enhance this for pupils and to extend an enhanced learning to the local community. It is also clear that community education as community schools is relatively recent. A more detailed study might show the relationship between when the commitment was made and what it was then intended to do. One single charity, the CS Mott Foundation, founded by a philanthropist who was deeply impressed by Manley, has been essential in the gradual growth of US community schools: 'The Mott Foundation became the financial force which led to the expansion of the concept as a national effort' (Williams and Robins, 1980, p. 58).

CASE STUDY 2: COMMUNITY SCHOOLS IN ENGLAND AND WALES

The English and Welsh experiences are good examples of historical layering too. The first public education community school was Impington Village College, Cambridgeshire, opened in 1930. Its purpose was to stem the tide of rural depopulation. Henry Morris, Cambridgeshire's Director of Education, in his Memorandum of 1928 had sought to bring

Table 19.3 Examples of four broad types of community schools and districts; their structures, USA 1995

	Type 1: Denver Community Schools, CO	Type 2: Hood River County School District, OR	Type 3: Vaughn Learning Centre, LA	Type 4: Boca Raton Community HS, FL
Date inaugurated	1974	1975	1993	1971
Type of district	Urban	Rural	Urban	Urban
District population	467,000	18,200	3,485,398	936,657
CS paid staff:				
Full-time	32	2	55	161
Part-time	345	0	32	39
Annual budget $	2M	271K	4.5M	7.8M
Poverty level/school meal	61.8%	15%	100%	17%
Community characteristics				
African American	21.4%		4.2%	16%
White	30.6%	75%		71%
Hispanic	42.6%	25%	95.8%	10%
School district funding	10%	17%	98%	70%
Programme-generated funding	85%	80%		25%
Grants	5%	2%	2%	5%

all the educational, social and medical services under one roof in each of Cambridgeshire's villages (Rée, 1973). With support from the Carnegie Foundation he was able to open four colleges before the Second World War. After the war, the idea spread to other rural counties (states). It became a suburban initiative when community comprehensive schools were decided upon in Leicestershire. First old schools were designated – or retitled (Rogers, 1971). Later, newly built schools had the distinctive additional architecture of public access and adult activities. An alliance developed between architects and administrators in order to build a new type of school which looked neither like a hospital nor like a factory. The bold and fluent architecture made spaces less territorial and more sociable. A great impetus was given to new community school building by a national government circular in 1966, which encouraged dual-use school and community leisure facilities. Huge urban complexes were built, cost savings were made, and there were some very muddled arrangements for the management of these complexes (Fletcher, 1982). Whilst community schools were to realise potentials for the community, they were also to present considerable problems for professional management. Being open all hours for every day brought out storage, security and staffing problems which had not occurred before.

Throughout the 1970s and until the mid-1980s, local authorities (districts) continued to designate community schools and reorganise their adult education and youth work in line with a fuller use for schools and an increased explicit commitment to community development. Headteachers were hand-picked for their beliefs; a deputy headteacher had a community remit; staff were encouraged to include adults in their classes – as learners, as helpers and as experts in their own right. Unemployment and redundancies throughout the community were added pressures on the more systematic processes of parental involvement (Bastiani, 1989).

Community schools became a matter of policy for local authorities controlled by the Labour and Liberal Parties. Community education became a political football (Knightsbridge, 1992). In the previous decades it had been possible to secure all-party agreement for community schools and so remove community education from the political arena (see AMA, 1991). But, from the mid-1980s this was no longer possible: decentralised budgets, a national curriculum and rate-capping combined to exclude community education activity with the exception of forms of short-term intervention in cases of extreme hardship. As with the US schools, a few targeted programmes replaced the many simultaneous tasks of an organic process. Elsewhere community schools lapsed into little but their name. Cambridgeshire's community primary schools, laboriously designated over 18 years, were all dedesignated (Minty, 1993). Only in the new local governments of 1997, with their urban problems, were designations and mission statements likely to be made.

In England and Wales there was a series of historical shifts: advances, retreats, countermovements and moribund states (Clark, 1996). There has never been any national acknowledgement of all but the smallest fragments of programmes: home – school links and after-school clubs, for example. Nationally, there has been firm resistance to any recasting of school education as an integrated education from womb to tomb – an education for all: with a locally based and locally challenging curriculum; through local control of the school and its resources; and partnerships with other public and voluntary agencies which aim to maximise local welfare.

ARE COMMUNITY SCHOOLS DIFFERENT?

The claim made on behalf of a community school is that it has greater diversity and greater local responsibility. There are more varied classes and courses with a wider range of participants as both teachers and learners. Greater local responsibility is fulfilled by there being a direct concern with local needs and the participation of students and local citizens in the schools' management. The vast majority of pupils will be local parents and workers in a very short space of time after leaving school. There is a logic to them learning about the locality in school: 'The starting-point . . . is an investigation of possible needs, since the "success" or otherwise of a community school will rely heavily on how well it contributes to meeting them' (Hall *et al.*, 1984, p. 12). One difference which may be consistently found is in the curriculum, in that every subject refers to local conditions. In addition there are three further sets of programmes (see Table 19.4).

Table 19.4 Community education programmes at Gunnison Valley Elementary School, Utah in 1995

For special populations	*Intergenerational, Special needs, Special education, Title 1*
For children/young adults	Pre-school; summer child care enrichment programmes; recreation; drug education; parenting; academic alternative schools
For adults and families	Parenting; drug education; leisure classes; recreation; employment training (Edwards and Biocchi, 1996, p. 27)

In the 1970s Williams and Robins (1980) argued that there was a pyramid of progress from expanded use of school facilities right up through community development to total integration and that 'the problem seems to be in getting beyond the center barrier' (p. 61). The 'center barrier' is said to be that of seeking to attract local people in rather than seeking to send professionals out of the centre. Arnstein's (1971) ladder of citizen participation inspired professionals to plan their next steps in response to changes going on around them.

There is a school of thought that holds that all schools are community schools. The difference between ordinary schools and community schools may lie more in the ambition than in the achievement (Nisbet *et al.*, 1980). But school-based community educators do talk of specific barriers: around buildings; teaching roles; subjects and curricula; young people when in school; heads and senior staff and other sections of the community (Wilson, 1980). The efforts to take these barriers down create a different atmosphere or feeling to the place. Put another way, a welcoming feeling, adults in all kinds of roles, and a productive atmosphere are all pointers to the nature of a community school. However, the strongest indicators are about school governance (being run by the community) and community presence (being out in the community) with 'outreach activities' and a wide personal role for both staff and community members.

Architecture either strengthens or weakens these indicators:

> The school orientates around a social focus which is the heart of the school. This area is served by the canteen, has comfortable seating, noticeboards and bridges at the upper level. It becomes a bustling activity centre and meeting place. Off this space is an outdoor terrace with seating and planting. The school has become a real asset to the community with a number of spaces used out of school hours.
>
> (*Australian Schools 3*, n.d.)

> As the site is situated in an existing community[,] efforts were made during the planning to involve the community in the process. Numerous meetings were held and articles conveyed information in the local press. One interesting development from the local council was the plan for a system of mini parks to feed pupils into the school thus avoiding congested roads. The path system has been carried through the school integrating it into the neighbourhood.
>
> (*Australian Schools 2*, n.d.)

> The architect has often acted as a catalyst, articulating local needs and desires and helping to translate these demands into programmes and buildings sometimes working in a 'kitchen table' situation with local citizens' groups sponsoring 'charettes', public debates or workshops where local citizens sit with professionals and discuss local issues.
>
> (Parker, 1980, p. 303)

With all these differences unitary management of both the formal and informal functions becomes essential – 'perhaps the most crucial principle of all' (Wilson 1980, p. 128).

CASE STUDY 3: COMMUNITY COLLEGES AND UNIVERSITIES

Writings about community colleges in the US, England, Canada and Australia make infrequent reference, if at all, to other cases of community education (e.g. Cohen, 1996). Instead they have their own network and their own rationale as being further education centres which specialise in local conditions and in meeting local needs.

Community colleges are fast becoming global villages due to a variety of reasons: growth in numbers of international students on campus, regular exchange programmes for faculty and students, local business pressures to teach global education and the fact that community colleges know the value of building community. Community colleges educate America as no other institution is inclined to do; and they educate for the next century, not the last.

(Boyer, 1995, in Bakke and Tharp, 1995, p. 27)

The community colleges are sprung up in some developed regions (of China) such as Guandong Province and Jiangsan Province. Most of them are built with the local government's investment or collection money. To meet the demands of the local society, many practical professions and curricula are set up and lots of advanced professional personnel needed by the local enterprises are trained in these community colleges. Some colleges even invite the celebrities, famous scholars or professors to act as president or honorary president in their colleges. Most of the students are later generations of peasants of the same region or its neighbouring towns.

(Li Yixian, 1995, p. 4).

All of these features have their own distinctive expressions in accounts of community colleges in England (see Box 19.1).

The distinctiveness and separateness of community colleges can be found in tribal community colleges which have the explicit purpose of protecting and promoting tribal cultures.

Box 19.1 A community college and its partnerships

1   Bilston Community College, England

- was conceived and born in the community;
- has always had a deep involvement in the community;
- has developed as a result of the support of the community, mainly through partnerships.

Democracy, participation, equal opportunities, anti–elitism and anti–racism have been prominent characteristics of the College throughout its history.

2   From the outset, equal opportunities policies were regarded as integral to the open–access strategy. They established priorities as a response to the education and training needs of:

- unemployed school-leavers;
- the long-term unemployed;
- ethnic minority groups;
- the disabled;
- women returnees.

The emphasis has always been on targeting specific groups through partnership. The first new partnership after 1984 was with the Black Education Consortium: the College in partnership with two Asian and two Afro-Caribbean community organisations.

3   Traditional college partnerships – with schools for full-time students and industry for part-time day-release students – have little to offer in terms of advice, guidance or curriculum to people who enrol as individuals, mainly part-time. Representing the interests of people who enrol as individuals, and expressing their needs and aspirations, is the primary purpose of community partnerships.

Source: Adapted from Wymer, 1995, p. 9

Tribal community colleges in North America parallel the community colleges in Australia and the South Pacific that likewise are controlled by indigenous people. The agenda is for colleges and their communities to recapture lost history, songs, dances, language, tales, medicines and the healing arts. These are then utilized to contextualize and understand modern day experience, which is . . . alienating to indigenous communities.

(Cunningham, 1996)

And in Brazil:

The Academy of the Guarani has the restoration and further development of Indian knowledge as its aim and to pass this on both to members of the tribe and to other Brazilians. The villages are an actively relevant part of the academy: the academy visitors live and learn together with the Guaranis.

(Zimmer, 1991)

Community universities have been formed in India (Parikh, 1994) inspired by the teachings of Mahatma Gandhi. Most universities that have adult education teaching also have community education programmes and associated applied research:

In Colombia, the State plays a less centralist role, allowing policies and action to spring from the communities themselves. One such action is organized by the Universidade del Norte in Barranguilla which, in association with the Bernard Van Leer Foundation, introduced care programmes for children in poor areas . . . of many communities in Colombia's Atlantic Coast.

(Amar, 1996, p. 2)

There are tensions for universities and colleges and these focus upon the control of accreditation.

There is a tension and conflict between the desire for qualifications training and access to higher education and the strengthening of local groups and communities to enable them to move together in the search for justice and equality for all. The former tends, often but not always, to remove possible leaders from the community whilst leaving the social and economic situation unresolved . . . the majority of community education projects fall into this category. What makes them distinctive is the involvement of local people in the organisation, management and control of such programmes.

(Lovett, 1992, p. 4)

CASE STUDY 4: COMMUNITY EDUCATION CENTRES

School community centers have different names . . . they are called full service schools, community service centers, community school centers, family resource centers etc.

(Ringers and Decker, 1995, p. iii)

There are three kinds of centres which embody and express community education. These are:

- family centres;
- neighbourhood houses or centres;
- adult education centres.

The survival of community education centres has been secured by some spectacular examples of best practice – like Pen Green Centre for the under-fives and their families in the once-steel town of Corby, Northamptonshire, England (Whalley, 1994; see Box 19.2). Visitors see parents learning alongside their children; hear the hum of happy productivity; read the notices and inspirational slogans; enjoy an environment that combines a homeliness with explicit challenges to learn.

Renard (1995), the Co-ordinator of Labourie Community Education Centre on St Lucia, gives advice on community-run pre-school. Nunarwading North Neighbourhood Centre, Melbourne, Australia is more often known as 'the House' (Stewart, 1979). There a group of women were invited to research and document how they and other housewives learn. Judy Kiraly wrote:

> The book illustrates what those of us who are involved in community education believe: that effective learning can happen outside formal schooling; that a sympathetic environment and appropriate learning processes can unlock creative powers and give the confidence for creative expression.
>
> (Kiraly, 1979)

For Tom Lovett in the early 1970s, networking communities of interest – like churches, unions, sports clubs – was a way of bringing communities of residents into local action to improve local conditions (Lovett, 1971). He was not intent on helping interest groups individually – they were all on regional, national and international networks which could do that. The Neighbourhood was far harder to affirm and yet was in a much more obvious need (Lovett, 1975). Tom Lovett was quick to identify two flaws in his own work with local

---

Box 19.2 Pen Green Centre for the under-fives and their families, England

Pen Green is in Corby, Northamptonshire, a former steel town with a population of 52,000. It was set up in 1983 as part of a substantive under-fives initiative in an area of significant urban deprivation. It is jointly financed and jointly managed by the Education and Social Services departments with a staff of 25, which includes teachers, social workers, nursery nurses and support staff, and a budget of approximately £300,000. The Centre is situated in a 1930s former comprehensive school. The Centre has four major strands of activity:

- high-quality early years education and care;
- parent education and family support services;
- community health services;
- training and research.

The Centre has a comprehensive parent partnership programme and approximately 4,000 parents have been involved over a period of 13 years. Staff at the Centre have established a model of co-operative working that respects both the learning and support needs of parents, and children's right to high-quality early years education with care. This model of working with parents is underpinned by the belief that parents are deeply committed to their children's learning and development. We believe that parents have a critical role as their children's primary educator in the early years and young children achieve more and are happier when early years educators work together with parents and share views on how to support and extend individual children's learning.

The centre has become a 'one-stop shop' for families with young children in the local community.

Source: Adapted from Whalley and Arnold, 1996

communities. These flaws are parochialism and tokenism. Tokenism refers to just involving a few people, regulars, who can become mascots rather than leaders. Parochialism is more dangerous and more deceptive. To reinforce a local community is all too often to amplify its antagonisms: to gain solidarity through the strength of hostility.

To challenge these two enemies Tom Lovett helped to bring into being the Northern Ireland Learning Federation when he moved from Liverpool to Belfast (Lovett *et al.*, 1987). By working with local radio, many contrasting views were encouraged into open expression. The significant shock was that the broadcasting conferred an authority to authentic local speech and dialect. Rarely, if ever, had local people been heard in reflective speech rather than in reaction. In Lovett's work community interest groups have been brought into an adult education centre from which outreach work stretches to the edges of the Province. The Adult Education Centre offers daytime and residential courses on neutral territory with crèche facilities and the means to make media.

Tom Lovett's main influences were the Highlander Center in Tennessee and the kitchen meetings of Father Moses Coady in Newfoundland in the 1930s.

CASE STUDY 5: ADULT, YOUTH AND COMMUNITY DEVELOPMENT

In the latter part of the twentieth century, these three services were under severe pressure throughout the world. There have been cuts in financing, expectations of extending the work, and the displacement of long-term provisions by short-term contracts in New Zealand.

> During its short period of development, the Edgewater Community Education Programme has endeavoured to create new options for local residents through its large range of course options which are available, but more importantly, to encourage other groups and individuals to share what they have with others.
>
> (Galloway, 1980, p. 1)

The pressures have been signified by a sequencing of terms and an elision of their meanings. Adult education has been challenged by continuing education, by training, by lifelong learning as well as by community education. Introducing the British Colombian continuing education programme's manual, the Head of Service wrote:

> [S]ome of a programmer's most important and challenging work is in fostering not 'courses' but programs or processes involving liaison and advisory tasks in the community . . . Ministry policy also requires funding of community education programs and processes . . . to encourage participation by geographically, economically or socially disadvantaged adults.
>
> (D. Faris in Lund and McGechan, 1981, p. iii)

The pressures take different forms. In Fiji the pressure was to leave mainline ministries and to set up the Fiji Association of Non-Formal Educators. FANFE was established in 1985

> to bring together individuals, groups and organizations involved in youth, adult and community education programmes under a national co-ordinating body . . . [B]y focusing on the enhancement of children's and students' performance in school, FANFE has been able to convince parents' direct involvement and also support from the presenting community.
>
> (Carn, 1995, p. 1)

Projects are very often undertaken by NGOs (non-governmental organisations), particularly when the governmental services have either contracted or collapsed. Some respond to major movements of awareness, as with women's groups for self-defence and youth groups for local environmental action.

> A community needs assessment is an excellent means of involving the public in problem-solving and developing local goals. There is a tendency for people to resist change – frequently because they have inadequate information, or because they have not been involved in making decisions.
>
> (Butler and Howell, 1980, p. 3)

Churches and temples are widely involved in community education projects, particularly those to counter child prostitution, child slavery and the consequences of AIDS. For example, an AIDS widows' group being held in Doi Saket Temple, Chainguai Province, Northern Thailand, is allowed to use the temple as an office, and to learn vocational skills and discuss their problems there. The temple's Abbot sought charitable support for this group from aid agencies and from private benefactors (Pariyatsulthee, 1995).

COMMUNITY EDUCATION IN THE TWENTY-FIRST CENTURY

Predictions for the future of community education are neither new nor rare. Throughout the 1900s prediction was a common activity (Fletcher and Thompson, 1980). The titles of the World Conferences of the International Community Education Association also give a strong sense of how community educators have been focusing on the challenges that community education was facing (see Table 19.5).

The 1995 International Community Education Association Conference declared,

> We have a vision of a world community of self-reliant and self-sustaining local and regional communities in a new, democratic, world socio-economic order based on equity, justice, equality . . . as community educators we start where we are . . . we need a new educational order to awaken people's awareness of their capacity to bring about change.

Thus the 1999 World Conference has a theme of global and local environment. This will be the term which unifies community education in the twenty-first century (Ibikunle-Johnson, 1994).

My content analysis of some main English language literature in community education also reveals that some of the themes are specific to a certain decade of writings – for example, community education was viewed largely as an integral part of community action in the 1980s whilst the role of the state is a predominant concern of the 1990s.

Table 19.5 ICEA conference titles 1979–1995

No.	Conference title	Year
3rd	Here Come the 80's	1979
4th	Crisis and Response	1983
5th	Harambee (Pulling Together)	1987
6th	Developing the Global Village	1991
7th	Sustainable Development through Community Education	1995

The fields in focus within the content analysis are, in descending order:

1 curriculum
2 resources
3 funding
4 parents
5 policy and planning (district)
6 local education and the state
7 outreach activities and learning
8 assessment
9 accountability
10 child-centred learning (which was also of especial concern in the 1990s).

However, to categorise the top ten concerns in this way is not an attempt to create a sense that community education is an apolitical enterprise. Mentions of youth work and community development, adult learning and equal opportunities abound. Empowerment, with reference to underprivileged and marginalised groups and participatory learning and management are frequently mentioned, the latter especially in the 1990s. The assertion that community education is an essential ingredient for social change is also an underlying theme in the literature.

Discussion of the tension between the practice and theory of community education was a common theme in the period 1975–1995. Also common was the examination of the fallacies of community education in an attempt to dispel them, especially in the 1990s. However, the literature of the 1990s is more of a guide to the commentaries than it is to the content. Community education engages with change – and rolls with it.

Each of the following predictions draws upon patterns of development, but in different ways. There are seven main patterns:

1 the worldwide struggle with poverty;
2 the demographic changes of ageing populations and of surges in child births;
3 the depletion of resources requiring regional and local sustainability;
4 lifelong learning having widespread need and appeal;
5 compulsory education for children being firmly separated from voluntary learning and adult learning;
6 the devolution of responsibility for educational property;
7 concern over the decline of community and its 'social capital' (Putnam, 1993).

Predictions

● Community school districts in the USA and elsewhere, once established, will be sustained. Indeed, community schools will continue also to be advocated and designated in First World countries where they will be depicted as a positive response to deprivation – particularly when that is the deprivation of a single racial group, Hispanic, Afro-Caribbean or white.

● Those community schools that are dependent upon programmes – those being seen as experiments, as pilot schools and as pet projects – will continue to rise and fall: to be launched with a flourish and let down by the withdrawal of short-term funds and ill thought-out arrangements for their management.

- Community school districts and designated community schools will continue to be both the victors and the victims of charisma. This means that they will attract staff with strong personalities. They will also be suspect because of being dependent upon charisma. The general designation of community schools will be resisted, in part, because of their alleged need for certain kinds of staff. The thread of truth in this argument will be seen clearly when there is a succession crisis. Active community schools usually have a very low staff turnover. When their leaders do leave, they can go into decline because of their replacement's lack of vision and a weaker grasp of the complex organic and political strategies which community schools have (Morgan, 1986). Community schools are led as well as managed and mistakes are made, but they are also overcome.

- Community schools – their districts and their specific sites – are generally able to claim less graffiti and less vandalism than ordinary schools. They highlight the fact that such attacks are a hidden and additional tax on compulsory education. The reduction of damage, which otherwise costs millions every year, is attributed to two main causes, less disaffection and more loyalty amongst pupils along with less time during which the school is wholly unattended. Community schools are more continuously defended. However, part of this twentieth-century formula – openness – has broken down. Openness is a matter of calculated risks. On the one hand there is the matter of giving offence to those who feel that they can become members of the school through their voluntary participation. There is trust shown towards parents, volunteers, adult learners and empirical teachers (those who can teach through life experience as distinct from through training and qualifications). Participation engenders feelings of membership.

- On the other hand, there is the vulnerability of staff and students, the risk of confrontation, physical attack and murder, as happened at Dunblane in Scotland. This vulnerability demands that the community within the school be shut off from the dangers in the community at large. Community schools will be open, but not wide open, their edges and their entrances will be made secure and kept that way.

- Community schools (districts and their sites) will be largely urban phenomena. However, rural deprivation also pushes community schools into prominence (Dove, 1980). Through modern mass communications technologies, rural needs will become more urgent. A good case can be made for every school in rural areas being a community school. Similarly, reasons can be given for elementary (primary) schools all being community schools. The UN's Rights of the Child point in this direction. The oscillations in child birth-rates also favour community elementary schools. Either children are rare and precious and should be given every encouragement to stay within their community, or children are numerous and so need many adults both qualified and unqualified to care for them. Such oscillations are also periods of the underuse and then excess of demand for schools. As Parker (1980, p. 311) noted, 'If creative reuse of underused schools is a viable option, inter-departmental co-operation and consultation with local residents is essential.' But behind expressions of the value of the child is the shadow of doubt about the viability of the family. The following three quotations capture the problems between them.

> The traditional idea of a family is that of a married couple with children living with them. However, the prevalence of this type of family in society has declined as a result of changes in cohabitation, marriage, divorce and parenthood as well as the ageing of the population.
>
> (Pullinger and Summerfield, 1997, p. 9)

> The United States is graying. The largest transfer of wealth in history has shifted poverty from the bent backs of the aged to the small backs of children.
>
> (Education Commission of the States, 1997, p. 4)

> Early retirement, unemployment, divorce and low pay all affect the future of many of Europe's older citizens – many of whom expect, and have reason to expect, a better life in old age than their parents and grandparents.
>
> (Laczko *et al.*, 1989, p. 6)

- Community schools will do more and more to support the family and to be supported by families. By putting students and their families first, they will restructure the resources for community in the schools.

- Designation itself will be less problematic because of a factor with far-reaching consequences. Whilst the state will finance the compulsory basic education, in the twenty-first century community self-financing will become the norm (Bray with Lillis, 1988). *Harambee*, Swahili for 'pulling together', will spread from developing countries to developed countries through a sequence of rapid reductions in state expenditure. These reductions will be attributed in large measure to reduced natural resources and therefore reduced revenues. There will also be demographically based reasoning to the effect that fewer and fewer households are made up of adults with children. Parents with school-age children will be in the minority and living within a majority that is unwilling to subsidise their choice to have children.

> In the province of British Colombia there are 32 designated community schools . . . designated by school district and each has a full-time co-ordinator. The province supports the idea and policy but does not allot funds. The funding is all from the local boards.
>
> (Mitchell, 1982, p. 26)

The pressure upon parents and the local community directly to finance all but the basics will be intensified through local governance with substantial powers: community associations and community education associations will increasingly replace boards of governors. Conflicts between community associations and governors over ownership and control will be drawn out and difficult. Community education does propose both an immediacy to public ownership and an intricacy in how that ownership is exercised. Direct democracy is usually slower than business in its decision-making.

- Ownership struggles will be more short-lived in community education centres. They are surplus outposts when viewed from centralised control. So, too, they attract all manner of piecemeal financing through projects, grants and donations. Centres will become all-purpose centres attracting more and more elements of social, medical and cultural interests. Neighbourhood centres will offer many opportunities for economy: reduced travel for participants, reduced overheads for providers. Community education centres become adept at accommodating diverse interests and covering their own overheads in the process.

- Community colleges (within further education) will acknowledge neighbourhood centres but remain alien from schools, and especially secondary schools. Having developed their contribution to and support for local employment, leisure and culture, they will turn to developing the same relationships with the voluntary sector. Rather than strengthen their relationships with schools, they will increasingly form stronger ties with regional universities as they, in turn, seek to add community-relevant qualifications to their portfolios.

- Some community education centres will be directly in touch with each other instantly, particularly through IT and local radio. Good practice will be distilled, stored and retrieved as never before. Ecological awareness, both the opposition to poisonous pollution and the proposition of positive action, will become essentially an area of local initiatives.

- The national lead will be taken by Second World countries. Those countries which have been centralist communist and are becoming decentralist socialist can understand the ambiguity of community education and can use its tension constructively. They do not have a whimsical relationship with community. The civic ethic, the ethic of collective improvement, is the vital focus; namely that improvements for all secure improvements for anyone (Peck, 1993).

- The unifying force will come from Second World countries and the major charities will move from supporting community education at home to supporting community education in former communist states. Even so, it is doubtful if more than enabling legislation will be passed. Community education in the twentieth century kept up with the changes in context by changing the content of its programmes and by claiming that the central value was upon community expressions of needs. Programmes partially displaced the process and yet partially preserved it. In the twenty-first century, too, the common sense of community education will continue to inspire both education centres and educational campaigns – again most probably without becoming mainstream. Some leading practitioners would not agree. They find the contrast between mighty visions and modest gains irritating. They foresee a future in which so much has been achieved in the immediate details of everyday education.

> I have this vision of the future . . . I am living in a community in the year 2020 as a very old man. . . . I go from my bungalow amid the houses for the young in my wheelchair each day to the local college. There I am very friendly with my neighbour's 8 year old and with a 17 year old boy . . . We play chess there each Friday morning and I enjoy reading to my neighbour's child . . . In the afternoon the 17 year old, the 8 year old's sister, the local bank manager and half a dozen others are taking a modular course in mid-twentieth-century social development over an intensive two or three week period.
>
> (Brighouse, 1983, p. 12)

Such details are not the fine brush-strokes from a chocolate box picture of the future. They will have been hard fought for, hard won and will always need to be defended. Jommo writes pointedly about three decades of distress in Africa. He sees community education as synthesising both a positive tradition and a popular democratic future – an argument which can be extended from Africa to the rest of the world.

> Researchers are challenged to undertake investigations that can objectively root community education in the African traditional experience and knowledge. . . .
>
> African professionals must take the lead in systematizing critical analysis . . . which can help more community education from isolated group initiatives to a mass movement for genuine African people-centred democracy and community empowerment.
>
> (Jommo, 1996, p. 5)

● In any event, community education will be pursued through conflict and through its successful cases.

> [W]e need to maintain a vision of community education that goes beyond the individualism and reductionism of educational consumerism and link theory to practice, institutional to community-based action. In developing it we need to be clear about values, explore our 'limitations', identify space for 'limit-acts', look to create new alliances, build on small victories and continue to develop our praxis.
>
> (Johnston, 1992, p. 5)

> Community education is a concept. It is not a programme; it is not a curriculum; it is a philosophical approach to education and indeed to living. Unless a person has some form of commitment to that philosophy, long lasting results are unlikely.
>
> (Tierney, 1980, p. 30)

BIBLIOGRAPHY

Alexander, D. J., Leach T. J. I. and Steward, T. G. (1984) *A Study of Policy, Organization, and Provision in Community Education and Leisure and Recreation in Three Scottish Regions*. Nottingham: Department of Adult Education, University of Nottingham.

Allen, G., Bastiani, J., Martin, I. and Richards, K. (eds) (1987) *Community Education. An Agenda for Educational Reform*. Milton Keynes: Open University Press.

Allen, G. and Martin, I. (eds) (1992) *Education and Community. The Politics of Practice*. London: Cassell.

Amar, J. J. A. (1996) *Quality of Life and Child Development*. Working Papers in Early Childhood Development, Bernard Van Leer Foundation, The Hague, The Netherlands.

Armstrong, R. (1977) 'Towards the study of community action'. *Adult Education*. 45 (1), 21–26.

Armstrong, R. (1982) 'The needs-meeting ideology of liberal adult education'. *International Journal of Lifelong Education*, 4, 293–321.

Arnstein, A. (1971) 'A ladder of citizen participation in the USA'. *Journal of the Town Planning Institute*, 57 (4).

Association of Municipal Authorities (AMA) (1991) 'Looking at community education'. Coventry: Community Education Development Centre.

Australian Schools 2 (n.d.) Hampden Park Public School, New South Wales Government, Sydney.

Australian Schools 3 (n.d.) Billabong High School, New South Wales Government, Sydney.

Baird, N. (1996) 'A new and interesting way of teaching and learning for adults in the Solomon Islands'. *Community Education International*, October, 10.

Bakke, A. and Tharp, B. (1995) *Building the Global Community: The Next Step*. Des Plaines, IL: American Council on International Intercultural Education and the Stanley Foundation.

Bastiani, J. (1989) *Working with Parents: A Whole School Approach.* Windsor: NEFER/Nelson.

Boyd, J. (1977) *Community Education and Urban Schools.* London: Longman.

Bray, M. with Lillis, K. (1988) 'Community financing of education: issues and policy implications in less developed countries'. Oxford: Pergamon.

Bremer, J., Bennett, I., Kiers, D. and Laird, J. (eds) (1979) *1980 Plus. Community Participation and Learning.* 6 vols. Melbourne: Australian Association for Community Education and Planning Services Division of the Education Department of Victoria.

Brighouse, T. R. P. (1983) 'Some thoughts on educational politics and the community'. Paper given to Community Education Association, Birmingham, April 1983, 1–14.

Brookfield, S. (1983) *Adult Learners, Adult Education and the Community.* Milton Keynes: Open University Press.

Brookfield, S. D. (1987) *Developing Critical Thinkers.* Milton Keynes: Open University Press.

Butler, L. M. and Howell R. E. (1980) *Community Needs Assessment Techniques.* Western Rural Education Papers 44. Western Rural Development Centre, Oregan State University.

Carn, K. (1995) 'The role of the Fiji Association of Non Formal Educators (FANFE) in Effective Schooling through parental education and community support'. Paper presented at the 7th World Conference on Community Education. Jomtien, Thailand.

Clark, D. (1996) *Schools as Learning Communities. Transforming Education.* London: Cassell.

Cohen, A. M. (1996) 'Community colleges'. In Tuijnman, A. C. (ed.) *International Encyclopedia of Adult Education and Training.* Oxford: Elsevier, 631–618.

Community Education International (1991) 'The global village'. ICEA 6th World Conference report. Blackhurst, A. (ed.) Coventry: ICEA.

Community Education International (1995) 'Women in development'. Murphy, P. (ed.) Coventry: ICEA.

Community Education Network (1990) *Really Learning.* Vol. 10 (9). Sayer, B. (ed.) Coventry: Community Education Development Centre.

Cunningham, P. M. (1996) 'Community education and community development'. In Tuijnman, A. C. (ed.) *International Encyclopedia of Adult Education and Training.* Oxford: Elsevier, 56–61.

Dave, R. H. (ed.) (1982) [1976] *Foundations of Lifelong Education.* Oxford: Pergamon.

Decker, L. and Boo, M. R. (1995) 'Creating learning communities: an introduction to community education'. Fairfax, VA: National Community Education Association.

Devon County Council (1994) *A Devon Approach to the Community Education Curriculum.* Exeter: Devon County Council.

Dove, L. (1980) 'The role of the community school in rural transformation in developing countries'. *Comparative Education,* 16 (1), 67–79.

Education Commission of the States (1997) 'Transforming the education system: the 1997 Education Agenda'. Denver, CO: ECS Distribution Center.

Edwards, P. and Biocchi, K. (1996) *Community Schools across America: 135 Community/School Partnerships that Are Making a Difference.* Flint, MI: National Centre for Community Education.

Evans, N. (1985) *Post-education Society.* London: Croom Helm.

Evason, E. (1978) *Family Poverty in Northern Ireland.* London: Child Poverty Action Group.

Evason, E. (1991) *Against the Grain. The Contemporary Women's Movement in Northern Ireland.* Belfast: Attic Press.

Fletcher, C. (1982) 'The challenges of community education'. Nottingham Adult Education Research Reports, Nottingham University.

Fletcher, C. (1984a) *The Challenges of Community Education: A Biography of Sutton Centre 1970 to 1982.* Nottingham: Department of Adult Education, Nottingham University.

Fletcher, C. (1984b) *Community Education and Community Development International Encyclopaedia of Education.* Oxford: Pergamon.

Fletcher, C. (1987) 'The meanings of community in "Community Education"'. In Allen *et al.* (eds).

Fletcher, C. and Thompson, N. (eds) (1980) *Issues in Community Education.* Barcombe, Sussex: Falmer Press.

Fletcher, C., Caron, M. and Williams, W. (1985) *Schools on Trial.* Milton Keynes: Open University Press.

Freire, P. (1975) [1972] *Pedagogy of the Oppressed*. Harmondsworth: Penguin.

Freire, P. (1977) [1970] *Cultural Action for Freedom*. Harmondsworth: Penguin.

Freire, P. (1979) [1974] *Education for Critical Consciousness*. London: Sheed & Ward.

Freire, P. (1985) *The Politics of Education*. Trans. by D. Macedo. Basingstoke: Macmillan.

Galloway, I. (1980) 'Community education – people helping people'. *Edgewater Community News*, New Zealand.

Gregory, J. (1991) 'Harry Rée', Obituary. *ICEA Regional Newsletter. European Region* 7, 23.

Hagan, B. T. (1996) 'Community education in the Cook Islands'. *Community Education International*, October, 4–5.

Hall, P., Marks, C., Street, P. and Clifford, A. (1984) *Going Community for Secondary Schools*. Coventry, England: Community Education Development Centre.

Halsey, A. H. (1972) *Educational Priority*, Vol. 1. London: HMSO.

Ibikunle-Johnson V. O. (1994) 'The environment as an integrating concept in community education'. *Community Education International*, October, 5, 6.

Inayatullah (1994) *But Where Is the Literacy Plan?* Lahore: Pacade Pakistan Association for Continuing Adult Education, Annual Report.

Jackson, K. (1971) 'Community Adult Education – "The Professional Role"'. *Adult Education*, 44 (3), 165–168.

Jackson, K. (1980) 'Some fallacies in community education and their consequences in working class areas'. In Fletcher and Thompson (eds), 39–46.

Johnston, R. (1992) 'Praxis for the punch drunk and powerless'. *Community Education Network*, 12 (7), 3–5.

Jommo, B. R. (1996) 'Reflections on community education'. *Community Education International*, February, 3–6.

Keeble, R. W. J. (1981) *Community and Education*. Leicester: National Youth Bureau.

Kiraly, J. (1979) Foreword in P. Slattery, (ed.) *And Now It Flows: Release of Learning*. Melbourne: Numarwading North Neighbourhood Centre.

Knightsbridge, J. (1992) 'Lobbying: The principles, community education'. *Network* 12, (3), 5–6.

Laczko, F., Robbins, D. and Giannichedda, M. (1989) *The Family and the Local Community*. Working Papers, Evaluation Section No. 38, European Programme to Combat Poverty, Bath: Centre for the Analysis of Social Policy, University of Bath.

Li Yixian (1995) 'Community education in China'. Paper presented at the 7th World Congress on Community Education. Jomtien, Thailand.

Lovett, T. (1971) 'Community adult education'. *Studies in Adult Education*. 3, (1).

Lovett, T. (1973) 'Community Development – a network approach'. *Adult Education*, 46 (3), 157–165.

Lovett, T. (1975) *Adult Education, Community Development and the Working Class*. London: Ward Lock.

Lovett, T. (ed.) (1988) *Radical Approaches to Adult Education: A Reader*. London: Routledge.

Lovett, T. (1992) 'The challenge of change'. *Community Education Network*, l2 (2), 3–5.

Lovett, T., Clarke, B. and Kilmurray, A. (1983) *Adult Education and Community Action*. London: Croom Helm.

Lund, B. and McGechan, J. (1981) *CE Programmer's Manual*. Victoria: British Colombia Ministry of Education.

Lynch, J. (1979) *Education for Community. A Cross-Cultural Study in Education*. London: Macmillan Education.

Martin, I. (1987a) *Community Education: Towards a Theoretical Analysis*. In G. Allen *et al.* (eds) *Community Education*. Milton Keynes: Open University Press, 9–32.

Martin, I. (1987b) 'Education and community: Reconstructing the relationship'. *Journal of Community Education*, 5 (3), 17–22.

Midwinter, E. (1972) *Priority Education*. Harmondsworth: Penguin.

Midwinter, E. (1975) *Education and the Community*. London: George Allen & Unwin.

Minty, I. (1993) 'The de-designation of Cambridgeshire's community primary schools'. M.Phil. thesis, Cranfield University.

Minzey, J. and Letarte, C. E. (1972) *Community Education: 'From Program to Process'*. Midland, MI: Pendell Publishing.

Mitchell, G. (1982) 'Some profiles of community education in Canada'. *International Community Education Newsletter* 4 (2), 24–27.

Morgan, G. (1986) *Images of Organization*. London: Sage.

Munoz, B. and Garcia-Blanco, A. M. (1989) 'Community based education: Part One'. *Harvard Educational Review*, 54 (4).

Newman, M. (1979) *The Poor Cousin: A Study of Adult Education*. London: George Allen & Unwin.

Nisbet, J., Hendry, L., Stewart, C. and Watt, J. (1980) *Towards Community Education. An Evaluation of Community Schools*. Aberdeen: Aberdeen University Press.

Nornsis, M. J. (1993) *SPSS for Windows: Professional Statistics*. Release 6.0 SPSS, Chicago.

O'Hagan, R. (1988) *The Aims and Principles of Community Education*. Hind Leys, Leicestershire: Hind Leys Community College Council.

O'Hagan, R. (ed.) (1991) *The Charnwood Papers. Fallacies in Community Education*. Ticknall, Derbyshire: Education Now.

Parikh, R. (1994) *The Role of Universities in Linking Learning and Work*. Lahore: Pacade (Pakistan Association for Continuing Adult Education).

Pariyatsulthee, P. S. (1995) 'Monks and the prevention and solving of AIDS in community'. Paper presented at the ICEA 7th World Conference on Community Education, Jomtien, Thailand.

Parker, G. (1980) 'Community schools: An American perspective'. *Architectural Journal*, 13 August, 301–335.

Peck, M. S. (1993) *A World Waiting to be Born: Civility Rediscovered*. New York: Bantam Press.

Poster, C. and Krüger, A. (eds) (1990) *Community Education in the Western World*. London: Routledge.

Pullinger, J. and Summerfield, C. (1997) 'Social focus on families'. London: Office for National Statistics/The Stationery Office.

Putnam, R. (1993) *Making Democracy Work: Civic Traditions in Modern Italy*. Princeton, NJ: Princeton University Press.

Rée, H. (1973) *Educator Extraordinary. The Life and Achievement of Henry Morris*. London: Longman.

Renard, R. (1995) 'A case for community-run pre-schools and day care centres, St Lucia'. *Community Education International*, November.

Ringers, J. and Decker, L. E. (1995) 'School community centres: guidelines for interagency planners'. Mid-Atlantic Center for Community Education, University of Virginia.

Rogers, T. (ed.) (1971) *School for the Community. A Grammar School Reorganises*. London: Routledge & Kegan Paul.

Scottish Community Education Council (SCEC) (n.d.) *The Services of the Scottish Community Education Council*, Edinburgh: SCEC.

Sirindhorn, HRH Princess Maha Chakri (1995) Inaugural Address. ICEA 7th World Conference. Jomtien, Thailand.

Slattery, P. (1979) *Release of Learning and Now It Flows*. Nunawading, Vic.: Nunawading North Neighbourhood Centre, Australia.

Smith, M. K. (1994) *Local Education. Community, Conversation, Praxis*. Buckingham: Open University Press.

Stacey, M. (1991) *Parents and Teachers Together*. Buckingham: Open University Press.

Stewart, B. (ed.) (1979) *The House*. Nunawading. Vic.: Nunawading North Neighbourhood Centre, Australia.

Thorpe, R. (1985) 'Community work and ideology: an Australian perspective'. In Thorpe, R. and Petruchenia, J. (eds) *Community Work or Social Change*. London: Routledge.

Tierney, T. (1980) 'Some impressions of community education in the United States'. *Community Education* No. 3, Autumn, Education Department of South Australia.

Tight, M. (ed.) (1983) *Education for Adults. Vol. II: Opportunities for Adult Education*. London: Croom Helm, in association with the Open University.

Titmus, C. (ed.) (1989) *Lifelong Education for Adults. An International Handbook*. Oxford: Pergamon.

Wasi, P. (1995) 'Community and sustainable development'. Paper presented at the ICEA 7th World Conference on Community Education, Jomtien, Thailand.

Whalley, M. (1994) *Learning to Be Strong. Setting Up a Neighbourhood Service for Under-fives and Their Families.* London: Hodder & Stoughton.

Whalley, M. and Arnold, C. (1996) 'Working with parents'. Corby: Pen Green Centre.

Widlake, P. (1986) *Reducing Educational Disadvantage.* Milton Keynes: Open University Press.

Williams, R. (1976) *Keywords.* London: Fontana.

Williams, W. and Robins, W. R. (1980) 'Observations on the California case'. In Fletcher and Thompson (eds), 55–62.

Willmott, P. (1989) *Community Initiatives. Patterns and Prospects.* London: Policy Studies Institute.

Wilson, S. (1980) 'The school and community'. In C. Fletcher and N. T. Thompson (eds) *Issues in Community Education*, London: Falmer Press, 115–132.

Wymer, K. (1995) 'Bilston Community College and Community/Partnerships'. Presented at conference on The Community College in the Global Economy: A Limitless Future, Ryton Hall, Shropshire.

Zimmer, J. (1991) 'Developing Culture-sensitive tourism'. *Community Education International*, July, 3–5.

Part III

SUBSTANTIVE ISSUES

20

STANDARDS

What are they, what do they do and where do they live?

Dylan Wiliam

INTRODUCTION

Three school districts use the same mathematics test for assessing the achievement of students at the end of a school year in order to decide whether they have made sufficient progress to move on to the next grade. In this test, a mark of 50% has traditionally been regarded as indicating that a student should be allowed to progress, and a mark of below 50% indicates that the student needs to repeat a grade.

In school district A, the proportion of students achieving the notional 'pass mark' of 50% rose in the last year from 90% to 95%. In school district B, they have decided that a mark of 50% is not really adequate for further study, and so this year they have decided to raise the mark needed to progress to 55%, which has resulted in a situation in which the proportion of students achieving the mark necessary for progression has gone down from 90% to 80%. In school district C, due to demographic changes, there are 10% more students in the age-cohort than there were last year, and so, while the proportion of students who achieve the mark necessary for progression has not increased, the actual number of students achieving this mark *has* increased. In which of these school districts has the *standard* of mathematics achievement increased?

The answer is, of course, that it depends what one means by the term 'standard'. It could be argued that standards have increased in all three school districts. The term 'standard' can refer to a level of performance, or to the number or proportion of a particular cohort achieving that level. If we think of a standard as the level of performance, then the standard has increased in school district B, but has remained constant in the others. If we think of a standard as the proportion of the cohort that achieve a particular level of achievement, then standards would have risen in school district A and stayed the same in school district C (and on the basis of the data given, we cannot say what happened in school district B). Finally, if we think of standards as referring to the number of students achieving a particular level, then standards have risen in school district C and have probably risen in school district A (provided that there hasn't been a drop in the size of the age-cohort), and again, we cannot be sure what has happened in school district B. This ambiguity about the meaning of the term 'standard' is why politicians are able to claim that standards are falling whether the proportion of students achieving a particular standard goes down or up. If the proportion or number of the cohort achieving the standard decreases, then 'standards are going down' because fewer individuals achieve the standard specified. However, if the proportion or number of the cohort achieving the standard increases, then 'standards are going down' because the increase in success must have been because the 'standard' has been made easier!

These different conceptualisations of standards serve different purposes. For employers who want a more highly skilled workforce, they may well feel that what matters is the *number* of people achieving a particular level of skill or capability. However, many employers might actually be using test outcomes as a tool for selection, caring little about the actual content of the test, but using the test as an apparently fair way of selecting employees. For these users of test information, test scores are 'positioned goods' – their value lies in their scarcity and become less valuable as they become more widely distributed.

However, as well as being clear about what we mean by standards, we should also be concerned about their effects. How was the improvement in school district A achieved? Did the teachers narrow their teaching to focus more directly on those elements of the curriculum that were assessed in the tests? Was more time given to mathematics than other subjects, because of its importance for progression, so that 'standards' in other subjects declined?

The next three sections of this article address three fundamental questions about standards:

- What are standards and what do they do?
- Where do standards live?
- How can standards be compared?

WHAT ARE STANDARDS AND WHAT DO THEY DO?

It is a truism to say that human beings are not equally good at all things, and yet this simple truth creates fundamental problems for the assessment of human performance which are all too often ignored. As Howard Gardner's work (1993) has shown, people who are good at the kinds of activities that have traditionally been valued in educational settings may not be as adept in (say) interpersonal relationships. Within the narrow focus of scholastic achievement, students who are good at mathematics will not necessarily be as competent in music, languages or at sports. Within a single subject, students will not be equally good at all aspects; those who are good at geometry will not necessarily be as good at algebra and highly articulate students may not be able to show this articulacy in writing. Even with a narrowly defined aspect of a single subject, it is rarely the case that students behave consistently.

One response to this complexity is to throw up one's hands in horror and say that there are no useful generalisations that one can make – every detail of every aspect of human performance is unrelated to anything else. As Banesh Hoffman observed, 'To compress all our information about a single candidate into a single ranking number is clearly absurd – quite ridiculously irrational. And yet it has to be done' (Hoffman, 1962, p. 35). There are many occasions when it is necessary to make a complex, multidimensional distribution of achievement or ability more easily understood. At its most general therefore (at least within the field of educational assessment) a standard involves the selection of a particular aspect of a distribution of some attribute to stand as a proxy for some more complex underlying distribution.

Within a particular domain, the traditional method of setting a standard involves two steps. The first step is to construct a numerical scale that represents the extent of an individual's achievement within the domain. The simplest (and most common) way of doing this is by setting a test which samples the domain. The more items on the test that an individual gets correct, the greater the extent of that individual's achievement in that domain. If we think that particular aspects of achievement are more important than others, we can include more questions related to that aspect in our test, or we can weight scores on different items differently.

The second step is to choose a particular point on the score scale as representing the 'standard' in which we are interested. The effect of this is to tie a specific score on the test to a particular set of patterns of achievement. If, for example, we have a test of 100 items, weighted equally, and we set a 'passing score' of 50%, we are saying that we will regard a candidate who gets *any* 50 items correct as having reached the standard – there is a huge number of different ways of getting 50 items correct out of 100, but if we set our passing score at 50%, we are saying that we shall treat all candidates who get 50 items correct as having reached the standard. In this approach, the setting of a standard involves identifying a particular level of performance in a domain (the performance standard) with a particular score (the passing score). The important thing to bear in mind is that the choice of both the performance standard and the passing score is arbitrary (i.e. they require the exercise of judgement).

Passing scores are arbitrary

It is widely agreed that the choice of a particular passing score is arbitrary. As Kane observes:

> the tradition of requiring 70% correct on tests seems especially arbitrary, because we know that, for any group of examinees, we can probably make the items easy enough so that everyone gets more than 70% correct or difficult enough so that nobody gets more than 70% correct.
>
> (Kane, 1994, p. 426)

Setting the proportion of items to be achieved at (say) 70% is, when considered in terms of classical measurement theory, a rather bad idea because setting such a high cut-score is likely to result in far lower test reliability than, say, one set at 50%, due to a variety of factors including 'ceiling effects'. At first sight, therefore, setting a cut-score at 70% seems unjustifiable.

However, while a high cut-score might not be justifiable in *measurement* terms, it might well be appropriate in terms of the *consequences* of setting the standards in a particular way. For example, if we had a qualifying examination for airline pilots, we could, by careful choice of items, arrange that the same performance standard would equate to 30%, 50%, 70% or even 90% of the available marks. The technical concerns of psychometricians would suggest that 50% would be the best threshold to choose so as to maximise reliability. However, as Messick argues:

> Values are important to take into account in score interpretation not only because they can directly bias score-based inferences and actions, but because they could also indirectly influence in more subtle and insidious ways the meanings and implications attributed to test scores.
>
> (Messick, 1989, p. 59)

In the context of the qualifying of airline pilots, no matter what level of competence was actually associated with a 50% score, it is likely that the general perception would be that 50% would be an unsatisfactory score with which to qualify airline pilots, no matter what performance standard such a score indicated. Indeed, it may be that the public would be unhappy with any passing score below 100%.

As well as having implications for the values that are associated with particular assessment results, where standards are set can also have social consequences, as was well understood by the advocates of mastery learning (Bloom, 1968). For example, we could arrange for the threshold performance level on an end-of-topic test to be equivalent to any score we chose. However, if we set the 'mastery' score at 30%, then we might well produce students who had succeeded *without believing that they had done so*, possibly leading to disaffection and withdrawal by the learners.

Therefore while the setting of passing scores is arbitrary (i.e. requiring the application of judgement), the examples above show that the exercise of that judgement needs to balance technical considerations against value implications and social consequences (Messick, 1989).

Performance standards are arbitrary

There is much less agreement about whether performance standards are arbitrary. Kane (1994, p. 426) argues that: 'Some standards do not seem at all arbitrary; a requirement that a lifeguard be able to swim a certain distance in a certain time and then swim back pulling a struggling victim does not seem particularly arbitrary.' On the face of it, this is a plausible assertion, but it disguises a series of arbitrary decisions that have been made. How are we to set the distance over which the lifeguard is to swim and bring back the 'rescuee'? Even if we undertook a rigorous analysis of every single life-saving incident, either actual or possible, we would still have to make an arbitrary judgement. Do we define the performance standard at the 85th, 90th, 95th or 99th percentile? What about the effects of currents? How much struggling is the rescuee allowed to do during the test, and what is the trade-off between the amount of struggling, strength of current, and distance? Even if we can determine such a trade-off (based perhaps on the 'average' swimmer), such resolutions will advantage some swimmers at the expense of others. For example, stronger swimmers will be advantaged in a test of swimming against a strong current, with a strongly struggling rescuee. In contrast, weaker swimmers with greater endurance would be advantaged by a performance standard that emphasised longer distances with more passive rescuees. The performance standard itself incorporates a set of implicit values about the different aspects of performance that will penalise those that depart too far from the norm. The consequence of this is that the performance standard *normalises* the activity.

More worryingly, the performance standards, because they emphasise particular aspects of performance, can be manipulated. In one school district a new test was introduced, and scores in the district rose steadily over the next four years. However, when a random sample of the students was given the old test, which had been discontinued five years earlier, their scores were well below that of the last cohort to take the test (Linn, 1994). The improvement in scores had been achieved not by an overall increase in the students' achievement, but by a change in emphasis. In crude terms, the clearer you are about what you want, the more likely you are to get it, but the less likely it is to mean anything.

We can summarise these processes in terms of Samuel Messick's model for validity argument, shown in Figure 20.1. In this model, he distinguishes between the *basis* and the *function* of the assessment. The basis of the assessment is the source of justification of the assessment while its function is what we want the assessment to do.

We might select a particular 'standard' because it captures in a simpler way some important features of the distribution of achievement, ability, attitudes or whatever. In other words, we are interested in whether achievement of the standard allows us to draw justifiable conclusions about the more complex distribution which we want to simplify (the top left-hand cell of Figure 20.1). This is an issue of construct validity – the extent to which a particular measure (in this case the 'standard') allows us to draw inferences about some wider domain.

In choosing a particular standard, we are often guided by concerns of relevance and utility. In certain situations, we may have little idea about how to measure something (or it may be too expensive), but we can often find a measure that seems to correlate well with the thing we wish to measure but that is easier or cheaper to carry out. So, for example, while measuring an individual's capacity to benefit from a university education appears to be extraordinarily difficult (to define, let alone measure!), it is possible to find other measures that appear to correlate well. The validation of the use of indirect measures or 'proxies' corresponds to the top right-hand cell of Figure 20.1.

What we want from an indirect measure is that it should correlate well with that for which it is intended as a proxy. For example, many researchers have pointed out that the use of complex (and expensive) constructed-response assessments is unnecessary because individuals' scores on multiple-choice tests tend to correlate quite highly with scores on constructed response tests, so we might as well use the former, because they are cheaper and more reliable. However, there is no guarantee that correlations will remain high.

| | | **FUNCTION** | |
		Meaning	Use
BASIS	Evidential basis	Construct validity	Construct validity + relevance/utility
	Consequential basis	Value implications	Social consequences

Figure 20.1 Facets of validity argument
Source: Adapted from Messick, 1989

The performance standard, originally selected as an *index* of performance, because it is known to be a correlate of performance ('construct validity' in Figure 20.1) becomes the *definition* of performance. This shifts the values of teachers from the overall performance to the indices ('value implications' in Figure 20.1), and their practice is altered to reflect this new emphasis (social consequences). The result is that the correlational link between the performance and its indices is weakened. It becomes possible to improve scores on the index without increasing scores on the performance. This may result in an increase in overall or average performance, but may equally well just be a redistribution of attainment. Indeed, it is entirely possible for the index of performance (e.g. the proportion of students achieving a particular standard) to rise while the average performance of the cohort decreases. The use of such a *manipulable* performance indicator may be justified in terms of its meanings, but in 'high-stakes' settings in particular, the consequences of its use needs to be carefully investigated before adoption.

WHERE ARE STANDARDS?

Of course, by itself, being told that a certain proportion of a cohort has reached a particular performance standard means little. To make any use of standards, we have to interpret the performance of a particular group in some way. What does it mean that (say) 55% of a particular population achieved a certain standard? Is that good enough or not? What are we justified in concluding about someone's performance when we are told that they have reached a specified standard?

Traditionally, the way that performance against some standard has been interpreted has been by comparing the performance of an individual or a group against some other group of individuals. For example, until recently, the performance of every student taking the Educational Testing Service's Scholastic Aptitude Test was compared with a group of students used to set the standard for the test in 1941. This kind of *norm-referenced* interpretation is similar to the kinds of 'benchmarking' activity undertaken by commercial organisations in comparing their performance with that of their competitors. The trouble with such an approach is that all it requires is that we put individuals in a rank order, and it is very easy to put people in a rank order, without having any clear idea what they are in rank order *of.* Norm-referenced interpretations, like bench-marks, are frequently used when we have no clear idea what level of performance is actually required. A good example of this is countries that measure the success of their education systems by where they rank in terms of international comparisons, rather than by whether the system actually does what the country wants or needs it to do (in this context, it should be noted that the evidence for a link between industrial com-petitiveness and levels of achievement in national education systems is actually quite sparse – see the report from the OECD's Centre for Educational Research and Innovation, 1998).

Norm-referenced interpretations of assessment outcomes can be of benefit in making selection decisions, but in educational assessments, particularly those intended to support learning, it is far less important to know where an individual is in some rank order than it is to find out what they have learnt. For this reason, since the late 1960s, there has been a rapid increase in the use of assessments that allow users to draw conclusions about what specific things an individual might know, understand or be able to do.

The original impetus behind the criterion-referenced measurement movement was to specify educational outcomes in precise terms, rather than by vague curriculum statements and syllabuses. The trouble with traditional syllabuses was that while experienced professionals were usually able to interpret the syllabuses appropriately, they were of little help to less experienced teachers and students. However, the attempt to specify learning outcomes precisely appears to have led to one of two unfortunate outcomes. In some approaches, outcome specifications became longer and longer in an attempt to tie down the meaning of the learning outcome more and more precisely, resulting in systems that were quite unusable because of their bulk. In other approaches, precision was attained by focusing on only those aspects that were easy to define, resulting in an atomisation and narrowing of the curriculum. The result of the criterion-referenced measurement project is that it is now generally agreed that the range of learning outcomes that are appropriate for educational systems cannot be defined unambiguously. Statements of learning outcomes will always need to be interpreted, and consensus in those interpretations will require the exercise of professional judgement. But where does this professional judgement reside?

Of course, not all assessors exercising their professional judgement will agree at all times, but where there is agreement, the question then arises of how does such consistency emerge? The consistency is not generated by the provision of external criteria, since there are none, nor is it, in any real sense, achieved by reference to a norm group that different assessors have in common. It seems therefore that the only solution is that the consistency in teachers' judgement (where it exists) arises out of a shared construct of the standard in question; in other words the assessment is 'construct-referenced'.

It could be argued that construct-referenced assessment is just a form of norm-referenced assessment, and in one sense, all notions of standards are based on intuitive ideas of norms. Objectively, the performance standard of being able to high-jump 2 metres is of no more relevance than being able to high-jump (say) 10 metres. It is only by reference to a human population that the first is more interesting than the second, which led to William Angoff's assertion that 'we should be aware that lurking behind the criterion-referenced evaluation, perhaps even responsible for it, is the norm-referenced evaluation' (Angoff, 1974, p. 4).

However, there is an important difference in emphasis between norm- and construct-referenced assessments. In norm-referenced assessment the standard exists in the performance of the reference group. In construct-referenced assessment, whatever standard that exists does so in the heads of those involved in the assessment, who form a more or less coherent 'community of practice'.

The common criticism levelled against such a notion of 'standard' is that it is not 'objective', but the word 'objective' here can be interpreted in two ways. One meaning of the term 'objective' is that the level of performance sought is delineated in the form of performance objectives – a process that has been termed *objectification*. However, to say that an assessment is objective also means that it is free from subjectivity; i.e. that the grade a candidate is awarded does not depend on who makes the assessment. In construct-referenced assessment, objectivity is achieved not through objectification, but through inter-subjectivity.

HOW CAN STANDARDS BE COMPARED?

Although standards can be used as a guide to interpreting the test results for individuals on a single test or assessment, it is far more often the case that 'standards' are used in order to compare the performance of an individual or a cohort of individuals with others taking the same or a similar assessment at a different time, or a different assessment of the same subject, or even with those taking a different subject.

Perhaps the best-known examples of comparisons of standards within the same subject are the attempts to compare standards of achievement in different countries. The vast majority of these studies have focused on mathematics and science, but other studies have also looked at literacy, writing, geography, history and information technology.

Ever since international comparisons began, there have been critiques of their usefulness, and even of their meaningfulness. Aside from the cultural differences between countries, which many commentators maintain render international comparisons useless if not meaningless, there are four main sources of difficulty:

- population sampling
- curriculum coverage
- test translation
- test administration.

These are discussed below in turn.

Population-sampling difficulties

The validity of any conclusions based on a nation's score in an international comparison depends crucially on the fact that the sample of pupils actually taking the test must be a random sample from all the eligible pupils in the whole country. So, for example, if we are assessing the performance of 13 year olds, it is very important that the sample of pupils is a random sample of all 13 year olds in the country. In the Scandinavian countries, this is relatively straightforward. However, many countries such as the United States, France and Germany require students who have not made sufficient progress in a school year to repeat the year (a process called 'grade retention' in the US or *'redoublement'* in France). In France and Germany, as many as a quarter of all students may have repeated a year at some time before they reach the age of 13, so that to obtain a random sample of all 13 year olds, it is necessary to extend the sample to include classes where the majority of children are much younger. This aspect is not well controlled in many studies, with the result that countries who do not use 'grade retention' often appear to have a negatively skewed distribution of attainment compared to countries using grade retention.

Sampling is also difficult because there are often systematic differences between countries in the way that students are allocated to particular year cohorts. For example, in Germany the average age of students sampled in the Third International Mathematics and Science Study (TIMSS) middle school survey was 10 months greater than the average for England. Based on the growth in attainment between age 13 and age 14 found in the whole international sample, this would lead to scores in England being underestimated by approximately 23 points in mathematics and nearly 30 points in science, when compared with Germany.

Curriculum coverage

Apart from the belief that they are important for industrial competitiveness, there can be little doubt that one of the reasons that mathematics and science have proved the most popular subjects for international comparisons is the similarity in the curricula for these two subjects in different countries. However, these surface similarities can disguise quite deep-seated differences in emphasis and approach. For example, many countries restrict their primary school mathematics curricula to little more than arithmetic, and primary science is often little more than the more descriptive aspects of biology. Even when the same topic is covered in all countries, there are often substantial differences in emphasis, so that in one country, the topic of 'number' might emphasise computational techniques, while in another, more time would be spent developing students' ability to choose the correct arithmetical operation. Inevitably, the construction of a test for international comparison must therefore involve a deal of compromise. Because of the costs of marking, particularly for poorer countries, there is also a considerable pressure to make substantial use of multiple-choice items, which clearly advantages countries where students have experience of taking such items, and also tends to emphasise 'lower-order skills' such as knowledge recall, rather than 'higher-order skills' such as analysis or synthesis. In passing it should be noted that multiple-choice items *can* assess higher-order skills, but these items appear to be more difficult to develop (and are certainly not commonly encountered).

Test translation

A third source of difficulty, and one that is rarely discussed, is that of ensuring that versions of the tests in different languages are in fact comparable. It has often been observed that translation of a test from one language to another can result in an increase in the difficulty of the test, and for that reason, a process of *parallel development* has sometimes been advocated (Wiliam, 1994). If this were the only source of difficulty, this would not be an issue for interpreting the results of English students, since most of the item construction for inter-national comparisons is done in English. However, it is clear that test translations can also result in making the test item easier. For example, in Wales students can take their school-leaving examination (the General Certificate of Secondary Education or GCSE) through the medium of either Welsh or English. Jones (1993) showed that a GCSE examination question involving similar triangles was found to be easier for students taking the examin-ation in Welsh than in English (established by comparing scores on that question for stu-dents who had scored the same total on the rest of the paper). The reason for this appears to be that the Welsh word for 'similar' is encountered only in its technical sense, and therefore students seeing this word were cued to respond in a technical register. In the English version, because the word 'similar' also has a vernacular meaning, some students did not interpret 'similar' as a carefully defined geometric term, but instead responded by gauging whether the triangles were like each other in some intuitive sense. In this respect, English is at a particular disadvantage, since many technical terms in English also have vernacular meanings, while other languages have had to coin new technical terms, which tend not to have vernacular uses. While there are technical solutions to the problems of population sampling and curriculum coverage identified above, there is absolutely no solution to the problems of test translation: the connotations of a particular word in a particular language are unique, and no amount of test development can compensate for this.

Test administration

It is also clear that the circumstances under which a test is administered can have a substantial effect on the results. There is certainly evidence from TIMSS that the contexts in which the tests were administered differed from country to country. While there may be some exaggeration in the stories that students selected to take the tests in certain Pacific Rim countries were cheered by the whole school as 'representatives of the nation's honour', there is little doubt that students in some countries were encouraged to treat the experience much more seriously than in others. Since students score higher marks on tests where they believe that the result matters (in other words 'high-stakes' tests), this must have a bearing on the meaningfulness of international comparisons.

Another factor that bears on the validity of the results is student absence. No matter what steps are taken to ensure that the identified sample is a random sample from the population under study, some students in the sample will be absent on a given day. In TIMSS, the proportion of students absent from the mathematics test for 13 year olds varied from a frankly improbable zero out of the 11,695 students in the sample in Thailand, to 14% absence in Bulgaria. Since it is not safe to assume that the absent students would have the same average scores as those tested (for example, the absentees will include a disproportionate number of persistent truants and those with chronic illness, who would be likely to achieve lower scores than average had they been tested), these differences in attendance further complicate drawing any meaningful interpretations from international comparisons.

However, the problems of comparing different countries' performance in the same subject are almost trivial compared with the technical difficulties of comparing the performance of students in different subjects. Indeed, whether such a comparison has any meaning at all was poignantly raised by Robert Wood in his classic article 'Your chemistry equals my French' (Wood, 1987).

Comparisons between subjects

In an important paper Cresswell (1996, pp. 73–77) identifies six different definitions of the comparability of standards between different assessments:

- equal attainment definition
- 'no nonsense' definition
- same candidates definition

- value-added definition
- similar schools definition
- catch-all definition.

The 'equal attainment' definition requires simply that for two groups of candidates with the same attainment, the different assessments generate identical distributions of scores. This definition is, of course, circular, since we can only establish that two groups of candidates have the same attainment by giving them each an assessment that is a fair measure of their attainment. The 'no nonsense' definition regards different assessments as being comparable if they have identical distributions of scores or grades, while the 'same candidates' definition requires identical scores or grades when the same group of candidates is entered for each. The 'value-added' definition requires the distributions of results to be the same for groups of candidates who are matched in terms of ability and prior achievement, but who have studied different curricula and taken different assessments. The 'similar schools' definition requires identical distributions of scores for matched groups of students attending similar schools, while the 'catch-all' definition takes this several steps further by matching the groups in terms of ability, prior achievement, similarity of school, comparability of school assessment policies, teacher competence and student motivation!

As Cresswell points out, none of these definitions is satisfactory. Indeed, the intractability of the technical problems has led many experts in the field to assert that comparability of standards is essentially impossible to achieve. However, Cresswell argues that such attempts miss the point because they divorce the assessment process from the social setting in which it takes place, and the value judgements that are made in those social settings. He suggests that educational qualifications function as a kind of 'currency with which candidates buy entry into education and employment'. Just as banknotes have little intrinsic value, but derive their value as 'promissory notes', so educational credentials fulfil their function provided two results from different assessments of the same subject, or even from different subjects, represent achievement that is equally *valued*.

By making central the value that is placed on awards, many of the technical difficulties are obviated. Perhaps more importantly, the definition makes explicit that the comparability of standards is only relative to a community of interested users of assessment results, and the assessment system functions only to the extent that the interested users trust the judgements of the awarders.

This can be thought of as an example of what the philosopher John Searle has called social reality (Searle, 1995). He points out that social facts frequently come into being simply by the speech acts of suitably qualified or empowered individuals or institutions. For example, in England two people are deemed to be married by the pronouncement of a registrar or minister. Once that person has spoken, provided she or he is suitably authorised, there is no question about whether the couple really are married. In the same way, the award of a PhD is made by the speech acts of (usually two) examiners. Unlike the wedding of course, the examiners have to exercise a considerable amount of judgement in making the award. The extent to which this award is not just the subjective whim of the examiners depends on the amount of agreement within the community from which these examiners are drawn.

Searle neatly illustrates the power that speech acts, made by suitably qualified or empowered individuals, have to create social facts with a story about a baseball umpire who was asked, in effect, whether his judgements were objective or subjective:

> *Interviewer*: Did you call them the way you saw them, or did you call them the way they were?
> *Umpire*: The way I called them *was* the way they were.

Francis Fukuyama, an economist, has argued that the essential ingredient for the creation of prosperity in modern societies is *trust* because trying to write more and more explicit contracts that tie a supplier down more and more tightly to delivering a specific outcome wastes enormous amounts of time, and is ultimately impossible (Fukuyama, 1995). In the same way, Cresswell's definition of 'standard' makes plain that the key feature in setting and maintaining standards is that the users of test results and associated certificates trust those making the awards. This is because there is no way of establishing comparability of standards other than the professional judgement of a community of experts.

Assessment results are 'social facts'; like banknotes they depend for their value on the status that is accorded to them within a social system. As foreign currency markets have found out to their cost, it is not possible to create comparability by fiat (witness the variation between 'official' and 'real' exchange rates in countries like Russia, China and Burma). Similarly, all attempts to define 'standards' or 'equivalence' independently of the social setting in which they are created have failed, and, for the reasons discussed above, are indeed bound to fail. Two qualifications are comparable only to the extent that there are people who are prepared to *believe* that they are comparable.

In this respect the 'track record' of awarders creates something akin to what art historians call provenance, which is of crucial importance in establishing the credibility of the awards. Awarding bodies understand this very well, which is why they often appear cautious with new developments. Any new system of awards will be treated very suspiciously by users until their awards have similar provenance. And it will be almost impossible for any body seen to be subject to political influence to establish such trust.

SELECT BIBLIOGRAPHY

Black, P. J. (1997) *Testing: Friend or Foe? The Theory and Practice of Assessment and Testing*. London: Falmer Press.

Boyle, B. and Christie, T. (eds) (1995) *Issues in Setting Standards: Establishing Comparabilities*. London: Falmer.

Broadfoot, P. (ed.) (1996) *Assessment in Education: Principles, Policy and Practice* (special issue: *the IEA studies*), 3 (2).

Impara, J. C. and Plake, B. S. (eds) (1995) *Standard Setting for Complex Performance Tasks*. Hillsdale, NJ: Lawrence Erlbaum Associates.

Jaeger, R. M. (1989) 'Certification of student competence'. In R. L. Linn (ed.) *Educational Measurement*. Washington, DC: American Council on Education/Macmillan, 485–514.

Messick, S. (1989) 'Validity'. In R. L. Linn (ed.) *Educational Measurement*. Washington, DC: American Council on Education/Macmillan, 13–103.

REFERENCES

Angoff, W. H. (1974) 'Criterion-referencing, norm-referencing and the SAT'. *College Board Review*, 92 (Summer), 2–5, 21.

Bloom, B. S. (1968) 'Mastery learning'. In *Evaluation Comment*, 1 (2). Los Angeles, University of California at Los Angeles Center for the Study of Evaluation of Instructional Programs.

Centre for Educational Research and Innovation (1998) *Human Capital Investment: An International Comparison*. Paris, France: Organisation for Economic Cooperation and Development.

Cresswell, M. J. (1996) 'Defining, setting and maintaining standards in curriculum-embedded examinations: judgemental and statistical approaches'. In H. Goldstein and T. Lewis (eds) *Assessment: Problems, Developments and Statistical Issues*. Chichester, UK: John Wiley, 57–84.

Fukuyama, F. (1995) *Trust: The Social Virtues and the Creation of Prosperity*. London: Hamish Hamilton.

Gardner, H. (ed.) (1993) *Multiple Intelligences: The Theory in Practice*. New York, NY: Basic Books.

Hoffman, B. (1962) *The Tyranny of Testing*. New York, NY: Crowell-Collier Press.

Jones, D. (1993) 'Words with a similar meaning'. *Mathematics Teaching* (145), 14–15.

Kane, M. T. (1994) 'Validating the performance standards associated with passing scores'. *Review of Educational Research*, 64 (3), 425–461.

Linn, R. L. (1994) 'Assessment-based reform: challenges to educational measurement'. Paper presented at Angoff Memorial Lecture. Princeton, NJ.

Messick, S. (1989) 'Validity'. In R. L. Linn (ed.) *Educational Measurement*. Washington, DC: American Council on Education/Macmillan, 13–103.

Searle, J. R. (1995) *The Construction of Social Reality*. London: Allen Lane, The Penguin Press.

Wiliam, D. (1994) 'Creating matched national curriculum assessments in English and Welsh: test translation and parallel development'. *The Curriculum Journal*, 5 (1), 17–29.

Wood, R. (1987) 'Your chemistry equals my French'. In R. Wood (ed.) *Measurement and Assessment in Education and Psychology*. London: Falmer, 40–44.

21

LEARNING SUPPORT FOR PUPILS IN MAINSTREAM SCHOOLS

Policy context and practical implications

Sheila Riddell

INTRODUCTION

The purpose of this chapter is to explore the various ways in which schools have endeavoured to educate pupils identified as having greater difficulty in learning than their peers. Inevitably, the methods developed at different times reflect changes in understandings of the underlying causes of problems in learning. The chapter focuses on the UK context, contrasting experiences in Scotland and England, and draws attention to the various ways in which policies enacted in the wider educational arena have particular, if sometimes unintended, consequences for children with learning difficulties. The structure of the chapter is as follows. I begin by looking at the teaching of children with learning difficulties prior to the publication of the Report of Scottish HMI (SED, 1978) and the Warnock Report (DES, 1978). Subsequently I explore the changes brought about by these two reports. An account is then given of the impact of the marketisation of education in Scotland and England and divergences between the two systems which have emerged. One of the provisions of the 1993 Education Act for England was the implementation of a Code of Practice governing the identification and assessment of special educational needs. The effects of the Code of Practice, which came into force in 1994 (DfE, 1994a), are considered and comparisons are made with the delivery of learning support in Scotland, where the Code of Practice does not apply. Finally, a number of wider issues are considered, including gender and social class differences in the identification of learning difficulties and the provision of additional support. Ongoing tensions are identified, including the boundary between those receiving a Record of Needs (Scotland) and a Statement of Needs (England) and those deemed as requiring learning support but not the additional protection of a Record or Statement of Needs. In addition, I discuss the nature of the boundary between pupils who are identified as in particular need of learning support and those who are judged to be making reasonable progress without additional support. As I shall demonstrate, understandings of learning difficulties inevitably touch on much wider issues to do with beliefs about pupil ability, how children learn and the nature of teaching.

PROVISION FOR PUPILS WITH LEARNING DIFFICULTIES PRE-WARNOCK

Education for pupils with learning difficulties in the late 1960s and early 1970s was characterised by a fairly rigid division between those who were deemed to require special education and were likely to be placed in a special school and those who were in a mainstream school and were assumed able to access the mainstream curriculum. In Scotland, Regulations (SED, 1956) identified nine legal categories of 'handicap' for which special educational provision should be made. These were deafness, partial deafness, blindness, partial sightedness, mental handicap, epilepsy, speech defects, maladjustment and physical handicap. Ten categories were used in England. A child who was considered to have learning difficulties which fell within one of these categories had to be 'ascertained', a process conducted by a medical team for children whose difficulties were recognised prior to the start of their school education and by a multidisciplinary team for school-aged children. The regulations did not include pupils with milder learning or other difficulties, or whose difficulties stemmed from such factors as absenteeism or frequent changes of school; these children were to be educated alongside their peers within the mainstream school. The dominance of medical personnel in the assessment team and the focus on the child's deficits rather than abilities through the medical system of categorisation led to a system where children with widely different intellectual abilities were grouped together.

Even within mainstream schools, divisions were maintained between children of different abilities. Since the 1920s, children who had learning difficulties were referred to as backward or retarded and as many as 12 per cent in any year group were held back for a year, a practice which became less popular after 1945 but which none the less continued to be used in exceptional circumstances. In both primary and secondary schools, the lowest achieving 20 per cent of the age-group were often educated together in separate classrooms. The Schools (Scotland) Code (1956) specified that there should be less than 25 pupils in such classes. In primary schools, segregation within mainstream schools was questioned within the report *Primary Education in Scotland* (SED, 1965), which suggested that children with social and emotional difficulties might not be helped by isolation from their peer group. The report advocated a system of withdrawal for individual tuition in numeracy and literacy rather than permanent separation and this recommendation was implemented. In secondary schools change was somewhat slower. The Education (Scotland) Act 1945 reflected a view of innate differences in the abilities of pupils, establishing junior secondaries for the less able and senior secondaries for the more able. Within junior secondary schools, modified classes were established for the least able 20 per cent of the school population. The idea was that the innate ability of such pupils was unchangeable and so the school had to accommodate their needs, teaching them a simplified version of the curriculum taken by their more able peers. The schools built after 1945 had special rooms for this group of pupils. Accompanying these special arrangements was the idea that specialist teachers were needed to deal with this group of 'dull, retarded and problem children', as they were described by the Advisory Council on Education in Scotland in 1946.

The development of the professional role of the learning support teacher emerged gradually. In 1959, a specialist qualification for secondary schoolteachers of 'backward pupils' was introduced, and in 1972 a similar course for primary teachers was introduced. At about the same time, the title of such teachers was changed from teacher of backward or retarded children to remedial teacher. Notwithstanding this change of title, there was an under-supply of such teachers and their status remained low, tainted by the deficit model associated with the pupils they were assisting. Broadly speaking, the organisation of remedial teaching in Scotland and England was broadly similar, although of course in the grammar schools in England which survived comprehensive reorganisation, special teaching for pupils with learning difficulties was often non-existent, since such pupils were assumed to have no place in such elite institutions.

TWO REPORTS OF 1978: THE PROGRESS REPORT OF SCOTTISH HMI AND THE WARNOCK REPORT

Two reports were published in 1978 which challenged significantly the status quo in relation to the education of pupils with learning difficulties in mainstream schools. First, let us consider the report published by Scottish HMI entitled *The Education of Pupils with Learning Difficulties in Primary and Secondary Schools in Scotland* (SED, 1978). The overall thrust of the report was to question the received wisdom concerning the nature and origins of learning difficulties and what schools should do to help children who were experiencing such problems. HMI was highly critical of the permanent segregation of lower achieving children within mainstream schools. Such children should be educated alongside their peers but rather than expecting the child to accommodate to a curriculum which might be too difficult or to teaching methods geared to the average child, the onus should be on the mainstream teacher, assisted by the newly styled learning support teacher, to accommodate the needs of each child. This should be done through the use of differentiated teaching materials and appropriate pedagogy.

Looking at the proposals in some detail, it was argued that the focus of remedial education on 'basic skills and numeracy' was too limited. The concept should be broadened to include 'a wider and more diverse range of pupils including those who have trouble coping with these ideas and concepts . . . [and those] whose problems are the result of discontinuity . . . [i.e.] frequent absence or change of school' (para 4.2). HMI was also critical of the diagnostic techniques used (paras 4.4 and 4.5). Identification and assessment of learning difficulties was seen as too dependent on standardised tests of basic reading and number, as establishing 'the point of onset of difficulty' or uncovering 'deeper problems' (not necessarily educational) which could be the cause of poor performance on basic skills tests, leading to 'adverse effects on [pupils'] whole attitude to school'. The curriculum offered to pupils with learning difficulties was regarded as fundamentally flawed by HMI and new goals were delineated (paras 4.6 to 4.9). These included the following:

- curriculum aims should be the same for all pupils;
- pupils should not all have to study the same things, at the same pace, in the same way;
- objectives for pupils should take into account their age, aptitude and ability;
- the curriculum must sustain skill and interest and get pupils across the 'plateau of learning';
- demands on pupils for higher skill and interest must be not only appropriate but also sufficiently challenging;

- decontextualised activity, such as routine drilling, should be avoided;
- reducing or dropping aspects of the curriculum for individual pupils who require greater provision for the development of basic skills should not be at the expense of enjoyable or creative activities or those that offer experience of 'success', self-confidence and stimulating variety (cited by Munn [1994] drawing on Allan *et al.* [1991]).

In relation to pedagogy (para 4.10), an increase in 'discussion' and a combination of class, group and individual methods for both secondary and primary schools were called for. Rather than undertaking separate work with children experiencing difficulty in learning, the emphasis should be on the preparation of differentiated learning materials. In general, HMI recommended less use of whole-class teaching and more use of group and individual work. This is in interesting contrast with recent pronouncements by Scottish HMI (SOEID, 1996) which, in the light of Scotland's relatively poor showing in International League Tables, suggest a return to more direct teaching, possibly in the form of whole-class teaching. These more recent shifts in policy are discussed in more detail in a later section.

The key to rethinking provision for children with learning difficulties, HMI decided, was to refashion the role of the learning support teacher and her relationship to the mainstream teacher. The following four main roles for the former were indicated:

- to act as a consultant to staff and members of the school management team;
- to co-operate with class and subject teachers offering tutorial support and supportive help in their normal classes to pupils with learning difficulties in any areas of the curriculum;
- to provide personal tuition and support for pupils with severe learning difficulties in the process of communication and computation;
- to provide, arrange for or contribute to special services within the school.

A firm message to mainstream teachers, however, was that children with learning difficulties should not be seen as the sole responsibility of the learning support teacher, but primarily of the mainstream class teacher who would draw on the remedial teacher's knowledge and expertise without passing over ultimate responsibility. Despite this shared responsibility, the role of the learning support teacher was couched in extremely broad terms. Elaborating on the four main roles identified above, HMI indicated that the learning support teacher should carry out a number of other tasks including initiating and contributing to staff development; offering a haven for pupils with 'temporary emotional upsets' and for pupils being phased back into mainstream school after a period in residential or special schools; offering a facility in the school whereby pupils can be observed and assessed for a short but intensive period; offering special expertise in the use of micro-technology, information technology, particularly in relation to differentiation of the curriculum and the analysis and adaptation of published schemes. From their lowly origins as teachers of backward pupils, it appeared that learning support teachers were being urged to adopt one of the most challenging roles in the school. Recognising opportunities for the expansion of this market, colleges of education in Scotland (now incorporated into universities) upgraded their in-service training programmes, offering courses at certificate, diploma and masters levels. None the less, many teachers who adopted the mantle of learning support expert in school continued to lack a specialist qualification and questions remained as to whether they possessed the necessary power and authority to bring about radical change in school.

Further demands on learning support teachers flowed from the Warnock Report, which was published in the same year as the report of Scottish HMI but was a much weightier tome. Whereas the report of Scottish HMI focused exclusively on children with learning difficulties and implicitly separated this group from children placed in special schools, the Warnock Report sought to blur the distinction between the special and mainstream school populations. According to Warnock, up to 20 per cent of children were likely to experience difficulty in learning at some point in their educational career. In addition to children with pronounced, specific or complex difficulties (about 2 per cent of the population), the special educational needs population should include those:

- whose difficulties were mainly emotional or social or who could be awkward or disruptive in class;
- in 'remedial' classes whose difficulties stemmed from a variety of factors but who were all too often treated alike;
- whose difficulties were temporary or short-term, for example arising from frequent changes of schools;
- whose difficulties resulted from the language in which they were taught being different from the language they spoke at home.

Warnock recommended that the categorisation of children on the basis of their 'handicaps' should be abandoned and that the focus should be on identifying children's needs rather than their deficits. There was a commitment to involve parents in the assessment of children's needs and, since it was considered impractical and unnecessary to conduct a multi-professional assessment of all children with learning difficulties, a staged process was envisaged. Stages 1–3 would be school based, Stage 1 mainly involving class teachers and the headteacher and Stages 2 and 3 to be co-ordinated by the learning support teacher. Stages 4 and 5 were to involve a range of agencies including education, social work and health as well as parents and would culminate in the issuing of an official document (known as a Statement of Needs in England and a Record of Needs in Scotland) indicating how the education authority proposed to meet the child's special educational needs. Although the process of identifying and assessing special educational needs was co-ordinated by the psychological service, it was evident that the recommendations of the Warnock Report had particular significance for the learning support teacher, who was charged with assessing needs, ensuring that appropriate support was delivered, liaising with parents and monitoring and reporting on progress.

LEARNING SUPPORT POST-WARNOCK: THREE STUDIES

English junior school teachers' views of learning difficulties

In both Scotland and England, research was conducted which provides some insight into the ways in which the Warnock Report and the Progress Report of Scottish HMI were implemented. In England, hard on the heels of the Warnock Report, research was commissioned which investigated the role of teachers in assessing and meeting the needs of the 18 per cent of pupils in mainstream classes identified by Warnock as likely to have difficulties in learning (Croll and Moses, 1985). The research was based in junior schools and used interviews with teachers and detailed classroom observation. The researchers found that teachers generally agreed with Warnock that one in five children might experience learning difficulties. Teachers considered that four-fifths of this group were likely to have learning difficulties, characterised by reading problems. The next largest category of special educational needs consisted of behavioural difficulties and these children were also often poor readers. Despite the long-established association between pupils' social background and the occurrence of learning difficulties (Townsend and Davison, 1982), Croll and Moses found that although there was evidence of a higher concentration of special educational needs in some areas, none the less learning difficulties were not restricted to a few 'problem' schools. Teachers in just over two-thirds of schools in the study (61 in all) reported that between 10 and 30 per cent of pupils had special educational needs. Four schools had more than 30 per cent but no school had more than half of its pupils falling into this category. Twenty per cent of schools had 10 per cent or fewer pupils with special educational needs, but in only one school did this fall to 5 per cent or below, and no school reported an entire absence of pupils with special educational needs. In a recent follow-up study, Croll and Moses (1998) reported a much greater proportion of schools that nominated more than 30 per cent of their pupils as having special educational needs. This is a highly significant finding in relation to both awareness of special educational needs and the concentration of children with such needs in particular schools (see the section below on learning support and social disadvantage for further details).

In their 1985 study, Croll and Moses found great variance among teachers in a given school with regard to the proportion of children in their class with special educational needs. They noted that teachers did not apply the same criteria in identifying which pupils required additional support, but brought to bear a range of professional judgements. Overall, the researchers noted that teachers' perceptions appeared to reflect the sex of their pupils (boys are twice as likely to be identified as girls), the overall level of pupil performance (classes with higher than average levels of attainment have more pupils identified as needing additional support) and the age of pupils in the class (younger pupils within a class are more likely to be seen as having learning difficulties). The dominance of boys in receipt of learning support is a phenomenon that has been noted by other commentators (Daniels et al., 1994; Riddell, 1996). The researchers acknowledged the interplay between pupils' 'real' characteristics and teachers' perceptions of individuals and classes and suggested that the greater use of standardised tests by teachers might provide a firmer baseline for teachers' judgements. They also noted with some concern that junior school teachers attributed learning difficulties to innate pupil characteristics rather than to the school or the curriculum, promoting the view that teachers could do little to remedy this situation. This contrasts with the views of Scottish primary school teachers reported by Munn (1994), who had a much greater faith in the amenability of early learning difficulties to intervention (see below for further discussion of this point). The English junior school blamed behavioural difficulties on out-of-school factors and again saw these as being outside the school's control. Belying this perception that teachers could effect little change, observation of lessons led Croll and Moses (1985, p. 153) to the view that: 'Working in small groups with the teacher made much more difference to the involvement in curriculum tasks of children with special educational needs than it did for other pupils.'

In terms of their general approach to integration, most teachers appeared to offer a warmer welcome to children with physical and sensory impairments than those with learning or behavioural difficulties, the very children with whom junior school teachers were already familiar. Overall this study demonstrated that teachers felt reasonably positive about the idea of integration, but were at the same time wedded to the belief that most difficulties were either innate or caused by out-of-school factors, implying that the teachers' job was to manage and accommodate rather than remove learning difficulties. This was in contrast to the more optimistic but critical view of Warnock and Scottish HMI that schools and teachers do not play a passive role in relation to children and their difficulties, but are implicated both in creating and ameliorating them.

The role of learning support teachers in Scotland

A number of studies in Scotland have also shed light on learning support teachers' work post-Warnock. Munn (1994), describing research conducted in one Scottish region between 1988 and 1990 (Allan et al., 1991), suggested that understanding of learning difficulties and the role of the learning support teacher differed in primary and secondary schools.

In primary schools, teachers tended to believe that difficulties in pupils' learning were likely to be temporary rather than enduring and therefore focused their energy on ameliorating these problems. The learning support teacher's role was seen as essentially similar to that of the mainstream teacher, although whilst the latter had responsibility for the entire curriculum, the former concentrated energy on tutoring pupils in numeracy and literacy skills in the hope that they would catch up with their peer group.

In secondary schools, teachers no longer believed that difficulties were transitory and the aim of learning support teachers was to ease the social integration of pupils with learning difficulties into mainstream classes by helping mainstream teachers to cope. A common role for the learning support teacher was to act as an extra pair of hands or a learning technician, helping a small number of pupils to work in a way that would not unduly impede the progress of the rest of the class or tie up too much of the mainstream teacher's time. Learning support teachers wished to work alongside the mainstream teacher in planning lessons and producing differentiated materials, but a number of factors tended to militate against such practices. As well as problems in finding time for planning lessons, there was a perception amongst some subject teachers that learning support teachers tended to lack appropriate subject knowledge and were therefore unlikely to be effective in producing support materials. Munn concluded:

> Unless we are clearer about what we want integration to achieve, particularly in the conceptualisation of learning difficulties and pupils' attainments, and how to translate this into practical classroom strategies, then the role of learning support staff as a catalyst for changing the way teachers think about learning difficulties is likely to remain unfulfilled.
>
> (Munn, 1994, p. 212)

Scottish parents' understanding of specific learning difficulties and perceptions of learning support

The final study described in this section provides an account of Scottish parents' views of policy and provision for children with specific learning difficulties and contrasts these with the perceptions of local authority policy-makers. The study (Riddell *et al.*, 1994) was commissioned by the Scottish Office to explore the education of children with dyslexia, but allowed the researchers to tap into the perspectives on post-Warnock learning support held by one particular group of parents. Parents' views were sought by means of questionnaires designed to gather both quantitative and qualitative data concerning parents' understanding of the nature of specific learning difficulties (dyslexia) and their assessment of the effectiveness of the school's interventions. Contacted through voluntary organisations and the psychological service, parents of children with specific learning difficulties emerged as a relatively socially advantaged group compared with most parents of children with learning difficulties. The majority believed that their children's difficulties were physiological in origin and were quite different from, on the one hand, those who had what was described as a 'mental handicap', and on the other, children who had social, emotional and behavioural difficulties.

Key informant interviews were conducted with educational psychologists in each authority, the majority of whom felt that children with specific learning difficulties could not be readily distinguished from other children with learning difficulties, but should be seen as occupying different positions on a continuum of special educational needs. This view clearly differed considerably from that of parents, who wished to see their children as a quite discrete group and were irritated by psychologists who were unwilling to diagnose or recognise dyslexia. If they felt put off by a local authority psychologist, they were willing to pay for a private psychological assessment. Despite their commitment to a view of dyslexia as an innate condition, they none the less believed that their children's difficulties were more susceptible to either cure or remediation and, some suggested, should be prioritised over the needs of children who were less salvageable. They had very clear views about the types of teaching that would be useful to their child and were strongly opposed to the new directions indicated for learning support teachers following the Warnock Report and the Progress Report of Scottish HMI. Co-operative teaching in the classroom was regarded as a waste of time; what was needed was direct one-to-one tuition in literacy skills. Such tuition should take place outside the mainstream class and should use specialist teaching methods designed to address the typical range of neurological difficulties encountered by dyslexic children. Parents were likely to insist on a clear educational plan, specifying the amount and nature of learning support. They generally monitored both the support received and the child's progress. If the state system failed in its delivery of adequate learning support, then parents were willing to purchase tuition privately.

There was also some evidence of dyslexic children receiving privileged access to existing resources. For example, some specialist resources, such as a reading centre in one region, were used disproportionately by this group. Other research exploring learning support in schools varying in relation to their socio-economic status and level of measured effectiveness (Duffield, 1998) found that the most advantaged school had more learning support teachers than the poorest school, since it was able to claim a higher proportion of dyslexic pupils. This, of course, does not suggest an absence of children with dyslexia in the poorer schools, but simply that learning difficulties were so common it was not possible to distinguish one form from another.

Although parents of children with specific learning difficulties felt shortchanged by schools, teachers and learning support systems in place since the late 1970s, they were none the less experiencing some success in influencing the future shape of the system. The term dyslexia was rejected in the late 1970s and 1980s as overly medical, but in the early 1990s it experienced a revival in Scottish Office publications. In addition, initial and in-service teacher training programmes introduced modules and courses on dyslexia, sponsored by voluntary organisations boasting wealthy industrial and private patrons. Parents of children with specific learning difficulties were clearly not a representative group, but they none the less illustrated the ongoing support for an impairment-based view of special educational needs which Warnock had tried to banish. They also illustrated the way in which particular groups of parents of children with special educational needs were able to operate within an educational market, using parent power as the engine of change. Although concerned to promote the interests of their own children, none the less parents of children with specific learning difficulties were able to exert a strong influence within the wider arena of special educational needs.

THE CONSERVATIVE EDUCATIONAL REFORM AGENDA: CENTRALISATION AND DISPERSAL OF POWER

In this section I consider the context of the political and social agenda which shaped developments in special educational needs in the late 1980s and 1990s. Deakin (1994) provides an interesting account of the work of US economic liberals such as Milton Friedman and Friedrich von Hayek, whose ideas were transplanted and applied to the British context in the 1980s, bringing about a radical shift within both public and private sectors. According to Deakin, Friedman and von Hayek did not deny a role to the state, but saw state intervention as admissible for only two purposes: 'to police the boundaries of the market and to provide where necessary the essential minimum of resources that the market cannot for a variety of reasons secure for those in extreme poverty' (Deakin, 1994, p. 7). Planning was seen as tyrannical because of its interference with individual freedom of choice, while 'social justice' was regarded as meaningless because inequality arises as a result of the free play of market forces over which no individual exercises control.

These ideas proved to be extremely effective both in the US and the UK, informing sweeping, market-based reform programmes. In its third term of office, the former Conservative government turned its attention to the reform of education, convinced that higher standards needed to be achieved in order to secure the national economic competitiveness of the UK. The general policy repertoire was similar in Scotland and England, although there were differences in the way in which the legislation was enacted in the two countries. Tighter control and demands for accountability at the centre were accompanied by the devolution of power to schools and parents. Thus finances were delegated to schools, apparently giving headteachers and governing bodies more power. However, as a means of assessing their efficiency and effectiveness, schools were required to provide information on a range of performance indicators to central government and to parents, seen as playing a vital role in driving the market. Armed with information about school performance, parents were given the right to choose their child's school, thus, in theory, encouraging the growth of 'good' schools and causing 'bad' schools to wither and eventually die. Criteria for judging schools were not specified, and parents were given information on attendance, costs and special educational needs policy as well as external examination results. In practice, however, it was the latter measure which was generally used by parents in making judgements about a school's worth, and such concerns were fanned by the publication of school 'league tables' in the press. Consequently some researchers maintained that school choice led to a polarisation between schools and less social class heterogeneity (Gewirtz *et al.*, 1995), whilst others maintained that in some urban areas some schools became more, not less, mixed (Adler, 1997). Overall, however, there was a general consensus that for schools in the most socially disadvantaged areas, there was an outflow of pupils, accompanied by loss of funding and decline in the morale of teachers and pupils.

Particular consequences of these changes arose for pupils requiring learning and behavioural support. As schools became more conscious of the need to compete with neighbouring institutions to avoid a cycle of decline, greater attention was paid to conscious and unconscious marketing mechanisms. Pupils with learning and behavioural difficulties were perceived increasingly as unattractive customers, both requiring a great deal of the school's learning support and guidance resources and potentially damaging the school's reputation. Such pressures led teachers to define children as disturbed (i.e. needing specialist teaching outside the mainstream class) rather than disruptive (i.e. needing a more disciplined regime within the mainstream class) (Armstrong and Galloway, 1994). Pupils with physical or sensory impairments, particularly if accompanied by an auxiliary teacher, were welcomed with more enthusiasm, since they were perceived as representing a net gain rather than drain on resources. Although comprehensive schools may not select their pupils, none the less some headteachers and governing bodies exercised resourcefulness in ensuring that middle-class parents were actively drawn to their school (Deem *et al.*, 1995). In other areas, particularly on peripheral housing estates, the concentration of pupils with learning difficulties, often representing more than a quarter of the school population, posed considerable problems for schools. Since education authorities funded learning support on a per capita basis, poorer schools had resources spread far more thinly than their privileged neighbours. In educational priority areas or their equivalent, a small additional allocation of teaching staff might be made, but the headteacher was under no obligation to use this staff to increase learning support provision. Indeed, in the context of league tables it might make more sense to target the efforts of these teachers on the small number of higher-achieving pupils.

The effect of the school's socio-economic status on its delivery of learning support was evident in the study of four Scottish secondary schools conducted by researchers at Stirling University (Brown *et al.*, 1996; Riddell *et al.*, 1998). The school in the most advantaged neighbourhood used a wide variety of teaching methods in its classes (whole-class teaching, group work, individual work) and the full repertoire of learning support roles was apparent (co-operative teaching, individual tuition within the class, withdrawal for individual or group work, consultancy). In the less advantaged schools, teachers generally spent more time in class control, used more whole-class teaching sessions, and gave pupils less variety of tasks to undertake in the class. There was little withdrawal for individual tuition sessions, with the learning support teacher generally offering help to a small number of pupils with the most significant difficulties in the mainstream class. Pupils who would have had learning difficulties identified in the more advantaged schools were simply part of what counted as normal in the less advantaged schools.

Further consequences for pupils with learning difficulties may arise from the current UK government's concern with the UK's showing in International League Tables. This has led to a focus on the teaching methods that are likely to produce the biggest increase in average performance levels, rather than those that will be most helpful to pupils with greatest difficulties. A report by Scottish HMI (SOEID, 1996) on selection within schools argued that mixed-ability teaching may not be the most 'effective and efficient' form of classroom organisation because 'For many primary and secondary teachers, however, the time which has to be given to the management of learning in mixed-ability classes reduces the potential for direct teaching and has the effect of slowing the pace of learning' (ibid., p. 25).

Although there is undoubted concern over the performance of children with learning difficulties, this is driven by the desire to raise standards in such a way that the position of the UK in International League Tables will be improved. This is likely to lead to a focus on improving the performance of those seen as most salvageable. Children requiring significant input of resources for only marginal improvement may be seen as less worthy of investment. Earlier work by Croll and Moses (1985) suggested that children with special educational needs, compared with other children in mainstream classes, were likely to gain most from direct contact with the teacher in a small-group setting, but clearly this advantage is being reconsidered in the light of overall efficiency. The dominant message from HMI in this publication is that on average children learn fastest when grouped with children of similar ability. Ironically, in 1978 HMI was arguing strongly against the grouping together of children with learning difficulties, suggesting they would learn more by mingling equally with children of a wide range of abilities. There is evidently a danger that calls for greater effectiveness might be at the expense of children in greatest need of learning support.

The quest for improvement is also being pursued by the setting of targets in examination performance for individual schools. Here too there is a danger that the desire to overtake certain targets may be detrimental to the interests of children with learning difficulties. For instance, in Scotland by the year 2000 the expectation is that 85 per cent of the population will achieve five Standard grades at grades 1–2 or their equivalent. There is a clear possibility that in meeting such a goal, the remaining 15 per cent will be further marginalised.

THE CODE OF PRACTICE IN ENGLAND AND THE INDIVIDUAL RIGHTS APPROACH

England and Scotland have diverged over recent years in relation to their formal management of non-recorded special educational needs. Whilst Scotland has tended to leave much power with individual teachers and schools in terms of their responsibility for providing learning support to particular children, England has moved down the route of laying down procedures through the 1994 *Code of Practice on the Identification and Assessment of Special Educational Needs*. Although the Code has the status of Regulations and is therefore non-statutory, it is intended to provide clear guidance to schools in terms of their responsibility to pupils with non-recorded special educational needs and to parents in terms of the level of information and service they should expect from schools. The motivation for the introduction of the Code of Practice in England was probably twofold. First, there was concern about the growth in the proportion of children with Statements of Needs (4 per cent of the population in England compared with 2 per cent in Scotland). It was felt that parents were seeking a Statement because they felt that this was the only way of committing the school to taking action and allocating resources to meet the needs of children with learning difficulties. Second, there was a sense that the marketisation of education had led to a growth of awareness among parents of their rights and those of their children, and being dependent on the benevolence of the school without any service-level agreement was no longer satisfactory. Parents of dyslexic children through their voluntary organisations were particularly active in promoting the need for a Code of Practice.

The Code of Practice sets out an obligation for the school to provide parents with detailed information about policy and provision for special educational needs in schools, and lays out five stages in the assessment of special educational needs which must be undertaken, drawing on Warnock's earlier framework. The special educational needs co-ordinator (SENCO) is responsible for the first three stages of assessment and pupils from Stage 1 are required to have an Individual Educational Plan which must be reviewed annually. In addition to the maintenance of the Plan for each child, special educational needs co-ordinators are responsible for the strategic direction and development of special educational needs provision in the school, teaching and learning, leading and managing staff and the efficient and effective deployment of staff and resources. Early research on the role of SENCOs (Bowers and Wilkinson, 1998; Garner, 1996; Lewis *et al.*, 1996) suggests that SENCOs are finding their roles inordinately bureaucratic and complex and that mutual understanding between parents and schools has not necessarily improved. Croll and Moses (1998) provided initial findings of a study seeking to make comparisons with their 1981 study (Croll and Moses, 1985, see above) in relation to teachers' understandings of special educational needs over time. They suggest that between 1981 and 1998, there has been an increase of about 50 per cent in the proportion of the school population identified as having special educational needs and that since the implementation of the Code of Practice, this expansion has been particularly rapid. More than a quarter of children in mainstream primary schools are now identified as having special educational needs and these pupils tend to be concentrated in poorer areas. Although the bureaucratic procedures of the Code of Practice are implicated, Croll and Moses suggest that it is difficult to determine to what extent children are actually experiencing greater difficulty in school, due, for example, to greater levels of poverty, or whether the increase represents the emergence of previously unrecognised problems, such as attention deficit disorder.

CONCLUSION

In this chapter, I have tried to indicate key themes in the development of the conceptualisation of learning difficulties and the types of learning support which flow from these understandings. During the postwar period in the UK, there appears to have been almost a circular development. In the 1940s and 1950s firm views were held about innate and unchangeable abilities, rooted in the now discredited theories of psychologists like John Bowlby (see Kamin [1974] for further discussion of the science and politics of IQ). Since children were fundamentally unchangeable, the job of the school was to select, separate and instruct to the level deemed appropriate for the particular child's aptitude and ability. During the late 1970s and early 1980s, these views gave way to a more optimistic view that firm divisions between children on the basis of measured ability were unhelpful and that learning difficulties when they arose could be ameliorated by appropriate teaching methods and differentiation of the curriculum. Subsequently, the growth of the market within education has led to a withdrawal of attention from children with learning difficulties, whose parents are often socially disadvantaged themselves and not particularly adept at operating educational systems to their advantage. Within the field of special educational needs, however, there is evidence that middle-class parents are able to operate successfully as service consumers, while pressure from single-focus voluntary organisations has fuelled a return to a view of learning difficulties as within-child deficits.

In England, the privileging of some difficulties over others may be assisted by the Code of Practice, which put in place mechanisms for intense scrutiny of individual children whose degree of difficulty may be relatively minor. Meanwhile, concerns to maximise human capital through the efficient and effective use of resources means that special educational needs may again slip down the agenda of concern, since the type of intensive support needed to assist children with special educational needs may not produce benefits in terms of average performance reflected in international league tables.

In reviewing the development of learning support provision since 1945, different understandings of academic ability have been translated into different visions of the role of the learning support teacher. The postwar view of intelligence as a fixed and innate characteristic produced a system that segregated children with the most severe difficulties into special schools and those with less severe difficulties into classes or groups for 'backward' children. Teachers of these children were not enjoined to remove children's learning difficulties but rather to provide them with the basic skills that would help them to perform low-level work. By the end of the 1970s, this fixed view of intelligence had given way to a focus on the range of abilities of individual children, which would vary over place and time and be affected by a number of external factors, including the teaching and learning environment. The role of the mainstream teacher was seen increasingly in terms of meeting the academic and social needs of all children apart from the very small number of children with severe, low-incidence disabilities who might require very individualised and specialised opportunities to learn. Learning support teachers were seen as creating the conditions for whole-school support which would assist mainstream teachers in their work.

The official acceptance of this view of learning support coincided with the election of a Conservative government committed to the encouragement of market forces within the public sector. Measures to increase accountability and performance of the state education system were often devised without considering their impact on children with special educational needs and there were some moves back to viewing the learning support teacher as someone to contain children with learning difficulties so that the mainstream teacher could concentrate on the majority of pupils. Aspects of education policy that focused on the inclusion of pupils with learning difficulties in mainstream schools, such as mixed-ability teaching and comprehensive schooling, were subjected to particular attack as inefficient.

Some recent research and commentary (e.g. Dyson, 1997) argued for a much tighter focus on the links between social background and special educational needs, suggesting that learning support teachers alone should not be expected to solve the problems of pupils with learning difficulties, but should act as a resource to bridge understanding and awareness between pupils' home and school environments. Such arguments are particularly salient in the light of the growing body of evidence, based on longitudinal studies of the attainment of literacy and numeracy, that social and economic disadvantage has a dominant impact in basic skills development. Robinson (1997), for example, argues:

> There is no evidence from these longitudinal studies that such factors as primary class size, teaching methods, homework policy or the use of streaming or setting has any impact on the attainment of literacy and numeracy. In the 1970 cohort, experience of pre-school education also had no impact. On the other hand, the proportion of a primary school's intake which was from a middle-class background did have a significant positive impact for all pupils, which has implications for admissions policy. . . . Over the long run the most powerful 'educational' policy is arguably one which tackles child poverty, rather than any modest interventions in schooling.
>
> (Robinson, 1997, p. 3)

Such arguments do not deny a role for learning support teachers in remedying children's learning difficulties, but they do indicate the boundaries of this role. Understanding the multiple ways in which social environments, including schools and homes, both create and remedy learning difficulties offers an escape from child-deficit, school-deficit or home-deficit models, and begins to bridge the gap between medical and social models of disability. Within a UK context, the incoming Labour government has declared its commitment both to tackling social exclusion and to producing 'joined-up policy'. This is one area where there is clearly plenty of scope for both these goals to be pursued.

REFERENCES

Adler, M. (1997) 'Looking backwards to the future: Parental choice and education policy'. *British Educational Research Journal*, 23 (3) 297–315.

Allan, J., Brown, S. and Munn, P. (1991) *Off the Record: Mainstream Provision for Pupils with Special Educational Needs*. Edinburgh: SCRE.

Armstrong, D. and Galloway, D. (1994) 'Special educational needs and problem behaviour: Making policy in the classroom'. In S. Riddell and S. Brown (eds) *Special Educational Needs Policy in the 1990s: Warnock in the Market Place*. London: Routledge.

Ball, S. J. (1997) 'Policy, sociology and critical social research: A personal review of recent education policy and policy research'. *British Educational Research Journal*, 23 (3) 257–275.

Bowers, T. and Wilkinson, D. (1998) 'The SEN Code of Practice: Is it user friendly?' *British Journal of Special Education*, 25 (3) 119–126.

Brown, S., Riddell, S. and Duffield, J. (1996) 'Responding to pressures: A study of four secondary schools'. In P. Woods (ed.) *Contemporary Issues in Teaching and Learning*. London: Routledge.

Croll, P. and Moses, M. (1985) *One in Five: The Assessment and Incidence of Special Educational Needs*. London: Routledge & Kegan Paul.

Croll, P. and Moses, M. (1998) 'Special educational needs in the primary school: A comparison over two decades'. Paper presented to the British Educational Research Association Conference, Belfast, 27–30 August.

Daniels, H., Hey, V., Leonard, D. and Smith, M. (1994) 'Gendered practice in special educational needs'. In J. Holland (ed.) *Equality and Inequality in Education Policy.* Cleveland: Multilingual Matters.

Deakin, N. (1994) *The Politics of Welfare: Continuities and Change.* Hemel Hempstead: Harvester Wheatsheaf.

Deem, R., Brehony, K. and Heath, S. (1995) *Active Citizenship and the Governing of Schools.* Buckingham: Open University Press.

Department of Education and Science (DES) (1978) *Special Educational Needs: Report of the Committee of Enquiry into the Education of Handicapped Children and Young People* (The Warnock Report). London: HMSO.

Department for Education (DfE) (1994a) *The Code of Practice on the Identification and Assessment of Special Educational Needs: Regulations on Assessments and Statements.* London: HMSO.

Department for Education (DfE) (1994b) *Education (Special Educational Needs) (Information) Regulations.* London: HMSO.

Duffield, J. (1998) 'School support for lower achieving pupils'. *British Journal of Special Education*, 25 (3) 126–135.

Dyson, A. (1997) 'Social and educational disadvantage: Reconnecting special needs education'. *British Journal of Special Education*, 24 (4) 152–158.

Garner, P. (1996) '"Go forth and co-ordinate": What special needs co-ordinators think about the Code of Practice'. *School Organisation*, 16 (2).

Gewirtz, S., Ball, S. J. and Bowe, R. (1995) *Markets, Choice and Equity in Education.* Buckingham: Open University Press.

Kamin, L. J. (1974) *The Science and Politics of IQ.* Harmondsworth: Penguin.

Lewis, A., Neill, S. R. and Campbell, J. (1996) 'SENCOS and the Code'. *Support for Learning*, 12 (1) 3–9.

Munn, P. (1994) 'The role of the learning support teacher in Scottish primary and secondary classrooms' in S. Riddell and S. Brown (eds) *Special Educational Needs Policy in the 1990s: Warnock in the Market Place.* London: Routledge.

Pringle, M. L. K., Butler, N. R. and Davie, R. (1966) *Eleven Thousand Seven Year Olds* (First Report of the National Child Development Study). London: Longman.

Riddell, S. (1996) 'Gender and special educational needs'. In G. Lloyd (ed.) 'Knitting progress unsatisfactory'. *Gender and Special Issues in Education.* Edinburgh: Moray House Publications.

Riddell, S., Brown, S. and Duffield, J. (1994) 'Conflicts of policies and models: the case of specific learning difficulties'. In S. Riddell and S. Brown (eds) *Special Educational Needs Policy in the 1990s: Warnock in the Market Place.* London: Routledge.

Riddell, S., Brown, S. and Duffield, J. (1998) 'The utility of qualitative research for influencing policy and practice on school effectiveness'. In R. Slee and G. Weiner with S. Tomlinson (eds) *School Effectiveness for Whom? Challenges to the School Effectiveness and School Improvement Movements.* London: Falmer.

Robinson, P. (1997) *Literacy, Numeracy and Economic Performance.* London: London School of Economics and Political Science.

Scottish Education Department (SED) (1946) *Measures to Improve the Supply of Teachers in Scotland. A Report of the Advisory Council on Education in Scotland.* Edinburgh: HMSO.

Scottish Education Department (SED) (1956) *The Schools (Scotland) Code.* Edinburgh: HMSO.

Scottish Education Department (SED) (1965) *Primary Education in Scotland* (The Primary Memorandum). Edinburgh: HMSO.

Scottish Education Department (SED) (1978) *The Education of Pupils with Learning Difficulties in Primary and Secondary Schools in Scotland: A Progress Report by HM Inspectors of Schools.* Edinburgh: HMSO.

Scottish Office Education and Industry Department (SOEID) (1996) *Achievement for All: A Report on Selection within Schools by HM Inspectors of Schools.* Edinburgh: HMSO.

Townsend, P. and Davidson, N. (1982) *Inequalities in Health.* Harmondsworth: Penguin.

22

HOME-LEARNING AND SCHOOL-LEARNING IN THE TWENTY-FIRST CENTURY

Alastair Macbeth

Much, probably most of every child's significant learning is acquired outside school, especially in the home. Of a child's waking (learning)[1] life from birth to age 16, only about 15 per cent is spent in school. Even if we assume that school, professionally staffed and relevantly equipped, has more than a 15 per cent impact on a child's education, home is still a crucial learning centre for good or for ill. Besides directly teaching their child, parents are gatekeepers to the child's access to other family members, to peer group, to neighbourhood, to media such as books and television, and to society at large. Parents are also role models and usually establish influential affective bonding with their child, especially in the early years. Research across cultures has consistently shown a link between the nature of home background and a child's educational attainment. Recent understanding about how the human brain works suggests that conventional schooling is an imperfect learning mechanism, concentrating on but a few of a child's multiple intelligences and learning styles. There is also some tantalising evidence that children who have home-based education tend to out-perform schooled children. No longer can we brush aside home-learning.

We may distinguish between *home-based education* (sometimes called 'home–schooling', provided at home by that small minority of committed families who do not send their children to school) and *home-learning* which all children experience. Home-learning may be deliberate or not, may be well-informed or not, and may be moral or not; but it is powerful.

Home-learning, which the school-centred policy-makers of the twentieth century have chosen substantially to undervalue and to under-resource, could offer the most crucial challenge to twenty-first century education in the interests of economic advance and of personal equity. Schools have achieved much and this is not a deschooling text. Yet excessive reliance on institutions seems to have been the twentieth century's educational myopia. The glibly expressed but under-implemented term 'parent–teacher partnership' might be turned into a carefully crafted basis for children's learning in the new century. Home-based education (discussed more fully below) will be the solution for some families, but most will expect support from school-like institutions. Adaptation of those institutions and their integration with home-learning could become the priority concern of twenty-first century educationists, politicians, administrators and parents.

'Parent–teacher partnership' has been part of the rhetoric of educationists, politicians and even teachers' unions for years. Generally meagre have been resources of time, funding and legal backing to institute such partnership. Also usually missing has been application of a rigorous definition of the term 'partnership', such as that offered by Pugh (1989, p. 5): 'a working relationship that is characterized by a shared sense of purpose, mutual respect and the willingness to negotiate. This implies a sharing of information, responsibility, skills, decision-making and accountability.'

The information, responsibilities and skills of partners need not be the same; school-teachers and hometeachers (especially parents) have different but complementary contributions. A distinction may be drawn between educational *duties* (legal) and *obligations* (moral) as elements of responsibility, but both would be integral to effective partnership. Moreover, resources could be allocated to both partners, not just to schools. This chapter will endeavour to offer practical ways to implement both the model and the definition.

PARENT–TEACHER RELATIONS: THE INCOMPLETE TWENTIETH-CENTURY LEGACY

RESEARCH: THE UNHEEDED CRESCENDO

In the first half of the twentieth century the nature–nurture debate threw up investigations into the influence of home environment, especially on intelligence as measured by intelligence tests. A new wave of research examining the relationship between home background and in-school attainment followed. In 1979 Majoribanks offered a world-sweep analysis of such research and concluded that in-family learning is influential and that parents and teachers should act as partners in children's learning processes, but he warned that 'home–school programmes are extremely difficult to construct and implement' (ibid., p. 191).

Much subsequent research has concentrated on intervention programmes and has focused on systems to assist specific aspects of learning through the home such as literacy (Hannon, 1995; Wolfendale and Topping, 1996) and mathematics (Merttens and Vass, 1993). Valuable studies of in-family processes have been appearing (e.g. Durning and Pourtois, 1994; Pourtois, 1991; Ray, 1997; Tizard and Hughes, 1984) and techniques piloted. To represent the whole literature in the field with its strengths and weaknesses would be impossible in this brief space, but three generalisations are probably safe.

1 Research over the twentieth century has consistently suggested that the nature of homes and learning within them are important determinants of children's overall educational attainment, however defined and measured.
2 There is a dearth of contrary evidence.
3 The findings accord with common sense.

In addition, recent investigations about how the brain functions and how humans learn force a reconsideration of the nature of schooling. Rose and Nicholl (1997, p. 26) state 'More has been learned about the brain in the last ten years than in all previous scientific history.' Furthermore, in the light of growing understanding, they argue that since schools concentrate on linguistic and mathematical intelligences, they under-assist the other five intelligences which Gardner (1993) has offered as the 'multiple intelligences' of humans. It seems that learning is enhanced by being associated with emotions and real-life relevance, by challenges to work things out for oneself, by being consolidated in relaxation and other features found as much outside school as within it. Further, *constant* stimulus and use of the mind is important and since about 85 per cent of a child's waking life is experienced outside school, that implies limitations to children's learning if schooling is viewed as its essence. Meighan (1996), referring to 30 different learning styles, argues that a uniform approach 'is intellectual death to some, and often most, of the learners'. There is some emerging evidence (Meighan, 1997; Ray, 1997) that children who do *not* attend school but are educated at home tend to do better than their schooled peers both academically and socially. It would seem that the time has come to challenge the schooling lobby and to seek a joint school–family approach to education in the early part of the twenty-first century.

PROBLEMS WITH THE CONCEPT OF 'FAMILY'

A 1997 British government report on the state of the family recorded that the family remains at the heart of society, despite increases in divorce and co-habitation. Much depends on the meaning of 'family'. The provisional definition of family by Warnock (1985) as 'that collection of people among whom it is natural to bring up children' is accepted in this chapter. There is evidence of family life 100,000 years ago (Jones, 1997, p. 199) and of genetic disposition to protect and to prepare children. Families have been integral to societies across cultures throughout recorded history. If schools cannot replace that force nor 'compensate' for it, then surely it follows that home-learning should be reintroduced as a major, recognised and supported contributor to official systems of children's learning. The question is, how?

IMPEDIMENTS TO HOME–SCHOOL PARTNERSHIP

Impediments to home–school partnership are many. There has been a tradition for minor and educationally peripheral relations between parents and teachers; occasional written reports and parents' meetings, school-initiated homework, parents carrying out menial tasks in the school, parent representatives on bodies of school governance, social and fund-raising PTAs involving a minority of parents, and so on. Even where schools go beyond such minimal gestures and seek collaborative teaching of the child, response by parents may be patchy and in some cases incompetent or resistant. Difficulties seem to fall into six broad categories.

1 *Familial diversity*. Parents differ in competences, commitment, wealth, facilities, time available for their children and social pressures.
2 *Dearth of incentives and sanctions*. Parents cannot be controlled in the same way as schools are through curricula, teacher training, teachers' contracts and career patterns. State intervention in family life is kept to a minimum for fear of invasion of privacy or infringement of personal liberty.

3 *Perception of education as a professional task*. The teaching occupation has long sought the advantages of professional status. The more that teachers claim elite mystique, the more governments will expect of them, and the more parents will feel obliged to 'leave it to the professionals' and opt out of their responsibilities. This aggrandisement of schooling has distracted from children's other sources of learning.

4 *Teachers' contracts and training*. Teachers' contracts have included little requirement to act as partners with parents and their training has tended to reflect this failing.

5 *Diminished sense of obligation*. Economic pressures and government policies often encourage both of the parents in a two-parent family to sustain paid jobs. This seems to imply that it is right for parents increasingly to allow institutions to care for children and, regrettably, this is happening ever earlier in children's lives. The danger would seem to be that parents may be misled into thinking that institutions *can* provide the whole of their child's learning – i.e. their natural concern for their children may be falsely lulled and their sense of obligation may be reduced by a belief in the efficacy of professional provision. It might be argued that parents' sense of educational commitment should be re-emphasised.

6 *Practical impediments*. Poverty, social disadvantage, physical and mental handicap, single parenthood, demanding employment hours – these and a range of other stresses may reduce the capacity of some parents to contribute adequately to the home-learning of their children.

The relative failure of the 'compensatory' education movement shows us that schools and other state agencies cannot satisfactorily replace the home-learning factor and, as collaborative intervention programmes have indicated, the best hope lies in drawing parents into genuine joint educational provision. Any system for the future must make partnership actual, rather than nominal.

ATTRACTIONS OF SCHOOLS

Schools are factory-like institutions reflecting an industrial age, mostly offering standardized, mass-production procedures in classrooms cut off from normal life, with pupils grouped artificially by age and largely fed a common curriculum not always adaptable to individual needs. Yet schools have attractions which society would be unwilling to lose.

1 Schools are systematised and this assists effectiveness and generates confidence.
2 Schools are capable of providing something for *all* children, so that there is a perceived, if often spurious, sense of equality.
3 Schools are relatively inexpensive *per capita*.
4 Schools provide a child-minding service which is convenient to parents.
5 Schools offer expertise and equipment which many parents cannot provide, especially at secondary level.
6 Schools seem to relieve parents of educational responsibilities (an insidious effect).
7 Tangible and relatively controllable, schools can be pointed to as evidence that politicians have taken action.
8 Schoolteachers are generally committed people doing a constructive job in difficult circumstances.

With the exception of 6 (which is so damaging that it has to be reversed), the other features of the above list are likely to be reflected to some degree in any twenty-first century education system.

THE ISSUE OF EQUALITY

Equality of opportunity has been a theme of twentieth-century educational debate. Much educational inequality has its origins in families and that carries across into social and economic outcomes. If the problem to some extent lies in the family, so too must the solution. It is not equality merely to place children in schools or even to provide extras such as homework classes or study support centres away from home if what they return to at home is counter-educational. While public facilities such as schools must be as thorough as possible, we cannot expect them to compensate for home deficiencies. Pursuit of fairness for children means placing obligations on parents (as well as teachers) and that creates difficulties, both ethical and practical. Those who protest at increased responsibilities for parents, especially deploring the likelihood that the most disadvantaged and desperate parents would be asked to take on added pressures, must face the fundamental question: are we concerned here with the welfare of the child or the welfare of the parent? We may also recall the natural wish of most parents to assist their children. We may accept that a small minority of parents are uncaring, unalterably incompetent or both; but their existence should not be used as an excuse to avoid drawing the great majority of parents more closely into the formal education process. It may be that societies will have to do more in the short term to assist as well as to obligate disadvantaged families, and in the long term to instil into the populace that parenthood is a demanding and responsible task requiring preparation, commitment and educational effort. The limitations of the 'compensation' movement in the twentieth century make it clear that the twenty-first will have to tackle the issue of the home as a learning centre if it is to have equality of either opportunity or outcome on the agenda. Equality is incompatible with mere provision of schooling because education is more than schooling.

THE MOST PRESSING CHALLENGES FOR TWENTY-FIRST CENTURY EDUCATION

We are, therefore, confronted with a dilemma. Childhood learning must be optimised for all, but schooling is inadequate and the child's other main learning centre – the home – is difficult to influence, let alone control. The educational impact of the home carries across into wider community matters such as social cohesion, co-operation and concern for others on the one hand and crime rates, disaffection of the young and a range of other social ills on the other. In the twentieth century it has been notable that schools have been quick to blame parents for problems, but fail to acknowledge parental contributions which are beneficial to education. This distortion, fuelled by teachers' wish for professional status, is coming back to haunt schools as teachers are being made increasingly accountable and are being blamed for social failures beyond their competence to rectify. Only by bringing back the family into the recognised learning system can these difficulties be tackled in the twenty-first century.

Governments may seek mechanistic solutions, but the problem is substantially attitudinal – i.e. to do with a preparedness to act. There would seem to be three shifts in public perception which must preface social change:

1 a reduction in people's belief in the educational efficacy of schools;
2 an increase in public understanding of the remorseless power, for good or ill, of learning at home and parents' gatekeeper role concerning access to community learning sources such as TV, neighbourhood facilities, peer group, etc.;
3 a heightened sense of obligation among parents and status for home-learning activities.

TOWARDS A PARENT–TEACHER PARTNERSHIP

How, then, might children's education in the new century be approached in such a way that home-learning can play a recognised part in state provision? What options have been suggested by others and how might a cohesive system evolve which builds on the best of present practice? We may consider two learning stages of the young, followed by two possible phases of actions: immediate and longer-term.

TWO LEARNING STAGES

The following model suggests that in the earlier years (childhood) the home has more impact on children's learning than in later years (initiation to adulthood).

Figure 22.1 is a model and it does not claim any accurate measure of 'influence' since this

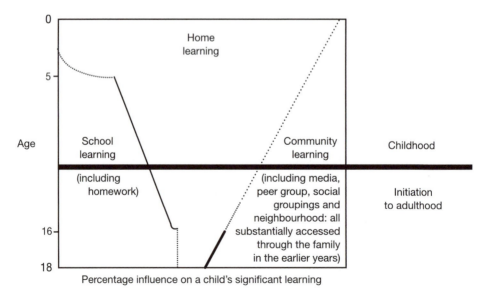

Figure 22.1 Sources of a child's significant learning in the twentieth century

384

will differ from child to child and culture to culture. 'Influence' is not the same as time in contact with a learning source. Thus, it is assumed that school, with its contact with the children for about 15 per cent of their waking life from birth to age 16, has more than 15 per cent of influence. The dividing line between childhood and initiation approximately coincides with that between primary and secondary schooling which is related to puberty, as is the word 'childhood'. However, the average age of puberty has dropped and it may be that psychological dependency is more relevant. Wherever the line is drawn, the essential point is that parents and family are educationally much more determinant in the childhood phase than during initiation to adulthood, though they remain important for the latter. Thus the roles of parents, of schools and of community agencies are different in each phase and the relationships between these adult sources also shift.

If it is accepted that there are two broad spans of a child's development with different educational emphases, what actions might be taken? Some might be applied rapidly while others might be viewed as longer term. Sections A and B below examine each in turn.

A. IMMEDIATE ACTIONS

Significant learning

In the new millennium we should de-emphasise the word 'education' and concentrate on 'significant learning'. Significant learning is taken to mean learning which both persists and has impact, for good or ill, on subsequent life (Macbeth, 1995, p. 48). The term avoids the convoluted and still unresolved discourse about what constitutes education. Significant learning may be acquired by deliberate action or by accident and may be moral or immoral, but it has an impact on children's future actions. It may be acquired in home, from the peer group, from public media, in the neighbourhood or in school. Unlike debates about the meaning of education which are teacher-centred (concerned with what it is proper to impart or do), significant learning is the intellectual product of the whole experience of childhood and adolescence. It is the learning, for better or worse, with which the individual is equipped on entering adult life. That is what matters.

Publicizing the limitations of schooling and the potency of home

An authoritative and highly public message from governments and professional groups in concert, continuously delivered through popular media and through schools, might contain the following points:

- Schools contribute to, but only partially provide, a child's significant learning.
- Much of every child's significant learning is acquired at home or through its agency, especially in the early years.
- The quality of home-learning affects the quality of school-learning and life development of the child.
- Parents, not teachers, are responsible for the child's education by law, while the task of

schools is to assist parents to fulfil that duty (and in any country where that is not the system, the law should be changed to make it so).

Mutual home–school support

Having accepted that the role of schools in children's learning is inevitably limited, though important, an additional message might be based on recognition that schooling is likely to be more effective if supported actively by home-learning and vice versa. Indeed, benign parental pressure on children could account for much of the seeming success of schools. Similarly, schools should recognise the importance of home-learning and lend it active support. Home–school partnership has to move from mere information exchange to a shared curriculum for each child.

Signed understandings

Parents and school should enter into a 'signed understanding' by which each partner acknowledges (a) that parents are legally responsible for their individual child's education; (b) that much learning happens at home; (c) that schools exist to assist parents; (d) that active family support for schooling may increase the child's likelihood of gaining maximum benefit from it (see Macbeth, 1989, 1995). This should not be a legally binding contract, but a statement that each party recognises the role of the other and each will support the other. It would emphasise obligations. Some agreements or compacts have been adopted or advocated (Jones *et al.*, 1992) but instead of focusing on home-learning and the service of schools to parents, many of these school-centred agreements have emphasised parental subservience to the school. In my view, practical issues such as homework conditions, backing for school rules and so on should appear, but they might be listed *after* the signature, whereas the signature should reflect understanding of the fundamentals given above. In return, schools should sign an undertaking to provide a professional service in partnership with parents.

Harnessing the 'curriculum of the home'

Most European countries have national curricula with these features:

- They aim to promote the all-round development of children.
- They aim to cover a wide range of knowledge, skills and attitudes with regard to intellectual, physical, moral, social and vocational learning.
- They embody the assumption that schooling will cover all facets of the curriculum.

Much of what is specified in school curricula is self-evidently also learnt from sources outside school. Chapter 3 of the Finnish curriculum framework (Finnish National Board of Education, 1994), for example, is devoted to the following: consumer education, traffic education, family education, health education, information technology skills, communication education, environmental education, entrepreneurship education and international education. Who can doubt that the family teaches these to a degree? The Scottish 5–14 Curriculum Guidelines include 'the development of the whole person', language, relations with others, beliefs, dealing with emotion, health education, moral values in life-situations, changes in society, advertising and the media, basic rights and responsibilities and 'understanding that family and friends care for them'. Again, home-learning is already an unacknowledged part of such a curriculum. Examples of such home-related learning could be taken from any national curriculum. To these obvious areas of overlap could be added examples from literacy, mathematics, social studies, motivation to learn and a range of other elements which not only *could* be learnt in all homes but, well or badly, *are* to some extent learnt at home.

The preposterous proposition that schools can 'educate the whole child' has, rightly, been attacked. In the new millennium politicians and educationists must accept that schools can only *contribute* to a child's learning and they must publicise the role of families. A useful start could be to copy the Danish Basic School Law of 1991 (sec. 2.1) which states:

> The task of the basic school is, *in co-operation with the parents*, to improve pupils' acquisition of knowledge, skills, working methods and forms of expression which *contribute* to the all-round, personal development of the individual pupil. [My italics]

The Norwegian school curriculum (Norwegian Ministry of Education and Research, 1990) devotes an introductory chapter to the contribution of parents. Such examples could become standard and could be reflected in teacher training, teachers' contracts and materials designed for parents. Building on the official curriculum, schoolteachers could ensure that parents are constantly made aware of the content of the school's teaching *in advance* of its application (through literature, class meetings, telephone chains, electronic conferencing, or whatever become the favoured future means) and should be informed what parents can do, so that home-learning might reinforce school learning.

Standard rights

Parental choice of school, parental representation on each school's board of management, information flow between teachers and parents, the encouragement of parents' associations (as distinct from PTAs) and regular class meetings of teachers and parents with children in the same class to discuss the coming curriculum – all these could easily be standard features and they already exist in many western countries.

B. LONGER-TERM ACTIONS: A FLEXIBLE PARENT–TEACHER PARTNERSHIP

Any future approach to children's learning might include:

1 the short-term features listed in section A above;
2 replacement of schools with school-like learning centres to interact with and to supplement other learning sources, providing a professional service to parents and their children;

3 Local Parent Resource Centres;

4 an arrangement by which families can, with state funding, take on as much home-schooling to replace facets of schooling as they wish and as their circumstances allow *and be encouraged to do so*;

5 some diversity of curricula, allowing for more exploratory learning and choice within a framework of basics;

6 increased use of electronic media and distance education techniques;

7 recognition of emerging evidence from the fields of brain research, genetics, and other sources about how we learn;

8 a resource-backed emphasis on parental care for very young children;

9 a switch in emphasis of educational research away from school-learning to home-learning;

10 revised contracts and terms of service for schoolteachers to enable them to work in partnership with parents;

11 a fresh approach to training schoolteachers (and, perhaps, also hometeachers).

Today's schools face attacks based on new evidence about how the brain works and on arguments that schools, as currently organised, are inappropriate for fast-changing future societies, especially in the light of advances in information technology. Marshall (1997), for example, argues that 'the schools we have today must be transformed because they simply are not capable of developing the kind of learner required for . . . the next century'. She refers to 'a new global economy and ultimately a new global civilisation' for which 'Generative learning and the creation of knowledge are the core competences', features which are not developed by current schools 'where many children and adults have become creatively and emotionally anorexic'. She lists 12 'erroneous assumptions' underpinning schooling and concludes, 'What all these assumptions point to is the view of a powerful teacher and a powerless learner and a "one size fits all" system that stifles our natural desire to learn' (Marshall, 1997, pp. 36–39). Abbott (1997), writing about The 21st Century Learning Initiative, condemns the innovation-suppressing nature of the conventional classroom and calls for ways to assist children to become independent learners earlier.

The above are quoted, not as incontrovertible authorities, but as indicators of current futurologists' new ammunition against schools. The majority of such attacks seek a solution in some sort of community learning process which would rely on goodwill as much as system. However, we know enough about schooling to begin to adapt it and enough about home-learning to build upon it in a way that would suit each family's circumstances. The following elements of shared curriculum, distance learning, electronic communication, home education, flexischooling and parent schools might already have demonstrated their worth sufficiently to enable a shift on a wider front.

A shared home–school curriculum

Above I argued that parents could be encouraged to understand the school curriculum and to reinforce it at home. However, it would be possible to go further and pass over to homes some elements of the formal curriculum. The nature of curricula has been challenged.

Although Toffler (1970) may have misjudged the pace of change in education, his basic thesis still deserves respect, as do his proposals for children's learning. In essence he argued that societies are altering at an accelerating speed, substantially due to advances in technology, and that their inhabitants must learn to cope with such change – 'cope-ability' as well as capability.

> It is no longer sufficient for Johnny to understand the past. It is not even enough for him to understand the present, for the here-and-now environment will soon vanish. Johnny must learn to anticipate the directions and rate of change. He must, to put it technically, learn to make repeated, probabilistic, increasingly long-range assumptions about the future. And so must Johnny's teachers.
>
> (Toffler, 1970, p. 346)

Others, such as Holt, have questioned the compartmentalisation of curricula into subjects and Meighan (1997) advocates a 'catalogue curriculum' from which parents and children might choose, including set courses (as in current national curricula) and the facility to branch out in other ways, though within a structure. He cites the Duke of Edinburgh Award Scheme as an example and the American *City as Schools* initiative and he notes that the catalogue approach is already normal at pre-school and post-school institutions. Pourtois *et al.* (1996) have argued that a child's learning might be constructed in terms of four groups of needs: affective needs, cognitive needs, social needs and value needs. They then present these in terms of challenges to parents with regard to providing for these educative needs in the family. Brighouse (1996, pp. 64–65) has suggested that there should be four distinct but related curricula: a national curriculum (broad outline); a more detailed school curriculum; a home curriculum (emphasising parental rights and responsibilities); and the pupil's personal curriculum.

These perspectives might contribute to the evolution of a shared home–school curriculum for the childhood phase. It might be stylised as shown in Figure 22.2.

There is constant pressure on school curricular time. Whenever a new topic is introduced, something else has to shrink. By accepting the home as a learning centre for part of the curriculum, that pressure can be relieved and schools can concentrate on what they do best – the transfer of cognitive knowledge – while much social and attitudinal learning can substantially be provided by or shared with other, especially family-related and media-borne, means. For example, a range of social skills to do with human relationships, some aspects of language and number, and various daily survival activities (food, health, traffic sense, etc.) can be initiated by parents who, in turn, can relate their teaching to both everyday practice and to in-school learning. They can be assisted by schools, Local Parent Resource Centres, advisory booklets, videos, neighbourhood meetings of parents at an informal level and other sources. A few families will find it hard to cope, but that is not a reason to ignore the power of home-learning for the majority.

Understanding and respect for world religions can be incorporated in moral education based on television and/or computer-based programmes or provided in printed form to be shared by parents and their children at home, as can the growing field of values education. Sport is another case in point. It can be required in some form, but it could be a parental responsibility to ensure that some sport/exercise be pursued by the child with the aid of evening and weekend facilities and specialist assistance, some of which can be school-based. Home assistance with literacy and numeracy for younger children is already

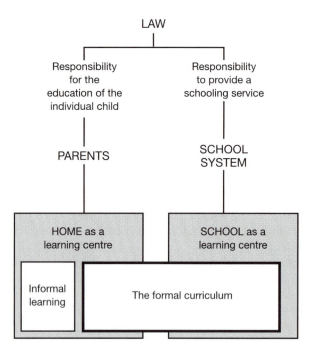

Figure 22.2 Model of shared home–school curriculum

becoming rapidly accepted. A range of other possibilities is explored under 'flexischool-ing' below.

The question arises: who should be the agents to assist parents in their teaching tasks? School itself can be that service to parents. Alternatively, a combination of non-school agencies (Local Parent Resource Centres) and neighbourhood parent self-help groups linked to schools could take on the task, but mediated through class meetings of parents with children in the same class, so that schoolteachers can update parents on the coming school curriculum and how families can reinforce it at home. A National Home Learning Service (i.e. central advice) might disseminate mass publicity and assist the Local Parent Resource Centres. The system could be funded and administered separately from schools (with special account taken of the more disadvantaged families) but could supplement school provision. This would be an extension to all families of the admirable home-assistance experiments already carried out in disadvantaged areas of several cities. However, care would have to be taken to ensure that it is not a rigid 'home curriculum', but something closer to Meighan's 'catalogue curriculum', involving families and children in choices and home initiatives. This system could provide adult education for parents as needed, along with other forms of inter-generational learning, for example with regard to computer use. It would also enable schools to concentrate on a more restricted curriculum, relating it to the complementary work of parents as their partners. An integral element to such a system should be the capacity for each family to negotiate the extent to which it would draw on professional services, an issue I return to under 'flexischooling' below. Time is a factor and those who choose to have children should be expected to find it.

There is evidence that the early teens is the time when we especially begin to develop certain higher-order thinking such as judgement, altruism, compassion and a sense of justice. The impact of homes and community in this process is obvious.

As the young person enters the initiation phase, so parent–teacher partnership might gradually change into a parent–teacher–student planning process. After age 16, there could be a contract between the student and various life-skills and learning agencies. The use of adult 'mentors', neither the young person's schoolteachers nor parents, to advise on educational, employment and personal matters, could become a feature.

Distance learning and the electronic factor

Toffler (1970) predicted that, just as parents would increasingly work from home, so children would one day partly obtain formal educational provision at home, linked electronically to school-like organisations but with some activities on site. A quarter of a century later, this is becoming a possibility. Taylor (1995) predicts that 'pervasive global digital communications utilities' will transform our 'networked homes' over the next decade or two. Hargreaves (1997) has asserted 'technology gives easy access to all the information that the home-based student needs and parents are so much better educated now that they know both what their children need and how to access it.' The pace of electronic change is formidable and parents (and homes as work-stations) will increasingly be integral to its educational applications.

Yet there are impediments. Although 93 per cent of households in Britain had telephones in 1996, only a quarter had computers (Office for National Statistics, 1998). Add to that the lack of compatibility between computing systems, the rapidity with which equipment becomes obsolete, the relative unreliability of both hardware and software (books don't 'crash'), and the 'fast–slow paradox' (Taylor, 1995) by which software and systems technologies are not keeping up with hardware advances. It is sometimes assumed that distance learning is inextricably linked to electronic communications. The latter may come to transform the former, but there is no necessary link. Distance provision goes back to the nineteenth century (e.g. Pitman's postal courses) and in Britain most distance courses at the end of the twentieth century are still largely paper-based, even at university level. Yet the techniques of distance education are increasingly accepted in tertiary sector education and are officially envisaged for younger learners (Department for Education/Scottish Office, 1995). Politicians on both sides of the Atlantic have urged that every child should have access to a lap-top. This electronic leap could be in conjunction with parents, many of whom could acquire computer skills either with or from their children. Brighouse (1995) has envisaged, as part of his proposed 'University of the First Age', that secondary school pupils might supplement conventional schooling in a diversity of locations, some of which would be computer-based backed by a tutor system. Electronic, distance and other methods are likely to change the nature of schools quite soon anyway. With those changes will come new roles for parents.

Home-based schooling

Home-based schooling (sometimes called home-schooling or home education) has a commendable track record but has been granted little support from the school-oriented establishment. In essence it consists of parents declining to send their children to school and providing learning at home – or, rather, *extending* learning provision from home since much learning happens there anyway and since home-schoolers make considerable use of the wider community. Starting with a wafer-thin proportion of children, it has grown to as high as 3 per cent in some places (Meighan, 1997) and there is evidence that home-schooled children tend to achieve more academically (Ray, 1997) and to be more socially confident than their schooled peers (Shyers, 1992). The legal situation differs from country to country and the response of authorities can vary. There is a clear case for state subsidy of home-schooling to enable more families to undertake it or, at the very least, to make the costs to parents tax-deductible. A corollary to state funding would presumably be state inspection, but that should be adaptable and should recognise a wide range of approaches as valid. Although organisations exist to help families to do it (e.g. Education Otherwise and the World-wide Education Service), home-schooling requires much dedication and time, some funds and a degree of confidence and competence which only a limited proportion of parents could offer, so it is bound to remain a minority activity, though Ray (1997) predicts a marked increase in the USA.

Flexischooling

Flexischooling, however, offers possibilities for widespread application. There are variants but, in essence, parents opt into elements of schooling and make other provision themselves. The in-school element might either be aspects of learning which a given family feels unable to provide either through lack of equipment or inability to master specialist subjects, or it may be determined by the employment demands on parents' time, so that a child might, for example, attend school some days or weeks, not others. As Meighan (1997, p. 56) puts it, 'School becomes one of many resources, such as libraries, radio, television, computers, etc., to be used when the child and parent choose, according to a contract between them and the school.' For administrative reasons the school is likely to want some planned basis for the arrangement, though as competition between schools increases, a 'drop-in' system might emerge. Toogood (1987), arguing that flexischooling 'may contain the seeds of a whole revised education system more appropriate to the needs of the time', points out that 'in home-based flexischooling the day-to-day responsibility for the curriculum is retained by the parent'. A voucher system could play a part in enabling parents to widen flexischooling through the use of more than one learning centre according to curricular needs and school specialisms on offer.

Parent schools

These are schools set up by groups of parents sharing a similar philosophy and in that sense parents also retain responsibility for the curriculum, but in a corporate way. Parents may also help to teach in the schools. Denmark's 'little schools' have existed for decades and about 11 per cent of Danish pupils attend them; American 'charter schools' are increasing in number. The state can subsidise (up to 85 per cent of costs in the Danish case) parent-run schools without having to control them, apart from occasional inspection.

Choice

Parental choice is integral to such schemes: choice between schools (or not school), choice within a 'catalogue curriculum' and choice of mix. Already the heated debates which once surrounded the introduction of choice between state schools seem quaint and dated as parental choice increasingly becomes the norm. However, the quasi-market arguments by which choice is intended to put pressure on schools to compete and so become more efficient have tended to distract from the liberal, democratic and educational arguments not only for choice between schools but for choice within schools, and for choice between non-school alternatives and mixtures of provision. Reasons for parental choice also rest on the responsibility placed upon parents by law for the education of the child, but this legal right of parents gives insufficient attention to the part which young people themselves can, do and should contribute to the choosing process. The added bonus which the home-schooling, flexischooling and parent school movements offer is recognition of how important choice will be in the future. As technology makes more and more information readily available and as knowledge itself expands to burst the bounds of set curricula, so we return inevitably to the view expressed 30 years ago by Toffler that learning how to choose must become central to the future-oriented learning process of young people.

MODIFYING THE FEATURES OF OUR CURRENT SYSTEMS

The argument above has been one of modification rather than replacement of schools. Ancillary parts of our present systems would have to adapt also. Boards of school management would have responsibility to ensure that, from the professional end, the home–school partnership was operating. Toffler suggested a 'Council of the Future' for every school, ensuring that provision was geared to a society that is changing, a function which could be taken on by existing boards. Parents' associations might replace conventional Parent Teacher Associations (PTAs), abandon fund-raising and concentrate on curricular issues, especially through a structure of class units (Macbeth, 1989, chapters 6 and 7). Teachers' contracts and teacher training would have to be updated and a new code of professional practice, based on partnership with families, might be created and enforced by general teaching councils. Bodies responsible for national curricula should restructure those curricula for choice-based, joint home–school delivery, while publishers of books, videos, CD-ROMs and other learning materials might be encouraged to present their products for a shared curriculum. Both commercial and government-sponsored, parent resource-and-advice centres should be normal features of neighbourhoods and could, for example, be attached to community organisations (e.g. Citizens' Advice Bureaux) as often as to schools.

According to the General Household Survey (1996), the proportion of British women with children under 5 working full-time has risen from 5 to 16 per cent since 1983. There is some evidence that institutional daycare of the very young may be less satisfactory than maternal care (Morgan, 1996; Tizard and Hughes, 1984). The daycare trend, especially for under-fives, might be reversed and incentives such as pension credits might be given for one or other partner to remain as home-educators for at least part of the working week. There might be an expansion of after-school clubs for older children, thereby allowing parents to work. There might also be unpaid but state-pensionable 'parent days' for those with older children being flexischooled. Extension of education for parents in how to optimise home-learning for children might be a common element of lifelong learning. There might also be recognised roles for grandparents and other adult family members.

SOCIAL EXPECTATIONS

The above have been examples of possible actions. Such initiatives may be challenged in their detail and more astute minds may construct better systems. If improvements can be made on the practical procedures, that would be welcome, but the fundamentals should not be obscured by criticism of details. Those fundamentals would seem to be:

1 government publicity that schools, although importantly helpful, can only provide a limited contribution to childhood learning;
2 creation of social acceptance (more than mere awareness) that families are providers of and gatekeepers to most childhood learning and that important educational obligations accompany parenthood;
3 establishment of shared, choice-based, home–school curricula and shared teaching.

Greater public scrutiny of and control over (yes, call it censorship if you will) anti-social elements of the mass media might accompany this home–school effort and it is surely time that greater control over the moral standards in the public media is reconsidered.

In essence, the future should move from a vision of learning founded on a factory model of schooling to one that is more based on a combination of natural learning, technological advance and future social and individual needs, and mediated in the early years through homes, supported by school-like learning centres and other agencies.

NOTE

1 There is evidence of *consolidating* learning in sleep, but it is doubtful if acquisition of new learning occurs in sleep (Rose and Nicholl, 1997, pp. 48–49).

REFERENCES

Abbott, J. (1997) 'The 21st century learning initiative'. *Education 2000 News*, Letchworth Garden City: Education 2000.

Brighouse, T. (1995) 'Competition, devolution, choice and accountability: An education authority view of the need for diversity and equality'. In A. Macbeth, D. McCreath, and J. Aitchison (eds), *Collaborate or Compete? Educational Partnerships in a Market Economy*. London: Falmer Press, ch. 4.

Brighouse, T. (1996) 'Avoiding failing the future – the need to go beyond the National Curriculum'. *RSA Journal*, CXLIV, 5470.

Department for Education, Scottish Office, Welsh Office and Department of Education for Northern Ireland (1995) *Superhighways for Education*. London: HMSO.

Durning, P. and Pourtois, J. P. (eds) (1994) *Éducation et famille*. Brussels: De Boeck.

Finnish National Board of Education (1994) *Framework Curriculum for the Comprehensive School 1994*. Helsinki: Painatuskeskus.

Gardner, H. (1993) *Multiple Intelligences: The Theory in Practice*. New York: Basic Books.

Hannon, P. (1995) *Literacy, HOME and School: Research and Practice in Teaching Literacy with Parents*. London: Falmer Press.

Hargreaves, D. (1997) Quoted in 'High-tech vision of schools in the home'. *Sunday Times, 8 June*.

Jones, G., Bastiani, J., Bell, G. and Chapman, C. (1992) *A Willing Partnership: Project Study of the Home–School Contract of Partnership*. London: RSA.

Jones, S. (1997) *In the Blood: God, Genes and Destiny*. London: Flamingo.

Macbeth, A. M. (1989) *Involving Parents: Effective Parent–Teacher Relations*. London: Heinemann Educational.

Macbeth, A. M. (1995) 'Partnership between parents and teachers in education'. In A. Macbeth, D. McCreath, and J. Aitchison (eds) *Collaborate or Compete? Educational Partnerships in a Market Economy*. London: Falmer Press.

Majoribanks, K. (1979) *Families and their Learning Environments: An Empirical Analysis*. London: Routledge & Kegan Paul.

Marshall, S. P. (1997) 'Does education and training get in the way of education?' *RSA Journal*, March, 36–39..

Meighan, R. (1996) 'The next learning system: alternatives for everybody, all the time'. *Education Now*, feature supplement, Winter.

Meighan, R. (1997) *The Next Learning System: And Why Home-schoolers are Trailblazers*. Nottingham: Educational Heretics Press.

Merttens, R. and Vass, J. (1993) *Partnerships in Maths: Parents and Schools*. London: Falmer Press.

Morgan, P. (1996) *Who Needs Parents?* London: Institute of Economic Affairs.

Norwegian Ministry of Education and Research (1990) *Curriculum Guidelines for Compulsory Education in Norway*. Oslo: Aschehoug.

Office for National Statistics (1998) *General Household Survey 1996: Living in Britain*. London: HMSO.

Pourtois, J.-P., (ed.) (1991) *Innovation en éducation familiale*. Brussels: De Boek.

Pourtois, J.-P., Desmet, H. and Lahaye, W. (1996) *Do I Educate My Child Properly?* Mons: Centre de Recherche et d'Innovation en Sociopédagogie familiale et scolaire.

Pugh, G. (1989) 'Parents and professionals in pre-school services: Is partnership possible?' In S. Wolfendale (ed.) (1989) *Parental Involvement*. London: Cassell, ch. 1.

Ray, B. D. (1997) *Strengths of Their Own: Home Schoolers across America*. Salem, OR: NHERI Publications.

Rose, C. and Nicholl, M. J. (1997) *Accelerated Learning for the 21st Century*. London: Piactus.

Shyers, L. (1992) 'A comparison of social adjustment between home and traditionally schooled students', *Home School Researcher*, 8 (3).

Taylor, J. (1995) 'The networked home: domestication of information'. *RSA Journal* CXLIII, 5458, April.

Tizard, B. and Hughes, M. (1984) *Young Children Learning: Talking and Thinking at Home and at School*. London: Fontana.

Toffler. A. (1970) *Future Shock*. London: Pan Books.

Toogood, P. (ed.) (1987) *Flexischooling*. Bideford, Devon: A Dialogue in Education.

Warnock, M. (1985) Speech given at the Community Education Development Centre Family Education Conference, Sept.

Wolfendale, S. and Topping, K. (1996) *Family Involvement in Literacy: Effective Partnerships in Education*. London: Cassell Education.

23

PEACE EDUCATION
A review and projection
Betty A. Reardon

THE NATURE OF THE FIELD: MULTIPLE APPROACHES, COMMON PURPOSES

As I write these reflections on the substance and evolution of peace education, it seems to me that the field, which I have observed from within for some 35 years, is on the brink of an unprecedented major advance into public acceptance. Peace education, which for so long has seemed marginal (as seen from mainstream education) may, after all, have a significant future. Like any reflection on a varied, often controversial, field, this essay is written from a particular personal perspective and is not without substantive bias or pedagogical preference. While my experience in peace education is perhaps more international than national, my opinions and perspectives are, of course, affected by US citizenship and European American cultural identity.

To contemplate the future of peace education it is necessary to comprehend what is meant by the term itself, the evolution of the substance it comprises, and to analyse the particular needs for further development of the field. The practices and perspectives that comprise the field are varied and not fully consistent one with the other. Indeed, there is an apparent reluctance to define it precisely, perhaps because it is a multidisciplinary field found in a wide range of learning environments practised by educators with varying concerns and perspectives. This lack of definition may have served to preserve the element of creativity which has been a source of pride among practitioners. It may in part be due to a lack of the organisational structure that characterises other fields, such as professional associations and specific departments in schools of education. Peace education has been limited to only a very few such departments that have had insufficient influence on mainstream education. In professional associations it has also been marginalised. While there are citizens' organisations that espouse, encourage, even facilitate the practice and some professional organisations that have within them groups devoted to sharing experiences and informing their colleagues of the needs for and educational possibilities of peace education, yet there are no major national or international peace education organisations, and only recently has peace itself and specific preparation for it become a major focus of UNESCO.

The lack of definition, however, is most likely because peace education has sprung up in many parts of the world, often independently of efforts in other countries, and has been developed in various subject areas. Yet the field has evolved, in some few cases, even flourished and developed in the various forms which seem to defy clear and precise definition that can be universally applied. Impelled by a range of socio-political concerns, by the varied professional specialisations of the practitioners, and the distinct, particular historic circumstances that have led to the emergence of a variety of approaches and issue focuses, there is not one standard field but a variety of subfields loosely held together by a few common purposes. It is from those purposes that I shall attempt, for the purposes of this chapter, to derive a definition that will offer some descriptions of the major practices, their perspectives, assumptions and goals, within the context of the historical circumstances that led educators to adopt them. I shall also offer comments on some of the historical context and public issues surrounding their introduction into the schools.

If asked what purpose practitioners of each approach to peace education are pursuing through their particular pedagogies, most responses will indicate that a major goal is a more humane society, be that on a community, national or local basis. There is, as well, a shared assumption that such a society derives from positive, mutually beneficial relationships among the members of the society, regarded both corporately and individually. Another common assumption seems to be that peace can only obtain under the existence of the fundamental precondition of mutually advantageous circumstances. This assumption extends to the belief that all concerned need to understand what constitutes such circumstances and seek to maintain them. Further, most would also agree that in the contemporary world such circumstances are limited in even the best cases and absent in most cases. We live in a world of disparities where few enjoy advantages, a world of peacelessness. As educators, most would also argue that unless their respective populations are intentionally educated to understand and to pursue what is mutually beneficial to their own groups and diverse other groups and individuals, in no case will a society experience these circumstances which, for the purposes of this discussion, will be called 'peace'.

Peace, then, is possible when society agrees that the overarching purpose of public policies is the achievement and maintenance of mutually beneficial circumstances that enhance the life possibilities of all. Such an agreement is sometimes identified as universal respect for human rights. It is also interpreted as an agreement to renounce the use of violence within the society, and to develop non-violent processes for dispute settlement and decision-making. Such agreements are, however, seldom fully and universally realised even within the national boundaries of democratic societies that enjoy a generally peaceful order. But at least at the level of publicly declared national values, if not daily practice, such societies espouse the human rights of their citizens and legally prohibit violence among them. There is no general, firmly held agreement on these principles at the level of world society, and some peace educators hold this to be a contributing factor in the widespread breakdown of the agreement within national societies, or more accurately, nation states and 'former' nation states. Few would hold that peace could exist in the absence of a consensus on respect for human rights and prohibition of violence. Thus, although seldom articulated in these particular terms (indeed, clear statements of conceptual definitions and social learning purposes are rare in many educational practices, even those of greater conformity and commonality in content and approach), the hope of strengthening human rights and reducing violence in the global society informs all the varied approaches to peace education, the absence of a consensus on definition notwithstanding.

Some will note that the two fundamental aspects of this stipulated definition of peace are reflective of the definitional distinctions peace researchers have made between 'negative peace', the absence of war, and 'positive peace', the presence of justice and other peace values.[1] Some will probably also be aware that most who practise peace education are to some degree advocates of holism, both philosophically and pedagogically, or as might be said by the academic peace researchers (some peace research is conducted by activists), in analysis and in policy application. Still others might say 'in theory and in practice'. Holists would argue that each of these categories is integral and essential to the other. It is this holistic approach to education that characterises the advocates of comprehensive peace education, who see a place for all the various teaching approaches as essential to an integrated framework of education for peace that comprehends both negative and positive peace. As will be discussed below, the holistic and comprehensive approaches are gaining ground as potentially the most effective routes to achieving the common purposes of all the approaches, especially when taking into account the recent historic circumstances that must be addressed by peace education. The trend is reflected in UNESCO's most recent policy statement on the field, the 1994 *Declaration and Integrated Framework of Action on Education for Peace, Human Rights, and Democracy* (to be dealt with in greater detail in the discussion of current trends and future directions).

In reviewing the historical evolution and practical development of the approaches, a common assumption about the essential nature of education can also be discerned. Given what all have attempted to do in introducing their respective approaches, they have assumed that two primary related functions of education are to provide *knowledge about* particular subject matter and develop *capacities for* addressing the subject in thought and action. From these assumptions a common if not consensually or professionally agreed upon definition of peace education can be derived that can serve to construct a working definition and provide a vantage-point from which to review the various approaches to the field. Peace education can be defined as: the transmission of knowledge about requirements of, the obstacles to, and possibilities for achieving and maintaining peace; training in skills for interpreting the knowledge; and the development of reflective and participatory capacities for applying the knowledge to overcome problems and achieve possibilities. This, then, is a definition that includes all the approaches and one that can be used not only for review and categorisation, but also as the basis for creating a curricular relationship among them which could comprise a holistically conceived, substantively comprehensive form of peace education.

It should be noted that comprehensive peace education also connotes a developmental approach which argues that peace education should be included in the curriculum of all grade levels and developmental stages, and in all subject areas. As such it is learner-centred, but the centring takes place with the focus of an interactive relationship between teacher and learner(s) in the learning process. Most practitioners of peace education assert that a learning process compatible with the concerns and developmental level of the learners is as important to effective pedagogy as is the subject matter to be learned.

Among the various approaches to education *for* peace are some included in the realm of international education (later global education and/or world studies). Some take the form of multicultural education, and some more recent efforts evolved from environmental education. Each has a substantive base in a discipline. In the aforementioned approaches, the disciplines are respectively international relations, cultural anthropology and environmental sciences. Each was also derived in response to a perceived need for the citizenry to be informed about matters perceived as potentially or actually problematic: the emergence of a more complex system of international interdependence; demographic and social changes that initiated or intensified racism, religiously based strife, ethnic tensions and conflicts; and the growing severity of environmental degradation. Each of these approaches also would fall into the area of 'education *for* peace',[2] that is education to create some of the preconditions for the achievement of peace.

Other approaches to peace education might be called 'education *about* peace', education for the development and practice of institutions and processes that comprise a peaceful social order. These approaches include: 'creative' or 'constructive' conflict resolution training; human rights education; and peace studies, which as practised in elementary and secondary schools, is generally designated as 'peace education', what is meant by the more narrow, traditional view of the field. Conflict resolution has its roots in jurisprudence, behavioural psychology, sociology and social change initiatives such as the American civil rights movements.[3] It became a distinct field of university education and research in the 1950s and has been slowly but steadily growing to a level of some academic significance since then. It became a component of school peace education in the United States in the 1980s and in the 1990s began to be practised in other countries, particularly those in 'post-conflict situations'.

Human rights education is a later entry into the schools and the universities, the first university programmes outside law schools being established in the late 1970s and early 1980s. The field, however, did not come to the schools so much as a translation of the substance of university courses and research as a response to what was seen as a virtual crisis in human and social relations, manifest in political repression, socio-economic deprivation, racism and sexism. While it placed some emphasis on the international standards, mainly the Universal Declaration of Human Rights, it focused more on the fundamental concept of human dignity and the problems and possibilities of the interpretations the various cultural traditions and legal systems gave to the concept.

Peace education, when so called in schools and the few universities in which it appears in the curriculum, is perceived and defined somewhat differently by the general field of education than it is by the practices I would identify as components of the field of 'peace knowledge' (comprising peace research, peace studies and peace education).[4] For the most part the subject matter which peace education transmits is derived from the field of peace research. This, like conflict resolution, emerged in the 1950s from the work of individual researchers, mainly in the social sciences, in various parts of the world, but predominantly in Europe. Called in its early days 'polemology' and/or 'irenology', it formally took the generic name of peace research when the International Peace Research Association was established in 1964. Peace research has entered the universities through institutes that conduct research and courses that teach the substance and methods of the field to future researchers. It also informs peace studies, which have been introduced into university curricula mainly, but not exclusively, through the social sciences, and mostly in the United States. Some universities have multidisciplinary peace studies programmes which offer degrees. This chapter, however, will deal with peace education as an aspect of the field methodologically concerned with instructional approaches as learning modes appropriate to the general education of large numbers. Hence it pursues its purposes primarily but not exclusively in elementary and secondary schools, in all parts of the world. Most of the experiences recounted here, however, took place in the United States or in 'international' settings and through 'transnational' initiatives.

Within the more narrow self-defined field of peace education there are also various approaches, interpretations and some contention about what does and should constitute the field. For the purposes of this essay the stipulated qualifier will be planned and guided learning that attempts to comprehend and reduce the multiple forms of violence (physical, structural, institutional and cultural) used as instruments for the advancement or mainten-ance of cultural, social or religious beliefs and practices or of political, economic or ideo-logical institutions or practices. As the earlier broader definition serves to categorise and interrelate all approaches to peace education, both *for* and *about* peace education, this definition serves the same purposes for the narrower, self-defined field of traditional 'peace education', which is the major focus of this chapter. Thus, greater attention will be given to the historical evolution, practices and purposes of education *about* peace (emphasising knowledge and skills of peace-making, especially traditional peace education) than to educa-tion *for* peace (emphasising attitudes towards and awareness of global problems and human diversity). While both are indispensable components of comprehensive peace education, most traditionalists would argue that without the particular capacities and skills that com-prise the learning objectives of the traditional field, no specific approach is adequate to the achievement of the goals implicit in the general definition. Thus traditional peace education has become the core of what I would call 'essential peace education', as I would call education *about* peace, 'supportive peace education'. It is distinguished mainly by the aforementioned substantive attention to one or more forms of violence.

THE VARIED PURPOSES AND PEDAGOGIES OF EDUCATION *FOR* AND *ABOUT* PEACE

Education *for* peace is primarily concerned with knowledge and skills related to 'the requirements of and obstacles to ... the achievement of peace'. Of all the approaches included here (i.e. international, multicultural and environmental education), international education has the longest history. The major educational goal of global or international education[5] is imparting knowledge and skills about the international system and global issues. The apparent assumption underlying this goal is that a well-informed public is essential to citizens' calling for and supporting policies that are more likely to lead to peace. Some thought of this approach as education for world citizenship. They saw that citizenship as participation in or expressing opinions on the international policy-making of the citizens' respective national governments, supporting the United Nations, and exercising overall responsible national citizenship within a framework of global responsibility. Much of this education was thus devoted to cultivating understanding of foreign policy and developing a global perspective, but not all of it cultivated the critical stance traditional peace educators assumed to be necessary to the purposes of achieving peace. An exception to this was those curricular efforts that taught a structural and values analysis of the international system, and those forms of 'development education', a subset or alternative approach to global education that guided students through an enquiry into the economics of poverty and global disparities.

The goals pursued by multicultural education are in the areas of the attitudes, the perspectives, and the knowledge required for peoples of different cultural backgrounds and traditions to interact with one another on positive and constructive terms. Multicultural education has three main sets of roots: one in education for international understanding, another in anti-racist education and one in education for religious tolerance. The fundamental cognitive objectives are detailed knowledge of one or more other cultures as a means to comprehend that there are various ways to be human and experience the world. The attitudes to be cultivated are tolerance of ways of life distinctly different from one's own, respect for the integrity of other cultures, and an appreciation of the positive potential of cultural diversity. Multicultural education is widely practised in American and European schools and to some extent is being introduced in other areas experiencing ethnic tensions and conflicts. It is often introduced only for purposes of reducing such tensions in schools or communities, but even when not self-consciously practised as education *for* peace, it makes a contribution towards that goal.

Multicultural education is also closely related to human rights education in that it teaches respect for other cultures and ways of life so as to lead to respect for the fundamental humanity of peoples of all cultures. This fundamental respect will militate against prejudice and discrimination and lead the learners to expect that all should be accorded fair treatment and that groups need not fear or be on guard against others simply because of cultural, religious or ethnic differences which in themselves pose no threat. Multicultural education has involved study of the cultures of other nations and of cultural and racial groups within multi-ethnic societies. It is a popular approach with internationally minded schools around the world, such as the UNESCO Associated Schools. It has also been adopted in areas affected by significant demographic changes, often due to world problems and conflicts.

The fundamental purpose of environmental education is the transmission of knowledge about the pervasive and dangerous threats to the global environment, the degradation of local and community environments, and the interrelationships between local and global environments. On the basis of this knowledge it seeks to cultivate a commitment to the preservation of the environment and the development of a sense of environmental responsibility, particularly for one's immediate or community environment. With regard to this purpose, practitioners of environmental education have been among those who promote activism within and outside the schools as a mode of participatory learning that appears to be an effective means to educating for various forms of social responsibility. Students are encouraged and guided in 'environment-friendly' behaviours and initiatives, often taking specific responsibility for the quality of the environments of their schools and communities.

Environmental education can be considered an approach to education *for* peace when it argues the preservation of the environment to be an essential prerequisite to all human endeavours, including the achievement of peace. All environmental education is not truly peace education. Some of it is still conducted within a framework that views the environment as the surroundings of or venue for human activity. Few curricula or programmes address such issues as the impact of war and 'defence' preparation on the environment, and few make the links between poverty and environmental degradation. None the less, a number of leading international peace educators and some environmental educators have begun to make these links.[6] Those environmental educators who encourage consideration of the Gaia hypothesis that the Earth is a single, self-regulating system have, in fact, made some significant contributions to recent developments in peace education, namely, ecological thinking (discussed in a later section of this essay).

Environmental education comes closer to education *about* peace when it takes an eco-logical, living-system perspective and when, in combination with development education, it addresses issues of sustainability. The question of preserving environmental sustainability raises some of the structural issues that researchers working in the area of 'positive' peace explore. This research, and some of the education that it inspires, demonstrates relation-ships among and between large-scale development such as the industrialisation of agri-culture, increased economic burdens on the poor, and environmental erosion. Such research is used to make the case that global economic structures give rise to 'structural violence', that is, avoidable harm done to economically vulnerable groups. Environmentalists who claim that some economic policies and development practices have led to irreversible dam-age to the environment, argue that they constitute a form of 'ecological violence', avoidable harm to the biosphere. Educators who introduce consideration of these arguments, and those that arise from the atmospheric pollution, land destruction, water contamination and excess consumption of mineral resources resulting from military activity, are clearly in the camp of education *about* peace, because they state the problematique addressed in their curricula in terms of violence, the fundamental concern of essential and traditional peace education.

Education *about* peace is 'essential peace education' in two respects. The substance it addresses is about what peace *is*, its essence, and it assumes that without knowledge of what it comprises, peace cannot be pursued, much less achieved. Certain knowledge is essential to peace. At present three approaches could be categorised as essential peace education: human rights education, conflict resolution and traditional peace education. It is these three approaches which are becoming the integrated core of comprehensive peace education.

All three are primarily concerned with avoiding, reducing and eliminating violence, and each emphasises one of those three possibilities. Human rights educators argue that respect for human rights would encourage individuals, groups, even corporate entities such as the state to avoid inflicting intentional, unnecessary harm on any human being. Some would extend this avoidance to the living environment. Conflict resolution educators hold that a broader repertoire of behavioural skills for dealing with conflict would result in a significant reduction of the violence that they assert occurs for lack of knowledge of or skills of non-violent conflict-processing and resolution. Traditional peace educators have come to believe that, at least, socially sanctioned state violence could be eliminated by the establishment of global structures and procedures for dealing with such war-producing conflicts as power differences, political struggles and economic competition. Some even argue that such institutions could help reduce other forms of social and political violence.[7]

It is important to emphasise here that the peace knowledge field has identified various forms of violence. In addition to the politically organised violence of war and various forms of repression, and the structural violence of neo-colonial economic institutions, there is social violence such as racism, sexism and religious fundamentalism, the cultural violence of patriarchal institutions, blood sports, the glorification of violent historical events in national holidays and the banalisation of violence in the media. And now, all of these forms of violence are being seen in their totality as a 'culture of violence and war'.[8] While there are various ways of conceptualising and defining violence, for the purposes of peace education, an effective definition has been 'intentionally inflicted harm that is avoidable and unnecessary to the achievement of just and legitimate purposes'. Such a conceptual framework comprehends all of the forms of violence above and explicates the purposes of the three main forms of essential peace education.

While there are some peace educators who have long approached education about positive peace through the study of human rights, it is only in the last decade that the field has become a distinct and growing educational practice, formally recognised as such by UNESCO in the Montreal Declaration of 1993.[9] Human rights education is undertaken in all parts of the world and in all spheres of education. It was given a significant impetus when the United Nations General Assembly declared a Decade of Human Rights Education in 1995. While it focuses much of its attention on the international human rights standards, it is not transmission of knowledge of the covenants and conventions that forms the primary goal of human rights education. The field seeks to engender such knowledge complemented by action skills for the implementation of the standards, familiarity with remediation procedures, and capacities to challenge states and other political actors to assure the human dignity of all members of human society. Essentially it hopes to develop a general, societal acceptance of human dignity as a fundamental principle to be observed throughout society, and to ensure that all people are aware that they are endowed with rights that are universal, integral and irrevocable. It also seeks to demonstrate the relevance of human rights concepts, issues and standards to a broad range of human and social problems. Some practitioners are advocating a holistic approach to human rights education which is consistent with the perspectives and purposes of comprehensive peace education.[10]

Conflict resolution education comprises efforts to impart knowledge and understanding of conflict processes, and the distinctions between constructive and destructive processes so that the constructive may prevail over the destructive. The most widespread form of conflict resolution education is skills training as applied to conflicts that occur in schools and the everyday life of students. Such education also takes place in corporations, nongovernmental organisations and other such groups who wish to increase their effectiveness and avoid the waste of productive time of employees and members in conflicts that could undermine the health and effectiveness of an entire organisation. In schools it has also been used to deal with discipline problems and to develop community and a sense of efficacy among students.

The goal of most resolution processes is the determination of an outcome that will end the immediate conflict so as to meet the perceived needs of both or all parties to the conflict. More recently, however, the underlying social and political factors are considered in the approach being taken by those practitioners who seek to develop capacities to derive longer-range, 'transformative' solutions that address root causes such as structures, fundamental social norms or political values that play into conflict formations. The separations between traditional peace education and conflict resolution become less distinct as these issues are addressed. So, too, there is some convergence between human rights education and conflict resolution; a few practitioners adopt human rights principles as guidelines for assessing desirable outcomes to be sought in the resolution process. Some are also turning their attention to post-conflict situations, wherein processes of reconstruction and reconciliation are seen as extensions of the resolution process, taking a wider view of conflict resolution as a component of a broader peace-making process.

Traditional peace education has always been concerned with the broader peace-making process. Some practitioners have included conflict resolution as one of various essential skills necessary to both citizens and policy-makers if war is to be eliminated and other forms of violence are to be delegitimised. Traditional peace education began with a concern that learning should be developed to avoid war. A few even spoke of abolition as a goal of both the peace movement and peace education which was conceived as a component of that movement. In many respects peace education has continued to be more closely tied to the peace movement than the other realms of peace knowledge, namely peace research and peace studies. At present peace education draws its inspiration and support mainly from the communities served by the schools in which it is practised.

Because peace education is practised in the schools, it is not only concerned with community standards and social factors that affect public education, it also unfolds in the environment that produces the adherents of social movements, the local community. Indeed, peace education came into the schools more as the consequence of citizen action and the particular concerns of individual teachers than of educational policy. Citizens' groups in association with nongovernmental organisations appealed to individual schools and local school boards for the introduction of some of the approaches discussed here. Some of these organisations also provided resources and services to teachers to facilitate this introduction. Some, such as Educators for Social Responsibility (founded by teachers in the United States) offered in-service teacher education programmes that were school and community based and often supported by contributions from peace movement members and organisations.[11] The importance of this citizen action in the dissemination of peace education is seldom recognised, but it is unlikely that the field could have developed to its present point without this involvement. It also accounts for some of the controversy that has surrounded the field throughout its history.

CHANGING HISTORIC CIRCUMSTANCES: ISSUES AND CONTROVERSIES

While most who identify themselves as peace educators have had, from time to time, at least one professional foot in one of the various approaches described here, the term peace education generally applies to those whose primary work is in traditional or essential peace education. My professional work has been based there with some considerable experience, as well, in world order studies and human rights education, leading me to the comprehensive approach and to ecological and co-operative peace education. More recently, I have begun to explore educating for a culture of peace as the organising framework most conducive to what I see as the needs and possibilities of peace education in these 'millennial' years. As the categories and definitions offered here derive largely from the geographic and cultural ground on which I work, my view of the evolution and future of the field is conditioned by an admittedly subjective perspective on the historical evolution of peace education since the 1960s. I have included here only those developments that I, personally, perceive as being significant influences on the field.

Traditional peace education has deep historical and broad geographical roots. Some of them are so entwined with the history of non-violence, that some researchers claim that religious teachings regarding personal behaviour and social obligations that prohibit violence are in fact forms of peace education, making the field perhaps the oldest form of social education. In this century it has been associated with child-centred education and 'progressive' education, Maria Montessori and John Dewey both having been advocates of peace education. Several educators and peace researchers, most notably Clint Fink, Aline Stomfay-Stitz, David Smith and Terry Carson, have researched this history and published some of their findings.[12]

Traditional peace education is, thus, a field that predates the theories and circumstances which have determined contemporary curriculum and educational practice and the various forms of education for and about peace, many practices of which seem unaware of the roots and earlier achievements of the field. However, as it has evolved in the period since the close of the Second World War, peace education, particularly in the United States, has reflected this theory along with the historic conditions that inspired the various forms presented here as the landscape which surrounds it. The most significant of these forms of postwar essential peace education have been war prevention, non-violence, world order studies, nuclear education, comprehensive peace education and ecological and co-operative education. The latter I consider to be the latest phase of comprehensive peace education. All were the consequence, as were the various forms of education *for* peace or 'supportive peace education', of educators' responses to particular historic conditions and/or forms of organised violence, and, in the case of essential or traditional peace education, of strategic and security doctrines and policies.

Peace education as such did not appear in school curricula for a number of years after the war, although service agencies and education groups such as those sponsored by the Quakers consciously conducted some of their efforts under the label. International university education was more in currency, and was developing along the lines noted above of education to develop a public that would be better informed about word affairs and foreign policy. As the Cold War developed, some of these efforts in the United States were openly education for understanding 'the national interest' and in many cases 'anti-communist education'. While many educators specifically interested in education for peace emphasised 'international understanding and co-operation' and encouraged study of the United Nations, it was not until the 1960s that the critical approach to these issues that characterised peace education became part of the curriculum reform movement that was affecting educational practice in Europe and the United States. Indeed, some of this reform was in response to the demand for a more rigorous substantive curriculum in the hard sciences and social sciences to assure a population well prepared to compete in the international power stakes of the times. However, there was also a call to continue the progressive education tradition of enquiry, critical thinking and problem-solving. Peace educators defined war as a world problem and asserted that enquiry and critical skills were required to solve it. The intention to develop these capacities led to that period's phase of peace education, education for the prevention of war. This was an approach that was followed in the universities that had established courses or programmes in peace studies as well as in the schools.[13]

Buoyed by the wave of educational innovation in the social sciences and renewed calls for peace, war prevention education came into the schools in the form of anthologies about war, simulation games demonstrating the costs of war, and some of the alternative courses of action that might be used to avoid war.[14] The year 1963 was pivotal in this phase of peace education because of the promulgation of Pope John XXIII's encyclical letter, 'Pacem in Terris' and President John F. Kennedy's commencement address at American University, 'Toward a Strategy of Peace', in which he announced the Nuclear Test Ban Treaty. Thus, two major world authorities had called for an all-out effort to achieve peace, providing the basis for some good curriculum material and validating and legitimising the efforts of peace educators. For a short time the barriers of suspicion and censorship, which had become inhibiting factors in the development of peace education, were lowered a bit.[15] This period lasted until the end of the decade, when a very different climate had quite different effects on the schools than on the universities.

The escalation of the war in Vietnam led to the student unrest and 'teach-ins' on university campuses, which resulted in a proliferation of peace studies programmes. However, the early public support for the war made it more difficult to engage in war prevention education in the schools. Peace education, not only in the United States but in Europe as well, became even more an avenue for the development of critical thinking and brought ethical issues into those few classrooms in which it continued to be practised. (In spite of the climate, many teachers, not all with the support of their administrations, raised issues associated with the war in their classes.) Although it was in many respects a setback for peace education, this, the forerunner of the 'low-intensity conflicts' that were to become the primary form of warfare in the succeeding decades, many of them proxy wars in the power struggle between the United States and the Soviet Union, brought significant new substantive and methodological developments to the fields of traditional and essential peace education.

It was a setback because, rationalised as a war against the spread of communism, to defend democracy and 'Western Values' against another totalitarian onslaught, it invigorated some of the anti-communist sentiment that painted peace education with the colours of 'disloyalty' and lack of patriotism. In spite of the supposed tradition of the rights to dissent and criticism of public authority that were usually cited as fundamental to Western democracy, criticism and resistance were censured, and critical education frowned upon.[16] Many school administrators found it prudent to encourage teachers to take up other less 'controversial' global problems than national security policy. Anything seen to undermine national security, including questioning the analyses and policies of the security establishments, was suspect as undermining 'our way of life'. The tensions and conflicts of the larger society also affected the peace and global education movements themselves. The collaboration of the 1960s gave way to differences and separations, that together with issues of funding, served to fragment the American movement.

The negative attitude towards critical peace education was also aroused by the pedagogies that were becoming part of the reforms taking place in social education, which saw its own splits and controversies. The Freirean dialogic method, which appeared in the 1970s and was rapidly embraced by peace educators, was thought by more conservative elements of the public and some in the educational establishments to be a faddish diversion from teaching the 'basics', the fundamental subjects and skills. Values education came under special fire, not only for raising criticism about public issues, but also for challenging students to examine fundamental private and personal values hitherto deemed to belong exclusively to the instructional realm of the students' families and religious institutions, and not to that of the schools.

It was in this area of values that some of the most important strides were made in essential peace education, both methodologically and substantively. Ethical and moral issues were confronted on several fronts: the legality of an undeclared war; questions of individual responsibility raised by dissent against the war policy and resistance to military service on the basis of law and conscience; both selective resistance to particular wars and general resistance on the basis of general conscientious objection. The morality of war had long been a component of traditional peace education, especially among those who taught the philosophy and practice of non-violence, and in religiously based schools, particularly Quaker and Catholic institutions. Now it was raised in some non-religious settings, using not scripture and the 'just war' doctrine, but the Nuremberg Principles as the basis for moral reflections. Another issue merged questions of structural and organised violence as the assertions regarding the underlying economic motivations for the war were examined, raising questions about the morality of neo-colonialism and such questions as were posed in the international political discourse by the call for a New International Economic Order (NIEO).

Study of the war in Vietnam strengthened somewhat, but only temporarily, efforts initiated by some law education projects to introduce elements of international law into the curricula of social education.[17] A more substantial development was the introduction of the issue of individual responsibility in the international system, especially important to the youths in secondary schools who were facing decisions regarding military service. Some peace educators felt morally obliged to help them sort through these issues with sound ethical analysis based on knowledge of the nature of the war, principles of international law, such as the Nuremberg Principles, and personal morality.[18] Individual and political morality were not the only ethical issues raised. Questions of economic justice and the lifestyles of the affluent were also brought into the enquiry, as what some argued to be the underlying economic motives for the war were explored, bringing to a personal and communal level the global structural issues emerging from discussion of the NIEO.

While essential and critical peace education was hardly popular, those who continued the practice developed some significant new dimensions to the field. Not all critical peace educators were pacifists, nor did they all question the institution of war itself. Those who did, including and especially those who taught the philosophy and practice of non-violence and those in religiously oriented schools (such as the Catholics and the Quakers), had long considered the ethical and moral issues raised by war itself.[19] Study of the Vietnam war, for which the primary basis of dissent and resistance was moral and legal principles, brought the ethical dimension more integrally into the field, even in the US public schools.

The enquiry was extended not only to questions of individual responsibility in the international system, raised by the issues of selective resistance to military service in illegal or immoral wars and fundamental conscientious objections facing many of the youths of secondary school age, it also examined the wider question of the responsibilities of all in societies where the high standard of living of large numbers of the population were attributable to the imbalance in global economic structures which researchers had classified as violent. As noted above, some ethical criticism was extended to the economic institutions and motives that were argued to be the underlying basis of this and other 'neo-colonial' struggles. Questions of the world economy and the 'lifestyles' of the affluent nations became integral to the values issues explored by peace education. Pope Paul's axiom, 'If you want peace, work for justice' was translated into the terrain of peace education under the assertion that teaching *about* or *for* peace, necessitates teaching *about* and *for* economic and social justice. Here was another instance in which human rights, economic and social structures were linked inextricably to essential peace education, as the structural, institutional and values dimensions of peace education were clarified and systematised in the world order approach. In this way the world order approach, like the ethical issues of low-intensity conflict and neo-colonialism, became a distinct approach to essential peace education.[20]

While most essential peace education has always been values-oriented, world order education took a particularly values-explicit and specific approach. This approach to peace education derived from a peace research methodology designated as 'world order enquiry' devised by the World Order Models Project (WOMP), a transnational peace research project established in 1968 by the Institute for World Order, then called the World Law Fund. The methodology comprised research into the potential designs of an alternative international system which could achieve the realisation of a set of fundamental or 'world order' values which these researchers argued to be, in one form or another, universal values: peace, social justice, economic well-being, ecological balance and political participation.[21]

Instructional methods and school curricula were developed using some of the research devices employed by WOMP. The core of these curricular developments were the 'world order values'. Since the world order approach to peace education was an enquiry openly and explicitly values-, systems- and future-based, world order enquiry was less practised than the war prevention approach. The older approach, from the point of view of the advocates of world order enquiry, had moved a bit too much from the consideration of the prevention of war as such, to an enquiry into the possible resolution of one war, the American intervention in the war between North and South Vietnam. From this perspective the war prevention approach was more concerned with foreign policy issues than with alternatives to the institution of war. World order enquiry led students through study of various cases of international conflict, including Vietnam, reflecting on the institutional requirements of resolution and termination not only of the particular conflict but also on the possibilities for resolution and prevention of similar future conflicts becoming violent. World order studies was fundamentally a values-based enquiry into the changes in the international system which could assure a more peaceful, just and ecologically viable global society.[22]

As all traditional critical and essential peace education was inhibited by the war in Vietnam, so too the intensification of the ideological and power struggles of the Cold War from 1978–1982 was especially obstructive to the advancement of the system-challenging and values-explicit approach of world order studies. In the early 1980s, however, the changes in strategic doctrine and the development of the 'Strategic Defense Initiative' that increased the possibilities of the use of nuclear weapons, led to a new, more widely practised and less publicly challenged form of traditional or essential peace education yet to reach the schools: nuclear education. Nuclear education and the founding of Educators for Social Responsibility (ESR) in the United States in 1982 and Teachers for Peace in Europe in 1984 inspired more vigorous, organised teachers' action than ever before.

Educators for Social Responsibility and International Teachers for Peace were generally similar in their curricular concerns, but had somewhat different stances on the politics of the issues they faced. Some European educators saw the task of the movement to be as political as it was educational. While the degree of political emphasis varied from country to country, it could be said that more classroom teachers preferred the emphasis to be on curricular matters, focusing efforts on persuading ministries as well as individual schools to undertake the emerging forms of peace education. Some who were not actually teachers believed that the educational tasks went beyond the schools, requiring education of the general public in the manner of other citizens' movements. These differences in the European movement (International Teachers for Peace was the product of a gathering of various national Teachers for Peace organisations in a conference which has taken place biennially since 1984) led to some controversy within the organisation and eventually to a change of name to International Educators for Peace.

In recent years International Educators for Peace have exerted efforts to mobilise educators for peace in regions of the world other than Europe, holding regional congresses in Senegal, Mexico, the United States and Canada. While the effort has helped to legitimise peace education, as has the support from teachers' unions, it has not initiated the production of materials or the development of pedagogical practice or theory as have the Peace Education Commission of the International Peace Research Association or Educators for Social Responsibility. However, some of its members have undertaken their own independent and collaborative curricular and training initiatives.

In the United States the movement initiated by Educators for Social Responsibility, founded in Massachusetts in 1982, placed most of its emphasis on curriculum development, in-service teacher education and building collaborative contacts through exchanges or joint conferences with Soviet Educators. The nuclear arms race was perceived to be part and parcel of the Cold War ideological and political struggle between the two super powers, a competition which had led to the demonisation of the opponent on both sides of 'The Iron Curtain'. ESR thus focused their curricular development work on two crucial areas that had considerable effect on critical and essential peace education: the nature and potential consequences of nuclear warfare and understanding, not so much the Soviet political system as had been emphasised by the 'anti-communist' education of the 1960s and 1970s, as the Soviet peoples in general and the Russians in particular. They produced a range of highly 'teacher-friendly' materials on both subjects.[23] While not without their share of resistance and controversies, these materials were generally well received by many concerned teachers and parents.[24] Nuclear education found its way into schools at all levels and in many subject areas, as did the particular form of education intended to increase understanding between the peoples of the United States and the Soviet Union as a major effort to avoid nuclear war. The efforts towards US–Soviet understanding were subject to some of the usual Cold War criticisms and accusations of eroding the need for resistance to communism and Soviet power. There was also some resistance to the study of nuclear war by parents who did not want their children subject to the possible trauma of instruction about the explicit and horrifying effects of nuclear weapons. None the less there was strong enough popular support for efforts to avoid nuclear war; this was reinforced by the policy assertion by some security analysts that such a war could be won and might be necessary. All this ushered in a new wave of peace education into schools where it never had been before.

Nuclear education was one component of an area of peace education that had few adherents and fewer practitioners, namely disarmament education. Disarmament education seemed to produce an even more negative response, especially from the security establishment, than the critical peace education practised during the war in Vietnam. This probably stemmed from two reasons in particular, 'national security issues' and an inability to distinguish between education and advocacy. The nuclear arms race among the super powers and nuclear powers was augmented by a parallel race in conventional arms that was consuming nations on both sides of the ideological divide, as well as the developing nations. These races were rationalised by the claimed imperatives of national security. The global arms race escalated to unprecedented proportions as virtually all nations accepted the notion that their national security depended on access to large numbers of sophisticated weapons. Whereas there was some adherence to the notion of arms control, the idea of disarmament *per se*, of reducing or eliminating any significant volume of weapons, flew in the face of conventional notions of security. Second, but no less significant, was the reluctance of security establishments to have national security policy subject to open public examination or debate. It was in their view a matter for experts which average adult citizens, much less adolescent students, were not competent to discuss or challenge. Enquiry into the arms race and exploration of alternatives to it, especially proposals regarding substantive disarmament, were considered to be challenges to national security policy and advocacy of changes that would lead to vulnerability. The concept of enquiry into and evaluation of alternatives as a form of political education as distinct from political action was not understood. Enquiry into issues and problems of disarmament was deemed to be a political contamination of 'objective' education.

Although the United Nations made some major efforts to change this climate with Special Sessions on Disarmament in 1978 and in 1982, and in spite of a history of various arms control agreements, national governments continued to guard jealously their autonomous, often secretive, control of security decisions. Making the case for education fared no better. In 1980 UNESCO, in fulfilment of a provision of the Final Document of the 1978 Special Session of the UN General Assembly on Disarmament, held a World Congress on Disarmament Education that produced a much overlooked, but still significant Final Document of its own: *The Final Document of the World Congress on Disarmament Education* (UNESCO, 1980). The document outlined the substance and dimensions of disarmament education and, in linking it to various other forms of peace education, anticipated the conceptualisation of comprehensive peace education that informs the 1994 UNESCO *Declaration and Integrated Framework of Action on Education for Peace, Human Rights and Democracy*, and tried, apparently without success, to clarify the distinction between education and advocacy. It was not until a decade later when the International Association of University Presidents in association with the United Nations Department for Disarmament Affairs established a Commission on Disarmament Education that the theme re-entered the discourse on peace studies and peace education.[25] However, even these efforts by so distinguished an educational association did not advance the cause of disarmament education in the schools. Teachers, seemingly convinced of the caveat that it was a highly technical matter into which enquiry required the knowledge of experts, chose instead to embrace conflict resolution as a more 'teacher-friendly' form of education *for* disarmament (see note 2 regarding education *for* and education *about*). Even peace educators themselves were ambivalent in their stance towards disarmament education, some claiming that it was but another fragmentation of the field as exemplified by the various forms of education *for* and *about* peace. As a distinct approach it would not strengthen the field.[26]

Long a component of essential peace education during the later 1980s and through the 1990s, conflict resolution education became the leading form of peace education, having been promoted and facilitated by various educational organisations, agencies and some NGOs.[27] Active training programmes now exist in many parts of the world, frequently established as an antidote to social or political violence in society and/or to violence and disciplinary problems in the schools. At the university level more degree programmes in peace and conflict studies were established during these years. University programmes were built on conflict theory, while school curricula emphasised practical skills and situation-specific conflict resolution. As noted earlier, much of the training was conducted within the framework of strategic non-violence. Citizen training and teacher preparation in conflict resolution skills were introduced, often by American and European practitioners into various areas where political conflicts and struggles for justice were becoming violent or had already erupted into violence.

Comprehensive peace education, conceptualised so as to accommodate aspects of traditional peace education with both nuclear and disarmament education, advocates conflict resolution training as a skill development component of a cross–curricular approach to peace education at all levels of elementary and secondary education. The approach, as noted earlier, seeks to integrate relevant aspects of education *for* and education *about* peace into a common conceptual framework, with its foundation in the purposes of essential and traditional peace education and its pedagogies derived from a developmental concept of learning and social change. It was to some degree a response to the problem of fragmentation and proliferation of approaches to peace education. The substance of comprehensive peace education derives primarily from various efforts at transnational co-operation among peace educators, most notably those undertaken by members of the Peace Education Commission of the International Peace Research Association in the years since its founding in 1992. Comprehensive peace education is a product of wider educational trends as well as the historical evolution of peace education. It owes much to the emergence of holism as a general principle of learning and curriculum development which gained more advocates among educators during the 1980s.[28]

Much of the methodology proposed as comprehensive peace education has its roots in the alternative systems, system change and system transformation approach of world order enquiry. However, comprehensive peace education stretched the notion of system transformation beyond the structural and social implications of general and complete disarmament and global governance to the realms of culture and consciousness, which had little or no currency in the realms of peace research and peace knowledge before the 1990s. The pedagogy of this approach remained true to its dialogic and Freirean roots as it incorporated aspects of the methods of discourse emerging from feminist scholarship and education that were becoming more widely practised in universities, and were beginning to have some effect on secondary schools. Feminist scholarship was another source of its holism.[29]

An initiative in which Norwegian educators brought together American and Soviet (later identified as Russian and Ukrainian) educators to collaborate on common projects and exchanges produced a later version of comprehensive peace education, namely ecological and co-operative education. The ecological element is a form of holism that uses metaphors of living systems as an alternative to thinking in structural terms that separate human actions from the environment. Ecological thinking conceptualises human and social actors as integral components of the larger living systems in which they are embedded. The co-operative aspect seeks to develop the particular skills of co-operation across lines that traditionally separate human and social actors in order to better equip learners to preserve and enhance the living systems essential to their survival. This approach takes a global perspective, comprehending human political and economic diversities, along with the commonalities inherent in a single species striving for survival on one planet.[30]

When the Project on Ecological and Co-operative Education first convened in Oslo in 1988, the American participants comprised advocates of both nuclear education and comprehensive peace education. This collaboration was to some degree made possible by the earlier co-operative efforts which Educators for Social Responsibility had initiated between Soviet and American educators. Although some of the participating Soviets and Americans had earlier been advocates of disarmament education, they did not consider it a viable ground for their collaboration even in the waning years of the Cold War. They undertook the exploration of the grounding of their collaboration with a view to practical possibilities and the educational needs of global society. They encountered one another not only as Norwegians, Soviets and Americans but as global citizens all.

In this exploration of subject matter and methodology which could inform a project to be embraced by both American and Soviet educators and, equally as important, not to be subject to 'discouragement' by their respective governments, a distinct approach to comprehensive peace education was devised that brought together all of these influences with the trend towards more proactive (and potentially critical) environmental education. In choosing the term 'ecological', the participants not only elected environment as their common global problematique, but they were, as well, seeking to develop a holistic living-systems approach that would explore environmental issues within the dimensions discussed above: an approach that related the subject to peace (as noted in the previous description of environmental education as a component of essential peace education) and one that could form the foundation of a pedagogy that would facilitate a form of thinking beyond the structural systems type of world order enquiry. They sought to develop a form of ecological thinking conceptually based on metaphors and models derived from natural, living systems; one that viewed the evolution of human social systems as a form of subsystem of the larger planetary system.

It seemed that such a form of thinking based on a reverence for life was more conducive to the change in consciousness necessary to the envisioned transformation of the global social system. Ecological and co-operative education seeks a merger of ethical and ecological principles that marry the moral purposes of peace education to the intellectual and cognitive tasks of its social and political purposes. Some argue that ecological thinking also comes closer to the spiritual aspects of peace-making, which are believed to be a source of the notion of human unity and universality that takes the biological reality of one human species into the realm of human consciousness, wherein the seeds of transformation must be sown. Such a mode of thinking and education has a strong affinity to the growing concept of a culture of peace, which is now becoming a kind of short-hand description of what peace educators see as the goal of global transformation. It is a form of thinking that transcends

413

culture and disciplines, seeking a fundamentally human perspective on education for a planetary future.

All three areas of peace knowledge, however, have from their inception been multidisciplinary, interdisciplinary and, in more recent times, transdisciplinary, too, as practitioners have made the argument that existing peace education, even as a widely included subject in schools and universities, was far from adequate to the task it had undertaken. Peace, they argued, called for nothing less than a transformation of human society and all its institutions, including education, which in turn necessitated a transformation of human consciousness. In other words, peace as a universal subject matter was not enough. Peace in its multiple forms and manifestations should become the core, the very purpose of all education. As such it must pervade the educational experience in content, pedagogy, school management and school community relations. It should become the ethos of the school culture.[31]

THE NEXT PHASE: EDUCATING FOR A CULTURE OF PEACE

No other idea has informed peace education with such profound transformational potential as the concept and vision of a culture of peace. While some approaches such as world order studies have promoted a values-centred enquiry which challenges the ethics of the dual moral standards applied to the domestic and global realms under the existing international system, none, not even human rights education, has yet taken the peace enquiry into the deeper realms of human values and human consciousness. Indeed, each of the approaches that evolved from essential peace education has attempted to probe fundamental values questions and has involved ways of thinking that tended towards holism. Comprehensive peace education aspires to the development of a pedagogy that can contribute to the evolution of a global, humanist consciousness. Feminist approaches have challenged core social and cultural values in their explorations of the links between patriarchy and war and the systemic sexism and violence of the war system. Ecological approaches have brought us to a planetary perspective that enables peace educators to present the world to their students as one living system, in a manner that awakens an awareness of human spirituality as the manifestation of humanity's integral relationship with that living system – an approach that opens the way for reflection on the cosmology from which cultures of war and violence have evolved. But none of these newer phases, even those that are undertaking to apply postmodernism to peace education,[32] have produced a pedagogy or an educational scheme of the transformational dimension necessary to a culture of peace.

The military modes of pursuing national interest and other social goals (which world order enquiry described as a war system) have come to be recognised by many more peace educators as the international structures that arise from and are sustained by a culture of war. Recently this more comprehensive and systematic analysis is becoming more widely applied to the discourse on peace.[33] However, even these efforts, taking place in an atmosphere in which peace studies flourishes in more colleges and universities and peace education becomes more widely accepted and practised in the school, have not confronted the real challenge of cultural change. Indeed, in the discourse of transcultural collaboration on many global concerns, culture remains an untouchable, sacrosanct area of the human condition.[34]

Even those who have offered the analysis of the relationship between culture and the war system[35] have not adequately probed the role of consciousness in the formation of the culture of war, and no peace educators have fully addressed the role of education in the formation of consciousness and socialisation for war.[36] Those who quoted the UNESCO constitution that 'wars begin in the minds of men' as a rationale for peace education, interpreted it as referring to the importance of adequate information, rational thinking and tolerant attitudes. Few challenged any of the fundamental cultural assumptions of education, the organisation of the school and the specific processes of the dominant form of pedagogy. Fewer still probed the role of education in the development of consciousness. There seemed to be an assumption that education is cultivated within a consciousness that is immutable. Exploration of consciousness remained the purview of psychology, philosophy and theology, but not education. Additionally the links between education and school reform of the 1960s waned in succeeding decades, and Freirean principles were given enough lip-service in the mainstream to have lost the vigour of their challenge. Those who continued to uphold the critical tradition seemed to assume that critical reflection and the dialogic method were adequate to the task and continued to direct the critical dialogue at economic and security systems and social values rather than at the culture itself. All of these assumptions need to be examined, probably challenged, by those who would educate for a culture of peace.

Given the particular nature of the current problems of violence and the unprecedented opportunities presented by the growing attention to the concept of a culture of peace, in particular, questions of the development of consciousness, and human capacities intentionally to participate in the evolution of the species and the reconceptualisation of culture should inform the next phase of peace education which might now address the 'heart of the problem'. A culture of peace perspective promises the possibility to probe these depths, the 'heart', the self concept and identity of the human species and the cosmologies from which these concepts and the dominant modes of thinking of a culture of violence arise. Now, as never before, all of education needs to be concerned about the question of what it is to be human and how formal curriculum can facilitate the exploration of that question so as to prepare learners to participate in social change, politico–economic reconstruction, transformation of culture and consciousness. Clearly, this requires profound changes throughout all educational systems, but most especially it demands equally significant developments in peace education, a new concept of purpose, a more fully developed pedagogy, broader dimensions than even comprehensive, feminist or ecological and co-operative education have envisioned.

The historic circumstances in which the next phase of peace education is unfolding are significantly different from those that form the approaches and phases described here. Yet the fundamental problematique remains at the core of the peace education task: the development of learning that will enable humankind to renounce the institution of war and replace it with institutions more consistent with the visions and values being articulated in the body of international standards intended to guide relations among people as persons and peoples as corporate groups, states and otherwise. (There is, for example, no clearer statement of the norms of a peaceful society than the Universal Declaration of Human Rights.) A culture of peace approach, however, illuminates more clearly the full extent of the task. Had peace educators been better students of history, we might have understood from the outset of our work that significant change in human behaviours and human institutions cannot be achieved without change in the cultures which give rise to and are shaped by the behaviours and institutions.

What most needs to be understood among those who pursue peace knowledge – researchers, academics and educators – is that the institutional problematique will no longer suffice. Nor will the augmentation of the field by new disciplines, even when those disciplines are integrated into a holistic, comprehensive approach. If we are going to lead our enquiry into the realms of what it is to be human and how the violence manifest by human beings and human institutions can be overcome, then we must develop new questions for the enquiry, based on the new institutional structures and cultural values and practices. We must review and assess our common intellectual past as a community of learners, to determine which aspects can help us to build a new foundation, and which would be useful to carry into the common future, the shared human culture which we seek to devise. Educators, more than most, should understand how we are both shaped by our cultures and how we shape our culture in the light of the values we hold and the images of the possible and desirable that guide our communal endeavours and elicit our social norms.

Thus it is that peace education must, at last, move into what many of us have been advocating for years (I fear without fully understanding the fundamental meaning of the term), namely a transformational mode, a mode that will bring about a profound change in both the form and the substance of human cultures. This is a mode which requires us to be not only prescriptive but prophetic. But it also requires a new generation of peace educators who can rally around this task as those of us involved in the history and the evolution of past concepts and approaches to peace education have done over the last four decades. We need a new generation of the global community of peace educators who co-operated and differed and, sometimes, conflicted in their endeavours to develop peace education in a global perspective, authentically rooted in their own societies and cultures. We need a generation that is aware of this history, even appreciative of its contributions, but unfettered by it (as some who produced the present modes of peace education sought to liberate their curricula and pedagogy from the limits of educational practices they believed served to support and replicate the war system). Those who formed transnational communities of peace educators in the earlier days of the international peace education movement were inspired and instructed by the values, the perspectives and ideas of their colleagues from other parts of the world. They were able to develop cross-cultural and global perspectives that were more varied, more 'down to Earth', humanly diverse perspectives than the more common image and metaphor of the Earth seen from the Moon, powerful and instructive as it was. We knew that few of our students would leave this planet, that the majority of them would never see it even from an airplane. But all need to perceive of themselves as sharing a single planet with millions of others with whom they have a common species identity, and who, like them, depend upon the health of that planet, seen or not in full, for their survival. To come to this perspective, to experience how diverse we could be and still hold common human and educational values, we needed contact with one another. With few resources and even fewer of the communications media that now enable some of us to be in daily electronic conversation across the globe, we somehow managed, because we knew this was the most effective way to learn what we needed to understand to do the work to which we were committed. For me the most meaningful of these experiences have been in the Peace Education

Commission of the International Peace Research Association and the International Institutes on Peace Education.[37]

Our conversations were sometimes informally woven into other international events where some were able to meet. Sometimes, opening our homes and sharing our airline mileage or piggy-backing on another trip, we would hold our own sessions. Events such as six people from five countries meeting at Casanovia College in New York State in 1971, which produced a curricular framework of a common value base and the shared planetary home, called global community education, occurred over the years. Among them the meetings of the Peace Education Commission at the Summer School held annually in Sweden in the early 1970s by the International Peace Research Association; the regular visits of American teachers to the Soviet Union, and Soviet teachers to the United States in the 1980s even before the end of the Cold War by Educators for Social Responsibility to enable them to work on common projects; the small meetings in homes and schools in Norway, Russia and the United States which produced the ecological and co-operative approach to peace education; the annual sessions of the International Institutes on Peace Education held regularly in various parts of the world through the 1980s and 1990s in which these networks shared their methods and materials to introduce other educators to the field; the collaborative projects which have been devised by a few participants in the Congresses of Educators for Peace in Europe, North America and Africa – all these were the venues in which we forged a network of personal and professional solidarity and through which we conducted the conversations from which the international peace education movement and its fruits emerged. There is, I am convinced, a need for such networks among young peace educators who will carry their conversations into the next century.

With the knowledge and media available to them, such a network would be able to explore in the depth and breadth necessary, the possibilities for a culture of peace and the learning that will be required to prepare this and succeeding generations to develop and preserve it. It is to be hoped that the pedagogic and cultural innovations devised by this new generation would be in a truly ecological mode, life-aware and nurturing continued change towards experiencing the ever unfolding possibilities of life and peace. I suspect that such a living-systems approach to the task may be essential to a culture of peace.

The purpose of this chapter is not to prescribe the terms and the questions of the networks and enquiries advocated here. Rather I have tried to set out a general framework of the conceptual perspectives, the development of pedagogical purposes, and the historic conditions in which they evolved, to apply to this reflection and assessment of peace education. With this framework in mind, I shall note some of the concepts I have suggested elsewhere as relevant to education for a culture of peace.[38] I still hold that the primary purposes of peace education should be the development of peace-making capacities.[39] In the context of present conditions I would suggest that the purpose of the new phase should be the development of capacities of cultural invention, knowing that these capacities must be developed within the context of the present historic circumstances, an age characterised by traumatic change and a lack of normative direction in social and political policies. This is not to say that there are not strong, normative concerns energising global movements, such as those devoted to concerns of a healthful environment, human rights, gender justice, poverty, demilitarisation, disarmament and peace. These movements, however, have of necessity generally taken an oppositional stance to policy establishments rather than a transformational stance towards systems and the culture that produces them. Some of these establishments are in the hands of segments of their respective societies who hold to a particularist form of thinking that reinforces cultural separatism and religious fanaticism – conditions that form a significant obstacle to cultural change, as well as to recognition of the unity of humanity and gender justice. Other establishments are in the hands of the pro-moters of globalisation, which poses a distinct and perhaps greater obstacle to human unity, economic justice and cultural integrity. It is not an easy time to educate for a culture peace, but it is an opportune one.

Peace education faces less resistance than ever before in the period covered by these reflections. The culture of peace concept steadily gains currency in both the discussions and the articulation of goals and purposes of civil society, and international agencies. While some governments have taken the standard position of not acknowledging the relevance of the concept or its purposes, and some have actually resisted and rejected its introduction into anything other than the realms of UNESCO's fields of competence, the member states of UNESCO have accepted the focus on a culture of peace as one of the main organising principles of the agency's work. Consequently there is both interest and legitimation, two conditions peace education advocates and practitioners have struggled to achieve. There is an opportunity not to be missed. Combined with the foundation that has been laid down over the past four decades and in a prophetic framework, these conditions invite a new generation to begin the conversation advocated here.

The conversation needs to look not only to the manifestations and proposed alternatives to a culture of violence, but most especially it needs to probe beneath the manifestations to the deep culture. It needs, as well, to explore the root values and worldviews of the culture of violence and the proposed alternatives. These need to address behaviours and strategies that are self-consciously transformational rather than oppositional. The latter mode is one that peace education and the larger movement find difficult to transcend. The oppositional mode was formulated by the circumstances that faced peace advocates of all types. But it is too limited for a transformational process or the prophetic role that peace education should share with other social sectors that form the visions and values of society. The prophetic role demands a visionary mode that could guide the conversation to envision transformed and peaceful institutions and practices, especially in education, to ask not what kinds of schools could form and maintain a culture of peace, but rather, 'Are schools the most effective route for societies to educate and socialise?', thus moving beyond changes in organisation and methodology to challenge the very institutions that comprise educational systems.

Such probings and enquiries I deem to be more transitional than transformational. They are what I conceptualise as elements of the process of recognising and moving out of present cultures into spaces where transformed cultures can be intentionally cultivated. It is this conceptualisation which leads me to suggest some 'transitional capacities', human abilities to change themselves and societies, which the peace education of the near future should cultivate. Among a wide range of possibilities five capacities seem to me to be especially relevant. All are grounded in and adapted from earlier and current learning purposes of education *for* and *about* peace. Each is now coming to new stages of relevance to the central task, and their conceptual parameters are being extended to meet present challenges. The five transitional capacities I would recommend to be considered for the initiating phase of the new peace education conversation are:

- ecological awareness;
- cultural proficiency;
- global agency;
- conflict competency and
- gender sensitivity.

Ecological awareness is the capacity not only to manifest concern for the health of natural and humanly constructed environments but to appreciate being, and to live as an integral part of the larger living world. It is knowing that the human species is unique and essential, yet interrelated to and interdependent with all the other organs of the living system of planet Earth. Such an awareness would be the opening to significant changes in relationships at all levels of the planetary social systems; changes that could initiate transformational processes in all spheres. While ecological and co-operative education seeks to cultivate understanding of this principle, transitional education should strive to teach how to internalise and live by it.

Cultural proficiency also moves multicultural education into new spheres, emphasising capacities to live with, in and through other cultures, as a way of becoming more human, more in touch with one's birth culture, more aware of one's human identity, and fully appreciative of the multiple possibilities for how to be human. Such an appreciation could form the basis of an enquiry into what it is to be human, what are the universals, the positives and negatives that I have argued we must deal with as we strive towards a culture of peace. If human rights education were to educate to enter the transitional mode, it would start to raise such questions, so as to cultivate the ground from which a strong and flexible commitment to the universality of human dignity might grow.

Global agency is the capacity required to be a global citizen. It can be cultivated in ways more practical than ever, now that civil society is a global force recognised throughout the world as an important component of the international political system. It is an arena in which world order thinking can be practically applied as citizens seek to change the institutions of the war system and to abolish the war itself, a necessary but not sufficient condition for a culture of peace. Core institutional changes are the beginnings of transformational change. Global agency is the means to bring about such essential changes in global systems.

Conflict competency is the ability to engage constructively in the controversies and contentions of the kind of structural and policy changes the abolition of war will require. Skills of conflict resolution and, as noted earlier, conflict transformation will be just as essential to the pursuit of these changes as they are now to the struggle for justice. The ethics and skills of non-violence combined with conflict-processing and reconciliation are perhaps the most essential transitional skills.

Gender sensitivity, the capacity to appreciate the differences and special qualities of being male or female, of understanding how culture has transformed biological differences into gender identities and gender roles, is the key capacity to enhance transitional capacities into transformational ones. Gender differences, and the privileging of masculine roles, while manifest in myriad ways, is a universal that cuts across all cultures. It is the lens through which the cultivation of human inequalities can be seen most clearly. It is a paradigm through which we can learn how differences in human perspectives conditioned by different experiences can reveal both humanly destructive and humanly enhancing possibilities. Peace knowledge and its various forms have helped us to understand much about what is humanly destructive. Culture of peace knowledge needs to help us to conceptualise and pursue what is humanly enhancing.

A culture of peace seen as a culture of human enhancement can provide the starting-point for this new phase of peace education, just as war prevention and elimination comprised the starting-point of the older phases. The transition must take us from the view and framework of eliminating war and overcoming violence to envision peace and creating the culture in which it can be achieved. I hope we can welcome a varied and vigorous new generation of international peace educators into the conversations that will exploit to the fullest these times of unprecedented challenge and opportunity.

POSTSCRIPT

Subsequent to the completion of this essay two significant developments have occurred which bear noting. One is the emergence of still another approach to peace education, which its practitioners call coexistence education.[40] The other was the launching of the Global Campaign for Peace Education at the Hague Appeal for Peace Civil Society Conference in The Netherlands in May 1999.[41]

NOTES

1 Defining the distinction between negative and positive peace is generally attributed to the Norwegian peace researcher Johan Galtung, one of the first and most prolific researchers in the field.
2 The distinctions between education 'for' and 'about' a social goal were made in the case of disarmament education in the background paper, 'The current status of disarmament education', prepared by UNESCO for their World Congress on Disarmament Education, Paris, 1980.
3 The civil rights movement in the US was also deeply influenced by the philosophy and practice of non-violence, a subject area which has been given some limited space of its own in university peace studies programmes, but enters school curricula mainly through conflict resolution and practices of classroom management.
4 The term 'peace knowledge' was used as a comprehensive description of the various learning, research and action practices related to peace, in order functionally to distinguish each from the others and to demonstrate the interrelationships among them that make it possible to define them as one field of knowledge. 'The pedagogical challenges of peace education', *Peace Studies Newsletter*, 17, June 1998, The Journal of the Peace Studies Association of Japan.
5 International education and the term 'education for international understanding' no longer have the currency they did in the first three decades following the Second World War. 'Global education', which evolved from these approaches, is now the more widely used term.
6 Among those who are interlinking environment with peace education are the Finnish educator Ritta Wahlstrom ('Promote commitment to peace and environmental responsibility', *Peace Environment and Education*, 3, (1), 1992), and the Swedish educational researcher, Ake Bjerstedt. During Bjerstedt's tenure as Executive Secretary of the Peace Education Commission of the International Peace Research Association (PEC) he published the PEC newsletter under the title of *Peace, Environment and Education* published by R. and D. Grove, Preparedness for Peace, School of Education, Box 23501, S-2000, 45 Malmo, Sweden.
7 Arguments that the institution of war contributes to the severity and perpetuation of other forms of violence are put forth by some peace researchers and critics of 'the military option'. Especially

notable among them are feminist peace researchers and women peace activists. See for instance the *Report of the Consultation on Women and Peace of the International Peace Research Association*, Gyor, Hungary, 1982, and the *Report of a United Nations Expert Group on Gender and the Agenda for Peace*, UN Division for the Advancement of Women, New York, 1994.

8 The concept of a culture of violence and its antidote, a culture of peace, were first conceptualised in the 1980s by the Peruvian peace researcher, Felipe McGregor, S.J. This concept inspires UNESCO's Culture of Peace Programme undertaken in 1993.

9 This *Montreal Declaration and Plan of Action* was formulated at a world conference on human rights education organised by UNESCO in Canada in 1993. It is the basis of UNESCO policy and activity in the field.

10 A holistic approach to human rights education is the basis of the work of the People's Decade for Human Rights Education (PDHRE), an NGO which catalyses human rights education throughout the world. It was the major lobbying agent in persuading the United Nations to declare a Decade for Human Rights Education, 1995–2005. PDHRE also formulated a definitional statement incorporating purposes and goals of human rights education. (526 West 111th Street, New York, NY 10025, USA.)

11 Educators for Social Responsibility is one of a number of national and international organisations that have encouraged peace education. Some focus more attention on substantive and contested issues than others. Among those that have been especially active are the International Council for Adult Education, the World Council for Curriculum and Instruction, International Educators for Peace and others.

12 Clint Fink's work, which traces the history back several centuries, has been published in several issues of the journal of the Consortium on Peace Research, Education and Development, *Peace and Change*. Aline Stomfay-Stitz covers two centuries of American peace education in *Peace Education in America, 1828–1990*, Scarecrow Press, Metuchen, NJ, 1993. Terry Carson and David Smith devote a considerable portion of their comprehensive work on peace education to the modern history of the field, *Educating for a Peaceful Future*, Kagan & Woo Limited, Toronto, 1998. It should be noted that this work also offers an interpretation of the categories and development of peace education that differs on some points from this one; as does the volume edited by Robin Burns and Robert Aspeslagh, *Three Decades of Peace Education Around the World*, Garland Publishing, London, 1996.

13 The first peace studies programme in the United States was established at Manchester College, a Church of the Brethren institution, in 1948 and the next at Manhattan College, a Catholic college, in 1963 in response to the papal encyclical of that year, 'Pacem in Terris'. Soon afterwards the programme at Bradford University was established in UK, to be followed by others in universities in England, Ireland and Australia. In Europe the University of Peace in Belgium and the Inter-European University in Austria and the Centre in Dubrovnik all offered peace studies. The University for Peace was established in Costa Rica in 1980, and offered several master's level courses.

14 Among the most widely used of the simulation games to teach about war prevention were 'Guns or Butter' developed by William Nesbitt for the Foreign Policy Association, 'Conflict', a simulation of a disarmed world, and 'Confrontation', based on the Cuban missile crisis, the latter two developed by Gerald Thorpe for the Institute for World Order. The two agencies were among the many independent agencies seeking to influence curriculum during these years of change and reform.

15 The papal encyclical 'Pacem in Terris' and President Kennedy's address at the American University 'Toward a Strategy of Peace', both of 1963, were published in a curriculum unit for senior high schools, *Let Us Examine Our Attitude toward Peace*, World Law Fund, New York, 1968.

16 While peace educators in the United States and other Western countries did not meet the same fate as Paulo Freire, (the Brazilian educator who developed a method of critical literacy education that came to be widely used to raise consciousness about unjust socio-economic structures causing his exile from his own country), it often took considerable commitment and courage to continue critical peace education in the face of pressure against it. Not all were able to stand their ground.

17 Some of the law education agencies in the United States, such as the Constitutional Rights

Foundation, also developed materials to include some international human rights law as well as American Constitutional law in the school curricula.

18 The World Law Fund with the aid of Robert Low, a classroom teacher who developed a unit on the ethical issue related to the Vietnam war, produced a unit, 'The Individual and the International System', Random House, New York, 1972, to enable teachers to introduce the Nuremberg Principles and other international legal precedents into inquiries into ethical aspects of war. More recently a new generation peace educator has argued the centrality of the Nuremberg Principles to all general education for citizenship. Dale T. Snauwaert, in 'International Ethics, Community and Civic Education', *Peabody Journal of Education*, 78 (1995), 119–138, raises issues that once again have currency for peace education as a consequence of war crimes tribunals related to the genocidal wars in Bosnia and Rwanda.

19 Catholic schools, some in social doctrine classes and some in citizenship or social education classes, studied the papal encyclical 'Pacem in Terris'; others studied the Augustinian 'just war' theory, which was especially relevant during the Vietnam war period. Pacifism is fundamental to Quaker religious beliefs and thus part of Quaker education. They, along with other 'traditional peace churches', also offered students counselling on decisions regarding military service.

20 Similar economic and ethical issues arise today in the age of 'globalisation' referred to by analysts of the left and some peace researchers as 'neo-liberalism', i.e. the economic and strategic dominance of the 'advanced nations' is extended through the spread of free-market capitalism. Globalisation is an issue now addressed by human rights education and peace education, creating another strong link between the two fields.

21 The value of political participation was contested and did not always appear on the list. In later listings of 'world order values', positive identity appeared in its place, a value now more current in peace education than it was when world order studies were being developed for the secondary schools in the 1970s.

22 The methodology devised for secondary schools is best illustrated by a curriculum unit by Jack Frankel *et al.*, *Peacekeeping: Can We Prevent War?*, Random House, Inc., New York, 1975.

23 ESR produces and distributes a wide range of materials. They regularly publish a catalogue. At the time of writing, they are developing curricula on the abolition of nuclear weapons.

24 In some instances parents and teachers, fearful of the possibilities of nuclear war, joined in common initiatives and organisations such as the Vermont group, Parents and Teachers for Peace.

25 Subsequently this Commission established by the International Association of University Presidents added the terms Peace and Conflict Resolution to its title, now being called the IAUP/UN Commission on Education for Disarmament, Peace and Conflict Resolution.

26 These issues were discussed by Stephen Marks in 'Peace development and human rights education: The dilemma between the status quo and curriculum overload', *International Review of Education*, 2 (3), 1983.

27 Children's Creative Response to Conflict began in the 1970s in the United States. The Conflict Resolution Network has been functioning in Australia since the 1980s and during the post-Apartheid period in South Africa, university-based schools services and teacher training have been undertaken. A regional affiliate of Educators for Social Responsibility, ESR Metro initiated a programme in the mid-1980s which spun off a programme which has worked with schools and done in-service training throughout the United States and in other countries.

28 Two works by Douglas Sloan, *Toward the Recovery of Wholeness*, Teachers College Press, New York, 1984, and Douglas Sloan (ed.) 'Toward an Education for a Living World', a special issue of *The Teachers College Record*, 84, (1), Fall 1982, are useful examples of holism and its early application to peace education.

29 Feminism gained a narrow but tenacious foothold in peace research in the 1980s, beginning with the 1983 Consultation on Women, Militarism and Disarmament, sponsored by the Peace Education Commission of the International Peace Research Association.

30 The ecological/co-operative approach was introduced in a book produced by the Norwegian-American-Soviet project, *Learning Peace: The Promise of Ecological and Co-operative Education*, State University of New York Press, Albany, NY, 1995.

31 Arguments about the centrality, holism and transformational tasks of peace education are made in Betty A. Reardon, *Comprehensive Peace Education*, Teachers College Press, New York, 1988.

32 See Lennart Vriens, 'Postmodernism, peace culture and peace education' in Robin J. Burns and R. Aspeslagh (eds) *Three Decades of Peace Education*, Garland Publishing, London, 1996 and Dale Snauwaert.

33 The organisers of the Hague Appeal for Peace sponsored a series of teach-ins on the war system on university campuses in the United States as preparation for the participation of youth in the May 1999 conference, held to observe the 100th anniversary of the founding of the International Court of Justice in the Hague. Peace education of this kind is a point in the Hague Agenda for International Peace and Justice issued by the conference.

34 The human rights movement frequently encounters resistance to the implementation of international standards on the grounds that they are not appropriate to the culture of the resisting society. Cultural resistance is specially strong in the case of the human rights of women.

35 Johan Galtung, *Peace by Peaceful Means*, Sage Publications, New York, 1996.

36 Some, such as Douglas Sloan and Dale Snauwaert, whose primary work has not been in peace education, have explored development and consciousness and at least suggested its relevance to peace education. One of the first American works in the field, *Education for Annihilation* by William Boyer (1973) was a virtual denunciation of the way in which the education system educated for war. There have long been those who argued that the competitive nature of most schooling was education for war.

37 The experience and work of the Peace Education Commission and its intellectual history are recounted in Robin Burns and Robert Aspeslagh, *Three Decades of Peace Education Around the World* (op. cit.). The volume also contains key theoretical works authored by members of the Commission through the 1970s, 1980s and 1990s, the International Institutes.

38 'Educating the educators: The education of teachers for a culture of peace', a paper prepared for a panel on Educating for a Culture of Peace at the World Conference on Higher Education, UNESCO, Paris, October 1998. To be published in *Peace, Environment and Education* (see note 6) and in a collection of the Culture of Peace Panel papers edited by Eudora Pettigrew, Chairperson of the International Association of University Presidents/United Nations Commission on Disarmament Education.

39 See Betty Reardon, *Comprehensive Peace Education*, chapter 7. Teachers College Press, New York, 1988.

40 See Eugene Weiner (ed.) *The Handbook of Interethnic Coexistence*, Continuum Publishing, New York, 1998.

41 Readers may address enquiries about the Global Campaign for Peace Education to the author at Teachers College, Box 171, Columbia University, New York, NY 10027, USA or <bar19@columbia.edu>.

SELECTED BIBLIOGRAPHY

Barash, David P. (1991) *Introduction to Peace Studies*. Belmont, CA: Wadsworth Publishing Company.

Bjerstedt, Ake (n.d.) *Peace Education in Different Countries*. Department of Educational and Psychological Research, University of Lund, School of Education, Box 23501, S-20045, Malmo, Sweden (all of the University School of Education publications are available from this address).

Bjerstedt, Ake (n.d.) *Peace Education: Toward Specification of Educational Objectives*. Malmo: Department of Educational and Psychological Research, University of Lund, School of Education.

Bjerstedt, Ake (n.d.) *Towards a Rationale and a Didactics of Peace Education: Notes from a Set of Swedish Research and Development Studies in Progress*. Malmo: University of Lund, School of Education.

Bjerstedt, Ake (ed.) (1993) *Peace Education: Global Perspectives*. Stockholm: Almsvist & Wiksell International.

Borrelli, Mario and Haavelsrud, Magnus (1993) *Peace Education within the Archipelago of Peace Research 1945–1964*. Tromsø, Norway: Arena Publishers.

Boulding, Elise (1988) *Building a Global Civic Culture: Education for an Interdependent World*. New York: Teachers College Press.

Boyer, William (1973) *Education for Annihilation*, published by author, Sisters, OR.

Brock-Utne, Birgit (1989) *Feminist Perspectives on Peace and Peace Education*. Athene Series, New York: Teachers College Press.

Burns, Robin Joan and Aspeslagh, R. (1996) *Three Decades of Peace Education Around the World*. London: Garland Publishing, Inc.

Carpenter, Susan (1977) *A Repertoire of Peacekeeping Skills*. Washington, DC: Consortium on Peace Research Education and Development.

Carson, Terry (ed.) (1985) *Dimensions and Practice of Peace Education*. Alberta: University of Alberta Press.

Carson, Terry and Gideonse, H. D. (eds) (1987) *Peace Education and the Task for Peace Education*. Bloomington, IN: WCCI (World Council for Curriculum and Instruction).

Carson, Terry and Smith, David (1998) *Educating for a Peaceful Future*. Toronto: Kagan & Woo.

Drew, Naomi (1987) *Learning the Skills of Peacemaking*. Jalmar Press.

Gordon, Haim and Grob, Leonard (1988) *Education for Peace, Testimonies from World Religions, Peace and Justice Traditions of the Major Faiths*. Maryknoll, NY: Orbis Books.

Graves, Norman J., Dunlop, James, and Torney-Purta, Judith V. (1984) *Teaching for International Understanding, Peace and Human Rights*, Paris: UNESCO.

Haavelsrud, M. (1975) *Education for Peace: Reflection and Action*. Surrey, UK: IPC and Technology Press. The Proceedings of the First World Conference of the World Council for Curriculum and Instruction held at the University of Keele, UK, September, 1974.

Haavelsrud, Magnus (1981) *Approaching Disarmament Education*. Guildford, UK: Westbury House.

Haavelsrud, Magnus (ed.) (1993) *Disarming: Discourse on Violence and Peace*. Tromsø: Arena Publishers.

Haavelsrud, Magnus (1996) *Education in Developments*. Tromsø: Arena Publishers.

Hall, Mary Bowen and Mansfield, Sue (1986) *Why Are There Wars? Powerful Ideas for Teaching Writing Skills: Grades 5–8*. Glenview, IL: Scott Foresman.

Harris, Ian M. (1988) *Peace Education*. Jefferson, NC: McFarland and Co.

Henderson, George (ed.) (1973) *Education for Peace Focus on Mankind*. Washington, DC: ASCD (Association for Supervision and Curriculum Development).

Hicks, D. (1988) *Education for Peace*. London: Routledge.

Hurst, John (1986) 'A Pedagogy for Peace.' *World Encyclopedia of Peace*. Oxford: Pergamon Press.

Johnson, David W. and Johnson, Roger T. (1991) *Teaching Students to Be Peacemakers*. Edina, MN: Interaction Books, Co.

Keefe, Thomas and Roberts, Ron E. (1992) *Realizing Peace: An Introduction to Peace Studies*. Ames, IA: Iowa State University Press.

Lantieri, Linda, and Patti, Janet (1996) *Waging Peace in Our Schools*. Boston, MA: Beacon Press.

Levin, Diane E. (1994) *Teaching Young Children in Violent Times: Building a Peaceable Classroom*. Philadelphia: New Society Publishers.

McGinnis, James (1992) *Educating for Peace and Justice: Religious Dimensions*. St Louis, MO: Institute for Justice and Peace.

McGinnis, James and McGinnis, Kathleen (1981) *Education for Peace and Justice*. St Louis, MO: Institute for Justice and Peace.

Nuclear Arms Education in Secondary Schools (1985) sponsored by the National Council for the Social Studies; the Social Studies Development Center of Indiana University; and the Johnson Foundation.

O'Hare, Padraic (ed.) (1983) *Education for Peace and Justice*. San Francisco: Harper Row.

O'Reilly, Mary Rose (1993) *The Peaceable Classroom*. Portsmouth, NH: Boynton/Cook Publishers, Heinemann.

Ray, Douglas (ed.) (1988) *Peace Education: Canadian and International Perspectives*. London, Canada: Third Eye.

Reardon, Betty (1982) *Militarization, Security and Peace Education*. Valley Forge, PA: United Ministries in Education.

Reardon, Betty (1988a) *Comprehensive Peace Education: Educating for Global Responsibility*. New York, NY: Teachers College Press.

Reardon, Betty (ed.) (1988b) *Educating for Global Responsibility: Teacher-Designed Curricula for Peace Education. K–12*. New York, NY: Teachers College Press.

Reardon, Betty (1995) *Educating for Human Dignity*. Philadelphia, PA: University of Pennsylvania Press.

Reardon, Betty and Nordland, Eva (1994) *Learning Peace: The Promise of Ecological and Co-operative Education*. Albany: State University of New York Press.

Smoker, Paul, Davies, Ruth, and Munske, Barbara (eds) (1990) *A Reader in Peace Studies*. Oxford, New York, Frankfurt, Seoul, Sydney, Tokyo: Pergamon Press.

Schneidewind, Nancy (1987) *Cooperative Learning, Cooperative Lives*. New York, NY: W. C. Brown.

Sloan, Douglas (ed.) (1983) *Education for Peace and Disarmament: Toward a Living World*. New York, NY: Teachers College Press.

Stine, Esther *et al.* (1983) *Education in a Global Age, Public Education Policy Studies*. Dallas, TX: United Ministries in Education.

Stomfay-Stitz, Aline M. (1993) *Peace Education in America, 1828–1990: A Sourcebook for Education and Research*. Metuchen, NJ: Scarecrow Press.

Thomas, T. M. *et al.* (1988) *Global Images of Peace and Education*. Ann Arbor, MI: Prakken.

Toh Swee-Hin and Floresca-Cawagas, Virginia (1989) *Peace Education: A Framework for the Philippines*. The Philippines: Phoenix Publishing House.

UNESCO (1974) *Recommendation concerning Education for International Understanding, Co-operation and Peace Education relating to Human Rights and Fundamental Freedoms*. Paris: UNESCO.

UNESCO (1980) *Final Document of the World Congress on Disarmament Education*. Paris: UNESCO.

UNESCO (1983) *Education for International Co-operation and Peace at the Primary School Level*. Paris: UNESCO.

UNESCO (1994) *Declaration and Integrated Framework of Action on Education for Peace, Human Rights, and Democracy*. Geneva: UNESCO.

Wahlstrom, Ritta (1991) *Growth towards Peace and Environmental Responsibility: Theory into Practice*, 67. Institute for Educational Research Publication Series B, International Institute for Educational Research, University of Jyvaskyla, Finland.

Wilson, G. K. (1982) *A Global Peace Study Guide*. London: Housmans.

24

FEMINISM AND EDUCATION

Madeleine Grumet and Kate McCoy

Curriculum is commonly understood as a course of study or a syllabus. Even though these encoded versions of curriculum, which exclude student activity, pedagogy and classroom discourse, seem superficial, even they have the power to reveal what we think about the world and how we think about it. Every time a syllabus is drawn up and a list of topics to be covered is developed, the author of this work is saying *this* piece of the world, and not *that*, is worthy of notice. Curriculum – of any sort – provides an index to what matters to someone who has the power to determine that it should matter to someone else. When curriculum is conceived as comprehending all the aspects that constitute a particular educational experience – selection of the phenomena to be studied, of representations of that phenomena, of modes of operating on that phenomena, of social interactions, assessment – then its capacity to reveal how we live and think is even greater.

The relationship of feminism to curriculum is profound, for what it means to be a man or a woman has a great deal to do with how human beings think about and experience our worlds. Our sex endows each of us at birth with a set of possibilities related to our anatomy, our hormones, our capacity to procreate. These differences between men and women assume different meanings in different times, different cultures, in different families. Just as the small child learns to discriminate mama from the lady next door, learns not to run into the street, and learns to discriminate a dog's bow-wow from a cat's meow, that child is also learning that he or she is male or female, and what being male or female means to the people with whom he or she lives. Whereas the sex of a person may be identified by physical characteristics, the gender of a person is constituted by this person's understanding of what it means to be male and female, (sometimes called the sex/gender system) and that understanding is utterly intertwined with other fundamental understandings that the child gathers around her as she moves into personhood.

The sex/gender system saturates all aspects of curriculum. It runs like a fine but everpresent thread through our understandings of what constitutes knowledge, what students are capable of learning, who is competent to teach them, what activities are necessary to the development of understanding, what literatures and materials are important, and how learning should be assessed. The sex/gender system influences our ideas about the role the parents of young children should play in their education; how teachers should work with students and with each other; how schools should be governed, financed and evaluated.

For centuries the sex/gender thematic in education has been denied because it has been associated with those aspects of our lives – our sex, our erotic relations, our procreative relations – that have been consigned to the area of experience that we call 'private'. The disciplines of education and the process of schooling are all wedged right into the fracture in culture and thought that feminist scholarship and politics have revealed: the split between the public and the private. It is telling that whereas the word 'public' functions as a noun in this phrase and in everyday speech, the word 'private' rarely is seen as a noun outside the context of this opposition, except when it refers to a military recruit, or serves as a euphemism for genitalia.

It is characteristic of our gendered society that the private should function as an index to unnameable contents, an adjective to an absent noun. Feminism has taken up the task of naming the private, taking an inventory of its contents, and of exploring the relation of this category to the public, its putative antonym. Because schooling and education are the processes through which persons move from the domain of family (the private) to the domain of work and knowledge (the public), the experience of education has served to strengthen the opposition of these categories.

Once feminists had revealed these categories as cultural constructions, rather than natural or universal necessities, feminist educators began to address the ways that schooling and informal education have contributed to the construction of these categories. In addition feminist educators have explored the processes through which these categories of private and public are taken up by children so that they shape the ways that they (and their teachers and parents) view culture, knowledge, identity and human relationships.

Because education is an event and a responsibility, as well as a field of study, feminist education scholars have linked their analyses of domestic, political, aesthetic and institutional cultures to strategies for change. Schools perform significant functions of socialisation as they teach children to learn and accommodate to the codes, mores and skills of the workplace and the state. But schools serve a liminal as well as a functional role in our societies: they are places where we *prepare* young people for the responsibilities of adult life, abstracting those responsibilities from their pressing contexts of use, and re-presenting them to children in the curriculum. The context of curriculum provides some space from the insistent demands of existence that everyday life presents: a dispensation that schooling shares with aesthetic experience. For while curriculum, like art, addresses real everyday life, it stands at a remove from the pressure of subsistence activity, and so permits playful and creative thought. It is this space that invites the critique of feminist educators and the redesign of relationships of learners to one another, and to knowledge. It is this space that invites schools to liberate both girls and boys from the restrictions of narrow conceptions of what it is to be female or male, restrictions that limit what they know and can do, or perhaps, even more significantly, what they can imagine.

ACCESS AND EQUITY

Initial efforts to develop a feminist critique of education addressed issues of equity and sexual discrimination and gender stereotyping. This approach, sometimes characterised as liberal feminism, is based on an analysis of rights and access. Supported by the conviction that all human beings have the capacity for a wide range of talents and activities, equity activists insist that women gain access to jobs and experiences that give them the opportunities to develop their interests and skills without being limited to occupations or activities construed as feminine or domestic. This liberal agenda is situated primarily in the public sphere. Committed to giving women and girls access to the rights, responsibilities and opportunities located in schools, industry and government, this project addresses the family, or the realm of the private, only when it articulates its interest in public settings, such as the courts, the welfare system and schools. Then the liberal agenda works to ensure fair treatment of women and girls in these negotiations and the protection of their civil rights as well as their rights to have equal access to schooling and work.

In education the issues of access and equity initiated a review of curriculum materials to make sure that they mirrored a broad range of life possibilities for women and girls. In what has been called the 'reformist' agenda, feminist scholars studied readers, and children's literature and romance novels to assess the frequency and substance of the presentation of female characters and interests. Their studies revealed portrayals of women as passive, dependent and dull (Pinar *et al.*, 1995). Boys were portrayed as adventurous problem-solvers, while girls were portrayed as tentative and fearful. Rarely were women presented in any productive labour other than housework and childcare.

This concern about the images of women in educational texts and materials may be related to a behaviourist approach to education as well as to themes in social psychology: a conviction that children are influenced by the images for their development that they see in the world that surrounds them. The work in role theory developed by Goffman in the 1960s (Goffman, 1961) had heightened our sensitivity to the power of media and of social expectations in influencing the aspirations and self-confidence of students. In an effort to bring women out of obscurity and into curriculum, materials that portray women as active agents, resourceful and productive in public society, were developed in the fields of history and literature as well as in children's literature. Women were included in illustrations in mathematics and science textbooks and problems, and examples were situated in contexts that would attract the interest of girls and young women. In what may have functioned as a precursor to what we now call the study of popular culture, feminist educators alerted parents, teachers, publishers and television producers to the significance and influence of the images that they construct for the imaginations of young children. The work of Selma Greenberg, on non-sexist nurturing of young children (Greenberg, 1978); the groundbreaking publication by Women on Words and Images (1974); *Dick and Jane as Victims: Sex Stereotyping in Children's Readers*, (1975); Steffere's work on the images of women in early readers (Steffere, 1975); and Linda Christian-Smith's research on female readers (Christian-Smith, 1988, 1990) contributed to this critique of sexism in the images that society offers young children for their gendered futures.

A simplistic interpretation of this project to develop non-sexist curriculum materials imputes inordinate power to sexist images, as if they, in themselves, have the power to determine the character and self-understanding of anyone who beholds them. This behaviourist notion has to be balanced with a conception of curriculum that involves teaching and the interpretation of materials, not just the presentation of materials themselves. The study of literature or of historical or philosophical texts is not constituted merely by the reading of these texts. A discourse of criticism that seeks to understand a particular text by studying its relation to its own time, the situation of its readers, as well as the imaginary world that it projects, is essential to any reading. Without this understanding of hermeneutics and pedagogy, concerns about the images of women and girls in curriculum degenerate into a form of political correctness which censures images that do not fit the model of development held by a school system or its teachers.

This interest in the representation of women in curriculum materials has been extended in studies of the ways that the academic disciplines exclude or discourage the participation of women and girls. For example, a 1971 study of 13 popular United States history textbooks indicated that material related to women constituted no more than 1 per cent of any of the books, and that the experience of women was either totally absent or trivialised. (Trecker, 1971). A 1989 study of literature taught in high school English classes in the United States revealed that of the ten books most frequently taught, only one was authored by a woman, and none was written by a member of a minority group (AAUW, 1995).

In the 1970s more than one hundred projects investigated the redesign of the academic disciplines, and as the field of women's studies developed, centres such as the Wellesley College Center for Research on Women became important to support the ongoing critique of sexist education and to develop new approaches to and materials for instruction (McIntosh, 1983). Other projects in the 1970s to develop non-sexist instructional materials included the Feminist Press and the federally funded Women's Educational Equity Program.

Sexism, expressing academic exclusion, stereotyping and preference, was seen to be functioning through the following forms and processes: research methodologies that ignore or suppress data; avoidance of enquiry related to women's lives or interests; research on men generalised to women; presentation of value-laden research as if it were objective; biases against new or transformative ideas or methods; privileging of highly rationalistic and technological paradigms for argument and enquiry; social and political networks dominated by male scholars which maintained the status quo (Pinar *et al.*, 1995).

Critiques of curriculum in the fields of mathematics and science were particularly cogent, for research indicated that boys achieved higher scores than girls in standardised tests in these areas and that more boys selected these areas for advanced study in college and graduate school than did girls. The 1992 study commissioned by the American Association of University Women and researched by the Wellesley College Center for Research on Women (AAUW, 1995) reported that no gender differences were found in the problem-solving abilities of elementary and middle-schools girls and boys, but that small to moderate differences, favouring male students, appeared in high school. In 1990 the National Science Board found that the number of boys and girls taking mathematics courses was approximately the same but diverged when students registered for calculus, with 7.6 per cent of boys, but only 4.7 per cent of girls enrolled (AAUW, 1995). The American Association of University Women's report concludes that the gender gap in mathematics achievement is closing but that the gender gap in science is not. While gender difference in the number of science courses taken is small, difference in the courses selected is not; girls are inclined to take biology, but not physics or advanced chemistry, which are courses favoured by boys. A 1991 survey administered by the Council of Chief State School Officers reported that boys comprised 60 per cent of the students in first-year high school physics, and 70 per cent of second-year students.

Greater than differences in achievement are differences in the career aspirations of boys and girls in the fields of mathematics and science. A study of the career plans of Rhode Island high school seniors revealed that 64 per cent of the boys who had taken physics and calculus expected to major in science or engineering in college, as opposed to just 18.6 per cent of the girls who had taken these courses with them (AAUW, 1995).

There has been rich and interesting research developed to examine the reasons for these differences in interest and achievement in mathematics and science. One study points to the different exposure of boys and girls to mechanical and electrical phenomena: by third grade 51 per cent of boys and 37 per cent of girls had used microscopes, and by eleventh grade 49 per cent of boys and only 17 per cent of girls had used an electricity meter (AAUW, 1995). Fennema and Sherman (1977) have suggested differences in early experiences of sports and physical activity as a factor in competence in spatial relations, while Sheila Tobias (1981) has addressed girls' lack of confidence and anxiety in responses to mathematics. These studies of mathematics and science in the lives of young girls sensitised educators to the particular kinds of experiences and discourse these disciplines contain.

Presentations of the disciplines as cultural discourses, prepared the way for the work of Sandra Harding (1986, 1991), Donna Haraway (1991) and Evelyn Fox Keller (1985) as they analysed the social networks and existential stance that sustain the disciplines of mathematics and science in industry, in research, and in the public imagination.

The critique of curriculum has not been limited to texts, tests and lab experiences. Criticism of sexual discrimination in academic tracking, classroom discourse and classroom interaction led to the awareness of the ways that opportunities have been withheld from women (Frazier and Sadker, 1973; Bull, 1974; Sears and Feldman, 1974; Serbin and O'Leary, 1975). This awareness contributed to the passage of Title IX of the 1972 Education Amendment in the United States, which denied federal monies to any educational institution practising sexual discrimination.

Studies by Sadker and Sadker (1994), Klein (1992), and the report of the American Association of University Women (1995), *How Schools Shortchange Girls*, indicate that equity issues are far from resolved despite the passage of Title IX. For instance, more boys are referred to special education classes than are girls. These referrals, motivated perhaps by a desire to exile disruptive children, may deny girls with genuine learning difficulties the opportunities to receive special help. In addition, extra-curricular activities play a role in reinforcing intellectual activities as well as in forming the social groups that support academic work. Until recently these activities have been sex-specific, with sports teams supported for male students but overlooked, underfinanced and poorly equipped for females.

In 1990 the National Education Association, after a review of more than 100 sex and race equity programmes, developed a checklist of actions that constitute sexual bias in the classroom. Included were double standards for males and females, condescension, tokenism, denial of achieved status or authority, backlash against women who succeed in improving their status, and divide-and-conquer strategies that praise individuals as better than others in their ethnic or gender group.

(AAUW, 1995, p. 110)

Projects such as these noted above, that diminish gender stereotyping in educational materials or provide equal access to facilities and educational opportunities, conform to Donovan's (1978) summary of the tenets of liberal feminism: faith in rationality, confidence in individual conscience, conviction in the similarity of male and female rationality, a belief in education as a force to change society, and the doctrine of natural rights. Liberal feminism does not question the meaning of gendered identities. It takes up the challenge of equity, securing for women the rights and privileges that men have exercised.

THE MATERIALIST CRITIQUE

Marxist-socialist feminists have joined the discussion of access and equity, but have brought to that discussion consideration of social class experience and its intersection with gender. They have been critical of androcentric Marxism's refusal to acknowledge the domestic work of women as real labour (O'Brien, 1981). The Marxist paradigm recognised only labour that had exchange value; consequently because housekeeping and child-rearing were forms of unpaid labour, the work of women was overlooked in Marx's theory. By incorporating women into the Marxist paradigm and insisting on the analysis of domestic labour, many Marxist-socialist feminists have worked to bridge the private–public schism in Marxist theory and educational practice.

The denigration of women's work in households and families has extended to the work of the female professions; women's work as teachers and as nurses has been undervalued and underpaid. Lather (1987) and Grumet (1995) have examined the work of teaching as an extension of domestic labour. This critique addresses the ways in which women's role in households is arrogated to the human relationships, structure of labour, and sense of occupational affiliation associated with teaching. The effort and thought, preparation and physical labour that women provide for their families are often invisible to family members who consider it necessary, natural and unremarkable. As the feminisation of teaching took place around the time of the Industrial Revolution, the practice of hiring women to replace the men who had been the school masters (but were now leaving the classrooms of villages and hamlets for employment in the factories of the cities) was rationalised with a sentimental celebration of women's maternal gifts. In addition to women's putative love for children and capacity to care for them, women were lauded for their modesty and self-abnegation, and these qualities were valorised as traits of the proper teacher (Grumet, 1988). Not only was the labour of care attributed to women as a quality intrinsic to their sex, it was also associated with their unpaid and unacknowledged domestic labour, and therefore, inadequately compensated.

The Marxist-socialist critique has also addressed the school experience of girls as influenced by their economic and social class status. Significant work includes McRobbie (1978) on working-class girls' reinforcement of the public/private split; Valli (1986) on women in the clerical workplace; and Weis (1990) on the effects of de-industrialisation on the study of cultural reproduction. Leslie Roman articulated a feminist materialist epistemology, emphasising research practices with women to develop their own strategies for studying and changing their worlds and to recognise the interplay of race, class and gender in experiences of oppression (see Roman and Christian-Smith, 1988).

EDUCATIONAL LEADERSHIP

The expectation that women would extend the care and concern for their families to their pupils rationalised a system that paid them little, and subordinated them to the leadership of male administrators and community boards of education. It ignored their ideas and leadership in issues of curriculum, school organisation or governance. The sentimentalisation of teaching camouflaged the intellectual achievement and assertion that constituted the good teaching that women practised behind the classroom doors.

Exclusion of teachers from the governance processes of the school was exacerbated by a structure of school time, school space and curriculum predicated on a model that segregated each teacher and her pupils from every other classroom, replicating a system of separate and isolated nuclear households. Collective planning, analysis and action were proscribed activities, as Kathleen Weiler (1988) has noted in her study of the structural constraints of schools and the political efforts of feminist educators.

Despite the great strides that female educators have taken to assume leadership in their schools and communities, a 1990 study of women in school leadership in the United States indicated that they constituted only 27.7 per cent of school principals and 4.8 per cent of district superintendents (AAUW, 1995).

The recent publication of a number of introductory texts and collections of articles on feminism and education attests to the continued significance of feminist thought and practice for education today (Biklen and Pollard, 1993; Stone, 1994; Weiner, 1994; Weis and Fine, 1993).

NARRATIVE, IDENTITY AND CURRICULUM

The struggle of Marxist-feminists to connect public and private labour mirrored the project of consciousness-raising that developed in the 1960s and the 1970s, and was expressed in the women's movement slogan 'the personal is political'. In professional meetings and in everyday life, women met to speak and study what had been kept secret in their lives. The history, function and cultural processes of the separation of the public and the private were explored in the significant works of Dorothy Dinnerstein (1976), *The Mermaid and the Minotaur*; Nancy Chodorow (1978), *The Reproduction of Mothering*; Jean Bethke Elshtain (1981), *Public Man, Private Woman*; and Mary O'Brien (1981), *The Politics of Reproduction*.

What distinguishes these feminist critiques from the liberal agenda is a dialectical understanding of identity, which recognises that every identity is a partial and tentative expression of both maleness and femaleness and that maleness and femaleness are themselves terms that depend on each other for their very existence and character. As a result, whereas liberal feminism tends to address change in public structures, other forms of feminism link that change to the social, cultural and psychological experiences in everyday life that constitute actors' sense of their gendered identities and life possibilities.

The relation of narrative to curriculum rests on a notion of curriculum that embraces the learner as well as the course of study. In this sense, curriculum is not merely a course of study, but a set of experiences. Moreover, the meanings that these experiences hold for any specific learner will depend on the perspectives, information, former experience and emotional attitudes that the learner brings to the curriculum experience. The invitation to write narratives of educational experience is an invitation for the learner to articulate what it is that he or she brings to curriculum. The process of that writing reveals the rich context in which the meaning of curriculum is embedded. It returns curriculum to the world of the student's experience and thus acknowledges the active role of the learner in making sense of the world, of schooling and of texts. Psychoanalytic studies of gender have asserted that one's sense of being male or female develops at the same time as language. It is not separate from the experiences in families and schools that shape the way we know the world and feel comfortable acting in it and questioning it. Just as consciousness-raising invited narratives that revealed the ways that gender expresses itself in family and public life, educational autobiographies may also reveal the ways that gender influences the ways that men and women experience education.

Psychoanalytic and object relations theories, as well as the scholarship in political economy developed in this era, moved the feminist analysis of educational experience from the liberal emphasis on rights and power to the discussion of desire (Taubman, 1982). Influenced by Lacan, this analysis of desire lodged power in the imagination, asserting that it accrued to certain people or to people who were male or tall or mature because of the projections of others, as they associated power, privilege, superiority and resources with men and not with women. As analysts studied the motives for these attributions, consciousness-raising invited women to come together in their everyday lives to talk about their experiences and to see how they had been complicit in the arrangements that oppressed them. The autobiographical voice was invited not only to speak in public of the experience considered private, but in the process of that speaking – which served to resymbolise experience – to formulate a story and a theory that would extend the knowledge and experience of private life into the public life of communities, knowledge and government. Feminist curriculum theorists recognised sexuality and desire to be themes in consciousness that are influenced by the sex/gender system and related to the ways in which we know the world and respond to its presentation in curriculum. They have therefore worked to respect the specificity and variation in the ways that women experience their sexuality, and have made efforts not to generalise the experience of heterosexual women to lesbian and bisexual women and girls (Rich, 1980).

The autobiographical turn in education encouraged articulation of students' and teachers' accounts of their own educational experiences, stories and meanings which had been largely effaced in an archive dominated by quantitative achievement measures and historical and sociological records of the evolution of intricate and bulky bureaucracies. In the early work of Pinar and Grumet (1976), autobiographical analyses of educational experience were sought as means to focus on the specificity of educational situations and histories, as well as to draw out negations of constraints into images for the future. Janet Miller (1990) worked with teachers to elicit their understandings of their work; she was interested in building school communities from groups of teachers whose reflections would generate a common project. Connelly and Clandinin (1988) approached autobiography as a method to encourage teachers' reflexive grasp of their teaching, drawing out images that expressed the ways they understood and constructed curriculum within the context of the school.

An important contribution of autobiography to curriculum is its phenomenological turn, its capacity to address experience as it has appeared to the author. No written account can be free of ideology or of the knowledge systems that have influenced our stories about teachers, parents and nature. Narratives of educational experience may provide sketches of phenomena – such as the experience of participating in a play, or travelling to a distant land, or experiencing the death of parent – which provide a contrast between the experiences of daily life and the ways in which these phenomena are coded and arranged for understanding in courses on theatre, geography, or psychology or medicine.

This contrast may serve a number of purposes: first of all, it denaturalises curriculum, reminding students that curriculum is an artefact, and that its terms are generated by and belong to a cultural discourse that is political and cultural. Second, it reveals the links that exist between the student's own experience in the world and the formal curriculum, by showing them to be two language systems working to encode similar phenomena. Third, through reciprocal readings, the narratives and the texts of the disciplines that correspond to them, can be used to provide critical perspectives on each other.

Autobiographical work in education is a strand in qualitative studies of education, where the perspective of the researcher is woven into an ethnography, denying the emptiness of the eye that sees and describes only other people's realities. In the accounts of so-called research 'subjects', autobiographical texts are joined to other accounts, empirical/quantitative, or ethnographic, to ensure their participation in the account that is being constructed to stand for their experience. Expression has also become a theme in school governance as site-based management schools invites the active participation of teachers and parents, elevating their points of view from a subordinated process of frustrated grumbling or passive assent to the processes that determine policy.

Post-structuralist critics of autobiography have expressed suspicions of all these writing selves. Critics have challenged the spurious unity of the narrating self and its linear psychology. Accompanying the logic of its narrative, is, they assert, a naïve conflation of viewpoint and truth, as if the risk of confession and discomfort of disclosure were sufficient to confirm the veracity and authority of its judgements (Willinsky, 1989). This critique challenges the reliance on reflexivity that came to dominate the discourse of teacher education and development in the 1980s (Schon, 1987), as well as educational research in the 1990s (Lather, 1991). Lacking theoretical scaffolding as well as identification of educational aims, reflexivity, on its own, can dwindle into the paralysis of infinite regression or self-absorbed trivia (Grumet, 1990; Lenzo, 1995; Orner, 1992).

Feminist educators have pointed to the irony that post-structuralism arrived to erase the speaking self just at the moment when women had seized the podium (Brodribb, 1992). This sardonic observation is accompanied by a serious concern that the activist and political expressions of feminism will not survive the assault on the psychological self, which, for all of its questionable cohesion, supports and sustains the social identities capable of social action. McCoy (1997), drawing on Butler (1992) and Spivak (1993), maintains that

434

foundational critiques, such as those challenging the notion identity, are significant if they reveal the presuppositions that constrain action and open in-between spaces where different sorts of action are imaginable.

GENDER, COGNITION AND CURRICULUM

The conflict between identity and possibility is expressed in debates about what it means to be a woman, and relatedly, the particular contributions that women have made, and can make, to education. This theme was announced in the important work of Carol Gilligan (1982), *In a Different Voice*. In that work she criticised Kohlberg's research on moral development, asserting that young women understand and make judgements about ethical dilemmas differently from the young men who were the subjects of Kohlberg's research. Positing a context-specific and improvisational attitude as feminine, Gilligan inspired many researchers and theorists to identify what is particular to feminine thought. *Women's Ways of Knowing* (Belenky *et al.*, 1986) followed by critiquing the progressively decentred trajectory that signified maturity in William Perry's work on cognitive development. Nel Noddings (1984) identified the feminine standpoint with the ethic of care and articulated the pedagogical implications of responsive and responsible practice that she associated with the maternal interests of women. Grumet (1988) addressed reproduction as a theme in consciousness and suggested that orientations towards knowledge and pedagogy were linked to the reproductive experiences of men and women. All of these approaches have been challenged as essentialist when understood to be ascribing attitudes, abilities or commitments to women on the basis of their sex.

Essentialist rationales surface in feminism in education because of the field's commitment to equity and social action. In an attempt to reorder the politics of schools so that female students and teachers find them to be places that support their interests and development, generalisations about those interests may be inevitable. Feminist critique perpetually examines such assumptions, loath to replace old stereotypes with new enlightened ones.

The function of generalisation has been a theme and concern for those who study feminist pedagogies. Some have worried about the influence of ideology on students and classroom discourse, while others have argued for methods that encourage the expression of each student's individuality (Culley and Portuges, 1985). For once discourse is studied to analyse how students and teachers express themselves and how that expression fosters or inhibits what others feel free to say and think, then no ideology, no matter how open or inclusive, can ensure that the experience of classroom instruction and interactions will realise its principles. What are the conditions that will allow a student to speak honestly, from her own experience, about her response to and questions about the object that is being studied? How can the conversations that take place in small study groups be elaborated and projected into the discursive space of the lecture? How can the rivalries and exclusions that erupt in social discourse be understood by students and teachers and handled so that they do not constrict expression and learning?

Frances Maher and Mary Kay Tetreault (1994) examined the effects of feminist pedagogies on classroom discourse, and Jo Anne Pagano (1990), in *Exiles and Communities*, analysed the sources of pedagogical authority. Elizabeth Ellsworth (1989) addressed the sexist assumptions of critical pedagogy, a progressive pedagogy bent on challenging the biases and presuppositions of students, in a challenging piece in the *Harvard Educational Review*, 'Why Doesn't This Feel Empowering?'. A collection of essays edited by Luke and Gore (1992) examined a variety of feminist responses to critical pedagogy.

Just as feminist scholars work to lift the weight of generalisations drawn from the experience of men that have been applied to the lives of women, so too they work to prevent the experience of white, middle-class women and girls from being generalised to women and girls of other economic classes, races and ethnicities.

Working with Linda Alcoff's (1988) concept of 'positionality', 'in which people are defined not in terms of fixed identities, but by their location within shifting networks of relationships, which can be analyzed and changed', Maher and Tetreault (1994, p. 164) analysed the discourse of classrooms where feminist curriculum and pedagogy were enacted. In the classrooms that they observed, student and teacher perspectives that issued from identity-specific experiences were presented or withheld according to the participant's experience of the dynamics of the instructional setting: his or her perception of its environment, curriculum, teacher and other students. Their research points to the complexity of associating students' interests with their identities, and reminds us that the classroom is a social and communicative event that is saturated with subjectivity as well as the ascriptions that constitute the social identities of class, race, sex, religion and ethnicity.

CURRICULUM RESEARCH AND FEMINIST POLITICS

Feminist scholars have contributed to the methodological literature on research in education. The most significant work is that which has questioned the power relations inherent in the binaries that structure traditional research paradigms (researcher/researched; knower/known; subject/object; etc.) and that which has responded to these questions by articulating new approaches to the conception, conduct, validation, representation and utilisation of research in education. Patti Lather maintains that the emancipatory project of feminist scholarship repudiates a disinterested stance towards research and explores the problematics of validation and representation arising from the juxtapositions of feminist and post-structural theories, political commitments and the lived experiences of research participants (Lather 1991; Lather and Smithies, 1997). The autobiographical turn in feminist scholarship, already discussed, has been significant to the methodological literature in its insistence on the privileging of research participants' experiences and voices. Other significant methodological contributions have been made by Middleton (1987), in her life histories of feminist teachers; McWilliam (1994), by integrating teacher education and critical research practices; Ladsen-Billings (1994), in her articulation of an Afrocentric feminist epistemology; Pillow (1997), by her rethinking of policy studies on teenage pregnancy; and St Pierre (1997), by analysing unusual kinds of data in her research with older southern women.

The work of Shirley Brice Heath is significant because it nests a study of literacy instruction in classrooms in a consideration of the literacies that the children in these classrooms have experienced within their familial and community cultures. This work situates schools in a rich world of affiliations and communities and marks the paths that each child in the study walks between the institutions and language systems that we have named 'public' and 'private'. Studies of children's everyday experiences of the disciplines, such as the mathematical operations embedded in the experience of going to the grocery store as presented in *Everyday Cognition* (Royoff and Lave, 1984) or the literacy experiences involved in going to church or in leaving notes for the family members presented in *Ways with Words* (Heath, 1983), provide portraits of learning that link public and private representations of knowledge. While not explicitly feminist, these studies incorporate analyses of domestic and family experiences, enlarging the scope of enquiry to address those domains previously exiled from formal enquiry.

COLLABORATION

Feminist acknowledgement of affiliation has undermined the prevalence of the myth of competitive individualism in learning, developmental constructs, and research. The feminist critique of the Cartesian subject, – split off, isolated, paralysed with doubt – challenges conceptions of creativity and intellectual achievement that extend these values into our classrooms. Classroom pedagogies requiring collaboration have developed through the classroom practices of process writing, where students are gathered together to act as each other's readers, editors and critics (Reagan *et al.*, 1994). Entitled – sometimes – 'cooperative learning', the development of study groups both in and outside school has been seen as supporting the achievement of the groups that have used them. Collaboration is seen to support teachers, as well as students, when teachers are enabled to work together to develop curriculum that bridges their classrooms, disciplines and grade categories. It is interesting to note that the model for process writing in the classroom was the National Writing Project, a staff development process that brought teachers together to share their writing so that they could offer one another encouragement, attention and critique. In the reform of classroom practice, professors in colleges and universities and teachers in elementary and secondary schools can join in common cause: for the ethic of individualism still dominates the college classroom, its structures for student work and its approaches to the assessment of that work. Dissertations are still tied to individual authorship, even though the problems of schooling require multiple and related research perspectives, and the work of faculty members is suspect if tenure and promotion reviews reveal a preponderance of co-authored articles.

Collaboration within and across institutional boundaries offers the promise of significant change in educational practices and structures. It requires acknowledgement of the role that each social relation plays in the cultural processes that educate children and it invites participants in the various domains – family, publicly funded schools, higher education, government, industry and community-based organisations – to identify common concerns as they respect each other's specific responsibilities, expertise and perspectives. Feminists who are working to share their work across the divisions of race, ethnicity, class, sexual preference and religion may be well suited to provide the leadership in the effort to support these collaborations, so necessary to educational reform.

REFERENCES

Alcoff, L. (1988) 'Cultural feminism versus post-Structuralism: the identity crisis in feminist theory'. *Signs*, 13 (3), 418–419.

American Association of University Women (AAUW) (1995) *How Schools Shortchange Girls. The AAUW Report. A Study of Major Findings on Girls and Education.* Washington, DC: AAUW, Educational Foundation, National Education Association.

Belenky, M., Clinchy, B. M., Goldberger, N. R., and Tarule, J. M., (1986) *Women's Ways of Knowing: The Development of Self, Voice, and Mind.* New York: Basic Books.

Biklen, S. K. and Pollard, D. (ed.) (1993) *Gender and Education.* Chicago: NSSE, University of Chicago.

Brodribb, S. (1992) *Nothing Mat(t)ers: A Feminist Critique of Postmodernism.* North Melbourne, Vic.: Spinifex Press.

Bull, J. (1974) 'High school women: Oppression and liberation'. In J. Stacey, S. Bereaud and J. Daniels (eds) *And Jill Came Tumbling After: Sexism in American Education.* New York: Dell.

Butler, J. (1992) 'Contingent foundations: Feminism and the question of "post-modernism"'. In J. Butler and J. Scott (eds) *Feminists Theorise the Political.* New York: Routledge. 3–21.

Chodorow, N. (1978) *The Reproduction of Mothering: Psychoanalysis and the Sociology of Gender.* Berkeley, CA: University of California Press.

Christian-Smith, L. (1988) *Becoming Feminine: The Politics of Popular Culture.* New York: Falmer Press.

Christian-Smith, L. (1990) *Becoming a Woman through Romance.* New York: Routledge.

Connelly, M. and Clandinin, J. (1988) *Teachers as Curriculum Planners: Narratives of Experience.* New York: Teachers College Press.

Culley, M. and Portuges, C. (1985) *Gendered Subjects: The Dynamics of Feminist Teaching.* Boston: Routledge & Kegan Paul.

Dinnerstein, D. (1976) *The Mermaid and the Minotaur: Sexual Arrangements and Human Malaise.* New York: Harper & Row.

Donovan, J. (1978) *Feminist Theory.* New York: Frederick Ungar Publishing Press.

Ellsworth, E. (1989) 'Why doesn't this feel empowering?' *Harvard Educational Review*, 59 (3), 297–324.

Elshtain, J. B. (1981) *Public Man, Private Woman: Women in Social and Political Thought.* Princeton: Princeton University Press.

Fennema, E. and Sherman, J. (1977) 'Sex related differences in math achievement, spatial visualisation and affective factors'. *American Educational Research Journal*, 14, 51–71.

Frazier, N. and Sadker, M. (1973) *Sexism in School and Society.* New York: Harper & Row.

Gilligan, C. (1982) *In a Different Voice: Psychological Theory and Women's Development.* Cambridge, MA: Harvard University Press.

Goffman, E. (1961) *The Presentation of Self in Everyday Life.* Garden City, NY: Doubleday.

Greenberg, S. (1978) *Right from the Start.* New York: Houghton-Mifflin.

Grumet, M. (1988) *Bitter Milk: Women and Teaching.* Amherst: University of Massachusetts Press.

Grumet, M. (1990) 'Voice: The search for a feminist rhetoric of educational studies'. *Cambridge Journal of Education*, 20 (3), 277–282.

Grumet, M. (1995) 'At home and in the classroom: The false comfort of false distinctions'. In M. Ginsberg (ed.) *The Politics of Educators' Work and Lives.* New York: Garland Publishing, Inc., 55–72.

Haraway, D. (1991) *Simians, Cyborgs, and Women.* New York: Routledge.

Harding, S. (1986) *The Science Question in Feminism.* Ithaca, New York: Cornell University Press.

Harding, S. (1991) *Whose Science? Whose Knowledge?: Thinking from Women's Lives.* Ithaca, New York: Cornell University Press.

Heath, S. B. (1983) *Ways with Words: Language, Life and Work in Communities and Classrooms.* New York: Cambridge University Press.

Keller, E. F. (1985) *Reflections on Gender and Science.* New Haven, CT: Yale University Press.

Klein, S. (ed.) (1992) *Sex Equity and Sexuality in Education*. Albany, New York: SUNY Press.

Kohlberg, L. (1984) *The Psychology of Moral Development*. New York: Harper & Row.

Ladsen-Billings, G. (1994) *The Dreamkeepers: Successful Teachers of African-American Children*. San Francisco: Jossey-Bass.

Lather, P. (1987) 'The absent presence: Patriarchy, capitalism, and the nature of teacher work'. *Teacher Education Quarterly*, 14 (2), 25–38.

Lather, P. (1991) *Getting Smart: Feminist Research and Pedagogy with/in the Postmodern*. New York: Routledge.

Lather, P. and Smithies, C. (1997) *Troubling the Angels: Women living with HIV/AIDS*. Boulder, CO: Westview Press.

Lenzo [McCoy], K. (1995) 'Validity and self-reflexivity meet poststructuralism: Scientific ethos and the transgressive self'. *Educational Researcher*, 24 (4), 17–23.

Luke, C. and Gore, J. (eds) (1992) *Feminisms and Critical Pedagogy*. New York: Routledge.

McCoy, K. (1997) 'Killing the father/Becoming uncomfortable with the mother tongue: Rethinking the performative contradiction'. *Educational Theory*.

McIntosh, P. (1983) *Interactive Phases of Curricular and Personal Re-vision: A Feminist Perspective*. Wellesley, MA: Wellesley College Center for Research on Women. Working Paper, no. 24.

McRobbie, A. (1978) 'Working class girls and the culture of femininity'. In Women's Studies Group (ed.) *Women Take Issue: Aspects of Women's Subordination*. London: Hutchinson, 96–108.

McWilliam, E. (1994) *In Broken Images: Feminist Tales for a Different Teacher Education*. New York: Teachers College Press.

Maher, F. and Tetreault, M. K. T. (1994) *The Feminist Classroom*. New York: Basic Books.

Middleton, S. (1987) 'Schooling and radicalisation: Life histories of New Zealand feminist teachers'. *British Journal of Sociology of Education*, 8 (2), 169–189.

Miller, J. (1990) *Creating Spaces and Finding Voices: Teachers Collaborating for Empowerment*. Albany, New York: SUNY Press.

Noddings, N. (1984) *Caring: A Feminine Approach to Ethics and Moral Education*. Berkeley: University of California Press.

O'Brien, M. (1981) *The Politics of Reproduction*. Boston: Routledge & Kegan Paul.

Orner, M. (1992) 'Interrupting calls for student voice in "liberatory" education: A feminist poststructuralist perspective'. In C. Luke and J. Gore (eds) *Feminisms and Critical Pedagogy*. New York: Routledge, 74–89.

Pagano, J. A. (1990) *Exiles and Communities: Teaching in the Patriarchal Wilderness*. Albany, New York: SUNY Press.

Pillow, W. (1997) 'Decentering silences/troubling irony: Teen pregnancy's challenge to policy analysis'. In C. Marshall (ed.) *Feminist Critical Policy Analysis I: A Primary and Secondary Schooling Perspective*. London: Falmer Press.

Pinar, W. and Grumet, M. (1976) *Toward a Poor Curriculum*. Dubuque, IA: Kendall/Hunt.

Pinar, W., Reynolds, W., Slattery, P. and Taubman, P. (1995) *Understanding Curriculum: An Introduction to the Study of Historical and Contemporary Curriculum Discourses*, New York: Peter Lang.

Reagan, S. B., Fox, T. and Bleich, D. (1994) *Writing With: New Directions in Collaborative Teaching, Learning, and Research*. Albany, New York: SUNY Press.

Rich, A. (1980) 'Compulsive heterosexuality and lesbian existence'. *Signs: Journal of Women in Culture and Society*. 5 (4), 631–660.

Rogoff, B. and Lave, J. (1984) *Everyday Cognition: Its Development in Social Context*. Cambridge, MA: Harvard University Press.

Roman, L. and Christian-Smith, L. (eds) (1988) *Becoming Feminine: The Politics of Popular Culture*. London: Falmer, Press.

Sadker, M. and Sadker, D. (1994) *Failing at Fairness: How America's Schools Cheat Girls*. Toronto/New York: Maxwell Macmillan.

Schon, D. (1987) *Educating the Reflective Practitioner: Toward a New Design for Teaching and Learning in the Professions*. San Francisco: Jossey-Bass.

Scribner, S. (1997) *Mind and Social Practices: Selected Writings of Sylvia Scribner* (E. Tobach, ed.). Cambridge/New York: Cambridge University Press.

Sears P. and Feldman, D. (1974) 'Teacher interactions with boys and with girls'. In J. Stacey, S. Bereaud and J. Daniels (eds) *And Jill Came Tumbling After: Sexism in American Education*. New York: Dell.

Serbin, L. and O'Leary, K. (1975) 'How nursery schools teach girls to shut up'. *Psychology Today*, 9, 56–58.

Smith, D. (1990) *Texts, Facts, and Feminity: Exploring the Relations of Ruling*. New York: Routledge.

Spivak, G. C. (1993) *Outside in the Teaching Machine*. New York: Routledge.

St Pierre, E. A. (1997) 'Methodology in the fold and the irruption of transgressive data'. *International Journal of Qualitative Studies in Education*, 10 (2).

Steffere, B. (1975) 'Run, mama, run: Women workers in elementary readers'. In E. Maccia, M. Estep and T. Shiel (eds) *Women and Education*. Springfield, IL: Charles C. Thomas.

Stone, L. (ed.) (1994) *The Education Feminism Reader*. New York: Routledge.

Taubman, P. (1982) 'Gender and curriculum: Discourse and the politics of sexuality'. *Journal of Curriculum Theorizing*. 4 (91), 12–87.

Tobias, S. (1981) 'The mathematics filter'. *National Forum: Phi Kappa Phi Journal*, 61 (4), 17–18.

Trecker, J. (1971) 'Women in US history high school textbooks'. *Social Education*. 35 (3), 249–60.

Valli, L. (1986) *Becoming Clerical Workers*. Boston: Routledge & Kegan Paul.

Weiler, K. (1988) *Women Teaching for Change: Gender Class and Power*. South Hadley, MA: Bergin Garvey.

Weiner, G. (1994) *Feminisms in Education: An Introduction*. Philadelphia: Open University Press.

Weis, L. (1990) *Working Class without Work: High School Students in a De-industrializing Economy*. New York: Routledge & Chapman Hall.

Weis, L. and Fine, M. (eds) (1993) *Beyond Silenced Voices: Class, Race, and Gender in United States Schools*. Albany, New York: State University of New York Press.

Willinsky, J. (1989) 'Getting personal and practical with personal practical knowledge'. *Curriculum Inquiry*, 19 (3), 247–264.

Women on Words and Images. (1974) 'Look, Jane, look. See sex stereotypes'. In J. Stacey, S. Bereaud and J. Daniels (eds) *And Jill Came Tumbling After: Sexism in American Education*. New York: Dell.

25

DAPPLED AND IRREPRESSIBLE

The kaleidoscope of multiculturalism
in education

Devorah Kalekin-Fishman

INTRODUCTION

Glory be to God for dappled things –
    For skies of couple-colour as a brinded cow:
. . . .
All things counter, original, spare, strange:
    Whatever is fickle, freckled (who knows how?)
        With swift, slow; sweet, sour; adazzle, dim;
He fathers-forth whose beauty is past change:
        Praise him.
            (Gerard Manley Hopkins, 'Pied Beauty')

Basically, Hopkins' images evoke the ordinary with the added insight that homely 'pied' things combine into a magic filigree. Like the figured rhyme and rhythm that lead the reader to see the wonder in the overly familiar, the idea of multiculturalism prods us to look at educational commonplaces from a wholly new point of view. In this essay we can begin to unpack some of the descriptive and prescriptive complexity of schooling in today's world.

Our interest lies in the subtle effects of cultural differences on ordinary educational practices, what are considered problems in this context, and the kinds of resolutions proposed. By definition the topic varies from place to place, for its conceptualisation hinges on a prescriptive philosophy and on a historically evolving educational policy, as well as on conventions of pedagogy, curriculum and organisation in education.

After presenting a working definition of culture on which to base a discussion of multiculturalism, we allude to evidence of the prevalence of multiculturalism in education throughout the world. We then look at some inevitable consequences, at how problems allegedly induced by multiculturalism in the schools are defined, and at some of the strategies summoned to deal with them. We then move on to how the literature on multiculturalism in education approaches issues in teaching and in teacher education. Finally, we cite bases for a critical look at the project of multiculturalism in education.

CULTURE AND MULTICULTURALISM

As an all-embracing term, culture can be grasped as both an attribute and a definition of a group. In the conceptualisation of Goodenough (1981), culture is defined in cognitive terms as learned and shared standards which are both 'inside' and 'outside' conscious awareness. Amalgams of feeling, thought and behaviour that distinguish one group from another and the (individual) member(s) of one group from those of another are transmitted from generation to generation as an integral constituent of the process of enculturation-socialisation. What at one time appeared to be an academic issue – that of what is meant by the term 'society'; how to define the limits of a 'group' – is being solved through existential imperatives. Populations are mixed, and in the daily encounters of people who have different conceptions of how to live, there are frequent crises. It is the compound of such conceptions and their motley articulation in action to which we give the name 'culture'.[1]

Despite the contention that throughout human history, cultures flower through group contact and exchange (Wax, 1995), our time is emphatically characterised as an era of diversity and transformation. Under the umbrella term of multiculturalism, the vocabulary of societal homogeneity has given way to a plethora of terms indicating the ongoing conglomeration, conjunction and occasional amalgamation of groups within politically differentiated units.

Multiculturalism is actualised in several ways (see Banks, 1995). Because of the ways in which state territories have been determined since the early part of the century, the population within state borders is often composed of majority and minority groups that differ in their mother tongues, and/or in religious allegiances. Some minorities are formed as an outcome of migration. In search of better economic conditions, migrants may choose to stay put in places where work is available, and they consciously accept the burden of being different. In these cases, the political and economic structures enforce awareness of the position of being 'other'. Differences may be maintained and even heightened as groups that inhabit a shared territory compete for resources; so 'clashes of cultures' tend to intersect with macro-political tensions.

There is, however, also a kind of 'closet' multiculturalism as the presumption of an all-embracing national culture is increasingly recognised as little more than a catchword. Even among members of the 'majority' and the 'locals', it is almost impossible to identify a single unifying culture. There are cultures of poverty and cultures of affluence; rural cultures and urban cultures. It is well documented that the cultures engendered by 'internal' structures of race, gender and poverty pose problems in unexpected ways (Smith, 1987, 1993).

Whatever its specific characteristics, multiculturalism is a social fact in the Durkheimian sense. It is, therefore, of interest to examine how this fact is framed in educational systems, what difficulties encountered by educational personnel are attributed to multiculturalism, what kinds of solutions are documented in recent literature and how they are evaluated theoretically. This will give us a basis for suggesting what is in store for multiculturalism in education as the millennium turns.

DIFFERENCE AS A CHALLENGE

Because of the pervasiveness of demographic diversity, educational institutions throughout the world are called upon to serve multicultural populations (Davidson and Jennett, 1994; Markou, 1994; Miller and Tanners, 1995; Mpofu, 1997; Root, 1996; Rumbaut, 1990; Smith, 1995). The challenge is manifold. For one thing, when the apperception of groups as being of diverse cultural origins is confirmed, so to speak, by a conventional marker, there is still uncertainty as to what configurations of capacities, understandings or behaviours are implied by the distinction. As a result, there is no justification to generalise recommendations. Still, the imputation of multiculturalism indicates inevitable challenges to education.

The need to deal with a multicultural population in the schools implicitly queries the validity of the institutionalised educational enterprise, minimally in terms of organisational forms and discourse. The customs and the habits that are 'normally' taken for granted come up against questions and alternative practices (Frykman and Loefgren, 1996). The 'ceremonies, symbols, and rituals', the 'great public routines of the school', which are of primary educational importance (Williamson, 1979), are also put in question by the very presence of groups with different cultural backgrounds.

Similar difficulties arise in connection with subject matter lore. The recognition of multiculturalism in a population is likely to put in question the choices of content in the curriculum and in the conceptions of what constitutes essential knowledge. In one sense, culture would seem to provide a common foundation for the learning required in schools. After all, 'through culture humans have a learned system for defining meaning, and in given situations of practical action, often seem to have created similar meaning interpretations'. But in a multicultural reality, there are justified doubts as to whether that foundation is shared. Furthermore, the 'system for defining meaning' and the creation of 'similar interpretations' may or may not be on the level of consciousness, and they can never be completely explicated. Thus, while some differences among cultures can be located, others are hidden from view, and similarities are not always what they seem. As a matter of fact, similar actions and even similar vocabularies may mask underlying differences (Erickson, 1986, p. 126).

Multiculturalism in education constitutes an ongoing puzzle and a serious practical challenge. The puzzle is exacerbated because cultural knowledge is by no means monolithic or ahistorical (Shore, 1991). 'Every cultural model [has] at least two moments of birth – one public and conventional, and the other a subjective appropriation and integration of a conventional form by a particular subject' (ibid., p. 22). As the authorised channel for enabling 'subjective appropriation' of what is presumed to be an authentic and integrated body of knowledge, institutions of education bear a weighty burden. A central issue is the definition of the goals of multicultural education, and connections with how problems are defined. The diverse approaches to multiculturalism lead to different articulations of the problems, and diversified directions for seeking resolutions.

GOALS OF MULTICULTURAL EDUCATION

A recently circulated 'Citizens' Public Trust Treaty' (Lunde, 1999) calls on governments 'to reduce military budgets by at least 50 per cent and to use the savings to guarantee the right to education', along with rights to shelter, health care, a safe environment, sound employment and peace. This call accords with the generally accepted identification of leaders in education with ideals of democracy and their public assertions in favour of the valorisation of ethnic difference (Auernheimer, 1996; Debeauvais and King, 1992). There are, however, different perspectives on how to formulate educational goals in a multicultural society. The diversity is concealed by listing goals under the legend of 'integrating different groups into the "wider" society'. Overall, the notion resonates with a reformist bias and an aspiration to egalitarianism. Yet, the term 'integration' may indicate quite different objectives – from the extreme of eradicating all differences as in the 'melting pot' model (Glazer and Moynihan, 1963) through the bare acceptance of diversity, to embracing the celebration of a thoroughly pluralistic society (Murray, 1992; Ray and Poonwassie, 1992).

Perspectives are anchored in different views of what constitutes a worthy goal. From a functionalist perspective, true democracy is based on a meritocracy, and schools are an objective agency with a duty to classify students according to their potential for contributing to society. Functionalists insist that multicultural education should be based on the approved cultural canon (Arthur and Shapiro, 1995; Bloom, 1987; Hirsch, 1987). Conflict theorists contest this claim and berate schools for using their 'goods' to reinforce inequalities. Radical approaches to multiculturalism insist that the task of multicultural education is activism, that is, to combat bigotry and discrimination (Giroux, 1992; McLaren and Welch, 1997). Among many, problems are defined in the macro in terms of cultural hegemony and social exclusion. Researchers point to specific expressions of racism and genderism (Connolly, 1994). There is widespread concern that just as the minority culture is overwritten so to speak, by the culture of the dominant, economic and social needs are also neglected (Boyd, 1996; Mpofu, 1997). Not paying attention to religious penchants of excluded cultural groups is considered a particular danger (Ghosh et al., 1995; Simel, 1996; Smolicz, 1994). It is claimed that on the level of the micro, these problems encounter constraints in the school organisation and in the classroom, both in pedagogy and in interaction (Fong and Gibbs, 1995; Gutierrez et al., 1995; Sardo-Brown and Hershey, 1995).

Still another approach emphasises the need to examine how schools affect the consciousness of individuals and their ongoing construction of the school world (Apitzsch, 1997; Knapp and Wolverton, 1995). In their view, the goal of multiculturalism in education is to prevent the scholastic *exclusion* of individuals. The stand for *inclusion* implies the coming to terms with, even the boosting of, different kinds of 'abnormalities' or 'eccentricities' whatever their sources. The distinctions noted do not rule out additional approaches.

DEFINING PROBLEMS: SPECIFICS IN SCHOOLS

In the schools, problems are defined by their relationship to various realms of the educational enterprise: instruction, interaction, organisational strategies and policy.

Instruction

Fundamental to the educational institution are assumptions that the knowledge imparted in the school is necessary for preparing the child for adult life, and that the principles held to be sacred in the school are necessary (if not sufficient) for ensuring the development of character. Teachers regularly track achievements of learning by constantly posing queries related to the material. They also collate scores on relatively informal tests and in the more formal examinations. Such scores classify students on scales of achievement as defined by the entire educational system. Cultural differences in norms of formal com-munication are usually overlooked in these connections (Macias, 1987; Minami and Ovando, 1995).

For many children, entry to school signals a sharp discontinuity in the process of encul-turation (Benedict, 1938) – 'an abrupt transition from one mode of being and behaving to another' (Spindler, 1974, p. 308). Confirmation is found in their academic records. It is almost a truism that 'minority groups do less well in academic achievement than dominant groups'. For this statement, Ogbu (1987, p. 256) cites work in Great Britain, Israel, Japan, Sweden and the United States of America. The results are clear and raise questions on various levels. Some researchers discuss the issues in terms of intelligence as an innate characteristic (Jensen, 1969). A second line of analysis is that of the representations teachers have of different groups. These are images that operate as self-fulfilling prophecies to flag both teachers' instructional activities and their interpretation of what is carried out as learning in the classroom (Henry, 1963; Mehan, 1979; Wolcott, 1982). Still others deal with achievement as evidence of different levels of motivation which become apparent in pupils' conscious exercise of choice (Gibson, 1987).

Teachers also see problems when there are failures in the realm defined as the domain of the formation of character. Failure here is disclosed not through scores for products of learning, but rather through the discernment of inadequate learning habits. These are tracked in how students do homework assignments, and in the consistency or inconsistency of class attendance. Further 'tests' are whether or not students appear in class with requisite equipment (pencils, pens, notebooks, rulers, drawing boards, calculators and so on) and how efficient they are in following instructions for tasks assigned to be done in class. A student's character is also judged by the kinds of snacks the child brings to school, her dress, her willingness to volunteer for service as defined by the school, as well as by the attitudes of her parents and their availability for consultation (Delgado-Gaitan, 1987; Finnan, 1987). According to Ogbu (1987; 1995), the core issue is that of the degree to which the minority group accepts the dominant culture. He points out that newcomers and immigrant minor-ities are more likely than non-immigrant minorities to accept school values and heel to the criteria that formal education imposes.

Interaction

Although the rules are at best explicated only in part, educational personnel have complex understandings of the kinds of rules that are requisite in the interaction of students among themselves in the schoolyard and in the classroom. Overt problems arise in the language of communication. Children of immigrants and children who come from homes in which minority languages are spoken may have difficulty in making themselves understood, as well as in understanding children who are comfortable with the language dominant in school. Differential competence and incompetence, in handling conventions of communication often present problems (Habermas, 1986). Beyond the skills identified with communicative rationality are those of situated expressivity – grasping, for example, what is meant as praise and what as ridicule; knowing when it is appropriate to be offended, and how. Of utmost importance are the control of repartee and the ability to foretell its effects – how offence can be expressed acceptably; what execrations are admissible in children's interchanges. In the large, students have to demonstrate their control of the kinds of games peers play, and the rules considered valid in a particular milieu. The etiquette of student–student interaction in the classroom is a subtle barrier to intercultural encounters. Included among the super-ficially negligible rules are conventions of seating, of turn-taking, of voice modulation, of calling attention to oneself; a tangle of linguistic and paralinguistic behaviours over which the teacher may have little power despite her convictions about what is 'right' (Banks, 1993).

Issues in educational organisation and in policy-making

Mismatches of culture and organisation are signalled in different ways. The features of school governance may not correspond to the norms of a minority culture, as evidenced in family organisation and in familiar political units. Distributions of time and space are salient areas of difference. Misunderstandings are likely to arise in connection with the distribution of time over the school day, and over the school year. Acceptance of the distribution of space within the area of the school and in distinguishing between 'inside' and 'outside' is not a foregone conclusion. Modes of formal and informal communication between school and home may be problematic, as may be the kinds of reactions considered 'normal' in each milieu. Overarching are the problems of policy-making, and the degree to which policies take multiculturalism into account. Policies may be insensitive to the variety of cultural models that govern learning and behaviours in the school system (Hanson and Avery, 1993; Kalekin-Fishman, in press; Wolcott, 1987).

In every locality, definitions of problems underlie the types of strategies adopted.

STRATEGIES FOR SOLVING PROBLEMS

Strategies for solving problems, derived from the crossing of definitions and goals, include research-based recommendations for policy strategies, as well as findings on programmes related to curriculum, and on ways and means in teacher education.

Policy

Basing recommendations on research findings, educationists' writings generally point out that existing policies are not satisfactory. The compelling moral basis for policy recommendations is a faith in the egalitarian universalism underpinning of a liberal humanistic education. It is widely feared that this doctrine is often abandoned and consequently policy works to undermine the healthy development of national and personal identity (Carter *et al.*, 1993; Gewirth *et al.*, 1993–1994). Government policy-makers are exhorted to institutionalise multiculturalism (Troyna, 1985), while affirming principles of equality of opportunity (Hampel, 1989). This can be done by adopting policies that constrain exposing students to local and international mixes of cultures (Wagenaar and Subedi, 1996), that actively promote cultural understanding, cultural competence and cultural emancipation (McCarthy, 1990).

Where multiculturalism is defined in terms of internationalism, there is a need for *global* education. Proposed strategies include the 'modification of the total school environment'. Students should be enabled 'to experience equal education opportunities and develop [the] knowledge, skills, and attitudes [requisite] to recognize the interdependence of nations and understand the interconnected political, economic, and social problems of an interdependent world' (Wahlstrom and Clarken, 1992, p. 1). When detailed as a local phenomenon, it is asserted that policy decisions must encompass the 'whole school'. This requires consideration of factors as diverse as parent participation, regulations of admission and placement, support services, school climate, teacher empowerment and school finance (Sileo *et al.*, 1996).

Curriculum

Diverse constructions of curricula have led theoreticians to advance programmes in the fields of moral education, attitude change, language, subject matter content and classroom management.

An approach that views multicultural education as a problem for moral education presents models for discussing racism, minority group relations and human rights. Workshops to encourage the creation of a multifaceted self, and celebrations that include the feelings and allegiances of 'others' are described at length (Cross *et al.*, 1978; Houser, 1996; Junn *et al.*, 1995; O'Connor, 1991; Suina and Smolkin, 1995). Specific plans are propounded for teachers who undertake to overcome intercultural conflict or violence, to promote interethnic unity, to achieve integration in class and to meet diverse needs (Calderon and Farrell, 1996; Lustig, 1997; Postiglione, 1998; Wang *et al.*, 1995; Wlodkowski and Ginsberg, 1995; Ziglio and Maniotti, 1995). Attitudes, it is suggested, can be formed and changed through judicious fostering of play and through extensive reliance on aspects of education in the arts (Dimidjian, 1992; Srivastava, 1996; Vold, 1992). The conscious mobilisation of empathy to deal with problems that arise in the classroom is singled out as an effective pedagogical tool (Sandhu *et al.*, 1991).

Many researchers are convinced that the most important aspect of the curriculum is children's control of language skills (Chiang, 1993; Christian and Mahrer, 1992; Kalantzis and Cope, 1990; Kalantzis *et al.*, 1986; Krishnamurti, 1986; Luchtenberg, 1994, 1995a, 1995b; Mathuna and Singleton, 1984; Olneck, 1993; Paribakht, 1987; Skutnabb-Kangas and Phillipson, 1985). While most of the research deals with how to ensure children's acquisition of the dominant school language; there is also intense concern with achievements in acquiring a second or a foreign language, and in the efficient use of verbal and non-verbal communication. Preservation of the language of the home is an issue that is drawing increasing attention as well. Research evidence supports the idea that a secure knowledge of the mother tongue (different from the school language) is likely to further a pupil's self-esteem and motivation to realise her academic potential.

Examples of subject matter content presumed to contribute to the furtherance of the goals of multiculturalism are ethnic studies (according to the recognised minority groups in the state), women's studies, as well as chapters in history and civics courses focusing on multiculturalism in its local interpretation. There are programmes for exploring literature in a multicultural framework, and for demonstrating that science is a multicultural project. In organising multicultural classrooms, furthermore, teachers are advised to maximise the potential for realising goals of multiculturalism by implementing techniques of co-operative learning (Arnold, 1995; Krugly-Smolska, 1996; Michigan State Dept. of Education, 1990; Patrick, 1991; Perotti, 1990a).

Teaching and teacher education

In discussions of multiculturalism in education, the cultivation of appropriate knowledge, attitudes and practices in the preparation for teaching are central issues. Among the efforts are: programmes for acquiring knowledge about 'other' groups; field experiences in multi-cultural educational settings so that students can devote more 'awareness, time, and value to cross-cultural issues' during their training (Bassey, 1996, p. 37; Salcido *et al.*, 1995); and intensive workshops for developing human relations skills (Reed and Diez, 1989; Solomon and Levine-Rasky, 1996). A proposed trajectory of professional training includes the probing of one's own identity; the acquisition of knowledge about the maze of diversity in language and literacy acquisition; acquaintance with a repertoire of teaching techniques; and the capacity to select a teaching style. Analysed as a process of overcoming 'unconscious racism', more neutrally, social distance, student-teachers can, according to research, be guided to achieve mature cross-cultural abilities. In addition, it has repeatedly been emphasised that to ensure success in the field after certification, in-service teachers have to be empowered and rewarded (Clark *et al.*, 1996; Corson, 1991; Martin and Williams-Dixon, 1994; Zeichner, 1991, 1995).

CRITIQUES

In tracing the history of theoretical and practical concern with multicultural education, Banks (1995) contends that the identification of multicultural education research and theory with social reform is rooted in a wide-ranging ideological consensus. His claim is borne out by the sheer quantity of related work – both in the academe and in the field. The monu-mental *Handbook of Research on Multicultural Education* (Banks and Banks, 1995) bears witness to the massive investment in programmes and in research. It is impossible to escape the conviction, however, that the issues are far wider than the net that the *Handbook* casts.

Despite evidence of intensive pressure for promoting multiculturalism in education, the general tone of the literature is one of scepticism.

In society there are different approaches to what multicultural education has to accomplish. Clearly, the need to embrace diversity is of overwhelming importance for leaders in industry, government and the military. Political and economic interests, however, are not necessarily identical with the moral and pedagogical proclivities of teachers and teacher educators. An emphasis on a pluralistic understanding has led, especially in Europe, to a search to realise the goal of *inter*-cultural education (see, among others, Singh, 1997). Thus, multiculturalism has deep material significance for meeting the provocation of the twenty–first century when multicultural education will be the vehicle for advancing peace in the world through the ineluctable macro-processes of globalisation (Michael, 1997). Since these processes will be felt in every corner of the globe, school systems have to discover how to adapt 'to the new requirements imposed by the multicultural, multi-denominational, and often multi-ethnic context of society. . . . The concern is no longer merely . . . to take into account the specific needs of one category of pupils' (Perotti, 1990b, p. 1). At the same time, it is clear that the desired conceptualisation is commonly impeded by political problems that can be shaped by bureaucratic inertia, family structures, and the passive if not active resistance of the professionals involved (Borman and O'Reilly, 1992), whose personal definitions of the issue often constitute an obstacle.

Theoretical descriptions of the effects of multiculturalism in education highlight the dissension. Critical theorists (Giroux, 1991; Kalantzis and Cope, 1990) centre on social structure as the stumbling block to the integration of student groups of diverse origins. Research shows that students from groups that are excluded from the realms of the powerful, do elaborate gratifying styles of living. These are interpreted as signs of how deprived classes are forced into resigned acceptance of conditions that are to their detriment (Willis, 1977, 1978). But there is also research that shows that schools can escape the perpetuation of differences by exploring the kinds of codes (for knowing and for living) that govern students' lives (Bernstein, 1996). This kind of study is necessarily, however, slow and uncertain. A highly trenchant basis for critique is the claim that by taking on programmes related to multiculturalism, educational systems are actually working against their own proclaimed goals. Extending contact between different cultural groups and spreading knowledge of different ways of life, constitute ways and means of homogenising school populations. Ironically, then, success of the educational means for combating prejudice and discrimination is likely to impair the capacity of society to capitalise on the advantages of diversity (Blau, 1994).

In sum, tensions among the different tenets related to what, why and how to proceed under prevailing conditions have to be reviewed from a highly informed perspective. There does not seem to be a consensus, apart from recognition of the usefulness of preserving and rewarding difference. Lighting on strategies will be possible only if goals are articulated in detail and practices constantly tested.

NOTE

1 Definitions of culture are of widely different types. Among them are: attempts at a thorough description of all its elements; attempts to rely on exhaustive descriptions of norms and values; references to imagined and 'real' commonalities in history and tradition; and so on. Recent writings tend to define culture as a composite of cognition and action (Cole and Scribner, 1974; Goodenough, 1981; Holland and Quinn, 1987; Kroeber and Kluckhohn, 1952; Shweder and LeVine, 1984).

REFERENCES

Apitzsch, U. (1997) 'Can adults learn intercultural learning? Three reflections on the building of supportive attitudes'. *Pädagogik*, 49 (3), 49–52.

Arnold, F. W. (1995) 'Developing and teaching a cultural pluralism course in one of America's "uneasy salad bowls"'. *Teaching Sociology*, 23 (2), 94–110.

Arthur, J. and Shapiro, A. (eds) (1995) *Campus Wars: Multiculturalism and the Politics of Difference*. Boulder, CO: Westview Press.

Asumah, S. N. and Hlatshwayo, S. (1995) 'The politics of multicultural education in South Africa: Vogue, oxymoron or political paralysis?' *Western Journal of Black Studies*, 19 (4), 284–292.

Auernheimer, G. (1996) 'Intercultural education: A reply to the thesis of F. O. Radtke'. *Zeitschrift für Pädagogik*, 42 (3), 425–430.

Banks, J. A. (1993) 'The canon debate, knowledge construction, and multicultural education'. *Educational Researcher*, 22 (5), 4–14.

Banks, J. A. (1995) 'Multicultural education: Historical development, dimensions, and practice'. In: J. A. Banks and C. A. M. Banks (eds) *Handbook of Research on Multicultural Education*. New York: Macmillan, 3–24.

Banks, J. A. and Banks, C. A. M. (eds) (1995) *Handbook of Research on Multicultural Education*. New York: Macmillan.

Bassey, M. O. (1996) 'Teachers as cultural brokers in the midst of diversity'. *Educational Foundations*, 10 (2), 37–52.

Benedict, R. (1938) *Patterns of Culture*. New York: New American Library.

Bernstein, B. (1996) *Pedagogy, Symbolic Control, and Identity: Theory, Research, Critique*. London: Taylor & Francis.

Blau, P. M. (1994) 'The paradox of multiculturalism'. Paper presented at the 33rd Congress of the International Sociological Association, Bielefeld, Germany, July.

Bloom, A. (1987) *The Closing of the American Mind: How Higher Education Has Failed Democracy and Impoverished the Souls of Today's Students*. New York: Simon & Schuster.

Borman, K. M. and O'Reilly, P. (eds) (1992) 'Politics and the schools'. *Educational Foundations*, 6 (2).

Boyd, D. (1996) 'Dominance concealed through diversity: Implications of inadequate perspectives on cultural pluralism'. *Harvard Educational Review*, 66 (3), 609–630.

Calderon, J. and Farrell, B. (1996) 'Doing sociology: Connecting the classroom experience with a multiethnic school district'. *Teaching Sociology*, 24 (1), 46–53.

Carter, B., Green, M. and Sondhi, R. (1993) 'The one difference that "makes all the difference?": Schooling and the politics of identity in the UK'. *European Journal of Intercultural Studies*, 3 (2–3), 81–89.

Chiang, L. H. (1993) 'Beyond language: Native Americans' nonverbal communication'. Paper presented at the 23rd Annual Meeting of the Midwest Association of Teachers of Educational Psychology, Indiana, October.

Christian, D. and Mahrer, C. (1992) *Two-way Bilingual Programs in the United States, 1991–1992*. Washington, DC: Center for Applied Linguistics.

Clark, E. R., Nystrom, N. J. and Perez, B. (1996) 'Language and culture: Critical components of multicultural teacher education'. *Urban Review*, 38 (2), 185–197.

Cole, M. and Scribner, S. (1974) *Culture and Thought: A Psychological Introduction*. New York: John Wiley.

Connolly, P. (1994) 'All lads together?: Racism, masculinity and multicultural/anti-racist strategies in a primary school'. *International Studies in Sociology of Education*, 4 (2), 191–211.

Corson, D. (1991) 'Realities of teaching in a multiethnic school'. *International Review of Education*, 37 (1), 7–31.

Cortesao, L. and Pacheco, N. (1990) 'Why is intercultural education absent from Portuguese educational realities?' Paper presented at the Congress of the International Sociological Association, Madrid.

Cross, D. E., Long, M. A. and Ziajka, A. (1978) 'Minority cultures and education in the United States'. *Education and Urban Society*, 10 (3), 263–276.

Davidson, B. and Jennett, C. (1994) *Addressing Disadvantage*. Canberra: Council for Aboriginal Reconciliation.

Debeauvais, M. and King, E. (1992) 'Outcasts of the year 2000: A challenge to education in Europe'. *Comparative Education*, 28 (1), 61–69.

Delgado-Gaitan, C. (1987) 'Traditions and transitions in the learning process of Mexican children: An ethnographic view'. In: G. and L. Spindler (eds) *Interpretive Ethnography of Education: At Home and Abroad*. Hillsdale, NJ: Lawrence Erlbaum Associates, 333–359.

Dimidjian, V. J. (ed.) (1992) *Play's Place in Public Education for Young Children*. Washington, DC: National Education Association.

Erickson, F. (1986) 'Qualitative methods in research on teaching'. In: M. C. Wittrock (ed.) *Handbook of Research on Teaching*. New York and London: Macmillan, 119–161.

Finnan, C. R. (1987) 'The influence of the ethnic community on the adjustment of Vietnamese refugees'. In: G. and L. Spindler (eds) *Interpretive Ethnography of Education: At Home and Abroad*. Hillsdale, NJ: Lawrence Erlbaum Associates, 313–329.

Fong, L. G. and Gibbs, J. T. (1995) 'Facilitating services to multicultural communities in a dominant culture setting: An organizational perspective'. *Administration in Social Work*, 19 (2), 1–24.

Franchi, A. (1987) 'Sociocultural aspects of the integration of the Spanish child in a multiethnic environment'. *Revista Internacional de Sociologia*, 45 (2), 273–287.

Frykman, J. and Loefgren, J. (1996) *Force of Habit: Exploring Everyday Life*. Lund Studies in European Ethnology I. Lund: Lund University Press.

Gewirth, A., Haroutunian-Gordon, S. and Neiman, A. M. (1993–1994) 'The moral basis of liberal education'. *Studies in Philosophy and Education*, 13 (2), 111–124.

Ghosh, R., Zinman, R. and Talbani, A. (1995) 'Policies relating to the education of cultural communities in Quebec'. *Canadian Ethnic Studies*, 27 (1), 18–31.

Gibson, M. (1987) 'Punjabi immigrants in an American high school'. In: G. and L. Spindler (eds) *Interpretive Ethnography of Education: At Home and Abroad*. Hillsdale. NJ: Lawrence Erlbaum Associates, 281–310.

Giroux, H. A. (1991) 'Democracy and the discourse of cultural difference: Towards a politics of border pedagogy'. *British Journal of the Sociology of Education*, 12 (4), 501–519.

Giroux, H. A. (1992) *Border Crossings*. New York: Routledge.

Giroux, H. A. and McLaren, P. (eds) (1989) *Critical Pedagogy, the State, and Cultural Struggle*. Albany, NY: SUNY Press.

Glazer, N. and Moynihan, D. (1963) *Beyond the Melting Pot*. Cambridge, MA: MIT Press.

Goodenough, W. (1981) *Culture, Language, and Society*. Menlo Park, CA: Benjamin-Cummings.

Gutierrez, K. D., Larson, J. and Kreuter, B. (1995) 'Cultural tensions in the scripted classroom: The value of the subjugated perspective'. *Urban Education*, 29 (4), 410–442.

Habermas, J. (1986) 'On hermeneutics' claim to universality'. In: K. Mueller-Volmer (ed.) *The Hermeneutics Reader*. Oxford: Basil Blackwell, 294–319.

Hampel, B. (1989) 'Social analysis or ideology? Themes, tensions and contradictions in a selection of major government statements on multiculturalism'. *Journal of Intercultural Studies*, 10 (1), 1–12.

Hanson, K. and Avery, M. P. (1993) 'Value diversity in schools: A model for systemic restructuring'. Paper presented at the Annual Meeting of the National Middle Schools Association, Portland, Oregon, November, 1993.

Hayhoe, R. (1986) 'Penetration or mutuality? China's educational cooperation with Europe, Japan, and North America'. *Comparative Education Review*, 30 (4), 532–559.

Hegedus, A. I. and Forray, K. R. (1990) 'The role of multicultural education in Hungary: A research in Romology'. Paper presented at the Congress of the International Sociological Association, Madrid.

Henry, J. (1963) *Culture Against Man*. New York: Random House.

Hirsch, E. D. (1987) *Cultural Literacy: What Every American Needs to Know*. Boston: Houghton Mifflin.

Holland, D. and Quinn, N. (eds) (1987) *Cultural Models in Language and Thought*. Cambridge, UK: Cambridge University Press.

Hollinsworth, D. (1992) 'Cultural awareness training, racism awareness training or antiracism: Strategies for combating institutional racism'. *Journal of Intercultural Studies*, 13 (2), 37–52.

Hopkins, G.M. (1953) 'Pied Beauty'. In: W. H. Gardner (ed.) *Poems and Prose of Gerard Manley Hopkins*. Harmondsworth: Penguin.

Houser, N. O. (1996) 'Multicultural education for the dominant culture: Toward the development of a multicultural sense of self'. *Urban Education*, 31 (2), 125–148.

Jensen, A. R. (1969) 'How much can we boost IQ and scholastic achievement?' *Harvard Educational Review*, 39 (1), 1–123.

Junn, E. N., Morton, K. R. and Yee, I. (1995) 'The "gibberish" exercise: Facilitating empathetic multicultural awareness'. *Journal of Instructional Psychology*, 22 (4), 324–329.

Kalantzis, M. and Cope, B. (1989) 'Pluralism and equitability: Multicultural curriculum strategies for schools'. *Curriculum and Teaching*, 4 (1), 3–20.

Kalantzis, M. and Cope, B. (1990) *The Experience of Multicultural Education in Australia: Six Case Studies*. Wollongong, NSW: Centre for Multicultural Studies, University of Wollongong.

Kalantzis, M., Slade, D. and Cope, B. (1986) *The Language Question: The Maintenance of Languages Other than English*. Canberra: Department of Immigration and Ethnic Affairs.

Kalekin-Fishman, D. (in press) 'Knowledge, belief, and opinion: A sociologist looks at conceptual change'. In: W. Schnotz, M. Carretero and S. Vosniadou (eds) *New Perspectives on Conceptual Change*. London: Routledge.

Knapp, M. S. and Wolverton, S. (1995) 'Social class and schooling'. In: J. A. Banks and C. A. M. Banks (eds) *Handbook of Research on Multicultural Education*. New York: Macmillan, 548–569.

Krishnamurti, Bh. (1986) 'A fresh look at language in school education in India'. *International Journal of the Sociology of Language*, 62, 105–118.

Kroeber, A. and Kluckhohn, C. (1952) *Culture*. New York: Anchor Books.

Krugly-Smolska, E. (1996) 'Scientific culture, multiculturalism and the science classroom'. *Science and Education*, 5 (1), 21–29.

Luchtenberg, S. (1994) 'Perspectives on bilingual education in Germany'. *Journal of Intercultural Studies*, 15 (2), 73–84.

Luchtenberg, S. (1995a) 'The concept of the multicultural society as a basis for education and instruction: The Australian approach'. *Zeitschrift für Pädagogik*, 41 (6), 987–1006.

Luchtenberg, S. (1995b) 'Intercultural communicative competence: A challenge in multicultural and anti-racist education'. *European Journal of Intercultural Studies*, 6 (2), 12–23.

Luke, C. (1994) 'Feminist pedagogy and critical media literacy'. *Journal of Communication Inquiry*, 18 (2), 30–47.

Lunde, T. (1999) 'Citizens' Public Trust Treaty'. Document circulated on the Progressive Sociologists' Network (e-mail), Jan. 1.

Lustig, D. F. (1997) 'Of Kwanzaa, cinco de Mayo, and whispering: The need for intercultural education'. *Anthropology and Education Quarterly*, 28 (4), 574–592.

McCarthy, C. (1990) 'Multicultural approaches to racial inequality in the United States'. *Curriculum and Teaching*, 5 (1–2), 25–35.

McLaren, P. (1997) 'Unthinking whiteness, rethinking democracy: Or farewell to the blonde beast: Towards a revolutionary multiculturalism'. *Educational Foundations*, 11 (2), 5–39.

McLaren, P. and Welch, S. (1997) *Revolutionary Multiculturalism: Pedagogies of Dissent for the New Millennium*. Boulder, CO: Westview Press.

452

Macias, J. (1987) 'The hidden curriculum of Papago teachers: American Indian strategies for mitigating cultural discontinuity in early schooling'. In: G. and L. Spindler (eds) *Interpretive Ethnography of Education: At Home and Abroad*. Hillsdale, NJ: Lawrence Erlbaum Associates, 363–380.

Markou, G. (1994) 'Intercultural education in multicultural Greece'. *European Journal of Intercultural Studies*, 4 (3), 32–43.

Martin, O. and Williams-Dixon, R. (1994) 'Overcoming social distance barriers: Preservice teachers' perceptions of racial ethnic groups'. *Journal of Instructional Psychology*, 21 (1), 76–82.

Mathuna, L. M. and Singleton, D. (eds) (1984) *Language across Cultures*. Dublin, Ireland: St Patrick's College.

Mehan, H. (1979) *Learning Lessons*. Cambridge, MA: Harvard University Press.

Michael, S. O. (1997) 'Models of multiculturalism: Implications for the twenty-first century leaders'. *European Journal of Intercultural Studies*, 8 (3), 231–245.

Michigan State Department of Education (1990) *Michigan Global/International Education Guidelines*. Lansing, MI: State Department of Education.

Miller, L. P. and Tanner, L. A. (1995) 'Diversity and the new immigrants'. *Teachers College Record*, 96 (4), 671–680.

Minami, M. and Ovando, C. J. (1995) 'Language issues in multicultural contexts'. In: J. A. Banks and C. A. M. Banks (eds) *Handbook of Research on Multicultural Education*. New York: Macmillan, 427–444.

Mpofu, E. (1997) 'Children's social acceptance and academic achievement in Zimbabwean multicultural school settings'. *Journal of Genetic Psychology*, 158 (1), 5–24.

Murray, D. E. (ed.) (1992) *Diversity as Resource: Redefining Cultural Literacy*. Alexandria, VA: TESOL (Teachers of English to Speakers of Other Languages).

Murray, S. R. (1997) 'Identity show and tell: Constructing racial biographies in the classroom'. Paper presented at the Annual Meeting of the American Sociological Association.

O'Connor, S. (1991) *'I'm Not Indian Anymore': The Challenge of Providing Culturally Sensitive Services to American Indians*. Washington, D. C.: National Institute on Disability and Rehabilitation Research.

Ogbu, J. U. (1987) 'Variability in minority responses to schooling: Nonimmigrants vs. Immigrants'. In: G. and L. Spindler (eds) *Interpretive Ethnography of Education: At Home and Abroad*. Hillsdale, NJ: Lawrence Erlbaum Associates, 255–280.

Ogbu, J. U. (1995) 'Cultural problems in minority education: Their interpretations and consequences: Theoretical background'. *Urban Review*, 27 (3), 189–205.

Olneck, M. R. (1993) 'Terms of inclusion: Has multiculturalism redefined equality in American education?' *American Journal of Education*, 101 (3), 234–260.

Paribakht, T. (1987) 'Investigating the complexities of communication in a second language'. Paper presented at the 5th Nordic Conference of Applied Linguistics, Jyvaskyla, Finland, June.

Patrick, J. J. (1991) 'The civic culture of the United States and its challenges to civic educators'. Paper presented at an international conference on 'Western Democracy and Eastern Europe', Berlin, October.

Perotti, A. (1990a) *Action to Combat Intolerance and Xenophobia in the Activities of the Council of Europe's Council for Cultural Co-operation, 1969–1989*. Strasbourg: Council for Cultural Co-operation.

Perotti, A. (1990b) *The Programme of Experiments in Intercultural Education from 1986 to 1991: Final Educational Evaluation*. Strasbourg: Council for Cultural Co-operation.

Postiglione, G. A. (1998) 'State schooling and ethnicity in China: The rise or demise of multiculturalism'. Paper presented at the 34th Congress of the International Sociological Association, Montreal, July.

Ray, D. and Poonwassie, D. H. (eds) (1992) *Education and Cultural Differences: New Perspectives*. Garland Reference Library of Social Science, Vol. 594. Hamden, CT: Garland Publishing.

Reed, C. and Diez, M. (1989) 'Empowerment for teachers in multicultural schools: Inviting the teaching–learning exchange'. Paper presented at the 3rd National Forum of the Association of Independent Liberal Arts Colleges for Teacher Education, Indianapolis, Indiana, June. 9 pp.

Root, M. P. P. (ed.) (1996) *The Multiracial Experience: Racial Borders as the New Frontier*. Thousand Oaks, CA: Sage.

Rosaldo, R. (1994) 'Cultural citizenship and educational democracy'. *Cultural Anthropology*, 9 (3), 402–412.

Rumbaut, T. G. (1990) 'Immigrant students in California public schools: A summary of current knowledge'. Paper presented at the Annual Meeting of the American Sociological Association.

Salcido, R. M., Garcia, J. A., Cota, V. and Thomson, C. (1995) 'A cross-cultural training model for field education'. *Arete*, 20 (1), 26–36.

Sandhu, D. S. *et al.* (1991) 'Cross-cultural counseling and neurolinguistic mirroring: An exploration of empathy, trustworthiness, and positive interaction with Native American adolescents'. Paper presented at the Annual Meeting of the American Association for Counselling and Development, Baltimore, MD, March.

Sardo-Brown, D. and Hershey, M. (1995) 'A study of teachers' and students' multi-cultural attitudes before and after the use of an integrated multi-cultural lesson plan'. *Journal of Instructional Psychology*, 22 (3), 259–276.

Shore, B. (1991) 'Twice-born, once conceived: Meaning construction and cultural cognition'. *American Anthropology*, 93, 9–28.

Short, G. and Carrington, B. (1996) *Educational Review*, 48 (1), 65–77.

Shweder, R. and LeVine, R. (eds) (1984) *Culture Theory: Essays in Mind, Self and Emotion*. Cambridge, UK: Cambridge University Press.

Sileo, T. W., Sileo, A. P. and Prater, M. A. (1996) 'Parent and professional partnerships in special education: Multicultural considerations'. *Intervention in School and Clinic*, 31 (3), 145–153.

Simel, D. L. (1996) 'Exclusionary Christian civil religion for Jewish and Islamic students in Bavarian schools'. *Comparative Education Review*, 41 (1), 28–46.

Singh, B. R. (1997) 'What education for a changing multicultural, multiracial Europe?' *European Journal of Intercultural Studies*, 8 (3), 279–289.

Skutnabb-Kangas, T. and Phillipson, R. (1985) *Educational Strategies in Multilingual Contexts*. Roskilde, Denmark: ROLIG Papir No. 35.

Sleeter, C. N. (1996) 'Multicultural education as a social movement'. *Theory into Practice*, 35 (4), 239–247.

Smith, D. E. (1987) *The Everyday World as Problematic: A Feminist Sociology*. Boston: Northeastern University Press.

Smith, D. E. (1993) '"Literacy" and business: "Social problems" as social organisation'. In: J. A. Holstein and G. Miller (eds) *Reconsidering Social Constructivism: Debates in Social Problems*. New York: Aldine de Gruyter, 327–346.

Smith, D. G. (1995) Organisational implications of diversity in higher education. In: M. M. Chemers, S. Oskamp and M. A. Costanzo (eds) *Diversity in Organisations: New Perspectives for a Changing Workplace*. Thousand Oaks, CA: Sage, 220–244.

Smolicz, J. J. (1994) 'Multiculturalism, religion, and education'. *Education and Society*, 12 (1), 22–47.

Solomon, R. P. and Levine-Rasky, C. (1996) 'Transforming teacher education for an antiracism pedagogy'. *Canadian Review of Sociology and Anthropology*, 3 (3), 337–359.

Spindler, G. D. (1974) *Education and Cultural Process*. New York: Holt, Rinehart & Winston.

Srivastava, S. (1996) 'Song and dance? The performance of antiracist workshops'. *Canadian Review of Sociology and Anthropology*, 33 (3), 291–315.

Suina, J. H. and Smolkin, L. B. (1995) 'The multicultural worlds of Pueblo Indian children's celebrations'. *Journal of American Indian Education*, 34 (3), 18–27.

Troyna, B. (1985) 'The great divide: Policies and practices in multicultural education'. *British Journal of Sociology of Education*, 6 (2), 209–224.

Vold, E. B. (ed.) (1992) *Multicultural Education in Early Childhood Classrooms*. Washington, DC: National Education Association.

Wagenaar, T. C. and Subedi, J. (1996) 'Internationalising the curriculum: Study in Nepal'. *Teaching Sociology*, 24 (3), 272–283.

Wahlstrom, M. A. and Clarken, R. H. (1992) 'Preparing teachers for education that is multicultural and global'. Paper presented at the Annual Meeting of the American Educational Research Association, San Francisco, CA.

Wang, M. C., Oates, J. and Weischew, N. (1995) 'Effective school responses to student diversity in inner-city schools: A coordinated approach'. *Education and Urban Society*, 27 (4), 484–503.

Wax, M. L. (1995) 'The irrelevance of multiculturalism'. *Sociological Imagination*, 32 (2), 119–125.

Williamson, B. (1979) *Education, Social Structure, and Development*. London: Macmillan.

Willis, P. (1977) *Learning to Labour*. Aldershot, Hampshire: Saxon House.

Willis, P. (1978) *Profane Culture*, London: Routledge & Kegan Paul.

Wlodkowski, R. J. and Ginsberg, M. B. (1995) 'A framework for culturally responsive teaching'. *Educational Leadership*, 53 (1), 17–21.

Wolcott, H. (1982) 'The anthropology of learning'. *Anthropology and Education Quarterly*, 13 (2), 83–108.

Wolcott, H. (1987) 'On ethnographic intent'. In: G. and L. Spindler (eds) *Interpretive Ethnography of Education: At Home and Abroad*. Hillsdale, NJ: Lawrence Erlbaum Associates, 37–57.

Zeichner, K. M. (1991) 'Contradictions and tensions in the professionalization of teaching and the democratization of schools'. *Teachers College Record*, 92 (3), 363–379.

Zeichner, K. M. (1995) 'Preparing educators for cross-cultural teaching'. In: W. D. Hawley and A. W. Jackson (eds) *Toward a Common Destiny: Improving Race and Ethnic Relations in America*. San Francisco, CA: Jossey-Bass.

Ziglio, L. and Maniotti, P. (1995) 'The foreign presence and initiatives for intercultural education in Trento's compulsory school'. *Studi Emigrazione*, 32 (119), 416–456.

26

MULTICULTURALISM

One view from the United States of America

Susan L. Melnick

INTRODUCTION

Multiculturalism characterises most of the world's educational systems, in both industrialised countries and developing nations, at the beginning of the twenty-first century. While the particular circumstances of diversity and pluralism vary within and among national communities, policy-makers and practitioners have been searching for ways to educate the children and youth who have previously been unserved, underserved or ill-served by the schooling to which they should be entitled as members of the international community.

Given major demographic and political changes around the world during the latter part of the twentieth century, there has been an increasing demand for an egalitarian philosophy for schooling the world's children to foster independence and dignity (Mitchell and Salsbury, 1996), a moral imperative for the reform of education writ large. Within this context, the United States serves as a case for the thoughtful consideration of the prospects, possibilities and problems associated with meeting the moral imperative. The intent here is to use the USA for comparative rather than illustrative purposes, for it is a country that, despite more than a century's efforts, falls far short of accomplishing the egalitarian goals for a free, universal and compulsory educational system. As Altbach, Arnove, and Kelly pointed out,

> a common question posed is, 'What can the study of other countries contribute to improved practice in our country?' Comparison often has a chastening effect, for in studying education systems around the world we discover the limitations and possibilities for schooling to foster fundamental reforms in a society. At the same time, comparison has a humanizing effect in that we come to realize the common problems that virtually all societies and school systems confront.
>
> (1982, p. 4)

It is this ameliorative strain in comparative education that undergirds the use of one country as a case for addressing an international concern.

This chapter provides a brief contemporary context for multicultural education in the United States, a brief historical context of its roots, and an explication of selected definitions and conceptual frameworks. It then explores three vexing questions that make current efforts to define and refine multicultural education as a reform movement problematic. If the answer to the question 'Who should go to school?' is 'Everyone's children', we are then vexed by answers to the questions 'What should be taught?', 'How should teachers teach?' and 'How should teachers be prepared to teach?'.

Three prior caveats must be made. First, constraints of space necessitate selectivity of topics covered and resources cited, and readers are encouraged to explore the fuller texts in the reference list. Second, while multicultural education as a defined area of study has developed over more than 30 years, the 1990s witnessed the publication of a number of noteworthy texts, such as the *Handbook of Research on Multicultural Education* (Banks and McGee Banks, 1995), *Multicultural Education: An International Guide to Research, Policies, and Programs* (Mitchell and Salsbury, 1996) and *Common Sense about Uncommon Knowledge: The Knowledge Bases for Diversity* (Smith, 1998), that warrant readers' fuller consideration. Third, the bodies of scholarship of several individuals over time merit readers' attention. Among them are the multiculturalists James Banks, Christine Bennett, Geneva Gay, Donna Gollnick, Carl Grant, Asa Hilliard, Sonia Nieto, Valerie Ooka Pang, Christine Sleeter and Ana Maria Villegas. Related work includes that of curricular theorists Michael Apple, Henry Giroux, Madeleine Grumet, Peter McLaren, William Pinar and William Schubert; historians Lawrence Cremin and David Tyack; philosophers John Dewey and Jürgen Habermas; sociologists Basil Bernstein and Nel Noddings; the incomparable Paolo Freire; and accounts by and about practitioners like Jessica Siegel (Freedman, 1990), Deborah Meier, Vivian Paley, and the African American teachers captured by Gloria Ladson-Billings and Michele Foster, for example, who struggled to provide an equitable education for all children in their care. Finally, readers are referred to other sections of this volume, including, but not limited to, the chapters on curriculum, anti-racism and feminism.

SETTING THE STAGE

At the beginning of the new millennium, the United States is faced with an unprecedented demand for new teachers to teach an increasingly pluralistic student population in public schools. Out of 3.1 million teachers in the US (National Center for Education Statistics, 1996) it is estimated that more than 2.2 million new teachers will be needed in the first decade of the twenty-first century. Further estimates suggest that the student population will become nearly one-half students of color – native, migrant and immigrant – with an increasing number of white immigrant children from the former Soviet Union and Eastern Europe. While some US schools are culturally insular, those in large urban centres already exceed the projected diversity. In public schools in Boston, Massachusetts in 1999, for example, 75% of the students were African American or Latino, with 9% Asian and 16% white (*Boston Globe*, October 28, 1998). Among the students of color, 35.6% spoke a primary language other than English, including Cambodian, Laotian, Chinese, Haitian Creole, Somali, Cape Verdean, Portuguese, Spanish and Vietnamese. These conditions and projections have created a two-pronged demographic imperative. First, while students of color have long been part of the educational landscape in the US (Cremin, 1990; Tyack and Cuban, 1995), their success rates in schools have been significantly below those of white students overall (Diaz, 1992) and especially when racial, socio-economic status/social class and native language factors interact. Evidence of past failure has precipitated the need for what Perry and Fraser called a 'struggle for redefinition' of schooling as white mainstream, a system built on white, Protestant, male, middle-class values:

> The story of this country, its mythology as an open, democratic society, is daily experienced as unbelievable ... [when] students of color sometimes constitute up to 80 percent of the student population of a district and 90 to 100 percent of many individual classrooms, and where their lives, cultures, and traditions are at best marginalized and at worst ignored or denigrated. ... The perennial question for the children of color ... in this country is whether the rhetoric of democracy makes sense if schools are organized around the principle of White political and cultural hegemony.
>
> (1993, p. 9)

Second, with the overwhelming need for new teachers, there are simply insufficient numbers of prospective teachers of color – and inadequate attractions in teaching compared with other career options – to radically alter current patterns of school staffing practices. In the coming years, students in US public schools will become increasingly different in background from their teachers, who will be largely white, middle class, female, and monolingual speakers of English (Melnick and Zeichner, 1998). As Gay (1990) noted, the changing demographic trends have the potential to create a significant 'social distance' between students and teachers. While she argued that teachers need to be 'affiliated' – that is, not necessarily of color but connected to their students and committed to making schooling relevant to their personal lives – Gay worried that the social, cultural and experiential gaps between teachers and students will 'make achieving educational equality even more unlikely in the existing structure of schooling' (1990, p. 61).

As US educators and policy-makers became aware of the projected demographic changes in the early 1990s, there was an increasing momentum for education reform strategies in pursuit of a singular goal: high and rigorous standards for teaching and learning. Threaded through the public, professional, and political discourse was an explicit concern for educating all students to the higher levels of understanding and competence once reserved for the privileged few. Darling-Hammond, Wise and Klein explained it thus:

> This new mission for education requires substantially more knowledge and radically different skills for teachers. ... If all children are to be effectively taught, teachers must be prepared to address the substantial diversity in experiences children bring with them to school – the wide range of languages, cultures, exceptionalities, learning styles, talents, and intelligences that in turn requires an equally rich and varied repertoire of teaching strategies. In addition, teaching for universal learning demands a highly developed ability to discover what children know and can do, as well as how they think and how they learn, and to match learning and performance opportunities to the needs of individual children.
>
> (1997, p. 2)

Given these circumstances, there is a growing consensus in the USA that educational opportunities and experiences must recognise and be responsive to the backgrounds, needs, interests and aspirations of an increasingly diverse student body. While not universally advocated (see, for example, Schlesinger, 1998), efforts to define and refine the principles of multicultural education are regarded by many educators and policy-makers as one promising route to addressing the USA's primary educational dilemma.

MAPPING THE CONCEPTUAL TERRAIN: WHERE DID MULTICULTURAL EDUCATION COME FROM?

Although the roots of multicultural education are traced by some (e.g. Gay, 1995) to the work of John Dewey and nineteenth-century progressivism, the issues related to serving the needs of a culturally pluralistic student population were more implicit than explicit (Semmel, 1996). While Dewey did not specifically attend to race, ethnicity, social class and gender at that time, he argued in *Democracy and Education* (1916) that a society should want a literate and skilled citizenry, not for economic reasons, but because these traits are the cornerstone of a democracy, where intelligent and informed citizens take an active role in their community (Semmel, 1996). Through the early years of the ethnic studies movement (the 1920s roots of the 1960s and 1970s movement), the intergroup education movement (1940s), and social reconstructionism (1950s), the tensions between educational assimilation and pluralism became apparent (Olneck, 1995). These early efforts to promote and preserve ethnic-group identity and reduce prejudice and discrimination challenged the myth of the USA as a melting-pot, an image coined by dramatist Israel Zangwill (1909). Recognising the broader social reality of assimilation and resistance within and among groups over time, these efforts specifically addressed the concern that assimilation had worked against the educational attainment of generations of children (Daly and O'Dowd, 1992). The rendering of the landmark Supreme Court decision of *Brown* v. *Topeka Board of Education* in 1954 forced the tensions to the front and ordered the official dismantling of the US educational system of apartheid through the elimination of separate schools based upon race. Over the years, however, efforts to desegregate schools have not necessarily led to the integration of diverse children, either socially or academically.

With the advent of the Civil Rights movement in the 1960s, there was a growing public awareness of the profound inequality of access to knowledge, skills, higher education and social mobility for working-class and minority students. A plethora of federal legislation ensued, designed to ensure that none of the then 48 states deny equal opportunity to any person on the basis of race, ethnicity, gender, national origin or native language. Within the broader social scope of rights, educational opportunity was in the forefront, and state education departments began to require the infusion of multicultural concepts in texts and curricular materials (Condianni and Tipple, 1980, cited in Daly and O'Dowd, 1992). Ethnic pride became a growing movement, and the injustice of unequal educational outcomes for poor, minority and working-class students could no longer be ignored. Although poverty, political disenfranchisement, repression and racism continue to characterise the lives of many historically oppressed peoples in the USA at the beginning of the twenty-first century, the Civil Rights movement of the 1960s and resultant legislation began to change the operative definition of 'equality of educational opportunity'. What was implicit in Dewey's simply stated claim – 'What the best and wisest parent wants for his [sic] own child, that must the community want for all of its children' (Dewey, 1900) – became an explicit demand.

The immediate response to the demands in the 1960s and early 1970s was the inclusion of ethnic studies classes, first in higher education and then in public primary and secondary schools, and the development of instructional materials. The subsequent general failure of these efforts was attributed to the fact that they had only adjunct rather than integral status in the curriculum, lack of relevant cultural knowledge on the part of educators and lack of measurable academic gains for students of color. In this aftermath of the Civil Rights movement, some educators came to understand institutional racism and victim-blaming (Ogbu, 1990; Ryan, 1971) as obstacles to educational equity (Banks, 1988), and curriculum organisation, tracking, family–school relations and classroom and school practices and policies became targets of reform. At the same time, women and persons with disabilities also sought inclusion. Matters of sexual orientation soon followed. Unanswered demands for recognition of cultural values, preservation of native languages, and greater understanding of the varied cultural and gendered contributions to a pluralistic society paved the way for a broader educational reform that became multicultural education (Daly and O'Dowd, 1992).

WHAT IS MULTICULTURAL EDUCATION?

The simple answer to this question is that multicultural education has no single definition. As Gay (1995) pointed out, the 'kaleidoscope' of available definitions reflects several positions: the scholarly perspectives of such diverse disciplines as anthropology, sociology and psychology; policies of state and local education agencies; professional, subject-matter and accreditation organisations; and experience-based statements of school practitioners. Banks' definition is one of the most encompassing: 'Multicultural education is an idea, an educational reform movement, and a process whose major goal is to change the structure of educational institutions' (1993a, p. 7). (It should also be noted that multicultural education is a field of scholarly and empirical study, which is beyond the specific purview of this chapter for explication.) As an *idea*, multicultural education is a set of beliefs and explanations that recognises and values the importance of ethnic and cultural diversity in shaping lifestyles, social experiences, personal identities, and educational opportunities of individuals, groups, and nations (Gay, 1995). As a reform movement, it is a 'process of institutionalizing the philosophy of cultural pluralism within the education system' (Baptiste, 1979, p. 172, cited in Gay, 1995, p. 28). As a process, multicultural education is a way of thinking, a decision-making style, and a way of behaving in educational settings that is pervasive and ongoing (Banks, 1993a). For Grant (1978), who terms it 'education that is multicultural', it is a different approach to the entire educational enterprise in all its forms and functions.

For others, multicultural education is an interdisciplinary instructional programme that has several process goals. Suzuki's definition is illustrative: multicultural education is a 'program that provides multiple learning environments matching the academic, social, and linguistic needs of students' (Suzuki, 1984, p. 305, cited in Gay, 1995). Such a programme has, as Gay describes it, multiple purposes, among which are: (a) to develop basic academic skills for students from different race, sex, ethnic and social-class backgrounds; (b) to teach students to respect and appreciate their own and other cultural groups; (c) to overcome ethnocentric and prejudicial attitudes; (d) to understand the socio-historical, economic and psychological factors that have produced contemporary ethnic alienation and inequality; (e) to foster ability to analyse critically and make intelligent decisions about real-life ethnic, racial and cultural problems, and (f) to help students conceptualise and aspire to a vision of a more humane, just, free and equal society, and acquire the knowledge and skills necessary to achieve it (Gay, 1995, p. 29).

Arguably the most inclusive definition of the early 1990s was Nieto's:

> Multicultural education is a process of comprehensive school reform and basic education for all students. It challenges and rejects racism and other forms of discrimination in schools and society and accepts and affirms the pluralism (ethnic, racial, linguistic, religious, economic, and gender, among others) that students, their communities, and teachers represent. Multicultural education permeates the curriculum and instructional strategies used in schools, as well as the interactions among teachers, students, and parents, and the very way that schools conceptualize the nature of teaching and learning. Because it uses critical pedagogy as its underlying philosophy and focuses on knowledge, reflection, and action (praxis) as the basis for social change, multicultural education furthers the democratic principles of social justice.
>
> (1992, p. 208)

When transferred from the realm of scholarship to state education-department policy designed to influence school and classroom practice, definitions tended to vary in their attention to idea, process, or programme. The following examples cited by Gollnick (1995, p. 55) suggest the range:

- The study of the meaning of culture, and relationship and influences between culture and education, with specific study of teaching, administration and effectiveness of schooling as they relate to multicultural school populations (Alaska, 1991).
- Interdisciplinary, cross-curricular education which prepares students to live, learn and work together to achieve common goals in a culturally diverse world. It does this by (a) enabling all students to be aware of and affirmed in their own cultural roots; (b) allowing all students to understand and value diversity; fostering appreciation, respect and understanding for persons of different backgrounds; and (c) preparing students to live fruitful lives in an increasingly global society with shifting and permeable borders (Kentucky, 1992).
- An interdisciplinary process rather than single program or series of activities. Concepts embraced by cultural pluralism, ethnic and intercultural studies and intergroup and inter-personal relations are included in this process. . . . The basic aim is to help students to accept themselves and other persons as having dignity and worth (Washington, 1992).
- Education that is multicultural is a continuous, integrated multiethnic, multidisciplinary process for educating all students about diversity and commonality. Diversity factors include but are not limited to race, ethnicity, region, religion, gender, language, socio-economic status, age and persons with disabilities (Maryland, 1993).

In reviewing a number of state policies, however, Gollnick and Chinn (1994) failed to find any definitions that matched their proposed goals, which approach Nieto's inclusive definition:

> All teaching should be multicultural and all classrooms should be models of democracy and equity. To do this requires that educators (1) place the student at the center of the teaching and learning process; (2) promote human rights and respect for cultural differences; (3) believe that all students can learn; (4) acknowledge and build on the life histories and experiences of students' microcul-tural memberships; (5) critically analyze oppression and power relationships to understand racism, sexism, classism, and discrimination against the disabled, young, and aged; (6) critique society in the interest of social justice and equality; and (7) participate in collective social action to ensure a democratic society.
>
> (cited in Gollnick, 1995, p. 55)

Given the rhetorical purpose of defining terminology and the variations among definitions, these definitions do not provide specific details for the design and implementation of multicultural education efforts. None the less, they are important in mapping the terrain to include curricular, instructional, administrative and environmental domains for school reform (Gay, 1995). Gay notes further that there is

> a high degree of consensus among multiculturalists on the major principles, concepts, concerns, and directions for changing educational systems to make them more representative of and responsive to the cultural pluralism in the United States and the world. Differences are located more in semantics, points of emphasis, and constituent-group orientations than in the substantive content of what constitutes the core and essence of multicultural education. . . . [Her analysis] demonstrates how each [definition for egalitarian educational initiatives] is a variation on the common consensus of (a) reforming education for the benefit of students who are underserved by schools, (b) being more inclusive and comprehensive by teaching the whole child, and (c) aligning schooling with the promises of democratic ideas.
>
> (1995, p. 40)

The need for specific details leads one to explore a sample of typologies, constructs, or conceptual frameworks related to multicultural education. Four had the greatest currency over the latter part of the twentieth century and, for many educators, continue to frame the work of the future: James Banks' Dimensions of Multicultural Education (1995); Carl Grant and Christine Sleeter's Five Approaches to Race, Class, and Gender (1988/1999); Banks' Approaches for the Integration of Multicultural Content (1993b); and Cornbleth and Waugh's Additive, Revisionist, and Transformative Multiculturalism (1995). They are described here in detail to show how far multicultural education has developed – or not developed.

The first conceptual organiser, Banks' Dimensions of Multicultural Education (1995), is a five-pronged typology. The first dimension, 'content integration', considers the extent to which teachers use examples, data and information from a variety of cultures and groups to illustrate key concepts, principles, generalisations and theories in their subject area or discipline. Although social studies education is Banks' field, he argued that all subject matters lend themselves to such integration.

The second dimension, 'knowledge construction', describes the procedures by which social, behavioural and natural scientists create knowledge and the manner in which the implicit cultural assumptions, frames of reference, perspectives and biases within a discipline influence the ways that knowledge is constructed within it. Banks argued that when this process is implemented in the classroom, teachers help students to understand how knowledge is created and how it is influenced by the racial, ethnic and social-class positions of individuals and groups.

The third dimension, 'prejudice reduction', describes the characteristics of children's racial attitudes and suggests strategies that can be used to help students develop more democratic attitudes and values. The fourth dimension, 'equity pedagogy', refers to teachers' use of techniques and methods that facilitate the academic achievement of students from diverse racial, ethnic and social-class groups.

The fifth dimension, 'empowering school culture', describes the process of restructuring the culture and organisation of the school so that students from diverse racial, ethnic and social-class groups will experience educational equality and cultural empowerment. Banks includes such aspects as grouping practices, labelling practices, the social climate of the school and staff expectations for student achievement.

In summarising his typology, Banks notes that the dimensions are 'conceptually distinct but interrelated and overlapping, rather than mutually exclusive. Consequently, some cases can be described only by using several of the categories' (1995, p. 5).

The second conceptual organiser, Sleeter and Grant's *Making Choices for Multicultural Education* (1988/1999), expands on earlier work by Gibson (1976) and Pratte (1983), whose efforts were seen as limited to race, ignoring social class and gender, and focused on cultural diversity more than social inequality (Sleeter and Grant, 1999, pp. 30–31). Drawing on their own work with novice and experienced teachers and extensive reviews of the multicultural education literature, Sleeter and Grant constructed a typology of five approaches found in use by educators in the latter part of the twentieth century.

The first approach, 'Teaching the exceptional and culturally different', aims to help students of color, low-income students and/or special education students achieve in society as it currently exists. This approach assumes that schooling in the USA provides opportunities for all students but that some require bridges between their backgrounds and the schools to help them achieve (Sleeter, 1992). Such bridges include the use of instructional strategies that build on students' learning styles, culturally relevant materials, use of students' native language to teach academic content and Standard American English, or various compensatory programmes to address students' perceived deficiencies. As Sleeter noted,

> Educators who favor this approach advocate changes in schooling that are mainly or solely for members of a particular group, such as students from the inner city, bilingual students, mainstreamed special education students, and immigrant students. . . . Advocates generally support much of the dominant discourse about the United States – that it is a free country with limitless opportunity, that its history is one of progress, and that only a few changes are needed to extend the American Dream to everyone.
>
> (1992, p. 53)

The second approach, 'Human Relations', attempts to foster positive interpersonal relationships among members of diverse groups in the classroom and to strengthen each student's self-concept. This approach assumes that US society at large is fair and open (Sleeter, 1992) and that disharmony among students is a result of individual and cultural misunderstanding. Concerned with how students feel about and treat each other, teachers advocating this approach focus on lessons about stereotyping, individual differences and similarities, and diverse contributions to society and are inclined to use co-operative learning to promote student relationships. As Sleeter noted,

> Much of what many schools do in the name of multicultural education is [this approach], such as ethnic fairs or special celebrations to feature a particular group. Usually the main purpose of such celebrations is affective . . . and seems to fit particularly well with Euro-Americans' conception of their own ethnicity.
>
> (1992, p. 54)

While the first two approaches are less critical of inequality in the USA, the next three highlight the degree to which inequity is embedded in social institutions. The third approach, 'Single-group studies', focuses teaching units on particular groups, such as ethnic studies, labour studies, women's studies or disability studies. The approach seeks to raise consciousness about a group by not only teaching its history, culture and contributions, but also exposing how it has been oppressed by the dominant group in society. While most educators are insufficiently knowledgeable about the enormous amount of information available on previously marginalised groups, Sleeter (1992) suggests that they can come to understand the degree to which other groups' perspectives challenge much of what they have taken for granted about the broader society.

The fourth approach, the 'multicultural' approach, aims to reconstruct the entire educational process to promote equality and cultural pluralism. Curriculum content is reorganised around perspectives and knowledge of diverse social groups, and tracking and ability grouping are challenged as mechanisms for institutionalising differential achievement and learning opportunity. This approach advocates a diverse teaching force, building on students' learning styles, critical thinking, and fostering native-language maintenance for non-native English speakers and multilingual acquisition for all students. Sleeter (1992) notes that this approach transforms everything in the school programme to reflect diversity and uphold equality.

The final approach, the 'multicultural and social reconstructionist' approach, builds on the third and fourth approaches and aims to teach students to analyse inequality and oppression in society and to help them develop skills for social action. The approach begins with contemporary social justice issues that cut across diverse groups and uses disciplinary knowledge to explore issues and create ways of effecting change. Grant and Sleeter liken this approach to Freire's notion of 'conscientization', where 'people learn to question society, see through versions of "truth" that teach people to accept unfairness and inhumanity, and become empowered to envision, define and work towards a more humane society' (1999, p. 109). While they argue the merits – and inadequacies – of all five approaches, Grant and Sleeter advocate the Multicultural and Social Reconstructionist approach, despite the inherent difficulties in pursuing such sweeping change in schools.

Two conceptual organisers, while more directly related to curricular reform in the service of multicultural education and understandably less sweeping than the Banks or Grant and Sleeter typologies, highlight the advantages and disadvantages of incremental change. The first, Approaches to the Integration of Multicultural Content – taken from Banks' approaches to cultural curriculum reform (1993b) – illustrates ways to integrate multicultural content into the curriculum. The 'contributions' approach showcases heroes, cultural components, holidays and other discrete elements related to ethnic groups on special occasions or celebrations but rarely during the rest of the year. Examples cited in Redman (1999) include celebrating famous Mexican Americans during the week of Cinco de Mayo (May 5); African American contributions during February (African American History Month in the USA); or studying ethnic foods with little attention paid to the cultures from which the foods come. The advantages include expedient ways for cultural integration and visibility of ethnic group heroes alongside mainstream counterparts. The disadvantages include promoting superficial understanding of ethnic cultures and reinforcing stereotypes and misconceptions (Redman, 1999, p. 155).

The 'additive' approach consists of the addition of content, concepts, themes and perspectives without changing curricular structures. The approach ranges from adding an ethnic studies course as an elective, leaving the core curriculum intact, to adding a book (e.g. by an African American author to a literature course) or an event (e.g. Japanese American internment during World War II to a history course) without the inclusion of necessary background knowledge or of the study of African Americans or Japanese Americans elsewhere in the curriculum (Redman, 1999, p. 155). While Redman notes that this approach makes it possible to add ethnic content to the existing curriculum structure, it tends to reinforce the marginal perspective of ethnic history and culture in the USA, promotes teaching students about ethnic groups from Anglocentric and Eurocentric perspectives, and fails to help students understand how the dominant and ethnic cultures are interconnected (ibid.).

In the 'transformation' approach, the basic goals, structure and nature of the curriculum are changed to enable students to view concepts, events, issues, problems and themes from the perspectives of diverse groups. An example of the approach is a unit on twentieth-century US literature which includes works by William Faulkner, Joyce Carol Oates, Langston Hughes, N. Scott Momoday, Saul Bellow, Maxine Hong Kingston, Rudolfo A. Anaya and Piri Thomas. Redman lists several advantages: it 'enables students to understand the complex ways in which diverse racial and cultural groups participated in the formation of US society and culture; helps reduce racial and ethnic encapsulation; enables diverse . . . groups to see their cultures, ethos, and perspectives in the school curriculum; [and] gives students a balanced view of the nature and development of US culture and society' (1999, p. 156). At the same time, Redman notes disadvantages, including the substantial curriculum revision, in-service training and identification and development of diverse materials required for implementation of this approach.

In the 'social action' approach, students identify important social problems and issues, gather pertinent data, clarify their values on the issues, make decisions and take reflective actions to help resolve the issue or problem. One example offered by Redman (1999) describes a class studying the treatment of ethnic groups in a local newspaper and writing a letter to the publisher suggesting ways to improve the treatment of ethnic groups in the paper. This approach helps students improve critical thinking, analytic, decision-making and social action skills and helps them develop a sense of political efficacy. The disadvantages Redman notes include the labour-intensity of teacher planning and lesson development, the potential difficulties with controversy in the community, and the reality that 'students may be able to take few meaningful actions that contribute to the resolution of the social issues or problem' (1999, p. 156).

The second curricular organising scheme is Cornbleth and Waugh's (1995) Additive, Revisionist, and Transformative Multiculturalism. While it is similar to Banks' in some ways, Cornbleth and Waugh offer their scheme for the selection and organisation of knowledge in history and social studies specifically. It is included here because it highlights the different conceptual and political–ideological positions with potentially different social consequences with which multiculturalists grapple.

'Additive multiculturalism' is similar to Banks' and Redman's definitions and illustrations of the contributions and additive approaches. Cornbleth and Waugh describe the limitations of its two forms – separate studies, and heroes and contributions: they 'maintain the conventional European-dominant historical narrative by "mentioning" only those "other" individuals and events that are deemed a proper fit; . . . heroes and contributions of whatever color, class, culture, or gender are selected because – by dominant or mainstream cultural standards – they are role models. They sustain rather than challenge the status quo; . . . and the individualist bias of [this approach] does not reach or reveal the institutional or structural arrangements in US and other societies that perpetuate inequity and relationships of domination-subordination' (1995, p. 36). At best, additive multiculturalism selectively enlarges the history conveyed within the existing curricular framework (p. 38).

'Revisionist multiculturalism' offers what Cornbleth and Waugh call a change in viewpoint, a different focus, or different themes for the story of America, its history, and its peoples. Similar to Banks' transformation approach representing the perspectives of diverse peoples, revisionist multiculturalism tells revised stories, but there are attendant limitations. As Cornbleth and Waugh note, 'While more inclusive than the older syntheses, they usually operate from a single interpretive framework or story line, . . . provid[ing] coherence at the expense of the diversity of the peoples and cultures whose stories are being told' (1995, p. 37). An alternative revisionist approach, multiple-perspectives, would sacrifice the single storyline and accommodate and highlight diversity, making the interests of various individuals and groups explicit rather than giving the appearance of being interest-free. Cornbleth and Waugh argue that this approach would present participants' voices directly and avoid a common limitation: 'Authorial interpretation of others increases the possibility of misrepresentation while implying that they are incapable of speaking for themselves' (ibid.).

Despite the appeal of this approach, there is no body of work of this sort available in the USA. Texts developed in the late 1990s commonly include such features as 'opposing viewpoints', but they are 'featured' outside the main text or included in supplementary readings and other materials (Cornbleth and Waugh, 1995, pp. 37–38). As with the additive approach, careful selection typically yields safe perspectives, either from the distant past or moderate in view or widely accepted, thereby offending few and not disrupting the *status quo*. At best, this approach alters and extends the narrative historical framework.

Unlike the two previous approaches, 'transformative multiculturalism' seeks to remake the framework by redefining history. One example of this approach is reciprocal history, which allows for racial/ethnic/cultural diversity and interconnections among diverse individuals and groups. According to Wynter, such history is not intended to simply round out standard, two-dimensional US history but to level its race- and class-biased hierarchy and reconceive it as a 'community of communities based on reciprocal recognition' (1992, p. 35, cited in Cornbleth and Waugh, 1995, pp. 38–39). According to Morrison, this approach is designed to give attention to how an Africanist presence, for example, has shaped both white America and American identity more generally, as well as how white America has constructed and portrayed Africanism and African Americans. While studies of racism typically examine its consequences for victims, ignoring racism's impact on its perpetrators, Morrison proposed to 'examine the impact of notions of racial hierarchy, racial exclusion, and racial vulnerability and availability on nonblacks who held, resisted, explored, or altered those notions. The scholarship that looks into the mind, imagination, and behavior of slaves is valuable. But equally valuable is a serious intellectual effort to see what racial ideology does to the mind, imagination, and behavior of masters' (Morrison, 1992, pp. 11–2, cited in Cornbleth and Waugh, 1995, p. 39). Reciprocal history argues that the histories of blacks and whites in the USA were inextricably connected and requires a reinterpretation of the ways in which various groups have influenced and learned from each other. For Cornbleth and Waugh, transformative multiculturalism demands the selection, organisation and use of knowledge that illustrates interconnections and mutual influences among diverse individuals and groups – a far cry from mere inclusion in or revision of the curriculum

(Cornbleth and Waugh, 1995, p. 40). Like the other higher order approaches, however, there are no comprehensive models to use as guidelines for curricular development.

Given the foregoing possibilities and problems associated with the conceptual terrain, a consideration of the prospects for the success of multicultural education in the new millennium requires attention to three vexing questions.

WHAT SHOULD BE TAUGHT TO A DIVERSE STUDENT BODY IN PUBLIC SCHOOLS?

Throughout the twentieth century, educators in the USA were vexed by the question of what should be taught. For curricular theorists, the debates raged across the traditionalist (e.g. Bobbitt, Tyler), conceptual empiricist (e.g. Popham, Gagne, Bruner), and reconceptualist (e.g. Giroux, McLaren, Pinar) boundaries. For philosophers and sociologists, the question was related to the multiple purposes of schooling. For policy-makers, it was both a political and economic question for a mandated educational system for its citizens and a competitive workforce for the global economy. For educators, the dilemma was closer to the classroom, focusing on accommodating community desires and deciding what was worthwhile content to teach children and adolescents. At the beginning of the twenty-first century, it is still unfinished business, a question with multiple parameters for the many stakeholders. For multicultural education specifically, it has three critical dimensions within this broader social context. First, what should be included in the curriculum, how should it be integrated, and where should it be located? (Banks, 1995, p. 5). Given the inherent inadequacies and difficulties in the conceptual organisers, questions of inclusion, integration, and location cannot be separated from more fundamental questions about the curricular demands of providing challenging learning opportunities for deep understanding for all students.

Second, what kinds of knowledge are most valid? Given the developments related to social constructivism in the 1980s and 1990s, the commitments to teaching for understanding (Cohen *et al.*, 1993) and the pursuit of high and rigorous standards for all students, the validity of Eurocentric canons, mainstream academic knowledge and school knowledge has been seriously challenged. Most curricular practice at the beginning of the millennium, however, is modal, and most knowledge, despite these developments, focuses on the transmission of the established canon with a small measure of the contributions and additive approaches as described by Banks (1993b). For multicultural education and critical theory, personal and cultural knowledge and multiple ways of knowing (e.g. Belenky *et al.*, 1986) show incontrovertibly that knowledge is neither objective nor neutral nor the exclusive domain of one social group, reflecting instead varying ideologies, human interests, values and perspectives (Habermas, 1971). A multicultural curriculum requires content and learning experiences that help students come to understand how knowledge is constructed in diverse ways, how particular human interests are reflected, and how to construct their own interpretations of reality (Banks, 1995, p. 12). Such a curriculum requires opportunities for students to actively construct knowledge through engagement in authentic tasks and problems, both disciplinary and social.

Third, what should be the form, content and processes of a curriculum that affords all

467

students opportunities to pursue equitable life chances and first-class citizenship in a multi-cultural, multiracial democracy? Given the *de facto* segregation that exists in many areas of the USA and the constitutional independence of the fifty state educational systems, multi-cultural curricular opportunities must be both responsive to local community needs and constrained and informed by national goals for educating all students (Perry and Fraser, 1993, p. 17). What this requires is making a conscious choice to embrace the egalitarian purpose of schooling, locally and nationally, and to invest the necessary resources, human and material, to develop the kinds of curricular and instructional materials and learning opportunities needed to finally address the egalitarian purpose.

HOW SHOULD TEACHERS TEACH?

Theoretical and conceptual developments of the late twentieth century, such as constructivism and teaching for understanding, demand a vast departure from modal practice which has historically characterised teaching in US schools (Cuban, 1984). To these ends, professional associations like the National Council of Teachers of Mathematics and federal agencies like the National Science Foundation have supported the development of curricular and instructional materials and extensive guidelines for effecting change in teaching practice. State Departments of Education have developed policies, standards, frameworks and curricular experiences for classroom implementation, and local school districts have invested in varying kinds of professional development for experienced teachers and mentoring for novices (See Chapter 42 by Feiman-Nemser and Norman) to meet the national guidelines and state and local mandates. In virtually every case, the diversity of the student body is mentioned prominently in the rationale sections of documents resulting from these efforts, and teachers are enjoined to do the right things to enhance educational opportunities and outcomes for diverse students. As Gay notes, however, the claims for making schooling more relevant, representational, and effective for diverse students are made without sufficient explanation for making the claims 'practically operational' (1995, p. 40). In her view, the lack of detail limits the potential for making teaching practice responsive to diverse students and fosters the use of contributions and additive approaches that lead to misinterpretations and distortions about what diverse students need to know and be able to do and how they might learn these things. The long history of inequality of opportunity for diverse students, and the extent to which teachers are directly implicated, suggests that educational practitioners need help in specifying the action or behavioural dimensions of the benchmark principles of multicultural education – child-centredness, social consciousness and civic responsibility, revisionist scholarship, educational equity and social reconstruction – before they can act responsibly upon them (Gay, 1995; Nieto, 1992).

If one were to combine the fundamental tenets of constructivism and multicultural education in teaching practice, what might it become? One possibility is Freire's notion of critical pedagogy. Concerned about the contradictions in the relations between teachers and students, Freire distinguished among three types of pedagogy: traditional, uncritically idealistic and critical. Traditional pedagogy assumes that the teacher is the knower and the learner is presumed to not know. The teacher, then, must transfer knowledge to the learner, who in turn 'receives' it. Freire viewed this pedagogy as an 'authoritarian, manipulative, "banking" pedagogy, which negates the possibility of democracy and distorts the lived experiences of the learners who are silenced and denied the opportunity to be authors of their own histories' (Freire *et al.*, 1997, p. xv). Uncritical idealist pedagogy celebrates the spontaneous acquisition of critical insight but denies that the learner may also internalise the ready-made categories of domination and subordination. Freire considered this kind of pedagogy a romanticisation of the child, which often led to the miseducation of students and abdication of responsibility on the part of teachers. He insisted that 'The teacher's authority ... is indispensable to the development of the learner's freedom. What may frustrate the process is the abuse of authority by the teacher, which makes him or her authoritarian, or the emptying of authority, which leads to permissiveness' (Freire, 1996, p. 163, cited in Freire *et al.*, 1997). In *Pedagogy of Hope* (1995), he argued for a pedagogy that is characterised by 'democratic substance' (Freire, 1995, p. 113). For Freire, this meant that critical pedagogy was practised by an educator who respects the 'educand' and is prepared to intervene, to dialogue, to offer his or her skills and insights, but never through the banking approach. As Freire *et al.* describe it,

> The term 'educand' challenges the objectification of the student as the passive receiver of the lessons provided by the teacher. The educand occupies the position of agent, of cognizing subject. As such the learner is not subordinate to the teacher ... but a participant in a dialogic exploration toward knowing and understanding. ... [Critical pedagogy] reveals, unveils, and challenges, by respecting the educands as subjects who can transform present realities and 'write' their future into existence.
>
> (1997, pp. xv–xvi)

Freire's notion of critical pedagogy demands a fundamental change in the relationships between teachers and students and a restructuring of schools as social institutions to support such thorough change. Teacher recognition of the importance of 'voice' (e.g. Majors, 1998; Nieto, 1992) and the responsible sharing of power with students (Kreisburg, 1992) are two building blocks towards achieving a more democratic form of education in the twenty-first century. Another is the enactment of Gutmann's (1987) principles of 'non-discrimination' and 'nonrepression' in classroom and schooling interactions. Two more are the principles of 'teaching to transgress' (hooks, 1994) and 'teaching against the grain' (Cochran-Smith, 1991). But without a radical shift in the definition of student agency, educators will never reach the transformative goals of multicultural education. Given most current views of students and their 'place', inside and outside schools, it is not surprising that there are no extant models demonstrating that curricular and instructional transformation are indeed possible.

HOW SHOULD TEACHERS BE PREPARED TO TEACH?

Preparing teachers for the twenty-first century requires a resolution to the problems that have plagued teacher education in the USA since the Civil Rights movement in the late 1960s. Smith, for example, concluded in 1969 that (1) teachers were unfamiliar with the backgrounds of their students and the communities where they lived; (2) teacher education programmes ordinarily did little to sensitise teachers to their own prejudices and values; and (3) teachers lacked the ability to perform effectively in the classroom in the service of all of their students. Smith's call for a major overhaul of teacher education programmes with respect to diversity and equity issues echoes into the new millennium. Despite state certification requirements to promote an understanding of diversity, the standards of the National Council for the Accreditation of Teacher Education for programme offerings, and teacher education guidelines from professional organisations like the American Association of Colleges for Teacher Education, most teacher education programmes acknowledge in principle the importance of pluralistic preparation, but in practice are best characterised as monocultural (Goodlad, 1990). Such programmes perpetuate the kinds of teaching practices which have historically benefited middle-class white students but have largely failed to provide quality instruction for poor and ethnic and linguistic minority students. Teacher candidates themselves, for the most part, come to teacher education with limited direct interracial and intercultural experience, with erroneous assumptions about diverse youngsters, and with limited expectations for the success of all learners (Melnick and Zeichner, 1998). They generally seek to avoid teaching in schools serving diverse students where the need is the greatest and the work is the most demanding (Grant, 1993; Zeichner and Hoeft, 1996). As Ladson-Billings pointed out, 'Their services are most needed in low-income schools, whose students come from races, cultures, and language-groups for whom these new teachers feel unprepared' (1990, p. 25).

The feelings of unpreparedness can be traced to two possible causes. First, most pre-service teacher candidates who will be expected to meet the demographic and moral imperatives have had little, if any, transformative multicultural education themselves. In addition, as O'Donnell noted,

> [While] the Civil Rights movement . . . may have been experienced by many of these students' parents, siblings, and relatives, . . . many [of these students] began their adolescence during the 1980s – an era that ushered in a period of intolerance for dialogue about the United States and its culpability in propagating domestic and international violence as well as rekindling an ethos of individualism, competitiveness, and greed. . . . [O]ur students have been privy to an onslaught of criticism addressed towards multiculturalism, pluralism, and the politics of difference (e.g. Bloom, 1987; D'Souza, 1991; Hirsch, 1987), as well as [having] witness[ed] the dismantling and demonization of hard-won civil rights initiatives such as affirmative action.
>
> (1998, p. 58)

As a teacher-educator, O'Donnell describes the challenges in teaching such students about race and racism and documents responses which range from denial to guilt to outrage. In his view, 'It is precisely this range of responses that creates and enables the possibility for transformation. It's the divergence of perspectives and lived experiences encountered within a dialogical framework that permits students the possibility to question themselves and their society' (ibid., p. 59). As Cochran-Smith notes, however, learning to teach diverse students requires more than confronting students' views about race. Prospective teachers must come to understand that '[teaching diverse students] is a matter of the knowledge, interpretive frameworks, and political commitments that guide and are guided by teachers' practices, social relationships, and questions about the immediacy of classroom life and larger issues of curriculum, instruction, and the purposes of schooling' (1997, pp. 29–30).

The second possible cause for feelings of unpreparedness can be traced to the faculty who have responsibility for preparing new teachers. The problem is that most teacher-educators are not like O'Donnell but like their students. They are limited in cross-cultural experiences and understandings, and they are overwhelmingly white, monolingual speakers of English, and culturally encapsulated (Ducharme and Agne, 1989; Villegas, 1993). Despite rhetoric to the contrary, efforts to reform US teacher education to address diversity is severely hampered by the cultural insularity of the bulk of the education professoriate (Melnick and Zeichner, 1997). Without concerted professional development in higher education, the faculty will simply be unable to help prospective teachers acquire the knowledge, skills and dispositions needed to teach diverse students.

In addition to the limitations posed by faculty inadequacies, there is also a general lack of broad institutional commitment to diversity in the higher education environments that prepare teachers. The degree of institutional commitment to diversity is evidenced in such things as an institution's hiring practices, student recruitment and admission policies and curricular offerings. Making issues of diversity central to the intellectual life of the broader institution legitimises efforts within teacher education programmes. Given the current makeup of teacher education faculty in the more than 1,200 institutions that prepare teachers in the USA, and the concerns about higher education reform in a time of diminishing resources and competing priorities, the prospects for widespread and immediate change are unlikely – without radical intervention.

In a five-year study of three teacher-education programmes that were considered exemplary in their attention to diversity issues, Melnick and Zeichner (1998) came to understand the problem as three-dimensional – one of selection of candidates, socialisation through curriculum and instruction, and institutional environment. Despite several promising strategies and the hard work of particular individuals for each of the dimensions of the problem (see Melnick and Zeichner, 1997; Zeichner, 1993; Zeichner and Hoeft, 1996), they concluded that there was little empirical evidence of widespread long-term success as a result of any of the approaches they uncovered. While some informants in their study reported longitudinal impact of their preparation on their teaching of diverse students, most evidence available is anecdotal. It is a conclusion that echoes the absence of models for implementing transformative multicultural education. Melnick and Zeichner (1998) noted that were they able to find confirming evidence of the success of approaches addressing the three-dimensional problem,

> There is still an underlying problem that demands redress . . . there is a profound separation in [the USA] that perpetuates the inequalities that shame this nation. Schools are not the sole reason why such inequities exist, but the failure to provide quality education for all students signifies a crisis that is intolerable in a democratic society. The issue of social justice is relevant not only for pluralistic settings for all areas of our country, for historic inequities affect – and diminish – us all, regardless of our 'neighborhood.' For teacher educators, the social crisis clearly means shouldering the responsibility for preparing teachers to teach diverse students in ways that we have not yet done. What will compel us to assume our responsibility?
>
> (1998, p. 93)

Any satisfactory answer to their question requires the same answers as the two prior questions: making conscious choices to educate teachers to teach a pluralistic student population; radically revising the curricular content and learning opportunities in teacher education; and practising a critical pedagogy in their work with novice and veteran teachers. For many teacher-educators in the early twenty-first century, these answers call for human behaviour that embraces Giroux's sense of the 'language of possibility', not an easy task in traditional academic settings nor within the political climate in the USA, but clearly an essential one.

UNFINISHED BUSINESS OR INTRACTABLE BARRIERS?

In the forethought to *The Souls of Black Folk* (1903), W.E.B. DuBois wrote:

> Herein lie buried many things which if read with patience may show the strange meaning of being black here in the dawning of the Twentieth Century. This meaning is not without interest to you, Gentle Reader; for the problem of the Twentieth Century is the problem of the color-line.
>
> (1903, p. 1)

If he were writing at the beginning of the new millennium, DuBois would say the same thing. While issues of culture, ethnicity, class, gender, language, disability, region, religion and sexual orientation are now prominent dimensions of the discourse, race, alone and in interaction with one or more of these dimensions, is still the most intractable barrier to educational access and equality in the USA. In whatever form(s) it may take, multicultural education for the twenty-first century is, in the end, a matter of intention and commitment. If we can develop technology that is arguably more intelligent than human beings, can we eradicate racism and solve the problem of educational inequality? Many of the approaches and examples described above hold promise for promoting more equitable and accessible learning opportunities for all children in the USA. In their current, underdeveloped form, however, they are in danger of being considered politically naïve or utopian by the unpersuaded (Semmel, 1996). For those traditionalists who desire to maintain their supremacy, they are considered dangerous and wrong, the route to 'disuniting' the country (Schlesinger, 1998). For those willing to take the challenge, however, the approaches demand an immediate explication and implementation and a willingness to continue to try until it is 'right' to answer the questions that vex a so-called democratic nation. As Tyack and Cuban noted:

> What is missing . . . is a generous vision of cultural democracy that builds on both difference and similarity in a pluralistic society. How can one go beyond the self-interest either of individuals or of separate groups in a nation where people are very unequal in wealth, power and prestige and in which racism is still rampant? How can schools become, as in John Dewey's vision, microcosms of a just, future society?
>
> (1995, p. 29)

The challenge is clear, to create educational reform that is truly responsive and educative for everyone's children, but it will be difficult to achieve without broader social reform to solve the ills of a society that are beyond the purview of the educational system. Within schooling, the challenge is to have the courage and conviction to act on a deep understanding of what Audre Lorde meant when she said, 'The master's tools will never dismantle the master's house' (1981, p. 99).

REFERENCES

Altbach, P.G., Arnove, R.F. and Kelly, G.P. (1982) *Comparative Education*. New York: Macmillan.

Banks, J.A. (1988) 'Ethnicity, class, cognitive, and motivational styles: research and teaching implications'. *Journal of Negro Education*, 57, 452–466.

Banks, J.A. (1993a) 'Multicultural education: characteristics and goals'. In Banks, J.A. and McGee Banks, C.A. (eds) *Multicultural Education: Issues and Perspectives*, pp. 2–26.

Banks, J.A. (1993b) 'Approaches to cultural curriculum reform'. In Banks, J.A. and McGee Banks, C.A. (eds) *Multicultural Education: Issues and Perspectives*, pp. 229–250.

Banks, J.A. (1995) 'Multicultural education: historical development, dimensions, and practice'. In Banks, J.A. and McGee Banks, C.A. (eds) *Handbook of Research on Multicultural Education*, pp. 3–24.

Banks, J.A. and McGee Banks, C.A. (eds) (1993) *Multicultural Education: Issues and Perspectives*, 2nd edn. Boston: Allyn and Bacon.

Banks, J.A. and McGee Banks, C.A. (eds) (1995) *Handbook of Research on Multicultural Education*. New York: Macmillan.

Baptiste, J.P. (1979) *Multicultural Education: A Synopsis*. Washington, DC: University Press of America.

Belenky, M.F., Clinchy, B.M., Goldberger, N.R. and Tarule, J.M. (1986) *Women's Ways of Knowing*. New York: Basic Books.

Bloom, A.D. (1987) *The Closing of the American Mind*. New York: Simon and Schuster.

Cochran-Smith, M. (1991) 'Learning to teach against the grain'. *Harvard Educational Review*, 61 (3), 279–310.

Cochran-Smith, M. (1997) 'Knowledge, skills, and experiences for teaching culturally diverse learners: a perspective for practicing teachers'. In Irvine, J.J. (ed.) *Critical Knowledge for Diverse Teachers and Learners*. Washington, DC: American Association of Colleges for Teacher Education, pp. 27–88.

Cohen, D.K., McLaughlin, M.W. and Talbert, J.E. (eds) (1993) *Teaching for Understanding: Challenges for Policy and Practice*. San Francisco: Jossey-Bass.

Condianni, A.V. and Tipple, B.E. (1980) 'Conceptual changes in ethnic studies'. *Viewpoints in Teaching and Learning*, 56 (1), 26–37.

Cornbleth, C. and Waugh, D. (1995) *The Great Speckled Bird: Multicultural Politics and Education Policymaking*. New York: St Martin's Press.

Cremin, L.A. (1990) *Popular Education and Its Discontents*. New York: Harper and Row.

Cuban, L. (1984) *How Teachers Taught: Constancy and Change in the American Classroom*. New York: Longman.

Daly, N. and O'Dowd, D. (1992) 'Teacher education programmes'. In Diaz (ed.), pp. 179–192.

Darling-Hammond, L., Wise, A.E. and Klein, S.P. (1997) *A License to Teach: Building a Profession for 21st-century Schooling*. Boulder, CO: Westview.

Dewey, J. (1956 [1900]) *The Child and the Curriculum* and *The School and Society*, reprinted in one volume. Chicago: University of Chicago Press.

Dewey, J. (1966 [1916]) *Democracy and Education*. New York: The Free Press.

Diaz, C. (ed.) (1992) *Multicultural Education for the 21st Century*. Washington, DC: National Education Association.

D'Souza, D. (1991) *Illiberal Education*. New York: Free Press.

DuBois, W.E.B. (1989 [1903]) *The Souls of Black Folk*. New York: Penguin.

Ducharme, E. and Agne, R. (1989) 'Professors of education: uneasy residents of academe'. In Wisniewski, R. and Ducharme, E. (eds) *The Professors of Teaching: An Inquiry*. Albany, NY: SUNY Press, pp. 67–86.

Freedman, S.G. (1990) *Small Victories: The Real World of a Teacher, Her Students, and Their High School*. New York: Harper and Row.

Freire, P. (1995) *Pedagogy of Hope: Reliving Pedagogy of the Oppressed*. New York: Continuum.

Freire, P. (1996) *Letters to Christina: Reflections on My Life and Work*. New York: Routledge.

Freire, P., Fraser, J.W., Macedo, D., McKinnon, T. and Stokes, W.T. (eds) (1997) *Mentoring the Mentor: A Critical Dialogue with Paulo Freire*. New York: Peter Lang.

Gay, G. (1990) 'Achieving educational equality through curriculum desegregation'. *Phi Delta Kappa*, 70, 56–62.

Gay, G. (1995) 'Curriculum theory and multicultural education'. In Banks, J.A. and McGee Banks, C.A. (eds), pp. 25–43.

Gibson, M.A. (1976) 'Approaches to multicultural education in the United States: some concepts and assumptions'. *Anthropology and Education Quarterly*, 7, 7–18.

Gollnick, D.M. (1995) 'National and state initiatives for multicultural education'. In Banks, J.A. and McGee Banks, C.A. (eds), pp. 44–64.

Gollnick, D.M. and Chinn, P.C. (1994) *Multicultural Education in a Pluralistic Society*, 4th edn. Colombus, OH: Macmillan.

Goodlad, J. (1990) *Teachers for Our Nation's Schools*. San Francisco: Jossey-Bass.

Grant, C.A. (1978) Education that is multicultural: isn't that what we mean? *Journal of Teacher Education*, 29, 45–48.

Grant, C.A. (1993) 'The multicultural preparation of US teachers: some hard truths'. In Verma, G. (ed.) *Inequality and Teacher Education*. London: Falmer, pp. 41–57.

Grant, C.A. and Sleeter C.E. (1999) *Making Choices for Multicultural Education: Five Approaches to Race, Class, and Gender*, 3rd edn. Upper Saddle River, NJ: Merrill.

Gutmann, A. (1987) *Democratic Education*. Princeton, NJ: Princeton University Press.

Habermas, J. (1971) *Knowledge and Human Interests*. Boston: Beacon Press.

Hirsch, E.D. (1987) *Cultural literacy*. New York: Houghton Mifflin.

hooks, b. (1994) *Teaching to Trangress: Education as the Practice of Freedom*. New York: Routledge.

Kreisberg, S. (1992) *Transforming Power: Domination, Empowerment, and Education*. Albany, NY: SUNY Press.

Ladson-Billings, G. (1990) 'Culturally relevant teaching'. *College Board Review*, 155, 20–25.

Lorde, A. (1981) 'The master's tools will never dismantle the master's house'. In Moraga, C. and Anazaldua, G. (eds) *This Bridge Called My Back: Writings by Radical Women of Color*. Watertown, MA: Persephone Press, pp. 98–99.

Majors, Y. (1998) 'Finding the multivoiced self: a narrative'. *Journal of Adolescent and Adult Literacy*, October, 42 (2), 76–83.

Melnick, S.L. and Zeichner, K.M. (1997) 'Teacher education for cultural diversity: enhancing the capacity of education institutions to address diversity issues'. In King, J., Hollins, E. and Hayman, W. (eds) *Meeting the Challenge of Diversity in Teacher Preparation*. New York: Teachers College Press, pp. 23–39.

Melnick, S.L. and Zeichner, K.M. (1998) 'Teacher education's responsibility to address diversity issues: enhancing institutional capacity'. *Theory into Practice*, Spring, 37 (2), 88–95.

Mitchell, B.M. and Salsbury, R.E. (1996) *Multicultural Education: An International Guide to Research, Policies, and Programs*. Westport, CT: Greenwood Press.

Morrison, T. (1992) *Playing in the Dark*. Cambridge, MA: Harvard University Press.

National Center for Education Stastics (1996) *Out of the Lecture Hall and into the Classroom: 1992–93 College Graduates and Elementary/Secondary School Teaching*. Washington, DC: US Department of Education, August.

Nieto, S. (1992) *Affirming Diversity: The Sociopolitical Context of Multicultural Education*. New York: Longman.

O'Donnell, J. (1998) 'Engaging students' re-cognition of racial identity'. In Chavez, R. and O'Donnell, J. (eds), *Speaking the Unpleasant: The Politics of (Non-) Engagement in the Multicultural Education Terrain*. Albany, NY: SUNY Press.

Ogbu, J.U. (1978) *Minority Education and Caste*. New York: Academic Press.

Ogbu, J.U. (1990) Overcoming racial barriers to equal access. In Goodlad, J.I. and Keating, P. (eds) *Access to Knowledge: An Agenda for Our Nation's Schools*. New York: The College Board, pp. 59–89.

Olneck, M.R. (1995) 'Immigrants and education'. In Banks, J.A. and McGee Banks, C.A. (eds), pp. 310–327.

Perry, T. and Fraser, J.W. (eds) (1993) *Freedom's Plow: Teaching in the Multicultural Classroom*. New York: Routledge.

Pratte, R. (1983) 'Multicultural education: four normative arguments'. *Educational Theory*, 33, 21–32.

Redman, G.L. (1999) *A Casebook for Exploring Diversity in K-12 Classrooms*. Upper Saddle River, NJ: Merrill.

Ryan, W. (1971) *Blaming the Victim*. New York: Vintage.

Schlesinger, A.M. (1998) *The Disuniting of America: Reflections on a Multicultural Society*. Revised edition. New York: W.W. Norton.

Semmel, S.F. (1996) '*Handbook of Research on Multicultural Education*'. Book review. *Teachers College Record*, Fall, 98 (1), 153, 177.

Sleeter, C.E. (1992) *Keepers of the American Dream: A study of Staff Development and Multicultural Education*. London: Falmer Press.

Sleeter, C.E. and Grant, C.A. (1999) *Making Choices for Multicultural Education: Five Approaches to Race, Class and Gender*, third edition. Upper Saddle River, NJ: Merrill. First published 1988.

Smith, B.O. (1969) *Teachers for the Real World*. Washington, DC: American Association of Colleges for Teacher Education.

Smith, G.P. (1998) *Common Sense about Uncommon Knowledge: The Knowledge Bases for Diversity*. Washington, D.C: American Association of Colleges for Teacher Education.

Suzuki, B.H. (1984) 'Curriculum transformation for multicultural education'. *Education and Urban Society*, 16, 294–322.

Tyack, D.B. and Cuban, L. (1995) *Tinkering towards Utopia: A Century of Public School Reform*. Cambridge, MA: Harvard University Press.

Villegas, A.M. (1993) 'Restructuring teacher education for diversity; the innovative curriculum'. Paper presented at the annual meeting of the American Educational Research Association, Atlanta, GA, April.

Wynter, S. (1992) *Do Not Call Us Negroes: How 'Multicultural' Textbooks Perpetuate Racism*. San Francisco, CA: Aspire.

Zangwill, I. (1909) *The Melting-pot*. New York: Macmillan.

Zeichner, K.M. (1993) *Educating Teachers for Cultural Diversity*. Special report. East Lansing, MI: National Center for Research on Teacher Learning, Michigan State University.

Zeichner, K.M. and Hoeft, K. (1996) 'Teacher socialisation for cultural diversity'. In Sikula, J. (ed.), *Handbook of Research on Teacher Education*, 2nd edn. New York: Macmillan, pp. 525–547.

27

ANTI-RACISM
From policy to praxis

David Gillborn

Anti-racism is an ill-defined and changing concept. For some the term denotes any opposition to racism, ranging from organised protest to individual acts of resistance through a refusal to adopt white supremacist assumptions (Aptheker, 1993). For others anti-racism describes a more systematic perspective that provides both a theoretical understanding of the nature of racism and offers general guidance for its opposition through emancipatory practice (Mullard, 1984). The former, broad conception of anti-racism is among the most common understandings internationally, while in Britain the latter more specific usage is dominant. Anti-racism has achieved a degree of public recognition in Britain beyond that attained in most other countries. For this reason I shall begin by using the British case as a vehicle for describing anti-racism in education, especially in relation to the sometimes complementary, sometimes conflicting understandings of *multiculturalism*. I shall broaden the focus later in the piece, particularly with reference to newly emerging discourses of critical anti-racism and praxis.

In Britain, anti-racism was most prominent in social policy debates during the 1980s. Although this period saw a Conservative government re-elected to power at a national level throughout the decade, it was at the local level, especially through the work of local authorities, that anti-racism enjoyed its most influential period. Anti-racism in the 1980s came to denote a wide variety of practices, especially those associated with radical left authorities (such as those in London, Sheffield and Manchester), trades unions and organisations (such as the Anti-Nazi League) which attempted to mobilise young people in opposition to racist organisations like the National Front and later the British National Party (Solomos and Back, 1996). Education emerged as a particularly important arena for anti-racist debate. Although anti-racist policies were adopted in many spheres, it was in education that local policy-makers and practitioners (including teachers' trade unions) achieved some notable changes in policy and practice, although progress was by no means universal or unproblematic.

Attempts to challenge racism in British education have a long and troubled ancestry. Historically, schools and local authorities have been able to take advantage of a system that allowed for an unusually high degree of autonomy, freeing educationists to be among the most consistently active professional groups in the struggle against racism. In the 1980s and 1990s, however, these activities came under severe threat. Education emerged as a key ideological battleground; an arena where each new government initiative was assumed to have a natural consequence requiring further reform of an already shell-shocked system. A succession of reforms, for example, institutionalised a national system of testing linked to a compulsory (and overwhelmingly Eurocentric) curriculum. This added to the divisive effects of an education system that already operated in racialised ways that disadvantaged many minority pupils (Gillborn and Gipps, 1996; Gillborn and Youdell, 2000). In addition to its symbolic importance as a crucial field of social policy, therefore, education is especially significant because it provides a testing ground for many new initiatives and strategies. It highlights both the damage that can be done and the progress that is possible.

Always a target for right-wing critics, during the 1990s anti-racism increasingly came under attack from *left* academics who questioned the notions of identity and politics that underlay certain versions of anti-racist practice. Additionally, attempts to marketise the education system (e.g. by introducing direct competition between schools) and the adoption of a colour-blind rhetoric of 'standards' (that privileged average attainments and ignored race-specific inequalities) further diverted attention away from equal opportunities issues. Despite this hostile environment, anti-racism continues to feature prominently in research and policy debates, particularly at the level of the local state and in community activism. Always a highly controversial aspect of policy and practice, the search for distinctively anti-racist pedagogy and philosophy continues.

ANTI-RACISM AND MULTICULTURALISM

> For the conservative critics, it [multicultural education] represents an attempt to politicize education in order to pander to minority demands, whereas for some radicals it is the familiar ideological device of perpetuating the reality of racist exploitation of ethnic minorities by pampering their cultural sensitivities.
>
> (Bhikhu Parekh quoted in Modgil *et al.*, 1986, p. 5)

Right-wing critics have attacked even the most limited attempts to introduce multicultural elements into the formal curricula of British schools. John Marks (a member of several influential pressure groups and an official advisor to successive Conservative governments) contributed to a volume entitled *Anti-Racism – An Assault on Education and Value*, arguing that attacks on racism in education (regardless of their 'multicultural' or 'anti-racist' label) shared a common goal of 'the destruction and revolutionary transformation of all the institutions of our democratic society' (Marks, 1986, p. 37). At the other end of the political spectrum, during the 1980s many left-wing education critics devoted their time to a deconstruction of multicultural education, presenting it as a tokenist gesture meant to placate minority students and their communities while preserving intact the traditional curricular core of high status ('official') knowledge (Figueroa, 1995). Barry Troyna, for example, used the phrase '*the three S's*' (saris, samosas and steel bands) to characterise the superficial multiculturalism that paraded exotic images of minority peoples and their 'cultures' while doing nothing to address the realities of racism and unequal power relations in the 'host' society (Troyna, 1984). Godfrey Brandt's (1986) study *The Realization of Anti-Racist*

477

Teaching made a significant contribution to the development of the field at that point, summarising the anti-racist critique of multiculturalism and offering strategies for the development of an anti-racist pedagogy.

In many ways Brandt's work typified the dominant characteristics of 1980s anti-racist education in Britain, including a strident attack on multiculturalism and an emphasis on oppositional forms. Drawing heavily on the work of Chris Mullard (1982, 1984), Brandt argued that 'multicultural education can be seen as the Trojan horse of institutional racism. Within it resides an attempt to renew the structure and processes of racism in education' (Brandt, 1986, p. 117). He argued that whereas multiculturalists typically sought to *respond* to ethnic minorities' experiences, anti-racist teaching should accord minorities an active and central role: 'anti-racism must be dynamic and led by the experience and articulations of the Black community as the ongoing victims of rapidly changing ideology and practice of racism' (ibid., p. 119). Throughout his analysis Brandt was keen to foreground the oppositional nature of anti-racism: 'The aims of anti-racist education must be, by definition, oppositional' (ibid., p. 125). This strand was exemplified in the language that Brandt used, for example, by carefully contrasting the language of multiculturalism and anti-racism. According to Brandt, multiculturalism focused on key terms that shared a rather distant and liberal character, such as monoculturalism/ethnicism, culture, equality, prejudice, misunderstanding and ignorance; its process was characterised as providing information and increasing 'awareness'. In contrast, Brandt presented anti-racism in terms of a hard-edged, more immediate lexicon as concerned with conflict, oppression, exploitation, racism, power, structure and struggle: its process was described as '*dismantle, deconstruct, reconstruct*' (ibid., p. 121, original emphasis). These differences in language are not superficial, they indicated a conscious stance that distanced itself from previous multicultural concerns and adopted an openly political position that emphasised the need actively to identify and resist racism.

The oppositional language of anti-racism has been both a strength and a weakness. On one hand it has highlighted the dynamic and active role that schools and teachers can play in confronting racism; on the other hand, it has also provided ammunition to those cultural restorationists who would characterise any left-liberatory reforms as necessarily lowering academic standards, threatening the majority culture and de-stabilising society (see Apple, 1996; Ball, 1990). Additionally, the issue of language points to one of the most important weaknesses in much 1980s anti-racism; the dominance of rhetoric over practical applications.

In both the United States and Britain, under Reagan and Thatcher respectively, the 1980s witnessed increased centralisation of power, the dominance of market economics and attacks on state intervention in social policy areas such as public health, welfare and education. In Britain it was local authorities, usually controlled by the Labour Party (then in opposition nationally), who defended the need for state intervention and, in some cases, funded high-profile anti-racist campaigns. The Greater London Council (GLC) and the Inner London Education Authority (ILEA) were especially active – both bodies were eventually abolished by a Thatcher government. Despite the hostile national government, therefore, for most of the 1980s anti-racism retained a strong presence in some areas: many education authorities, for example, adopted multicultural and/or anti-racist policy statements. However, the impact of such policies was often negligible. Troyna argued that such policies continued to present 'race' and racism as 'superficial features of society; aberrations, rather than integral to our understanding of the way society functions' (Troyna, 1993, pp. 41–42). In this way, the policies deployed key terms, such as 'pluralism', 'justice' and 'equality', as 'condensation symbols' (after Edelman, 1964). That is, they functioned as textual devices that could generate widespread support (and reassure diverse groups that their interests were taken into account) when in fact their meaning was shifting and imprecise, so that power-holders were not constrained by any meaningful directives with clear practical consequences.

In Britain, therefore, the 1980s marked anti-racism's most prominent policy phase but produced uncertain achievements; although many local education authorities committed themselves to anti-racist positions, this was a field where rhetoric far outweighed practical action. As the decade came to an end, anti-racism was dealt what many commentators (mistakenly) interpreted as a wholesale critique from within; at the same time, left academics and cultural critics became increasingly vocal in their attacks on anti-racism: it is to these developments that I turn next.

LEFT CRITIQUES OF MUNICIPAL ANTI-RACISM

Most left critiques of anti-racism in Britain take as their focus a brand of high-profile, 'municipal' anti-racism (Gilroy, 1987) practised by certain Labour-controlled local authorities, most notably the GLC. Tariq Modood has been particularly critical of the emphasis on 'colour racism', arguing that this excludes minority groups whose most dearly felt identity concerns culture, not colour (Modood, 1996). Modood has argued against 'racial dualism', a view that splits society into two groups: white and black. Not only does this ignore significant social, economic, religious and political differences (between and within different ethnic groups), it also leads to a narrow definition of what counts as legitimate anti-racist politics:

> Media interest, reflecting the social policy paradigm of the 1980s, has been narrowly circumscribed by racism and anti-racism: ethnic minorities are of interest if and only if they can be portrayed as victims of or threats to white society.
>
> (Modood, 1989, p. 281)

Modood argued that this 'radicals and criminals' perspective played an important role in stifling peaceful protest against *The Satanic Verses* (Rushdie, 1988), thereby fuelling Muslim anger and encouraging 'the unfortunate but true conclusion that they would remain unheeded till something shocking and threatening was done' (Modood, 1989, p. 282). In a succession of critical pieces Modood argued that anti-racists should recognise that 'culture' is not a surface factor that can be dismissed as unimportant – as if minorities who do not see themselves in terms of colour are somehow deluded about where their true interests lie. Municipal anti-racism's constant privileging of 'colour', he argued, meant that it was bound to fail to connect with many minority populations:

> [I]n terms of their own being, Muslims feel most acutely those problems that the anti-racists are blind to; and respond weakly to those challenges that the anti-racists want to meet with most force. ... We need concepts of race and racism that can critique socio-cultural environments which devalue people because of their physical differences but also because of their membership of a cultural minority and, critically, where the two overlap and create a double disadvantage.
>
> (Modood, 1990, p. 157)

479

Modood's critique identified several weaknesses in the kinds of emphasis characteristic of the local state's attempt to challenge racism. In particular, the failure to acknowledge ethnic *culture*, as a genuine and vital part of shifting and complex ethnic identities, was revealed as a serious mistake in attempts to encourage wider political mobilisation around anti-racist concerns.

The absence of culture from many anti-racist agendas reflected the bitter disputes between multiculturalists and anti-racists in the late 1970s and 1980s. Modood's critique highlighted one of many negative consequences that arose because of the way the debate became polarised. However, we should not forget the historical reasons for anti-racists' unease about the political and epistemological status of culture. Paul Gilroy, for example, has attacked some anti-racists for accepting too readily 'the absolutist imagery of ethnic categories beloved of the New Right' (Cross, 1990, p. 3). Gilroy (like Modood) has attacked the simplistic assumptions that exposed much 'municipal anti-racism' to ridicule while failing to connect with the lived experiences and struggles of minority groups. At the same time, however, he took a rather different position on the politics of culture within anti-racism; a position that highlights the complexity of identity, 'race' and culture in contemporary society.

Paul Gilroy has been especially critical of the conceptions of 'race' and racism that underlie municipal anti-racism. He attacked the 'coat-of-paint theory of racism' that viewed racism as a blemish 'on the surface of other things' and never called into doubt 'the basic structures and relations of [the] British economy and society' (Gilroy, 1990, p. 74). He argued that such an approach effectively placed racism outside key debates, characterising it as a complicating factor of marginal importance rather than a central defining concern. In contrast, he sought to position racism 'in the mainstream' as 'a volatile presence at the very centre of British politics actively shaping and determining the history not simply of blacks, but of this country as a whole at a crucial stage in its development' (ibid., p. 73). He argued for a wider and more dynamic understanding of 'race' and racism; one that foregrounds the socially constructed nature of 'racial' categories and draws attention to their historically constituted and specific nature – an analysis that strongly echoed some of the most influential and insightful work by prominent cultural theorists in the US (see, for example, Omi and Winant, 1986). By accepting a fixed and simple notion of culture, therefore, municipal anti-racism had itself come to accept a spurious ideology of 'culturalism and cultural absolutism' (Gilroy, 1990, p. 82) that paralleled the position of the New Right. This development reflected several factors, not least a concern to support campaigns by minority groups and to highlight distinctive cultural identities and activities as a corrective to the deficit pathological models proposed by right-wing politicians and commentators (Apple and Zenck, 1996). By simply *inverting* the right's pathological view of minority culture, however, municipal anti-racism unwittingly repeated and sustained the basic culturalist analyses that presented 'culture' as if it were a fixed, ahistorical 'thing' rather than a constructed, contested and continually changing discourse. For example:

> 'Same-race' adoption and fostering for 'minority ethnics' is presented as an unchallenged and seemingly unchallengeable benefit for all concerned. It is hotly defended with the same fervour that denounces white demands for 'same race' schooling as a repellent manifestation of racism.
>
> (Gilroy, 1990, p. 81)

Paul Gilroy's attack on such policies highlighted their *essentialist* and *reductionist* character: although born of anti-oppressive aims, they actually committed the same errors that typified the racist thinking they sought to oppose. That is, such policies came to argue that there is some innate quality that characterises the true/authentic *essence* of a particular 'racial'/cultural group. This 'sad inability to see beyond the conservation of racial identities to [the] possibility of their transcendence' reinforced assumptions about inherent difference between cultural groups and trivialised 'the rich complexity of black life by reducing it to nothing more than a response to racism' (Gilroy, 1990, pp. 81, 83). Gilroy argued that just as they must adopt a more sophisticated understanding of 'race', so anti-racists had to break with limiting notions of 'culture' as in any way natural, homogeneous or fixed:

> Culture, even the culture which defines the groups we know as races, is never fixed, finished or final. It is fluid, it is actively and continually made and re-made. In our multicultural schools the sound of steel pan may evoke Caribbean ethnicity, tradition and authenticity yet they originate in the oil drums of the Standard Oil Company rather than the mysterious knowledge of ancient African griots.
>
> (Gilroy, 1990, p. 80)

Gilroy argued, therefore, for a conception of culture and 'race' politics that recognised the fluid, dynamic and highly complex character of the new cultural politics of difference (see also Goldberg, 1993, 1997; Hall, 1992; West, 1990). These arguments reflect a shift in social theory often associated with post-modern or post-structuralist approaches (see, for example, Aronowitz and Giroux, 1991; Thompson, 1992). At times such approaches can seem overly complex and removed from the lived reality of schools, teachers and students (Skeggs, 1991). However, many of the same points have been raised (in a more immediate and school-focused way) in relation to a racist murder, and the conditions that surrounded it, in a Manchester secondary school, called Burnage High. The episode and the subsequent inquiry represent a fault line in British anti-racist politics.

THE FAILURE OF SYMBOLIC ANTI-RACISM: LEARNING FROM BURNAGE

On Wednesday 17 September 1986, Ahmed Iqbal Ullah (a 13 year old Bangladeshi student) was murdered in the playground of Burnage High School, Manchester (England). His killer was a white peer at the same school. A subsequent inquiry, led by Ian Macdonald QC, investigated the background to the murder and presented a full report to Manchester City Council. Afraid of possible legal action by people mentioned in the report, the Council refused to publish the inquiry's findings. Following widespread 'leaks' and misreporting in the popular press, the inquiry team itself decided to publish their findings (Macdonald *et al.*, 1989).

> The committee of inquiry, composed of individuals with impressive antiracist credentials – Ian Macdonald, Gus John, Reena Bhavnani, Lily Khan – delivered a strong and, for some, an astonishing condemnation of the antiracist policies apparently vigorously pursued at the school, castigating them as doctrinaire, divisive, ineffectual and counterproductive.
>
> (Rattansi, 1992, p. 13)

The inquiry team were highly critical of the particular form of anti-racism that had been practised in Burnage; what they called '*symbolic, moral and doctrinaire*' *anti-racism*. It is a

481

form of anti-racism that is essentialist and reductionist in the extreme. Within such a perspective 'race' and racism are assumed always to be dominant factors in the experiences of black and white students, with the former cast as victims, the latter as aggressors. According to symbolic anti-racism:

> since black students are the victims of the immoral and prejudiced behaviour of white students, white students are all to be seen as 'racist', whether they are ferret-eyed fascists or committed anti-racists. Racism is thus placed in some kind of moral vacuum and is totally divorced from the more complex reality of human relations in the classroom, playground or community. In this model of anti-racism there is no room for issues of class, sex, age or size.
>
> (Macdonald *et al.*, 1989, p. 402)

The inquiry report documented the way this approach combined with several other factors (including the style of management and 'macho' disciplinary atmosphere in the school) to increase tension and damage relationships (between school and community; staff and students; students and their peers; teachers and their colleagues). While the report was damning in its criticism of Burnage's 'symbolic' anti-racism, it was absolutely clear about the reality of racism and the need for more sensitive and sophisticated approaches to anti-racism. Although this point was reflected in the first press coverage (in a local paper in Manchester), the national press took a rather different line, representing the report as 'proof' that anti-racism is a damaging extremist political creed. One national paper presented Ahmed as a victim, not of a white racist, but of anti-racism: 'Anti-racist policy led to killing' (*The Daily Telegraph* quoted in Macdonald *et al.*, 1989, p. xx). The distorted press coverage had a significant effect: in education and academia, the 'Burnage report' – though rarely read in detail – was frequently understood as an attack on anti-racism *per se* (see, for example, Rattansi, 1992). Such an interpretation does the report a major disservice. The inquiry team were careful to reject the press interpretation of events at Burnage and emphasised their continuing support for anti-racist education policies:

> It is because we consider the task of combating racism to be such a critical part of the function of schooling and education that we condemn symbolic, moral and doctrinaire anti-racism. We urge care, rigour and caution in the formulating and implementing of such policies because we consider the struggle against racism and racial injustice to be an essential element in the struggle for social justice which we see as the ultimate goal of education. . . . We repudiate totally any suggestion that the anti-racist education policy of Burnage High School led . . . to the death of Ahmed Ullah . . . [W]e state emphatically that the work of all schools should be informed by a policy that recognises the pernicious and all-pervasive nature of racism in the lives of students, teachers and parents, black and white, and the need to confront it.
>
> (Macdonald *et al.*, 1989, pp. xxiii–xxiv)

In its attack on essentialist and reductionist analyses of 'race' and racism, the Burnage report shared several key features with other left critiques of anti-racist theory and practice. Although the critiques have been generated by a range of writers with diverse agendas, several important lessons can be learnt.

THE CRITICAL REVISION OF ANTI-RACISM

The critical thrust of left academics like Gilroy and Modood in Britain has been echoed internationally by authors who emphasise the complexity and fluidity of 'racial' and ethnic categories (Carrim, 1995a, 1995b; McCarthy, 1990; Rizvi, 1993; Walcott, 1994). In the light of such theoretical advances, it is argued, anti-racism must grow into a more sophisticated and flexible strategy that moves away from the racial dualism of its past – what Bonnett and Carrington (1996) characterise as a model of 'White racism versus Black resistance'. However, much anti-racism continues to be characterised by a preference for rhetoric over practical application. Writing with reference to the Australian case, for example, Rod Allen and Bob Hill have commented on the 'lamentable absence of studies evaluating school-based programs to combat racism' (Allen and Hill, 1995, pp. 772–773). There may be several reasons for this. First, academics have a history of critique that enables them to perceive many shortcomings in practical strategies, but does not dispose them well to identifying things that work. This is particularly the case with sociologists, who have been especially active in developing theoretical approaches to anti-racism. Their disciplinary roots teach sociologists to be aware of the many constraints that shape, limit and frustrate attempts to reform the educational systems of advanced capitalist economies. Given their acute awareness of such limits, it can be difficult for them to move from a 'language of critique' to a 'language of possibility' (McCarthy and Apple, 1988, p. 31). More practically, research on anti-racism at the school level is likely to require careful and lengthy qualitative research that can prove expensive in terms of time and resources. Despite these problems, there is now a small, but growing, range of studies that attempt to identify, describe and (constructively) critique the development of anti-racist practice at the school level – including work from pre-school through to post-compulsory education. In Britain, for example, there are now studies of anti-racist practice in early years education (Siraj-Blatchford, 1994), primary schools (Connolly, 1994; Epstein, 1993), secondary schools (Gillborn, 1995; Troyna, 1988) and beyond (Neal, 1998; Troyna and Selman, 1991). The studies reveal the complex, politically explosive and often painful nature of anti-racist change. They demonstrate the futility of attempts to create an anti-racist 'blueprint' for school change, but point to the micro-political nature of change (Ball, 1987), where conflict may be more or less hidden, but consensus is always fragile and prone to destabilisation by events locally (such as a racist incident in the vicinity of the school), nationally (e.g. a scare story about 'political correctness' in the media) and globally (the Gulf War and Salman Rushdie affair, for example, galvanised Muslim communities in Britain and forced many schools to reappraise previous perspectives and practices: Gillborn, 1995; Parker-Jenkins and Haw, 1998).

Studies of anti-racist school practice show that advances are easier where there is wider institutional support for anti-oppression politics (at a local and/or national government level): nevertheless, even where the national government has never accepted anti-racism as a legitimate policy direction, considerable headway can be made at the school level (see Carrim and Gillborn, 1996). Meaningful school change requires the support of the headteacher/principal and cannot be won without the involvement of wider sections of the school staff, its pupils and feeder communities. Anti-racist changes threaten many deeply held assumptions and, in larger schools, it seems that small 'core' groups of staff may be needed to act as the vanguard for anti-racist developments: researching initiatives elsewhere, organising events, and pushing forward school policy. Making genuine links with local communities is a vital part of successful anti-racist change: such developments can be extremely difficult to engineer but once established, they offer schools an immense resource of support and continually argue the need for schools to deal with the complexities of racialised identities by challenging received stereotypes. Finally, students themselves can play a crucial role in pushing forward school-based, anti-racist change. The democratic participation of *all* students (including whites) strengthens anti-racist change where teachers come to realise the need to see beyond simple 'race' labels, to engage with the cross-cutting realities of gendered, sexualised and class-based inequalities that also act on and through the lives of young people.

Studies of anti-racist developments in school show that a concern with theory and practice need not be mutually exclusive. Although anti-racists' historical preference for rhetoric over practice has not always encouraged school-based developments, it is possible to reflect critically on some of the theoretical assumptions that have informed earlier approaches by focusing on the experiences, failures and advances of anti-racist practitioners. To take a single example, it has often been argued that anti-racism should adopt a theoretical position that defines racism as a whites-only activity, in order to 'acknowledge the asymmetrical power relations between black and white citizens' (Troyna and Hatcher, 1992, p. 16). A frequent observation among post-structuralist critics has been that such a view is essentialist and, paradoxically, refuses to allow minorities the same diversity and complexity of perspective recognised in whites. At a practical level such a position can be difficult to justify to white students without falling into the doctrinaire and morally condemnatory tone of symbolic anti-racism: put simply, white working-class young people rarely feel very powerful; to argue that their skin colour alone identifies them as beneficiaries of centuries of exploitation can destroy the credibility of anti-racism in their eyes. In contrast, it has been noted that some schools have, for reasons of pragmatism, adopted a standpoint that echoes the revisionist critics' point that '*racism and ethnocentrism are not necessarily confined to white groups*' (Rattansi, 1992, p. 36, original emphasis). This is not to say, of course, that racism is equally a problem for all groups: in 'the West' the dominant racist ideologies and the most frequent racists are white. Nevertheless, to deny that white students *can ever* be victims of racist violence is to devalue anti-racism. In schools that have adopted a wider understanding of racism, for example, it is still the case that the vast majority of students using racist harassment procedures are black; however, the acknowledgement that all students can, in principle, use the procedures has served to strengthen wider commitment to the developments and helped support the involvement of all student groups (Dei, 1996b; Gillborn, 1995). Pragmatism is no panacea – it has too often served as an excuse for doing nothing to challenge racism: the point here is that anti-racism (as both theory and practice) can learn from the complex and changing realities faced by students, teachers, parents and other community members. Anti-racism is not a *gift* bestowed by intellectuals and liberals; it is a vital, developing and changing combination of activism and opposition that must continually involve diverse groups and be sensitive to its own limitations in vision and action. The best anti-racism seems likely to reflect a dynamic mix of experience and critical reflection – *praxis*. The need to focus on developments at the school level does not militate against further theoretical developments in this field.

OPPOSING RACISM AND STAYING 'CRITICAL'

The adjective 'critical' is seemingly one of the most frequently used terms in contemporary social science, running a close second to 'the almost ritualistic ubiquity of "post" words in current culture' (McClintock, 1995, p. 10). In many cases, 'critical' is invoked as a descriptor to signal a break with previous assumptions about an issue or approach while maintaining a sense of uncertainty, avoiding closure about the necessary form of future analyses and/or actions. Critical social research, for example, 'tries to dig beneath the surface. . . . It asks how social systems really work, how ideology or history conceals the processes which oppress and control people' (Harvey, 1990, p. 6). Critical social research may take many forms but is not bound by the limits of conventional positivist assumptions about what counts as 'scientific' rigour, since such assumptions may themselves be implicated in the very processes of oppression that are at issue (Troyna, 1995). Similarly, 'critical multiculturalism' has been proposed – though adherents differ about the precise meaning of the term (cf. Berlant and Warner, 1994; Chicago Cultural Studies Group, 1994; May, 1994, 1999; McLaren, 1994, 1995; Nieto, 1999). It has also been argued that a *critical anti-racism* should learn from past errors (such as the Burnage tragedy) to position a more complex and contextualised understanding of racialised difference at the centre of attempts to oppose racism in the policy and practice of education (Carrim and Gillborn, 1996; Carrim and Soudien, 1999; Dei, 1996a; Gillborn, 1995). The emerging, contested and varied approaches that are sometimes described as 'critical race theory' similarly display a wide variety of perspectives, pedagogy and praxis but often share a determination to identify, name and oppose racism in its many diverse forms: recognising that racism is a deeply ingrained feature of capitalist societies; challenging claims to legal, academic and political neutrality; and pursuing a complex and contextually sensitive understanding of the construction of knowledge/identity boundaries (see Matsuda *et al.*, 1993; Tate, 1997). Whatever nomenclature is adopted, the processes are frequently difficult, always opposed and sometimes pursued at considerable personal cost (see Banks, 1998; Grant, 1999).

To some readers such debates about terminology might seem trivial or obsessive. It has been argued, for example, that the 'unhelpful dichotomisation of multicultural and antiracist education' in Britain (May, 1999, p. vii) diffused anti-oppressive efforts during the height of Thatcherism and still detracts from shared agendas. But as Nazir Carrim and Crain Soudien (1999) have argued, in relation to education in South Africa, there is frequently a qualitative and historically significant difference between interventions informed by multiculturalism and anti-racism. In the UK, South Africa, Canada and Australia, for example (where multiculturalism versus anti-racism debates have attained prominence), the former have frequently been associated with exoticised, superficial approaches more concerned with lifestyles than life chances (Troyna, 1993). To argue that multiculturalism can conceivably be as critical, oppositional and dynamic as anti-racism may be to underestimate the historical and practical dangers in concepts, such as 'culture' and 'multiculturalism', that have too often been framed in unidimensional and fixed ways that are irreconcilable with the decentred and anti-essentialised view of identity, knowledge and power at the heart of critical anti-racist praxis (Dei, 1996b). As Carrim and Soudien have noted:

> A critical antiracism, which incorporates a notion of 'difference' would, therefore, work with complex, non-stereotypical and dynamic senses of identity, and would 'talk to' the actual ways in

485

which people experience their lives, worlds, and identities . . . the use of culturalist language in the schools we report on tends to be assimilationist. . . . These 'bad' multiculturalist practices essentialize cultures, homogenize and stereotype people's identities and do not address the power dimensions of racism. . . . [The] possibility of 'good', critical multicultural practices is indeed conceivable . . . but we do not have evidence of this existing in any of the South African experiences, either historically or in the contemporary situation.

(Carrim and Soudien, 1999, pp. 154–155, 169)

What is perhaps of central importance in these debates is the requirement to remain critical, not only of others, but of our own attempts to understand and oppose racism. An examination of anti-racist policy and practice demonstrates clearly that there is no blueprint for successful anti-racism – no one 'correct' way. What succeeds at one time, or in one context, may not be appropriate at a later date or in another context. Racism changes: it works differently through different processes, informs and is modified by diverse contemporary modes of representation, and changes with particular institutional contexts. Anti-racism must recognise and adapt to this complexity. In practice this means facing up to the complexities of racism: identifying and combating racism will always be difficult. Racism is often entrenched in commonsense understandings about 'ability', 'aptitude', 'the right attitude', etc. Race is a constant presence in policy and pedagogy – even when it appears absent (Apple, 1999). When legislation adopts a de-racialised discourse, for example, by espousing a desire to help 'all' children regardless of ethnic origin, the consequences of reform have almost invariably been to remake differences that further entrench and extend all too familiar patterns of exclusion and oppression (Gillborn and Youdell, 2000). Although anti-racism has enjoyed more prominent periods, therefore, the need for anti-racist research, analysis and practice is as great as ever. It is to be hoped that anti-racism can win wider acceptance and affect more meaningful change in the future than has been achieved generally in the past.

REFERENCES

Allen, R. and Hill, B. (1995) 'Multicultural education in Australia: Historical development and current status', in James A. Banks and Cherry A. McGee Banks (eds) *Handbook of Research on Multicultural Education*. New York: Macmillan, 763–777.

Apple, M. W. (1996) *Cultural Politics and Education*. Buckingham: Open University Press.

Apple, M. W. (1999) 'The absent presence of race in educational reform', *Race Ethnicity and Education*. 2 (1), 9–16.

Apple, M. W. and Zenck, C. (1996) 'American realities: Poverty, economy, and education', in M. W. Apple (1996) *Cultural Politics and Education*. Buckingham: Open University Press.

Aptheker, Herbert (1993) *Anti-racism in US History: The First Two Hundred Years*. Westport, CT: Praeger.

Aronowitz, S. and Giroux, H. A. (1991) *Postmodern Education: Politics, Culture and Social Criticism*. Oxford: University of Minnesota Press.

Ball, S. J. (1987) *The Micro-Politics of the School: Towards a Theory of School Organisation*. London: Methuen.

Ball, S. J. (1990) *Politics and Policy Making in Education: Explorations in Policy Sociology*. London: Routledge.

Banks, J. A. (1998) 'The lives and values of researchers: Implications for educating citizens in a multicultural society', *Educational Researcher*, 27 (7), 4–17.

Berlant, L. and Warner, M. (1994) 'Introduction to "critical multiculturalism"', in D. T. Goldberg (ed.) *Multiculturalism: A Critical Reader*. Oxford: Blackwell.

Bonnett, A. and Carrington, B. (1996) 'Constructions of anti-racist education in Britain and Canada', *Comparative Education*, 32 (3), pp. 271–288.

Brandt, G. L. (1986) *The Realization of Anti-Racist Teaching*. Lewes: Falmer Press.

Carrim, N. (1995a) 'From "race" to ethnicity: shifts in the educational discourses of South Africa and Britain in the 1990s', *Compare*, 25 (1), 17–33.

Carrim, N. (1995b) 'Working with and through difference in antiracist pedagogies', *International Studies in Sociology of Education*, 5 (1), 25–39.

Carrim, N. and Gillborn, D. (1996) 'Racialized educational disadvantage, antiracism and difference: countering racism at the school level in South Africa and England'. Paper presented at the annual meeting of the American Educational Research Association, New York, April.

Carrim, N. and Soudien, C. (1999) 'Critical antiracism in South Africa', in S. May (ed.) *Critical Multiculturalism: Rethinking Multicultural and Antiracist Education*. London: Falmer Press.

Chicago Cultural Studies Group (1994) 'Critical multiculturalism', in D. T. Goldberg (ed.) *Multiculturalism: A Critical Reader*. Oxford: Blackwell.

Connolly, P. (1994) 'All lads together?: Racism, masculinity and multicultural/anti-racist strategies in a primary school', *International Studies in Sociology of Education*, 4 (2), 191–211.

Cross, M. (1990) 'Editorial', *New Community*, 17 (1), 1–4.

Dei, G. J. S. (1996a) *Anti-Racism Education in Theory and Practice*. Halifax: Fernwood.

Dei, G. J. S. (1996b) 'Critical perspectives in antiracism: An introduction', *Canadian Review of Sociology and Anthropology*, 33 (3), 247–267.

Edelman, M. (1964) *The Symbolic Uses of Politics*. Urbana: University of Illinois Press.

Epstein, D. (1993) *Changing Classroom Cultures: Anti-Racism, Politics and Schools*. Stoke-on-Trent: Trentham.

Figueroa, P. (1995) 'Multicultural education in the United Kingdom: Historical development and current status', in J. A. Banks and C. A. M. Banks (eds) *Handbook of Research on Multicultural Education*. New York: Macmillan.

Gillborn, D. (1995) *Racism and Antiracism in Real Schools: Theory. Policy. Practice*. Buckingham: Open University Press.

Gillborn, D. and Gipps, C. (1996) *Recent Research on the Achievements of Ethnic Minority Pupils*. London: HMSO.

Gillborn, D. and Youdell, D. (2000) *Rationing Education*. Buckingham: Open University Press.

Gilroy, P. (1987) *There Ain't No Black in the Union Jack*. London: Hutchinson.

Gilroy, P. (1990) 'The end of anti-racism', *New Community*, 17 (1), 71–83.

Goldberg, D. T. (1993) *Racist Culture: Philosophy and the Politics of Meaning*. Oxford: Blackwell.

Goldberg, D. T. (1997) *Racial Subjects: Writing on Race and America*. London: Routledge.

Grant, C. A. (ed.) (1999) *Multicultural Research: A Reflective Engagement with Race, Class, Gender and Sexual Orientation*. London: Falmer Press.

Hall, S. (1992) 'New ethnicities', in J. Donald and A. Rattansi (eds) *'Race', Culture and Difference*. London: Sage.

Harvey, L. (1990) *Critical Social Research*. London: Allen & Unwin.

McCarthy, C. (1990) *Race and Curriculum: Social Inequality and the Theories and Politics of Difference in Contemporary Research on Schooling*. Lewes: Falmer, Press.

McCarthy, C. and Apple, M. W. (1988) 'Race, class and gender in American educational research: Towards a nonsynchronous parallelist position', in L. Weis (ed.) *Class, Race and Gender in American Education*. Albany: State University of New York Press.

McClintock, A. (1995) *Imperial Leather: Race, Gender and Sexuality in the Colonial Contest*. London and New York: Routledge.

Macdonald, I., Bhavnani, R., Khan, L. and John, G. (1989) *Murder in the Playground: The Report of the Macdonald Inquiry into Racism and Racial Violence in Manchester Schools*. London: Longsight.

McLaren, P. (1994) 'White terror and oppositional agency: Towards a critical multiculturalism', in D. T. Goldberg (ed.) *Multiculturalism: A Critical Reader*. Oxford: Blackwell.

McLaren, P. (1995) *Critical Pedagogy and Predatory Culture*. London and New York: Routledge.

Marks, J. (1986) '"Anti-racism" – revolution not education', in F. Palmer (ed.) *Anti-Racism – An Assault on Education and Value*. London: Sherwood Press.

487

Matsuda, M. J., Lawrence, C. R., Delgado, R. and Crenshaw, K. W. (eds) (1993) *Words that Wound: Critical Race Theory, Assaultive Speech, and the First Amendment*. Boulder CO: Westview.

May, S. (1994) *Making Multicultural Education Work*. Clevedon: Multilingual Matters.

May, S. (ed.) (1999) *Critical Multiculturalism: Rethinking Multicultural and Antiracist Education*. London: Falmer Press.

Modgil, S., Verma, G. K., Mallick, K. and Modgil, C. (eds) (1986) *Multicultural Education: The Interminable Debate*. Lewes: Falmer Press.

Modood, T. (1989) 'Religious anger and minority rights', *Political Quarterly*, July, 280–284.

Modood, T. (1990) 'British Asian Muslims and the Rushdie affair', *Political Quarterly*, April, 143–160.

Modood, T. (1996) 'The changing context of "race" in Britain', *Patterns of Prejudice*, 30 (1), 3–13.

Mullard, C. (1982) 'Multiracial education in Britain: from assimilation to cultural pluralism', in J. Tierney (ed.) *Race, Migration and Schooling*. London: Holt, Rinehart & Winston.

Mullard, C. (1984) *Anti-racist Education: The Three O's*. Cardiff: National Antiracist Movement in Education.

Neal, S. (1998) *The Making of Equal Opportunities Policies in Universities*. Buckingham: Open University Press.

Nieto, S. (1999) 'Critical multicultural education and students' perspectives', in S. May (ed.) *Critical Multiculturalism: Rethinking Multicultural and Antiracist Education*. London: Falmer Press.

Omi, M. and Winant, H. (1986) *Racial Formation in the United States: From the 1960s to the 1980s*. New York: Routledge.

Parker-Jenkins, M. and Haw, K. F. (1998) 'Educational needs of Muslim children in Britain: Accommodation or neglect?' in S. Vertovec and A. Rogers (eds) *Muslim European Youth: Reproducing Ethnicity, Religion, Culture*. Aldershot: Ashgate.

Rattansi, A. (1992) 'Changing the subject? Racism, culture and education', in J. Donald and A. Rattansi (eds) *'Race', Culture and Difference*. London: Sage.

Rizvi, F. (1993) 'Race, gender and the cultural assumptions of schooling', in C. Marshall (ed.) *The New Politics of Race and Gender*. London: Falmer Press.

Rushdie, S. (1988) *The Satanic Verses*. London: Viking.

Siraj-Blatchford, I. (1994) *The Early Years: Laying the Foundations for Racial Equality*. Stoke-on-Trent: Trentham.

Skeggs, B. (1991) 'Postmodernism: what is all the fuss about?', *British Journal of Sociology of Education*, 12 (2), 255–267.

Solomos, J. and Back, L. (1996) *Racism and Society*. Basingstoke: Macmillan in association with the British Sociological Association.

Tate, W. F. (1997) 'Critical race theory and education: History, theory, and implications', in M. W. Apple (ed.) *Review of Research in Education, vol. 22*. Washington, DC: American Educational Research Association.

Thompson, K. (1992) 'Social pluralism and post-modernity', in S. Hall, D. Held and T. McGrew (eds) *Modernity and Its Futures*. Cambridge: Polity Press.

Troyna, B. (1984) 'Multicultural education: Emancipation or containment?' In L. Barton and S. Walker (eds) *Social Crisis and Educational Research*. Beckenham: Croom Helm, 75–92.

Troyna, B. (1988) 'The career of an antiracist education school policy: Some observations on the mismanagement of change', in A. G. Green and S. J. Ball (eds) *Progress and Inequality in Comprehensive Education*. London and New York: Routledge, 158–178.

Troyna, B. (1993) *Racism and Education: Research Perspectives*. Buckingham: Open University Press.

Troyna, B. (1995) 'Beyond reasonable doubt? Researching "race" in educational settings', *Oxford Review of Education*, 21 (4), 395–408.

Troyna, B. and Hatcher, R. (1992) *Racism in Children's Lives: A Study of Mainly White Primary Schools*. London and New York: Routledge.

Troyna, B. and Selman, L. (1991) *Implementing Multicultural and Anti-Racist Education in Mainly White Colleges*. London: Further Education Unit.

Walcott, R. (1994) 'The need for a politics of difference', *Orbit*, 21 (2), 4–6.

West, C. (1990) 'The new cultural politics of difference'. Reprinted in S. During (ed.) *The Cultural Studies Reader*. London and New York: Routledge.

28

ENVIRONMENTAL EDUCATION
A time for re-visioning

Christopher Oulton and William Scott

Our purpose in writing this chapter is, first, to critique established ways of thinking about formal environmental education, and then to comment on what the priorities for environmental education programmes might now be. Our principal contention is that the influence of socially critical thinking over environmental education has led to its being theory-led and problematic for school practitioners. We argue that teachers, schools and communities need to contribute to theory themselves through their own collaborative practice, and to do this in a multiplicity of ways which are determined by their own contexts and needs.

For three decades there has been intense activity in environmental education stimulated by international bodies, facilitated by NGOs and mediated through national and regional activities, governments, national associations, regional forums and local groups (see, for example, IUCN, 1970; UNESCO-UNEP, 1976, 1978, 1987). It is, however, unclear what we have achieved, and how far we have moved towards a more environmentally educated, concerned and responsible citizenry as envisaged by Stapp *et al.* (1969), or indeed whether such a goal is appropriate (Fien, 1993a). The increasing influence on environmental education of the sustainability debate, stimulated, *inter alia*, by the World Conservation Strategy (IUCN *et al.*, 1980), the World Commission on Environment and Development (1987), the publication of *Caring for the Earth* (IUCN *et al.*, 1990), and the United Nations Conference on Environment and Development (UNCED, 1992) has also contributed to a shifting of position and perspective, and many issues remain unresolved, as witnessed in the publication of *Education for Sustainability* (Huckle and Sterling, 1996) which demonstrates some seemingly unbridgeable divisions in the worldviews of the theorists of environmental education, in their ideas for the future, and in their notions of strategies to achieve them. In the meantime, schools and teachers struggle to find their own path through a bewildering mixture of often contradictory advice and guidance, and amid doubts about their effectiveness and progress.

There have been persistent critical commentaries about the effectiveness of environmental education programmes (Ham and Sewing, 1987; Hungerford and Volk, 1990; Samuel, 1993; Volk *et al.*, 1984; Walker, 1997) and little evidence that this has had a sustained effect, beyond schools, on the ways that people act in their adult lives. How can we explain this when so much effort has been expended in development, research and teaching? Many answers have been proposed focusing on school curriculum and organisation, teacher education, and the complexity, contradictions and ambitious goals of environmental education. The rest of this chapter looks at certain aspects of this important question.

The work of the ENSI programme (ENvironment and Schools Initiative: OECD, 1991) has been a significant influence on environmental education. The programme promoted an action research approach (Elliott, 1991, 1995) and its aims and principles specified a theory of learning that is associated with 'active engagement in finding and implementing solutions to real-life problems that fall within the sphere of students' personal experience' (Posch, 1996, p. 358). Posch (1994a, 1994b, 1996) has drawn on the ENSI experience to write about the problems of introducing environmental education into curriculum and school organisational structures which have been designed for an education that has other priorities. He has provided glimpses of school practice which suggest that, whilst ENSI's theory of learning has had some limited utility, it has failed to overcome existing curriculum and school structures militating against the systemic introduction of environmental education into schools. But is this necessarily the best way to view this issue?

Walker (1997, p. 155) offers an alternative perspective in her analysis of the Australian experience of the ENSI programme. In her discussion of why research in environmental education seems to have had 'so little influence on . . . environmental education in schools', Walker examines Robottom's (1993) analysis of the Australian ENSI programme where the effectiveness of environmental education in the ENSI schools was to be determined on the basis of a set of criteria relating to environmental education of a 'more socially critical kind' (Robottom, 1993, p. 64) drawn from socially critical theory (see Fien, 1993b; Huckle, 1991; Robottom, 1987). Walker (1997, p. 157) argues that the lack of success of the ENSI programme in Australia was due to 'a formidable list of requirements' which had to be met before success could be claimed, including:

- the recognition of a shared, community-based environmental problem which is solvable by school students;
- school and parental agreement that the environmental problem will become the focus of the curriculum;
- committed teachers, school principal and community;
- a preparedness on behalf of the teachers, students and community participants to confront their own values and the values held by others;
- a teacher with specific expertise in relation to the problem, or an outside expert.

These requirements, or conditions, necessarily flow from the tenets of socially critical theory and have two problematic consequences: the first is that what counts as environmental education is narrowly defined; the second is that even when you accept the narrowness of the definition, it is hard to meet the conditions. Walker (1997, p. 157) goes on to argue that socially critical theory, whilst being potentially useful in analysing contexts, is not a 'practical theory' in the sense that it can contribute to 'a practical solution of the problems' found in schools because it 'falls short of viable strategies for social action', and because 'schools are structured in such a way that they cannot accommodate the radical social change required by the theory'. Thus schools only succeed where such challenging conditions can be met. Our contention is that the issue is not whether schools need to change in order to accommodate the theory, but how schools working with their communities can be helped to take greater responsibility for their own work; i.e. to determine the most appropriate theories to develop for themselves.

In her analysis, Walker draws on Robinson (1994, pp. 57–60), who sees such socially critical thinking depicting practitioners and students as passive victims of wider economic forces. The heart of the critical theorists' message is that the purpose of environmental education, rooted in emancipatory action research (Fien, 1993b; Huckle, 1983; Robottom, 1993), is to show teachers and students how to resist such forces and to work towards social transformation which then becomes the purpose of schooling. Walker goes on to elaborate on Robinson's problem-based methodology (Robinson, 1993), which she claims sets out to provide an alternative framework and strategies for practitioners and researchers to work together in schools in order to pursue a developmental strategy which is informed but unconstrained by external theories, and which allows schools to develop their own ideas.

The ideas underpinning a critical education *for* the environment, built up through the 1980s, have exerted an extensive influence outside the United States over theorising about, and research into, environmental education. This domination has not been without conflict, as evidenced, for example, through the politics of method and the so-called paradigm wars (Connell, 1997; Gage, 1989; Gough, 1987, 1989, 1993; Mrazek, 1993; Robottom and Hart, 1993a, 1993b, 1995), in the growing influence of post-modern thinking (see Gare, 1995 for a lucid conflation of post-modern and green ideas), and by ideological tensions between the so-called deep-green and red-green positions which are exposed in the continuing debate between Huckle (1996) and Sterling (1996).

Critical research and critical theory are terms that refer to a research methodology and to a loose grouping of social theories (Robinson, 1993, p. 227). Critical research is attractive to many educational researchers because it is seen to overcome what they consider to be the limitations of positivist and interpretive positions. Critical researchers reject what they see as the claims to value and political neutrality of positivist versions of empirical enquiry, arguing that such a stance only serves to hide values and interests which can be served (perhaps unwittingly) by such approaches. The question for them is *which* values are promoted by research, not whether a piece of research can be value-free. Further, the goal of critical research, and of the critical theories that inform and underpin it, is to promote a particular politics, i.e. one devoted to what Braybrooke (1987, p. 68) describes as the 'emancipation . . . of social classes from oppression or contempt; emancipation of people throughout society, from ideas that inhibit rationality'. Thus, there is a contradiction built into socially critical theorising about environmental education: namely that, if research or development has to be underpinned by specific and specified values, how can practitioners have autonomy, and learners be free to evolve their own value positions? These we see as necessary conditions for environmental education.

Robinson (1993, p. 227) critiques the critical theory approach to research, claiming most of it falls short of its practical promise for four reasons:

1 the scope of the problems it tackles is too large;
2 its critical analyses fail to show how particular actors in particular circumstances can act to resolve their situation;
3 its educative strategies frequently omit reference to powerful groupings;

4 it gives too little emphasis to the development of an effective theory and practice of interpersonal and organisational change.

Walker (1997) acknowledges this in the context of environmental education and argues that the approach is ineffectual because it lacks an appropriate theory of implementation through which practitioners and researchers can make improvements to practice. This point is echoed by Gare (1995, p. 104) writing about how radical Marxists 'appear to provide people with little guidance for overcoming the destructive imperatives of capitalism they have identified'. A criticism of critical theory must be that, whatever the problem, the solution is a priori always of the same form and that, because of this, critical theory finds it difficult to provide solutions to complex and diverse (environmental) educational problems in schools. See Robinson (1993, pp. 234ff.) for a further discussion.

The environmental education goals of the socially critical theorists draw heavily on Habermas's (1978, pp. 370–371) contention that there are three forms of 'knowledge-constitutive interests': (a) a 'technical interest', (b) a 'practical interest', and (c) an 'emancipatory interest'. This analysis has been very powerful in its effect on how environmental education has been conceptualised and enacted, especially in the genesis of a critical education *for* the environment. Debates about the ways in which environmental education might he conceptualised are long-established and continuing. The distinctions between education *about/in/for* the environment first mooted as primary classes by Lucas (1979), but preceded by Watts's (1969) characterisations of education *about* the environment and education *from* the environment, has provided a framework within which conceptualising about environmental education has occurred.

However, we distrust the neat symmetrical analysis which equates Habermas's three forms of knowledge with Lucas's three primary classes of environmental education: viz. technical = *about*; practical = *in*; emancipatory = *for*). In such analyses, education *about* the environment 'emphasises teaching facts, concepts and generalizations about environmental patterns, processes and problems' (Fien, 1993b, p. 40); education *through* the environment is seen as using the environment 'as a medium for education' (ibid. p. 42); and education *for* the environment 'represents an integration of a socially critical orientation in education and eco–socialist environmental ideology' (ibid., p. 43). The critical theorists make such analyses carefully in order to valorise their goal of a '*critical* education for the environment'. See Fien (1993b, p. 40, Table 2.5: derived from O'Riordan [1989, p. 85]) for an example of how such analyses rest on particular assumptions about the relationship of educational and environmental ideologies. The reality on the ground has always been much messier, but the result has been that, for too many writers and theorists (whether critical or not), education *for* the environment has become synonymous with environmental education.

In order to boost the claims of the 'for' approach, it has proved necessary to downgrade other ways of viewing and interpreting environmental education, and this has marginalised many schools' work. This was certainly not the intention of Lucas's paper, which saw a balanced environmental education comprising his primary classes in combination. In terms of environmental education research, another neat symmetrical analysis has resulted in the identification of *about* with positivism, *in* with interpretivism, and *for* with a critical approach (for example: Robottom and Hart, 1993b, p. 26, Table 2.1). Once again, this merely serves the purposes of particular groups and is constraining to school practitioners and researchers alike. Connell (1997, pp. 124–129) explores the debate about approaches to environmental education research and takes issue with the notion that all empirical-analytical approaches can be dismissed as 'behaviourist and/or traditional positivist in nature', and with 'attempts to establish which methodological research approach is *the* most desirable for environmental education' (our italics), and which other approaches should not be pursued. This would cover such claims as 'clearly environmental education research should be grounded in the alternative emerging paradigm and not in the positivist "applied science" paradigm which is antagonistic to the very nature of environmental education' (Robottom and Hart, 1993a, p. 54).

These are not new criticisms of the claims to exclusivity of the *for* approach, nor of its usefulness as an idea. Gough (1987, p. 50), for example, has challenged its anthropocentric tendencies and its patronising nature ('Who are we to say what is "good for" the environment, and which environment is *the* environment, anyway?'), while Payne (1995a, 1997) has questioned the usefulness and appropriateness of the continuing uncritical use of the preposition 'for' by setting out to problematise the word from the perspective of a 'critical ecological ontology for educational enquiry'. Payne (1995a, p. 1) concludes that 'for' ought to be enriched through phrases such as 'being for' and 'for education', i.e. that we ought now to be espousing education 'for being for the environment' because of the power which this has to 'shift the locus of accountability and responsibility for environmental consequences to humans and their individual and collective actions', and 'redress the possible . . . theoretical hegemony in practices of a critical education primarily *for* the environment' which he sees as 'overly idealistic and emancipatory imperatives typical of critical theories'. Payne (1995a, p. 21) calls for an environmental education which is socially affirmative. This echoes the work of the MUVIN project (see below, and also Payne [1995b]).

Limiting the value given to the *in/about* approaches has had the unfortunate effect of narrowing what is allowed to count as environmental education. What we advocate here agrees with Walsh's (1984, p. 22) view that 'there are many benefits to be gained from an education "about the environment" approach, particularly if the only alternative to this approach is for no environmental studies to be attempted at all'. We see that 'in and about' approaches can be valued of themselves, *and* as precursors to other ways of approaching the field. We do not believe that they are 'valuable only in so far as they are used to provide skills and knowledge to support the transformative intentions of education *for* the environment' (Fien, 1993b, p. 16). As the use of the 'for' construction becomes more sloganised, valuable opportunities are lost, not only to reassert the value of the *for* component and to think beyond the limitations currently imposed upon it, but also to restore a sense of perspective to the notion of being critical. We need to be clear: we are not arguing here against critical approaches *per se*, far from it; but we feel that it is time that environmental education maps showing the relationship of educational and environmental ideologies were redrawn to reflect different understandings, and in a way that doesn't privilege particular ways of bringing critical arguments to bear.

Our discussion of the role of socially critical theory and the dominance it has acquired over ways of thinking about environmental education leads us to warn against the idea that one perspective can offer a valuable way of looking at all contexts, and can provide resolutions of all problems. Although a socially critical approach can be a valuable analytical tool, it is necessary to look beyond this if we are interested in finding ways of resolving problems faced by teachers and schools in implementing and effecting environmental education, and in bridging the gap between schools and communities, or as Smith (1992, pp. 2–3) would argue, between curriculum and community. An emphasis on links between schools and communities leads us back to sustainability issues, and to Local Agenda 21 (LA21) where schools as key institutions in the community can play a pivotal role (UNCED, 1992).

Environmental education is characterised by a rhetoric of action-taking. Education *for* the environment, whether critical or not, is explicitly aimed at an amelioration, conservation and/or improvement of widely varying contexts and circumstances which can only be realised *through* action. But what action? What forms of action matter in this regard? Is everyone capable of taking action, even at a young age? Are some actions more worthwhile than others? Is action-taking essentially an individual or collective act? Should schools 'act'? Should they act alone? Should they encourage or require action through the curriculum – and if so, what forms of action are approved or tolerated? What are the ethical limits to action, and how are they arrived at? These are examples of a set of questions that need to be addressed in communities as part of a deliberative process (Dillon, 1994) so that appropriate goals can be established. The work arising from the MUVIN project (environmental education within the Nordic countries: Brieting and Janniche, 1995) allows us some insights into this notion of action and what it has to offer environmental educators.

Jensen and Schnack (1997) discuss the concepts of 'action' and 'action competence', drawing on extensive work on the MUVIN project at the Royal Danish School of Educational Studies (see, for example, Brieting and Neilsen, 1996; Jensen, 1995; Jensen and Schnack, 1994). Action and action competence bring together the purposes of school education and the nature of the ecological and environmental crises facing societies across the world. The development of action competence ideas is partly a reaction to what is seen as a widespread tendency, first, to foster crude behaviour modification programmes in environmental education, and second, to rely on individualism as a means of effecting change (see Robottom and Hart, 1995). The former are seen as anti-educational, and the latter as anti-societal; the combination of the two is seen as a recipe for ineffectiveness and a sense of hopelessness in the face of the urgent need for change and a need for an involved citizenry. Action competence is also a reaction against what is seen as an overly academic school curriculum which is disempowering because of its tendency to divorce the content and praxis of the curriculum from the realities of everyday life, treating the former as abstractions, and seeing the latter as of marginal interest only. Crucially, however, with action competence the efficacy of what pupils do in schools has to be judged on educational criteria; i.e. it is not the purpose of schools, or of the educational experiences offered in schools, to 'solve the political problems of society' or to 'improve the world with the help of . . . pupils' activities' (Jensen and Schnack, 1997, p. 165). The importance of 'concerns about the environment' in schools is that they are 'coupled with a corresponding concern for democracy', and the essence of action and action competence is a democratic commitment to be participants in the continuing shaping of society, and the capability to participate as shapers on their own terms and in their own ways.

For Jensen and Schnack, the characteristic feature of an action is not that something happens, but that there is intention in the actor(s). They make the point that a goal of behaviour change is not the same as a goal of action competence, and it is important to distinguish what is suggested here from 'training in action skills', which is part of 'educating for a change in behaviour' (Hungerford and Volk, 1990, pp. 8–21). Action competence is a set of capabilities which equip individuals with the ability to act in whatever way they choose: actions are not predetermined, as with behaviour-change strategies, but are commensurate with the liberal democratic goals of environmental education as set out, for example, in the Tbilisi Declaration (UNESCO–UNEP, 1978), as is the avowal that 'it is not the task of the school to improve the world by means of children's activities. Actions must be judged in relation to their educational value.' Thus a distinction is drawn between education which is for pupils and/or society and that which might in some fashion be 'for the environment'.

These ideas on action competence are a significant reinterpretation of the aims of environmental education, although it might be argued that distinguishing between action and activity again serves only to narrow down what counts as environmental education. Jensen and Schnack assert that activities fall short of action unless they are focused on the resolution of a problem which pupils themselves regard as important; i.e. that the limitations of the task in question are balanced by its being part of a more substantial goal. This, along with their differentiation between direct and indirect environmental actions, imposes an external rigidity on schools' own ideas, and we doubt the point of such narrowness. However, an education for action competence has resonances with the *education for participation* cited by Agyeman *et al.* (1996, p. 193) in their discussion of Local Agenda 21 (LA21) developments within Scotland. Agyeman *et al.* make the point that 'Education for participation in LA21 will only achieve its potential when it is targeted as much at community and environmental professionals as at communities themselves. It must be a two-way process.' To this we would add that, where they are present in a community, schools, their educational and other professionals, and learners must also be involved within developments, otherwise 'the need to activate a sense of common purpose' (UNCED, 1992, ch. 27) will be frustrated.

In this chapter we have argued that for too much of the past 20 years, particular ways of viewing and doing environmental education have sought dominance over the field; exclusivity has been the order, but the only result has been ineffectiveness. Too many school practitioners' efforts have been effectively disqualified by theorist-arbiters. The result has been a stifling of innovation and disempowerment. We have also argued that socially critical theory, which in many parts of the world in recent years has been the dominant way of viewing environmental education, has had the effect of leading into a cul-de-sac and that the only way forward is to adopt an approach that encourages schools and teachers, working with their communities to find their own ways of interpreting and enacting environmental education. For some, a socially critical perspective may well be helpful; others may wish to adopt approaches that have, at their core, an education which promotes free social action unfettered by particular groups' *a priori* assumptions about the nature of that action in particular circumstances, the goals to be achieved, or the theoretical framework within which work might fit. We support a multiplicity of approaches to teaching, research and development, and encourage the use of a range of techniques which suit the context, rather than seeing one particular view as appropriate whatever the circumstances. We seek to encourage diverse ways of conceptualising environmental education and sustainability, and through this to encourage confidence and action. We also look forward to an environmental education where each methodological approach and corresponding paradigm 'can contribute to meeting valid research goals of environmental education' (Connell, 1997, p. 129). Connell cites Jacknicke and Rowell (1987) and Soltis (1984), supporting their call for

> an associated community of researchers in education where not all researchers do all kinds of research but all do what they do well and where methodologies are selected to meet clearly identified research needs, balanced with a clear understanding of the social, political and philosophical contexts in which the techniques are located
>
> (Connell, 1997, p. 130)

One of our purposes was to set out a vision of what the priorities for formal environmental education programmes might be; Connell (above) encapsulates this in terms of research, but we would go further: put simply, we advocate a community of practitioners (teachers, students, managers, researchers and people across the community) in which not every group approaches environmental education in the same way, but where what is done is done well, and where approaches are selected to meet clearly identified goals suited to the social, political and philosophical contexts in which the education takes place. In other words, we argue for a multiplicity of approaches, carefully and communally deliberated on, to deliver the educational goals deemed appropriate and necessary by communities. Such a strategy will be 'multiparadigmatic' (or 'clumsy': Thompson, 1990) and cross-disciplinary in that it will be informed by a combination of traditions and ideological persuasions which together will offer more than any one of them could alone. This will necessarily be a reflexive and iterative process which will need time to develop and deliver its goals.

ACKNOWLEDGEMENT

The authors are grateful to Andrew Stables and Steven Gough for their helpful comments on drafts of this chapter.

REFERENCES

Agyeman, J., Morris, J. and Bishop, J. (1996) 'Local government's educational role in LA21', in J. Huckle and S. Sterling (eds) *Education for Sustainability*, London: Earthscan.

Braybrooke, D. (1987) *Philosophy of Social Science*, Englewood Cliffs, NJ: Prentice-Hall.

Brieting, S. and Janniche, P. M. (1995) *MUVIN-DK; Background Information for Schools in Denmark Participating in 'Nordic Environmental Education in 1994–96'*, Copenhagen: Ministry of Education/The Royal School of Educational Studies.

Brieting, S. and Neilson, K. (eds) (1996) *Environmental Education Research in the Nordic Countries*, Copenhagen: The Royal School of Educational Studies/Research Centre of Environmental and Health Education.

Connell, S. (1997) 'Empirical-analytical methodological research in environmental education: response to negative trend in methodological and ideological discussions', *Environmental Education Research*, 3 (2), 117–132.

Dillon, J. T. (ed.) (1994) *Deliberation in Education and Society*, Norwood, NJ: Ablex.

Elliott, J. (1991) *Action Research for Educational Change*, Milton Keynes: Open University Press.

Elliott, J. (1995) 'Environmental education action research and the role of the school', in *Environmental Learning for the 21st Century*, Paris: OECD.

Fien, J. (1993a) (ed.) *Environmental Education: A Pathway to Sustainability*, Geelong: Deakin University Press.

496

Fien, J. (1993b) *Education for the Environment: Critical Curriculum Theorising and Environmental Education*, Geelong: Deakin University Press.

Gage, N. (1989) 'The paradigm wars and their aftermath: A "historical" sketch of research on teaching since 1989', *Educational Researcher*, 18 (7), 4–10.

Gare, A. E. (1995) *Postmodernism and the Environmental Crisis*, London and New York: Routledge.

Gough, N. (1987) 'Learning with environments: Towards an ecological paradigm for education', in I. Robottom (ed.) *Environmental Education: Practice and Possibility*, Geelong: Deakin University Press.

Gough, N. (1989) 'From epistemology to ecopolitics: Renewing a paradigm for curriculum', *Journal of Curriculum Studies*, 21 (3), 225–242.

Gough, N. (1993) 'Narrative enquiry and critical pragmatism: Liberating research in environmental education', in R. Mrazek (ed.) *Alternative Paradigms in Environmental Education Research*, Troy, OH: North American Association for Environmental Education.

Habermas, J. (1978) *Knowledge and Human Interests* (2nd edn), trans. J. J. Shapiro, London: Heinemann.

Ham, S. and Sewing, D. (1987) 'Barriers to environmental education', *Journal of Environmental Education*, 19 (2), 17–24.

Huckle, J. (1983) 'Environmental education', in J. Huckle (ed.) *Geographical Education: Reflection and Action*, Oxford: Oxford University Press.

Huckle, J. (1991) 'Education for sustainability: Assessing pathways to the future', *Australian Journal of Environmental Education*, 7, 43–62.

Huckle, J. (1996) 'Realizing sustainability in changing times', in J. Huckle and S. Sterling (eds) *Education for Sustainability*, London: Earthscan.

Huckle, J. and Sterling, S. (eds) (1996) *Education for Sustainability*, London: Earthscan.

Hungerford, H. and Volk, T. (1990) 'Changing learner behaviour through environmental education', *Journal of Environmental Education*, 21 (3), 8–21

IUCN (1970) *International Working Meeting on Environmental Education and the School Curriculum – Final Report*, Gland: IUCN.

IUCN/UNEP/WWF (1980) *World Conservation Strategy: Living Resources Conservation for Sustainable Development*, Gland: IUCN.

IUCN/UNEP/WWF (1990) *Caring for the Earth: A Strategy for Sustainability*, Gland: IUCN.

Jacknicke, K. G. and Rowell, P. M. (1987) 'Alternative orientations for educational research', *The Alberta Journal of Educational Research*, 33 (1), 62–72.

Jensen, B. B. (ed.) (1995) *Research in Environmental and Health Education*, Copenhagen: Royal Danish School of Educational Studies.

Jensen, B. B. and Schnack, K. (1994) *Studies in Educational Theory and Curriculum Vol. 12: Action and Action Competence as Key Concepts in Critical Pedagogy*, Copenhagen: Royal Danish School of Educational Studies.

Jensen, B. B. and Schnack, K. (1997) 'The action competence approach in environmental education', *Environmental Education Research*, 3 (2), 163–178.

Lucas, A. (1979) *Environment and Environmental Education: Conceptual Issues and Curriculum Interpretations*, Kew, Victoria: Australian International Press.

Mrazek, R. (ed.) (1993) *Alternative Paradigms in Environmental Education Research*, Troy, OH: North American Association for Environmental Education.

O'Riordan, T. (1989) 'The challenge for environmentalism', in R. Peet and N. Thrift (eds) *New Models in Geography*, London: Unwin Hyman.

OECD (1991) *Environment, Schools and Active Learning*, Paris: OECD.

Payne, P. (1995a) *Phenomenological Inquiry for Environmental Education: Directions and Challenges for 'a Critical Ecological Ontology'*. Paper presented at the Northern Call for the Environment conference, Binna Burra, Australia, November 1995.

Payne, P. (1995b) 'Environmental education as ontological enquiry', *Australian Journal of Environmental Education*, 11, 83–105.

Payne, P. (1997) 'Embodiment and environmental education', *Environmental Education Research*, 3 (2), 133–154.

Posch, P. (1994a) 'Changes in the culture of teaching and learning and implications for action research', *Educational Action Research*, 2, 153–160.

Posch, P. (1994b) 'Networking in environmental education', in OECD/CERI (ed.) *Evaluation and Innovation in Environmental Education*, Paris: OECD.

Posch, P. (1996) 'Curriculum change and school development', *Environmental Education Research*, 2 (3), 347–362.

Robinson, V. M. J. (1993) *Problem-based Methodology: Research for the Improvement of Practice*, Oxford: Pergamon.

Robinson, V. M. J. (1994) 'The practical promise of critical research in educational administration', *Educational Administrative Quarterly*, 30 (1), 56–76.

Robottom, I. (1987) 'Towards inquiry-based professional development in environmental education', in I. Robottom (ed.) *Environmental Education: Practice and Possibility*, Geelong: Deakin University Press.

Robottom, I. (ed.) (1993) *Policy, Practice, Professional Development and Participatory Research: Supporting Environmental Initiatives in Australian Schools*, Geelong: Deakin University Press.

Robottom, I. and Hart, P. (ed.) (1993a) *Research in Environmental Education: Engaging the Debate*, Geelong: Deakin University Press.

Robottom, I. and Hart, P. (1993b) 'Towards a meta-research agenda in science and environmental education', *International Journal of Science Education*, 15 (5), 591–606.

Robottom, I. and Hart, P. (1995) 'Behaviourist environmental education research: Environmentalism and individualism', *Journal of Environmental Education*, 26 (2), 5–9.

Samuel, H. (1993) 'Impediments to implementing environmental education', *Journal of Environmental Education*, 25 (1), 26–30.

Smith, G. A. (1992) *Education and the Environment: Learning to Live with Limits*, Albany, NY: SUNY Press.

Soltis, J. F. (1984) 'On the nature of education', *Educational Researcher*, 13 (9), 5–10.

Stapp, W. *et al.* (1969) 'The concept of environmental education', *Journal of Environmental Education*, 1 (1), 30–31.

Sterling, S. (1996) 'Education in change', in J. Huckle and S. Sterling (eds) *Education for Sustainability*, London: Earthscan.

Thompson, M. (1990) *Policy Making in the Face of Uncertainty*, London: Musgrave Institute; Geneva: International Academy of the Environment.

UNCED (1992) *Agenda 21*, Geneva: United Nations Conference on Environment and Development (UNCED).

UNESCO-UNEP (1976) The Belgrade Charter, *Connect*, 1 (1), 69–77.

UNESCO-UNEP (1978) The Tbilisi Declaration, *Connect*, 3 (1), 1–8.

UNESCO-UNEP (1987) *International Strategy for Action in the Field of Environmental Education and Training for the 1990s*, Paris: UNESCO.

Volk, T., Hungerford, H. and Tomera, A. (1984) 'A national survey of curriculum needs as perceived by professional environmental educators', *Journal of Environmental Education*, 16 (1), 10–19.

Walker, K. E. (1997) 'Challenging critical theory in environmental education', *Environmental Education Research*, 3 (2), 155–162.

Walsh, M. (1984) 'Environmental education: A decade of failure but some hope for the future', *Australian Journal of Environmental Education*, 1 (1), 21–24.

Watts, D. (1969) *Environmental Studies*, London: Routledge & Kegan Paul.

World Commission on Environment and Development (1987) *Our Common Future*, Oxford: Oxford University Press.

SELECT BIBLIOGRAPHY

Background reading

CEE/DEA/RSPB/WWF-UK (1998) *Key Concepts of Education for Sustainable Development: First Annual Report*, Reading: Council for Environmental Education.

Fien, J. and Spork, H. (1993) *Trends and Issues in Environmental Education: Study Guide and Reader*, Geelong: Deakin University Press.

Greenall Gough, A. (1993) *Founders in Environmental Education*, Geelong: Deakin University Press.

Hungerford, H., Peyton, R. and Wilke, R. (1980) 'Goals for curriculum development in environmental education', *Journal of Environmental Education*, 11 (3), 42–47.

Lucas, A. M. (1980) 'Science and environmental education: Pious hopes, self-praise and disciplinary chauvinism', *Studies in Science Education*, 7, 1–26.

Pike, G. and Selby, D. (1988) *Global Teacher, Global Learner*, London: Hodder & Stoughton.

Robottom, I. (ed.) (1995) *Environmental Education: Practice and Possibility*, Geelong: Deakin University Press.

Smyth, J. C. (1995) 'Environment and education: A view of a changing scene', *Environmental Education Research*, 1 (1), 3–20.

Sterling, S. (1992) *Coming of Age: A Short History of Environmental Education (to 1989)*, Walsall: National Association of Environmental Education (NAEE).

UNESCO/Government of Greece (1997) *Educating for a Sustainable Future: A Transdisciplinary Vision For Concerted Action*, Paris: UNESCO.

Eco-philosophy

Bowers, C. (1993) *Education, Cultural Myths and the Ecological Crisis*, Albany, NY: SUNY Press.

Caduto, M. J. (1985) *A Guide on Environmental Values Education: Environmental Education Series No. 13*, Paris: UNESCO.

Devall, W. and Sessions, G. (1985) *Deep Ecology*, Salt Lake City: Gibbs Smith.

Dickens, P. (1992) *Society and Nature: Towards a Green Social Theory*, Philadelphia: Temple University Press.

Fox, W. (1990) *Towards a Transpersonal Ecology*, Boston, MA: Shambala.

Goodin, R. E. (1992) *Green Political Theory*, Cambridge: Polity Press.

Jencks, C. (1992) *The Postmodern Reader*, London: Academy Editions.

Lovelock, J. E. (1979) *Gaia: A New Look at Life on Earth*, Oxford: Oxford University Press.

McKibben, B. (1990) *The End of Nature*, London: Viking.

Marshall, P. (1992) *Nature's Web – an Exploration of Ecological Thinking*, London: Simon & Schuster.

Orr, D. (1992) *Ecological Literacy: Education and the Transition to a Postmodern World*, Albany, NY: SUNY Press.

Pepper, D. (1993) *Ecosocialism: From Deep Ecology to Social Justice*, London: Routledge.

Ross, A. (1994) *The Chicago Gangster Theory of Life*, London: Verso.

Skolimowski, H. (1981) *Ecophilosophy*, London: Marion Boyars.

Van Matre, S. (1990) *Earth Education: A New Beginning*, Martinsville: Institute for Earth Education.

Sustainability

Carley, M. and Christie, I. (1992) *Managing Sustainable Development*, London: Earthscan.

Hopkins, C., Damlamian, J. and López Ospina, G. (1996) 'Education for sustainable development', *Nature and Resources*, 32(3), 2–10.

Jacobs, M. (1991) *The Green Economy: Environment, Sustainable Development and the Politics of the Future*, London: Pluto Press.

Kerry, Turner R. (1993) *Sustainable Environmental Economics and Management*, London: Belhaven Press.

Marien, M. (ed.) (1996) *Environmental Issues and Sustainable Futures: A Critical Guide to Recent Books, Reports and Periodicals*, Bethesda, MY: World Future Society.

Meadows, D. H., Meadows, D. L. and Randers, J. (1992) *Beyond the Limits: Global Collapse or a Sustainable Future?* London: Earthscan.

Merchant, C. (1992) *Radical Ecology: The Search for a Livable World*, London and New York: Routledge.

Milbrath, L. (1989) *Envisioning a Sustainable Society: Learning Our Way Out*, Albany, NY: SUNY Press.

Pearce, D., Markandya, A. and Barbier, E. (1989) *Blueprint for a Green Economy*, London: Earthscan.

Redclift, M. (1987) *Sustainable Development: Exploring the Contradictions*, London: Routledge.

Smith, G. (1992) *Education and the Environment: Learning to Live within Limits*, Albany, NY: SUNY Press.

Sterling, S. (1993) 'Environmental education and sustainability: a view from holistic ethics', in J. Fien (ed.) *Environmental Education: A Pathway to Sustainability*, Geelong: Deakin University Press.

UNESCO/World Bank (1998) *Organizing Knowledge for Environmentally and Socially Sustainable Development*, Washington: World Bank.

Research methodology and method

Cantrell, D. C. (1993) 'Alternative paradigms in environmental education research: the interpretive perspective', in R. Mrazek (ed.) *Alternative Paradigms in Environmental Education*, Troy, OH: NAAEE.

Carr, W. and Kemmis, S. (1986) *Becoming Critical: Education, Knowledge and Action Research*, London: Falmer Press.

Fien, J. and Hillcoat, J. (1996) 'The critical tradition in research in geographical and environmental education research', in M. Williams (ed.) *Understanding Geographical and Environmental Education*, London: Cassell.

Gough, N. (1993) 'Narrative enquiry and critical pragmatism: Liberating research in environmental education', in R. Mrazek (ed.) *Alternative Paradigms in Environmental Education*, Troy, OH: NAAEE.

Guba, N. L. (1990) *The Paradigm Dialogue*, Newbury Park, CA: Sage.

Hart, P. (2000) 'Requisite variety: The problem with generic guidelines for diverse genres of inquiry', *Environmental Education Research*, 6(1), 37–46.

Lincoln, Y. S. and Guba, E. G. (1985) *Naturalistic Enquiry*, Newbury Park, CA: Sage.

Patton, M. (1990) *Qualitative Evaluation and Research Methods*, Beverly Hills, CA: Sage.

Reid, W. A. (1981) 'The deliberative approach to the study of the curriculum and its relation to critical pluralism', in M. Lawn and L. Barton (eds) *Rethinking Curriculum Studies: A Radical Approach*, London: Croom Helm.

Reid, A.D. and Gough, S.R. (2000) 'Guidelines for reporting and evaluating qualitative research: What are the alternatives?', *Environmental Education Research*, 6(1), 59–91.

Robinson, V. M. J. (1993) 'Current controversies in action research', *Public Administration Quarterly*, 17 (3), 263–289.

Robottom, I. (1992) 'Matching the purposes of environmental education with consistent approaches to research and professional development', *Australian Journal of Environmental Education*, 8, 133–146.

Ecofeminism

Di Chiro, G. (1987) 'Environmental education and the question of gender: A feminist critique', in I. Robottom (ed.) *Environmental Education: Practice and Possibility*, Geelong: Deakin University Press.

Gough, A. (1997) *Education and the Environment: Policy, Trends, and the Problems of Marginalisation*, Melbourne: Australian Council for Educational Research.

Merchant, C. (1980) *The Death of Nature: Women, Ecology and the Scientific Revolution*, San Francisco, CA: Harper & Row.

Merchant, C. (1990) 'Ecofeminism and feminist theory', in I. Diamond and G. F. Orenstein (eds) *Reweaving the World: The Emergence of Ecofeminism*, San Francisco, CA: Sierra Club Books.

Mies, M. and Shiva, V. (1993) *EcoFeminism*, London: Zed Books.

Plumwood, V. (1991) 'Nature, self and gender: Feminism, environmental philosophy and the critique of rationalism', *Hypatia*, 6, 3–37.

Rodda, A. (1991) *Women and the Environment*, London: Zed Books.

Shiva, V. (1989) *Staying Alive: Women, Ecology and Development*, London: Zed Books.

Spretnak, C. (1990) 'Ecofeminism: Our roots and flowering', in I. Diamond and G. F. Orenstein (eds) *Reweaving the World: The Emergence of Ecofeminism*, San Francisco, CA: Sierra Club Books.

Teacher Education

Board of Teacher Registration (1993) *Environmental Education: An Agenda for Pre-service Teacher Education in Queensland*, Toowong: Queensland Board of Teacher Registration.

DEA (1999) *Training Teachers for Tomorrow*, London: Development Education Association.

HE21 (1999) *Sustainable Development Education: Teacher Education Specification*, London: HE21 Project.

Hungerford, H. R., Volk, T. L., Dixon, B. G., Marcinkowski, T. J. and Archibald, P. C. (1988) 'An environmental education approach to the training of elementary teachers: A teacher education programme', *International Environmental Education Programme; Environmental Education Series No. 27*, Paris: UNESCO-UNEP.

Marcinkowski, T. J., Volk, T. L. and Hungerford, H. R. (1990) 'An environmental education approach to the training of middle level teachers: A prototype programme', *International Environmental Education Programme; Environmental Education Series No. 30*, Paris: UNESCO-UNEP.

Oulton, C. R. and Scott, W. A. H. (1995) 'The environmentally educated teacher: An exploration of the implications of UNESCO-UNEP's ideas for pre-service teacher education programmes', *Environmental Education Research*, 1 (2), 213–232.

Scott, W. A. H. (1994) 'Diversity and opportunity: Reflections on environmental education within initial teacher education programmes across the European Union', in F. G. Brinkman and W. A. H. Scott (eds) *Environmental Education into Initial Teacher Education in Europe (EEITE) 'The State of the Art'*, ATEE Cahiers No. 8, Brussels: Association of Teacher Education in Europe.

Scott, W. A. H. (1996) 'The environmentally-educating teacher: A synthesis of an implementation theory for pre-service courses', *Australian Journal of Environmental Education*, 53–60.

Stapp, W., Caduto, M., Mann, L. and Nowak, P. (1980) 'Analysis of pre-service environmental education of teachers in Europe and an instructional model for furthering this education', *Journal of Environmental Education*, 12 (1), 3–10.

Tilbury, D. (1992) 'Environmental education within pre-service teacher education: The priority of priorities', *International Journal of Environmental Education and Information*, 11 (4), 267–280.

Wilke, R. J., Peyton, R. B. and Hungerford, H. R. (1987) 'Strategies for the training of teachers in environmental education', *International Environmental Education Programme; Environmental Education Series No. 25*, Paris: UNESCO-UNEP.

UNESCO-UNEP (1990) 'Environmentally educated teachers: The priority of priorities?' *Connect* XV (1), 1–3.

29

ENVIRONMENTAL EDUCATION IN CHANGING TIMES

Ian Robottom

PRELIMINARY STATEMENT: WHAT IS DISTINCTIVE ABOUT THE FIELD OF ENVIRONMENTAL EDUCATION?

There have been many recent developments at the levels of policy, practice and organisation that raise new issues for the field of environmental education – issues not countenanced to the same extent even ten years ago, and in the light of which we should regard past definitions as problematic. For example, recent international meetings have asserted a strong social change agenda for environmental education that challenges the adequacy of the field's historical disciplinary relationships. The approach in this essay will be to present a sample of contemporary international developments in policy and practice in environmental education and then to consider some of the larger-scale issues which shape and constrain the relationship between policy and practice in this field.

As a starting-point in providing a perspective on what is distinctive about the field of environmental education, we shall consider some of the contemporary discourses in environment and environmental education that form the policy context within which environmental education practices are conducted.

The United Nations Conference on Environment and Development (UNCED)

Over 170 countries participated in the United Nations Conference on Environment and Development (UNCED) – also known as the Earth Summit – held in Rio de Janeiro, Brazil in June 1992. Parts of UNCED's Agenda 21 provide a contemporary policy perspective on the field of environmental education:

> Education, including formal education, public awareness and training should be recognised as a process by which human beings and societies can reach their fullest potential. Education is critical for promoting sustainable development and improving the capacity of the people to address environmental and development issues. While basic education provides the underpinning for any environmental and development education, the latter needs to be incorporated as an essential part

of learning. Both formal and non-formal education are indispensable to changing people's attitudes so that they have the capacity to assess and address their sustainable development concerns. It is also critical for achieving environmental and ethical awareness, values and attitudes, skills and behaviour consistent with sustainable development and for effective public participation in decision-making. To be effective, environment and development education should deal with the dynamics of both the physical/biological and socio-economic environment and human (which may include spiritual) development should be integrated in all disciplines, and should employ formal and non-formal methods and effective means of communication.

(UNCED Plenary 1992, section iv)

This influential international report of the UNCED conference demonstrates the complexity of contemporary constructions of environmental education, and goes on to assert an unmistakable social agenda for a field which historically had sustained somewhat stronger physical/biological connotations. UNCED encourages a form of education that addresses questions of ethics, values, and access and equity; it encourages multi-sectoral public participation in decision-making and analysis of the causes of major environment and development issues in a local context; and it encourages co-operation to redress existing economic, social and gender disparities and to assert the rights of indigenous peoples.

Further recommendations about environmental education were tabled at the International Forum of Non Government Organisations (NGO) held in parallel with UNCED at Rio de Janeiro, Brazil, on 9 June 1992. These recommendations form part of the Treaty on Environmental Education for Sustainable Societies and Global Responsibility which was accepted in a plenary meeting of the International Forum of NGOs and Social Movement on 12 June 1992 (NGOs International Forum, 1992, p. 4). The Treaty recommended *inter alia* that:

Environmental education . . . should be grounded in critical and innovative thinking in any place or time, promoting the transformation and reconstruction of society . . .

Environmental education is both individual and collective. It aims to develop local and global citizenship with respect for self-determination and the sovereignty of nations . . .

Environmental education is not neutral but is values based. It is an act for social transformation . . .

Environmental education must involve a holistic approach and thus an interdisciplinary focus in relation between human beings, nature and the universe . . .

Environmental education should treat critical global issues, their causes and interrelationships in a systemic approach with their social and historical contexts. Fundamental issues in relation to development and environment, such as population, health, peace, human rights, democracy, hunger, degradation of flora and fauna, should be perceived in this manner . . .

Environmental education should empower all peoples and promote opportunities for grassroots democratic change and participation. This means that communities must regain control of their own destiny . . .

Environmental education values all forms of knowledge. Knowledge is diverse, cumulative and socially produced and should not be patented or monopolised . . .

Environmental education must stimulate dialogue and co-operation among individuals and institutions in order to create new lifestyles which are based on meeting everyone's basic needs, regardless of ethnic, gender, age, religious, class, physical or mental differences.

(NGOs International Forum, 1992, pp. 1–2)

In these documents, it is clear that there was recognition at UNCED that environmental issues are not exclusively scientific issues – that empirical information alone will not permit their resolution. There is recognition that, fundamentally, most environmental issues are concerned with quality of life matters. Importantly for the field of environmental education, these can be seen as involving philosophical questions (of the 'ought' and 'should' kind) that can only be engaged through extensive community debate addressing a range of social (historical, political, cultural, ethical and religious) issues. There is also a clear 'social transformation' prescription for the field of environmental education.

Ecologically sustainable development (ESD)

The UNCED conference is an instance of an international discourse on the topic of sustainability (referred to sometimes as sustainable development or ecological sustainability) that has obvious implications for the field of environmental education. The Australian *National Strategy for Ecologically Sustainable Development* (Commonwealth Government, 1992) provides another international perspective on the field of environmental education. This document has the following stated goal for national ecologically sustainable development: 'development that improves the total quality of life, both now and in the future, in a way that maintains the ecological processes on which life depends' (Commonwealth Government 1992, p. 8).

Three core objectives are identified:

- to enhance individual and community well-being and welfare by following a path of economic development that safeguards the welfare of future generations;
- to provide for equity within and between generations;
- to protect biological diversity and maintain essential ecological processes and life-support systems

(Commonwealth Government, 1992, p. 8).

Guiding principles directing sustainable development in Australia are outlined:

- decision-making processes should effectively integrate both long- and short-term economic, environmental, social and equity considerations;
- where there are threats of serious or irreversible environmental damage, lack of full scientific certainty should not be used as a reason for postponing measures to prevent environmental degradation;
- decisions and actions should provide for broad community involvement on issues which affect them

(Commonwealth Government, 1992, p. 8).

An interest in individual and collective quality of life issues, patterns of economic development that support the principle of intergenerational equity (especially recognising the need to preserve the welfare of future generations), broad community involvement, and the preservation of biological diversity and life-support systems are fundamental to the international discourse of (ecologically) sustainable development. Yet this discourse is not without its critics.

Some of the critiques of the emerging international interest in educating for sustainable development concern the close links between economic development and the environment stressed by advocates of sustainable development, in which the environment is presented as a constraint that must be dealt with in maintaining current or future economic development aspirations. On this view, the 'old' modernist perspective on human dominion and control over nature is only slightly softened to a notion of environmental management (with economic interests determining the nature of appropriate management). Critics of education for sustainable development (see Sauvé, 1999) see it more as a progressive form of modernity (maintaining the status of scientific and economic knowledge and rationality) rather than as a genuine reform underpinned by a change at epistemological, ideological and ethical levels. Still other critics (see Huckle, 1999) point out, in rejoinder to Sauvé, that 'the global environmental crisis cannot be separated from the global economic crisis and any analysis of the causes and possible solution to environmental problems should start from this fact' (p. 40). The modernity/post-modernity tensions experienced by contemporary environmental education are evident in the debate concerning education for sustainable development.

National policies in environmental education

Support for the view that environmental education is concerned with both biophysical and social issues is evident in the policy statements of a number of countries active in the field. For example, the Australian government, embarking on a course towards a national curriculum, has produced a national statement on Studies of Society and Environment, which asserts a strong social agenda including a major role for values in environmental education as demonstrated here:

> Values play a part in studies of society and environment in three important ways.
>
> First, they are an object of study. When students consider people and their actions within societies and environments, they investigate and analyse the values and beliefs that influence them. As social and environmental participants themselves, students learn to subject their own values and actions to careful scrutiny . . .
>
> Second, values influence what is selected for study. No curriculum is value-free or value-neutral and so, because of the diversity and changing nature of values held by Australians, it is important to identify areas of agreement on what values should influence studies in this learning area . . .
>
> Third, certain values are a result of study. Through their studies of society and environment, students come to value diversity in viewpoints, curiosity in questioning, thorough and balanced investigations, logically developed and well corroborated argument and justification . . .
>
> Three clusters of shared values, significant in this and other learning areas, have been identified . . . They are democratic process, social justice, and ecological sustainability.
>
> (Curriculum Corporation, 1994, pp. 5–6).

The values that this national statement espouses (democratic process, social justice, ecological sustainability) resonate strongly with the values underpinning the two contemporary international discourses sampled above – those of the UNCED conference and sustainable development.

Similar values are espoused in Swiss reports and policy statements. The Swiss Confederation comprises 26 cantons, which enjoy considerable autonomy in the field of education, so there is considerable diversity in the interpretation of environmental education expressed across the country. This diversity is evident in extracts from a number of current Swiss documents on environmental education presented in the Swiss national report to the recent Environment and School Initiatives Project co-ordinated by the Organisation for Economic Co-operation and Development:

> Ecological education is not simply a subject or topic, but on the contrary a pedagogical principle, a way of looking at things and thinking about them . . .

> Environmental education is not concerned solely with biology, i.e. the natural sciences, but also covers a great many other disciplines such as civil education, health, traffic, energy, agronomy and agriculture (mesology) . . .

> At the forefront of environmental education is the problem of the relationship of man and his natural environment, but also with the man-made environment . . .

> Environmental education transmits not only scientific knowledge or know-how, but also awareness, attitudes and behaviours. It calls upon the ethical conscience as well as man's affective and aesthetic development . . .

> The curricula and teaching resources for the disciplines or subjects concerned should take greater account of current problems or issues concerned with the environment . . .

> In a pluralist society it is essential that controversial subjects or problems should not be passed over in silence. Taking them into account in education enables the pupils to form their own opinion and contributes to civil education.

> (Kyburz-Graber *et al.*, 1995, pp. 6–7)

There are clear resonances between several of these Swiss policy statements and the prescriptions from UNCED: the view that environmental education entails more than a scientific orientation to problem-solving; a recognition of the importance of social relationships and issues of a civic, aesthetic and ethical nature; and an interest in bringing a social education perspective to the study of controversial environmental issues. Policy statements in Finland echo the same sentiment regarding the essentially social nature of environmental education:

> To the Finns, environment is very much a social matter, basically determined by how people interact with each other. To them, it does not really make sense to isolate the physical aspects of the environment from the social ones. Problems of physical environment can never be solved unless you also find solutions to the problems of social environment.

> (Eide *et al.*, 1993, pp. 8–9)

Another distinctive feature of environmental education is that above all, and perhaps like no other 'subject', it is diverse. Much environmental education curriculum is constructed from an investigation of environmental issues (sometimes through text – this is referred to by some as 'education *about* the environment'; sometimes through the senses – this is referred to by some as 'education *in* the environment'; sometimes through active critical enquiries – this is referred to by some as 'education *for* the environment'). Moreover environmental issues differ in content and form in different localities: there are different geographical and demographical features, different stakeholders, different proposals for change, and different vested interests at work. Environmental issues, and the environmental education based on an exploration of environmental issues, are necessarily contextual.

Whether or not we adopt a realist ontology with respect to the biophysical environment, environmental issues can be seen as historically, socially and culturally constructed, and their meaning and significance are related to those historical, social and cultural contexts. Add to this 'environmental diversity' the kind of 'educational diversity' referred to by Scott (1994) – where he claims that in environmental education there are several elements of diversity including the practice (pedagogy), interpretation of terms, and readiness and ability to incorporate environmental education into courses – and environmental education can be seen as being 'doubly idiosyncratic'.

The diversity and contextuality of environmental education can be exemplified with reference to a number of 'vignettes' of environmental education practice worldwide:

- In an Amsterdam state school, pupils learn about the effects of traffic (road construction and road use) on nature. They learn about the relationship between exhaust gases and nutritious matter, the effect of over-manuring on bio-diversity and the effects that the (re-)development of regions of ecological and scenic value can have on the survival or extinction of species. They learn this by computer-simulation model, comparison in the field between a nutrient-poor pasture and a nutrient-rich pasture, and by applying that knowledge in the study of several cases presented in newspaper articles. When they have sufficient background information to judge the ecological effects of traffic, they complete this unit by choosing their own means of transport (Keurentjes *et al.*, 1994).

- In the far north of Australia, a primary (elementary) environmental education programme is based on an investigation of water quality and natural features and resources within a remote mining community comprising Western European and indigenous Australian people with vastly differing appreciations of the value of the natural environment (Andrew and Robottom, 1995).

- A group of schools in Ireland carried out a project that centred on the study of hedgerows. The aims were: to study the flora of hedgerows in the vicinity of the four participating schools; to find out if hedgerows are disappearing in the areas under study; to investigate the policy and practice of local authorities, farmers and other groups towards hedgerow management. The schools developed a computerised database of their findings (OECD, 1994).

- In Canberra, Australia's capital, a secondary environmental education programme comprises a drama-based exploration of issues of power and domination among teachers, students and environments within the setting of a fairly uniform, middle-class government city (Andrew and Robottom, 1995).

- In Scotland, a class of 10 year olds conducted a survey of the school grounds and its users with a view to establishing what changes were most sought. The class divided into groups with responsibility for gardening, wildlife, landscaping, play, publicity and fund-raising. They sought material help from local businesses, parents and friends, and received practical help from a Further Education College. They wrote a mission statement and embarked on a course of action including planting trees and shrubs and establishing nursery beds, containers, rockeries, seating areas, murals and playground games (Scottish CCC, 1993).

The distinctiveness of environmental education

The foregoing suggests that the field of environmental education is concerned with a range of substantive topics relating to:

- *conventional ecological subject matters* such as population, pollution, resources, degradation of flora and fauna, biological diversity, and ecologically sustainable development; and
- *social issues* including considerations of intergenerational equity, health, peace, human rights, ethnicity, gender, age, religious, class, physical or mental differences – in short, matters concerning democratic process, social justice and quality of life.

As a consequence of the issues-based nature of the field of environmental education, these substantive topics, and the educative moments within which they are considered, are highly diverse and necessarily contextual.

While it is clear that there are important questions of an empirical nature that can be considered within both these categories, there are also questions of a philosophical nature that environmental education sets itself, especially in relation to the category of 'social issues'. It is argued that the distinctiveness of environmental education resides in its interest in exploring, in specific educational contexts, a range of philosophical questions concerning the social issues associated with the interrelationships of humans and environments – in particular, the ways in which democratic process, social justice and quality of life are constructed, achieved and sustained within specific environmental contexts.

ENVIRONMENTAL EDUCATION: PROFESSIONAL AND ORGANISATIONAL ISSUES

The distinguishing characteristics of environmental education give rise to a number of professional and organisational dilemmas for the field – dilemmas which need to be negotiated now the field has entered the next century. These are outlined below.

The inevitability of professional dilemmas in environmental education

If it is recognised that the distinctive feature of environmental education is that it engages important social questions of a philosophical kind concerning the political, social, cultural, ethical and religious implications of environmental change proposals, and if it is also recognised that as a field, environmental education is necessarily contextual, then it can be anticipated that environmental education practice is itself political and tends to become politicised. In brief, teachers and students are likely, in environmental education, to become involved in environmental politics. The social/political issues being investigated as part of studies of environmental issues tend, for sound educational reasons linked to accessibility and credibility, to be very 'close to home' as teachers and students engage in a form of 'investigative journalism' into local, current matters of interest and concern to themselves. Professional dilemmas arise for teachers of environmental education in deciding how far to pursue these enquiries within their own communities when the investigations might have implications for colleagues, neighbours, relatives and friends (Andrew and Robottom, 1995). The professional dilemmas associated with the philosophical and contextual nature of the substantive issues being studied remain a significant issue for teachers of environmental education, notwithstanding the existence of international policy statements (for example, from the United Nations Conference on Environment and Development) and national curriculum statements (for example, from the Australian government in its statement on Studies of Society and Environment) which support this kind of environmental education.

Environmental education and science education

One of the relationships that shapes the ways in which environmental education is conducted in educational institutions is that between environmental education and science education. Environmental education has assumed different guises in the curriculum of different schools and centres. For many people there is a strong relationship between environmental education and science education. Some see an important role for science in the resolution of environmental issues. For others, environmental issues are self-evidently socially constructed, involving strong social and political values, and environmental education is seen as a kind of social education. In a sense both science education and social education claim a relationship with environmental education, with science education historically having the stronger hold, as is the case in Switzerland: 'Environmental education is still limited mainly to the natural science disciplines: the social and ethical aspects of the environmental problems not being dealt with' (Kyburz-Graber et al., 1995, p. 7) Yet the epistemology of science (and also expressed in much of science education) may be inappropriate for the field of environmental education (Robottom, 1983).

While environmental education must certainly concern itself with investigating the empirical questions posed in all environmental issues, its distinctive concern with the political, social, cultural, ethical, religious implications of environmental change proposals entails the adoption of a post-empiricist perspective on environmental issues in which the role of science in investigating environmental issues is seen as much less important than social and philosophical forms of enquiry. Unlike science education, environmental education acknowledges the socially constructed nature of much of its subject matters, and sees the role of education as the investigation of the ways in which knowledge is constructed, including a critique of the way that power relationships of various kinds shape the processes of knowledge construction.

The view of knowledge adopted in environmental education is an expanded one: knowledge is not just what is generated by scientific and other experts and encoded in textbooks of some kind; it is not just the kind of awareness one can develop through direct contact with aspects of the environment; it is both of these and more, and includes the outcomes of critical enquiries that teachers and students themselves conduct – the knowledge that is generated by and emerges from the educative work of participants in a community of enquirers.

One of the challenges for the field into the next century would appear to be this: if the newly emerging social agenda of the field is to be adequately addressed in environmental education in the future, there needs to be a new structural relationship between environmental education and other disciplines within the curriculum. This strong social agenda is suggestive of a different relationship with other disciplines: the 'objective', quantitative enquiries of applied sciences, while adequate in addressing the empirical issues to do with ecological subject matters, may prove to be inadequate to the task in environmental education of addressing the philosophical issues concerning such subjective, qualitative constructions as democratic process, social justice and quality of life. The positioning of environmental education within a social education framework would appear to have greater epistemological coherence than a continuing relationship with science education.

Central vs. community control

In many parts of the world, centralised control over curriculum development is commonplace. In countries such as South Africa, England, Canada and Australia, there has been a movement towards greater central control over curriculum development, with the introduction of national or state/provincial curricula. One of the issues for the field of environmental education is the apparent tension between a form of education that is distinctively contextual in its enquiries and subject matters (being based on investigations of local, current and often controversial environmental issues whose meaning and significance reside in particular communities and settings), and a form of educational organisation that vests control over curriculum development processes within a central bureaucracy. Commenting on the then imminent educational restructuring within Australia at the time of the introduction of a national curriculum, Gough warned that:

> Centrally prescribed goals are hazardous policy instruments for effecting any form of educational change and hold particular risks for environmental educators. Such statements tend to foreclose debate on the nature, purpose and practices of environmental education and supplant local innovations and variations with uniform prescriptions. Moreover, the hierarchical and antidemocratic patterns of authority and decision-making embedded in [centrally-located curriculum agencies'] mode of operation are incompatible with the collectivist and communitarian ideals of environmental education.

> (Gough, 1991, p. 113)

The 'social agenda' of environmental education presents another reason for questioning whether increased central control over education is 'good for' the field of environmental education. We considered earlier the UNCED NGO prescription that environmental education ought to be concerning itself with pressing social issues and indeed with social transformation. The relationship of education and social change has been raised explicitly and recently in South Africa, for example. But as Tandon and Buzzati-Traverso (a key figure in the UNESCO-UNEP Environmental Education Programme of the 1970s) have warned us, the political role of educational bureaucracies can be contrary to the very social transformation that is becoming part of the environmental education agenda:

> Control over knowledge production systems, dissemination and use of knowledge, and access to knowledge historically have been used in different societies to continue the systems of domination of the few against the many, to preserve the status quo and to undermine the forces of social transformation.

> (Tandon, 1988, p. 6)

510

At any one time, the educational system – whether based on religious dogmas and practices or on rational thought – has tried to divulge, sustain and perpetuate sets of social values. The process has occurred sometimes openly, at other times through devious channels. If you consider the world today and examine the diverse educational systems, you can clearly identify competing ideologies: those which are attempting to hold on to recognised and almost undisputed values, and those which have launched a major strategy for conquering the world and men's [*sic*] minds.

In other terms, behind any educational process lies a philosophy, a moral philosophy, for the people who exert power and are in charge of educational institutions share certain values, which they wish to disseminate in order to ensure the prolongation, if not the indefinite survival, of the system they are devoted to.

(Buzzati-Traverso, 1977)

That is, while there is growing recognition of the responsibility for environmental education to be an agent in social transformation, political interests within educational bureaucratic systems may actually frustrate the achievement of this aim. The tension between 'central' and 'community interests' in environmental education is an issue that is currently being worked through in several countries and poses another major challenge for the field.

CONCLUSION

This chapter describes the distinctive features of environmental education with reference to a sample of contemporary policy developments in the field. The 'social transformation' agenda of environmental education and its necessarily contextual character are examined. The essay considers some larger-scale professional and organisational dilemmas in environmental education, including issues concerning the referent discipline for and locus of control over environmental education. A distinction is drawn between environmental education and science education, and the tension between community interests and central interests in environmental education is described. In a sense, as we approach the next millennium, these issues in the field of environmental education can be seen as expressions of the larger global tension between modernity and post-modernity that characterises our contemporary social and intellectual life. These issues are presented as an 'agenda' to be negotiated and reconciled within the field as it enters the next century.

REFERENCES

Andrew, J. and Robottom, I. (1995) *Environmental Education across Australia*. A core programme of the National Professional Development Program. Geelong: Deakin University Press.

Buzzati-Traverso, A. (1977) 'Some thoughts on the philosophy of environmental education'. In UNESCO, *Trends in Environmental Education*. Paris: UNESCO.

Commonwealth Government (1992) *National Strategy for Ecologically Sustainable Development*. Canberra, ACT: Australian Government Publishing Service.

Curriculum Corporation (1994) *A Statement on Studies of Society and Environment for Australian Schools*. A joint project of the States, Territories and the Commonwealth of Australia. Carlton, Victoria: Australian Education Council.

Eide, K., Norris, N. and Kelley-Laine, K. (1993) *Environmental Education Policies in Finland – A Review*. Helsinki: Ministry of Education National Board of Education.

Gough, N. (1991) 'A do-it-yourself guide to dismantling Trojan horses', *Australian Journal of Environmental Education*, 7, 112–116.

Huckle, J. (1999) 'Environmental education – between modern capitalism and post-modern socialism – a reply to Sauvé'. *The Future of Environmental Education in a Post-modern World?* Proceedings from an online colloquium sponsored by the *Canadian Journal of Environmental Education*, 40–45.

Keurentjes, E. *et al.* (1994) *From Case to Case: A Dutch Contribution to the OECD Project Environment and School Initiatives of the OECD Centre for Educational Research and Innovation (CERI)*. Enschede, Netherlands: National Institute for Curriculum Development.

Kyburz-Graber, R., Gingins, F. and Kuhn, U. (1995) *Environment and School Initiatives in Switzerland*. Zurich: VDF Hochschulverlag AG an der ETH Zurich.

NGOs International Forum (1992) *Environmental Education for Sustainable Societies and Global Responsibility*. ICAE Environmental Education Programme, Sao Paulo, Brazil, and the International Council for Adult Education, Toronto, Canada.

OECD (Organisation for Economic Co-operation and Development) (1993) *Evaluation and Innovation in Environmental Education*, eds. M. Pettigrew and B. Somekh, Paris: OECD.

OECD (1994) 'Environment and Schools Initiative in Ireland: European Action for the Environment'. Unpublished report to the Organisation for Economic Co-operation and Development, Paris, France.

Robottom, I. (1983) 'Science: A Limited Vehicle for Environmental Education?', *Australian Science Teachers Journal*, 29 (1), 27–31.

Robottom, I. (1987) 'Two paradigms of professional development in environmental education', *The Environmentalist*, 7 (4), 291–298.

Sauvé, L. (1999) 'Environmental education – between modernity and post-modernity – searching for an integrating educational framework'. *The Future of Environmental Education in a Post-modern World?* Proceedings from an online colloquium sponsored by the *Canadian Journal of Environmental Education*, 1–19.

Scott, W. A. H. (1994) 'Diversity and opportunity – reflections on environmental education within initial teacher education programmes across the European Union', in F. G. Brinkman and W. A. H. Scott, *Environmental Education into Initial Teacher Education in Europe (EEITE): the 'State of the Art'*. AATEE Cahiers No. 8, Brussels: Association of Teacher Education in Europe.

Scottish CCC (1993) *Environment and School Initiatives (ENSI) Project in Scotland – The Final Report*. Edinburgh: Scottish Consultative Council on the Curriculum.

Tandon, R. (1988) 'Social transformation and participatory research', *Convergence*, XXI (2/3), 5–15.

UNCED Plenary (1992) 'Promoting education, public awareness and training', in *Agenda 21*, Chapter 36, United Nations Conference on Environment and Development, Rio de Janeiro, Brazil. (Advanced unofficial copy), Section IV, obtained from the Pegasus Network.

30

THE NEW ENVIRONMENT OF MEDIA EDUCATION[1]

Oliver Boyd-Barrett

WHAT IS MEANT BY 'MEDIA EDUCATION'?

The term 'media education' has gained wide currency. At one time it signified a particular approach: an approach to teaching *about* media rather than teaching either *in* media (production) skills, or teaching *through* the media (e.g. educational television); an approach to media that had its own place as a subject in the curriculum, or which was consciously applied across the curriculum, but which was comprehensive, tied neither to a particular medium (such as film or television) nor exclusively to a particular academic tradition (e.g. sociologically inflected media studies). The term was a *contested* one, in competition with others, including film studies, media studies, or English. Care was advisable in using it, for fear that for the listener it might have particular significations.

Media education as defined by the British Film Institute in the 1980s and 1990s, however, is comprehensive and consensual:

> Media education seeks to increase children's critical understanding of the media – namely, television, film, radio, photography, popular music, printed materials and computer software. How media texts work, how they provide meanings, how media institutions and industries are organized, and how audiences make sense of media products, technologies and institutions – these are the issues that media education addresses. It aims to develop systematically children's critical and creative powers through analysis and production of media artefacts. This also deepens their understanding of the pleasure and entertainment provided by the media. Media education aims to create more active and critical media users who will demand, and could contribute to, a greater range and diversity of media products.
>
> (Bazalgette, 1989, p. 1)

This definition is specifically about education for children, but could be applied to a media-related education in higher education and for adults. For its time, it is unusually comprehensive in its view of what constitutes 'the media', incorporating both print and the electronic media, including computing. It seems to focus on media *products*, and in its insistence on computer *software* rather than hardware or computer networking, and given the exclusion of telephony, it is still partial in its compass of media technologies. Whereas the term 'printed materials' appears studiously neutral with respect to the kind of content which these might represent, the expression 'popular music' indicates a view of media education as being about popular media texts as opposed to those 'canonical' texts which are usually the province, for example, of literature and music studies. Some proponents of media education would argue that this is unnecessarily limiting, and that media education is about concepts and analytical skills applicable to *all* media and mediated communication.

The BFI definition takes no position on other long-standing controversies: for example, whether media education should be taught across the curriculum, as a separate subject, or as part of English. It does encompass both critical understanding and creative production. Its key questions are articulated more in the language of social science and linguistics than of literature and aesthetics. It seems carefully to avoid taking a position with respect to the media themselves, until the very last sentence, with its veiled suggestion that media could be more diverse than they currently are.

THE HISTORY OF MEDIA EDUCATION

The BFI definition was developed within the context of its campaign to persuade government to include media education in the national curriculum, which was introduced to England and Wales by the Education Reform Act of 1988. While the BFI Royal Charter requires it to 'foster study and appreciation of cinema, television and video', its campaign adopted a pro-active role on behalf of most media.

David Buckingham (1997) has identified four major phases in the development of media education. For the most part, these are phases in thinking or theorising about media education – and in attitudes to the media within education. Our knowledge of actual classroom practice for any of these phases, on the other hand, is scanty, although it is probably better for phase (4) than for the others. In recent years there have been more systematic attempts to accumulate case studies of good practice. Buckingham's categories are UK-bound, but arguably the UK has been a leading influence for media education theory worldwide. Buckingham's phases are as follows:

1 The Leavisite phase associated with the Cambridge tradition of F. R. Leavis, whose principal aim was to teach children to discriminate between good and bad art, and to inoculate children against the products of commodified mass culture. This has its origins in the 1930s (associated with the literary journal, *Scrutiny*).
2 The cultural studies phase grew out of a tradition inaugurated by Raymond Williams, Stuart Hall and others, whose emphasis was on the appreciation of the popular arts and a reformulation of the concept of 'culture' to signify 'living' art (often in the sense of being rooted in the everyday life of communities) as opposed to 'processed' (commodified) art. This originated in the 1960s.
3 A phase associated with the BFI journal, *Screen Education*, which was much influenced by neo-Marxist structuralism, focusing on the role of the media as ideological tools, and on the consequent necessity to 'demystify' their ideological work, especially through the analysis of media language and representation. This had its origins in the 1970s.
4 A more recent phase, particularly associated with the 1980s, is the media education phase,

more open-minded than its predecessors as to how readers actually 'read' media texts, and whose focus is much more on children and children's learning, having a more positive attitude to the integration of critical theory and creative production.

These phases are not altogether linear; they overlap and run in parallel. As Buckingham notes, they should be considered in the light of broader changes in society and in education. Running throughout them all, he claims, is a tension between enthusiasts who wanted to establish a link between media education and democratisation, and conservatives whose attitudes to media were suspicious and defensive. The 'democrats' saw in media education a way of introducing children to critical study of the same media products which surrounded them in the home, believing that this would link education with life as actually lived, and would contribute to democracy in society by helping people to become more critically aware of the role of the media and their powers of persuasion.

The conservatives, on the other hand, were more concerned about culture (in particular the perceived erosion of 'high' culture, and the – malign – influence of American culture), about morality, and about politics. They saw the media as alien to refined and civilised thought, brash and commercial (American), corrupting of behaviour (encouraging sex and violence). Yet such 'conservative' preoccupations could be found on both the political left (e.g. Frankfurt School) and right (Leavis); the left also worried about the role of the media in developing 'false' beliefs and ideologies, i.e. beliefs and ideologies that did not correspond with the 'real' interests of the majority (often defined as their 'class' interests), essentially revealing a 'transmissional' view of media communication that was increasingly in conflict with the findings of research.

Buckingham's phases are not watertight. He attributes 'discrimination' and 'inoculation' philosophies to the first phase, but alternatively we may see 'discrimination' growing up in reaction to 'inoculation' approaches. These concepts in the context of media education were first developed by Murdock and Phelps in their now classic 1973 study of teacher attitudes to media, and probably still the most sophisticated of its kind. The 'discrimination' which Leavis urged between high culture and mass culture was rejected by Hoggart and others, who were more concerned to distinguish between the culturally authentic and the manu-factured culture of (many) mass media products – the 1945 *Daily Mirror* (+) against the *Daily Express* (–), the *News of the World* against the *Sunday Pictorial*, although the basis of such judgements, in retrospect, look shakily subjective, with their claims to understand the mood, instincts and tastes of 'ordinary people'.

Buckingham's phases are cross-cut by more continuous tensions which put into some doubt his principles of categorisation. These tensions include those between practical work and theory; between creative doing and critical understanding; between literary-oriented work and social scientific investigation; between a popular education for academic failures and a rarefied subject for subversive intellectuals; between instruction in media production skills and using the media to cultivate literacy or other skills; between the media regarded as tools for self-expression and the media deployed as resources for textual reconstruction; between simulation of mainstream media performance and radical explorations of new forms; between a transmissional, one-way teaching about media industries or operations and an approach to media education that stresses children's existing experience; between media education as *knowledge* and media education as *process*; teaching *about* the media as opposed to teaching *through* the media; between teaching media through a single medium such as film or television or newspapers, and including all these and more within a comprehensive analytical framework.

WHO TEACHES MEDIA EDUCATION, FOR WHOM?

In the period leading up to the introduction of a national curriculum in the wake of the 1988 Education Act, considerable effort was invested by the BFI, lobbying the government and the educational community to support the inclusion of media education in the new curriculum. The outcome was not particularly successful, and amounted mainly to a requirement within English that children at Key Stages 3 and 4 (ages 11–16) should study ' "a range of media texts" and to make judgements about how they present their messages' (Dickson, 1994, p. 23).

The 1992 national curriculum order for English stipulated that media education should be included, and 95 per cent of all respondents to a BFI survey (Dickson, 1994) said that their teaching included planned elements of media education (as opposed to only 58 per cent in a previous 1988 survey). Changes proposed for introduction in 1995, however, did not contain any requirement to study the media *per se*; rather, the media are seen as significant only in the context of developing verbal language through reading, writing and listening. Thus by 1996, Learmonth and Sayer (1996) conclude, 'media education as such is not in the national curriculum and is not routinely inspected by OFSTED' (the national body charged with inspecting schools). At Key Stages 3 and 4 (ages 11–16), however, the Programme of Study stipulates that pupils should be introduced to a wide range of media, and be given opportunities to analyse and evaluate such material, which should be of high quality and represent a range of forms and purposes, and different structural and presentational devices.

To make sense of these evaluations one has to distinguish between the use of media as a resource for the attainment of English language achievements, and the study of media in their own right, incorporating analysis of their production, content and reception in broad political, economic, social and cultural contexts. Even if the view of media within English was to be sustained principally on the basis that the media represent a range of means for self-expression, it is obvious that this would entail much more than conventional language skills. The concept 'media education', as now generally applied, encompasses the study of media production, content and reception, in their full context from the viewpoint both of critical analysis and of production; its view of language goes far beyond the encoding and decoding of spoken and written forms. While such a view does inform some of the teaching within English that occurs, it is given no space within the national curriculum.

The future prospects within compulsory education are limited, first of all, because media education has been ascribed mainly (but weakly) to the sphere of English, yet is here hindered by philosophical differences of approach to media between media education as defined above and traditional English teaching. Buckingham (1992) argues that English is primarily defined and organised in terms of activities and practices, whereas media education gives much more sociological emphasis to agencies and audiences, and to critical 'readings' of media texts, often to the exclusion of 'writing'. English is concerned with the 'humanising' effects of certain kinds of texts (usually printed texts) which it recognises as 'literature'. Second, central government interest in media within education has been consistently cautious, notably cool in recent years, with the important exception of information technology, which by contrast is celebrated because it is connected with national economic benefit and with the advance of science. Such coolness to media education has been stubbornly persistent despite the ever intensifying role of media throughout society, affecting central institutions of politics, economics, the judiciary and the monarchy, amongst other things. Even as the Conservative government in the 1980s under Prime Minister Margaret Thatcher ushered in a radical policy of media deregulation, which has increased the commodification and commercialisation of media and media products to the detriment of non-entertainment goals and public service broadcasting, it resisted the extension of serious analysis of media within education, and at least one minister of education (John Patten) rubbished the very project of media studies in higher education. In this time, therefore, it is hardly surprising that the advance of media education has been far short of spectacular.

Within the United Kingdom, the BFI survey of primary, secondary and tertiary institutions by Peter Dickson (1994) shows that most institutions (86 per cent) teach media education within English and that 67 per cent of the institutions teach media education in other areas, including media studies, communication studies, theatre and drama, art and design. Media education at primary level is strongly associated with English, and in two-thirds of secondary schools is concentrated in English, but only in around one-third of colleges. At secondary level (11–18 years), nearly three-quarters of respondents devote at least 10 per cent of their time to media education in English.

Fifty-five per cent of institutions claim to have policy statements about media education – interpreted by Dickson (1994, p. 4) as a 'sign of commitment to a subject area which has no national profile in cross-curricular themes or dimensions'. Uses of literary adaptations are particularly common, but the report notes there is a 'substantial interest in media as a subject of study in its own right'. The production of media texts features in the work of around half of those institutions dealing with media in national curriculum work at Key Stages 3 and 4 of the curriculum. In commenting on his findings, Dickson worries that media education within English 'is likely to be undermined and underfunded', tending to be designated for the less academic at Key Stage 4.

In their survey of good practice in media education, Learmonth and Sayer (1996) note that there are no national standards against which achievement in media education can be assessed in Key Stages 1, 2 and 3 (ages 5–11). While there are examples of adventurous and exciting media education work in primary schools, some teachers need support in understanding media theory at an appropriate level and in handling practical work. In secondary schools, much media education is undertaken by English departments, which not unreasonably have other priorities; the quality of practical work is found to be uneven, with limited experience of extended audio-visual projects at Key Stages 3 and 4, for example, but there is more opportunity at earlier stages of the curriculum wherever media education is taught. Assessment of pupils' learning in media education is rarely undertaken. There is too much dependence on the enthusiasm of individuals or small groups, with little hope of embedding the subject successfully without clear strategic planning as part of a coherent, school-wide planning. The support of heads, governors and parents is essential. The authors note that teachers consistently express a need for continuing training, particularly in practical skills, but are less aware of a need to become more confident in using a conceptual framework to underpin their teaching. Provision of training, however, is being undermined by cut-backs in government support for in-service training.

WHAT IS MEDIA EDUCATION ABOUT?

The modest acknowledgement of media within the national curriculum notwithstanding, there exists no national consensus for the teaching of media in the UK. While the UK has a formidable record in theorising about media education, it can boast of only a very uneven record in doing it and, until very recently, an extremely poor record in evaluating what is actually done inside classrooms.

In lobbying for the inclusion of media education within the national curriculum, the BFI had proposed a general framework, broadly applicable and inoffensive (which has informed various BFI teaching materials and the BFI/OU course, *Media Education*, 1992). As indicated above, the history of media education has been turbulent and often political. It represents a marriage of film studies, literary theory and sociology of the media. The attempt to establish a respectable aesthetics of cinema in the 1950s and 1960s, much influenced by 'auteur' and 'genre' theories as applied, especially, to non-mainstream and often subtitled 'continental' film of France and Italy, was very text-focused, and often antagonistic to mainstream cinema. Whatever its limitations, the generation of film studies prepared the way for later endeavours to take television seriously. Outside the circle of film studies' enthusiasts, the prevailing characterisation of film and television as a popular medium led to an attitude that other than in the case of specialised GCSE and 'A' level courses, the study of film and television was best suited for the less academically able children who, since the raising of the school-leaving age to 16 in 1973, had grown in significant numbers. Media studies was seen as a 'soft option' that might help pacify a restless and conscripted army of non-academic teenagers.

Between this target population and the heady intellectual debate within the BFI's *Screen Education* there was an immense chasm. The intended beneficiaries of media education belonged to an anti-academic subculture soon to be identified by the RSA's 'capability' movement as the most in need of (now revalued) practical skills or 'competency' or 'capability'. But teachers looking for inspiration in the BFI's journal would have found cerebral, sometimes inaccessible debates on radical screen theory, dealing with such issues as the ideological work of film, and the positioning of audiences, much influenced by the work of structuralists such as Althusser and Lacan, semioticians such as Barthes and Eco, and the work of Hall and others at Birmingham University's Centre for Cultural Studies.

The influence of *Screen Education* is commonly asserted rather than investigated by many who write about media education. Except, possibly, with reference to the relatively small numbers sitting for examinations in film studies or media studies at the age of 16–18, I think this source of influence should be weighed against others. *Screen Education* was but one forum for the development of cultural studies – in particular, of popular culture, a movement which was spearheaded largely by humanists with a background in language, literature and film studies. Social science approaches were not much in evidence and this may help account for the 'transmissional' models of communication that sometimes lay behind the